INTEGRATIVE ASSESSMENT
A GUIDE FOR COUNSELORS

Andrew Gersten

Antioch University, New England

Boston   Columbus   Indianapolis   New York   San Francisco   Upper Saddle River
Amsterdam   Cape Town   Dubai   London   Madrid   Milan   Munich   Paris   Montreal   Toronto
Delhi   Mexico City   São Paulo   Sydney   Hong Kong   Seoul   Singapore   Taipei   Tokyo

Vice President and Editorial Director: Jeffery W. Johnston
Senior Acquisitions Editor: Meredith D. Fossel
Editorial Assistant: Krista Slavicek
Vice President, Director of Marketing: Margaret Waples
Marketing Manager: Christopher Barry
Senior Managing Editor: Pamela D. Bennett
Senior Project Manager: Mary Irvin
Senior Operations Supervisor: Matthew Ottenweller
Senior Art Director Cover: Jayne Conte

Cover Designer: Karen Salzbach
Cover Art: Fotolia
Full-Service Project Management: S4Carlisle Publishing Services
Composition: S4Carlisle Publishing Services
Printer/Binder: STP Courier
Cover Printer: STP Courier
Text Font: 10/12, Times LT Std

Credits and acknowledgments for materials borrowed from other sources and reproduced, with permission, in this textbook appear on the appropriate page within the text.

Every effort has been made to provide accurate and current Internet information in this book. However, the Internet and information posted on it are constantly changing, so it is inevitable that some of the Internet addresses listed in this textbook will change.

Library of Congress Cataloging-in-Publication Data
Gersten, Andrew.
   Integrative assessment: A guide for counselors / Andrew Gersten.
      p. cm.
Includes bibliographical references.
ISBN-13: 978-0-13-503485-9
ISBN-10: 0-13-503485-X
   1. Psychological tests.   2. Counseling psychology.   I. Title.
[DNLM: 1. Psychological Tests.   2. Counseling—methods.   3. Mental Disorders—diagnosis.
   4. Needs Assessment.   BF 176]
   BF176.G47 2013
   150.28'7—dc23

                                                    2012014871

10 9 8 7 6 5 4 3 2 1

www.pearsonhighered.com

ISBN 10:   0-13-503485-X
ISBN 13: 978-0-13-503485-9

Dedication

To my family: Jo, Ben, and Sarah. Thank you for giving me the support and space to complete this project.

ABOUT THE AUTHOR

Andrew Gersten is a private practitioner specializing in the assessment and treatment of children with emotional and behavioral disorders. He received his doctorate in clinical psychology in 1987 from the Illinois Institute of Technology. Since his internship training at the University of Massachusetts Medical Center Developmental Clinic in 1986, he has provided cognitive and psychological assessments to children—preschool through adolescence. He has worked in community mental health as a therapist, assessor, and supervisor and has consulted to elementary and middle schools on school climate, behavioral program development, and special education services. In addition, Andy is a teacher, presenter, supervisor, and researcher. He has been teaching in counseling programs for over 19 years. Andy is currently adjunct faculty at Antioch University New England, where he has been teaching Assessment: Principles and Methods, and Psychopathology: An Ecological Approach since 2008. Prior to Antioch he was an Associate Professor of Counseling at Rivier College, Nashua, New Hampshire, where he taught graduate students in school and mental health counseling and teacher education programs. He has presented at regional and national counseling and psychology conferences on various topics, including DSM-5, counselor intentionality, school counseling models, and interpersonal problem solving. Andy has co-authored several articles on the effects of shiftwork on sleep and well-being and counselor intentionality. His current research focus is the development of intentionality in counselor trainees. Andy is a member of the American Counseling Association, Association of Counselor Education and Supervision, New Hampshire Psychological Association, and American Psychological Association. He can be reached at *dragersten@comcast.net*.

PREFACE

My intention in writing this book was to address one basic question: What assessment principles and methods do all helping professionals need to know, in order to apply them in a culturally sensitive and ethically sound manner? An overarching premise in the fields of counseling and psychology is that assessment is an information-gathering and analyzing process in which different types of methods and sources of information are relied upon. Consequently, my and others' perspective is that both traditional, formal, standardized tests and informal methods are valued, each with its own benefits and limitations. Although these two broad categories have equal value, the level of training required to use them is not equivalent. Some types of psychological tests—intelligence, achievement, and personality—to be used competently require a greater degree of education and training than a text like this and one assessment course can provide. Furthermore, the creation and revision of psychological tests has accelerated exponentially in the past 30 years, so much that some of the tests that you will read about may already or soon be replaced with a revised edition. The emphasis here, however, is on those procedures that are client- and counselor-friendly. That is, this text presents assessment approaches and instruments—unstructured interviews, informal and formal observations, and brief self-report questionnaires—that do not require advanced training, are easy to use, score, and interpret, and have added benefit relative to their costs. Keeping in mind this focus, it is also necessary to incorporate and discuss fundamental assessment concepts such as ethical standards specific to the assessment process, psychometric theory, and cultural considerations when using formal standardized instruments. The term *psychometric* refers to the measurement of psychological constructs and includes terms such as *reliability, validity, norm-,* and *criterion-referenced* tests. Thus when you encounter a given client, you will better able to gather, integrate, and communicate information gained from informal and formal approaches so as to be an effective helper.

I made a discovery while teaching in masters counseling programs for almost 20 years. I had read and used excellent resources that focused on interviewing and observing, and others that focused on psychological testing—but I was looking for a graduate text that did justice to both approaches. I saw a need shared by graduate students, trainees, early career professionals, supervisors, and counselor–educators for one practical guide that would bridge the gap between the two types of counseling assessment texts currently on the market. As a text designed to integrate both informal and formal assessment procedures, it was necessary to provide a more comprehensive and balanced discussion of both methods than typically occurs in other texts of this nature. A counselor's assessment of a client can be analogized to a photographer taking a picture. Although the photographer's subject may be the same with each snapshot, different lenses—35mm, zoom, and wide angle—each capture the image in a different way, but collectively they enrich and enhance one's understanding of the subject matter. The tendency, however, in traditional assessment texts has been to view assessment through mainly one lens: psychological testing. And yet an unstructured interview is *the* assessment method used most often by counselors and other helping professionals. In addition, there was a need to discuss topics that again tend to be neglected in books about psychological testing but are vital assessment concerns: suicide potential and dangerousness to others, substance use, and the quality of the counseling relationship. Those types of assessments are part of helping professionals' ongoing work regardless of setting or specialty area: education, community, mental health, rehabilitation, vocational, and so on. Therefore, this book is intended to help emerging and new practitioners understand the assessment methods that are available to them and then apply this new knowledge in the field.

The chapter sequence that follows is based on the following premises: 1) both informal and formal methods have merit and neither one should be considered superior to the other; 2) assessment is an ongoing process, not something that occurs only at the outset of a counseling process or intervention and then is completed; and 3) in order to assess in a professional, responsible manner, one must have a grounding in the ethical standards that shape the process. Furthermore, it has been my experience that many students find it easier to become acclimated to and assimilate information about psychological testing and complex tests when they are exposed to informal approaches before psychometric theory and measurement concepts.

Readers are introduced in Chapters 1 through 5 to the multiple reasons why we assess ethical standards and concepts, interviewing, and observations, and Chapters 6 and 7 cover measurement concepts, reliability, and validity. Specifically, Chapter 1 lays out the seven interrelated reasons why assessment occurs: defining problems and diagnoses, conceptualizing cases, screening for risk, planning interventions, monitoring client progress, evaluating outcomes, and providing therapeutic benefit. Chapter 2, on ethics, focuses on informed consent, competency, including test user qualifications, and test security. Chapters 3 and 4 are devoted to interviewing: skills and the content of the initial interview. The initial assessment interview is presented from a risks and resources framework for understanding presenting problems, and includes a discussion of assessing clients' readiness for change. Chapter 5, on observations, covers both informal and formal observations (mental status evaluations, functional behavior assessment, and direct observation coding schemes) along with how counselor bias can impact this process.

Following the first seven chapters, more traditional topics are taken up in Chapters 8 and 9: personality and interest tests and assessing psychopathology. Chapters 10–12 are devoted to topics that often receive less coverage in other assessment texts: Chapter 10 discusses standardized measures for assessing emotional and behavioral problems in children and adolescents, and Chapters 11 and 12 focus on combining informal and formal methods for evaluating suicide and dangerousness to others, and substance use. Chapter 13 focuses on theories of intelligence, cognitive ability, and achievement tests, and Chapter 14 is devoted to assessing the therapeutic relationship, a concept that is often presented elsewhere but without a means to formally assess it. In addition, sections of these chapters are devoted to cultural issues that impact the understanding and use of formal standardized assessments. Ultimately, the knowledge gained from an assessment needs to be helpful to our clients. The final chapter, Chapter 15, *Putting It All Together*, includes a section on communicating assessment results to clients. All of these chapters contain practical assessment information that can be applied during field placements and beyond.

This text is intended for graduate students, emerging helping professionals, and those already in the counseling fields who need more guidance in how to apply the various assessment tools we have. As both a practitioner and teacher, I have found the case study context helpful when learning new material or reinforcing previous knowledge. All the chapters, with the exception of the introductory and reliability–validity chapters, open with a case that is a composite sketch, so to speak, based on my 30-plus years in the field, and these cases are used to illustrate how a particular assessment principle or method can be applied to that client. The case study approach is woven throughout by providing a practitioner's voice, providing Practice Suggestion boxes, giving guidance in the use of assessment methods and specific instruments, and at times illustrating through sample dialogues. The Reflection Questions and Experiential Exercises contained at the end of each chapter will provide you with opportunities to assimilate and apply concepts and methods that will facilitate your use of assessment strategies in the field. Hopefully you will find this to be a valuable resource, one that you will come back to as you continue in your professional helping endeavors.

A note about terms used in this book is needed. Throughout, I use the terms *counselor* and *helping professional.* Counselors are but one branch of the professional helping tree that also includes psychologists, social workers, marriage and family therapists, and other allied health and human service professionals. This text is designed for any current or emerging helping professional. In addition, the racial–ethnic labels used when discussing test norms and cultural considerations are those used in the language of a test manual, test review, or journal article. Therefore, you may see inconsistency in usage—e.g., Black versus African American—across or within chapters since there is variation among the sources from which the terms are drawn.

ACKNOWLEDGMENTS

It goes without saying that even as the sole author on a project of this magnitude, this was a team effort. A number of individuals shaped this textbook in various ways. Several former teachers and mentors instilled in me a passion for scientific curiosity and discovery, and a commitment to understanding and helping people. Professor William Revelle, whose lab at Northwestern University I had an opportunity to assist in, instilled in me an appreciation for measurement and an understanding about the relationship between personality, physiology, and individual performance; Professor Donald Tepas, who mentored me through my graduate school research and dissertation at the Illinois Institute of Technology; and my internship assessment supervisors Dr. Marty Young at the University of Massachusetts Medical Center Child Development Clinic and Dr. Bob Andrews at the Worcester Youth Guidance Clinic. All of them provided me with a scaffold from which I was able to build an assessment textbook.

I also thank the reviewers of this first edition: Lorie S. Blackman, Oregon State; Cynthia Campbell, Northern Illinois University; Laurie Ann Carlson, Colorado State University; Robert D. Colbert, University of Connecticut; Jon C. Crook, Texas Wesleyan University; Shannon Dickson, CSU Sacramento; Lane Fischer, Brigham Young University; Richard Halstead, Saint Joseph College; Patrick Hardesty, University of Louisville; Kristin K. Higgins, University of Arkansas-Fayetteville; Larry C. Loesch, University of Florida; Trevor Milliron, Lee University; Mittie T. Quinn, George Mason University; Clarrice Rapisarda, UNC Charlotte; Donna Sheperis, Delta State University; Michelle L. Slater, University of North Florida; Zachery B. Sneed, University of North Texas; Sue Stickel, Eastern Michigan University; Jeremy R. Sullivan, University of Texas at San Antonio; and Robert Walrath, Rivier College. A debt of gratitude is also owed to the many individuals who read chapter drafts and provided kind words and insightful feedback: Shannon Hodges, EdD, Niagara University; Diane Kurinsky, PhD, Antioch University New England; Joseph Fish, PhD, Child Health Services—Manchester, New Hampshire; and Val Draskovich, LMHC, private practice, and all my colleagues whom I haven't met but participated with in the blind peer review process from initial proposal to the final manuscript.

At Pearson, I also owe a debt of gratitude to my editor, Meredith Fossel, who was steadfast with her encouragement and guidance, which an insecure new author greatly needed, and to Mary Irvin for all her technical and production assistance. Finally many thanks to my daughter, Sarah Gersten, and my former graduate student Anne Thompson, MEd, for their editorial assistance and compilation and checking of references.

BRIEF CONTENTS

CONTENTS

1

INTRODUCTION TO PSYCHOLOGICAL ASSESSMENT

Chapter Objectives

After reading this chapter, you should be able to:

■ Understand models and principles guiding the assessment process.

■ Identity the purposes of an assessment.

■ Identify the different assessment methods.

■ Understand where and when assessment is performed.

■ Explain historical factors that shape the field and current trends.

OVERVIEW

Is this a book about psychological testing? In part, yes. You may be thinking, "But I'm a counselor—or educator or some other type of helping professional—not a psychologist. Why do I need to know about psychological tests?" The answer is that testing is a common assessment practice that counselors, psychologists, and other helping professionals rely on to help them better understand and effectively serve their clients. This book, however, is more than a survey of different psychological tests and how they are used; it is about assessment. *Assessment* and *psychological testing*, although often used interchangeably, mean two different things (Fernández-Ballesteros, 2002; Matarazzo, 1990; Meyer et al., 2001). Assessment is a process; psychological testing is one of several assessment strategies or tools. To equate the two confuses the concept with its component. This would be analogous to saying traveling is flying. There are many ways to travel—by car, foot, plane, boat, even mentally—flying being just one of several useful methods, each with its own set of advantages and limitations. Similarly, there are different kinds of assessment methodologies, each with its respective benefits and limitations, *testing* being only one of them. The others include observing, interviewing, measuring, and reviewing records.

Why then are the terms *psychological testing* and *assessment* often equated, and why are some textbooks and journal articles ostensibly about assessment but are essentially discussions of only tests? Perhaps it is because testing is the only tool, among many that a helping professional has in his or her tool kit, that has been simultaneously prized and vilified. Tests have been valued because they help professionals gain knowledge and understanding of individual differences that they might not get otherwise, and because the information gleaned can be used in beneficial ways. Test results can be used to inform an educational plan for a student so that more effective teaching can take place. A test may also help a clinician determine the best treatment approach for a client or help an employer select the most suitable job applicants. Simultaneously, testing has been attacked for how it has been both used and misused, which has resulted in some individuals' civil liberties and freedoms being curtailed (Dawes, 1994; Matarazzo, 1990). For example, when the results from a personality test are presented in a courtroom and a parent's involvement with his or her child is severely limited because of the findings from that test, its merits and the testing process are scrutinized and potentially restricted. Historically, testing was the exclusive domain of psychologists because of their role in the development of modern tests. If a person or group of persons needed to be evaluated, screened, or assessed, they were sent to a psychologist who administered a test to make a decision about their future. In some cases the results of those early tests had a profound impact: the manner and setting where some children were educated; whether or not military service was an option. Over the past 50 years, the use of psychological tests in noncounseling contexts, (e.g., courtrooms and employment centers) has continued to significantly affect people's lives. This is perhaps part of why the terms *testing* and *assessment* have been used synonymously.

Assessment is no longer the exclusive province of psychologists. Not only do counselors and other helping professionals engage in it, but we all do it in our daily lives. Before ever reading this book you will have conducted myriad assessments without perhaps realizing it, literally from the day you were born. What is it that we do from the moment of birth onward that makes us assessors? We gather information, evaluate it, and come to conclusions or decisions based on that analysis. The infant hears a voice, analyzes its tone, pitch, and rhythm, and concludes, this is my mother. Based on that judgment the infant may turn in the direction of the voice and smile. Later on, the infant is a toddler looking around the room, and not seeing his or her mother, concludes, she has left me. That conclusion brings on distress. These assessments are rudimentary and intuitive, but nevertheless information from the environment is taken in, analyzed in some fashion, and acted upon. Jumping ahead to high school, a rising senior asks the question, Which college is right for me? The senior may perform a more sophisticated kind of process to answer that question. She or he decides to consult a variety of sources—friends, a college's website, the school counselor, a college guidebook—and then organizes in some way all that information in order to decide among the thousands of available options which one will be a good fit. Each source may provide the student with unique information and perspectives that help paint a picture of a good fit. The sources might all provide very similar information, so the student is confronted with a basic assessment problem: How much information should I gather and what if different places say different things? What if the information from one source conflicts with another? The task could become overwhelming. Somehow the information needs to get winnowed down and filtered. For example, the guidebook, the friend, and the college website each provide somewhat different perspectives on one piece of vital information: the degree of difficulty in getting accepted. Whose information and perspective should the student rely on? The divergent information makes the decision more complex and difficult. Beyond this example, children and adults routinely engage in assessment when they informally size up people or situations. Is this someone I can trust? How do I feel about going to this party? Why didn't my friend text me back? Does it make sense to go home for the holidays? There are countless other questions one can pose from everyday experience, the answers to which reflect an assessment process. Some of those questions may even pop into your mind as you read this paragraph. All of these questions and examples illustrate that assessment is part of human nature and is fundamentally a process consisting of several steps.

Professional psychological assessments are a multistep process that begins with a question. For example, What is this client's diagnosis? Which treatment will this person benefit from? Is this student making progress toward his or her individualized education plan objectives? The first step in answering those and other assessment questions is for a counselor to gather information from some source and then organize and synthesize it in some fashion. The process then moves on to an evaluation or analysis step and ends with a judgment, conclusion, or decision. That final step will guide what the helper does next. So, what distinguishes the assessments done by laypersons throughout their lives from assessments done by professionally trained helpers? The purpose of this chapter is to describe the nature and purpose of professional counseling assessments; present an overview of the principles that serve as the foundation for the assessment process and the methods that counselors and other helping professionals utilize; introduce the requisite professional skill set; and discuss how assessment has evolved.

THE NATURE AND PURPOSE OF COUNSELING ASSESSMENTS

The term *assessment* has been defined differently over the past century, but a relatively recent conceptualization, which was the work product of a multidisciplinary committee representing the fields of psychology and education, is generally accepted by those disciplines and the counseling field. Simply stated, assessment is a process of gathering and integrating information from multiple sources in order to make inferences about a person or program (American Educational Research Association, American Psychological Association, & National Council on Measurement in Education [AERA, APA, & NCME], 1999). The sources from which information might be collected are varied—from observations of a client to the client's responses to interview questions; from informal questionnaires to formal tests. The inferences an assessment process is designed to address are also diverse and stem from a particular question. The question could be a diagnostic one: "Does Brian have an attention-deficit-hyperactivity disorder?" It could be predictive: "Is Brian likely to harm himself next week?" Furthermore, a counselor might wonder, "What among several treatment options—individual counseling, family, medication, or some combination—is this elementary school girl who is depressed and anxious likely to benefit from?" Similarly, the counselor might ask a client, "How will we be able to tell if counseling is helping you?" These typical assessment questions suggest there are different reasons why counselors engage in this process.

Assessment Purposes

Two broad approaches govern psychological assessment practice: the *nomothetic* and the *idiographic* (Hunsley & Mash, 2008). The **nomothetic** model is concerned with how an individual compares with relevant others on some domain such as intellectual ability, personality trait, or psychopathology severity. That comparison is made with some kind of formal standardized measure such as an intelligence or personality test. Consequently, formal standardized methods of assessment—tests, measures, and questionnaires—come out of this nomothetic tradition and are used to gather quantitative information about an individual in relationship to others. This approach also focuses on generalizations that can be made about a person across situations based on the information gleaned from a test or measure. According to this approach, an individual who is found to have high intellectual ability based on some standardized test is likely to demonstrate that same level of intellectual aptitude in different places. On the other hand, the **idiographic** approach stresses understanding the unique qualities, abilities, or psychological makeup of the person. The idiographic tradition relies more on informal procedures, such as unstructured interviews or client diaries, to understand the nuances, subtleties, and unique aspects of a client's emotional, cognitive, and behavioral experiences. The idiographic approach does not preclude, however, the use of formal measures in order for the counselor to help his or her client gain a better understanding of self. For any given client, the assessment can, and often does, include a combination of nomothetic and idiographic approaches.

Experts in the field of psychological assessment have described seven fundamental, interrelated purposes for assessing individuals or groups regardless of the overall approach (Finn & Tonsager, 1997; Hersen, 2003; Hunsley & Mash, 2008; Spengler, Strohmer, Dixon, & Shivy, 1995):

1. Defining problems and diagnoses
2. Conceptualizing cases
3. Planning treatment
4. Tracking client progress
5. Screening
6. Evaluating intervention outcomes
7. Intervening

An understanding of those reasons enhances helping professionals' ability to conduct effective and beneficial assessments.

Defining Problems and Diagnoses

All counseling clients come with a problem or set of problems. Even in those situations where a client arrives not "owning" a problem, as is often the case when counseling is mandated legally, or is there because a family member "requires" it, the primary task for the counselor is to understand the nature of the presenting problem(s). How a problem is conceptualized will ultimately determine how the client and counselor responds to it. A person may come, for example, to an initial counseling session stating, "I haven't been myself for awhile. I have been tired and just can't seem to get going, nothing interests me anymore." What do those statements mean? When did the person begin feeling this way and how often does this occur? Through a series of questions and perhaps other procedures, the assessing professional can begin to get a fuller contextual understanding of client problems. The process of helping clients put problems in context will focus on when the problem began, how frequently it occurs, how severely or intensely it is experienced, what factors may be associated with its occurrence, and what has been tried so far to alleviate it. When clients and counselors have a mutual understanding of the problems and an agreed-upon plan for resolving them, the counseling or therapeutic relationship is strengthened (Asay & Lambert, 1999; Bordin, 1979; Norcross & Wampold, 2011). And when compared to other factors—technique, theoretical orientation, and therapist experience—it is the quality of the counseling relationship that has been consistently shown to have the largest impact on client improvement (Lambert & Barley, 2001; Orlinsky, Ronnestad, & Willutzki, 2003; Prochaska & Norcross, 2010; Wampold, 2001). Problem descriptions, however, are not the same thing as a formal diagnosis.

Clarifying Diagnosis

A constellation of problems and symptoms can also be defined formally with a taxonomy: a classification system. Although multiple diagnostic systems exist for categorizing psychopathology—c.f.

International Classification of Diseases and Related Health Problems (ICD), World Health Organization (1992); *Achenbach System of Empirically Based Assessment*, Achenbach (2011); *The Psychodynamic Diagnostic Manual*, American Psychoanalytic Association, Alliance of Psychoanalytic Organizations (2006)—the one utilized most often by counselors and other professionals in the United States is the *Diagnostic and Statistical Manual of Mental Disorders* (DSM) (American Psychiatric Association, [APA], 2000) currently in its fourth edition (DSM-IV). The fifth edition is due out in 2013 (APA, 2010). The current DSM system classifies individuals on five different dimensions, or axes as they are called in the DSM: I–clinical disorders, II–Personality Disorders and Mental Retardation, III–medical conditions, IV–psychosocial stressors, and V–overall functioning. Therefore, one purpose and outcome of an assessment would be to provide DSM-IV diagnoses. Despite the revisions to the DSM since the introduction of the multiaxial system in 1980 and better criteria for establishing the presence of a disorder, the relevance of these diagnoses for treatment planning and interventions has been considerably lacking (First, 2010; Reed, 2010; Widiger, 2008). Although clinicians in graduate programs throughout the United States and other countries are trained to use the DSM, its conceptual base and categories only loosely match the ways in which mental health professionals frame the nature of problems they typically see in a mental health setting (Flanagan & Blashfield, 2010). However, in mental health settings, unlike in other counseling settings, a formal DSM diagnosis is required in order for third parties—government, commercial insurers, and managed care organizations—to pay for mental health services. Notwithstanding these limitations of the DSM classification system, it can be a vehicle for improving communication between professionals, is necessary for research and reimbursement, and revisions to it are aimed at improving its clinical utility (First, 2010). Ideally, a diagnostic system is clinically useful when a strong relationship exists between a specific disorder and both assessment and treatment. One of the goals in the ongoing revision process to the DSM is to get closer to that ideal.

In an educational context, students are evaluated informally and formally for a variety of reasons, one of which is diagnostic classification. School psychologists and other professionals may assess a child to determine if a disorder is present that is affecting the learning process. In order to make that determination, the child is likely to be assessed with cognitive ability and achievement tests (see Chapter 13). One result of that testing, when combined with other information gathered about the child from teachers and parents, may be the diagnosis of a learning disability, educational handicap, or some kind of development disorder such as autism. That classification, in theory, like a mental illness diagnosis, can provide an understanding of why a child is having difficulty learning and provide a path toward educational interventions that can improve the child's chance for success.

Assessment is done routinely in educational contexts for nondiagnostic purposes as well. Teachers give reading, spelling, math, and other types of tests to see if their students are meeting curriculum benchmarks, and school personnel administer standardized tests to assess the level of performance of groups of students.

Problem descriptions and formal diagnoses provide a partial picture of what an individual is experiencing. What is needed to complete the picture is a theory about what has caused and possibly is maintaining the problem set or disorder. Case conceptualizing is an assessment process from which a theory is developed.

Conceptualizing Cases

Like problem definition, case conceptualization is a task fundamental to all counseling professionals regardless of the work setting: school, mental health, community, rehabilitation, or organizational. Case conceptualization incorporates problem definition and expands upon it by developing a hypothesis about why a particular client is experiencing a problem. Simply stated, it is the clinician's working theory about the client and what is going on. More formally, it can be defined as a process of integrating and synthesizing client data—presenting problem, history, observations, records, and psychological testing (if available) to develop a hypothesis of the factors causing and maintaining the current problems (Porzelius, 2002). Notice the similarity in definition between case conceptualization and assessment in general. This is because case conceptualization can be thought of as a specific assessment task, a mini-assessment. The counselor's case conceptualization is an explanatory statement that speculates on the specific factors that are connected to the presenting problems, symptoms, and concerns. These case conceptualization factors include development, modeling and learning history, culture, life stressors, physical conditions, and personality traits (Porzelius). The conceptualization will consider which factors may have played a role in causing the presenting problems and which ones are contributing to its ongoing maintenance. Causal and maintenance factors, however, may or may not be the same for any given client. Take the example of a woman who experienced a trauma, sexual abuse at the age of 9, and 10 years later is reporting symptoms of a post-traumatic stress disorder. Some of those symptoms (nightmares and hyper-vigilance) may stem from the trauma experiences, whereas other difficulties and problems—emotional numbness and detachment, trouble trusting men, and anxiety about sexual activity—may be a result of not only the original trauma, but ongoing thoughts, reactions, and coping strategies as well. The initial or tentative hypothesis can be confirmed, modified, or rejected as more information about a client is gathered (Spengler et al., 1995). Perhaps the initial hypothesis for this fictional female client was that she is having these problems because of a childhood trauma. Additional assessment indicates that this is a woman who also has introverted and emotionally unstable personality traits. The clinician expands his or her initial hypothesis in order to incorporate this new information and theorizes that both the sexual abuse history and certain personality traits are contributing to the ways in which the client is experiencing her current symptoms and problems. To summarize, assessment of presenting problems is concerned with *what* and *how* questions, and case conceptualization with the question *why*.

Once a case conceptualization has been developed, even if it is a preliminary and tentative one, as is typical in the counseling field, a course of action is then decided upon. That action plan is most likely to be effective when helper and client collaboratively agree upon it. A question then arises, "How is the plan working?"

Planning Treatment

Another fundamental reason to assess any client is to develop an action or treatment plan. Careful, comprehensive assessment can guide treatment at the macro and micro levels (Spengler et al., 1995). At a macro level, counselors and clients make decisions about overall treatment goals and the ways to achieve them—for example, the treatment modality: individual, group, or family. The macro level can also include community resources such as AA or NA, Al-Anon, legal aid, educational advocacy, and so on. Once treatment has unfolded, information can be gathered to enable clients and clinicians to judge its helpfulness. Assessment can also guide what a counselor does within a session. The process can help clinicians and clients decide not only on overall goals, but which ones to focus on within a particular session. Furthermore, clinicians will continue to assess within sessions in order to 1) evaluate the working hypothesis developed in the case conceptualization, 2) form new impressions about a client, or 3) judge the effectiveness of a particular technique or intervention. Assessment at that level is likely to be simple and informal and may come in the form of an open-ended question such as "What was that relaxation exercise like for you?" It can also occur more formally by having a client complete a questionnaire or rating scale. A collaborating clinician integrates this new information from either informal or formal procedures and uses it to continue to monitor and evaluate how the intervention is going.

Tracking Client Progress

Throughout the counseling process and at the end of it, assessment procedures can be used to address two essential questions: Is the counseling helping and Is my client making progress? Both informal procedures and formal ones, such as standardized questionnaires, can be used to answer those questions. Of the latter procedure, there are hosts of client- and counselor-friendly questionnaires that can be used for measuring and tracking client changes during counseling (Meier, 2008). The changes that formal questionnaires can evaluate range from degree of symptom relief to perceptions about the therapeutic relationship; from perceptions about interpersonal relationships to overall functioning. These measures are described in detail in Chapters 9, 10, 11, 12, and 14. It can be difficult at times for counselors to determine at the outset of counseling whether or not a particular approach is a good fit for a client, especially given the lack of evidence favoring any one therapy model (Asay & Lambert, 1999; Imel & Wampold, 2008). By assessing client progress or the lack thereof, counselors and clients can discuss whatever changes may need to be made in the overall treatment approach. Regular and ongoing assessment of the client's perception of change can help to avert therapy failures (Lambert & Shimokawa, 2011), an overlooked topic that has gained increased attention in professional journals and books since the 1980s (Lambert & Ogles, 2004; Whipple & Lambert, 2011).

Screening

Screening is used as part of secondary prevention efforts in medicine, education, and mental health. The goal of a prevention screening process is to identify individuals from the general population who are already at risk for developing a treatable condition. Physical health care screening happens routinely for identifying at-risk individuals for all sorts of conditions: hypertension, diabetes, and colon cancer, for example. Since 1991 there have been annual events where individuals in the community, workplace, and military can get screened for some common mental health disorders such as depression, anxiety, alcohol abuse, and eating disorders (Screening for Mental Health Inc., 2011, *www.mentalhealthscreening.org*). According to Screening for Mental Health Inc., thousands of organizations worldwide have screened over a million people ever since the first national screening day, which was devoted to depression. Individuals who participate in these and other screening efforts are likely to complete a standardized questionnaire, either in person or online, similar to the ones described in Chapter 9. Typically the higher the score on the screening instrument, the greater the likelihood that a person is at risk for a particular condition such as depression or hypertension. Once a screener identifies someone as being at risk, information about further assessment and intervention is usually provided to the individual. As part of the 2010 comprehensive U.S. health care bill, the Affordable Care Act, many insurance plans will be required to cover prevention screening beginning in 2014 (U.S. Department of Health and Human Services, 2011). The disorders and problems that can be screened at no cost to the individual or family include autism and other developmental disorders, childhood behavioral disorders, depression, domestic violence, and adolescent substance use.

EVALUATING TREATMENTS AND PROGRAMS   Assessment tools are also used routinely to gauge the effectiveness of treatments, interventions, and programs delivered to groups of individuals: clients, students, employees, and community members. Typically, pre and post measures are obtained as a way of judging the overall impact a program or intervention had on a group. An employer-sponsored 10-week program promoting healthier lifestyles in its employees would likely have an assessment component to it. Employees might be asked, prior to the lifestyle program commencing, to fill out a questionnaire about exercise, sleep, and dietary practices. The same questionnaire would be given to the group at some point after the program had concluded, and the pre and post responses would be compared. In addition, this hypothetical questionnaire could be given at the same points in time to a comparison group of employees who did not participate in the intervention as a way of evaluating whether, on average, there were different kinds of changes between the two groups.

Similarly, standardized measures can be used to evaluate the practices of the clinicians or program providers. One goal of this type of assessment is to judge the feasibility and acceptability of programmatic changes or interventions (Ey & Hersen, 2004). The feasibility, acceptability, and value of a program can be judged in terms of cost (materials, training time and demands, client time to complete questionnaires), perceived degree of difficulty in implementation, and the perceived benefits for both program providers and recipients. For example, the author participated in a project at a local community mental health center clinic where the clinical director wanted to change the way clinicians conducted their initial assessments, or what are known as intakes. The clinicians were a multidisciplinary group of mental health counselors, psychologists, social workers, and substance abuse counselors. The plan was for all new adult clients, prior to the intake interview, to complete a 90-item standardized questionnaire, the Symptom Checklist-90-Revised (SCL-90-R) (see Chapter 9). The SCL-90-R asks how bothersome a range of symptoms, feelings, physical sensations, thoughts, and behaviors have been during the past week. Parents of minors completed an alternative questionnaire about their child's behaviors, feelings, and symptoms, over a six-month period, the Child Behavior Checklist (CBCL) (see Chapter 10). The clinical staff participated in two hours of in-service training to learn how to instruct clients on completing the SCL-90-R and CBCL and how to score and interpret them. After one month, the clinicians were asked about their attitudes, feelings, and perceived value of incorporating these assessment instruments into the intake procedure. The results of that questionnaire helped guide the director and the clinicians to make some modifications in the overall screening and intake procedures used at the center as well as how and when in the assessment process the SCL-90-R and the CBCL would be used.

Intervening

Not only is assessment an information gathering and analyzing process, it is a form of intervention. Assessment and intervention can be thought of as synchronous and synergistic processes whereby each one informs the other. How does that work? Let's take the example of a counselor asking during the fourth session, "On a scale of 1 to 10, how nervous are you today, 1 being not at all and 10 being the worst nervousness you have ever experienced?" And the client replies, "A 2." It may seem clear that this question is an assessment because the clinician is gathering information about the severity of the client's emotional state. But how is this simultaneously an intervention? Implied in the question is the notion that emotions, like nervousness or anxiety, fluctuate in intensity and severity. Therefore, this question can potentially promote client insight—the intervention part—by helping the client to see that his or her nervousness can vary;

rather than being an all-or-nothing state. With that realization, the client and counselor can explore what may be going on that makes today a "2," especially given that the nervousness was "unbearable" at the first appointment. This new information can then shape subsequent counselor assessments within the session. The counselor may ask, "What is it you are doing differently on days when nervousness is a 2 versus those when it is a 10?" Consequently, a feedback loop is created: assessment–intervention elicits client responses that inform the next assessment–intervention action.

In a similar vein, the act of providing feedback about data gathered from the assessment process, either moment to moment within a session or after a formal procedure like testing has been completed, can have a therapeutic impact on clients. Finn (2007) and Finn and Tonsager (1997) have described this as the therapeutic model of assessment and have contrasted it with a purely information-gathering paradigm. In their model, providing clients with assessment feedback can have a number of therapeutic benefits that are shared with overall counseling goals. These include 1) developing empathy and enhancing the therapeutic relationship, 2) enhancing self-esteem and reducing feelings of isolation, 3) promoting new ways of understanding self and others, helping clients apply new insights to alleviate problems, 4) valuing a collaborative approach to goal setting and problem solving, and 5) increasing client motivation to actively participate in the process (Finn & Tonsager, 1997). According to this model, as stated earlier, assessment is an ongoing collaborative process between client and assessor–therapist, and the clinician is a participant–observer in the process. This approach to assessment clearly values the idiographic model: the client's subjective experience and unique perceptions, characteristics, and beliefs. This goal of understanding the individual client's subjective experience is rooted in the humanistic and existential counseling approaches developed by Carl Rogers (1951, 1961) and others (Bugental, 1990; May & Yalom, 2000), which have profoundly influenced how counselors and others currently practice. Rogers, in particular, recognized that all human beings have a need to gain knowledge of self and be understood and accepted, and this became part of the necessary and sufficient conditions of his person-centered theory. The theory states that when a therapist helps a client achieve knowledge of self and empathically communicates to the client a shared understanding of client self, feelings, and attitudes, that client will grow and change. Similarly, this premise underlies the therapeutic assessment model (Finn, 2007; Fischer & Finn, 2008). The empathic delivery of data gathered from the assessment process is one of several ways in which the therapist–assessor can help clients to understand themselves more completely and thereby set the stage for promoting client change.

What evidence exists to support this therapeutic model of assessment? A number of published case studies with adults (Ackerman, Hilsenroth, Baity, & Blagys, 2000; Fischer & Finn, 2008; Newman & Greenway, 1997) and youth (Smith, 2010) have provided empirical support for its purported benefits. For example, one study found it helped to decrease client symptoms and increase feelings of self-esteem and hopefulness. Another study demonstrated its positive impact on clients staying with the treatment and the therapeutic alliance. One other research project involving a small group of children and families found a significant decrease in child symptomatology and enhanced family functioning as reported by children and mothers. In addition, mothers demonstrated a significant increase in positive emotion and a significant decrease in negative emotion pertaining to their children's challenges and futures.

Finn and his colleagues have contrasted their view of assessment with the test-and-tell approach. That is, the assessor assumes a detached role, administers questionnaires and tests, and provides a diagnosis or personality description to facilitate communication between professionals. This is the essence of the nomothetic tradition discussed earlier. They believe, however, that their approach and the nomothetic can coexist and complement one another. They echo a perspective that Allport (1937), one of the key contributors to the field of personality assessment, expressed 60 years earlier: the information-gathering nomothetic and idiographic therapeutic assessment models are complementary and interdependent. Therefore, psychological assessment does not need to be a dehumanizing process, a view once expressed by some humanistic and existential theorists. Although assessment, especially testing, has been criticized as a procedure that "misses the person for the scores," this is a somewhat narrow and traditional perspective. Both approaches to assessments are aimed at promoting client well-being, increasing understanding of self and others, and identifying treatments that can reduce suffering and promote growth. This perspective is shared by the author and is a foundational principal for this text. Hopefully, you too will share it by the time you have completed your assessment coursework.

Now that the seven purposes of assessment have been described, a discussion of assessment principals and methods can take place. Like all counseling endeavors, the assessment process is guided by a core set of philosophical viewpoints and ethical standards. Those perspectives provide a framework for the selection and application of specific assessment tools a professional helper will utilize.

GUIDING ASSESSMENT PRINCIPLES

Three overarching principles guide all counseling assessments, regardless of setting and purpose: 1) valuing and using a multimethod, multisource approach, 2) valuing a multicultural and ethically sensitive approach, and 3) understanding referral questions and contexts. Although each guiding part of this assessment framework will be discussed separately, they too are interrelated.

Valuing a Multimethod Multisource Approach

Any one assessment strategy, be that an interview, test, or observation, can be conceptualized as a lens through which a clinician can view a client. A single lens can provide a detailed but incomplete picture. A more comprehensive view and understanding of a client comes about through the use of multiple lenses: a multimethod, multisource procedure. As Figure 1.1 illustrates, any assessment method can gather information from different sources: the client, a family member, another professional, or the counselor. For example, when a child is referred for mental health counseling, information about the child's concerns, interests, feelings, and perceptions can be gathered by interviewing the child, the parents, and a teacher. In addition, the child could

Method					
	Interview		Observation		Test-Measure
Source	informal	formal	informal	formal	
Client					
Significant Other					
Counselor-therapist					

FIGURE 1.1   Multiple Methods and Sources for Gathering and Obtaining Information

complete a self-report rating scale, and parents and teachers could rate the child's behaviors on another questionnaire. A similar process of obtaining pieces of information from different people could happen in the case of an adult seeing a career counselor. Often, career counselors assess a client's personality to help the client understand the potential fit between one's personality traits and the features of certain jobs. Both the client and a spouse or other family member who knows the client well could complete similar tests that would paint a broader and more in-depth portrait of the client.

Valuing a Multicultural and Ethically Sensitive Approach

When counselors and other helpers engage in assessment activities, they are guided by ethical standards and an awareness of how cultural factors can impact the process. The American Counseling Association's (ACA) Code of Ethics (ACA, 2005) and the ethical codes of related disciplines (psychology and social work) include sections pertaining to assessment activities, each one to a lesser or greater level of detail. As with other sections of ethical codes, the ones relevant to assessment are meant to be aspirational guidelines. When professionals are involved in any aspect of assessment, from selecting procedures to integrating data, it is critical that the following principles, which govern all aspects of the ethical codes, are adhered to: promoting human welfare, respecting diversity, and respecting clients' rights and integrity. The users of assessment methods need to understand how cultural factors—age, gender, race, ethnicity, religion, and sexual orientation—can impact one's response to or performance on any assessment procedure. For example, imagine an 8-year-old boy, Dumaka, who along with his parents came to the United States from Nigeria not speaking English. Two years later, Dumaka has developed proficiency in English but is having difficulty in his fifth-grade classroom. His teacher is unsure, based on his school performance—homework assignments, classroom participation, quizzes, and tests—what he is learning, particularly in math. A referral is made to the pupil assistance team to determine if he has a learning disability. Although Dumaka can now read and understand English well, it is not is his primary language. The person who is going to assess his learning styles and cognitive abilities needs to take this into account when considering the choice of English-language tests available and be cognizant of the possibility that low test scores may reflect a language barrier and not a deficit in the measured abilities. The impact of language and other cultural factors is especially important, as will be discussed further later on, when test results are interpreted and decisions made that could have profound consequences for the individual student, client, employee, or group undergoing an assessment. Even when alternative language versions of a test or measure exist, translation does necessarily mean the parallel versions are equivalent. A multiculturally sensitive assessor is aware of that notion and strives to understand the potential differences and limitations of a translated test.

Much of the controversy surrounding the use of standardized tests in the United States has had to do with the notion that some tests are biased against members of certain minority groups. It is not that some tests are inherently biased but rather that the inappropriate use of them can potentially harm people (AERA et al., 1999). In light of that recognition, a division within ACA, the Association for Assessment in Counseling (AAC) produced Standards for Multicultural Assessment in 1992 and published a second edition 11 years later (AAC, 2003). This document addresses the challenges test users face when assessing multicultural populations. Cultural competency in this context refers to having an understanding of how culture, race, and ethnicity can contribute to the very traits, choices, and behaviors that are being assessed and how that awareness can lead to more beneficial counseling services (AAC, 2003).

Understanding Referral Questions and Contexts

All helping professionals, regardless of their role and setting, engage in an assessment process, especially when services are initially sought, and throughout the course of counseling. Whether one is a career counselor in a college counseling center, a school counselor in a public elementary school, a therapist at a community mental health center, or a psychologist in private practice, a common concern is deciding whether or not a client's problems or difficulties can be addressed with the available services. A foster parent may seek out the elementary school counselor because of concerns about her foster daughter's behaviors, but the girl's needs may be more complex and require more intensive therapy than the school counselor can provide. A middle-aged man may seek treatment from an addiction clinic because of compulsively searching the Internet for pornography but the clinicians there work solely with substance abuse. More typically, a mental health counselor is contacted by someone looking for medication and the counselor is unable to prescribe. Conversely, the presenting problems are such that the helper decides there is a fit between the available services and a potential client's needs and goals. These mini-assessments are usually conducted via telephone screenings or through an initial interview. Sometimes it is not clear until the end of an initial interview whether there is a fit between what the client is seeking and what the helper can provide. Therefore, a common role for professional helpers during the initial contact with a person seeking services is that of an assessor.

Once it is decided that helper and client will continue working together, assessment will continue either informally or formally, and the context of that assessment shifts. As discussed earlier, another purpose of assessment is to track client progress over the course of counseling and evaluate again once the process ends. This can be done through informal or formal means or a combination of the two. Client progress could be tracked with both a personal diary and a standardized symptom checklist, for example.

One other general context for understanding the process occurs when an individual is referred to a helping professional for a specific type of assessment or evaluation. When that happens, often the counselor's job is to shape the referral question in order to provide a meaningful assessment. Effective assessment depends upon specific referral questions and understanding the context in which it will take place (Groth-Marnat, 2003). Sometimes the referral question is broad and ambiguous: "What's wrong with this person?". A more helpful question is one that is more narrow and focused: "Does Suzy have a learning disability?" An even better question is one that poses a problem in search of solution. For example, a teacher might come to the school counselor or school psychologist and state with concern and curiosity, "Suzy has been having trouble learning to read, and maybe I'm just not reaching her. Is there a way to find out how she learns so that I can adapt my teaching methods to her needs so she can read better?" Knowing at the outset the specific question(s), the assessment process can be designed and conducted in such a way that problems can be better understood and potential interventions identified.

By shaping and focusing the referral question, the assessor is also clarifying his or her professional role with respect to the client and the referring person, agency, or organization. Sometimes, depending on the referral question and context, the assessor's role may be narrowed to that of a diagnostician. More often, in educational, mental health, primary care, and forensic contexts, the assessor's role will be broader. Therefore, the professional who is called upon to conduct only an assessment, needs to explicitly communicate to the client and referral source the nature of this involvement. The assessor should clarify at the outset 1) the length of the assessment and the methods that will be used: tests, interviews, telephone contacts, and so on; 2) whether or not a report will be produced and, if so, who will receive it; 3) if recommendations

will be made and, if so, how those recommendations will be communicated to client and referral source (in person, via a report, or electronic communication); 4) that the assessor's role does not include an ongoing counseling relationship. One complex scenario that illustrates the importance of clarifying the nature of the assessment and the assessor's role is the mental health professional who is asked by a representative of the legal system, a guardian ad litem (GAL), for example, to assess a child's emotional well-being and make recommendations about contact with parents after a divorce. To begin, the mental health professional helped the GAL focus a broad concern about emotional well-being. In this case the question became "Is there evidence that Renee, a 7-year-old girl, was experiencing symptoms of a trauma because of domestic violence she witnessed?" The GAL also wanted recommendations from the mental health professional that she could include in her final custody evaluation report to a judge. The GAL was looking for guidance regarding Renee's visiting her father, who was living in a separate apartment, and whether therapy was needed since the parents were divided about this. The GAL expected that the mental health professional would complete a report outlining recommendations, but it was not the role of the mental health evaluator to render an opinion about custody. This was clarified in their discussion prior to the assessment commencing and would need to be communicated to Renee's parents along with the other limits of the evaluator's role. The evaluator informed the parents that even though assessment interviews that would resemble therapy sessions would take place with Renee, this contact would be more limited in time and scope and would not continue once the evaluation was completed. At any point in which an assessment is requested by a third party, it is the responsibility of the professional to communicate and clarify the purpose of the assessment, how it will be conducted, what will be communicated to whom, and the limits of the assessor's role.

Once the assessor helps the referring party to articulate an effective assessment question, the process of considering and selecting appropriate assessment methods to provide some answers begins. Given that there is a wide array of tools available, it is helpful to have a basic understanding of the general categories of assessment methods and strategies to select from.

ASSESSMENT METHODS AND STRATEGIES

Although the preceding discussion of assessment principles has referenced specific assessment methods, a more comprehensive description of these informal and formal approaches is needed. Four broad categories of assessment methods exist: interviewing, observing, testing and measuring, and reviewing. Of the four, tests and measures contains the greatest number of specific assessment methods and it is the one most often researched and throughout history has been the most controversial.

Interviews

An unstructured informal interview is the most common assessment method used by all counselors (career, community, mental health, school, and rehabilitation) as well as other helpers. In mental health settings, the prototypical unstructured interview is also known as an intake interview. There are two additional types of interviews—*semistructured* and *structured*—both of which are more formal because the content of the questions and the order in which they are asked is already established. Structured interviews resemble surveys and typically have a scoring system. They are used primarily for research purposes or to help clarify a formal diagnosis such as those contained in the DSM or ICD systems. Unstructured interviews tend to be more client centered in that they allow the clinician more flexibility regarding topic coverage and how much depth to go into in any one area. Although structured and semistructured interviews can seem more assessor-centric, their value is in the consistency and comprehensiveness they provide. In terms of consistency, the likelihood that two or more clinicians using the same structured interview will arrive at a similar diagnosis is much greater than for those using an unstructured approach.

Observations

Like interviewing, observing can be done both informally and formally. Counselors, when engaged in assessment, typically begin with informal observations about a client's appearance, emotional expression, speech, physical movements, and interactions with the assessor. Those observations are also part of a more structured observation process, a *mental status evaluation* (Morrison, 2008; Trzepacz & Baker, 1993). In addition to those observations, a mental status evaluation focuses on cognitive process such as perception, memory, attention, and verbal reasoning. Collectively, the informal observations and mental status observations help clinicians to formulate a case conceptualization and diagnosis.

Formal observations about clients can also be made using coding forms. These forms identify discrete behaviors which an observer counts the frequency of during a predetermined time schedule. Observation forms have been developed and used primarily with children in educational and psychiatric types of settings (schools, day-cares, therapeutic schools, residential facilities, and hospitals). Formal methods for observing and coding the behavior of adults is used less often, and usually when done, it occurs in institutional settings such as hospitals or rehabilitation facilities. Behavior observation coding methods and mental status evaluations are discussed in depth in Chapter 5.

Tests and Measures

The terms *tests* and *measures* are often used interchangeably and are often associated with other terms such as *personality tests*, *questionnaires*, *inventories*, and *rating scales*. A psychological test can be defined as an objective and standardized procedure with items designed to measure a *sample* of behavior that purportedly represents a person's trait, ability, or psychological functioning (Anastasi & Urbina, 1997; Kaplan & Saccuzzo, 2005). Like psychological tests, measures are objective and standardized, and when they quantify a sample of behavior they are in essence psychological measures (McIntire & Miller, 2007). Therefore, they both are psychometric devices. *Psychometric* refers to the measuring and quantifying of psychological phenomena: abilities, traits, and characteristics. So what, if anything, differentiates a test from a measure? A primary distinction concerns the kind of response expected of the client. Psychological tests have a method for evaluating correctness and a set of right and wrong answers; standardized measures often explicitly state there is no right or wrong answer. Second, tests are used to evaluate and describe in detail a person's underlying ability, trait, or characteristic more than a measure does. Measures are more limited in the information they provide: the frequency, severity, or intensity along a specific domain (e.g., depression symptoms, self-esteem, or substance usage). Third, the term *test* has been reserved for and is still used with those types that came first: intelligence scales (e.g., *Wechsler Intelligence Scales, Stanford-Binet Intelligence Scales* [see Chapter 13]) and personality tests (e.g., *Minnesota Multiphasic Personality Inventory* [see Chapter 8]). Notice the word *test* is not used in the names of these "tests," but rather the term *scale* or *inventory*. The term *measures* has been used with questionnaires, rating scales, checklists, or inventories

that can be completed by the client or someone knowledgeable about the client (e.g., a parent, teacher, or spouse). Despite these differences, both tests and measures share a larger commonality: a standardized administration and scoring process.

STANDARDIZATION PROCESS   What is it that makes tests and measures standardized assessment tools? There are several factors to consider. First, everyone who takes a psychological test or fills out a questionnaire or rating scale is given the same instructions, same set of questions or items, and the same sequence of items. Therefore the administration procedure, unlike an unstructured interview, does not vary from person to person. Second, tests and measures have an established objective scoring system for the questions and items. Although, some subjective judgment can be involved in how to score some responses on certain types of tests, primarily cognitive ability and projective. The latter include various picture-story tests and the Rorschach inkblot test. Third, as part of the development process, tests and measures are given to a selected sample of people who are then referred to as the normative or standardization group. Individuals who later take that test have their scores evaluated against the average performance of the normative sample. To put it another way, the normative group serves as the reference point for making inferences about an individual's score as to whether it is normal or pathological, average or atypical. This is the essence of the nomothetic approach to assessment.

RELIABILITY AND VALIDITY   Another commonality of psychometric devices is that their strengths and limitations can be judged quantitatively on the basis of two foundational concepts: reliability and validity. *Reliability* refers to the stability of a measuring device (Anastasi & Urbina, 1997). There are several ways in which a procedure could be stable but perhaps the easiest to understand is retest stability: each time a person's ability, trait, or characteristic is measured, the test produces approximately the same result. Validity, on the other hand, refers to the degree to which a test or procedure measures what it purports to (Anastasi & Urbina). Like reliability, there are several types of validity, and perhaps the easiest to understand is the concept of content validity. For example, cognitive ability tests are deemed valid to the extent that they contain items experts in the field recognize as being representative of thinking skills and processes such as memory, pattern recognition, and verbal reasoning, rather than an unrelated concept such as psychopathology. The reliability and validity of any test or measure can be quantified with a statistic known as the *correlation coefficient*, and the value of that correlation is one criterion by which the effectiveness of any psychometric device can be evaluated (Hunsley & Mash, 2008). These two psychometric concepts will be taken up in much greater detail in Chapter 7.

PROCESSES AND CONTENT   Tests and measures can be sorted into subcategories on the basis of either the process or the content. Tests, in particular, can be based on verbal or nonverbal processes or a combination of the two. Verbal tests require that the test taker answer questions orally, and nonverbal tests generally require a motor response—for example, copying shapes, arranging blocks to match a model, or pressing a computer key in response to a stimulus. These tests are not, however, exclusively nonverbal in that the instructions are usually administered orally, though in some limited circumstances, the directions can be pantomimed.

Another process dimension is speed versus power. Some tests contain subtests that are timed, in which fast, accurate responding results in better performance. Other tests are untimed but are considered power tests because the items get increasingly more difficult, and the further one successfully continues, the stronger the ability, theoretically.

The administration format can differ as well. Most tests used in mental health settings are given on an individual basis, whereas some tests used in educational settings or to evaluate learning potential, like the SAT, are administered to a group. In terms of the process, one other general type is tests that involve reading multiple-choice or forced-choice questions and require a written or computer-based response versus tests that ask open-ended questions.

The content of tests and measures can be uni- or multidimensional. Many cognitive ability tests contain multiple subtests or scales, each one measuring a different dimension of cognitive ability: memory, verbal reasoning, quantitative skills, visual–spatial reasoning, attention, problem solving, and abstract reasoning. Similarly, a personality test may assess different traits—introversion, conscientiousness, and flexibility, for example—each one measured by a separate scale within the test. Conversely, a measure may be unidimensional in that only one concept is evaluated, such as self-esteem. In general, unidimensional measures tend to be shorter in length and multidimensional tests tend to be relatively longer. A measure may contain as few as four items, such as the *CAGE*, an alcohol-abuse screening tool, or as many as 567 questions as is the case with the *Minnesota Multiphasic Inventory-2* (MMPI-2). From a practical perspective, tests and measures that are brief and can provide as much clinical information as similar but longer instruments are more beneficial assessment tools because they pose a lesser burden on clients and counselors. Regardless of whether an instrument is multidimensional or unidimensional, it is usually grouped with other instruments that assess related concepts.

Personality   Standardized inventories, questionnaires, and rating scales are used to measure both what are considered normal and pathological, or maladaptive, personality traits. Some personality tests measure dimensions of normal, and others pathological traits, but currently there are not tests that attempt to measure both, with one exception, the *MMPI-2*. In general, when taking a personality test of either type, the individual will read a statement—for example, "I like going to lively parties"—and answer the degree to which he or she agrees with that statement. These standardized personality measures are also referred to as self-report questionnaires because the individual is responding to the items based on that person's view of self. Some self-report personality instruments are part of a broader assessment package that contains a parallel other-report version. In those versions someone who knows the client well—spouse, partner, close friend—will respond to items that are essentially the same as those on the self-report version by giving their perception of the client.

Interests, preferences, and values are considered by some researchers and scholars (Armstrong, Day, McVay, & Rounds, 2008; Blake & Sackett, 1999; Holland, 1999; Savickas, 1999) to be a circumscribed aspect of personality that is expressed in work, hobbies, and leisure. Interest measures are considered one of three separate but related categories of career counseling assessment measures that also include values, abilities, and career planning or process (Whiston, 2009). An assessment of interests and values is typically conducted in the context of career counseling that often takes place in educational, workplace, or private practice settings.

Psychopathology   Procedures for assessing psychopathology are thought of as *objective* or *projective* types. Objective tests and measures have content that is readily and easily associated with different aspects of psychiatric conditions: anxiety, depression, psychosis, and so on. These instruments usually have a list of items that are similar in language to the criteria in DSM-IV for a particular disorder, and they are designed to measure the frequency, intensity, or severity of symptoms, and the features of the disorder. All self-report measures specify a time frame for the person filling it out to reflect upon: one or two weeks, several months, or an entire lifetime.

Projective instruments are based on the assumption that when given an ambiguous stimulus—inkblots or pictures—an individual will form a perception and response that is a manifestation of unconscious feelings, attitudes, interpersonal styles, and concerns. The oldest and most frequently used projective tests are the Rorschach and the Thematic Apperception Test (TAT), ranking fourth and sixth respectively in a survey of clinical psychologists test usage (Camara, Nathan, & Puente, 2000). The TAT belongs to the class of projectives called picture-story tests, in which the individual is shown a card where an interpersonal scene is depicted and is asked to tell a story.

Cognitive Tests   Cognitive ability tests, as noted earlier, are multidimensional and vary both in terms of their content and process. The specific cognitive skills, the manner in which they are assessed, and the emphasis placed upon a particular ability is what distinguishes one test from another. Some of these tests, like the Stanford-Binet and Wechsler Scales, produce an IQ score and traditionally have been called intelligence tests. At the present time there is considerable overlap in the dimensions of cognition that are assessed with tests that produce IQ scores and those that do not (see Chapter 13). Procedures that evaluate cognitive concepts such as memory, attention, and visual–spatial skills are also known collectively as neuropsychological tests.

Related to the concept of cognitive ability is the notion that as an individual develops and acquires education, aptitude for a particular kind of knowledge is obtained. Aptitude and achievement tests are primarily used in educational and vocational settings because they measure aptitude and knowledge within a particular subject matter: reading, writing, and arithmetic.

Reviewing Records

One additional assessment strategy that counselors and other helpers have at their disposal is the review of any existing records. As part of the initial information-gathering process, it is typical to inquire of clients, students, family members, and others whether any previous evaluations have been conducted. When previous evaluations have been done, the current assessor may want to review the written reports. Many kinds of reports may be available for review: intake assessments, treatment summaries, psychological evaluations, psychoeducational evaluations, report cards, speech and language evaluations, occupational therapy reports, medical notes and reports, and legal documents (forensic evaluations, probation, parole and guardian reports). It is, in the author's view, a more helpful practice to review reports during the integration phase of the assessment rather than before observing, interviewing, or testing a client. Why? If a clinician has read about a client's abilities, traits, strengths and weaknesses, and diagnosis prior to the initial meeting, that previous information is likely to produce a priming effect. That is, human beings can be primed to perceive and respond to new information about objects or people in selective ways because of the associative nature of memory (Buonomano, 2010). For example, if a previous evaluator concluded that John was learning disabled, the current assessor is more likely to notice things about John that are consistent with that label. Consequently, reading a report prior to an assessment is likely to color the clinician's efforts to gather new information through a neutral, unbiased lens. Because an objective approach to assessment is considered one of the many competency criteria an assessor needs to possess, it is best to review records at the integration phase of the assessment process.

OVERVIEW OF PROFESSIONAL ASSESSMENT SKILLS AND COMPETENCIES

Knowledge, Skills, and Attitudes

What are the requisite knowledge, skills, and attitudes one must possess to use assessment instruments in a professionally competent and ethically sound manner? A related question is, Who gets to decide those standards? Competency is an ethical standard to which counseling and related disciplines (psychology, social work, and medicine) expect their members to adhere. From an ethical perspective, professionals engage in activities and practices only for which they have had the requisite education and training and do not practice beyond the boundaries of their competency (ACA, 2005; APA, 2002). With regard to assessment competencies, there is a set of knowledge, skills, and attitudes necessary for using assessment procedures in a responsible, professional manner. Who then determines these core assessment competencies? Professional organizations and committees and task forces within those organizations have taken primary responsibility for establishing specific assessment competencies. Groups within both ACA and APA have independently and collaboratively put forth substantive guidelines pertaining to one specific assessment method: testing. The Association for Assessment in Counseling produced *Responsibilities of Users of Standardized Test,* the "RUST document" (AAC, 2003), and it is similar in scope and content to the guidelines multi-disciplinary groups have put forth. Furthermore, regulatory bodies (state licensing boards) may or may not include certain assessment practices, such as diagnosing, within a profession's scope of practice. A scope of practice describes the parameters of what a professional is legally able to do. The ethical and responsible use of tests and other assessment methods will be discussed more fully in the following chapter.

These guidelines and regulations recognize there are multiple ways in which an individual may use a test: administration, scoring, interpretation, construction and development, and conducting research. In general, a competent test user understands why a particular instrument is being selected and for what purpose. An attitude of objective inquiry is a noteworthy aspirational goal but assessors, being human, may unwittingly go about the process of making inferences from assessment results in a biased fashion. An awareness of one's biases and how they can affect the assessment process can be considered another kind of competency.

Clinical Judgment and Decision Making

The end product of any assessment is some kind of decision. The assessor may need to decide whether or not, on the basis of all the information gathered, to classify an individual; recommend a course of treatment; or conceptualize the presenting problems from a particular perspective. Integrating all the relevant information in order to come up with a working hypothesis about a client is a very complex task. Not only is this task complicated, but it is prone to human error. When it comes to decision making, a task that involves forming judgments or inferences, human beings often are unwittingly biased. We tend to demonstrate particular kinds of cognitive biases when we are asked to make inferences or form conclusions about others. Many studies, from the fields of behavioral economics to social psychology, have identified these biases or cognitive shortcomings of the mind's inferential processes (Buonomano, 2010; Nisbett & Ross, 1980), and the neuroscientific explanations for them are now better understood (Buonomano). Helping professionals, despite their training, cannot escape their basic humanness and are equally likely to unwittingly arrive at judgments and conclusions in a biased fashion (Dawes, 1994; Garb, Lilienfeld, & Fowler, 2008). All of us rely on cognitive maps or shortcuts to reduce large amounts of complex stimuli and information to a more manageable and understandable degree. These mental maps are necessary in order to make sense of the world around us, especially our interpersonal one, but their use can lead to errors in judgment about situations and people we are observing and evaluating.

Given that human beings can be biased and error prone in making decisions and arriving at conclusions, is the assessment process inherently flawed? In a general sense, that is not the case. More specifically, however, when clinicians use certain types of methods for the purpose of diagnosing psychopathology or making predictions about future behavior, the validity of their judgments is suspect according to a number of research studies. For example, research has shown that clinicians don't typically adhere to diagnostic criteria when making diagnoses from unstructured interviews or make inferences about psychopathology based on certain personality test scores that are not empirically supported (Dawes, 1994; Garb et al., 2008). The concept of assessor bias and guidelines for minimizing it is taken up in greater detail in Chapter 5.

A willingness to continuously self-reflect in order to identify personal biases that may affect the assessment process is a necessary professional attitude to maintain. For example, is there a particular group of people for whom I tend to overlook psychopathology when it exists? Conversely, do I have an inclination to see deviance in certain individuals or groups when the behavior in question is normal? Raising these questions and developing an understanding of what contributes to those potential biases is part of what makes for a multiculturally competent professional.

Finally, an attitude of valuing transparency and collaboration is helpful. What does this mean? A transparent assessor explains his or her thinking to clients. As much as possible, the assessor can share with the client the rationale for exploring an interview topic, administering a questionnaire, or making a referral for testing. Furthermore, as alluded to earlier, when a client has been referred by someone else for an assessment, the assessor's understanding of that referral question and the assessment methods is discussed with the client. This is also necessary from an ethical perspective. This is the concept of informed consent: providing an individual with sufficient information about the procedures to be used and the benefits and risks, in order for that person to make an educated and voluntary decision to proceed. Having said that, there are times in forensic settings where an assessment is involuntary; nevertheless, the individual can be told ahead of time what will take place. Collaboration involves checking in with clients about methods to be used and feedback given to them. For example, a collaborative helper may ask, How does that sound to you? What do you think about that? Does what I've said make sense to you? How do you feel about that recommendation?

Understanding of the theory underlying specific assessment methods, tests and measures' technical properties, the benefits and limitations of a given procedure, and the concept of decision-making bias is a necessary but not sufficient knowledge set for competent assessment practice. Assessment methods do not spring up in a vacuum, and having an understanding of how, when, and where these procedures evolved is another critical part of using them in a knowledgeable and professional manner.

EVOLUTION OF ASSESSMENT: ACROSS CONTINENTS AND TIME

The act of assessing—gathering, synthesizing, and analyzing information to make a decision—is part of our nature. It is in our DNA so to speak, and it has enabled us to survive and evolve over tens of thousands of years. The very first humans needed to determine whether a newly discovered berry was edible or poisonous; the person arriving at the cave a friend or foe; and which rocks could be converted to tools. Any discussion of the evolution of formal assessment practices needs, however, to be cursory in a text like this. An initial understanding of current professional assessment practices can be gained from a review of some of the nodal events and key figures that shaped and influenced this discipline. Furthermore, assessment, like other aspects of counseling, does not develop in research labs divorced from social and political contexts. Many of the societal concerns and controversies that have surrounded assessment and testing practices over the past 50 years, particularly in the United States, appear very similar to the ones voiced in different cultures over two millennia.

Ancient Practices

Formal methods for measuring human abilities and aptitudes date back to ancient Greek and Chinese civilizations (Bowman, 1989; Dubois, 1970). The Chinese used tests of both mental and physical abilities to identify men who, on the basis of their score, were expected to perform well in various civil service roles. Most likely it was during the period 200–100 BCE that Chinese society instituted written examinations for a similar purpose of selecting males for governmental positions. These tests focused on a range of abilities, including literacy, verbal cleverness, writing, and other subjects (Bowman). Men who succeeded on these exams gained not only titles but more power within the society's civil services. Interestingly, some of the same controversies and debates associated with current intelligence and other psychological tests—the effect of class on test performance, the social opportunities afforded by testing, examiner bias, and whether or not memory should be considered an aspect of mental ability—came about in Ancient China (Bowman). During the Middle Ages, different types of mental tests were suggested for other purposes such as assessing individuals' ability to study in a university, and European universities institutionalized the practice of using exams for granting degrees (Dubois).

Early Pioneers and Sensory Tests

The roots of current assessment procedures can be traced back to developments that were occurring in the 19th century in the fields of medicine, education, experimental psychology, and biology. As has often been the case in the history of assessment, individuals representing related but distinct disciplines influenced the development of specific assessment instruments, and those instruments have been used by professionals representing the applied branches of those fields. In the middle of the century, two French physicians, Esquirol and Seguin, developed procedures for classifying and training individuals deemed mentally retarded. Their work grew out of a societal need at the time to differentiate mental retardation from insanity. Although each physician had a different approach to understanding mental retardation—Esquirol focused on the use of language and Seguin experimented with sensory and muscle training techniques—their respective contributions foreshadowed current tests of intellectual and cognitive abilities (Anastasi & Urbina, 1997).

MEASURING INDIVIDUAL DIFFERENCES   Toward the end of the 19th century an experimental psychology laboratory was flourishing in Leipzig Germany under the direction of Wilhelm Wundt. He and his students designed experiments where abilities such as reaction time and sensitivity to various sensory stimuli were measured. Although Wundt and his colleagues were less interested in assessing individual differences and more concerned with general principles of human behavior, they recognized the importance of standardization procedures, which became a defining element, as noted earlier of tests and measures (Anastasi & Urbina, 1997). One of Wundt's doctoral students was James M. Cattell, who brought the study of individual differences to the United States—much to the chagrin of his advisor. Cattell is credited with being the first to use the term "mental test" in a professional journal (Anastasi & Urbina, p. 36). He believed that intelligence could best be measured with simple cognitive tasks such as reaction time and sensory discrimination. Cattell's perspective was influenced by an English physician and scholar named Sir Francis Galton. Galton was considered one of the founders of the scientific study of individual differences and was particularly interested in questions regarding the heritability of human traits (DuBois, 1970). He developed a series of tests for measuring physical and mental traits such as weight discrimination, breathing capacity, and memory. His most important contribution to the emerging field of psychological measurement was recognizing the need for a method of showing the relationship between two variables (DuBois). Galton went on to provide substantial financial support to Karl Pearson, who developed the correlation statistic that is used to quantify the relationship between two variables, which is the psychometric foundation of the concepts of reliability and validity (see Chapter 7).

BIRTH OF INTELLIGENCE TESTING   Another Frenchman, Alfred Binet, an experimental psychologist, broadened the focus of his physician compatriots to the testing and teaching of children with mental retardation. His early professional career, however, was not devoted to the assessment of children but rather on hypnosis and the use of magnets to alter perceptions, hallucinations and emotions (Matarazzo, 1972). After this work was discredited by his professional colleagues, Binet turned his attention to studying the mental processes and development of children. His interest in children with mental retardation came about, in part, from his appointment by the French Minister of Public Instruction to find ways to educate these children. After a number of aborted attempts to devise a system for assessing intelligence, which included handwriting analysis, Binet and his colleague Théodore Simon produced the first mental ability test in 1905. The Binet-Simon scale contained 30 problems or subtests that included sensory and perceptual tasks that were arranged in order of difficulty (Matarazzo, 1972). Binet and Simon challenged this earlier perspective that viewed sensory perception and discrimination abilities as the markers of intelligence, and proposed that verbal reasoning and comprehension skills were more important determinants of one's intelligence. In addition to sensory tasks such as "recognizing the difference between a square of chocolate and a square of wood," their tests involved "defining common words by function," "telling how two common objects are alike," and "defining abstract terms" (Matarazzo, 1972, pp. 38–39). By broadening the definition of intelligence, they spawned a scholarly debate over the nature of it and how best to measure it, a debate that is still being waged (McGrew, 2009).

　　Binet and Simon considered their scale to be a work in progress and it did not have an objective scoring system. Despite that limitation, the test underwent two subsequent revisions—the second being substantive and the next one mostly superficial. A major change to the second edition was the establishment of age-level scores and a more objective method for deriving them. These scores were based on the performance of a group of children ages 3 to 13 (Matarazzo, 1972). This was probably the first known use of a normative group from which future test takers' performance would be compared. Along with a standardized process for administration and scoring, the use of a normative group is an essential element of all psychological tests.

　　Across the Atlantic, Lewis Terman, a Stanford University psychologist, developed a revision of the original Binet-Simon Scale. This test became known as the Stanford-Binet, which is now in its fifth edition (see Chapter 13). Terman's contributions to the field of intelligence testing included the intelligence quotient, or IQ score (the ratio between mental and chronological age), and the importance of a larger, more representative standardization group.

In addition to being scholars and theoreticians, Binet and Simon were practitioners who were sensitive to the social uses and potential abuses of a test designed to measure intelligence. Binet in particular recognized that psychological assessments should be used to aid a client or individual in making a decision and that professional guidelines and safeguards governing the use of assessment procedures need to be in place in order to protect the rights of individuals (Matarazzo, 1972). Although he was not alone in recognizing that the onus for responsible assessment practices lies both with the test user and the larger professional societies, it wasn't until decades later that professional guidelines for the responsible and ethical use of assessment procedures were formally established. A multidisciplinary committee representing the American Educational Research Association, the American Psychological Association, and the National Council on Measurement in Education published in 1966, and revised in 1974, *Standards for Educational and Psychological Tests and Manuals* (APA, AERA, & NCME, 1974). An impetus for revising the 1966 *Standards* was a realization that members of minority groups—Spanish-speaking children and Black job applicants—were being adversely impacted by the misuse of existing tests. Rather than acquiescing to a position that favored a moratorium on testing, the joint committee thought it made more sense to develop standards for the process of constructing and using assessment procedures, since unfairness is not inherent in the procedures but is a function of their misuse (APA, AERA, & NCME).

Developments in the 20th Century

At the outset of World War I, the United States was interested in having a way to identify the mental fitness of soldiers. The American Psychological Association formed committees to help in this effort, and the president of the association, Robert Yerkes, appointed himself chair of one committee to devise a system that could quickly classify and select large numbers of military recruits (Geisinger, 2000). This committee, which included Terman and Arthur Otis, who had already created a group intelligence test, developed the Army Alpha and Army Beta tests. The latter version was intended for foreign-born recruits who didn't speak English and Americans who were illiterate. The tests helped the military make placement decisions and, as a result, the practice of legitimately screening large numbers of individuals by a single test in one setting had been established. The practice of screening millions of potential college and graduate school students with tests like the SAT, ACT, and GRE and employers' use of personality and other types of tests to assess job applicants can be traced back to the U.S. Army's Alpha and Beta tests.

During World War I there was also a need to evaluate the psychological fitness of recruits. Robert Woodworth developed a self-report questionnaire that contained items focused on psychiatric symptoms such as fears and phobias. The individual filling it out would respond either yes or no and it was hoped that this would be a tool for screening out "disturbed" men from military service. The questionnaire was not ready, however, until the war ended, but it became the prototype for later tests of personality traits, vocational interests, and emotional adjustment even though it lacked basic psychometric properties.

The war marked a transition point in the evolution of assessment in the United States. The initial focus on screening mental and cognitive abilities had shifted to measuring psychological adjustment, psychiatric symptoms, and vocational interests for a wide range of purposes. Over the next 25 years, tests for diagnosing psychopathology, describing personality traits, and identifying vocational and career interests were developed. This included the posthumous publication of Herman Rorschach's *Psychodiagnostics* in 1932, which described his experiments involving the "interpretation of accidental forms" (Rorschach, 1932/1975, p. 15), or what became known as the inkblot test; the *Strong Vocational Interest Blank* in 1927 and the *Minnesota Multiphasic Inventory* in 1943.

Rorschach, a Swiss psychiatrist, originally conceived of his test as a research and theory building tool to better understand the nature of mental processes and personality. His experiments with 10 symmetrical inkblot cards, some monochromatic and some colored, led him to see its usefulness as a diagnostic tool. The inkblot test was considered a kind of psychological x-ray in which unconscious perceptions, attitudes, and emotions could be revealed through an association task—that is, the percepts the inkblot images are connected to. In addition, Rorschach believed his test was also a method for assessing intelligence and personality types based on Carl Jung's typology.

His was not, however, the first association test designed to uncover unconscious processes. Emil Kraepelin, a German physician who coined the term *dementia praecox* (dementia of the young), or what we now call schizophrenia (Walker, Bollini, Hochman, Kestler, & Mittal, 2008), developed a word-association test in 1892 (Anastasi & Urbina, 1997). In that test, patients were presented with a word, rather than a visual image, and asked to report whatever additional words came to mind. Having a test, such as the Rorschach, that could help differentiate between normal individuals and those with schizophrenia, manic-depressive illness, neurosis, and organic brain disease (the major conditions medicine was concerned with then) met an important clinical and social need. Psychoanalysis had become accepted as a treatment for neurosis, but individuals with other disorders were typically institutionalized, and a powerful clinical tool could help pave the way for less costly and more humane forms of treatment.

The developers of the MMPI, Starke Hathaway, a psychologist, and J. Charnley McKinley, a neuropsychiatrist, had a less ambitious but very practical goal: to develop an empirically based personality assessment instrument that could "aid in the routine psychiatric case work-up of adult patients and as a method for determining the severity of the conditions" (Dahlstrom, Welsh, & Dahlstrom, 1972, p. 4). It was also hoped that the test could serve as an objective measure of psychotherapy progress. Hathaway and McKinley wanted an instrument that would be an improvement over the existing personality inventories, of which there were only a few (e.g., the Woodworth Personal Data Sheet), which they considered to be too transparent and unreliable. Although the MMPI (now in its third revision) was originally designed to assess psychiatric conditions and psychological traits based on late 19th and early 20th century conceptualizations, it has been used for a number of other purposes in multiple contexts over the past 70 years, including employment, medical, and forensic.

Current Practice: Trends and Technological Advances

From those auspicious beginnings, the number of tests mushroomed to the present situation where there are several thousand that are used for a variety of purposes. The sheer volume of tests and measures can be staggering to both novice and seasoned clinicians. Many of the current psychological tests are in their second, third, or even fourth editions. In fact, some of the tests you will read about may already have been replaced by a newer version. Once a test is published, the developers of it undertake the process of considering what changes may need to be made to correct possible flaws. Why are the tests continually revised? One reason is the need to correct limitations in the test that subsequent research has identified, and another is the need to improve and expand the use of it (Ranson, Nichols, Rouse, & Harrington, 2009). Ranson et al., describe three kinds of problems that drive the revision process, according to the assessment literature. The first is a realization that items on the test have become outdated because they have little if any relevance to the current generation of test takers, or cultural trends have altered the meaning of a word and therefore the item. An example of that might be, "I enjoy going to parties that are lively and gay," an item that was on the original Minnesota Multiphasic Personality Inventory (MMPI). The MMPI was developed in the 1930s and revised in 1989, and by then the meaning of the word "gay" had changed considerably. Another problem that prompts test revision is when a normative sample that was once useful is no longer valid for the purposes in which the test is being used. A test that was normed with a psychiatric population, for example, might be used later in organizational and employment settings and therefore a more representative normative sample is desired. Finally, in this era of the Internet, test items are easily accessible and once that happens, the administration of the test is altered. That is, those who have gained familiarity with the test items via the Internet take the test from a different vantage point than those who do not, and consequently scores on the test for the former group may, in part, reflect previous knowledge of the test items. Furthermore, tests may be revised because theory and statistical analyses may suggest that the concept the test items were designed to measure has changed, or the items on a scale within the test measure a concept that is somewhat different than what the scale was designed to measure. This was the case, for example, with the latest revisions to the Wechsler Intelligence Scales. The concept of working memory had not been assessed with prior editions of the test, but research indicated that it was an important but neglected aspect of cognitive ability that ought to be included in the next version. When tests are revised, the users of them have an ethical and professional obligation to use the most current version (AERA, et al., 1999).

An important theme that emerges from this history is that the construction and revision of assessment tools is a circular process that reflects social needs and values as well as ongoing research, as Figure 1.2 illustrates. Initially, societal needs and values along with theoretical and research development coalesce to produce an assessment instrument. The instrument is then applied in a context for which it was intended. Once the application process begins, so does the need for revision. This revision can have a subsequent impact on social values and theory underlying the concept the instrument is measuring. And the cycle continues. A more recent example of this taken from the counseling and psychology fields is the development and revision of the *NEO Personality Inventory* (NEO-PI) and its proposed application to DSM-5 personality disorders. Personality disorders have been problematic from both a social and clinical perspective. Those who are diagnosed with those disorders tend to require greater and therefore costlier treatment, including hospital care, are more likely to become involved in the legal system, and in

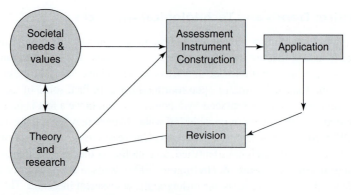

FIGURE 1.2   Assessment Instrument Construction and Revision Process

some cases can pose a greater harm to self and others. Therefore, society has a vested interest in the proper assessment and treatment of personality disorders. Clinically, however, psychometric study of "normal" personality traits has been completely split off from research into personality disorders as they have been conceptualized in the DSM and elsewhere. The dimensional approach to personality traits embodied in an instrument like the NEO-PI (revised) is being field tested for the DSM-5 revision process and represents, for the first time, the application of personality trait theory and tests to psychiatric disorders.

A related theme is one of assessment instruments providing both benefits and negative consequences to individuals and groups. Like any other tool, when handled properly they can be put to constructive uses but when mishandled the recipient is likely to suffer. As assessment procedures have advanced, individuals have benefited from them because their use can level the playing field with respect to job and education admissions. No longer is obtaining a job or school acceptance based solely on factors such as social status, income, or group membership. Assessment procedures, especially tests, help identify, based on abilities and other traits, which individuals are more likely to succeed and/or fit with the demands of the role, and therefore brings a greater degree of objectivity to the selection process. Similarly, assessment can help identify, in a neutral fashion, who is in need of treatment and can fit the treatment approach to the needs and concerns of the client. Conversely, when misused, these very same procedures can have profound negative consequence, from invasion of privacy to infringement of civil liberties and freedoms; from denial of appropriate services to stigmas associated with certain labels. An example is the use of an assessment method for which it was not designed, as has happened with the practice of using the Rorschach and human figure drawings for the purpose of detecting child sexual abuse. If a clinician concludes that a child was sexually abused, on the basis of those test results, and that conclusion is an erroneous one, the consequences for the alleged victim and abuser can be very detrimental in terms of stigma and curtailment of civil liberties. A large-scale review of studies addressed the validity of these two projective approaches for detecting child sexual abuse and concluded there was little support for using them for that specific purpose. The study's conclusion consequently recommended that clinicians should refrain from using them in that context (Lilienfeld, Wood, & Garb, 2000).

Finally, the same kinds of technological advances that have impacted all of us have shaped assessment practices as well. Computer technology has affected all the various stakeholders: test developers, users and consumers, researchers, clinicians, governmental agencies, and insurers. The Internet, in particular, has enabled a more democratic assessment process. A number of brief tests and questionnaires can be found easily through search engines such as Google, and an individual can complete them and get immediate feedback. For example, by entering "personality questionnaires" in Google, the first page alone revealed seven separate sites at which anyone could take some kind of personality test or questionnaire. Depending on the site, that feedback may come with a cautionary note about the feedback, but usually not a way to judge the science behind it. At least one large national health insurance company expects that clients will complete a brief symptom and functionality questionnaire either prior to or after an initial mental health visit, and then the clinician is expected to fax the questionnaire to the insurer. In addition, many assessment instruments, including cognitive ability and achievement tests, personality and psychopathology questionnaires and inventories, and structured interviews, can be scored by a software program, and interpretative reports can be generated. It is incumbent upon the assessing clinician to integrate computer-generated interpretations with other information gathered about the client, acknowledging that those reports are based on a prototypical case, not the assessed individual.

Summary and Conclusions

Assessment is a multifaceted process that involves gathering information from various sources in order to make an inference about a person or a decision. For example, a clinician might infer on the basis of assessment data that a client has major depression; a school counselor might decide that a student would benefit more from a social skills group than from traditional individual play therapy; or a human resource director might conclude that candidate A is a better match for the job than candidates B, C, and D. Counselors and other helping professionals reach conclusions and make decisions on the basis of both informal and formal methods. These methods include observing, interviewing, testing, measuring, and reviewing.

Historically, testing has been equated with assessment, but the chapter emphasized that it is just one of several assessment procedures, each with its set of advantages and limitations. The choice of a particular procedure or combination of them is guided by an understanding of the reasons why assessment takes place. These include inferring a person's diagnosis, conceptualizing how current problems and client history are related, quantifying and describing traits and abilities, screening at-risk individuals and groups, selecting an appropriate course of action, monitoring the effectiveness of a treatment, and intervening. Conceptually, intervention and assessment go hand in hand; they are complementary, interrelated processes whereby each one informs the other.

The act of gathering and integrating information about people and situations is a long-standing human activity of daily life. This basic human task, even when enhanced through training, can be undercut by certain kinds of unconscious, inferential biases. Consequently, an important aspect of professional development is engaging in self-reflection in order to understand how one's unique biases as well as those shared by others can impact the assessment process. This is the case regardless of the type of assessment procedure being used. An understanding of one's biases is not, however, adequate preparation for using assessments tools competently. Professional associations have devised sets of knowledge, skills, and attitudes that counselors and helpers need to possess in order to assess in an effective and ethically sound manner.

As assessment tools have evolved and the focus of the problems the tools were designed to solve has shifted, it has become clear that they are works in progress. Those tools are just as much a reflection of societal needs and values as they are theoretical developments and research endeavors. In the hands of a knowledgeable and well-trained helper, these tools can provide important benefits: enhancing understanding of self and others, promoting psychological and behavioral change, identifying appropriate treatments or educational plans, and matching individuals to organizations. Like any other tool, harm can result when misused, and this can include curtailment of civil liberties, stigmatization, or denial of needed services.

Reflections Questions and Experiential Exercises

1. What are the seven reasons for conducting an assessment?
2. Which kinds of formal assessments have you received? What was that experience like for you?
3. What are the two broad approaches to assessment?
4. What are the four main categories of assessment methods?
5. What makes a method standardized?
6. Knowing what you know about yourself, which aspects of an assessment might you feel comfortable with and which parts might challenge you?
7. Over the course of the next week, pay attention to when and how you make assessments, evaluations, or judgments in your daily life. What information did you use to reach your conclusion and how was your assessment process affected by your mood?

2

ETHICAL AND LEGAL CONSIDERATIONS: PREPARING FOR THE ASSESSMENT

Chapter Objectives

After reading this chapter, you should be able to:

■ Understand the relevant sections of the various professional codes of ethics pertaining to assessment practices.

■ Identify ethical issues that are commonly encountered during assessment.

■ Explain how the concepts of informed consent, competency, and confidentiality apply to the assessment process.

■ Explain what is meant by a *qualified test user*.

■ Identify the pertinent ethical and multicultural issues related to selecting and interpreting tests.

It is 8:30 Monday morning and Melanie is headed out of her office to meet a new client, Brian, for an intake interview. In addition to thinking about what Brian will be like—easy or hard to engage, open and forthcoming or guarded, and his readiness for change—Melanie is making sure she has the forms she needs to write up her assessment and she is reviewing in her mind what she needs to tell Brian about the assessment process, the limits of confidentiality, and the phone-screening information she has in hand. Melanie is also considering having Brian complete the SCL-90-R (see Chapter 9), which would help her get a handle on Brian's problems and diagnosis as well as establish a baseline measure of his symptoms in order to gauge his progress during counseling. She is thinking that the SCL-90-R is one of several questionnaires that could be helpful to her in understanding Brian but she is unsure if she is qualified to use it. The mental health clinic where she works has recently started using a number of questionnaires with clients and the clinical director has strongly encouraged all of the clinicians to routinely use two questionnaires as part of the intake process. But Melanie is still unclear which ones she can use and which ones she cannot. She decides to hold off on giving the SCL-90-R to Brian until she has completed the intake interview and has had a chance to discuss further assessment options with her supervisor.

OVERVIEW

Practical and ethical considerations shape the assessment process, as is the case with all counseling endeavors. Melanie is faced with all sorts of pragmatic issues: everything from how much time to allot for the assessment to how she will balance note-taking and listening; whether or not she should review prior records, if they exist, before meeting Brian, and what she will say to him about the assessment process. The question of how Melanie will go about informing Brian about the assessment process is as much an ethical question as it is a clinical and practical one. She is also faced with two additional important questions. First, "Of the many assessment tools available, which ones am I qualified to use?" Second, "How will I go about ethically using an instrument for which I *am* qualified to administer?" The answers to questions regarding informing clients about the assessment process and who is qualified to use tests are guided by professional codes of ethics and standards.

Codes of ethics are created and promulgated by professional associations: the American Counseling Association (ACA), American Mental Health Counselors Association (AMHCA), American Psychological Association (APA), American School Counselor Association (ASCA), National Association for Social Work (NASW), and others. In fact, according to Ken Pope's website (***www.kspope.com***), one of the leading authoritative resources on professional ethics, there are over 100 professional associations worldwide that have established codes of ethics and standards of practice for counseling, assessment, and forensic evaluations. Ethical codes are based on general moral principles—autonomy, beneficence and nonmalfeasance, integrity, respect for human dignity, and social justice—and contain specific sections regarding counseling and assessment practices that provide descriptions and guidelines as to what constitutes ethical behavior. They are periodically revised reflecting changes in practice standards, professional and community norms, legal decisions, technological changes, and ethical dilemmas encountered by practitioners (e.g., dual relationships in rural settings [Corey, Corey, & Callanan, 2007]). There are important similarities and differences among the professions' codes, particularly with respect to assessment. One similarity, for example, is that the ACA, AMHCA, APA, and ASCA ethical codes devote an entire section to assessment. An example of an important difference is the content and language of the various codes regarding making diagnoses. Although laws influence certain aspects of the codes, they are not legal documents, nor are they the product of state licensing bodies. In essence, the codes are meant to guide, not prescribe, professional behavior for the protection of the clients. The codes serve a secondary purpose of improving professional practice standards (Corey et al.). Students and trainees are often disappointed in discovering that ethical codes, despite being shaped by important core values such as respect for human dignity and welfare (ACA, 2005; AMHCA, 2010; APA, 2002; ASCA, 2010; NASW, 1999) have a lot of ambiguity and often don't answer the question "What should I do in this situation?"

Surveys of practitioners representing various disciplines have found that ethical questions and dilemmas related to assessment occur fairly regularly. One of the first surveys to systemically address this issue with a group of psychologists found ethical dilemmas related to assessment were the sixth-most-frequent category, tied with sexual concerns, colleague conduct, and research, from a list of 23 "ethically troubling incidents" categories (Pope & Vetter, 1992). Other categories of concern in order of frequency of occurrence included confidentiality, dual relationships, payment issues, teaching and training concerns, and forensic. Typical assessment concerns the Pope and Vetter survey identified were 1) the use of tests by those lacking proper qualifications and 2) drawing improper inferences from assessment data. More recent surveys of school psychologists and multicultural counselors (Dailor & Jacob, 2011; Sadeghi, Fischer, & House, 2003) have produced similar findings: ethical dilemmas related to assessment issues are quite common and they can be challenging to resolve. Furthermore, in this national sample of school psychologists, over one-third reported witnessing in themselves or others, assessment practices that directly violated ethical standards (Dailor & Jacob). The types of violations were similar to the concerns identified in the Pope and Vetter survey as well as other behaviors such as testing a client in a nonprivate setting such as a library or hallway. Collectively, these surveys indicate that ethical problems are not abstract concerns divorced from the day-to-day practice of professional assessments; they are realities that trainees and practitioners will encounter.

Students and professionals need grounding in the ethical standards in order to be equipped to deal with ethical dilemmas or potential violations as they arise.

In addition to the codes of ethics of the professional organizations, other resources also guide ethical practice and decision making in the assessment process, particularly when standardized tests are used. Keep in mind, as was discussed in Chapter 1, that assessment is the overall process whereby different methods are used to integrate data about an individual or system, and testing is just one of the methods used in that process. Three separate committees, which became known as the Joint Committee on Testing Practices (JCTP), representing the American Educational Research Association (AERA), APA, and the National Council on Measurement in Education (NCME) published a set of standards for all participants in the testing process to have criteria by which tests and testing practices can be evaluated (AERA, APA, & NCME, 1999). Their most recent publication, *Standards for Educational and Psychological Testing*, completed in 1999, built upon work that was initially begun by a committee of APA in 1954 and three subsequent revisions by APA, AERA, and NCME over the ensuing decades. The JCTP also produced *The Rights and Responsibilities of Test Takers: Guidelines and Expectations* (1999) and *Code of Fair Testing Practices in Education* (2004); both are available free at ***http://www.apa.org/science/ programs/testing/committee.aspx*** and are intended for lay and professional audiences.

This chapter will focus on the sections of the codes of ethics from ACA, AMHCA, APA, ASCA, and NASW that pertain to the assessment process and upon which clinicians, students, and trainees draw when making decisions about assessment practices such as whether to administer a test or what assessment information can be shared with other professionals. The purpose of this chapter is to familiarize students, trainees, and clinicians with those relevant sections of the different ethical codes and discuss the professional and ethical issues that arise when helping professionals are engaged in assessment practices. The relevant sections of the various codes of ethics that will be discussed include **Informed Consent in Assessment, Competence to Use and Interpret Assessment Instruments, Instrument Selection and Interpretation,** and **Confidentiality and Test Security**. Integral to the concepts of professional competency and instrument selection and interpretation is the question about who is qualified to administer and interpret psychological tests. A solid understanding of these ethical concepts and standards will shape your behavior with clients as well as influence the values you hold regarding the assessment practice. It will also help prepare you to deal with ethical concerns as they arise in work settings.

ETHICAL CONSIDERATIONS

Informed Consent in Assessment

Informed consent was originally, and still is, a legal concept, but it has become an ethical value as well. Within professional codes of ethics, informed consent sections are based on moral principles regarding client autonomy, rights, and dignity. Simply put, informed consent means that clients have a right to certain information upon which they can then make educated decisions about the benefits and risks of the services they will receive. Therefore, in order to make informed decisions, relative to the assessment process, the client needs the information prior to the process beginning, and needs to have the capacity to make that decision. Capacity is one element of the legal concept and involves being able to understand the information presented and make rational or sound decisions based on the information given (Corey et al., 2007). Those who are deemed legally and ethically able to make informed decisions regarding health care, in general, and assessment services, in particular, are adults of "sound mind." Minors are typically viewed as not being capable of giving consent in mental health settings. Which health and mental health services minors can legally consent to are typically decided by each state and in some states, Virginia for example, a minor can consent to psychotherapy (Koocher & Keith-Spiegel, 1998). Occasionally, some adults are deemed to lack the capacity to consent to mental health services and may have a guardian appointed to them who, like minors, can consent to assessment and treatment services. Adults who are legally found to be incompetent and therefore lacking in capacity are often those with severe cognitive or intellectual limitations. Assessments that are conducted with minors in educational settings may not need parental or guardian consent depending upon the nature of the assessment and relevant state laws. Even when a client lacks the capacity to make decisions, the ACA, APA, and NASW codes of ethics stipulate that the professional still seek the clients' agreement and involve them in the decision-making process *as much as possible* (ACA, 2005; APA, 2002; NASW, 1999). A second element of the legal aspect of informed consent is that the client assents to receive services voluntarily (Corey et al., 2007). They are not pressured or coerced to make a decision about the services they may receive. There are some clients, however, for whom assessment is mandated by a court. In those cases there still remains an ethical obligation to inform the client of the process and the limits of confidentiality. This would involve explaining to the client what information will be released to the court or its representative and how that information will be shared (i.e., verbally, in writing, electronically, or some combination of methods).

There is common ground amongst the various codes of ethics with respect to the need to obtain informed consent from clients *prior* to the assessment process. The language used in the different codes reflects some important differences, however, in what type of information should be provided to clients before the assessment process unfolds. The APA Code of Ethics, Section 9.03: Assessment, makes a fairly general statement: "Psychologists obtain informed consent for assessments, evaluations, or diagnostic services" (APA, 2002, p. 1071). The ACA Code of Ethics has more explicit and stronger language, and the level of detail in the ACA code provides greater guidance to counselors than the APA code gives to psychologists (see Box 2.1).

Similarly, the AMHCA Code of Ethics states, in Section D: Assessment and Diagnosis, "Mental Health counselors provide the client with appropriate information regarding the reason for assessment, the approximate length of time required, and to whom the report will be distributed" (AMHCA, 2010, p. 11). The various codes also differ in whether informed consent needs to be provided in writing, only orally, or both. Some state laws and licensing board regulations

---

BOX 2.1
ACA Informed Consent

"Counselors explicitly explain to clients the nature of all services provided. They inform clients about issues such as but not limited to the following: the purposes, goals, techniques, procedures, limitations, potential risks, and benefits of services" (ACA, 2005, p. 4). The ACA code goes on to say:

Prior to Assessment, counselors explain the nature and purposes of assessment and the specific use of results by potential recipients. The explanation will be given in the language of the client (or other legally authorized person on behalf of the client), unless an explicit exception has been agreed upon in advance. (p. 12)

now require that clients receive written informed consent. In New Hampshire, for example, all licensed mental health professionals are required to post a "Mental Health Bill of Rights," which states that clients have a right to *documented* [italics added] informed consent (New Hampshire Board of Mental Health Practice, 2002). In addition to being the required thing to do, written informed consent may have a salutary effect. The limited research that has been done regarding written informed consent has found it has a beneficial impact on client's perceptions of the counselor (Miller & Evans, 2004).

INFORMED CONSENT AND DIAGNOSING   One purpose of an assessment is to provide a diagnostic opinion or judgment. Although most codes of ethics do not explicitly discuss the implications of a diagnosis for a client within the context of informed consent (the ACA Code of Ethics being an exception), it is prudent to inform clients when a diagnosis will be given and the potential consequences for the client. The ACA Code of Ethics, A.2.b states, " . . . Counselors take steps to ensure that clients understand the implications of diagnosis" (p. 4), and Section E.5 Diagnosis of Mental Disorder states, "Counselors may refrain from making and/or reporting a diagnosis if they believe it would cause harm to the client or others" (p. 12). Most initial assessments in mental health settings are conducted, in part, for the purpose of a diagnostic evaluation with the diagnosis being documented and released to insurance companies, the government, or other third parties. The recognition and acknowledgment of the potential harm to clients when diagnostic information is released to third parties was the basis for including a subsection, "Refraining from Diagnosis," in the revised 2005 ACA Code of Ethics (Kaplan et al., 2009). The following case illustrates one potential consequence of a client being diagnosed with a DSM disorder.

Jenny, a 29-year-old new mother, began experiencing depression symptoms following the birth of her daughter. Her lack of motivation and reoccurring suicidal thoughts posed a serious risk for Jenny and her baby. Jenny sought help at a local mental health clinic. Upon completion of the intake assessment she was diagnosed with a postpartum major depression. She was informed of her diagnosis but not the potential implications of the diagnosis. Jenny continued in treatment at the clinic with a combination of an antidepressant and therapy. Within three months she was symptom free and functioning well in her role as a mother. One year later Jenny applied for life insurance but was denied coverage because of her history of depression. Jenny, through a good deal of persistence and assertiveness, ultimately was able to get life insurance.

Although the ACA Code of Ethics does discuss informing clients about diagnoses and their potential consequences, it does not state specifically what steps should be taken with clients like Jenny and other clients to inform them of possible consequences. And to date, the other professional codes remain silent on this specific issue. Furthermore, a clinician is not going to know until after the assessment process has been completed, which can take several meetings, whether the client has a serious disorder for which the diagnosis could have negative implications. Nevertheless, a clinician might consider a sequence of discussions around the potential impact of receiving a diagnosis.

Once a diagnostic evaluation has been completed and a diagnosis given, several steps can be taken so that the clinician acts in accordance with ethical guidelines. First, the clinician can inform the client of the diagnosis, what it is and the treatment options, counseling, medication, self-help strategies, and so on. A discussion of those options with their respective advantages and limitations can follow. Second, a discussion of who will have access to that diagnosis, for example, third-party payers, and the potential consequences of that diagnostic information being released can take place. Third, the clinician and client could explore and collaboratively strategize about

> ## PRACTICE SUGGESTION
> ### Providing Informed Consent
>
>
>
> *"This initial assessment is for the purpose of determining whether you or a member of your family is in need of and would benefit from counseling or further assessment services. I am going to ask you a series of questions and have you fill out a brief questionnaire [procedure] so that I can gather as much information as possible about your problems, history, and background in order to figure out how I or someone else here at the clinic can be of help to you [purpose]. We will meet for about one hour and I will be taking notes as we talk. Also information about your presenting problems, including a diagnosis, will be sent to _____ (your insurance company or other third-party payer). You should be aware that in some cases a mental health diagnosis can affect you in the future. In addition to difficulty obtaining certain kinds of insurance, some diagnoses can affect employment with certain occupations. Do you have any questions about what will happen or about my training or experience before we begin?"*

potential steps to take, such as the client contacting an insurance company or employer to find out what would be the impact of having a psychiatric diagnosis. Alternatively, they could explore not releasing the diagnostic information and using alternative pay sources such as the client paying the fee. By engaging in this discussion, the clinician is acting in the spirit of the informed consent standard. Having said that, the vast majority of clients in mental health settings are generally not concerned with the potential short- and long-term consequences of receiving a psychiatric diagnosis but are more focused on telling their stories and getting help. In many cases, the Practice Suggestion: Providing Informed Consent will be an adequate way to provide informed consent in the case of a specific issue of an assessment culminating in a diagnosis.

The process of providing information to clients so that they can make educated decisions about the assessment process is a balancing act. Clients need enough information to understand the process and its benefits and potential risks while at the same time not be overwhelmed with so much information that they perceive the assessment as being too risky, and opt out. They also need to have the process explained, including tests that may be used, in language they can understand, free of professional jargon. How can a clinician frame an assessment and act in accordance with the relevant codes of ethics as well as any applicable state laws? One way is to have succinct written and verbal statements that cover the assessment process: purpose, task or procedures, length of time, and client questions.

INFORMED CONSENT AND TESTING   The language in the Practice Suggestion could be modified and presented in client-friendly language when assessments involve the use of specific tests such as intelligence or personality. For example, Joshua, an 8-year-old boy, is about to undergo intellectual ability testing (see Chapter 13). The evaluator explains to him prior to administering any tests:

"For the next hour and a half I am going to ask you questions, and other times you won't need to talk, just do things with your hands and a pencil. Some of the questions may be like things you have been asked in school and others will be different. We are doing this so that I can understand better how you learn things and what is easy and hard for you so I can help your parents and teacher to help you better in school. Do you have any questions?"

A few sentences like that can orient the client to the testing process, alerting him or her to what is going to happen and provide an opportunity to raise any questions about the process. Again the idea is to explain in client-friendly language the purpose of the assessment and the tasks involved. Furthermore, when a client is provided with some basic information about the process ahead of time, he or she is more likely to have a vested interest in the assessment and cooperate with the clinician's approach than clients who have procedures sprung upon them.

When testing is being done as part of an assessment, then further information will need to be provided to the client and parent or guardian. Clients should be told as part of the informed consent process that they will be given feedback about the assessment and any tests they take. Knowing up front that feedback on the assessment and test results will be given is another piece of information that may help a client decide whether or not to go through with the process. The various ethics codes are consistent in asserting the right of clients to obtain feedback about an assessment and test results, unless the nature of the assessment (e.g., a forensic evaluation) precludes it. The ACA Code of Ethics Section E.1.b: Client Welfare states, for example, "They [counselors] respect the client's right to know the results, the interpretations made, and the bases for counselors' conclusions and recommendations" (ACA, 2005, p. 12). If an assessment or test report is going to be generated, then the client and guardians should know that and be given information on how the report will be used, and must provide their consent to have the report released. In order to consent to a release of test data, the clients need to understand precisely what information will be sent and what may be withheld (see Confidentiality and Test Security later in the chapter). The clients and/or their parents or guardians should understand that decisions made about the client—to create an individualized education plan or social security disability eligibility, for example—will be impacted by the clinician's report but are not the provinces of the tester.

As was discussed briefly in Chapter 1 and will be discussed at various points later on in this book, the process of providing assessment feedback to clients is not only an ethical requirement but has a number of therapeutic benefits. Research and clinical experience has shown that clients who are given assessment feedback experience validation, enhanced motivation to change, greater optimism and self-efficacy, and an accelerated rapport-building process (Allen, Montgomery, Tubman, Frazier, & Escovar, 2003).

Competence to Use and Interpret Assessment Instruments

TEST USER QUALIFICATIONS AND PRACTICES   Melanie, the counselor in the chapter case study, needs to make a decision about incorporating a test or standardized measure into her initial assessment of her client. Her inclusion of standardized measures into a comprehensive assessment process is guided by both an understanding of what can be accomplished by using them and the ethical and regulatory guidelines pertaining to the use of psychological tests. (The term *test* will be used in this section since that is the term ethical and regulatory guidelines use.) As you may recall from the previous chapter, a test can be defined as a standardized procedure for measuring a human characteristic—personality, intelligence, degree of psychopathology, and so on—by obtaining a sample of behavior designed to reflect the characteristic in question. Ethical and regulatory guidelines address who is qualified to use specifics tests, the development and potential bias of tests, and how test results are used. Who is qualified to use a specific test is a complicated question (see Figure 2.1) and the answer to which is unsettled.

Melanie, like any other test user, would need to consult the three sources identified in Figure 2.1 to determine if she is qualified to administer, score, and interpret the test she would like to include in her assessment. Having consulted those guidelines and statutes, she might

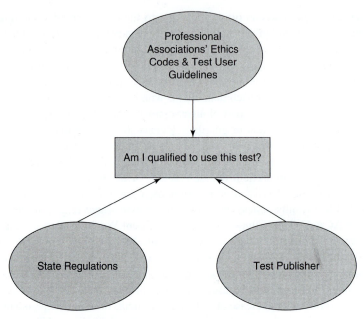

FIGURE 2.1   Organizations That Establish Test-User Qualifications

decide, for example, that she is qualified to administer, score, and interpret a rating scale designed to measure some aspect of psychopathology, such as depression, but not another construct, such as intelligence. Test-user qualification criteria are embedded in the broader ethical standard of competency.

COMPETENCY   The ACA, AMHCA, and APA codes of ethics have two sections relevant to test user qualifications, **competency** and **assessment**. Competency is an aspirational goal and value shared by the different professional disciplines. Counselors and psychologists "practice only within the boundaries of their competence, based on their education, training, consultation, professional and supervised experience" (ACA, 2005, p. 9; APA, 2002, p. 1063). Applying the spirit of competency to the practice of administering and interpreting tests and standardized measures is complicated because the requisite education, training, and supervised experience are not delineated in any of the professional ethics codes. The ACA Code of Ethics does additionally state in Section E: Evaluation, Assessment, and Interpretation, "Counselors utilize only those testing and assessment services for which they have been trained and are competent" (p. 12), but again neglects to provide guidance on what constitutes adequate training or a competency standard for using tests. In the ACA code subsection "Competence to Use and Interpret Assessment Instruments," what constitutes competency is discussed further, but again in a broad manner: "Counselors . . . have a thorough understanding of educational, psychological and career measurement, including validation criteria, assessment research, and guidelines for assessment development and use" (p. 12). The other codes of ethics—APA, AMHCA, ASCA, and NASW—use similarly broad and at times vague language regarding assessment competency. If the ethical codes of the respective professional organizations do not provide more explicit criteria about what constitutes a qualified test user, what about other places within the professional organizations?

The professions of psychology and counseling have made major strides toward creating assessment competency frameworks that can help practitioners, supervisors, and educators determine whether an individual is qualified to administer, score, and interpret standardized measures. During the past decade a task force of the APA (Turner, DeMers, Fox, & Reed, 2001), a conference group sponsored by a sister organization, National Council of Schools and Programs of Professional Psychology (NCSPP, 2007), and ACA (2003) produced documents with more specific assessment competency criteria. The APA task force recommended that test users acquire knowledge and skills in the following areas: psychometric principles and concepts including descriptive statistics, reliability, validity (see Chapters 6 and 7), and normative interpretation of test scores; ethical and legal issues pertaining to test usage and interpretation including the ability to explain test results to diverse audiences; the impact of cultural variables on test selection and interpretation; and the effects of disabilities on test administration and interpretation (Turner et al.).

In addition to that core knowledge base, a qualified or competent test user in a health care setting, including mental health, would have opportunities to develop and practice testing skills under the supervision of experienced professionals. Essentially these guidelines establish a minimum standard that test users should meet. NCSPP has put together a developmental competency model for the overall education and training of psychologists, and assessment is one of seven competencies identified. The model describes knowledge, skills, and attitudes a psychologist in training is expected to achieve at three stages: beginning practicum, beginning internship, and degree completion. This developmental model can be applied to counselors in training as well. Within the assessment competency are four domains, including psychological testing. These competencies (NCSPP, 2007 pp. 6–7) are as follows:

Assessment Competencies

Knowledge of constructs and theories underlying tests and testing methods:

- Basic psychometric concepts such as reliability and validity
- Strengths, weaknesses, and limits of applicability of standard intellectual and personality measures
- Methods of norming tests and implications for test usage with diverse populations

Skills include:

- Ability to identify appropriate measures and sources of information for the purposes: diagnosis, case conceptualization, treatment planning, or monitoring
- Ability to administer and score personality measures and to begin the process of integrated interpretation under supervision
- Ability to understand and convey results from individual tests
- Ability to identify and adapt assessment methods for unique individuals and systems, with supervision

Attitudes include:

- Respectful objectivity and inquiry when conducting an assessment
- Respect for the value of psychological testing and assessment
- Commitment to looking at the short-term and long-term usefulness of one's assessment work
- Willingness to develop competency in administration and interpretation of new or revised tests that can be incorporated into the assessment process

This set of knowledge, skills, and attitudes can be considered the requisite qualifications one needs to competently administer, score, and interpret standardized measures. Similarly, the International Test Commission (ITC) has published *Guidelines for Test Use* (ITC, 1999), a document outlining responsibilities and competencies of test users. The ITC guidelines are based on earlier efforts by multidisciplinary groups and publications such as the *Standards for Educational and Psychological Testing* (AERA, et al., 1999). These guidelines are designed to bring about a greater degree of uniformity in testing practices, particularly performance-based user competency criteria, and to identify who is granted access to specific tests. Like the NCSPP's competencies, ITC's specify the knowledge and skill sets a responsible test user ought to possess. In that sense they are not meant to be a new set of user criteria and guidelines, but an attempt to weave together common elements of existing standards from which local entities and practitioners can use for benchmark comparison purposes (ITC).

The practical application of assessment and test user competencies can be illustrated by the use of two very different tests—*Wechsler Intelligence Scale for Children*–4th Ed. (WISC-IV) and the *Beck Depression Inventory–II* (BDI-II). The most important knowledge set the test user would need to consider is the theoretical construct underlying the test. One would need a course in theories of intelligence to competently administer and interpret the WISC-IV. That theoretical framework would provide an understanding of the strengths and limitations of an intelligence test like the WISC-IV so that the user could be competent in interpreting IQ scores and appropriately conveying the meaning of those scores to clients, family members, and other relevant parties. On the other hand, a depression inventory, to be used competently, requires an understanding of different constructs—psychopathology in general, and depression in particular. Psychopathology courses are part of any master's program in counseling or psychology, whereas intelligence courses are more commonly found in doctoral level programs. Therefore, if the potential test user has not had coursework in the underlying construct of the test, then he or she would not be qualified to administer, score, and interpret it.

Beyond an understanding of the construct, the user may need specialized training in the administration of the test. The WISC-IV, like most intelligence tests, has administration procedures that vary for each part of the test, and those procedures require significant supervised practice in order to follow the established administration protocol. On the other hand, a depression inventory like the BDI-II, and most of the measures covered in this book, require no specialized training to administer and some are essentially client administered measures or what are referred to as self-report scales or inventories. Furthermore, the scoring of psychopathology measures like the BDI-II is straightforward and a simple clerical task. On the other hand, the scoring system for the WISC-IV and other intelligence tests is complicated and requires professional judgment for some items.

The remaining competencies described above (knowledge of psychometric and measurement concepts including norms, reliability, validity, and standard scores, and cultural factors and attitudes) would be applicable for the WISC-IV, the BDI-II, and any other standardized test or measure. Psychometric concepts are what differentiate formal, standardized measures from informal, nonstandardized ones. Therefore, in order to competently use any standardized assessment instrument, a clinician needs to have a solid understanding of psychometric and measurement concepts in order to judge the appropriateness and usefulness of a test for a specific client with a given set of presenting problems. Furthermore, the evaluation of a test's legitimacy for a specific client rests on an understanding of the limits to which test scores and interpretations apply to individuals who differ from the standardization or normative group on one or more significant factors.

The interpretation of test scores is of particular concern when those scores are being used as part of a diagnostic process. When tests are used to label or categorize individuals, then an understanding of psychometric concepts is critical because the assessor needs to understand how to interpret the individual client's results in the context of how some normative group performed. (This will be discussed at greater length in Chapter 6). On the other hand, many tests are used not for diagnostic purposes, but instead for treatment monitoring or tracking purposes, and therefore the individual client is not being compared to some group but rather to his or her own baseline over the course of counseling. A test like the WISC-IV is likely to be used for the purpose of making diagnostic determinations (e.g., "learning disability" rather than monitoring treatment). The BDI-II, on the other hand, could be used for both diagnostic and treatment monitoring purposes.

The NCSPP competencies and the practical application of them are in accord with the various professional associations' codes of ethics regarding assessment competency and more clearly describe the requisite knowledge base and skills. The extent to which these concepts are covered in any given counseling or psychology program will vary, and the process for determining whether or not a trainee has achieved these competencies will also vary considerably. Continued efforts to develop user qualification guidelines and standards should be based on competency-based models, rather than on degree and professional license (Frauenhoffer, Ross, Gfeller, Searight, & Piotrowski, 1998). Test-user competency criteria also need to be aligned with test publishers' standards.

The major publishers of psychological tests—Multi-Health Systems, Pearson, Psychological Assessment Resources, Psychological Corporation (a subsidiary of Pearson), and Western Psychological Services—have established three test-user qualification levels, and each specific test is assigned a user level. Test-user qualifications and the designation of a particular test as being a level one, two, or three test was a by-product of the Test User Qualifications Working Group (TUQWoG) (Anastasi & Urbina, 1997). The TUQWoG was a collaborative effort of test publishers and committees of national professional organizations. Level 1 (A-tests) is the minimum training required, and the subsequent levels (B and C tests) presume knowledge and training at the prior level. Level 1 may not require any specialized training other than familiarity with the test manual. Level 2 typically requires that the user have completed training or coursework in assessment or measurement at the graduate school level or have equivalent supervised experience in test administration and interpretation. Like the ethical guideline regarding competency, however, the specific number of courses and the course content required is not delineated. Nor is "equivalent supervised" experience defined. One major publisher, Pearson, recently adopted a parallel qualification system, Q1 and Q2, whereby those with a degree or license in health care can purchase tests (Q1), and formal training and supervised experience in assessment ethics, interpretation, and psychometrics is required for the second level (Pearson, 2010). The third level usually requires the user to meet level 2 standards and have a doctorate degree or licensure in the appropriate discipline. Furthermore, some publishers require that the users of certain tests obtain additional qualifications involving advanced training with the particular test. A number of standardized measures exist, however, such as the therapeutic alliance ones discussed in Chapter 14 and some self-report psychopathology questionnaires that are not distributed by publishing companies and do not have a user level associated with them. Counselors and other professionals could utilize these measures as long as they judged themselves to be competent but do not have to concern themselves with publisher user qualifications.

A problem that arises from publisher qualification criteria is inconsistency both within and across companies. Several examples of these inconsistencies can be found by reviewing publisher catalogues and websites. For example, Publisher A may decide that a common child depression inventory is a level 2 test, whereas an adult depression inventory is a level 3. Both inventories measure the same construct, have very similar scoring and interpretation systems, and yet there is no clear reason why the two tests are at different user levels. Or two different publishers sell very similar child behavior rating scales but one company has determined rating scale A to be at a level 2 and rating scale B to be at a level 3, though again, for all intents and purposes, the constructs being measured, the administration, scoring, and interpretation training needed, are virtually the same. Another example is a test that would require greater training and education to administer, score, and interpret, a test of nonverbal intelligence (TONI) e.g., has the same user qualification level as a simpler tool, a behavior questionnaire. Fortunately, these examples of inconsistencies are the exception rather than the rule, but they occur often enough to be a source of concern and confusion for students, trainees, and professionals.

As indicated in Figure 2.1, the third source of information regarding test-user qualifications comes from state regulatory boards. The educational, training, supervisory, and professional experiences required for obtaining licensure or certification as a helping professional—Licensed Mental Health Counselor, Licensed Clinical Social Worker, Licensed Psychologist, Marriage and Family Therapist, Psychiatrist, School Counselor—are determined at the state level and vary from state to state. States regulate both the qualifications necessary to obtain a professional license or certification as well as the discipline's scope of practice.

Within each state a discipline's scope of practice may or may not include assessment and diagnosis, and the statutes governing assessment practice tend to be fairly broad. Almost all states include assessment and diagnosis within the scope of practice for masters' level mental health disciplines. Across state regulatory agencies there is, however, wide variability regarding psychological test usage (Dattilio, Tresco, & Siegel, 2007). Their comprehensive survey of U.S. and Canadian psychology licensing boards found that two-thirds of the states or provinces have a law prohibiting nonpsychologists from conducting psychological testing. That percentage, however, reflected states that prohibit the practice of psychological testing as well as those states and provinces that only protect the term "psychological testing." Fewer than half the states and provinces restrict the actual practice (Dattilio et al.). What that means is that other mental health professionals could use standardized measures as part of an assessment process and not violate state law as long as the end product (i.e., the assessment report) was not titled a "psychological evaluation" or "psychological report." Several isolated legal challenges have occurred in a few states over who is qualified to administer specific psychological tests, and the rulings have been mixed, favoring both the exclusive rights of psychologists to use psychological tests, and a broad right for all mental health disciplines with the appropriate training and supervision (Dattilio et al., 2007; Frauenhoffer et al., 1998). Interestingly, among the 20 states and provinces the survey found did not restrict psychological testing to psychologists, there was little difference among the types of tests whose usage is restricted. For example, an equal number of states or provinces did not restrict the use of intelligence tests and inventories, yet intelligence tests require much greater education, training, and supervision to competently administer, score, and interpret. Another survey of a relatively small group of professional counselors and social workers from four states found a wide range of the types of psychological tests—from intelligence to unidimensional rating scales—being administered and interpreted by those two professional groups, though significantly less so than psychologists (Frauenhoffer et al.).

Needless to say, much work still needs to be done in bringing consistency to the scope of assessment practice and identifying which types of tests can be used by trainees and professionals representing different disciplines. As professional organizations take the lead role in developing objective behavioral assessment competencies, publishers and state regulatory boards are likely to refine their guidelines and statues to be in accordance with professional standards. Until such time, more professional turf battles may be waged. Debates over who is qualified to administer psychological tests are similar to previous arguments over who is qualified to provide psychotherapy, and current ones about who is qualified to prescribe psychotropic medications. Often these debates are long on professional identity concerns and short on scientific data.

One organized response to state regulatory restrictions regarding test usage is the Fair Access Coalition on Testing (FACT), an educational nonprofit corporation founded in 1996. FACT's mission is to advocate for access to testing services for all professionals with the appropriate training and competencies (FACT, n.d.) In particular, FACT monitors restrictions on assessment practices that have been imposed by state licensing boards. They will help professionals by following legal cases and gathering information to testify on behalf of professionals and clients who have been adversely impacted by restrictive laws. In addition to their advocacy work, FACT board of directors in 2000 voted to adopt the ITC International Guidelines for Test Use. Additional information about FACT and the cases it has followed can be found at *www.fairaccess.org*.

Once a trainee or practitioner decides he or she is competent to administer, score, and interpret a particular test, what else do the respective codes of ethics say about the use of tests? Like competency guidelines, the ethical codes of counseling and psychology have developed general standards for selecting and interpreting a specific test for a particular client regardless of whether that client is an individual, family, group, or organization.

Instrument Selection and Interpretation

The ethics codes of ACA, APA, AMHCA, and ASCA identify, to a greater or lesser degree, five issues an ethical practitioner needs to consider when choosing a test. Ethical practitioners select instruments that:

- are appropriate for the intended purpose *What is the purpose*
- are appropriate given the client's language preference
- have established reliability and validity
- have normative information relevant to the client
- are not obsolete

Appropriate use of a test is a minimum standard, and, with the myriad of available tests, not a difficult standard to meet in most situations. Practically speaking, appropriate use means selecting a test that was designed to measure the construct in question: intelligence tests to assess intellectual function, personality tests to measure personality traits, psychopathology scales to diagnose psychopathology, and so on. An extreme example of inappropriate test usage would be assessing a child's cognitive abilities with a test designed to measure different aspects of psychopathology and personality, such as the Rorschach inkblot test. A more complex and ethically grayer area would be using a test that may have some relevance to the assessment question but was not originally designed to answer the referral question. One example of this ethically questionable area involves the use of personality tests in evaluating parenting abilities as part of custody evaluations. A court may be interested in having an individual's parenting abilities evaluated in order to make a determination about custody and visitation. There is, however, no existing instrument designed to predict an individual's parenting abilities and only one, the *Parenting Stress Index,* which is designed to identify parents who may be at risk for dysfunctional parenting practices.

Instead, personality tests are sometimes used that can assess the presence of severe psychopathology but don't directly answer the question, How good a parent is Mr. Smith? Severe psychopathology can certainly impact one's role functioning, including parenting, but that does not necessarily mean that one is unable to parent effectively during the course of the disorder. Making inferences about an individual's parenting skills from a score on the *Parenting Stress Index* would be acceptable practice, whereas judgments about parenting based solely on a personality test would be ethically questionable. From an ethical perspective, it is imperative that the clinician clarify with the referring party what questions can and cannot be answered with a given test and the overall assessment process, and not mislead others into believing that a test designed for one purpose is appropriate for another.

Appropriateness also pertains to the fit between the clients preferred language and the language of the test. Most psychological instruments currently in use in the United States were developed in English, though a number of the more common ones (e.g., *Wechsler Intelligence Scales* and the *Child Behavior Checklist*) have been translated into other languages and normed with specific cultures. It would be unethical, for example, to administer an English intelligence test to someone whose primary language is Spanish and then make inferences about the person's intellectual capabilities based on test performance, when the performance may likely reflect a language barrier, not cognitive weaknesses.

Beyond selecting tests that are appropriate for addressing the referral question and the client's language, responsible test selection means choosing assessment instruments that have established reliability and validity. As you may recall from the previous chapter, reliability refers to the internal consistency and stability of a test, whereas validity is a measure of the degree to which a test assesses what it purports to. For example, does a test designed to measure intellectual skills indeed evaluate the abilities experts in the field would call intellectual ones? In order to judge a test's reliability and validity, one must have a solid understanding of those two measurement concepts. A test's reliability and validity can be established in various ways (see Chapter 7), and the various codes of ethics do not specify how or to what degree reliability and validity need to be established. Therefore, saying a test is "reliable and valid" is a minimum standard since one could potentially choose a test for which no reliability or validity has been demonstrated, at least by accepted scientific standards. A higher ethical standard would be to choose only those tests with the highest levels of reliability and validity. Work has recently begun, in developing evidence-based criteria for judging a test's reliability, validity, and published norms (Hunsley & Mash, 2008). Using Hunsley and Mash's three-level framework, a clinician could evaluate a test as having excellent, good, or merely adequate reliability, validity, and norms, and use only those that are good or better. Whether or not the next revision of the respective codes of ethics will reflect this, or similar criteria, for test selection and interpretation, remains to be seen.

As will become apparent in Chapters 8–14, many tests have gone through revisions and the ethical practitioner stays abreast of those developments and avoids or refrains from using tests that have become "obsolete" (ACA, 2005; AMHCA, 2010; APA, 2002). How to judge a test's datedness, is not something the codes address, but general guidelines are provided in *Standards for Educational and Psychological Testing* (Adams, 2000). Often a test revision is driven by a recognition that a more culturally diverse standardization group, upon which test norms are based, is needed, as well as research developments pertaining to the construct the test measures. Once a revised version is available for use, standard practice would be to use only the current version unless clinically it makes sense to use the earlier version. For example, a client's symptoms were measured at intake with version 1.0, and now counseling has ended and the clinician wants to measure progress but version 1.2 is available. The clinician may want to rely on version 1.0 the second time symptoms are measured so that changes are a reflection of the client's progress, or lack thereof, and not the result of a slightly different instrument.

Clearly a number of factors need to be considered when choosing assessment instruments in order to practice in an ethically responsible fashion. Attention to instrument purpose, appropriateness and client relevance, psychometric properties, and datedness is critical when considering a range of alternative measures. Ethical considerations do not, however, end with the issue of test selection. The inferences, interpretations, and conclusions a practitioner makes based on a client's test performance and scores are both a clinical process and an ethical issue.

One of the primary purposes of assessment is to make inferences about a client's abilities, functioning, and psychological well-being. The ethics codes caution practitioners to not stray too far from the test data, and use multiple sources of data, when forming judgments and conclusions. The APA cautionary guideline says, "psychologists base the opinions contained in their recommendations, reports, and diagnostic or evaluative statements, . . . on information . . . sufficient to substantiate their findings" (APA, 2002, p. 1071). Similarly, the ACA Code (2005) states that multiple cultural factors—age, color, gender, ethnicity, sexual orientation, religion, and socioeconomic status—should be considered when interpreting tests results and that those results are kept in "proper perspective with other relevant factors" (p. 13). The ASCA code (2010) goes one step further and cautions school counselors when using assessment instruments and making interpretations from them when a population of interest is not "represented in the norm group on which an instrument is standardized." These sections of the respective codes stress the importance of considering cultural diversity and contexts when engaged in the assessment process. For example, a client who experienced the death of a family member recently and was showing signs of grief and depression might be given the *Beck Depression Inventory–II* (BDI-II), a self-report checklist (see Chapter 9), to complete as part of the assessment. If the clinician concluded, solely on a high score on the BDI-II, that the client had a diagnosis of major depression, that conclusion would be problematic from an ethical as well as an integrative assessment perspective. Even though high scores on the BDI-II are highly correlated with the diagnosis of major depression, the high score alone should not be the sole basis of a diagnosis, especially when contextual and cultural factors, not psychiatric illness, may be accounting for the client's problems and symptoms. Similarly, a clinician should not conclude that a child has an attention deficit–hyperactivity disorder, based exclusively on the results of parent and teacher questionnaires such as the *Behavior Assessment System for Children* (see Chapter 10). In both examples, even though the assessment instruments have been found to have excellent reliability, are well validated, and have norms that support their use in these hypothetical cases, the ethics codes are clear about having sufficient information upon which to make judgments and render opinions. Although how much information one must gather before making a judgment or an evaluative opinion is debatable, the use of test scores for making diagnostic judgments, without evaluating those scores in light of a host of other variables—culture, history and background information, observations, context of the assessment, psychosocial stressors, degree of functional impairment—is unethical and clinically unwise.

USING TECHNOLOGICAL ADVANCES IN TESTING   Technological developments over the past three decades have enabled the creation and widespread use of test interpretation software and automated reports. Consequently, revisions to the respective ACA and APA codes of ethics added language to address the ethical issues these advances have brought. Now both sets of codes have assessment subsections pertaining to assessment scoring and interpretation services. Counselors and psychologists who offer computerized scoring and interpretation services and software have an ethical obligation to demonstrate, as with all assessment instruments, their "purpose, norms, validity, reliability, and applications of the procedures [assessment services]" (ACA, 2005, p. 13; APA, 2002, p. 1072). Furthermore, counselors and psychologists who make interpretations about client performance and functioning based on automated or computer-generated assessment reports have an ethical obligation to ensure that those interpretations are valid for the client being assessed. Computer-generated interpretation reports tend to be somewhat generic. Therefore, the clinician has an ethical responsibility to take that report and integrate it with other information about the client that results in a set of statements and judgments that reflect a holistic assessment, rather than adopting uncritically a computer report as being a valid set of statements about a client's personality, psychopathology, or cognitive functioning. Technology has also enabled tests to be administered via the Internet, but the latest revisions of the respective ethics codes do not specifically address Internet testing.

The Internet has spawned a proliferation of new self-report tests and created wider access to some old ones. As with other technological advances, Internet testing has its advantages and disadvantages. On the one hand, it enables easier, quicker, and less costly testing, which is particularly helpful for those clients in rural areas who may need to travel a considerable distance to undergo an assessment. On the other hand, the ease of transmitting psychological and assessment information and actual tests over the Internet has led to a number of ethical challenges. Those challenges have been summarized by a task force of the APA that was convened for the purpose of addressing Internet-based testing (Naglieri et al., 2004). The task force's main conclusion was that regardless of whether a test is administered via paper and pencil in an office, or over the Internet, the same ethical considerations discussed above regarding informed consent, a test's psychometric properties (reliability, validity, and norms), the interpretations drawn from tests, and the use of obsolete tests, still apply. The task force elaborated on four central challenges that are specific to Internet-based testing (Naglieri et al.). The first is the practical matter of informed consent when Internet testing occurs. It is important from the outset to clarify the limits of a professional relationship established through the Internet (i.e., what type, if any, access the client will have to the tester, and how test feedback will be provided to the client). In addition, there needs to be some way to verify that the client is able to give consent (e.g., not a minor). A second issue is one of quality control. Currently, consumers are being offered a sizable number of tests whose reliability and validity is either unknown or questionable as well as access to obsolete tests (Naglieri et al.). Third is the interpretation challenge that Internet administration raises. Interpretations drawn from a test that was designed and standardized for office paper-and-pencil administration may not readily translate to computer-based administrations. The greater anonymity provided with Internet testing can affect how an individual responds to test items and questions. Therefore, scores on certain types of personality and psychopathology tests may even be higher because of a greater willingness to disclose information in a more anonymous setting. Since an individual's scores on normative tests are being compared to some reference group in order to make judgments about normality, new benchmarks may be needed for Internet administration of a given test. Without those Internet-based standards, any interpretation of an Internet-administered test, even the same version of an in-person test, should be done with caution. A fourth challenge, also related to informed consent, stems from the fact that a large number of potential test takers whose primary language differs from the test, can take it via the Internet, but the inferences a clinician can make as a result of that language difference are limited. Furthermore, there is the related issue of how to inform those who may reside in a country and culture other than the one in which a test was developed and standardized, that the score they obtained can have a different meaning than it does for the normative population.

Perhaps the greatest challenge with the creation of the Internet is how to maintain a test's integrity and security when the process of putting a test on the Net is so simple. Tests, like books, music, and films, are copyrighted, but that does not prevent the illegal dissemination of tests anymore than it does for other mediums.

Confidentiality and Test Security

A trustworthy, confidential relationship is the cornerstone of all counseling services, and yet confidential communication between counselor and client is not absolute. The codes of ethics of all the professional counseling–related disciplines have long recognized that the ethical and legal obligations to keep client communications confidential can be circumvented when a client poses a serious and imminent danger to self or others, or when a client, or client's parent or guardian, elects to release confidential information to others. In the area of assessment, third parties—courts, government agencies, educators, insurance companies, and employers—will want access to confidential information revealed during the assessment process. This is where the ethics of informed consent and confidentially intersect. Adult clients and the parents or guardians of minor clients have the legal right to authorize that information obtained through the counseling process in general, and assessment in particular, be released to third parties. That right is what is known as "privileged communication." That is, the client, not the counselor, holds the right to decide what information will be released to others. From an ethical perspective, the counselor wants to make sure that the client is fully informed and understands what information will be released and to whom, and the potential implications of that disclosure. The ACA Code of Ethics, Informed Consent in Assessment, states, for example, "Counselors consider the examinee's welfare, explicit understandings, and prior agreements in determining who receives the assessment results" (ACA, 2005, p. 19). Although clients or their representatives can authorize assessment information to be released, counselors and psychologists can still make professional judgments about which test data will be released to third parties. For example, a clinician could decide that in the case where a parent is ordered by a court to undergo personality testing as part of a custody evaluation, that the clinician will release his or her interpretation of the test but not specific scores, nor certain historical information that was revealed during the evaluation that is irrelevant to the referral question and could adversely impact the client.

A clinician exercising his or her professional judgment and discretion, when releasing assessment information, is supported by another segment of the assessment sections of the respective codes of ethics. The "Release of Test Data" section of the APA Code of Ethics states, "Psychologists may refrain from releasing test data to protect a client/patient or others from substantial harm or misuse or misrepresentation of the data or the test . . ." (APA, 2002, pp. 1071–1072). The "misuse and misrepresentation of the data" phrase recognizes that individuals and organizations who receive test scores and are not knowledgeable about psychometric concepts and the meanings attached to scores on any given test, can misunderstand the data, or worse, distort and make invalid inferences from it. Therefore, psychologists are guided to be cautious and mindful about the nature of the test data released and to whom it is going. Counselors have a similar standard, "Release of Data to Qualified Professionals." This standard indicates that even when clients authorize the release of test information, the "data are released only to persons recognized by counselors as qualified to interpret the data" (ACA, 2005, p. 12). This can be a challenging standard to adhere to at times because knowing whether or not the recipient of the test data is qualified to understand it can be tricky. The case study of Joshua (see Chapter 13), who underwent intelligence testing to determine whether he had a learning disability, illustrates how this ethical standard can be applied. Joshua was evaluated by a psychologist independent of the school district because the district's psychologist was unavailable. Joshua's mother signed a release for the test report to go to the school so that the special education team would have the information it needed to make a determination about a learning disability. The evaluating psychologist also believed it was necessary for the school to get the report, for the same reason, but advised the mother that the report be released only to the school's psychologist, rather than to the entire special education team, because the psychologist was not sure if some of the team members, which included the classroom teacher, would be able to understand the test scores. By having a narrow release, to another professional, the psychologist was able to follow both ethical guidelines: satisfying the client's right to have assessment information released, and refraining from releasing information to persons unqualified to interpret it.

Although a psychologist or counselor may decide to release test *data* to a client or a qualified third party, test *materials* are legally and ethically protected from release. Among the association codes referenced throughout the chapter, the APA Code of Ethics makes the clearest distinction between test data and test materials. *Data* refers to "raw and scaled scores, client/patient responses to test questions or stimuli, and psychologist's notes and recordings concerning client/patient statements and behavior"; *test materials* refers to "manuals, instruments, protocols, and test questions or stimuli" (APA, 2002, pp. 1071–1072). Test materials, if released, could undermine the integrity of the tests. If test questions and stimuli become publically available, then the conditions under which the test is administered could significantly change and therefore affect performance. A test where one knows the questions ahead of time is a different type of test, and one's performance therefore might simply be a reflection of memorization and not other learning processes, attitudes, beliefs, or emotional reactions. Furthermore, as noted above, test materials are copyrighted, and reproduction and distribution of them without the publisher's permission would be illegal. That has not stopped the practice of selling a variety of copyrighted test materials on eBay, Amazon, and other Internet sites (Erard, 2004). It had been pretty clear that the copying and distributing of test materials without permission was both an ethical and legal violation until the Health Insurance Portability and Accountability Act (HIPAA) went into effect in 2003 (see the following) and muddied test security practices.

LEGAL ISSUES

Since the mid-1960s, court decisions and federal legislation have impacted certain aspects of assessment. Sometimes legal regulations support and buttress ethical standards and at other times they conflict. When, however, laws and ethical standards are inconsistent, counselors face a dilemma. Counselors and other mental health professionals have an ethical duty to take whatever steps are necessary to try and resolve ethical and legal conflicts. Educational and vocational assessments are the two areas that have been affected by case law and legislation, and these decisions have resulted in regulations that reinforce and give legal teeth to the principles and standards of the various professional ethical codes.

Individuals with Disabilities Education Act (IDEA)

The Individuals with Disabilities Education Act (IDEA) (see Chapter 13), formerly public law 94-142, the Education for All Handicapped Children Act, is one example of a law that is consistent with, and has supported and strengthened, assessment ethics regarding test selection and interpretation. IDEA is congruent with assessment ethics in requiring that the assessments of children for diagnostic purposes be done in the child's native language or form of communication and use a process that includes multiple sources of data and is valid (U.S. Department of Education, 2004). Revisions to the IDEA regulations came about, in part, from a California court decision (*Larry P. v. Riles,* 1979) and other court decisions that ruled that IQ tests were "racially and culturally" biased against Black and other minority children. The circuit court, in the *Larry P. v. Riles* case, concluded that Black children had been inappropriately diagnosed as mentally retarded and assigned to educable mentally retarded classrooms because an IQ score was the sole basis for the diagnosis and a disproportionate number of Black children had been labeled as mentally retarded as a result. That decision generated extensive research on whether or not tests, particularly intelligence tests, are biased. Several large research reviews have concluded that intelligence tests are not culturally and racially biased and would not account for inappropriate classifying of minority students as learning disabled or mentally retarded, but that conclusion may be premature because those reviews were based mostly on studies of outdated intelligence tests (Skiba et al., 2008). Although under IDEA it is permissible to use intelligence and other ability tests as part of an assessment of learning disabilities, a single test cannot be the sole criterion upon which an educational diagnosis and program is made. Furthermore, the intention of IDEA, in mandating that clinicians use information from various sources—tests, teacher reports and observations, response to prior interventions, and parent and child interviews—is to reduce individual professional bias and increase shared accountability for diagnosis and interventions (Bersoff & Hofer, 2008).

Supreme Court Rulings

Similarly, in the areas of employment and personnel decisions, Supreme Court rulings and the 1964 Civil Rights Act have impacted the manner in which test results are used in those contexts. When tests are used to determine job competency and qualifications, the test cannot unfairly disadvantage one group more than another. In 1971 the Supreme Court ruled, in the case of *Griggs v. Duke Power Company*, that the use of intelligence tests for determining job promotions is illegal if the test has an adverse impact on one racial group (i.e., systematically and negatively affects one group more than another) (Miller & Evans, 2004). The *Griggs v. Duke Power Company* case involved 13 African American men who claimed that the company's use of a so-called intelligence test, which Duke Power had created, for promotion purposes, was discriminatory. One impact of that court ruling and others (*Albemarle Paper Company v. Moody* and *Washington v. Davis*) is that tests can still be used for personnel decisions as long as the items and questions on the test are "job-related" (Kaplan & Saccuzzo, 2005; Miller & Evans, 2004). That is, the burden is on the employer, and anyone hired by the employer to administer and interpret the test to demonstrate its validity for personnel decisions with respect to a particular job. Many of the subtests on traditional intelligence tests, for example, may not have any direct bearing on the skills and aptitudes necessary for successful performance with a certain job. Therefore, from a legal perspective, only those tests that directly measure the skills and qualities pertinent to the job in question can be used. Again these various rulings were congruent with the sections of the ACA and APA codes of ethics that speak to using only tests for which validity and reliability for specific populations and *purposes* have been demonstrated.

Health Insurance Portability and Accountability Act (HIPAA)

One area where laws and ethics appear to be at odds and have created confusion is the extent to which the Health Insurance Portability and Accountability Act (HIPAA) (U.S. Department of

Health and Human Services, 2009) has affected test security. HIPAA was enacted in 1996 and went into effect in 2003 and was designed primarily to ensure greater privacy and protections for health insurance subscribers, including the ability to maintain insurance following a job change or loss. There are several important provisions of HIPAA that affect counseling and mental health services in general, but the one area that has raised concern among assessment professionals is whether clients are entitled to receive copies of test questions and items. Under HIPAA regulations, patients have a right to review and duplicate their records (Bersoff, 2008). A client's record can contain both the "raw test data" and the test materials. Clients can therefore have access to their test answers and answer sheets, if those exist, but it remains unclear if under HIPAA they have a right to the tests themselves, which are copyright protected. Several test publishers have issued clarifying statements that test materials, items, and questions are trade secrets and copyrighted, and that the protected health information section of HIPAA does not apply to these materials. One publisher, Harcourt, has cited a Health and Human Services (HHS) ruling that testing professionals would not be in violation of HIPAA for refusing to allow clients to copy test materials (Pope, 2009). In many instances, however, the raw test data and test materials are not separated and both could be released if the client requests it (Erard, 2004). For example, on some intelligence tests and most self-report questionnaires, the test items or questions and the answer sheet with client responses are one in the same. Steps can be taken, however, so that client information is released without the accompanying test items, questions, and stimuli in order to maintain test security and integrity (Fischer, 2004). Whether HHS' ruling is the last word on HIPAA and test security remains to be seen, and how much it may erode test security and copyright laws will probably be determined by future court cases. Additionally, there has been debate about whether or not HIPAA regulations are even applicable in non–health care settings such as forensic and educational (Rogers, 2004).

Family Educational Rights and Privacy Act (FERPA)

In educational settings, the federal law governing the privacy and accessing of educational records, including assessment data and reports, is the Family Educational Rights and Privacy Act (FERPA) (U.S. Department of Education, 2011). FERPA, enacted in 1974, applies to all schools that receive federal funds—which is the case for almost all public schools but generally does not apply to private and parochial schools. The spirit of the regulation is to protect the privacy rights of children and their parents, both custodial and noncustodial. In essence, FERPA supports the ethical concept of confidentiality and provides parents with a legal right to access and inspect educational records; amend them if the record contains misleading or inaccurate information; and restrict release of education records (U.S. Department of Education, 2011). The last right, however, is not absolute and there are certain exceptions. One exception is that educational records can be released to school officials who have a "legitimate educational interest." According to the U.S. Department of Education (2011), it is up to individual schools to determine the criteria for what constitutes a school official and a legitimate educational interest; FERPA does not define either term. Therefore, parental consent is not required to release educational records to a school official who has a legitimate interest in viewing them. Counseling notes kept in the course of providing treatment to a student who is not a minor, are not, however, considered in the definition of educational records. Those notes would need parental permission to be released to anyone else. When students become 18 they too are accorded the same rights as their parents have under FERPA.

Summary and Conclusions

Ethical principles and standards developed by professional associations that guide and shape all counseling endeavors apply to the assessment process as well. Throughout the assessment process, the principles of beneficence and promoting client welfare are important to keep in mind. From those principles flow three specific standards—informed consent, confidentiality, and competency—which have direct bearing on how clinicians interact with clients before, during, and after the assessment process. A thorough understanding of these standards enables clinicians to conduct assessments and use specific methods, such as psychological tests, in an ethically sound manner.

Of the three standards, competency is the one with the greatest complexity and ambiguity. It is an aspirational standard that does not specify the type and amount of training one needs in order to responsibly use assessment methods, particularly tests. Work is underway, however, to flesh out the necessary training to competently perform assessments. Competency to use one assessment method, psychological testing, is a challenging issue. A problem for the field of assessment is that there are incongruities between those entities who share responsibility for who is considered a "qualified" test user. Test publishers have adopted a three-tier system for broadly designating the type of training a test user must have. That system has inconsistencies both within and across publishing companies so that two tests with very different levels of complexity, and training needed to administer, score, and interpret the test, are given the same user level. And as yet these test levels are not aligned with professional association developmental assessment competencies. To complicate matters, each state licensing board defines a scope of practice for the various counseling disciplines, which may or may not include one of the primary purposes of assessment, performing diagnostic evaluations, depending upon the discipline.

The competent test user needs to also be aware of and adhere to ethical standards for selecting and interpreting tests. Responsible testing involves selecting tests that are appropriate for the intended purpose, have acceptable reliability, validity, and norms, and are no longer out of date. Regardless of whether a test is an A-, B-, or C-level test, the ethical test user needs to possess a fundamental understanding of psychometric concepts (see Chapter 7). It is this knowledge that helps a clinician determine the relevancy and limitations of what a particular test can reveal about a client given his or her history and cultural background. In addition to ethical standards, court decisions and legislation have impacted how tests are used, particularly in the areas of educational and vocational testing.

Reflection Questions and Experiential Exercises

1. How will you provide informed consent to a client prior to an assessment?
2. What kind of assessment data can you release to others and when can you do that?
3. This chapter discussed the ethics of limiting the scope of your professional activities to those skills and procedures you are competent to perform. How will you decide whether or not you are competent to use various assessment methods? What might you do when faced with an assessment situation that seems to be beyond the limits of your competency?

Case Vignette

Melanie is a recently licensed mental health counselor working in a local agency that provides physical and mental and social services. Her boss, the clinic director, recently attended a workshop that discussed and promoted the advantages of using a new brief questionnaire, the PROQ-1.0, to track client progress and outcomes over the course of counseling. The PROQ-1.0 is available from the authors, not a test publisher, and therefore has not been given a test level. The director is strongly encouraging Melanie and all the other mental health clinicians to use the PROQ-1.0 with all new clients. Melanie asked her boss for a copy of the PROQ-1.0 manual. The manual has a technical information section that describes the questionnaire's reliabilities and how those reliabilities were determined. The manual also provides information about the questionnaire's validity with different outpatient groups. Melanie is counseling mostly male Latino and African American clients and occasionally Caucasian clients, all of whom have substance abuse or dependence as the primary problem along with anxiety and depression. Melanie agrees with her director that it would be beneficial to have a standardized measure to track

client progress but wonders how she can use the PROQ-1.0 with her clients and still act in accordance with the code of ethics she is following.

4. Discuss in small groups the following questions:
a) What ethical questions does this case vignette raise?
b) How could Melanie go about using the PROQ-1.0 and act in accordance with assessment ethics regarding informed consent, test selection, and interpretation?
c) What might be her other options if she wants to have a standardized way to track and measure client progress during counseling but does not think the PROQ-1.0 would be appropriate for her to use with her clients?

3

INTERVIEWING ADULTS AND YOUTH: PRINCIPLES, METHODS, AND SKILLS

Chapter Objectives

After reading this chapter, you should be able to:

■ Describe the three types of interview methods and understand their advantages and limitations.

■ Understand the fundamental interviewing skills and their practical application.

■ Identify strategies and techniques that can be used with young children to facilitate their engagement in the interview process.

Brian dragged himself out of bed Monday morning after a difficult weekend. He finally decided it was time to take the advice of his primary care physician and get into counseling, especially since he was not sure if the medication he was taking was helping. He found the card his doctor had given him underneath a pile of magazines and placed a call.

Telephone Screening

Brian, a single, 27-year-old Hispanic male, called the Maple Street Behavioral Health Clinic to make an appointment to see a counselor. He told the telephone screener that "there is just a lot going on right now" and that his doctor had suggested he talk to someone. He reported that he is "snappy all the time," has "trouble getting going" and hasn't been "sleeping well," and has had "a case of the jitters" for "a long time." When asked if he was having thoughts of harming himself, he quickly responded, "No, it's not that bad."

After obtaining that brief description of the problem, the screener requested some basic demographic and insurance information. An appointment for an intake interview was scheduled for later that week.

Presenting Problem

At the intake session, Melanie Grenvue, the intake clinician, reviewed the clinic's informed consent form with Brian to see if he understood it and had any questions. "I'm all set," he replied. Melanie went on to ask if he had any questions about her training or background. "Are you a psychiatrist?" Brian asked. "I'm a Licensed Mental Health Counselor," she said, and went on to briefly explain how that is different from a psychiatrist.

After the preliminary discussion, Melanie opened the intake interview by asking, "How are you hoping I can be of help?"

Brian, who appeared tired and lethargic, hesitated and then replied frankly, "I don't know; this wasn't really my idea."

"Whose idea was it?" Melanie asked.

Brian quickly responded, "My doc and my girlfriend; they think I should be here."

Melanie inquired further, "What do you think about their suggestions that you come here?"

"They think I have a problem with my temper and I guess I've not been sleeping much lately. I've just got a lot going on right now."

"A lot going on? Tell me more about that."

"I don't know what to say—things are not going well with my girlfriend, they're givin' me a hard time at work, and I'm just getting pissed off a lot lately."

"You mentioned that your primary care doctor and your girlfriend are concerned about your temper. What makes them think you have a problem with your temper?"

"Well, after she got me so pissed off, I slapped her, and I've blown up a couple of times at work."

"Blown up, what do you mean?" Melanie clarified.

"Sometimes I swear at people and I've punched my computer screen a couple times."

"When did this start happening?"

"I've kinda had a temper since I was a little kid; I got into fights at school when kids made fun of my accent."

"So given what you've told me so far, do you think you have a temper problem?"

"I wouldn't be losing it if people would just stop gettin' me mad," Brian replied.

Melanie went on to gather additional information about Brian's "temper" problem, its frequency, when it occurs, and what is happening when it doesn't occur. She also clarified the nature of his sleep problem. For the past two years, Brian has been having trouble getting to sleep at night and since his girlfriend broke up with him a month ago after he slapped her, he has had even more trouble falling asleep and has become more quick-tempered at work. Later on in the interview, Brian also mentioned that he's been getting tense a lot and he's not "hanging out" as much.

OVERVIEW

The purpose of this chapter is to describe commonly used counseling interview methods and discuss fundamental interviewing skills with an emphasis on practical tactics. The types of interviews and interviewing skills discussed in this chapter are typically utilized with adults and adolescents. Special considerations are needed when interviewing young children, and those modifications and additional strategies for engaging children in the assessment process will also be discussed.

There are three types of interviews: unstructured, semistructured, and structured. Typically, unstructured interviews are used as the initial information-gathering process in most counseling settings. Of the three types, **unstructured interviews** allow the counselor the maximum flexibility with respect to which topics to cover and how much depth to go into in any one area. They also are more client centered in that the counselor can shape and guide the interview to fit the concerns, needs, demographics, and interpersonal style of the client.

Structured and **semistructured interviews** consist of a prescribed set and sequence of questions, similar to a survey. For example, a structured interview question might be, "In the past year, have you experienced a depressed (sad or down) mood?" And if the answer is yes, the follow-up question might be, "How often do you experience a depressed or sad mood: rarely, sometimes, often, or almost all the time?" Structured interviews also have a system for scoring question responses, and those scores are typically used for making diagnostic decisions. Given, however, the nature of these interviews—very lengthy and highly directive—structured interviews have been criticized as being more research-centric than client centered. Recent studies (Hoyer, Ruhl, Scholz, & Wittchen, 2006; Suppiger et al., 2009) have found, contrary to common clinical opinion, that semistructured and structured interviews are as acceptable and helpful to mental health clients as traditional unstructured intake interviews.

TYPES OF INTERVIEWS

Unstructured Interviews

Although there are various unstructured interview formats, the prototypical type is the initial, or intake, assessment used in most mental health settings. Relative to other assessment methods, the unstructured clinical interview is the one most commonly used by psychologists (Watkins, Campbell, Nieberding, & Hallmark, 1995). Because of managed care policies and practices, it continues to be relied upon as well by other professionals as the primary assessment tool in clinical settings (Piotrowski, 1999). The intake interview (often referred to as just "intake") is a helpful way to begin with a new client in most counseling settings, including educational and organizational ones because it can more easily be adapted for the concerns, culture, and interpersonal style of the client than structured interviews. Furthermore, since there is flexibility in interviewing content and style, the intake is better suited for developing and building rapport with clients. As will be discussed later, rapport building is a key element of counseling interviews because the greater the rapport, the greater the likelihood that clients will communicate openly and thoroughly. Traditionally, the intake interview has been categorized as an *unstructured* interview because what follows after the clinician's opening question is highly variable and dependent upon the presenting problems or concerns as well as the interpersonal styles of the client and clinician. It is the intention of this and the next chapter to describe a process that provides a greater degree of structure and focus to initial counseling interviews.

Practically speaking, intakes generally range in length from 60 to 90 minutes. In many cases, a one-session intake of this length will be sufficient for addressing presenting problems, client background information, and risk and protective factors related to the presenting problem. In some cases, however, the problems and client history are of such complexity that two or more intake sessions will be needed before a treatment plan can be established.

In most mental health settings, a diagnosis will be required after the initial intake session in order to receive insurance or government reimbursement for the service, even if the counselor is very uncertain about a diagnosis. Fortunately, the DSM system has a couple of ways for recording diagnostic uncertainty—indicating that a diagnosis is "provisional" or using the "Not Otherwise Specified" (NOS) category associated with most diagnostic categories—and the diagnosis that is documented after only one intake session can be revised as additional information warrants.

Intake interviews typically begin with an exploration of the client's presenting problems. Exploring the client's concerns and presenting problem begins with the opening question, which can be phrased in various ways (see Chapter 4), one being "What brings you here today?" Most counseling clients, particularly in mental health settings, are coming because of multiple problems. A majority of mental health clients, for example, present with problems and symptoms related to both anxiety and depression, and a significant number, like Brian in the chapter case study, have substance abuse problems as well.

It is also essential that the client's **readiness for change** is assessed along with the presenting problems. Where a client is at, in terms of readiness for change, will affect both the initial interview process and subsequent treatment decisions. Client readiness for change is based on the stages of change model developed by Prochaska, DiClemente, and Norcross (1992) (Prochaska, Norcross, & DiClemente, 1994). Clients can enter counseling anywhere along a continuum of change, from denying the existence of a problem to acknowledging it and needing help in maintaining changes already implemented. A client's readiness for change has been identified as a critical variable to be assessed in order to effectively help clients, irrespective of their presenting problems (Hill, 2004). A more detailed discussion about the assessment of client readiness for change will take place in the next chapter.

Additional topics that are typically inquired about during intake interviews include family history and other interpersonal relationships, educational and work histories, previous mental health treatments, health status, and substance usage (Morrison, 2008). The approach that is advocated here is to gather additional information within a risks and protective factors framework—that is, those factors in the client's current life and history that serve either as a resource for problem resolution or an impediment toward progress. How a clinician can use that framework to gather additional client background information will also be discussed in greater detail in the following chapter.

Semistructured and Structured Interview Schedules

Semistructured and structured interviews differ from unstructured intake interviews in several fundamental ways. By standardizing the interview process, the researcher or clinician can be sure that all interviewees are asked the same questions in the same way. In fact, structured interview questions are designed to be read just as they are written (Rettew, Lynch, Achenbach, Dumenci, & Ivanova, 2009). Of the two structured approaches, semistructured interviews can be more easily modified to fit the needs of a particular client, presenting problems, and the setting in which the interview takes place because they tend to have more open-ended questions and the question sequence can be modified. Semistructured interviews are a useful assessment method when a client is new to a clinic, school, hospital, or other counseling setting because they allow for greater flexibility than a structured interview schedule, while at the same time providing an organized information-gathering process.

Along with the multiaxial diagnostic system that was introduced with the third edition of the DSM in 1980 came structured interview schedules for various disorders. The various interview schedules that exist are designed to identify whether an individual has a DSM diagnosis. Most of the interviews that are currently being used are aligned with the fourth edition of the DSM, designated as DSM-IV, or the text-revision version (DSM-IV-TR). The diagnostic criteria for all the DSM disorders are the same, however, with the two versions; only changes to the narrative portion of the text were made in DSM-IV-TR. Structured interviews can be very broad in scope, designed to identify most major categories of DSM disorders and a specific diagnosis within a category, for example major depression versus bipolar disorder type I within the Mood Disorders category. One commonly used broad-based interview is the *Structured Clinical Interview for DSM-IV Axis I Disorders* (SCID). Other schedules may be specific to a certain category of disorders such as anxiety disorders. An example of this is the *Anxiety Disorders Interview Schedule for DSM-IV: Lifetime Versions* (ADIS-IV-L). These interview schedules contain separate modules that are specific to a particular disorder, and the interviewer has some flexibility in deciding whether to use the entire interview or just certain modules.

The overall format of most structured interviews is based on a flowchart or decision tree model where the response to a particular question determines which subsequent questions or modules will be presented to the interviewee. Most of the questions are based on or match DSM-IV diagnostic criteria, particularly the requisite symptoms. For example, a sample question from the Structured Clinical Interview for the DSM-IV Axis I Disorders (SCID PTSD Module) (First, Spitzer, Gibbon, & Williams, 1996) asks, "How did you react when (trauma) happened? (feel afraid, feel terrified or helpless?)." The questions in other structured interviews will also match or relate to the wording of diagnostic criteria for specific DSM-IV disorders.

A scoring system is used with structured interviews both for individual questions and the total interview. Total scores are used for determining whether or not an individual has a diagnosable DSM condition such as major depression. In the previous example, the individual's emotional reaction to the traumatic event is scored on a 3-point scale. A 1 is given if the interviewee denies feelings of fear, terror, or helplessness, 2 if there is some fear but not terror or helplessness, and a 3 if the response is true, that the interviewee experiences much fear, terror, or helplessness. Different scoring systems can be found both within an interview and among the various schedules.

The length of time required to complete structured interviews is highly variable and depends upon the schedule used, whether or not all modules are used, and whether or not the client indeed has one or more diagnosable conditions. The interviews can range, on average, from 45 to 60 minutes (Ey & Hersen, 2004), which is no longer than a typical intake interview. A list of the commonly used structured interview schedules for DSM-IV disorders can be found in Table 3.1.

Structured interviews have been used much more frequently in research settings because of their enhanced ability to provide diagnostic agreement than does an unstructured interview method (Rettew et al., 2009). Even when some clinicians are engaged in a diagnostic evaluation, they are more likely to rely on an unstructured interview, rather than a semistructured or structured interview as part of the diagnostic process (Handler & DuPaul, 2005). There are several reasons why practicing professionals tend to favor unstructured over more structured interviews. Some have raised concerns that the latter are too formal and interfere with rapport building. An additional criticism is that they don't allow the clinician to probe in greater detail about problems or concerns the client is having. Finally, there is the added cost and time to undergo the training that is required to administer a structured interview schedule. Like psychological tests, the required training time and cost depend upon the particular interview schedule. They can, however, be useful diagnostic methods in counseling settings when other methods—unstructured interviews, standardized tests, and observations—do not adequately clarify a diagnosis. In clinical settings, structured interviews have been used for diagnosing adult attention deficit–hyperactivity disorder (ADHD), major depression and bipolar disorder, anxiety disorders, eating disorders, schizophrenia, substance abuse, and some personality disorders. Furthermore, a skilled interviewer can incorporate the fundamental principles and techniques discussed earlier into a structured interview to facilitate rapport building (Rogers, 2001). A study conducted in Europe in various clinical settings found that, indeed, clients have very positive feelings and attitudes toward undergoing a structured interview (Suppiger et al., 2009).

Structured and semistructured interviews were designed for the purpose of identifying or clarifying a DSM diagnosis by asking specific questions pertaining to the DSM criteria set for a given disorder. That is where their advantage over intake interviews lies: the ability to determine where the requisite symptoms, symptom severity, and functional impairment are present. On the other hand, there is nothing inherent in an unstructured clinical interview that would preclude its use for diagnostic purposes. The problem is that the two approaches—standardized interview schedules (structured or semistructured interviews) and clinical intakes (unstructured interviews)—can produce very different outcomes. A recent large-scale meta-analysis of 38 international studies and almost 16,000 patients found that overall level of agreement between the two interview approaches in terms of deciding upon a DSM-IV diagnosis was well below generally accepted standards for stating that two different interview types produce similar outcomes (Rettew et al., 2009). Their analysis found that level of agreement between a clinical interview and standardized interview schedule varied depending upon the disorder in question and setting (inpatient versus outpatient), but the only disorder for which there was an

Table 3.1 Semistructured and Structured Psychiatric Interviews

Name	Disorders or Information Identified	Admin Time (minutes)
Structured Clinical Interview for DSM-IV-TR Axis I Disorders Research Version, Patient Edition (SCID-I/P)	Anxiety, Mood, Schizophrenia, Substance Use, Adjustment, Eating, and Somatoform Disorders	45–90
Structured Clinical Interview for DSM-IV Axis II Personality Disorders (SCID-II)	DSM-IV Personality Disorders and Depressive Personality and Passive–Aggressive personality Disorder	120
Diagnostic Interview for Personality Disorders	DSM-IV Personality Disorders	120
Structured Interview for DSM-IV Personality Disorders (SIDP-IV)	DSM-IV Personality Disorders	120
Diagnostic Interview Schedule for The DSM-IV (DIS-IV); Computerized DIS-IV	DSM-IV Axis I Disorders	75
Diagnostic Interview Schedule for Children Version IV (DISC-IV)	Attention Deficit-Hyperactivity, Conduct and Oppositional Disorders; Mood and Anxiety Disorders	45–120
Kiddie Schedule for Affective Disorders and Schizophrenia for School Age Children (K-SADS)	Mood Disorders and Schizophrenia	35–150
Schedule for Affective Disorders and Schizophrenia (SADS)	Mood Disorders and Schizophrenia	90–120
Anxiety Disorders Interview for DSM-IV (ADIS-IV, Lifetime Version, Revised Version)	Anxiety and Mood, Somatoform and Substance Use Disorders	120–180
Clinician Administered PTSD Scale (CAPS)	Post-Traumatic Stress Disorder	30–60
Global Appraisal of Individual Needs (GAIN)	Substance Use Disorders and Background Information: physical health, family-living arrangements, and risk factors	60–120
Addiction Severity Index (ASI)	Substance use: family and treatment history	45–90
Eating Disorder Examination	Eating Disorder Symptoms and Related Psychopathology	45–75
Interview for Diagnosis of Eating Disorders, 4th Version (IDED-IV)	DSM-IV Eating Disorders	unspecified

acceptable level of agreement was anorexia nervosa. In other words, if two clinicians were to interview the same client, but one used an unstructured interview and the other an interview schedule, they would be very likely to come up with different conclusions: the client has or does not have a diagnosable condition, or agreement that a disorder is present but disagreement about which disorder. Which procedure led to the correct decision? Like many researchers, those who conducted the meta-analysis were unable to either identify the reasons for the disagreement, or be in a position to advocate that one method be universally adopted in clinical settings (Rettew et al., 2009). Each approach has its strengths and limitations, and the task of the assessor is to understand a method's weaknesses and recognize that information gathered by one method, an interview, may need to be integrated with other sources (e.g., family member) and methods (e.g., clinician observation) in order to make a diagnosis. The relative advantages and disadvantages of the three interview formats are summarized in Table 3.2.

Because of their focus on DSM diagnoses, structured interviews do not typically address the situational, interpersonal, psychological, systemic, and cultural factors associated with presenting client problems. Furthermore, there are many counseling situations where obtaining a DSM diagnosis is not necessary because having it would not influence the course of treatment. Many clients enter counseling because of problems related to life cycle or developmental transitions, reactions to acute or chronic stressors, family or other interpersonal difficulties, or mild anxiety and depression symptoms that are of insufficient number, severity, and duration to indicate a disorder. In those cases, an unstructured interview such as an intake can be a more helpful

Table 3.2 Interview Formats Advantages and Disadvantages

Interview Formats	Advantages	Disadvantages
Unstructured	Flexible, can be customized to fit the needs and concerns of the client Useful for case conceptualizing Go into as much depth as needed; requires minimal training, and no additional costs No set time frame to complete	Inefficient process for arriving at DSM-IV-TR diagnoses May miss important information Low interclinician agreement
Semistructured	Combines the flexibility of unstructured interviews with the format of structured ones; includes open and closed ended questions; questions are predetermined but order can vary depending upon client and presenting problems and concerns	Limited to diagnostic interviews; requires additional training and cost to use competently; lacks reliable scoring system
Structured	Useful for determining DSM-IV-TR diagnoses; particularly complex ones such as autism, ADHD, bipolar disorder, and personality disorders Includes a standardized scoring system Relatively good interclinician diagnostic agreement	Lacks flexibility; requires significant additional costs: training materials, and time to administer; format fits better with research than clinical purposes; limited to diagnostic evaluations and too directive for some clients

starting place because it meets the needs of the client better and allows the counselor and client to develop a greater contextual understanding of the problem and the factors triggering and maintaining it. Regardless of the content area to be explored in an initial interview, there are fundamental interviewing principles and techniques that enhance the effectiveness of any assessment interview, including structured and semistructured ones.

FUNDAMENTAL INTERVIEWING PRINCIPLES AND TECHNIQUES

An assessment interview, like a counseling session or the overall course of counseling, can be conceptualized as a multistage process. One way to conceptualize the assessment interview is as a process consisting of three phases: socializing and providing information, gathering information, and closing. The first two phases will be discussed in this chapter and the third one in the following chapter.

An understanding of these three phases will help the counselor guide the client through the interview in order to accomplish several goals: 1) developing a contextual understanding of the presenting problems, including potential causes and maintaining factors; 2) forming a therapeutic relationship to facilitate client disclosure; and 3) developing a preliminary action plan. Given what needs to be accomplished and the amount of information that needs to be collected, sometimes more than one interview session is necessary before an action or treatment plan can be agreed upon.

Socializing and Providing Information

The initial stage of socializing and providing information begins the moment counselor and client meet. There is a greeting and brief conversation about some relatively neutral topic such as the process of getting to the appointment or the weather. Although it is a social exchange, it is still an opportunity for the counselor to make some preliminary observations about the client. How is the client dressed? How does the client respond to the counselor's greeting? How much information is spontaneously shared? What, if any, emotion is being expressed? Brian, the client in the chapter's opening case study, was dressed casually in blue jeans and T-shirt. He had a tattoo on his left forearm and beard stubble on his face, as if he had not shaved in several days. He was sitting impassively in a chair when the counselor greeted him but was eager to shake hands after the counselor introduced herself.

The social stage will conclude with the framing of the interview. The frame signals that the social exchange has ended and that the work of gathering information is about to begin. In addition, the frame is an opportunity to provide and discuss informed consent (see Chapter 2) by explaining the parameters of the interview, its purpose, and tasks involved. In most organizations and facilities, clients will be given written information about the services they will receive. It is, however, clinically and ethically advisable to review this information at the outset of an assessment interview even if the client has already received information in writing. Since it is a client's first experience with the agency or organization and many clients are uncomfortable or anxious in the beginning of an assessment interview, it helps to provide informed consent multiple times in different ways. Presenting informed consent orally, as was illustrated in the previous chapter, gives the client an opportunity to ask questions of the interviewer about the process before it begins, and tends to ease any initial discomfort. The framing statement accomplishes three important goals: 1) communicates a transition to the information-gathering stage, 2) provides the opportunity to discuss informed consent, and 3) allays client anxiety. Any communication from the interviewer that can ease a client's discomfort can go a long way toward developing rapport.

DEVELOPING AND MAINTAINING RAPPORT   Effective interviewing incorporates fundamental counseling attitudes and skills, which Rogers (1951; 1961) and others, more recently Hill (2004), Ivey and Ivey (2007), and Kottler (2010) have discussed at length. Empathy is a quality that Carl Rogers identifies as a fundamental and essential counseling concept. It consists of both an attitude and an emotional response. An empathic attitude is a willingness to see what it is like to walk in someone else's shoes and understand their worldview from a nonjudgmental perspective. To be empathic, a counselor does not necessarily feel what the client is feeling. When, however, an understanding of a client's circumstances, problems, and history occurs, there is often a warm connection or bonding that is experienced by the counselor and client. Communicating this nonjudgmental understanding to a client is as important when conducting assessment interviews as it is during counseling sessions.

Maintaining a respectful, empathic attitude toward clients is essential for rapport building. The development of rapport between clinician and client accomplishes several goals. First and foremost, when a client perceives the counselor as warm, empathic, and caring, trust begins to be established, which allows for more client self-disclosure. Clients who experience their counselors as trustworthy and caring are more likely to reveal information about themselves (Hill, 2004), including sensitive topics such as family history of mental illness, substance usage, and suicidal thoughts. In addition, through the development and maintenance of rapport, the counselor and client are better able to collaborate in the exploration of client problems and factors affecting those problems. Clients are more likely to respond with more than just the facts if they are forming a connection with a sensitive, caring interviewer. For example, a client might be asked a basic question such as "When did these problems begin?" If there is little or no rapport between counselor and client, then the client is apt to provide a quick, nonreflective response such as "A while ago" and passively wait for the next question. On the other hand, if rapport is present, the client is more likely to engage in some reflection and consider what was going on in his or her life at the onset of the problems and disclose this knowledge to the interviewer. All theoretical models of counseling recognize the importance of empathy, and the interviewer who can demonstrate that at the outset is in a better position to facilitate client reflection and disclosure. This relates to the final goal of rapport building and maintenance: setting the stage for further engagement. Regardless of what comes next—additional assessment interviews, continuing counseling with the interviewer or another professional, or engaging in some other type of action—those whose first encounter with the counseling process consists of warmth, empathy, and connection are more apt to continue. Although the phenomenon of dropping out of counseling after only an intake interview has rarely been studied, it appears to be a significant problem. The existing research suggests that anywhere from 7% to 25% of clients with either a DSM disorder or significant self-reported problems may not continue with treatment (Chiesa, Fonagy, Bateman, & Mace, 2009; Pekarik, 1992), and one major reason for that is dissatisfaction with the therapist (Pekarik). An understanding of why rapport building matters is a necessary first step toward effective interviewing. Applying that understanding within the time constraint of an initial assessment interview is both an art and a skill.

Rapport can be achieved through the use of nonverbal attending and verbal helping skills such as restatements, reflection of feelings, and summarizing (Hill, 2004; Ivey & Ivey, 2007). Those skills are useful for communicating empathy and thereby strengthening the emerging relationship between clinician and client. A range of nonverbal attending skills lets the interviewee or client know that the counselor is listening nonjudgmentally to what is being said and provides reassurance that this is a safe place to disclose. Nonverbal skills such as head nods, maintaining eye contact, an interested facial expression, a relaxed open posture, and a moderate tone and rate of speech will promote rapport building and encourage further openness on the part of the interviewee. In addition, empathy can be communicated and trust can be fostered through the use of minimal nonverbal encouragers such as "um-hmm" (Hill, 2004).

More verbal skills such as restatements, paraphrasing, summarizing, and reflection of feelings share a common underlying counselor intention: communicating understanding to the client in order to strengthen the therapeutic relationship (Hill, 2004). When a counselor feeds back to a client what has been heard and seemingly understood, an emotional connection or bond develops. Those emotional bonds are the building blocks of rapport, and rapport is a necessary step for creating and strengthening the relationship. Although assessment interviews are fairly directive processes infused with an abundance of questions, the skillful interviewer will intersperse these relationship-building communication skills along the way.

Rapport building can also occur through the act of "small talk." This happens during the greeting stage of the interview. Before engaging in the business of the interview, small talk with the client (e.g., commenting on the parking or the weather) can send a message that we are two human beings who have come together for a particular purpose. If the client has an opportunity, even if brief, to experience the counselor as an ordinary person rather than an aloof professional, rapport is more likely to develop.

The intentional interviewer stays mindful of his or her use of language during all three stages of the interview. During the framing of the interview, for example, the intentional counselor is cognizant of incorporating certain words and excluding others. The framing statement shown earlier used the question "How are you hoping I can be of help?" The use of the word *help* is deliberate. It challenges negative preconceived notions about counseling that many people hold. Rather than analyzing, treating, or restraining you, I'm going to try and help you. Someone who is perceived as a helper is easier to connect and relate to than one viewed as a powerful authority figure.

Although interviews, particularly semistructured ones, rely mostly on the use of questions to gather information, it is important to weave summarizations, reflections, and restatements into the interview process. The blending of questions with other types of helping skills not only fosters for clients a sense of being heard and understood, it reduces the possibility that the interview will be perceived as an interrogation. It is important to be cognizant of the number of consecutive questions asked without a break. If too many questions are asked in a row, without restatements or reflections, not only might clients feel like they are being interrogated, but an unhelpful dynamic is also created. When counselors go through a long series of interview questions without providing empathic communication back to the client, an active passive dynamic occurs in which clients sit back and wait for the next question, and tend to give shorter answers to the subsequent questions. On the other hand, interviewing is an information-gathering process that necessitates the need for many questions. Clearly, interviewing is a balancing act. The most effective interviewers are those who can seamlessly build and maintain rapport while at the same time gathering the information from which case conceptualizations and treatment plans will follow.

Gathering Information from Adolescents and Adults

USING QUESTIONS   When using an unstructured process it is important for the interviewer to consider what it is he or she wants to learn about the interviewee or client because question type and phrasing will determine the kind of answer one receives. In general, there are two types of questions used in interviewing: open-ended and closed. An **open-ended question** typically produces a more expansive response from the interviewee than a closed question. Questions that begin with *what, when,* or *how* are examples of open-ended. **Closed questions** will most often generate a one-word or short-phrase response and lessen the chance that the interviewee will disclose more than the initial brief reply. Closed questions begin with words such as *did, can,* or *is*. An example of a closed question is, "Did you have this temper problem at your previous job?" The answer to that might simply be yes or no, and thus narrows the range of client responses. On the other hand, the question "*When* did you first notice having a temper?" is open ended—to which, Brian, the client in the case study, might reply, "When I was in high school and that's when my mother was always yelling at me about my grades."

One objective of any assessment interview is to have the client share a lot of information about a variety of topics—problems or concerns, history of problems, self, background information, relationships and support systems—and open-ended questions are generally more effective than closed ones for accomplishing that goal. Therefore, counselors and other helping professionals will want to utilize mostly open-ended questions during intake interviews.

Having said that, there are times when the most efficient way to get the information needed is to ask a closed question. One such situation is when the interviewer wants to determine whether a specific risk factor, problem, or symptom is present. For example, when assessing Brian's substance use, the clinician could ask the close-ended question "Have you ever used any drugs other than alcohol?" If Brian's response is yes, then a follow-up open-ended question would be helpful: "What other drugs have you used?" On the other hand, if Brian responds to the initial closed question about substance usage negatively, then the interviewer could either explore further his alcohol use or move on to another topic. In addition, the directive statement "Tell me more" has been categorized as a kind of open-ended question (Hill, 2004) and is another useful way to explore client statements or as a follow-up to positive answers, such as "Yes, I've used other drugs." It is important for the interviewer to be intentional about the type of question he or she will use at each point during the interview. The intentional clinician is aware of and understands his or her purpose in choosing either an open or closed question at any given point in the interview.

The concept of the inverted pyramid, or triangle, often applied to journalistic writing, can also be a metaphor for effective interviewing. An inverted triangle is one in which the wide base is at the top and the tip is at the bottom:

$$\nabla$$

In journalism, the upside-down pyramid approach suggests leading off with the headline, or main idea, of the story and working down with more specific supporting details. When interviewing, it is also helpful to gather the headline and then obtain the rest of the story. Therefore, an overall interviewing strategy is to begin with fairly broad questions that enable the widest amount of information about a particular topic to be gathered, and then ask more specific and narrower questions to gather the details of the story that is emerging from the client. Open-ended questions that begin with *what, when,* or *how* cast a fairly wide net and are therefore helpful interview starters. Closed questions may be useful filler questions for obtaining important details related to the main story or problem set as it emerges. The inverted triangle approach to interviewing can be illustrated with a standard opening question such as "What brings you here today?" "What brings you here" is both broad and neutral. It allows for a wide range of possibilities to emerge—everything from "My probation officer told me I had to come to counseling" to "I'm just not feeling like myself anymore, I'm so stressed out I'm not sleeping well anymore." Once those topics are identified, the interviewer can narrow the focus to one of them and explore it in greater depth. This process can be repeated for any specific area such as the ones to be discussed in the next chapter.

In addition to paying attention to the types of questions that can be used during an interview, it is important to understand how the interviewer's choice of words and phrases will shape client answers. One area to be especially mindful of is professional language and jargon that many clients may not comprehend or will understand differently than the clinician. This can be illustrated by two different questions used to assess a history of trauma such as sexual abuse. The word *abuse* has many different connotations and meanings for many individuals, and the types of actions that one might consider abusive vary widely. Therefore, if the clinician asks, "Have you ever been sexually abused?" the reply might well be no, even though the client may have experienced something that a mental health professional might consider abusive. On the other hand, a clinician could forgo the word *abuse* entirely, and ask, "Was there ever a time when someone touched you in a way that made you uncomfortable?" If the interviewee responds affirmatively, one can follow up with "Tell me about that." By asking about uncomfortable touch, the context and details of that experience can be identified in a way that potentially differing definitions of abuse would prevent. Similarly, the choice of language is critical in what seemingly would be as straightforward as asking about family history of psychiatric disorders. Often clients are unsure about whether family members were diagnosed with a specific disorder by a mental health professional. They might, however, report that a relative had a "breakdown" or had "lots of problems" or was "always depressed." Brian could be asked, for example, "Is there anyone in your family with a history of depression?" His response would depend upon his understanding of the term *depression*. Instead, he could be asked more generally, "Has anyone else in your family or your parents' families ever had similar problems?" That question is more likely to prompt him to reflect on whether or not family members have had problems—such as with temper, alcohol use, sleep, or concentration—than a question that requires him to think about whether or not someone was ever diagnosed with a disorder. These examples illustrate that the choice of language used in asking questions is as important as the overall question type. What is asked and how it is phrased will ultimately influence the information the interviewer receives.

Knowledge of question types and an awareness of the choice of language can be considered two aspects of effective interviewing skills. What about things not to do? Should certain interviewing styles and questions not be used? Yes, and it is equally important to understand tactics that tend not to be helpful during an assessment interview.

STYLES OF QUESTIONING TO AVOID It is best to avoid the use of *why* questions during assessment interviews. Questions such as "Why did you do that?," "Why did you feel that way?," or "Why are you here?" are not helpful for two reasons. First, *why* questions suggest the client is cognizant of his or her motivation for doing something. Most often awareness of one's motivations is something that comes about through the process of counseling but typically is not readily and easily known at the outset. Therefore, it is best to avoid asking questions during an initial or intake interview that a client will be hard pressed to answer. *Why* questions may have their place in the counseling process but only after a solid therapeutic relationship has been developed and the client is actively involved in seeking understanding of self. This leads to the second reason not to use *why* questions during an assessment interview. *Why* tends to elicit defensiveness in many people. When individuals become defensive, they also become guarded and consequently disclose less information than when they feel open and nondefensive. Since one goal of an interview is to help the interviewee to talk openly and freely about him- or herself, *why* questions tend to be counterproductive.

Clients are also likely to have difficulty and be less open when asked simultaneously two or more questions. There is a common tendency for counselors in training, in their eagerness to gather information, to pose a two- or three-part question. For example, a counselor could ask, "When did your problems begin? Was that before you went to college? What was going on with your family then?" It is best to ask one question at a time and allow a client to respond before asking a follow-up question; otherwise the interviewee can feel like he or she is being bombarded with questions. People tend not to like having questions fired at them and will likely shut down if they perceive the process as interrogation rather than one of information exchange.

When clinicians are anxious or feeling pressured to get through a large agenda of questions, the interview process can be rushed. The author has observed in graduate student trainees a tendency to not allow clients adequate time to answer one question before moving on to the next one. This tends to happen when an interviewer feels pressure to get it all done in the allotted time. One way to reduce the chances that the interview becomes a pressured grilling is to keep in mind that it is neither necessary nor possible to ask every conceivable question in a single interview session. Often, information gathering will need to occur with a series of assessments interviews. Other than a concern about a client posing a serious risk of harm to self or others, there is not information that is so critical to gather that it cannot wait until the next interview.

Effective pacing of interview questions will also be guided by careful observation of client nonverbal communications and active listening skills. Does the interviewee appear tense and short-winded in response to questions, or comfortably expansive? Reading the interviewee's body language and amount of disclosure will also help to ensure that adequate time to reflect on and respond to interview questions is given. Beyond question type and style, what other fundamental concepts are necessary to understand in order to conduct effective assessment interviews?

FACILITATING CLIENT DISCLOSURES AND ASSESSING CLIENT BEHAVIORS The continual use of active listening and attending skills is crucial for an effective interview. Active listening and attending, as discussed earlier, help to promote and maintain rapport. In addition, these skills enable the interviewer to read client behavior. Clients, through their responses to questions, are giving feedback to the interviewer. Is the client giving only terse, circumspect answers even when presented with an open question? Conversely, is the client eager and starting to tell his or her story even before being asked the opening question? Does the client seem to react in an uncomfortable, nervous fashion when a particular topic or question is raised? The skilled interviewer responds to client feedback and modifies the interview based on the verbal and nonverbal behavior of the interviewee. The client who responds with clipped, short answers may need to hear more validating and supportive statements from the counselor before moving ahead with further questioning. On the other hand, the verbose client may need some gentle interruption and focus so that other pieces of the story can be gathered. Clients whose anxiety does not seem to dissipate as the interview unfolds will need reassurance and validation that this first meeting is uncomfortable for many people. Empathic reassurances can help build trust and move the interview along so that the client is more willing to open up.

Client openness is also facilitated by interspersing interview questions with restatements and summarizations. If too many questions are asked consecutively, without a break, the client may not feel heard and understood. Clients who sense their concerns are not being understood are likely to reveal less and less about themselves as the interviewer tries, sometimes in vain, to gather more and more information. When that happens, the process has become adversarial, not collaborative. Since interviewing is both a skill and an art, there is not a precise number of questions that can be asked before an empathic summary statement is communicated. In general, it is helpful to respond with a restatement of the client's presenting problem before gathering more contextual information such as problem onset, frequency, and severity. Having said that, in some cases one or two clarifying questions are needed before the interviewer has an adequate sense of the problem in order to respond empathically. As the interview proceeds, the clinician will want to stay mindful of the number of questions that have been asked consecutively, and break up the questioning process with statements of validation, encouragement, and reassurance, as needed.

Another strategy for facilitating client openness is to introduce difficult and sensitive topics through normalizations and bridges. A **normalizing statement**, prior to posing a question, lets the client know that a routine question is being presented. For example, an interviewer could state to a child client, "This may sound like a funny question, but I ask all the kids who come to see me, is there anything you are feeling scared about?" Similarly, with an older client like Brian, Melanie, the interviewer, might preface a suicide assessment question with, "One of the questions we ask everyone who comes to our clinic is whether they have been having thoughts about killing themself this past week." The use of a normalizing statement prior to certain questions creates a more transparent process. By being transparent, the interviewer lets the client know his or her intention about why the question is being raised. In these two examples, the interviewer's intention is to screen all clients who come to the clinic for the presence of certain feelings or thoughts. Without the use of a normalizing statement before raising certain sensitive topics, the interviewer may inadvertently signal to the client that something that was said previously prompted this new question and possibly raise the interviewee's anxiety that something very unusual, troubling, or problematic has been disclosed.

Bridges, like normalization statements, foster transparency and bring a sense of continuity to the assessment interview. **Bridges** are linking statements that connect an assessment question to the client's stated concerns or problems. An example of this might be, "When we began talking today, you mentioned having difficulty with being snappy and blowing up (restatement of Brian's problem using his language). When people are having difficulty with angry outbursts, it's helpful to know if anyone else in their family or their parents' families have ever had a similar problem." Rather than introducing the topic of family mental health history with a more abrupt statement, such as "Now I'd like to ask you about your family history," the bridge helps the client understand the rationale for the question. That rationale could be expanded upon if the interviewer was sensing the client was somewhat hesitant to reveal information. For example, "It's helpful to know if anyone else in your family or your parents' families have ever had a similar problem, because some problems, like _____, can run in families and knowing that can give us a clue about what might be going on for you." Both normalization and bridging statements signal to clients that their concerns are being validated and that the information-gathering process is logically connected to those concerns.

PRACTICAL INTERVIEWING STRATEGIES   The nature of the initial interview process—asking many information-gathering questions—can make it appear more clinician driven than client centered. It may even seem to an outside observer looking in, that clinician and client are working at cross-purposes: the client has a story to tell and the clinician interrupts the story with a predetermined agenda. Client disclosure will be facilitated if the two interview participants are working in tandem rather than in dissonance. Although it is easier to remain client centered and collaborative during a counseling session than during an initial assessment interview, it is feasible and facilitative to do so.

Ultimately, interviewing is a balancing act. On the one hand, the interviewer needs to attend to, follow, and remain sensitive to the client's story, while at the same time sometimes

PRACTICE SUGGESTION
Practical Interviewing Tips

- Share with the client information you've received from a referral source.
- Review any prior records *after* the interview, not before.
- Prepare emotionally.
- Develop note-taking strategies:
  - ✔ Have several blank pages to write on: many times client information won't fit neatly into the allotted space on a preprinted intake form and the interview doesn't usually follow the sequence on the form.
  - ✔ Use a shorthand, with common abbreviations:
    - Sx—symptoms
    - Hx—history
    - Tx—treatment or therapy
    - Ct—client
    - ⬆—increased/improved;   ⬇—decreased/worsened
    - ▲—change
  - ✔ Develop your own shorthand system.
  - ✔ Jot down only the key phrases and facts.
  - ✔ Allow sufficient time after the interview to review your notes and add detail where necessary.
  - ✔ Differentiate client words from your own impressions and observations.

needing to interrupt or redirect the story in order to gather the additional pieces. Learning how to juggle listening and empathic communication with posing information-gathering questions takes time and practice.

There are, however, some practical interviewing tips which, based on the author's experience with interviewing and other assessment methods, such as psychological testing, can enhance the likelihood of the interview becoming a collaborative rather than counselor-centered endeavor. The following Practice Suggestion: Practical Interviewing Tipslists practical suggestions that can be used prior to, during, and after an initial interview.

In order to put these suggestions into practice, it is important to understand the rationale behind them. Any time a client is referred for counseling services, it is important for the interviewer to acknowledge awareness of the referral and assess the client's understanding of and attitude toward the referral. A brief conversation about the referral helps to create an atmosphere of transparency and openness—acknowledging that "we both know this is how you got here, but I (the interviewer) don't know your view of that recommendation." For example, Brian might be told, "I understand you were referred to our clinic by Dr. Jones." Following that statement he could be asked, "What is your understanding of Dr. Jones's recommendation that you come here?" Furthermore, an assessment of the client's attitude about the referral is a way to gauge his or her views about the helping process.

When prior client records exist, regardless of whether they are mental health, educational, legal, or medical, it is better to review those records after the initial interview rather than before it, for a couple of reasons. First and foremost, reading a record about someone prior to the interview will unwittingly create a bias toward the client. As was discussed in Chapter 1, a large body of psychology research has documented the existence of a confirmatory bias in human beings. When someone is given information about an individual prior to either reading a narrative about that person or observing the person engaged in a certain behavior, and then later asked to make judgments, evaluations, or conclusions about the target individual, those judgments and evaluations reveal a biasing effect. That is, information is attended to and recalled that is consistent with or confirms what the observer or reader has been told about the other person. Furthermore, both verbal and nonverbal behavior that is *inconsistent* with the prior narrative tends to be ignored. This unconscious biasing can happen even in those trained to be aware of such processes. For example, when graduate counseling students are given different background information about a client—history of anxiety, neutral information, history of resiliency—and then watch the client being interviewed, they tend to make observations about client behavior during the interview that is consistent with the background information they were given prior to watching a videotaped interview. Therefore, it is better to interview a new client from a neutral, objective position. Records can be later reviewed in order to assess to what degree the client's current presentation and report of his or her history is consistent or inconsistent with the record. In addition to the biasing problem, a prior record review may simply be an unnecessary time commitment on the part of the interviewer. In the event that a prospective client does not show for an initial assessment appointment, time would have been spent on someone who does not end up receiving services. Furthermore, the current problem and possible course of treatment may not necessarily be informed by someone's previous documented history and evaluations. It is more advantageous for the clinician and client to collaboratively decide whether the clinician's review of the record will be helpful once the initial interview has been completed and a course of action has been agreed upon, which may involve further assessment such as record review. When done that way, the purpose in reading the prior record is clear to both parties.

Emotional preparation involves getting ready and relaxed. Meeting a new client, let alone a group of individuals in the case of an initial interview with a family, can be awkward and uncomfortable. The added demands of gathering information, developing rapport, and establishing a treatment plan can intensify any initial discomfort or nervousness. Several preparatory steps can be taken to allay a clinician's initial discomfort with beginning the assessment of a new client.

1. *Check that You Have the Necessary Equipment:* Gather writing tools, paper, forms, list of questions, appointment cards, and names and contact information in case the client will be referred to someone else in your agency or another facility.

2. *Get Acquainted with the Physical Space:* Know the space where the interview will take place, such as where a clock is located, seating arrangements, and any furniture in the room that can become an obstacle for creating rapport, such as a large desk between two chairs. Consider the following questions: How quiet is the space? Are noise-dampening devices needed and turned on? What, if anything, is in the space that might pose a distraction to the client or you?

3. *Calm Yourself:* Any type of relaxation strategy can help to alleviate initial tension and anxiety. This can be anything from taking a few deep breaths to meditation, from visual imagery to self-talk. Reminding oneself about the purpose of the interview (*I'm here to gather information to figure out how I or someone else can be of help*) and reassuring oneself (*It's OK if I don't get all the information the intake form requires. I can arrange another interview if needed*) can help to alleviate nervousness.

4. *Keep Expectations Realistic:* Sometimes trainees and novice professionals put pressure on themselves to have an accurate diagnosis, case conceptualization, and treatment plan by the end of an initial interview. Although in some cases that is possible, it is more likely that at the end of an initial interview some tentative case conceptualization hypotheses will emerge along with the recognition that a number of topics still need to be explored.

5. *Remember to Listen:* Another element of clinician anxiety is worrying about what to say next. It can be helpful to realize that many of the questions an interviewer might ask often flow naturally from actively listening to the client's unfolding story—rather than to one's internal thoughts—and being aware of the unclear and missing pieces to the story. If the clinician is too caught up in his or her thoughts about what to do and say—*What should I say next? How should I ask that? What did my supervisor want me to ask?*—then listening to the client ceases and anxiety begins. One practical remedy is to come to the interview with not only the list of topics to cover, which sometimes is contained on an intake form, but specific questions as well. Then rather than feeling pressured to memorize a script, you can rest in the knowledge that the questions are at hand, if needed. This is what semistructured and structured interviews involve.

An understanding of these strategies and suggestions can help to develop effective interviewing skills. There is, however, no substitute for experience. These skills can be acquired and mastered both through listening and watching other interviewers as well as practicing the techniques described in the chapter. Interviews are often conducted in other contexts, and paying attention to how a radio or television host, for example, interviews a guest, and what seems to promote disclosure and what may not, can help you hone your skills. A more comprehensive discussion of interviewing strategies is beyond the scope of this chapter. There are, however, several excellent resources available for those interested in a more detailed, nuts-and-bolts discussion of interviewing techniques (see Appendix B: Additional Resources).

Gathering Information from Children

DIRECT INTERVIEW QUESTIONS   The initial interview with a young child—preschool through elementary school age—has four goals, three of which are essentially the same as for an interview with an adolescent or adult, and one is specific to the developmental needs of young children. The three similar goals include 1) building a therapeutic relationship; 2) engaging the child in the counseling process; and 3) determining what, if anything, the child wants help with. The fourth goal is to gain an understanding of the child's social and emotional development. Since adults almost always are the ones referring children to counseling, it is important to assess whether or not the child perceives him- or herself as having a problem that a counseling process could help with and, if so, whether the child's view of the problem matches the adult's perception. This is done by establishing the child's understanding of why he or she has been brought to the clinician's office. Unlike adults, who may be referred by someone else—physician, probation officer, or employer—young children vary widely in their understanding of why an adult caregiver thinks a referral to a helping professional is necessary. Adults may not agree with the referring person's rationale for the referral and may potentially be in a precontemplative stage of change, but they generally comprehend why someone else has suggested or mandated their involvement in counseling. Some young children are able to articulate why they are seeing the counselor and their statements match closely to the parent or other adult caregiver's view of the problem. A sizeable number, however, come with an incomplete, confused, or fundamentally different presentation of the presenting problems. One basic interview question that can help establish the child's understanding of the referral is, "How come your _____ (caregiver who brought the child) brought you here today to see me?" Sometimes a child will respond with a shrug, or a "Don't know." When that happens, a prompt to "take a guess" may help uncover the child's awareness of why he or she is seeing you. Once some answer has been supplied ("I have trouble listening to my teacher"), a follow-up question, as would be asked of an adult, can be helpful: "Do *you* think you have that trouble (or whatever problem statement the child has given)?"

Children as young as preschool age can be questioned directly during an initial interview about feelings and problems as well. When direct interview questions are used with young children, it is preferable to first engage them on topics they are more likely to have the ability and comfort level with answering, such as age or grade in school, name of teacher, family members, or fun activities. For example, a child might be asked, "What do you like to do for fun?" These areas are useful to explore initially, both because they are safer and easier topics to converse about, and they provide the clinician information about the child's verbal skills. In fact, it is better to engage a young child by asking first about these safer, easier topics before even getting to the question of how come he or she is here. If these initial questions reveal difficulty with verbal expression, then the clinician may be better off relying more on nonverbal techniques (see below). If, on the other hand, this initial inquiry suggests that this is a child with adequate verbal skills, then proceeding to a series of questions about feelings can be helpful. Furthermore, at this stage of an initial interview with a young child, it is better to interview about feelings rather than problems because most children have feelings and may want help with those. Problems are typically the concern of the referring adult, and the child may or may not share the parent's view, especially in the case of externalizing or acting-out behaviors (see Chapter 10).

When children are questioned directly about feelings, the format of the questions will need to vary depending upon the age of the child. Younger children (preschool and early elementary school age) tend to respond better to closed and multiple-choice questions than to open-ended ones. They can be asked about whether or not they are experiencing primary emotions such as fear, sadness, or anger. For example, the clinician can preface this exploration about feeling states by saying, "Lots of the girls and boys who come here have things they are scared about. Is there anything you are scared about?" Some children may also be able to report on the frequency of the fear: "How often do you get scared about . . .?" A child client could then be asked the same questions but substituting the other emotions for fear with feeling labels (such as mad and sad). Although a child may report one or more emotional experience, that does not mean he or she wants help with those feelings. It is important for the counselor to clarify whether or not the child indeed wants help with one or more feelings. This can be done straightforwardly by asking, "Would you like me to help you with your scary (or mad or sad) feeling?"

Those children with adequate verbal skills can be questioned about problems as well. Young children can be told, "Lots of the girls and boys who come here have a problem they get help with. Do you know what a problem is?" Some young children may not know and a simple explanation can suffice: "A problem is something that happens that you don't like, like your brother always taking your Lego pieces, or is something that is hard to do." Once it seems apparent that the child understands what is meant by *problem,* she or he can be asked, "Do you have a problem you want help with?" If the answer is yes, then a follow-up question is in order: "What is that?"

Children as young as preschool age typically have the verbal skills necessary to respond to interview questions like the ones described earlier, but the format of the questions needs to be revised. One example of modifying an interview question for a child can be illustrated with asking about problem severity. An adolescent or adult could be asked a scaling question in order to assess their perception of the severity of a problem. For example, "On a scale of 1 to 10, how severe is your _____ (problem), with 1 being not severe at all and 10 being the sever-est?" Preschool and early elementary age children do not typically have the cognitive capacity to understand a numerical ranking of problem severity because this involves a mathematical con-cept they typically have not yet acquired. On the other hand, most young children understand the concept of size. Therefore, rather than asking the child a scaling question, the clinician can use a visual and verbal approach. The counselor can use his or her hands to gesture size and ask, "Is this a small, medium, or big problem?" This is just one of many examples of the kinds of modifications in interviewing techniques that are needed when young children are clients.

The problem series questions, as with the feeling questions, can help establish whether or not the child wants help and whether that is something suitable to a counseling process. In addi-tion, this preliminary assessment can help the clinician discern what type of counseling makes sense, individual, family, group, or some combination of approaches. If the child identifies an internal problem—a difficulty with feelings—or a behavior he or she wants to change, then indi-vidual counseling could be helpful. On the other hand, if the child does not identify anything he or she wants help with or is wanting someone else to change (e.g., a parent to "stop getting super mad"), then a family or group approach may need to be considered.

One additional goal of the initial contact with a child, which is unique to children, is an assessment of the child's social and emotional development. The remainder of this section will focus on combining nonverbal techniques and questions in order to assess the child's perception of problems and develop some tentative hypotheses about social and emotional functioning, themes, and concerns. Collectively, nonverbal assessment techniques have been labeled projectives. As mentioned in Chapter 1, **projectives** are indirect assessment methods whereby a person reveals emotions, concerns, psychological themes, and interper-sonal styles through responses to ambiguous stimuli such as inkblots, pictures, or phrases. Projective techniques also include the use of drawings, storytelling, and symbolic play. A detailed discussion of how to assess children's social and emotional development using another methodology—objective standardized measures—will take place in Chapter 10. The exploration of presenting problems and assessment of social and emotional functioning in young children will require a combination of modified adult interview questions as well as nonverbal projective techniques.

NONVERBAL TECHNIQUES   The younger the child, the more nonverbal methods will be utilized in the assessment of presenting problems. When drawing and play materials are used as part of an initial assessment of a child's social and emotional functioning, the information gleaned from those methods should be integrated with other sources and methods to gain a comprehensive view of the child's perception of his or her problems and concerns. Given that children differ in their preferred modes of expression, it is advisable to have a variety of drawing materials and toys and figures available for assessment. However, turning one's interview space into a toy store is not only unnecessary but will create a hindrance to effective assessment.

The nonverbal methods most commonly utilized when assessing young children include drawings, dollhouse play, and human and animal puppets. Of these methods, only drawings have been standardized in terms of scoring and interpretation systems, but the reliability and validity of standardized drawings is relatively weak compared to other methods, so they should be used for engagement and possibly case conceptualization purposes but not diagnosing emotional and social maladjustment (Hojnoski, Morrison, Brown, & Mathews, 2006). The two kinds of drawings for which a variety of standardized scoring systems have been developed include Draw-A-Person and Kinetic Family Drawings. Like the other nonverbal methods, these types of drawings can be used informally, rather than formally scored, and can provide a rich understanding of a child's perceptions of self and family. Again, those initial hypotheses developed from drawings, regarding a child's perceptions of problems and other pertinent themes should be integrated with other sources of information. At times, these nonverbal methods allow the clinician access into the child's world in a way that direct questions may not. Furthermore, for those children who have difficulty expressing themselves verbally, drawings may be a more productive means toward understanding a child's perceptions than more traditional verbal techniques.

DRAWING AS AN ASSESSMENT TOOL   For those children who like to draw (and it is useful to ask that of the child client before embarking on a series of drawings), there are several types of drawings that can be helpful assessment methods. First, it is helpful to allow the child to draw a picture of whatever he or she wants to. That provides the child some control and freedom over self-expression. It is also helpful to tell the child, "You can draw me a picture of whatever you like and then I'm going to ask you to draw certain things." After the initial drawing, a child can be asked to make a series of problem-and-solution drawings (Mills & Crowley, 1986). The child is simply instructed to "draw a picture of a problem you are having." Next the child is instructed to "draw a picture of what that problem will look like when it is all better." Last, the child can be asked to "make a picture of how the problem got better or solved." Depending upon the child and his or her verbal skills, some brief discussion about the drawings can be done after all three are completed.

One of the most common childhood drawing assessment techniques is the Draw-A-Person (DAP). Although there are variations on how to instruct the child in this task, one common procedure to ask the child to "draw me a picture of a person" (Merrell, 2008). As mentioned before, scoring and interpretation systems have been developed for this procedure (Cummings, 1986; Naglieri, McNeish, & Bardos, 1991), *The Draw A Person Screening Procedure for Emotional Disturbance (Draw A Person: SPED)* (Naglieri et al., 1991) is intended to be just what the name suggests, an assessment instrument for screening children and adolescents for being at risk of having some kind of emotional disorder. However, it has been the experience of this author and others (Merrell, 2008; Schroeder & Gordon, 2002) that the Draw-A-Person is best used informally as a springboard for assessing the child's perceptions and feelings indirectly. When using the DAP informally, the clinician can ask the child a series of questions about the person in the drawing and make some tentative hypotheses about the child based on those answers. Those questions pertain to perceptions of gender, age, mood, and favorite activities. They include:

- Is this person a boy or girl?
- How old is he/she?
- How is he/she feeling?
- How come he/she is feeling _____?
- What does he/she like to do for fun?

The answers to those questions may indirectly reveal concerns the child may be having about feelings or self-perception. This is based on the projective theory that the child is creating through the drawing feelings and concerns related to self. Information gathered from the drawing and the child's responses to questions about it should be integrated with other sources of information that come more directly from the child or from knowledgeable adults in the child's life.

A modification of the DAP is to have a child make a series of drawings starting with a house, then a tree, and finally a person. Scoring and interpretation systems for the house and tree drawings have also been developed but are even more controversial than the DAP and are better used as warm-up activities for the person and family drawings.

The Kinetic Family Drawing (KFD) is one other type of drawing that the child can create and be asked questions about to potentially uncover family and interpersonal concerns the child may want help with. The basic instruction in the KFD is, "Draw a picture of everyone in your family, including you, doing something" (Burns & Kaufman, 1970). Young children are more likely to ask questions about how to do the KFD than the other types of drawings mentioned previously. Children sometimes inquire about whether it is OK to include certain people, and that decision is up to them. Additionally, they may ask what is meant by family, and whoever they think is part of their family can be included in the drawing. Sometimes children will hesitate with the drawing by stating "I can't draw well" or "I can only draw a stick figure." Providing reassurance and letting them know that whichever way they want to draw is acceptable is a helpful response. Like the Draw-A-Person technique, some scoring and interpretation systems have been developed for the KFD (Handler & Habenict, 1994), but it too can be used more informally. Once the drawing is complete, the clinician can review it with the child to find out who is in it and what each person is doing. Again, it is more advisable to use this technique to stimulate conversation about family relationships, conflicts, roles, communication and discipline patterns, and unmet needs, rather than scoring and interpreting it, given that studies of its validity, particularly cross-cultural validity, have produced mixed, nonsignificant, and counterintuitive results (Handler & Habenict).

Inferences about family relationships and roles can be made by inspecting the drawing. For example, the child's perception of close and distant relationships may be gleaned by identifying who is next to whom, the distance between members, and whether or not family members are doing something on their own or with another member. In addition, who is included in the drawing and who is left out, and the relative sizes of the figures may provide clues about the child's feelings toward family members and perceptions about who is considered important or powerful (Handler & Habenict, 1994).

SYMBOLIC PLAY ASSESSMENT   For those children who have trouble with verbal engagement and do not enjoy drawing, symbolic play can be another option for assessing perceptions of problems and concerns. Some children may spontaneously act out feelings and themes with dolls, puppets, and a dollhouse. On the other hand, some may need guidance and direction in order to reveal emotional and social concerns when engaged in symbolic play. When the child is engaged in symbolic play, he or she can be asked some questions about a doll or puppet figure that may provide some clues as to how the child is feeling and thinking about self and significant others. Like with the DAP, the child can be asked about how a doll or puppet figure is feeling, how come they have the feeling, and what the figure likes and does not like to do. Lastly, the child can be asked if there is something the symbolic figure wants help with. It is important to keep in mind, however, that whenever children communicate about a symbolic figure's emotions and actions, those communications may not represent how they are actually feeling or thinking about themselves.

OTHER PROJECTIVE TECHNIQUES   Two additional projective techniques that can be useful for engaging young children and assessing potential emotional and social concerns is the **sentence completion task** and the **three wishes** question. Like the DAP and KFD, scoring and interpretation systems exist for various sentence completion tasks but they can also be used informally. A sentence completion technique involves providing a stem phrase to a child, such as "I like people who . . ." and the child's task is to complete the sentence. Several different versions of sentence completion tasks have been developed, including informal nonstandardized and formal standardized ones, and typically they are 40 items in length (Merrell, 2008). A specific emotional or social theme may emerge from the child's responses. If that is the case, the child can be asked whether that is something he or she would like help with. In that way, the sentence completion task, like drawings, can be used to engage the child in the counseling process and elicit concerns that may not come about readily with direct interview questions. Of the formal sentence completion tasks, the *Rotter Incomplete Sentences Blank* is the oldest (Anastasi & Urbina, 1997) and most commonly used (Camara, Nathan, & Puente, 2000). Two more recent additions include *Hart Sentence Completion Test for Children* and *Washington University Sentence Completion Test* (Merrell).

The three wishes question is one additional way to indirectly infer whether or not a child has a concern. Simply, the child is asked, "If you had three wishes right now, what would they be?" A child's answers to the three wishes can be as varied as flavors of ice cream. Some children wish for material possessions or toys, others for certain powers or abilities, some want something interpersonal (e.g., "my parents to stop fighting"), and others simply don't know.

Many children will respond well to a mixture of nonverbal and verbal strategies. By following the child's lead and cues, the assessor can get a sense of which ones to rely on and when to use them. As is the case with working with adults, creativity, caring, and experience will help to make this a beneficial process.

Summary and Conclusions

This chapter focused on interviewing as an initial information-gathering assessment method. The main goal of an initial counseling interview is to develop a contextual understanding of a client's presenting problem and concerns, which leads to a preliminary case conceptualization and treatment plan. Three types of interviews were identified—unstructured, semistructured, and structured. The main focus was on the unstructured, or intake, interview. An intake interview allows the counselor maximum flexibility in deciding about which direction to go and how best to tailor the interview to fit the concerns and needs of the client. Semistructured and structured interviews have greater interclinician diagnostic reliability but are more limited than intake interviews with respect to gaining a contextual understanding of presenting problems and possibly rapport building. Regardless of the type of interview used, there are fundamental interviewing principles and skills that, when utilized, enhance the effectiveness of this assessment process. This chapter reviewed those essential interviewing tactics and techniques and illustrated their use in an intake.

The interviewing of preschool and elementary school age children requires modifications in the use of questions as well as the application of additional methods such as projective techniques that facilitate the engagement of the child. Nonverbal techniques included Draw-A-Person, Kinetic Family Drawing, other drawings, and symbolic play. The discussion of specific projective techniques included sentence completion and three wishes. Although standardized scoring systems exist for some of these procedures, the perspective here was on informal uses of these methods. When interviewing young children, careful attention needs to be paid to language, word choice, and nonverbal techniques that can help to uncover a child's perceptions, feelings, and thoughts.

Reflection Questions and Experiential Exercises

1. How will the process of developing and maintaining rapport with a client during assessment be similar to rapport building during therapy? How will the process be different?

2. When might you consider using a structured interview schedule?

3. Which interviewing skills do you think you are fluent in and which ones might you need to develop?

4. Of the various techniques for interviewing young children, which ones would you likely use and which might you not use?

5. Role-play in groups of three in an initial interview about presenting problems for approximately 10 minutes. One person can be the interviewer, the other the interviewee, and the third person can function as an observer. Upon completion of the interview, discuss which interview skills were used and how effective those skills were.

4

EXPLORING PRESENTING PROBLEMS, READINESS FOR CHANGE, AND RISKS AND RESOURCES

Chapter Objectives

After reading this chapter, you should be able to:

■ Understand how presenting problems are assessed using an unstructured interview process.

■ Understand the concept of readiness for change and how to identify a client's stage of change at the time of an initial assessment.

■ Explain the concept of risks and resources and how to gather information from this perspective.

■ Describe various ways to open an initial interview and the tasks of the closing phase.

Brian, the client from the case study in Chapter 3, was seen for an intake interview at the Maple Street Behavioral Health Clinic. He had reported concerns about his temper, his relationship with his girl-friend ending, trouble sleeping, and a "case of the jitters." In addition to the presenting problems that were identified in the previous chapter, Melanie, the intake clinician, obtained the following background information during the intake and a second interview the following week.

Brian's parents are from Costa Rica and he moved to the United States with his mother and younger sisters after his parents divorced when he was 12 years old. He has a sister who is 24 years old, who was adopted when Brian was around age 5. He also has an older half-brother. He had very little contact with his father, who remained in Costa Rica after Brian and the rest of the family came to the United States. Three years ago, his father died in a car accident.

Brian reports that at one time his mother was on antidepressants and that he has a maternal uncle who suffers from depression. Also, a paternal grandfather committed suicide.

Brian is now a sophomore at a local community college working on an associate's degree. Brian has been working as a machinist for six years and lately has noticed he has "difficulty paying attention at work" and "always feels tired."

OVERVIEW

The purpose of this chapter is to describe an interview process for gathering information about a client's presenting problems, readiness for change, current functioning, and psychosocial history. It will focus on a process for exploring and defining the presenting problems as well as identifying individual, familial, and environmental factors that can impact those problems. These factors can be thought of as potential risks or resources. Risk factors are those parts of an individual's life that may interfere with the alleviation of the presenting problem or possibly worsen it. Resources can also occur at any level (individual, interpersonal, and community) and can be thought of as factors that promote problem resolution. A risks and resources framework can be applied to an initial interview in order to provide a rationale for the information gathered and to organize what potentially can be an overwhelming amount of data. With that in mind, there are three goals of an initial assessment interview. The first goal is for both counselor and client to establish a comprehensive contextual understanding of the presenting problem. The second goal is to identify potential risks and resources. The third and final goal is to begin to formulate a case conceptualization, which will set the stage for planning further counseling and other potential interventions.

This chapter will also focus on practical strategies for collecting the necessary information. Specific questions to use during an initial assessment and a process for closing an intake interview will be addressed. Traditionally, the term "intake" interview has been applied to initial interviews done in mental health settings. This unstructured intake interview format can, however, be thought of as a prototypical initial assessment interview that can be applied in other various counseling settings: college counseling centers, K–12 schools, community and organizational settings, and rehabilitation. The chapter will conclude with a presentation of an interviewing skills evaluation checklist for students, trainees, and supervisors.

EXPLORING PRESENTING PROBLEMS

Clients, both younger and older, often describe their problems with vague idiosyncratic terms that mask the contexts in which those problems occur. Brian, for example, tells the intake screener that he has "a lot going on" and "a case of jitters." What do those statements mean? How might Melanie, the clinician, probe further to gain a fuller definition of his problems and the contexts in which they occur? Once informed consent has been reviewed and the client has been given an opportunity to ask questions about the process or interviewer credentials and training, the information-gathering stage of the interview commences. The information gathering begins with an exploration of the problems and concerns that have led an individual or family unit to seek out counseling services. Something as seemingly straightforward as inquiring about presenting problems and concerns has, however, multiple possibilities, each one having implications for how the interview unfolds. In structured interviews, the initial question is set and each interviewer asks it exactly the same way. In semistructured interviews, more latitude is given to the interviewer in framing questions. When using unstructured interviews, the clinician can exercise the most discretion in formatting questions. The intentional interviewer recognizes the different ways to begin a clinical interview and deliberately chooses one based on an understanding of how the opening question style can affect client responses.

The Opening Question

The purpose of the opening question is to communicate to the client that he or she is free to discuss a broad range of concerns while simultaneously creating a focus to the interview. One such opening—"What brings you here today?"—was briefly discussed in Chapter 3. The following are additional examples of opening questions, each having implications for client responses to the initial and subsequent questions:

- What would you like to talk about?
- What problems have brought you here?
- How are you hoping _____ (I/we or name of organization) can help you?

All four questions are broad and open-ended but each one sends a slightly different message. The second opening is the broadest; the client is being asked to discuss anything that comes to mind. That might appear to be a helpful way to begin, giving the client free rein to discuss whatever he or she needs to. What, however, might be problematic with that opening? By being so open-ended, the client may not understand that the purpose of an assessment interview is to focus on problems that can be addressed through counseling or some other kind of intervention: medication, support groups like Alcoholics Anonymous, exercise, or relaxation techniques. When asked "What would you like to talk about?," the anxious or guarded client may choose to discuss something—the weather, politics, a favorite movie—unrelated to the matter at hand and then need to be redirected. When that happens, the client is given a meta-message or communication about the initial question, which in essence says, Wait, what I said first is not quite true, you can discuss certain things, but not anything. Having begun that way, rapport building does not get off to a good start.

The third possibility, "What problems have brought you here?," reduces the ambiguity about what to talk about and yet remains a fairly broad opening. However, the word "problems" can be problematic for a couple of reasons. First, there are some clients who present at an intake interview but do not see themselves as having a problem, and the question suggests that they do. This can happen when someone else has recommended or required that they seek counseling. Second, this opening may suggest to all clients that the purpose here is to discuss only what is wrong and deficient, and by implication, with them. One way around this is to substitute a more neutral, less loaded term, such as *concerns*, for problem.

The opening "What brings you here *today*?" is another neutral, broad opening question that introduces a focus on current concerns and events that led to the client seeking counseling services. By introducing the word "today," the interviewer communicates a focus on present concerns. Having that focus in the question is more advantageous than the first possibility— "What would you like to talk about?"—because it helps to guide the client toward the information that will be necessary to gather: present concerns. It also eliminates the use of a more emotionally charged word, "problems." How the client responds to this question will be one way to gauge how he or she views the counseling process and his or her readiness to engage in the process.

A fourth way to open the interview is to ask, "How are you hoping _____ (I/we or name of organization) can help you?" It has been the author's experience that out of the four possible opening questions, this one evokes the strongest feelings and opinions, both positive and negative, among students and trainees. Why is that? With this opening, help is implied and client expectations are sought. Some trainees experience discomfort with the idea of taking responsibility for helping someone when they don't know ahead of time if that will be the case. On the other hand, many see the value in communicating to clients that this is a helping process. Since it is largely through the use of spoken language that rapport is established, one's choice of words makes a big difference. With whom would you prefer sharing your concerns and intimate details of your life: the person who has a helping orientation or a problem orientation? As Jerome Frank (1973, p. 42), an influential psychiatrist and psychotherapy researcher, concluded, "Thus success in therapy depends in large part on its ability to combat the patient's demoralization and *heighten his hopes of relief.*" This opening can convey a sense of optimism that things can get better, that relief is possible. The client's perception of the interviewer as hopeful and optimistic can have important therapeutic benefit and may be a major factor in accounting for the significant improvement many clients report after an initial interview (Snyder, Michael, & Cheavens, 1999). Furthermore, by asking "How are you hoping I, or we, can be of help?," client's expectations about counseling can be readily uncovered. Research has shown that with depressed clients, for example, expectations that a given treatment will be beneficial, regardless of whether it is psychological or pharmacological, is strongly correlated with improvement (Kirsch, 2010). Therefore, it is helpful to know at the outset what the client expects. Does the client want to be told what to do? Is he or she wanting the therapist to fix someone else, such as a family member? Does the client want symptoms to go away, or does he or she want help in understanding how a problem happened in the first place? In addition to assessing client expectations for counseling, this opening has the advantage of getting to goals right away. If the client goals are identified at the beginning of the interview, then the information-gathering phase of the interview can proceed in a more efficient way. When one knows where one is headed, it is easier to get there. Therefore, using an opening that includes the words *help* and *hope* has multiple benefits for both the client and counselor.

Ultimately, there is no one right way to begin an intake interview, but trainees and professionals will serve their clients better by understanding their intention for using a particular opening. Once the opening question has been posed and the client has begun to tell his or her story, a series of follow-up questions will emerge that will help to establish for both the clinician and the client a contextual understanding of the presenting problem and concerns.

Developing a Contextual Understanding of the Presenting Problems

The old adage that context is everything is never more apropos than in the assessment of presenting problems. A contextual understanding is necessary for appropriate intervention to take place. Furthermore, understanding context is important because many clients enter a counseling process with multiple problems and symptoms, each of which may have a different pattern and history. A series of questions will help to move clients along from initial fuzzy descriptions of a concern or problem to a story that takes on a certain shape as the interview unfolds. At the outset of an intake interview, clients tend to describe problems with global, vague phrases: "I have not been doing well," I haven't been myself lately," "I'm falling apart," and so on. Even when the initial problem presentation includes more specific phrases and terms such as *anxiety, depressed,* or *stress,* there is still much that requires elucidation. The task of an initial problem assessment interview is to create a contextual understanding of the client's problems and concerns in terms of their onset, frequency, duration, severity, and attempted solutions. Standard intake questions for assessing presenting problems are listed in Table 4.1. In addition, there are questions for assessing situational factors affecting problem frequency and severity, as well as eliciting information about strategies used for coping with the problem. Lastly, an effective initial interview will include a question designed to elicit from the client a statement about problem resolution or goals if that was not articulated in response to the opening question. As more context is created, both client and counselor are in a better position to address the presenting problem than they were before the interview started, and in that sense assessment becomes an intervention. If a series of interview questions promotes client insight; or relief that the presenting problem, when put in perspective, is not so overwhelming; or sets the stage for making behavioral change, then the act of assessing was an intervention. Assessment becomes intervention when it facilitates client change at the cognitive, emotional, or behavioral level.

Depending on the client, some of the information gathered through an unstructured intake interview will come spontaneously as the client tells his or her story. Other clients will need to be asked most, if not all, of the questions contained in Table 4.1 in order for a comprehensive understanding of their problems to emerge. The ones identified in Table 4.1 and discussed in this section reflect cognitive–behavioral (Beck, 1995; Meichenbaum, 1985) family systems (Haley, 1976) and solution-oriented (O'Hanlon & Weiner-Davis, 1989) models for understanding and resolving presenting problems. These models provide guides for developing contextual understanding of problems in the sense that they provide a framework for gathering and organizing inter- and intrapersonal factors affecting an individual's emotional, cognitive, and behavioral experiences.

Table 4.1 Interview Questions for Presenting Problems

Problem onset:

When did _____ (client statement of problem) begin?

When did this start happening?

When did you first start experiencing _____ (problem statement)?

When did you first notice that you were _____?

Problem frequency:

How often does _____ occur?

Problem duration:

How long does your _____ (problem, symptoms, mood, thinking) last?

Problem intensity/severity:

How severe has this _____ (problem description) been: a little, somewhat, very much?

On a scale of 1 to 10, how _____ are you feeling; 1 being very little and 10 being very much?

If you were to rate this problem on a scale of 1 to 10, 1 being not at all severe and 10 being extremely severe, how severe is this?

How severe has this _____ been over the past week (two weeks, or month)?

Situational factors affecting problem frequency and severity:

What is the difference between days where _____ is very severe and days when it is less so?

When is _____ at its worst? When is _____ at its least?

When do you have the most trouble with _____? When do you have the least trouble with _____?

What is your life like when _____ is not happening?

You said you were feeling (thinking, doing) _____. What prevents _____ from being worse?

Attempted solutions:

What did you do to try and solve _____ before you came here?

What sorts of things have you done to try and make _____ better?

Defining goals:

How will we know when _____ (the problem) is getting better?

What would you like to see going on in your life in a week, a month, three months that would tell you _____ is improving?

Who would notice if _____ got better?

What would _____ (other person[s]) notice if _____ got better?

Some of the questions in Table 4.1 are relatively straightforward and perhaps can stand on their own without further elaboration. The ones pertaining to problem onset, frequency, and duration are those kinds of questions that help to build a context and are fairly clear-cut. The questions listed in Table 4.1 can be thought of as a template, and the exact wording may need to be modified depending upon the age and cultural background of the client. The questions pertaining to problem intensity or severity, situational factors, attempted solutions, and goals require further explanation.

PROBLEM SEVERITY OR INTENSITY: SCALING QUESTIONS   Scaling questions are typically used to assess the intensity or severity of a problem, feeling, behavior, or bothersome thought. This type of question is similar to those used on standardized questionnaires or inventories. A scaling question provides a response choice for the client. The responses could be qualifying terms, for example, "a little" "somewhat" or "very much," or a numerical rating scale like 1 to 10 or 1 to 100; the higher the number the greater the intensity or severity. Since just about all clients do not experience their presenting problems as a 10 each moment of every day, factors that affect the frequency and severity of the problems are critical to ascertain. Typically, information about the situational variability of problems does not come about spontaneously from clients, and further interview questions will be needed to flesh out that additional context. Part of understanding the nature of a problem involves knowledge of what is happening when the problem is less severe. Effective assessment interview questions help not only to clarify the presenting problem but the ebb and flow of it as well.

EXPLORING SITUATIONAL FACTORS   The questions listed in Table 4.1 under the heading "Situational Factors Affecting Problem Frequency and Severity" are for the purpose of identifying factors that affect the dimensions of problems and concerns. These factors can be environmental, interpersonal, or intrapersonal in nature. For example, Brian could be asked during an intake interview, "What is the difference between those days when you find yourself getting 'snappy' a lot, and those days when that doesn't happen much?" His responses could be anything from "I don't know" to "It seems to happen most when I have trouble getting out of bed in the morning." Here, again, assessment becomes intervention. By asking this question, Brian has reflected and identified a possible trigger for his behavior when feeling irritated, and with awareness of that information lies the potential for change. From there, further assessment about trouble getting out of bed and its relation to his aggressive behavior can take place, which can lead to further intervention, and the cycle continues. Even if Brian is unsure of what distinguishes days with frequent irritable episodes from days with little or no episodes, important groundwork has been laid. The interviewer could respond to Brian's uncertainty with a follow-up question such as, "Do you think it would be helpful to figure out what may be making a difference?" If the answer is yes, then clinician and client could collaboratively discuss ways to uncover that connection. That uncovering, whether it happens in the initial interview or subsequent ones, could then identify environmental factors related to his trouble getting up in the morning—for example, nights out with his drinking buddies. Those uncovering steps could include anything from an additional assessment interview to engaging in counseling or from some type of self-monitoring—keeping a journal, log, or diary—to having him ask coworkers what they notice. If, on the other hand Brian's reply is no or noncommittal—"I don't know, I'm not sure"—then the interviewer probably needs to shift gears and go back to assessing client readiness for change before moving on to assessing risk and protective factors that will be addressed in the next sections.

ASSESSING PSYCHOSOCIAL STRESSORS   Stressful life events, be they negative or positive, can affect the onset and course of problems individuals and families experience. According to the transactional model of stress, it is not the events per se that produce stress, but rather a lack of fit between environmental demands and a person's perceived coping resources (Meichenbaum & Turk, 1982). An individual's appraisal of whether he or she has adequate resources to cope with the demands of an event, situation, or experience is what creates intrapersonal stress. If the demands stemming from a life experience—for example, a job change resulting in a longer commute, less flexible hours, and less autonomy—are perceived as threatening or overwhelming, the individual will likely experience and report stress. On the other hand, if the same change is seen as an opportunity or something one can cope with—more time to listen to my iPod, a more predictable work schedule, and less responsibility for making important decisions—then it is much less likely to be experienced as stressful. Potential stressors can be psychological, physiological, or environmental, and therefore any change in one's psychological well-being or development, health or living status, or other environmental changes has the potential to place added demands on a person. Within the DSM-IV-TR diagnostic system, a potential psychosocial or environmental stressor is conceptualized as a problem that can be "a negative life event, an environmental difficulty or deficiency, a familial or other interpersonal stress, an inadequacy of social support or personal resources . . ." (American Psychiatric Association, 2000, p. 31). In the multiaxial framework of the DSM system, psychosocial and environmental problems that affect clinical disorders are recorded on Axis IV; unless the stressor is the presenting problem, as in the case of post-traumatic stress disorder. In that case, the disorder (and the psychosocial or environmental problem that is part of the disorder) is coded on Axis I. One question that helps to identify psychosocial stressors that may be affecting the presenting problem is, "What changes have there been in your life in the past year?" The time frame in that question can be modified to shorter or longer intervals— 6 months or 2 years—depending upon the client and presenting problems. If a client seems unsure about what is meant by "changes" or asks, "Like what?" it can be helpful to provide an example or two from the DSM-IV-TR list of psychosocial stressors. These can include:

- *Economic–Occupational Changes:* job loss or promotion, pay increase, bankruptcy, obtaining welfare, work schedule, conflict with coworkers or boss
- *Family–Primary Support Changes:* death, birth, divorces, separations, family member or friend moving; remarriage, child maltreatment, and health problems
- *Environmental Changes:* housing, move, homelessness, changes in household membership, involvement with legal system
- *Educational Changes:* conflict with teachers or students, academic problems, inadequate academic resources
- *Traumatic Events:* child abuse, exposure to combat, natural disasters, victim of assault or other threatening crime, witnessing domestic violence, severe automobile accident, diagnosed with a life-threatening illness (American Psychiatric Association, 2000, p. 31).

Once specific stressors have been identified, the next step is to assess how the stressors have affected the presenting problem and the person's ability to cope with them. This can be accomplished with an open-ended question such as "What has _____ (stressor) been like for you?" This question has the potential for establishing a connection between stressful life events and the presenting problems or symptoms, as well as facilitates further discussion about coping resources.

Assessing Coping Strategies and Identifying Counseling Goals

Inquiring about steps the client has already taken to try and solve the problem or cope with a stressful event can provide an array of valuable assessment and intervention information. What can be learned by asking Brian, for example, "What sorts of things have you done to try and get over feeling jittery and snappy?" One is his efforts, prior to counseling, aimed at bringing about relief and resolution to his problems. If he identifies steps he has taken and things he has tried to do to fix his problems, the closer he may be to taking further action. This information is related to the concept of readiness for change, which will be discussed shortly. Another piece that can be gleaned from his answer is the quality of his problem-solving skills. Has he tired one thing and only one thing, or has he tried a few qualitatively different strategies? In general, individuals, including those as young as early elementary school age, who can identify multiple divergent solutions to a problem have better problem-solving abilities (Youngstrom et al., 2000). For example, when asked about solutions to a peer teasing him, a child could respond with multiple possibilities: "I could hit him, punch, or kick." This child did identify three possible solutions but each one is only a slight variation on the overall strategy theme: respond with physical aggression. On the other hand, the child might identify multiple and qualitatively diverse solutions: telling him to stop, telling the teacher, finding someone else to play with, or teasing back. Similarly, Brian might tell the interviewer he's been drinking or smoking marijuana to calm himself, variations on one problem-solving strategy: using drugs to relax. Alternatively, his problem-solving skills might reflect qualitatively different strategies: "telling myself not to let him get to me," "just doing my job," and "trying to get it out when I play hockey." Furthermore, Brian's answer to the attempted solutions question can provide clues about his level of insight, possible goals, and a potential starting point for further intervention. Knowledge of the prior steps Brian has taken to resolve his problems can shed light on his understanding of, or insight into, the nature of his problems. Then at the point in which the interviewer or another clinician makes a suggestion or recommendation, the client is more likely to carry it out if what is suggested closely resembles what has been tried before.

Just as important as understanding the nature of the presenting problems and a client's repertoire of coping strategies is the identification of counseling goals. When clinicians and clients have a clearer picture of where the client is headed, the decision about which methods to use to facilitate that arrival is made easier. Is the client looking for symptom relief, self-understanding, advice, coping tools, or something else? Sometimes an opening that asks about what the client wants help with gets to goal statements quickly. Other times, clients, despite that opening, will launch into the telling of their story and history and sidestep the question. When that happens, it is important before the initial interview ends to guide the client back to "What is it you are hoping can get accomplished through counseling? (or coming to _____ [name of facility])?" Clients sometimes have an easier time addressing goal identification when the question becomes more focused, as suggested in Table 4.1. Brian was asked, "How will you know in a month or two if your temper problem and jitteriness is getting better?" After pausing and seemingly unsure, he responded, "When I'm not shouting and swearing as much and don't feel like beating the crap out of that jerk I work for." His response provides a behavioral description of a goal: a goal that can be observed, measured, and attained, or G:OMA.

Sometimes goal identification is facilitated when clients are given a specific time frame to think about; other times visual metaphors or thinking about problem resolution from someone else's perspective can help. When clients are asked to visualize what they or someone else would see them doing when improved or feeling better, more concrete goal statements are often elucidated. These kinds of goal- or solution-oriented questions are designed to provide counselor and client with a clearer destination, which is especially important if the interviewer is not the one who will continue with the client in counseling. It is also possible that through asking a goal-seeking question, the client realizes he or she does not know what might be possible to accomplish through some type of counseling process. If time permits during an initial interview, some further discussion about that uncertainty and what in general people try to accomplish in counseling could take place.

Developing a contextual understanding of a client's presenting problems, concerns, or symptoms is the first step in an initial assessment interview. This task will vary in length of time depending upon the setting (inpatient, outpatient, educational), client (cultural background), and presenting problems. In outpatient settings it is typical that one to one-and-a-half hours will be devoted to this kind of interview. In many cases that will be sufficient time to gain a contextual understanding of the problems and identify treatment goals as well as to gather some, if not all, of the important background and historical information discussed later in this chapter. In some cases, particularly those involving children and those clients with chronic conditions, it may take two or three assessment interviews before a realistic plan of action can be developed. Although all clients present with one or more problems, not all acknowledge responsibility for their problems, or if they do, are ready to do something about it.

ASSESSING CLIENT READINESS FOR CHANGE

Overview of Stages of Change Model

When individuals, couples, or families enter a counseling process, they can be at very different places in terms of their readiness to actively go about making changes in their lives. In fact, many clients begin the process in a state of ambivalence: a part of one's self wants to make a change and another does not. Each part may have valid reasons for their position, which can then strengthen a sense of inertia. The idea that individuals and even groups and organizations can be at different stages of change at different times stems from a theoretical model that has impacted various assessment and intervention approaches.

The stages of change model posits six identifiable stages individuals can go through when addressing a problem or habit (Prochaska, Norcross, & DiClemente, 1994; Prochaska, DiClemente, & Norcross, 1992). Those stages have been conceptualized as being along a continuum of readiness for change and have been identified as the **precontemplation**, **contemplation**, **preparation**, **action**, **maintenance**, and **termination** stages. The model has influenced and shaped several effective therapeutic approaches—motivational interviewing, motivation-enhanced treatment, project match—for a wide variety of problems and disorders, including substance use disorders, obesity, psychiatric treatment adherence, HIV risk-reduction behavior, and dual-diagnosed disorders (Miller & Rollnick, 2002). Clients are likely to enter the counseling process in one of the first three stages and typically go back and forth between stages over the course of counseling or individual efforts to bring about change. Therefore, this section will focus on how to identify which of those first three stages a client may be in.

According to the model, clients who are in the precontemplation stage are least ready to make changes, and those in the action stage are furthest along in their readiness for change. Assessing where a client is, along this change continuum, can help the clinician to tailor an interview and subsequent interventions to match the client's position.

IDENTIFYING THE PRECONTEMPLATION STAGE   Clients who are in the precontemplation stage do not recognize or acknowledge that they have a problem and tend to externalize blame for their situation (Prochaska et al., 1994). Often, clients who are precontemplators enter a counseling process because either they were mandated by the legal system, or a family member coaxed, cajoled, or coerced them into seeking professional help. These clients are likely to present in a highly defensive style. In response to the question "What brought you here?" they typically respond by saying someone else—the judge, my wife, my parent—"said I should be here." They may also be vague and noncommittal about why the other person either ordered them into treatment or were so concerned about them to refer them for professional help. Unless asked specific directive questions, clients in the precontemplation stage are likely to spend a good portion of the assessment interview describing what's wrong with the person or persons who believe strongly that they have a problem.

Clients who present in the precontemplative stage present a serious dilemma for counselors and other professional agents of change. How do you help someone change who does not believe he or she has a problem? One overall strategy that has been advocated and researched and can be partially incorporated into an initial assessment is to ask questions that have the potential for shifting clients from the precontemplation to the contemplation stage, rather than trying to assess the nature of a problem the client does not own. The overall goal of an assessment with a client in the precontemplation stage is to determine whether the client is demonstrating a shift in beliefs and worldview that suggests movement into the contemplation stage. For those clients who are referred or mandated to counseling and do not acknowledge the existence of a problem within themselves, and tend to externalize blame—suggesting the problem lies within someone else—the questions in Table 4.2 can be helpful.

A discussion focused around the questions in Table 4.2 can sometimes shift a client's perspective from externalizing blame to acknowledging having a problem or concern. Other times, further motivational interviewing (Miller & Rollnick, 2002) will be needed for those who appear stuck in the precontemplation stage.

IDENTIFYING THE CONTEMPLATION STAGE   When an individual acknowledges and accepts having a problem but is ambivalent about changing the problem, the contemplation stage is occurring. Clients who are in the contemplation stage will take ownership for their problems and use language suggestive of that ownership, but simultaneously minimize the severity of the problem. For example, Brian stated partway through the interview, "I know my drinking gets out of hand sometimes but it's not like I'm showing up at work drunk." Further along in

---

▌ Table 4.2 Interview Questions for the Precontemplation Stage

- Why do you think _____ (person x) wants you to be here?
- What is your understanding of (referring person) sending you here?
- What would you need to change for _____ (person x or place y) to no longer be concerned about you?
- Does anyone else think _____ (behavior y) is a problem?
- How is _____ (person x) affected by your _____ (behavior y)?

Source: Prochaska, J. O., Norcross, J. C., & DiClemente, C. C. (1994). *Changing for Good: The revolutionary program that explains the six stages of change and teaches you how to free yourself from bad habits.* New York: Morrow.

the assessment interview, when a discussion of goals might take place, a client who is still in the contemplative stage will talk in a way indicative of that stage and some remnant of the previous stage. When Brian is asked, "How would you know if you are making progress toward controlling your temper at work?," he replies, "I don't know if I need to do something different, or if it's my boss's fault—if he would stop being such a prick, I wouldn't be losing it." Brian acknowledges a problem with his temper but continues to blame someone else for igniting it as if he has one foot in the precontemplative stage and another in the contemplative one. This kind of straddling highlights two important aspects of the contemplation stage. First is the significant shift in mindset from externalization of blame to some degree of problem acceptance. The internalization of a problem enables further assessment of the nature of the problem(s) to take place. Second is the commonality of ambivalence. Most people have mixed feelings and attitudes about personal change. On the one hand, they don't like and are bothered by the problems they are experiencing. They may even have several logical reasons for changing or letting go of a problematic behavior, emotional state, or way of thinking. On the other hand, it is commonplace for many individuals to have thoughts and feelings that reflect a desire to maintain the status quo. The idea of changing a problem, even a debilitating one, can be accompanied by worry, discomfort, and possibly fear, along with ideas such as "It's too much effort," "It won't matter," or "Things won't get better anyway." Consequently, many clients will spend a significant amount of time in the contemplation stage struggling with their ambivalence toward change. Counseling that extends beyond the initial assessment can be for the purpose of helping clients like Brian resolve their ambivalence in order to be in a better position to work on the presenting problems.

IDENTIFYING THE PREPARATION STAGE AND BEYOND   The preparation stage occurs when an individual has resolved his or her ambivalence about changing a problem and has begun to take some preliminary steps toward engaging in a committed process of change. These preliminary preparation steps typically involve gathering information and resources about a change process, either a self-help one or a professionally guided process like counseling (Prochaska, et al.,1992). For example, the person who is in the preparation stage with respect to a weight problem might begin gathering information about different diets and gym memberships. Similarly, if Brian is in the preparation stage with respect to his alcohol abuse, he might gather information about where the nearest AA meetings are located and speak with his primary care doctor about a counselor and get some phone numbers. Clients in the preparation stage are often able to describe what they've tried to do to resolve the presenting problem prior to entering counseling. And some of those strategies may have been effective in resolving the problems, even if only temporarily. Those clients are likely to be that much more ready than contemplative stage clients for engaging in sustained change-making efforts such as ongoing counseling. How long someone spends in the preparation stage before moving on to the action stage varies from person to person and problem.

Most clients who enter the counseling process begin in one of the first three stages: precontemplation, contemplation, or preparation. Occasionally, counselors may encounter a client at an initial interview who is already in the action stage. According to the stages of change theory, the action phase represents an ongoing commitment to and engagement in a change-oriented process (Prochaska et al., 1992). Those clients may be looking for support and help in maintaining involvement with a new behavior, program, or lifestyle. They may also be ready to make changes with the help of a professional counselor.

Fitting the Interview to the Stage of Change

A skilled clinician is able to adapt to the circumstances and the unfolding information he or she is presented with. Part of that flexibility involves a balancing act. The clinician needs the ability to attend to and empathize with the client's story and worldview while at the same time gathering more and more information, sometimes seemingly unrelated to the presenting story, in order to figure out how the individual clinician or organization can best help this client. Another aspect of clinician adaptation is fitting the interview to the stage of change the client seems to be in. Clinical lore and wisdom suggest that meeting the client at whatever stage she or he is in is the most helpful strategy.

By locating where along a continuum of readiness for change a client resides, the clinician can tailor the assessment interview accordingly. When a client presents in the precontemplation stage, it can be helpful to suspend a plan to gather more detailed information about history—educational, work, family, and interpersonal—and instead use the interview to explore the questions shown in Table 4.2. Clients who are in this stage are unlikely to see the need for detailed history-gathering questions and are likely to respond in defensive or guarded ways, which limits the quality of the information the clinician is trying to obtain. Furthermore, by not staying with where the client is at, especially if it's "I don't have a problem," the process can become adversarial, and it reduces the likelihood that the interview can help move the client to the next stage, contemplation. Similarly, modifications can be made in the assessment interview to fit the contemplative client. Brian's presentation, for example, suggests he is in the contemplation stage with respect to a drinking problem. He indicates that he does not get "drunk" at work but that at times his drinking can "get out of hand." Asking, "When does your drinking get out of hand?" can lead not only to a greater understanding about the variability of his substance usage, but also the consequences for himself and possibly others. One strategy Prochaska et al. (1994) have advocated using with people in the contemplative stage is decisional balancing—a type of personal and interpersonal cost–benefit analysis. This process involves evaluating the pros and cons of change for both oneself and others if that change were to occur. Decisional balancing questions can be incorporated into an assessment interview to help guide Brian to reflect further on his ambivalence while gathering further family and interpersonal history.

ASSESSING RISKS AND RESOURCES

Overview of Risks and Resources Framework

Once a counselor has developed a contextual understanding of a client's symptoms and problems and assessed readiness for change, the next task is to gather information about factors that may interfere with problem resolution and, conversely, those that may promote and support progress. As stated at the outset of the chapter, conditions that support coping strategies, facilitate problem resolution, or promote resiliency are considered **resource factors**. Conditions that hinder problem resolution or increase the likelihood that problems can worsen, or at best not improve, are considered **risk factors**. Risks and resources can be present at multiple levels: individual, family, community, and cultural. They can also be relatively new or longstanding, existing over multiple generations. For example, an individual resource factor might be a flexible problem-solving style. At the cultural level, a risk factor might be a shared group belief, existing for multiple generations, that seeking help from a professional counselor is a sign of personal weakness. The identification of risk and resource, or what has been termed "protective" factors that can affect both normal and pathological child development, has been a standard assessment practice for the past 20 years (Davies, 2004; Schroeder & Gordon, 2002). In addition, experts in the field of suicide and homicide assessments have described and used risk and protective factors models for evaluating a client's risk of harming self or someone else (Bryan & Rudd, 2006; Shea, 1998). Applying a risks and resources framework is an effective approach to initial counseling interviews as well. Within this framework, there are several fundamental questions for a counselor to keep in mind:

- What is the presenting problem or concern?
- What resources does the client currently possess to help alleviate or resolve the problem?
- What risks are present in the client's life that will lessen the chance that the problem will be resolved or increase the chance the problem could get worse?
- How do I gather information about risks and resources?
- How can I, or my organization (clinic, agency, school, or facility), be of help given the nature of these risks and resources?

Although this chapter implies a linear progression from presenting problem to risks and resources, the typical unstructured intake interview is a more recursive back-and-forth process. Some information about problems and their features may be gathered, then some history and background information is provided, then problem definition is addressed again, then further assessment of risks and resources is done. Some information about risk and resource factors may be disclosed spontaneously by clients during the course of the initial interview, and other information the interviewer will need to gather more actively.

One way to think about an individual's social and psychological history and background is as a set of facts and events that make up a biographical narrative. The intake clinician could ascertain, for example, where Brian grew up, how many siblings he has and his birth order, how far he got in school, his work history, and mental health history. When woven together, this history becomes Brian's story. Alternatively, another narrative could be information woven together about Brian and his presenting problems and factors that can help to alleviate the problems or interfere with their resolution. Typically, assessment and interviewing texts delineate the facts and events that are important to gather—the specific social, educational, and family history, mental and physical health histories, and additional background information—without a guiding framework for organizing and assimilating what can be an overwhelming amount of data. A risks and resources framework is one model that can help to guide and organize the collection of this large amount of background information and client history, because the information sought is directly related to problem resolution or stagnation.

It is helpful to use the kinds of bridges or linking statements discussed in the previous chapter when transitioning to inquiries about risks and resources. One concept that guides bridging statements is transparency. The transparent interviewer shares with the interviewee his or her thinking about the reason for the focus shift. Transparency is an effective interviewing tactic because it communicates to the interviewee that the problems have been heard but more information is needed to understand the full dimensions of the problems and their resolution. Furthermore, by being transparent, the interviewer is promoting a collaborative approach to the interview process. In essence, the interviewer is saying, "I have a reason for moving the conversation in this direction," and "What do you think about that?" Here are several examples of bridge statements and questions that emphasize transparency:

- When people are experiencing _____ (presenting problem), it is helpful to know about some things that could make the problem better or worse. Would it be OK for me to ask you some more questions?
- In order for me to better understand how I can help you with _____ (presenting problem), it is helpful for me to learn more about some areas of your life that could be affecting your _____ (client's statement of problem).
- There are some more questions we ask everyone who comes here so we can figure out how to help with _____ (client's statement of problem).

During initial interviews, a counselor will gather information about different categories of risk and protective factors (see Table 4.3). During unstructured intake interviews, the order in which this information is gathered matters less than an understanding of why the additional information being sought is relevant. A common place to start, however, is with the concept of social support versus isolation, because for many people this is disclosed during the course of discussing one's concerns and difficulties.

Table 4.3 Identifying Risks and Resources

Risks	Resources
Interpersonal and social:	
Social isolation	Supportive family relationships,
Significant interpersonal conflicts	friendships, and peers (classmates or colleagues)
Limited contact with friends	Community supports
Experienced trauma	
Intrapersonal:	
Poor problem-solving skills	Good problem-solving skills
Rigid thinking	Flexible thinking
Maladaptive coping skills	Adaptive coping skills
Negative educational experiences or behavior problems in school or the workplace	Spirituality and faith beliefs and practices
	Academic or work strengths
Health lifestyle:	
Inadequate sleep length and Exercise trouble initiating or maintaining sleep	Adequate sleep
No regular exercise	Adequate diet
Significant changes in appetite or weight	Regular exercise
Substance abuse including prescription drug abuse or noncompliance with a prescription	
Activities:	
Lack of involvement in fun or pleasurable activities	Involvement in fun or pleasurable activities

Interpersonal Relationships and Social Systems

SOCIAL SUPPORT VERSUS ISOLATION   Social support is one important protective factor to consider, especially given the substantial research demonstrating the palliative effect healthy, supportive interpersonal relationships can have on a number of health and psychological problems and conditions such as depression, alcohol abuse, stress, and immune functioning (Besser & Priel, 2005; Cohen & Herbert, 1996; Cohen & Wills, 1985; Pierce, Frone, Russell, Cooper, & Mudar, 2000). Perceived social support has also been shown to be related to one's increased likelihood to seek mental health services (Maulik, Eaton, & Bradshaw, 2011). On the other hand, individuals who are socially isolated or perceive themselves as such, are at greater risk for feeling sad, lonely, alienated, despondent, and demoralized. Whether it be in the form of a friendship, partnership, or collegial relationship, supportive relationships involve warm emotional connection and understanding. For some, social support is a fairly stable presence, such as for a couple who have been happily married for many years. For others, social support is fleeting; one day there is a best friend and the next day that friend is gone. Therefore, this part of the interview will explore both the history and nature of social supports in a client's life and the degree of stability. In general, during initial interviews, information about social supports will be gathered by a focus on the nature and quality of current family relationships, friendships, and other significant interpersonal relationships. This usually includes the nature of parental and sibling relationships, partners, spouses, and friends—the extent to which these relationships are perceived as supportive, conflictive, disengaged, or volatile. Information regarding the quality of previous significant relationships may also be gathered. One way to make a bridge to the topic of interpersonal supports and relationships is to ask the following question: "If you were not coming here to talk about _____ (client problem description), who else might you be talking to about this?"

The quality of interpersonal relationships, along with the frequency in which certain kinds of activities take place, can be explored with a series of questions. These questions are included in Table 4.4.

This discussion of relationships may also reveal losses that have occurred or changes in these relationships, both of which could be a source of stress for a client. How, Brian, for example, coped with his parents' divorce, his father's death, and the move from Costa Rica could be explored. A question such as "What was your parents' divorce like for you?" could reveal information about Brian's style of coping with stressful events as well as the degree to which he may still be impacted by significant changes in his life.

FAMILY HISTORY AND RELATIONSHIPS AND GENOGRAMS   One structured way to gather information about family relationships and history is through the use of a family diagram, or **genogram**. As an assessment tool, genograms can be useful for identifying family members over multiple generations, the nature of family relationships and significant family events, as well as gaining an understanding of familial patterns and beliefs systems (McGoldrick, Gerson, & Petry, 2008). A genogram is a diagram that can readily convey a wealth of information about an individual's family history and relationships, especially when it includes at least three generations.

Genograms are constructed with a set of symbols that connote gender, relationship quality, living arrangements, deaths, marriages, and separations. The basic genogram symbols are provided in Table 4.5. Before beginning to construct a genogram with a client, it is helpful to explain what this diagram will consist of and why it is being made. Having a visual representation of

Table 4.4 Interview Questions for Assessing Interpersonal Relationships

- Tell me about your friends.
- How often do you see your friends?
- What do you do with them?
- When do you and your (spouse, partner) spend time together?
- How do you feel about the time you spend with your friends?
- Is there someone in your life you consider a best friend?
- Is there anyone else you enjoy being with?
- What does your _____ (spouse, friend, parents) think about _____ (presenting concern)?
- Who do you find support from?

When interviewing elementary school age children and adolescents, the following questions can also be helpful:

- Who else do you know has problems with _____ (presenting problems)?
- Who is your best friend?
- What do you do with your friends (or name of best friend)?
- When do you see them?
- Where do you play with them (e.g., school, home, friends' home, neighborhood, community activity)?

Table 4.5 Basic Genogram Symbols and Recording Procedures

Gender and sexual orientation:

Male   Female

Heterosexual

Age is placed inside symbol; an X in the symbol indicates death

Gay   Lesbian   Bisexual

Relationships:

Line indicates marriage and shows year recorded; dashed line indicates living together, sexual relationship

Children: List in birth order, beginning with oldest on left

Line with one slash indicates a separation; line with two slashes indicates a divorce

Quality of interpersonal relationships:

Close   Hostile   Distant

family history and patterns can be especially helpful when a client's family history includes separations and divorces, blended family arrangements, or multigenerational patterns of trauma, illness, or psychiatric disorders.

A genogram is both an assessment tool and an intervention technique and therefore it can be viewed as one of many examples of the complementary and synergistic nature of assessment and intervention (McGoldrick et al., 2008). Genogram construction is a structured process by which information about relationships, patterns, and beliefs can be obtained while simultaneously facilitating client insight. As the client(s) participates in providing the information for the genogram, he or she may develop an awareness of how family patterns and relationships are affecting presenting problems, concerns, or emotional functioning. Brian's genogram is shown in Figure 4.1. While providing his family background information to Melanie, the intake counselor, who was co-creating his genogram, he saw more clearly how both his father and paternal grandfather had lost their marriages because of serious problems with alcohol and an uncontrollable temper. He also became more aware of the patriarchal beliefs he grew up with and how that affected some of his attitudes toward his girlfriend who broke off their relationship. With that insight he was more inclined to address his own difficulties with anger, alcohol, and relationships than he was at the outset of the intake.

Much has been written from a family systems perspective about genograms as an intervention tool, but further discussion of the intervention aspect of them is beyond the scope of

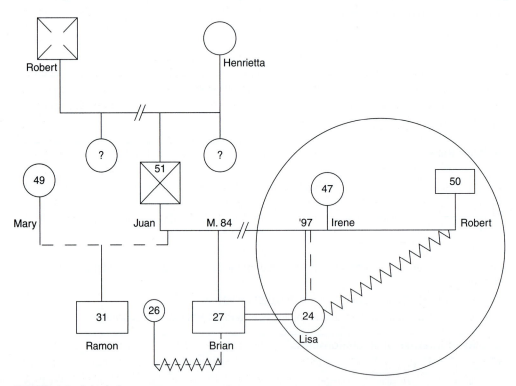

FIGURE 4.1 Brian's Genogram

this assessment text. For those interested in learning more about using genograms as interventions, *Genograms: Assessment and Intervention,* 3rd ed. (McGoldrick et al., 2008) is an excellent resource.

Another area to inquire about, whether through the genogram process or interview questions, is a family history of emotional and psychological problems and psychiatric disorders. One way to make a bridge to that information is to ask, "Has anyone else in your family ever had the same or similar problems?" A number of psychiatric disorders—schizophrenia, major depression, anxiety disorders, substance abuse and dependence, and some personality disorders—tend to have a familial component with genetics playing a role to some degree, depending upon the disorder. Having a parent, grandparent, or first degree relative with a psychiatric disorder places most individuals at greater risk for developing some DSM-IV psychiatric disorder, compared to those without that family history. Research has indicated that genetics is one, but not the only, contributing factor in the development of schizophrenia, depression, and substance abuse disorders (Smith, 2008) and to a lesser extent in some personality disorders (Lowe & Widiger, 2008).

History of Trauma

Clients often spontaneously disclose having experienced a traumatic event, whether as a child or as an adult, either when discussing the presenting problem or during an exploration of family history. This is often the case when the trauma is a natural disaster, witnessing a violent event or death, or an accident where serious injury occurred. However, an individual's experience of physical or sexual assault or child maltreatment may not be reported unless the counselor gathers that information. Clients may not disclose a history of any kind of abuse, particularly sexual, for several reasons. One is that the client may minimize the impact this kind of trauma can have on psychological, emotional, and interpersonal functioning, especially if it occurred during early childhood and the client is now a middle-aged adult. Another reason is that this kind of trauma, in particular, can evoke feelings of embarrassment, guilt, and shame, which are difficult to acknowledge and express for most people. Lastly, when abuse has occurred, family members or significant others may have given implicit or explicit messages to keep it secret. Given these reasons and the fact that a number of clients might not label a physical or sexual assault as abusive, it is better during an initial interview to avoid using the emotionally charged and idiosyncratic term *abuse* when inquiring about a history of assault or child maltreatment. Instead, the interviewer can begin the exploration by asking, "Has anyone ever touched you in a way that made you uncomfortable or that you did not like?" If the answer to that is yes, then several follow-up questions or directives are important:

- Tell me about that.
- What happened?
- When did that happen?
- Who besides me have you told about this?
- Are you having, thoughts, dreams, or memories about this that bother you?

An interviewer who asks this broad and ambiguous question about uncomfortable touch can receive a wide range of responses. This could include anything from "When my Aunt Sadie came to visit, she would kiss me and she had bad breath" to "My stepfather raped me when I was 12." When clients report a history of sexual or physical abuse during an intake, it is important to follow up with the questions listed above in order to determine whether the client has disclosed this to others and, if so, what happened when the previous disclosure occurred. The interviewer will also want to determine whether the client ever received professional help for that trauma and, if so, whether the client thinks that treatment was beneficial. If a prior traumatic experience has been previously dealt with successfully—that is, the problematic emotional and psychological consequences have been resolved—then the person may have developed some coping resources that could be applied to the problems or concerns that are the focus of the current assessment. On the other hand, if trauma experiences have not been adequately processed and assimilated, they still may be impacting the client's functioning and could become an additional focus of counseling. In that case, the client may be reexperiencing the trauma in some recurring fashion: intrusive, bothersome thoughts and memories; distressing dreams; or a sense or reliving the event through some perceptual distortion (flashbacks, hallucinations, or illusions). In the DSM-IV, re-experiencing a trauma in some way is the second criterion for making the diagnosis of post-traumatic stress disorder (American Psychiatric Association, 2000).

Experience with Other Social Systems

EDUCATIONAL HISTORY   Interviewers using a risks and resources framework will also explore educational history because it can provide clues about an individual's social and interpersonal functioning and intrapersonal strengths and weaknesses. Was school an area in which the person developed competencies and skills that could serve as resources for resolving the presenting problems? Did those competencies promote self-confidence and self-efficacy? Self-efficacy is the belief that my actions will produce a certain desired outcome. Alternatively, was school a continual struggle that negatively impacted the person's self-image? Perhaps one's experience was different at various developmental stages: preschool, elementary, middle, and high school. And what may have accounted for periods of success and times of difficulty? An interviewer can open up the topic of educational history by asking, "What was _____ (elementary, middle, high school or college) like for you?" Brian, for example, although he had struggled mightily with English and writing assignments in middle and high school, was a master at diagnosing and fixing car problems. Later on in counseling, he and the counselor explored how his diagnostic and problem-solving skills could be put to use in overcoming his substance abuse and relationship problems.

Intake interviewers are also likely to explore educational history, because that focus can potentially reveal patterns of behavioral problems, interpersonal difficulties, or a learning disability. The following questions can be useful when assessing a history of behavior problems:

- Was there ever a time in school when you were getting into trouble with teachers?
- Was there ever a time you refused to go to school?
- Did you ever get detentions or suspensions?
- Did you ever skip classes?

If the answer to any of those questions is yes, then probing further about when that was and what happened can fill in the missing pieces of that history. Often, this discussion of school history can segue naturally into gathering information about a client's history of making and maintaining friendships, relationship endings and losses, experiences with victimization such as bullying (either as the one bullied or the bullier), and interpersonal conflict resolution skills. What is important to consider at this stage of an initial interview assessment is how the client makes sense of her or his interpersonal history. How does the client go about explaining, for example, how a lack of friends in elementary school occurred. One explanation might be, "I was a very shy kid," and another, "I kept doing things that annoyed the other kids." Those are two very different explanations for a lack of friendships; each one helps to develop alternative client case conceptualizations.

Another perspective intake interviewers may focus on is academic performance. Sometimes information about a client's academic performance can elucidate problems with cognitive functioning. Some clients will present with one or more cognitive problems or symptoms: trouble remembering things, difficulty concentrating or paying attention, frequent forgetfulness, or being disorganized. Reviewing academic history and performance may help establish when those problems began and what they might be attributed to. One way to begin that exploration is to ask either "What kind of a student were (or are you) you?" or "How well did you do (are you doing) in school?" More specifically, the interviewer can ask about each developmental period, one question at a time: "What grades did you get when you were in _____ (elementary, middle, high school)?" Other areas to address include:

- Did you ever repeat a grade?
- Did you ever receive any kind of special services in school?
- Did you ever get tutored in a subject?
- Were you ever identified as having some kind of learning problem or disability?
- Did you graduate high school?
- Did you go to college?

Furthermore, one could have or have had a history of successful academic performance, overall, or in particular subject areas, that can reveal verbal, quantitative, visual–spatial, artistic, athletic, or musical strengths. Again, knowledge of these strengths can inform subsequent interventions. A client, for example, who has a fondness for reading and writing and did well ever since middle school in those areas might benefit from keeping a journal and reading a self-help book, both of which could supplement the counseling sessions.

WORK AND MILITARY HISTORY   A client's work and military history, if applicable, can also be assessed from a risks and resources perspective. What has a person's work experience been like? Has it been a source of fulfillment, meaning, and purpose, or has it been an arduous, unfulfilling task to get through? Information about a client's current job, what it entails, and how he or she feels about it can provide clues to whether it is a source of stress or fulfillment. Sometimes an exploration of work history may reveal that both kinds of experiences have occurred with different jobs. Knowledge about the person's job history can also provide clues about potential strengths he or she possesses such as organizational, managerial, time management, problem solving, conflict resolution, and so on. Similarly, job endings and how they occurred—layoff, firing, job change—and what the ending has meant for the client can be ascertained. Sometimes a series of brief employments at various places, or long stretches of unemployment can provide diagnostic clues since this is a pattern seen with people with schizophrenia or certain personality disorders (Morrison, 2008).

If a client is or has been in the military, it can be useful to identify what that experience has been like, as well as whether there has been exposure to combat directly or indirectly. Exposure to combat directly, or indirectly through prolonged contact with those who have, can be a traumatic experience for many, a trauma that may be reexperienced. As noted earlier, one of the criteria for post-traumatic stress disorder is that a traumatic event is reexperienced in some recurring way.

As with questions about educational and work history, probing about a client's military role and responsibilities can reveal potential strengths and psychological resources. It can also illuminate a pattern of interpersonal conflicts and behavioral problems. If a question such as "Have you ever served time in the military?" is answered affirmatively, these general follow-up questions would be helpful:

- What did you do?
- What was that experience like for you?
- How did you get along with the other people in your group?

The Role of Spirituality, Religion, and Faith

Another dimension of a person's life that can provide a source of comfort, psychological guidance, and at times functions as a social support is spirituality and religious life. If spirituality or religion is a positive and important aspect of a person's life, it can also serve as a potential coping resource for life stressors and emotional problems (Milstein, Manierre, & Yali, 2010). Recently, psychologists, along with a theologian and other professionals (Milstein et al.; Saunders, Miller, & Bright, 2010), described a framework for spiritually conscious and sensitive assessment approaches, which involve identifying the role spiritual and religious beliefs and practices have in clients' lives. Their overarching view is that a person's religious beliefs and practices can impact, either positively or negatively, his or her health status, emotional well-being, the presenting problem, rapport building, and the course of treatment. Therefore, counselors and other helping professionals will need to attend to this aspect of a client's life in order to conduct a comprehensive and culturally sensitive assessment. The spiritually conscious approach is embedded within a larger cultural diversity and ethical framework that recognizes and respects cultural differences, including religious ones. Counselors should also recognize that religion and spirituality are not a salient part of everyone's lives, and for them, additional assessment questions related to spiritual and religious beliefs would not be helpful. A range of questions can be incorporated into an initial comprehensive assessment for the purpose of identifying the connection between overall health and psychological functioning and spiritual and religious beliefs. Incorporating some questions about religious and spiritual beliefs, attitudes, and practices into an intake is a beneficial assessment practice given that an overwhelming majority of Americans believe religion is important in their lives and a smaller majority are members of or affiliated with a religious community (Gallup Organization, 2011; Jones et al., 2002). Furthermore, many clients desire and expect that their health care professionals will attend to and ask about their religious and spiritual life and views (Saunders et al.). Based on their review of the literature, Saunders et al. (2010, p. 359) have recommended asking the following series of questions of clients presenting for psychological or counseling services:

- Are you a religious or spiritual person? *(If the answer is no, then the remaining questions probably would not be asked.)*
- How important is spirituality or religion in your daily life?
- What gives your life purpose or meaning?
- Do you believe in a higher power?
- Are you part of a spiritual or religious community?
- Has the problem for which you are seeking help affected your religious or spiritual life?

- Has your current problem affected your relationship with your higher power?
- Are spirituality or religion important to this problem?
- Has your religion or spirituality been involved in your attempts to deal with this problem?
- Are members of your spiritual or religious community (such as a spiritual leader) potential resources for you in trying to deal with this problem?
- Is there someone you can talk to about spiritual or religious matters as they relate to this problem?
- Is there anything that I can do to help you access such resources?

Those clients who identify religion or spirituality as an important aspect of their lives may need an additional interview beyond the intake to address the breadth of questions listed here. The answers to these questions can, as with other intake information, identify potential strengths and inter- and intrapersonal resources as well as suggest possible directions for future counseling.

Assessing Healthy versus Unhealthy Lifestyles

Assessment of a client's physical and mental health history is also typically part of an intake interview because of the relevance for diagnosis, treatment planning, and prognosis (Morrison, 2008). This part of the interview will include an exploration of overall health status, chronic medical conditions, current and previous prescription medications, nonprescription drug usage (caffeine, nicotine, alcohol, marijuana, and other drugs), and adherence to previous treatments. A list of common health status–related questions is shown in Table 4.6. The purpose of exploring the questions in Table 4.6 is to determine whether or not the individual has a medical condition or problem that may be causing or is affected by the presenting problem, is creating additional stress, or is not being adequately managed. It is also helpful to inquire about compliance with and attitudes toward current and previous treatments, both physical and mental health. Attitudes and beliefs, either positive or negative, about previous treatments and helpers can certainly impact how someone may respond to future interventions. For example, if Brian had been on an antidepressant medication in the past and felt the side effects were worse than his depression symptoms, he may be reluctant to try another psychotropic medication. Certainly any prior history with mental health services in general, and counseling in particular, would be a fruitful topic for exploration. Prior experiences with helpers and counselors will shape attitudes, beliefs, and feelings about subsequent counseling processes. It can be helpful to begin that exploration by asking a fairly general open question such as, "What was that counseling or (therapy) like for you?" The interviewer can then follow up with additional clarifying questions, as needed, similar to the ones in Table 4.6.

The degree to which a client has a healthy lifestyle—adequate and restful sleep, adequate nutrition and diet, and sufficient exercise—is another topic typically assessed during intake interviews. A healthy lifestyle can be considered another resource or protective factor: it can help support emotional, cognitive, and behavioral change or provide a buffer against psychological distress. Alternatively, the extent to which someone does not get adequate sleep, nutrition, or exercise poses a risk for whatever else may be a presenting problem. And sometimes the lack of a lifestyle that promotes physical and psychological health can be the primary problem the client wants to address. In a recent study (Léger, Scheuermaier, Philip, Paillard, & Guilleminault, 2001), the relationship between one aspect of a healthy lifestyle—good sleep—and an individual's perceptions of general health, vitality, social functioning, and mental health were examined. The authors found that good sleepers, compared to those with chronic and severe insomnia, who

Table 4.6 Physical and Mental Health Status and History Questions

- How is your health?
  - When was your last physical?
  - Who is your primary care provider?
- Have you had any serious medical problems?
  - Do you have any chronic medical problems?
  - Are you being treated for a medical condition?
- Are you taking any prescription medication?

  If yes:

  - What is the medication(s)?
  - What are you taking it for?
  - Is it helping?
  - Who is prescribing it?
- Do you smoke cigarettes or use any tobacco products?
- Do you drink alcohol?

If the answer is no, accept that, but pursue specific drugs: caffeine and marijuana

If the answer to any of those questions is yes, then:

- *Assess Quantity:* How much _____ do you use in a week?
- *Assess whether drug usage has led to any problems: interpersonal, physical, legal, financial, etc.* Has anyone been concerned about your (drug/alcohol) use? *Or* What does _____ think about your drug/alcohol use?
- *Assess attempts to control usage:* Have there ever been times when you tried to stop or cut down your _____?
- Did you ever spend time in a hospital?
  - Have you been to see a counselor before?

If yes, explore that history:

  - Tell me what that was like.
  - What did you find helpful, not helpful?

did not have anxiety or depression, reported significantly better general health, vitality, and overall quality of life. Although there are individual differences in how much sleep and exercise and the kind of diets that will promote psychological and physical health, there are parameters that can be used to assess the adequacy of these areas.

SUBSTANCE USAGE   Although the assessment of substance use and abuse will be addressed more fully in Chapter 12, it is helpful to consider the screening questions that are listed in Table 4.6 and usually included as part of an intake interview. They are designed to help identify those who are indeed at risk for substance abuse or dependence, or the degree to which current substance usage poses a risk to the alleviation of current problems. It is helpful to conceptualize substance usage assessment broadly to include any kind of prescription or nonprescription drug a client may be using, the amount, and the physical, psychological, and relational consequences of the drug usage. Furthermore, the interviewer is more apt to hear an honest and open reporting about other drugs such as caffeine, nicotine, alcohol, marijuana, and so on when beginning with initial questions about overall health and prescription medication and then transitioning to questions about other kinds of substances that are often more difficult to talk about. It is also important to keep in mind that when a medication has been prescribed by a physician or other health care professional, that does not necessarily mean it is being used as intended. Noncompliance is fairly common and can include infrequent usage, overuse, or ineffective use such as taking it at the wrong time of day or with other substances.

SLEEP Sleep difficulties are common symptoms of anxiety, mood, and other disorders as well as being primary problems in need of intervention (Breslau, Roth, Rosenthal, & Andreski, 1996). Several brief interview questions can screen for the presence of both acute and chronic sleep difficulties. The most common sleep problem is insomnia—difficulty falling or staying asleep— which affects about one-third of American adults (Roth, 2005). When problems with initiating or maintaining sleep persist, individuals are also likely to report excessive fatigue, difficulty concentrating, memory complaints, slowed response time, increased risk for automobile accidents, somatic complaints, irritability, increased emotional sensitivity, and mental health problems (Ancoli-Israel, 2005; Dahl, 1996; Roth, 2005).

An interviewer can determine whether or not a client is suffering from insomnia by asking, "Have you ever had trouble falling asleep?" If the answer is yes, then two follow-up questions are in order: "When was that?" and "How often does that happen?" Similarly, an interviewer can ask, "Have you ever had trouble staying asleep?" Again, if a client reports having had or currently having that problem, follow-up questions about frequency and the length of time it takes to fall back to sleep are helpful.

When clients report problems either falling or staying asleep, or both, the interviewer can also explore thoughts and behaviors when not sleeping. Does the person lie in bed and ruminate, and if so, about what? Does the person get up and do something relaxing to try to get back to sleep? Is some internal or external stimuli (nightmares, worrisome thoughts, street noises, a crying child) causing the awakening or preventing sleep onset?

Clients who report that they are often tired, have trouble paying attention, or experience changes in emotional sensitivity or frequent moodiness may be suffering from insufficient sleep. Most adults require seven-and-a-half to eight hours of sleep, and young children and adolescents need even more to feel rested and to function well (Acoli-Israel, 2005). The typical sleep length requirements for children range from 11 hours at age 5, to 10 hours by age 12; and 8 hours by age 18 (Schroeder & Gordon, 2002). A significant number of children and adults, however, are getting less than adequate sleep. Multiple factors and conditions can contribute to children and adults having reduced sleep. These include medical conditions, irregular sleep schedules, shift work, jet lag, stress, anxiety and depression, and alcohol use.

EXERCISE Regular focused physical activity with some degree of exertion has a number of meaningful physical and mental health benefits (Hays, 1999). Canadian and American federal guidelines recommend that adults, ages 18 to 64, should get a minimum of 150 minutes per week of "moderate" physical activity, and youth need an hour a day (Canadian Society for Exercise Physiology, 2009; Centers for Disease Control, 2008). Health professionals have long recognized that exercise can decrease risk of heart disease and attacks, improve blood pressure and cholesterol levels, help with weight loss, help manage diabetes, and enhance sleep quality.

In addition, exercise has been found to have important psychological and emotional benefits as well. In reviewing the research on the relationship between exercise and psychological well-being, Hays (1999) found that in both clinical and nonclinical groups, exercise can reduce anxiety and depression symptoms and enhance self-concepts such as body image, self-efficacy, and sense of personal control. Consequently, incorporating questions about regular physical activity or exercise into an initial interview is necessary and easily accomplished. To some people, however, the word *exercise* may have a limited connotation, referring only to sports or strenuous exercise. Therefore the phrase "any kind of physical activity" may need to be substituted. In discussing the use of exercise as an adjunctive intervention in psychotherapy, Hays (1999, p. 243) recommended the following exercise history questions, some of which could be included in an intake interview:

- Do you currently exercise or do some kind of physical activity? *If the answer is yes, then:*
  - What do you do?
  - How often?
  - How do you feel when you are done exercising?
  - How long have you been doing it?
  - When do you _____ (client's stated activity)?
  - What do you like about exercising?

If the answer to the first question is no, then:

- Have you exercised regularly at some other time in your life? (*If yes, then:* What stopped you from exercising?)
- Do you have some interest in exercising now?

APPETITE AND WEIGHT CHANGES   Significant changes in appetite and weight over relatively short periods of time (days and weeks) are often signs of serious psychiatric disorders identified in the DSM-IV such as major depression, eating disorders, schizophrenia, and various medical conditions. Therefore, appetite change is another physiological symptom, along with sleep, energy, and libido changes, that is routinely assessed during intake interviews. One way to begin the assessment of appetite and weight changes is to ask, "How is your appetite?" If the answer is "not good" or something to that effect, then helpful follow-up questions can include:

- How often do you eat?
- Is this a change from what you typically eat?
- Are you eating less because you are trying to lose weight, or because you haven't felt like eating as often?
- Have you gained or lost weight over the past month? (*If the answer is yes, then ask,* How much?)

ASSESSING INVOLVEMENT IN INTERESTS AND FUN ACTIVITIES   Why is inquiring about interests, hobbies, and the engagement in pleasurable activities a part of assessing a healthy lifestyle? Engagement in enjoyable, playful, and self-fulfilling activities may satisfy a psychological need, perhaps not as basic as the needs for love, freedom, safety, and esteem, but nevertheless an important one. Although Maslow (1943) in his theory of human motivation did not explicitly posit fun as a need when describing the notion of self-actualization, others (Glasser, 2000; Wubbolding, 1991) have explicitly considered fun a basic human need—and humans are not the only species that spends time being playful, as any dog owner knows. Whether the pursuit of fun is a need, a desire, or integral to emotional well-being is likely to be debated by theoreticians for some time, but from a practical standpoint, assessment of that aspect of a client's life is as important as an understanding of sleep, exercise, and eating habits. Doing things that are fun can bring joy, happiness, laughter, comfort, and peace of mind. When the need for fun is not being met or, conversely, when it is compulsively sought, other problems can arise.

One's involvement or withdrawal from activities considered fun and enjoyable can provide diagnostic clues. Anhedonia, the loss of interest in activities once considered enjoyable and pleasurable, can be a symptom of depression. In fact, anhedonia is one of the two symptoms, the other being frequent depressed mood, which must be present in order for the DSM-IV diagnosis of a depressive episode to be made (American Psychiatric Association, 2000). Conversely, during a manic episode an individual typically experiences excessive involvement in certain kinds of pleasurable activities: sex, shopping, or spending money lavishly (APA, 2000).

In addition to diagnostic considerations, the involvement in fun, enjoyable activities can both meet a need and provide a means of coping. These pursuits can provide mental and physical distractions from troubling thoughts and feelings. Furthermore, involvement in these experiences can provide opportunities for mastery, enhancing emotional well-being, and social connection. Therefore, initial assessment interviews are likely to include the following questions:

- What do you like to do for fun? (*If the answer is,* I don't do anything fun, then follow up with, Was there ever a time you did?)
- How often do you do _____ (client's stated activities)?
- Was there a time when you were doing this more often?
- How do you feel when you are doing_____ (client's stated activity)?

CLOSING THE INTERVIEW AND PLANNING AHEAD

Summarizing

The closing phase of the initial interview is the time to summarize for the client what the interviewer has learned, and to plan ahead. Therefore, it is important to finish asking questions with enough time remaining in order to provide the client feedback and collaboratively develop a plan. The summary will typically consist of several parts. The first part of the summary generally includes a restatement of the presenting problems and concerns using behavioral descriptions based on the information gathered so far. Melanie, Brian's counselor, tells him at the end of the information-gathering phase of the intake:

> What I'm hearing is that you have concerns about your temper, how your relationship ended, whether your drinking may be affecting you more than you had thought, and whether some things from your past, such as your parent's divorce and your move to the United States, are still affecting you.

The counselor, during the next part of the closing, will assess the client's verbal and nonverbal reactions to the summary statement, looking for signs that the summary statement is on target. If some aspect of the summary statement does not match the client's view of the problems, then the client has an opportunity to modify the counselor's description. This may also be a time when information is given to the client about a diagnosis and why the counselor believes, based on the interview and information collected, that a particular diagnosis is justified. Sometimes the counselor will provide normative or developmental information to help the client understand that he or she is not alone with these concerns and troubles and the factors that may have played a role in the onset or maintenance of the problems. In essence, the counselor's emerging case conceptualization may be shared at this time. Once this information is shared, the stage is set for a collaborative discussion of an action plan and potential options.

Developing an Action Plan

The action plan can run the gamut from additional kinds of assessments to some type of treatment or steps the client will try to carry out. Further assessment options could include conducting another unstructured interview, administering a structured interview, giving a standardized test or measure, or developing a self-monitoring plan. All of these assessment options would have the shared purpose of gathering further information about the nature of the problem or risks and resources in order to clarify a diagnosis, help target additional symptoms or problems, develop a better case conceptualization, or aid in treatment planning. For example, before the intake interview concluded, Melanie was thinking, based on Brian's presenting symptoms and concerns, that he may be depressed, so she wanted to further assess that more systematically. She was considering having him complete the *Beck Depression Inventory-II* (BDI-II) (see Chapter 9). Melanie shared with Brian,

> You've mentioned problems with your temper, some sleep difficulty, and trouble getting going in the morning. When those things are happening all at the same time, there can be other problems and symptoms going on as well. I am thinking it would be helpful to have you fill out a questionnaire that would let us see what else might be going on. How does that sound?

Brian expresses a willingness to complete the BDI-II, and Melanie arranges a time and place for him to fill it out.

It is also possible and quite common that at the end of an initial interview the counselor is ready to discuss helping options with the client. A counselor in an employee assistance program might provide the client with a list of local mental health resources, how to contact them, and information regarding fees and insurance. In the case of Brian, Melanie felt she was ready to discuss options even though she was not yet confident about the diagnosis. She mentioned weekly individual counseling, regular exercise, a referral to the clinic's psychiatrist for a medication evaluation, and a men's depression support group her clinic was offering as possible ways that could help. Brian decided he would try counseling but wanted to know if he could come every other week and said "Nothing personal, but is there a male counselor I could see?" Melanie checked the list of counselors at her clinic who had time available, and there was a male counselor. Brian also thought he might start going back to the gym.

Clinician's Self-Assessment of the Interview and Interviewing Skills

Unstructured interviewing is the most common assessment method but is also a very challenging one to master. Effective interviewing requires a blend of empathy, caring, and reassurance along with opened-ended questions and follow-up probes while simultaneously attending in an unbiased and nonjudgmental fashion to the interviewee's expressions, reactions, mannerisms, and moods as the interview unfolds. Operating on parallel tracks can be difficult. Practice, review, and reflection can help one to develop any skill set, including interviewing. Reviewing one's interviewing skills is best accomplished through audio and/or visual recording of the interview, because relying only on one's recall of the interview will likely produce a biased and distorted account of what was said and how. The recording can be analyzed using the Practice Suggestion: Intake Interview Self-Assessment. The review can be first done independently and then collaboratively in supervision. The purpose of the review is to identify which skills were used, which were not, and the effect the skills had on helping the client to tell his or her story. It is also important to keep in mind when assessing one's own interview that there is only so much information that can be gathered in one sitting, and sometimes further relevant information will need to be collected in subsequent interviews or through other assessment means. The Practice Suggestion can also be used to identify information that still needs to be gathered and how it will be done. Furthermore, assessment is an ongoing process, not something done only at the outset of counseling. As more information is gathered and critically analyzed, case conceptualizations become refined, which ultimately drives the type of help a counselor will consider.

PRACTICE SUGGESTION
Intake Interview Self-Assessment

INTERVIEWING CONTENT AND SKILLS CHECKLIST

Interview Content & Skills	Not at All	Once	2–3 Times	More Than 3	Don't Know
Presenting Problem(s) Information Gathered:					
Problem: Onset / Duration / Frequency					
Changes in the past year					
Stressors (acute or chronic)					
Solutions tried to resolve the problems; coping strategies					
When problem occurs (least/most)					
Situations when problem not occurring					
Assessed Risks and Resources:					
Readiness for change stage					
Family history					
Educational, work, or military history					
Mental health/health history					
Trauma history					
Friendships and other interpersonal relationships					

(*continued*)

Interview Content & Skills	Not at All	Once	2–3 Times	More Than 3	Don't Know

Healthy vs. Unhealthy lifestyles:
    Diet
    Exercise
    Sleep
    Substance usage					

Role of spirituality, faith, or religion					
Involvement in pleasurable activities					
Interview Skills:					
Used rapport-building statements					
Used effective open questions					
Used closed questions that could be open					
Gave restatements or summaries					
Used normalizations					
Made bridges					
Asked two or more questions simultaneously					
Asked *why* questions					
Tailored the interview for the client					
Gave closing or summary statement					

PRACTICE SUGGESTION
Interviewing Self-Assessment Questionnaire

1. How did I develop and maintain rapport during the interview?
2. How effective were my questions?
3. How effective were my transitions between topics?
4. How was my closing of the interview?
5. If I were to do this interview again, what would I do the same and what would I do differently?

Summary and Conclusions

The unstructured interview is the most common assessment approach for developing a contextual understanding of a client's presenting problems and concerns, readiness for change, and risk and resource factors. Although the initial assessment interview, or intake as it is referred to in mental health settings, was the process described in this chapter, an intake style interview can be applied in various counseling settings: school, community, organizational, employee assistance, and rehabilitation. This chapter focused on questions an interviewer can ask to gather a comprehensive definition of a client's problem set. The stages of change model was also introduced, as well as a description given of how an interviewer can locate where, along a readiness for change continuum, a client resides. By identifying a client's readiness for change, the interviewer can tailor his or her questions to fit the client's needs and concerns.

This chapter described a risks and resources framework for gathering client background information. Risk factors are those inter- or intrapersonal components of a client's life—lack of social supports or unhealthy lifestyles, for example—that can worsen the presenting problem or prevent it from getting better. Resource factors are those internal and external areas of a client's life that can help to alleviate the presenting problems and can include social support, spirituality, adequate sleep, exercise, and strengths and abilities. Questions designed to identify those risks and resources along with specific techniques—for example, the genogram—were presented. This chapter also described the closing phase of the interview and what the interviewer tries to accomplish during this phase. The closing is an opportunity to summarize the presenting concerns, share with the client the emerging case conceptualization, and collaboratively plan the next step. That next step could involve further assessment using another unstructured process, a formal standardized method, or some type of intervention. Having said that, it is important to remember that assessment is not confined to the intake; once the intake ends, the assessment process is not over. Assessment is an ongoing process, with the amount and type being a function of the needs of the client and the presenting concerns.

Reflection Questions and Experiential Exercises

1. What are the advantages and disadvantages of the intake opening questions described in this chapter?
2. How will an interviewer's knowledge of the strategies a client used to solve the presenting problems before seeking professional counseling help the interviewer better understand the client?
3. Identify a habit you have or a problem you or someone else thinks you have. Identify which stage of change you are in with that habit or problem. What would you need to do to move to the next stage of change?
4. What are risk and resource factors? What is an example of each? What is one question an interviewer could ask to assess a risk and a resource?
5. In small groups of four to six people, brainstorm a list of questions for assessing a presenting problem. Then decide which stage or stages of change the question fits.
6. Role-play in groups of three an initial interview about a presenting problem. One person will be the interviewer, one the client, and the third an observer. The observer can use the checklist in the Practice Suggestion to guide the observation and provide feedback to the interviewer.
7. Using the evaluation checklist from the Practice Suggestion, rate yourself on an interview you did with a practicum or internship client.

5

OBSERVATIONS, INFERENCES, AND BEHAVIORAL ASSESSMENT

Chapter Objectives

After reading this chapter, you should be able to:

■ Understand the difference between informal and formal observations.

■ Identify the different aspects of a person's behavioral and emotional expression, and cognitive processes counselors typically observe.

■ Understand how counselors use formal observation systems.

■ Describe a mental status evaluation.

■ Explain the functional behavior assessment process.

Tanya came to the intake interview on a rainy Monday morning wearing a dress and was neatly groomed as if she were going on a job interview. Melanie, the intake counselor, greeted Tanya in the waiting room of the clinic and immediately began to take notice of Tanya's appearance, mannerisms, and style of speaking. Simultaneously, Melanie needed to hear Tanya's story, gather information about her concerns and background, and observe her behavior. What was it about Tanya that caught Melanie's attention? Tanya appeared obese, with dark hair and wore dark glasses despite the cloudy weather, and some makeup: lipstick and eye shadow. Relative to other clients with whom Melanie had worked, Tanya seemed easy to engage and was very verbal. She often maintained eye contact with the interviewer, except when she appeared to be searching for a word. In the beginning of the interview she seemed quite restless, often shifting her position in the chair, playing with her hair and adjusting her blouse. She did, however, appear more at ease and sat still as the interview progressed. By the end of the hour, much more about Tanya's presentation, emotional state, and psychological functioning had unfolded. What Melanie needed was a format for organizing and making sense of all the observations she had made.

OVERVIEW

Yogi Berra, the talented New York Yankees catcher who became equally legendary for his philosophizing, once said, "You can observe a lot by watching." Along with interviewing, observing is the most commonly used assessment method. As with interviews, observations can be done in an informal unstructured manner or formally with a coding and scoring system. Informally, a counselor might take notice of a client's eye contact and volume of speech over the course of an interview. More systemically a counselor could spend time in a classroom and measure the amount of time a student was on-task during a math assignment. Observations, whether made informally or formally, tend to be used as part of a more comprehensive assessment process such as a mental status evaluation or a functional behavioral assessment, both of which will be discussed in depth later in the chapter. Informal and formal observations are also integrated with other assessment data—interview information, tests results, and records—to develop a case conceptualization, diagnostic impression, or treatment plan. The purpose of this chapter is to describe what counselors and other professionals look for when assessing clients and some of the formalized systems for making and recording observations of individuals.

INFORMAL BEHAVIORAL OBSERVATIONS

Observations and Inferences

Upon meeting a client for the first time, a counselor begins the process of making behavioral observations. The **observation** data set comprises behaviors that can be readily seen and counted. This includes a client's appearance, clothing, hygiene, emotional expression, speech, movement, and interaction with the interviewer. Observations, however, are distinct from inferences. An **inference** is a speculation, judgment, or conclusion a counselor makes about a client, in part based upon what is being seen or heard. The distinction between observations and inferences can be illustrated with a group's response to a video of an intake session. After a group of counseling students were shown a video of an intake interview, several reported that Amanda, the client, sat with an open posture and gestured with her right hand when she spoke. Several other students said that Amanda "seemed nervous." In the first instance, observations were made because behaviors like gesturing and how one is sitting can be seen and counted, and two or more observers are likely to agree on what they are witnessing. The second statement reflects an inference about Amanda. Nervousness is an internal emotional state that cannot be seen by the outside observer. The counselor may see other behaviors that could suggest a nervous feeling—fists clenching and unclenching, frequent leg tapping, and rapid speech—but until Amanda states how she is feeling, those same behaviors could reflect something else: anger, a medication-induced state, or a habit when meeting unfamiliar people. Inferences are one step removed from the observations one can make, and consequently there is often less agreement among professional counselors at the inferential level than at the observational one. Professionals and trainees may even make widely divergent inferences about relatively small, discrete behaviors such as a client's smile (Scheflen, 1978). To put it another way, inferences are the end product of an assessment, and observations are the components of the assessment process, along with client self-reports, historical data, and testing results. This distinction between observations and inferences will help the interviewer or evaluator to stay focused on what is seen and heard while simultaneously beginning to formulate hypotheses about what observed behaviors may suggest.

Assessor Biases

Given the distinction between observations and inferences, it would seem that the counselor could go about the act of observing in a straightforward and accurate fashion. Counselors are not, however, cameras, and even a camera records behavior from only one angle or vantage point at a time. Human beings may miss things or see more or less of something than is actually occurring for different reasons. Several factors can account for making distorted observations, seeing something that did not occur, or not seeing something that did. One factor is the observer's emotional state. If the observer is anxious or too highly aroused or preoccupied with what to say next, client behavior can be missed. Simply stated, a relaxed and attentive assessor will make for a more accurate observer. A second and more difficult factor to overcome is the magnitude of the data the clinician is trying to process. In addition to making observations about the client's behavior, the counselor is processing client statements, prior information about the client, and the degree to which the observations and statements relate to what the counselor knows about human behavior. Rather than becoming overwhelmed by information, a natural human tendency is to simplify incoming data in order to make sense of it. Therefore, the assessing clinician is likely to selectively attend to client behavior and statements (Spengler, Strohmer, Dixon, & Shivy, 1995). The clinician's selective focus will mean that some of what is occurring in front of him or her may be missed or misread. What might account for what counselors selectively attend to and not? A wealth of social psychology research (Nisbett & Ross, 1980) has demonstrated how preconceptions and other kinds of biases can affect how observations about people are attended to, coded in memory, and recalled. So a behavior, seemingly as basic as a smile, may be viewed differently by different people depending upon their previously held views, beliefs, or theories about smiling, the individual person in question, or the situation eliciting the smile. That is why some look at the painting of the Mona Lisa and see a smile and others a frown. Which perception is accurate? Perhaps both perceptions are correct and maybe neither one. There can be multiple realities and ways of looking at someone's behavior that can reflect an interaction between the observer and the observed.

When a counselor goes to the next level and makes inferences and judgments based on prior observations, certain kinds of unconscious processes can be triggered that impact the assessment. A judgment or conclusion could be formed about anything—the client's emotional state during an interview, a set of observed behaviors, a thinking process. The unconscious processes that can impact those judgments have been termed cognitive errors, or heuristics (Nisbett & Ross, 1980). A **heuristic** is a cognitive strategy for solving problems, processing information, and making inferences and judgments. It is also a kind of a cognitive map or shortcut, in that it helps reduce a large amount of complex stimuli and information to a more manageable and understandable level. These mental maps are necessary for all of us to make sense of the world around us, especially our interpersonal one, engage in inductive reasoning, and form generalizations, but their uncritical use can lead to errors in judgment about situations and people we are observing and evaluating. These inferential errors have been found to occur in both laypersons and counseling professionals (Garb, Lilienfeld, & Fowler, 2008; Nisbett & Ross, 1980; Spengler et al., 1995).

When individuals, whether professionally trained or not, go about recalling their observations and making inferences from them, two heuristics come into play that can affect what the person remembers seeing: availability and representative (Nisbett & Ross, 1980; Spengler et al., 1995). The **availability heuristic** refers to the tendency to judge frequency and cause-and-effect relationships based on personal egocentric data that are easily accessible rather than on objective data. A common situation that illustrates how people use the availability heuristic and come up with distorted estimates of frequency is the new car owner judging how many of the same car have been recently purchased. A new Prius owner, for example, will inflate how many Prii there are and underestimate the number of any other type of car. What tends to happen is that each time a Prius is seen it is counted and stored in memory, unconsciously, and other types of cars are ignored. A more objective method for estimating the number of Prii on the road would be to consult an industry trade publication that collects data on car purchases. How might this cognitive simplification strategy apply in a counseling context? A clinician's experience with and recall of the symptoms of a certain disorder, attention deficit–hyperactivity disorder (ADHD), for example, is available and more easily accessible to him or her than normal childhood behaviors because of years of working in a children's mental health clinic. The clinician then is asked to come to an elementary school and observe the children from a third-grade classroom during recess. The clinician unwittingly applies the availability heuristic when watching the children play and erroneously concludes that there are more ADHD children on the playground than there actually are, based on that clinical experience. The features that make up ADHD are more salient and readily available to the clinician than are normative data on elementary school age behavior, and therefore these ADHD-like behaviors get counted more. Furthermore, that same clinician may attribute certain movements and behaviors in a particular child being observed to the condition ADHD because the features of that disorder are more salient for the observing clinician than are lesser known environmental and situational factors that may be causing the child's behavior that day.

The **representative heuristic** is a cognitive strategy that can be used to judge the degree to which a person or object belongs in a category, predict outcomes, and understand cause and effect (Nisbett & Ross, 1980). Counselors and other helping professionals are likely to utilize the representative heuristic when conceptualizing cases, assigning clients to a diagnostic category, or predicting a client's future behavior. The use of this mental strategy, particularly for categorizing, can be illustrated both in everyday and professional life. In daily life, people look at the features of a situation, object, or person to see how well those features resemble or fit with a category. That animal with reddish-brown fur, four legs, a long tail, and a certain size that just darted across my front yard—is it a squirrel or a chipmunk? If I did not get a good look at the fast-moving creature, I will compare the features of what was seen to what I know are the essential and representative features of different species or categories of animals to figure out what that was in my yard. One important piece of data that is often left out when making decisions about assigning a person or object to a category is the concept of *base rates*. That is, the percentage within a population that belongs to a category: racial–ethnic group, diagnostic category, or in this case, red squirrel and chipmunk populations in Northern New England. Knowing that far fewer red squirrels than chipmunks live in this part of New England, and therefore the probability of the animal being a chipmunk is far greater, would help determine which animal it likely was that invaded my yard. Research has shown, however, that base rates and probability estimates are often not used when making predictions or classifications (Dawes, 1994; Nisbett & Ross, 1980). This hypothetical animal classification story is analogous to what has happened at times with mental health professionals. Mental health professionals typically need to make decisions about diagnostic categories: how many and which features of a diagnostic category need to be present in order for a clinician to judge that the category in question is present. Studies have shown, as with the animal example, that clinicians have believed that particular observations are characteristic of a diagnostic category. What the clinician observes—for instance, lack of eye contact, emotional lability, and a loud angry tone of voice—is compared with what is known about the essential features or criteria of a diagnostic category. The clinician then searches his or her memory store of diagnostic categories and quickly compares what is being observed with what he or she recalls about the characteristics of the diagnoses to see if these observations match the relevant criteria. The problem with relying solely on the representative heuristic in this fashion is that it gets applied without consideration of base rate information, probability estimates, and other data (Dawes, 1994; Spengler et al., 1995).

A particular case of the representative heuristic, which clinicians and nonprofessionals alike are subject to, is the **illusory correlation**, a term coined by two researchers in the 1960s who were interested in exploring the kinds of inferences clinical psychologists made from projective tests (Nisbett & Ross, 1980). This is the process of thinking a characteristic, trait, or behavior of someone is correlated to a condition or event, such as psychopathology or childhood trauma, when in fact no or little statistical relationship exists. Laypersons and counseling professionals are more likely to erroneously conclude two things are correlated if they hold a prior belief, based on personal experience, about the existence of a relationship, like binge drinking and attending college. In other words, professionals, like others, are more likely to make judgments about correlations based on personal expectations and beliefs rather than on empirical evidence (Garb et al., 2008; Spengler et al., 1995). An example of this is the belief that certain aspects of human drawings are signs of psychopathology or experience: large eyes signifying paranoia and the inclusion of a tongue indicating a sexual abuse history. These correlations have been found to be virtually nonexistent and thus an illusion (Lilienfeld, Wood, & Garb, 2000).

Another kind of cognitive bias that we are prone to is a **confirmatory bias**, or a self-fulfilling prophecy. A confirmatory bias is the human tendency to take in information that confirms or supports one's preexisting theory and ignore contradictory evidence. This cognitive bias or mental map, like the others described earlier, tends to occur outside of a person's awareness; that is, it happens automatically and unconsciously. It is also one of the more heavily researched judgment heuristics that counseling professionals need to be aware of, otherwise they too will continue to utilize it unwittingly. For example, if a counselor comes to the conclusion, based on a client's response to interview questions and observations about that client, that she has a post-traumatic stress disorder, the counselor is apt to search for and store in memory any new information that supports that diagnostic judgment and ignore any evidence that would contradict it. Another example of when a confirmatory bias can occur in counseling settings is the common situation where prior information about a client—a record, evaluation, or referral information—is given to and looked at by a clinician before interviewing the client. Once absorbed, that information will prime the counselor to develop a theory or hypothesis about the client before meeting him or her. The hypothesis could be something like, "This is going to be a difficult client, someone who will try to manipulate, or has maladaptive coping skills." With that theory in mind, the counselor may unconsciously look for information and observations that can confirm the theory and ignore the pieces that don't fit with it. The author has found, not surprisingly, that graduate students, given different fictitious background descriptions of a client (one that involves neutral demographic information, one that suggests childhood psychopathology, and one suggestive of a resilient history) and then shown a video of the intake with the actual client, tend to report observations and inferences consistent with the prior history they received. Once impressions, inferences, judgments, or conclusions about someone are formed, there is a natural human tendency to resist modifying those conclusions even in the face of new data that would indicate the original hypothesis was wrong (Nisbett & Ross, 1980).

Information processing style is another factor that can affect the kinds of observation a clinician makes. Some people are better at processing visual stimuli, others auditory, and still others kinesthetic. During a counseling session, most information is coming to the clinician through the auditory channel, but a fair amount is also coming through the visual. In addition, those stimuli can be processed in a sequential fashion, one piece after another, or in a simultaneous or parallel manner (Das, Naglieri, & Kirby, 1994). A counseling interview is a parallel processing task: the clients' statements and behaviors need to be processed simultaneously. The act of listening and watching can be harder than it seems at times and even harder when combined with the acts of speaking and writing. To the extent that one is adept at processing auditory and visual stimuli simultaneously, the more accurate the observation method will be.

Similarly, how people in general, regardless of processing style, store and recall information is subject to unconscious bias. These biases are known as the primacy, or anchoring, effect and the recency effect. Simply put, when individuals are given a list of things to remember, what tends to get recalled more often and accurately is what was at the beginning and end of the list. Therefore, observations made about a client in the beginning of a session and the end are likely to be remembered more than what occurred during the middle unless what was observed seemed particularly unusual or unrepresentative or provoked an emotional response from the observer. Research has shown that emotionally charged events boost memory, but only to a point (Phelps & Sharot, 2008). When a situation is emotionally arousing, the gist of what happened is likely to be recalled better and more vividly than neutral events. The contextual details, however, of an emotional event may not be more accurately remembered despite individuals believing more strongly in the accuracy of those details. Furthermore, the confidence and conviction in one's memory leads to quick decision making and responding. Therefore, a clinician who has a particularly emotionally charged contact with a client may mistakenly "remember" parts of what occurred and make snap decisions such as a judgment or diagnosis about the client.

As natural and understandable as this tendency to reduce information overload through heuristics and other information management processes is, it can unwittingly lead to assessment outcomes that have ethical implications. These include inaccurate diagnosis, client stereotyping and other inappropriate judgments, and counseling recommendations that may be a poor fit for the client (Garb et al., 2008; Spengler et al., 1995). On the other hand, not all heuristics and mental shortcuts result in erroneous inferences and conclusions. Sometimes those strategies will lead to accurate judgments and predictions, but it is important to recognize the existence of the unconscious processes and the potential negative consequences of them for counselors and their clients.

How then can counselors and other professionals overcome these biasing tendencies or order to make valid and useful observations and inferences? Several general strategies involving certain knowledge, attitudes, and skills can help (see Practice Suggestion: Guidelines for Minimizing Observation and Inferential Biases). By keeping an open mind, developing a tolerance for ambiguity, checking out observations, inferences, and hypotheses with clients, colleagues, and supervisors, and trying out interventions that can test the accuracy of those hypotheses, the practice of observing and inferring can occur more effectively. These assessment attitudes and skills, as identified in the Practice Suggestion, can be strengthened through ongoing training, clinical experience, and supervision.

Mental Status Evaluation

So what exactly is a counselor looking and listening for during the first and subsequent times he or she encounters a client? Typically, counselors and other professionals make informal observations about a client's appearance, physical activity, emotional expression, speech and language, thought content and process, and attitude toward the examiner. Collectively, these observations about a client make up what is known as a **mental status evaluation** (Morrison, 2008; Shea, 1998; Trzepacz & Baker, 1993). Although the term *mental status* implies evaluating cognitive abilities and processes such as perception, attention, concentration, memory, and judgment, behavioral observations help to shape and inform an understanding of those cognitive processes, as well as overall emotional and psychological functioning. Therefore, the term *mental status evaluation* is a comprehensive method for assessing thinking, behavior, and emoting, which relies primarily on the observational method and, to a lesser extent, interviewing. It is an assessment process on which clinicians rely for gathering and organizing observations that can aid, like other assessment methods, in the case conceptualization, diagnostic, and treatment planning processes (Polanski & Hinkle, 2000). Consequently, a clinician who is equipped with a set of guidelines that describe what to pay attention to, such as the mental status format, will observe more effectively.

PRACTICE SUGGESTION
**Guidelines for Minimizing Observation
and Inferential Biases**

1. Avoid reading reports, evaluations, or other client information *prior* to an initial assessment of a client. Integrate that information after the assessment interview or observation session.
2. Keep in mind the difference between observations and inferences.
3. Attend to how observations of nonverbal behavior are in sync with or differ from client's verbal reports.
4. Be tentative about hypotheses generated, and be open to changing them as new observations and information are acquired.
5. Try not to rush the process of forming judgments and conclusions such as case conceptualizations and diagnoses.
6. Develop a tolerance for ambiguity and maintain a low level of confidence about initial ideas about a client.
7. Develop an awareness of your own biases, beliefs, and values that could color your observations and inferences.
8. Develop an awareness of your preferred information processing style and how that might impact the observation process.
9. Practice collaboration: check out your inferences with clients, colleagues, and supervisors. For example, "You moved on to another subject right after you started to mention how you were feeling nervous about getting into another relationship. Was that how you were feeling?"
10. Check out how observations and inferences match or are discrepant with other data obtained from or about the client: self-reports, test or questionnaire data if available, and significant others' reports. For example, a parent may report that her child is often in a negative mood but the counselor thinks of the child as happy, curious, and playful based on observations during a counseling session.
11. Change or confirm initial hypotheses based on supporting or contradictory information.

The mental status exam was originally used as a neurological screening tool but has become common practice in most mental health settings (Morrison, 2008). There are both informal unstructured and formal structured parts to this type of evaluation. As mentioned, the informal part includes observations about a client's appearance, emotional expression, speech, physical activity, and engagement with the interviewer. The formal part is similar to a structured interview with a scoring system that involves questions related to memory, orientation, language, abstract reasoning, and judgment. The formal part of the exam is often used for diagnostic purposes when there is a concern about cognitive problems, which occur in disorders such as dementia, severe depression, or schizophrenia. What follows is a discussion of the different categories of the informal and formal parts of the mental status examination, how this assessment method is conducted, and the hypotheses that can be generated from this information.

APPEARANCE   One of the first observations a counselor is likely to make about clients is their overall appearance. There are several aspects of appearance to consider: body stature and weight, appearance relative to chronological age, style of dress, grooming, hygiene, and marks on the body. Upon meeting a client for the first time, a counselor will make note of a client's physical characteristics. Tanya, the woman in this chapter's case study, appears to have a medium frame, and looks obese. The cause of her obesity could be due to several factors, and that information may come about later in the interview. Furthermore, her appearance seems to fit with her chronological age; that is, she does not seem much older or younger than her 39 years. Clients who appear considerably older than their age may have a chronic physical or mental health condition such as multiple sclerosis, alcohol abuse, or depression. A clinician's judgment of whether a client appears younger or older than his or her age is a subjective one but is often based on physical features such as hair color and style, skin condition, energy level, and dress (Trzepacz & Baker, 1993).

Attire and Hygiene   Another aspect of appearance is a client's dress and hygiene. How is Tanya dressed and groomed? Is she dressed formally in professional business attire or casually in sweatpants and a T-shirt? Does she look neatly groomed and dressed, or unkempt or disheveled? Sometimes a client's appearance can provide diagnostic clues, and it is also a reflection of cultural and personal factors: socioeconomic status, peer or community group affiliation, occupation, and identity expression. Tanya arrives at the initial interview wearing a dress and some makeup and is neatly groomed. Others, however, may show up looking disheveled, with messy hair, and exhibiting a body odor. Other odors may be noticeable as well: cigarette smell, alcohol, urine, perfume, or cologne. A person's lack of attention to dress and hygiene can be a sign of a condition such as major depression, and an unkempt, disheveled look can signify psychosis. Furthermore, someone like Tanya who later in the interview reports symptoms of depression—often feeling down, having trouble sleeping, and feeling guilty a lot—but is well dressed and groomed may have a less severe level of depression than one who cannot muster the energy and motivation to attire herself or himself neatly. Another aspect of a client's style of dressing includes the fit between the season and the clothing. Is the person wearing a jacket on a warm summer day or shorts on a cold December morning? Certain medications and disorders, like schizophrenia, can impact body temperature, which may be why someone appears over- or underdressed given the outer temperature. On the other hand, this can be a matter of cultural influence and style. Some folks wear wool caps in the summer and some teens walk around in shorts in the winter. In children, appearance, dress, and hygiene can provide further clues about a child's level of supervision and the possibility of neglect or abuse, peer group identification, and cultural background.

Body Marks   In addition to dress, grooming, and hygiene, the counselor can observe marks on the body that also may have relevance to diagnostic and case formulations. Does the client have any burns, scratches, scars, or cuts that might reflect self-injurious behavior? What about tattoos and body piercing? These are now pretty common in teens and young adults. On the other hand, it is unusual to see elementary school age children in most cultures with body piercing or tattoos. The counselor, therefore, will want to notice any marks on the body. What those marks may reflect can vary widely from person to person, but it is another piece of the observation set that potentially can help with an overall assessment of the client.

Level of Arousal   A client can present for an interview or counseling session at various levels of alertness and arousal. A person can appear rested, with a moderate degree of energy and be aware of and respond to environmental stimuli—sounds, sights, and smells—without being frequently distracted or seemingly preoccupied by them. This would be considered a moderate degree of arousal, along a continuum that has sleep or stupor—drifting in and out of wakefulness—at one end, and hyperarousal at the other end. Most clients will maintain the same level of alertness throughout an interview but at times may show unusual changes (Morrison, 2008). Some clients may appear to be tired, fatigued, and even drowsy, yawning frequently and occasionally closing their eyes. They are showing decreased arousal. The most direct cause of that would be sleep deprivation, but it can also be a manifestation of drug intoxication or a medical condition (Trzepacz & Baker, 1993). It is very rare for a client to fall asleep or become stuporlike during an interview; on the other hand, an observer might notice hyperalertness or vigilance to sounds and visual stimuli. Hypervigilance is a symptom of post-traumatic stress disorder. It also can be observed when someone is paranoid. When someone is hyperaroused, he or she may also exhibit a startle response, often in an exaggerated manner.

EXPRESSION OF EMOTIONS It is important for clinicians to pay attention to not only what clients say, but how they say it. Much of our communication is nonverbal, and most of our emotional state is conveyed through tone of voice, facial expression, gestures, and postures, rather than words (Duke, Nowicki, & Martin, 1996; Hill, 2004). Although emotions can be expressed in a variety of ways, the face is where we look first to understand what a person is expressing. What might a facial expression suggest about how a person is feeling? Some signs of emotional expression may be fairly obvious, such as teary eyes reflecting sadness, or narrowing eyes and eyebrows indicating anger. Others may be more subtle, such as an enigmatic smile. Facial expressions, gestures, and other external signs—voice tone, for example—that an observer notices in order to infer a person's emotional state is called **affect**. In addition to the face, body posture, muscle tension, and activity level can be further signs of a client's emotional state, what collectively is often referred to as body language—that is, what emotional state is being expressed through the body. There is a difference, however, between a person's affect and mood. A client's self-report of a feeling state is what is termed **mood**. Mood, therefore, is considered a subjective internal state, whereas affect is an external state that someone else can observe. The distinction between a client's stated mood and the observed feeling state is another aspect of the mental status evaluation (Morrison, 2008; Trzepacz & Baker, 1993).

Affect, Mood, and Topic Congruency At times, what the client reports and what the counselor sees will match, and at other times there can be a discrepancy. Sometimes a client may state he or she is feeling "OK" but appears tense and nervous. Other times a client may, for example, talk about feeling disappointed, hopeless, and sad, and his or her eyes and posture will match that self-report. Another way a client's affect may seem congruent or incongruent is with the topic at hand. Tanya discusses the loss of her father and the breakup of her marriage and reveals sadness in her voice and eyes. Her sad affect matches what she is discussing. Later in the same interview, she discusses things her current boyfriend does that annoy her and frighten her and yet she chuckles and smiles. At that point, her affect does not appear congruent with what she is describing about her mood and her current relationship. The degree to which a client's affect matches his or her mood and the focus of the conversation will be another element of the observational data set a counselor will obtain when interviewing a client.

Range and Intensity of Affect Over the course of an interview or counseling session, a client's affect, like mood, can change and have a range and intensity. Although a client may report several different moods or appear at times to be expressing different emotions, one feeling may be predominant. Tanya, for example, shows a mixture of irritability, sadness, and agitation, but her sadness is the overriding emotion. It is not uncommon for a person's affect to change over the course of an interview. A limited range of emotional expression is termed **constricted affect**. The observer will want to take note of which affects are shown, when the switch in expression occurs, and how abrupt the shift is. The phrase used to describe sudden rapid changes is **labile affect**, or **lability**. A complete absence of affect is termed **flat affect**. Generally, someone displaying a flat affect shows blankness, an almost complete lack of emotional expression in the face. A flat affect is rare, but is more commonly observed in people with schizophrenia (Morrison, 2008). A less severe form of limited affect is called blunted affect. **Blunted affect** is the term used to describe emotional expression that seems very diminished or muted, but not flat, as in the case of clients with post-traumatic stress disorder who report feeling numb (Trzepacz & Baker, 1993).

Judgments about the range and intensity of affect are also subjective. Clinicians do not base these judgments on set standards but tend to base them on experience with people both in counseling and noncounseling settings. As a result, a clinician has an affect data base in his or her head, so to speak, which enables distinctions between flat and constricted affect to be made. It is these kinds of observations and judgments that can be biased for the reasons noted earlier. Therefore, two or more clinicians watching the same interview of a client may come up with different impressions about the affect expressed.

MOVEMENT AND ACTIVITY LEVEL The type and extent of physical activity a client displays during an assessment can also provide diagnostic signs and case conceptualization information. A person who is anxious, for example, may show various kinds of motor activity or body movement: leg tapping, shifting of seating position, eye blinking, muscle twitching, and even perspiration. Conversely, someone with anxiety and other psychiatric disorders may sit very still as if in a frozen state (Morrison, 2008). Muscle twitching, rapid eye blinking, or another tic-like movement can also be due to a medication side effect or a disorder such as Tourette's. Another type of movement, hand tremors, is often related to neurological conditions such as Parkinson's, a side effect of antipsychotic medications, or someone withdrawing from significant alcohol use. Children with attention deficit–hyperactivity disorder may climb on furniture, move quickly from one object to another, or appear fidgety and restless.

Other kinds of gestures and movements are additional forms of nonverbal communication that suggest emotional experiencing. Someone who is highly agitated may get up and pace around the room. Others may sit still but gesture with their hands in an animated way, especially if they are angry. What happens at the beginning and end of the interview? Does the client extend a hand to shake hello or goodbye, or is parting more effusive, with the client hugging the interviewer? Movement, gestures, and activity level may shift over the course of a session and it is useful to note when those shifts occur and whether more disclosure seems to have a calming effect on heightened activity or just the opposite.

With young children—preschool through elementary age—additional areas to attend to include ease of separation from caregiver, exploration of the interview space, proximity to the clinician, and how play materials and other objects are manipulated. Children vary in their ability to separate from a parent or caregiver, and this will become readily apparent as the interviewer signals a move to the interview area. Some children will leave readily with a quick goodbye, some may need parental coaxing, and others may have so much difficulty that they cling to their parent. Upon entering the interview room, some children will move about comfortably and easily, exploring and handling the toys and other materials. Other children, particularly those who are anxious, may stand or sit, still and stiff, and will need a prompt to explore. As the child explores the room, the interviewer can also note the child's proximity to the interviewer. Some children, especially those with histories of attachment problems, may spontaneously sit in the clinician's lap or wrap their arms around, giving a hug. Others may seem to be so close at times, as if they lack an awareness of personal space. This is often the case with children with autism spectrum disorders and to a lesser extent attention deficit–hyperactivity disorder. Many children, on the other hand, will maintain a more comfortable and socially appropriate distance for being with an unfamiliar adult.

SPEECH The aspects of speech that a counselor can informally observe include rate, rhythm, volume or intensity, and fluency. These variations in speech have been termed **prosody** (Trzepacz & Baker, 1993). About one-third of emotional meaning is expressed in conversation through prosody, or what is also referred to as **paralanguage** (Duke et al., 1996). It is through the observation of a person's speech that inferences about thought processes can be made as well. Both the content of speech and style of speaking can reflect underlying thoughts, beliefs, images, and fantasies.

The interviewer, when conducting informal observations of speech, is likely to use his or her own personal experience as a barometer for judging the client's rate, rhythm, and volume. Rate of speech, the number of words produced per minute, is not usually measured, and even if it were, we don't have a standard from which judgments about fast or slow can be made. The same can be said about volume, so counselors do not measure decibel levels. Therefore, inferences about speech patterns are necessarily subjective. Someone, for example, who appears to the interviewer to be speaking rapidly may be judged by others to be a rapid speaker and is likely to have thoughts going through his or her head at a similar speed. A related phenomenon is **pressured speech**. Not only is the client talking very quickly, but they seem to be experiencing this urge or intensity to get the words out in order to move on to the next idea or thought, which is probably emerging into consciousness rapidly. Pressured speech is one sign of the condition called mania or a manic episode, which occurs in people with a bipolar disorder. Conversely, when speech seems halted or blocked, a person may be having trouble organizing his or her thoughts or losing track of them. This can happen for a variety of reasons—everything from fatigue to a psychiatric disorder such as major depression, and more commonly schizophrenia.

Different aspects of speech can also provide clues about a person's emotional state. Does the person appear to be using a conversational tone of voice, a loud shouting voice, or a quiet, soft-spoken one? Volume, for example, tends to become louder when someone is becoming emotionally aroused regardless of whether the specific feeling triggering the arousal is excitement, nervousness, anger, or agitation. On the other hand, fatigue and a low energy level, especially when one is depressed, may produce speech that is both low in volume and monotone. Voice inflection or tone, like affect, can take on a wide or constricted range through the course of an interview. Variations in tone and inflection can be noticed, and when they occur may provide some clues to what the client may be experiencing or thinking about. Tonal variation and rhythm will also be influenced by one's culture and region: a Southerner's accent versus a New Yorker's, for example.

Difficulties with fluency and articulation may stem from several factors. A client may speak a language that is not the primary one. A Spanish-speaking woman attempting to communicate in English, for example, may demonstrate these kinds of speech problems. Furthermore, language acquisition has a developmental component and therefore articulation errors may be within a normal range. On the other hand, they may reflect an underlying speech or communication disorder, a developmental delay, or possibly severe anxiety. In some cases, when a client is very tense or anxious, speech may become choppy or stuttering may occur.

Speech and Thought Processes   The final aspect of speech to observe is the degree to which it is focused, connected, and coherent. Speech that becomes disorganized, difficult to follow, and ultimately incoherent is a sign that the person's thinking is also that way. Speech that is disorganized, rambling, and hard to make sense of is most often a reflection of a thought disorder that occurs during a psychotic state or a condition like schizophrenia. That type of speech, and inferentially one's thinking, can also be a sign of severe and chronic substance abuse, dementia, or some other pathology affecting the brain (Morrison, 2008).

A client's speech may be coherent and organized around particular topics or themes but she or he tends to veer off in different directions. This is known as **tangential speech**. That phenomenon is part of normal daily conversation and usually the listener can see the connection between the initial topic and the tangent. For example, a client when asked, "When did these problems begin?" may answer, "When I left for college," then go on to remark that "the winters were really cold there and I didn't go out much." Tangential thinking can also occur when an individual has difficulty sustaining attention, is anxious, or is experiencing intrusive, bothersome thoughts.

When a person talks, his or her focus can shift rapidly and abruptly to another tangential topic or idea. This is known as **flight of ideas** (Trzepacz & Baker, 1993), and it is characterized by the person quickly moving from one seemingly related tangent to another. There is a logical connection between sentences but every second or third sentence introduces a new topic or theme and the connection is usually difficult for the listener to follow. Speech that not only reflects rapidly changing ideas but no logical connection between them is referred to as **loose associations** (Trzepacz & Baker, 1993). Furthermore, the connections may be based more on puns, word-plays, rhymes, or homophones than logic (Morrison, 2008). Loose thinking is a sign of psychosis or mania.

The most extreme form of a speech disruption is incoherency. The listener can make no sense of what the speaker is trying to communicate. Incoherent speech is rare, its occurrence is usually a sign of a person with schizophrenia or a degenerative induced psychosis as can happen in dementia (Morrison, 2008).

THOUGHT CONTENT AND PERCEPTION   Unusual thinking and perception may be noticeable to the interviewer as well. When the content of one's thinking is not based in some shared external reality, represents a false interpretation or perception of experience, and is rigidly adhered to, it is considered **delusional** (American Psychiatric Association, 2000). To be considered a delusion, the false belief would not be a reflection of a cultural norm (e.g., believing in paranormal phenomenon), nor would it be a reflection of developmental status (e.g., a preschool child believing in alien monsters). Delusions can vary in their degree of bizarreness, to the extent that they involve ideas completely outside the realm of ordinary life, but the cultural context needs to be considered when making that judgment (American Psychiatric Association, 2000). In counseling settings, clients may reveal various kinds of delusions, including paranoid, persecutory, grandiose, or referential. **Ideas of reference** refers to a person thinking that a story, message, or conversation was indirectly meant for him or her. For example, a client with ideas of reference would report that an opinion piece he had read in a news magazine last week was placed there for him. A delusional process can be subtle and may be discernible only through multiple interviews, while others may be fairly obvious. Delusions are generally signs of schizophrenia and less often a personality disorder. Jonathan Nash, a renowned physicist, suffered from schizophrenia, and his paranoid and grandiose delusions were portrayed in the film *A Beautiful Mind.*

Delusions are not the same, however, as obsessions. Like delusions, **obsessions** are ideas that a person may rigidly cling to but unlike them, obsessions are reality based and represent a way of thinking that is shared by others in one's culture, but in a more extreme way. Furthermore, the person who has obsessive thoughts will recognize the unrealistic or senseless nature of them, which is not the case with a delusional thinker. Obsessions tend to be experienced repetitively and are often reported as unwanted, repugnant, bizarre, and distressing (American Psychiatric Association, 2000). They tend to center around a specific theme: contamination, illness and health, responsibility, harm, sexual urges, aggression, and morals. Obsessions are usually a sign of an obsessive–compulsive or some other anxiety disorder, and sometimes depression (see Chapter 9).

Perceptual distortions can take the form of illusions and hallucinations. The latter is more indicative of severe psychopathology because, like delusional thinking, the person's perception is erroneous and there is no sensory stimulus to trigger it (American Psychiatric Association, 2000). An illusion, on the other hand, is based on some external stimulus, a shadow for example, being perceived as some other type of object, and an outside observer may be able to see how that perception was arrived at. Hallucinations can occur in any of the five senses—auditory, visual, tactile, gustatory (taste), and olfactory (smell)—but auditory ones are most commonly reported by mental health clients (American Psychiatric Association, 2000). It is common for people to experience false or hallucinogenic perceptions upon drifting off to sleep and awakening. They can also be experienced during some religious events. When hallucinations are perceived during those times, they are not considered signs of psychosis (American Psychiatric Association, 2000). Both auditory and visual hallucinations can be rated in terms of severity. Auditory hallucinations could range from hearing noises to complete sentences coming from two or more voices, and visual ones from blurred images to entire scenes (Morrison, 2008). Individuals who are having auditory hallucinations may appear as if they are talking to someone else in the room or continue to look at a spot in the room as if someone else with whom they were conversing was there. Often, however, merely observing a client will not be sufficient to determine whether a client is having or has ever had hallucinations. The interviewer will need to directly ask about the experience of hearing voices, or seeing things others have not seen, to accurately assess a history of hallucinations. A person may report "hearing voices," and the interviewer must discern whether the person perceives the voices as being internal or external. Many people may say that they have a "voice in their head" as a way to connote what one part of them is thinking. That is different than the perceptual phenomenon of a voice coming from outside one's head. When that occurs, the person usually perceives the voice as telling or commanding him or her to do something. Typically the nature of the perceived command is frightening to the person such as a command to harm oneself or someone else.

DEMEANOR AND ATTITUDE TOWARD THE INTERVIEWER   The one remaining aspect of informal observations that make up the mental status evaluation is the client's demeanor and attitude toward the interviewer. A client's approach to the interview situation and response style provide a clue about readiness for change. The counselor will want to consider the ease or difficulty in engaging the client, the client's response style, and level of participation in the process. Those clients who are open, easy to engage, cooperative, tend to elaborate on answers, and show some degree of reflection are usually in the preparation or action stage of change (see Chapter 4). Tanya, the client in the opening case study, was easy to engage and maintained eye contact throughout the interview. She was conversational and engaged in some chitchat prior to the interview questions. Furthermore, she willingly opened up about different aspects of her life. Other clients can be difficult to engage in the interview process. They tend to avoid making eye contact, and extracting information seems like pulling teeth; it does not flow out easily. Some clients may have difficulty cooperating with the interview process, and challenge the interviewer. For example, a client might ask, "Why do we need to talk about that?" In more extreme and rare cases, a client may appear argumentative and antagonistic toward the interviewer.

The ease or difficulty of engaging a client is related to response style. Clients who open up easily tend to elaborate on their answers with no or little prompting or encouragement needed from the interviewer; they are actively involved in the process. Furthermore, they are likely to produce spontaneous speech; that is, they disclose information based on what is being shared rather than sitting back and waiting for the next question. Conversely, some will remain fairly closed, exhibiting a passive style, only speaking in response to direct questions. In addition, answers to questions may be very limited, noncommittal, evasive, or circumspect, and the client may appear to be guarded and withholding of information. These clients are typically in the precontemplation stage of change.

Another aspect of response style is reflectivity. When Tanya responds with, "I hadn't thought about that before," she is showing that she is reflecting upon something the interviewer asked or she disclosed. As the interview unfolds, clients may make other statements or expressions that suggest they are thinking about what is being discussed. Some clients, however, may show little if any signs of reflection. Degree of reflection is also characterized as level of insight or awareness about one's thinking, emotions, or behavior.

FORMAL OBSERVATION ASSESSMENTS

Formal Mental Status Evaluations

Observations about a client's overall appearance, affect, physical activity, speech, thought process and content, and engagement with the interviewer are typically gathered in an informal, unsystematic fashion. Earlier, the assessment of thinking or cognition focused on content (delusions and obsessions) and process (connection of ideas and perceptions). Formal mental status exams assess other aspects of cognitive abilities and processes, which are not included in the informal mental status. This is done with a systematic and structured format. More specifically, the *Mini-Mental State Examination* (MMSE) (Folstein, Folstein, & McHugh, 1975; Folstein, Folstein, McHugh, & Fanjiang, 2001) or some variation of that traditional test of cognitive functioning, the *Modified Mini-Mental State Examination* (3MS) (Teng & Chui, 1987) is used to assess: 1) orientation, 2) attention and concentration, 3) language and comprehension, 4) memory processes, 5) abstract reasoning, and 6) visual–spatial perception.

Formal mental status tests typically include one or two questions or tasks to evaluate those different aspects of cognitive processing. The MMSE and 3MS are designed to evaluate a person's cognitive functioning at a point in time for the purpose of detecting thinking deficits that could be attributable to some type of pathology—dementia, traumatic brain injury, psychosis, or chronic substance abuse. Therefore, mental status tests can be considered screenings of cognitive functioning and underlying abilities. As screening tools, the MMSE and 3MS may indicate the need for more comprehensive assessment in any one or more of the areas assessed: language and verbal reasoning, memory, attention, and visual–spatial skills. These cognitive abilities are typically assessed more comprehensively with tests that are referred to as cognitive ability, intelligence, or neuropsychological tests (see Chapter 13).

The original MMSE was designed to aid in the differential diagnosis of elderly individuals admitted to inpatient settings and was found to be a valid measure of cognitive impairment often found in depression, dementia, delirium, or schizophrenia (Folstein et al., 1975). The 3MS was created in an effort to make up for some of the purported inadequacies of the MMSE—limited reliability and validity and assessing a narrow range of cognitive functioning (Teng & Chui, 1987). One study found, however, that it was not significantly different in its ability to correctly identify patients with Alzheimer's disease nor was it more clinically useful than the MMSE, despite the modifications (Tombaugh, McDowell, Kristjansson, & Hubley, 1996). Since its development, the MMSE and its modified versions have been used in non-inpatient settings—community- and clinic-based mental health and rehabilitation settings—with a wide range of age groups and clients, but they remain, primarily, as tools for detecting level of cognitive impairment when dementia and other neurological disorders are suspected, or to facilitate a differential diagnosis (e.g., dementia versus major depression) (Anderson, Burton, Parker, & Godding, 2001; van Gorp, Altshuler, Theberge, & Mintz, 1999). Although most professional counselors and other helping professionals will not conduct a complete formal mental status exam, different aspects of it can aid the diagnostic process, help monitor treatment for certain clients, and are required in some managed care settings (Polanksi & Hinkle, 2000).

ORIENTATION   The concept of orientation refers to a person's awareness of his or her name, the day of the week and month, year, and season, and where the interview is taking place (city, state, office, clinic, or hospital). It is part of the MMSE and other mental status exams. In addition, orientation to purpose is sometimes assessed. That is, what is the person's understanding of why the interview is taking place? Disorientation to person, place, and date can occur because of acute psychosis, drug-induced delirium, dementia, or some type of head injury. Therefore, some type of disorientation is more likely to be observed in hospital and crisis settings. The vast majority of clients seen in outpatient settings are oriented in these three ways, typically documented in clinical records as "oriented X3." Sometimes, a clinician will note that a client was oriented X4, meaning that the client was also oriented to the purpose of the interview.

ATTENTION AND CONCENTRATION   Typically, formal assessment of sustained attention or concentration is done either by a subtraction or spelling task or both. The subtraction task, commonly referred to as serial 7s, instructs the client to count backwards from 100 by 7s. After five responses the task ends. Some clients, however, have difficulty with the subtraction and since this is not meant to be a test of math aptitude, serial 3s can be substituted; that is, counting backwards by 3s rather than 7s. Spelling the word "world" backwards is another option for assessing the ability to sustain attention. Both tasks require a moderate degree of concentration to be successful, and inaccurate performance can be the result of various factors such as severe anxiety, serious depression, psychosis, or a neurocognitive disorder like dementia.

LANGUAGE AND COMPREHENSION   As with the assessment of attention and concentration, language and comprehension is evaluated with several brief tasks: word recognition, reading an instruction and carrying it out, and a writing sample. The mental status evaluator will point to several objects (e.g., different body parts, or objects in his possession, such as a watch or pencil) and ask the client to name them, in order to get a small sample of word recognition. Then the client is asked to read a brief instruction, for example, "Close your eyes" and follow that direction. In addition, a three-step direction will be provided for the client to read and do. Assessment of writing will be done by stating a phrase for the client to write and then asking for a sentence to be written spontaneously. These tasks help assess whether basic language and comprehension functions are intact. A more sophisticated assessment of language, understanding, and verbal reasoning focuses on abstract reasoning.

ABSTRACT REASONING The ability to think abstractly, as opposed to concretely, typically occurs toward the end of the elementary school years, according to Piaget's model of cognitive development, and can be assessed in a variety of ways. On the *Modified Mini-Mental State Examination,* abstract reasoning is examined with one task, commonly known as a similarities test based on the similarities subtest of the *Wechsler Intelligence Scales* (see Chapter 13). The similarities test presents several pairs of words and the person is asked to describe how the two words are alike. For example, how are "an orange and a tomato" alike? The specific abstract reasoning ability that is being assessed is categorization. Categories that have less to do with the physical properties of objects or behaviors and more to do with a common function or underlying concept or theme are considered more abstract. A person might respond to the orange–tomato comparison by saying "they are both round." Although correct, that answer reflects a more concrete response because the person is saying they are similar because they both belong to the round objects category. What might be a more abstract category? If you are thinking they are both fruit, you are correct. Recognizing that tomatoes and oranges are both fruit reflects an understanding of the concept of what it means to be fruit, which requires more advanced and elaborate thinking than recognizing a common shape. Another way to assess abstract reasoning is to ask the meaning of a couple of different proverbs (Morrison, 2008). Commonly used proverbs are "People in glass houses shouldn't throw stones" or "Strike while the iron is hot." Understanding proverbs, however, is much more a function of cultural background than is a similarities question. If the client gave a concrete answer to a proverb or seemed just not to get it, that could be due to cultural and language factors rather than to a limited ability to think abstractly.

MEMORY PROCESSES Memory processes can be divided into three types: immediate or working, short-term, and long-term (Mayer, 2003). Assessment of immediate and short-term memory was part of the MMSE and later modifications. Immediate recall is evaluated by having the client repeat back three words, for example, *apple, table,* and *penny,* which are presented 1 second apart. Short-term memory is then assessed by having the person recall those same words after several minutes. Although long-term memory is not assessed with the MMSE, some mental status evaluations will include it by asking the person to name the current and past three presidents. Unlike immediate and short-term memory, long-term memory is not typically impaired with dementia and other neurocognitive disorders, which is why it has not been part of formal mental status exams.

VISUAL–SPATIAL PERCEPTION The final part of the MMSE and other formal mental status evaluations is the assessment of visual–spatial perception. This typically involves presenting the person with two geometric shapes, such as two overlapping pentagons, and asking the person to copy it.

Guideline for Selecting and Using Mental Status Evaluations

In addition to the MMSE and 3Ms there are two other commonly used screening tests of cognitive functioning: *Neurobehavioral Cognitive Status Examination* (Logue, Tupler, D'Amico, & Schmitt; 1993) and *Cognitive Capacity Screening Examination* (Anderson et al., 2001). The selection of a particular test will depend upon several factors: age of the client, diagnostic need, the particular cognitive ability that is in question, the need to quantify cognitive impairment, and practical considerations. A test like the *Cognitive Capacity Screening Examination* is a more complex mental status test, covering more aspects of cognitive impairment than the traditional MMSE but has been found to be easy and quick to administer and has a standardized scoring system (Anderson et al., 2001).

In general, a formal mental status evaluation can be worked into an intake or initial interview. Client cooperation with the evaluation can be facilitated by an open explanation about what is to transpire. It is helpful to normalize the exam by mentioning, "I'm about to ask you a series of routine questions that we ask everyone who comes here that will help me better understand your thinking." The MMSE can be administered in 5 to 10 minutes, and the test and user guide is available from Psychological Assessment Resources.

Scoring systems exist for both the individual parts of mental status tests and the entire test. Various cutoff scores have been devised for these tests that set the boundary between normal and impaired cognitive functioning. For example, on the orientation portion of the MMSE, 1 point is allotted for each correct identification of time (day, date, month, year, and season) for a total of 5 points. On the MMSE, total scores greater than 26 are considered in the normal range (though 23 has been considered the cutoff score that differentiates normal from impaired cognitive functioning), 21 to 26 indicates mild cognitive impairment, 11 to 20 moderate, and 0 to 10 severe cognitive impairment (Folstein et al., 2001). The 3MS has a broader range of scores up to 100 (Teng & Chui, 1987). These cutoff scores need to be viewed with some caution because a low score can be due to psychological and cultural factors rather than cognitive impairment, and should not be used as the sole basis for concluding that a client is impaired (Albanese, 2003). Factors such as fatigue, age, education level, and race have been found to be related to differential performance on mental status exams (Albanese, 2003; Ward, 2003).

What about formal mental status exams for children? Both the informal and formal aspects of the mental status evaluation need to be modified when assessing children. Different assessment procedures such as art materials, toys, and puppets may need to be used during the mental status evaluation, depending upon the developmental level of the child, as was discussed in Chapter 3. Furthermore, it is imperative that the interviewer modify his or her language as needed, as well as possess a solid understanding of social, emotional, and cognitive development in order to effectively assess a child's mental status (Palmer, Fiorito, & Tagliareni, 2007).

The MMSE can be adapted for use with preschool and elementary school age with several developmental caveats to keep in mind. As with the adult version, attention and concentration can be assessed with serial 7s in elementary school age children and older. Alternatively, a child can be asked to "look carefully around the office for 10 seconds, then close your eyes and name as many items as you can remember" (Palmer et al., 2007, p. 66). Elementary school age children can typically recall 5 to 10 objects on that task. When assessing orientation, it is important to recognize that prior to age 8, many children may have difficulty understanding time of day and therefore should not be expected to be oriented to that. On the other hand, elementary school age children typically know the day of the week but may not be able to correctly identify the date. Immediate and short-term recall can be assessed in the same way as described earlier with adults, but the assessment of long-term memory can be modified by asking child to recall a favorite gift from a birthday or holiday or tell about something done during a vacation (Palmer et al., 2007). Along with information gathered from parents, caregivers, or other adults familiar with the child, these modifications in the formal mental status evaluation can help the clinician assess the child's cognitive functioning. There is not, however, a scoring system associated with these modifications of the MMSE for children as there is for adults.

To date the MMSE and 3Ms have been used in research studies (Rubial-Álvarez et al., 2007; Tombaugh et al., 1996) to gain a preliminary understanding of the applicability of using these screening tools in clinical settings in several different countries. These studies have shown that, not surprisingly, mental state exam scores are correlated with age and grade level. That is, as children get older and gain more education, their performance on these tests increases. There is not yet, however, sufficient normative data on preschool and elementary school age children that would enable scores on the MMSE or 3Ms to be used to screen for developmental and neurological disorders such as autism and attention deficit–hyperactivity disorder, in the way the scores are used with adults to detect dementia and other cognitive disorders.

A cautionary note about administering formal mental status exams to any client is necessary. In order for a counselor or other helping professional to use a psychological test in an ethically and professionally sound manner, several important questions need to be addressed. First of all, does the counselor have the requisite knowledge and skills to use this type of assessment tool? Second, what is it about this exam, beyond its title, that makes it a psychological test? Last, what kind of quantitative knowledge is necessary in order for the clinician to properly interpret scores on a mental status exam? The first question was discussed in Chapter 2, and the latter two questions will be the focus of the next two chapters.

Documenting Mental Status Observations

Mental status observations can be documented in different ways. In some settings a checklist format is used, in others a narrative, and sometimes a combination of both formats is used. What follows is a sample of a mental status narrative for Tanya, the client in the case study at the beginning of the chapter.

Tanya presented as a dark-haired obese female, who appeared to be her stated age. She came to the interview wearing a dress and eyeglasses. She was neatly groomed. She was easy to engage and was very verbal. At the beginning of the interview, she shifted her position in her chair and played with a button on her blouse while talking. She sat more still as the interview progressed and did not use her hand to gesture when she discussed emotionally laden topics such as history of child abuse. She often exhibited annoyed facial expressions and made comments expressing her annoyance during the cognitive portion of the evaluation. Furthermore, she would make comments suggestive of irritation such as "How the hell do I know?" Her speech was articulate, and there were no oddities or unusual mannerisms in her speech. She described her mood over the past two weeks as "yucky," and today her mood was also a negative one, which she described as "yucky" as well. She exhibited a restricted range of affect that was consistent with the topic at hand. Her predominant affect was one of irritability. She was able to maintain good eye contact with the examiner.

She was oriented times four. There was no evidence of auditory or visual hallucinations, though she complained of having visual images, memories, and possibly flashbacks of significant others in her life who are deceased. There was no evidence of delusions or disordered thinking. At times there was a self-referential quality to her thinking; for example, when asked what *domestic* means, she responded, "My cat." She reported fear of bridges and flying, but no other fears. She was able to immediately recall three out of four nouns, and short-term recall was three out of four nouns.

Behavior Observation Assessments

Formal systems for recording observations of children's behavior exist as well. Two of the most comprehensive methods for observing and coding behavior in school settings are part of large multirater assessment systems: the *Behavior Assessment System for Children,* 2nd Edition (BASC-2) (Reynolds & Kamphaus, 2004) and the *Achenbach System for Empirically Based Assessment* (ASEBA) (Achenbach, 2011). The BASC-2 contains a Student Observation System, and the ASEBA has both a Direct Observation Form and a Test Observation Form. The other components of the BASC-2 and ASEBA—parent, teacher, and self-behavior rating scales—are described in more detail in Chapter 10. The direct observation methods contained in the BASC-2 and ASEBA represent well-researched state-of-the-art formal observational assessments. These straightforward behavior observation systems are designed for use by paraprofessionals as well as professional educators and mental health professionals (Achenbach, 2011; Reynolds & Kamphaus, 2004). They can be used to aid in the diagnostic process, develop treatment plans, and evaluate how a particular intervention is working.

STUDENT OBSERVATION SYSTEM   The Student Observation System is designed for evaluating the classroom behavior of preschool through high school students and contains three parts: a behavior key and checklist, a time sampling observation procedure, and teacher–student interaction section (Reynolds & Kamphaus, 2004). The Behavior Key and Checklist contains 13 preestablished categories of behavior and one additional section to document unusual behaviors that are not contained in the checklist. Each category contains multiple examples of specific behaviors to help the observer know exactly what to look for as well as facilitating comparable behavior ratings across different observers. For example, the aggression category includes "kicking others," "hitting others with hand," "throwing object(s) at others," "destroying property," "pushing others," "stealing," and "other." The observer records the frequency of the behaviors listed in the checklist on a 3-point scale (not observed, sometimes, or frequently observed) after a 15-minute period and notes whether the behavior was disruptive. Those same behaviors can be documented in a more systematic fashion by noting whether or not the behavior occurred during a 3-second interval each at the end of each 30-second period for a total of 30 recordings. In addition, detailed observations of student and teacher interactions are documented after the 15-minute observation period.

DIRECT OBSERVATION FORM   The Direct Observation Form (DOF) has a more limited age range than the Student Observation System, ages 6 to 11, but can be used in multiple settings: classroom, recess, and group during a 10-minute period (McConaughy & Achenbach, 2009). The DOF contains two parts: ratings of on- versus off-task behavior and an 89-item problem list. The on–off task behaviors are rated during 5-second intervals after each minute of the 10-minute period, and the problem list is completed following the observation period. The majority of the items on the problem list correspond to the items on the teacher and parent behavior rating scales of the ASEBA (see Chapter 10). Each problem is rated on a 4-point scale, 0 to 3, with 0 indicating no occurrence and 3 meaning a behavior that occurred for at least 3 minutes or was of severe intensity and high frequency.

TEST OBSERVATION FORM   The Test Observation Form (TOF) is designed to aid the clinician who is giving a child a formal test like an intelligence or achievement test, in systematically noting and recording client behavior during the testing (McConaughy & Achenbach, 2004). The evaluator is expected to record in an open-ended fashion the child's behavior, and upon completion of the testing rate the occurrence of 124 problematic behaviors using the same 4-point scale and frequency criteria as the DOF. Although there are some items on the TOF that are similar to the items on the DOF, most of them have to do with behaviors more likely to be exhibited during a testing situation. These include behaviors such as "Giggles too much," "Avoids eye contact," "Complains of tasks being too hard or is upset by tasks," and "Guesses a lot; does not think out answers or strategies" (McConaughy & Achenbach, 2004). In addition, the front page of the TOF contains spaces to record the specific test that was administered, the length of testing time, whether the child was on medication during the evaluation, and demographic and educational data.

OBSERVER EFFECTS   How does the presence of an observer affect a child's behavior? A child's awareness of being watched can lead to some subtle and not-so-subtle changes in behavior.

Children are often aware of and sensitive to the expectations adults have for their behavior and may believe that the observer, as well, holds these norms. Consequently, whether the perception is accurate or not, a child may attempt, not always consciously, to conform to that perceived behavioral expectation or possibly violate it. This phenomenon has been demonstrated with adults as well through a myriad of social psychological experiments. This potentially can result in the experimenter-observer noticing behavior that is less typical and more due to the artificial nature of the situation: an adult who is not normally in that setting being present. What then can the observer do to increase the likelihood that the witnessed behavior is a typical sample of the target child? One strategy is to enlist the cooperation of the teacher, day-care staff, or an adult known to the child. The cooperating adult can make a general statement to the group that decreases the chance the target child will suspect he or she is being singled out for observation. That statement might sound something like, "Someone will be coming in later to see what we do in our classroom and what happens during _____ time (specific activity or subject)." A second strategy is to observe at least one other child than the target one. This has the added benefit of providing the observer with another set of behaviors from which the target child's can be compared and evaluated.

Observations of Couples and Families

Often, helping professionals will want to make observations about dyads and larger groups. Like other observations procedures, this can be done informally, formally, or with a combination of the two. Some of the areas a clinician will observe and track are similar to those with an individual: emotional expression, appearance of group members, and communication. When two or more individuals are being observed simultaneously, the helper will also want to pay attention to sequences of interaction and emerging patterns. For example, in a family consisting of two parents, a father and mother, and three children (two female teenagers and a male preschool child), is there a typical sequence that occurs each time the father speaks? Perhaps the young son moves closer to his mother, the eldest daughter rolls her eyes, and the younger one interrupts Dad, to which the mother responds with a scolding. Does the sequence happen exactly the same each time the father speaks or is there some variation depending upon the topic? Certain family systems models—structural and strategic (Breunlin, Schwartz, & MacKune-Karrer, 1992; Minuchin, 1974; Watzlawick, Beavin, & Jackson, 1967)—have described the potential connections between family sequences and family functioning, and identified problems. What might a family or group's communication patterns say about how they are organized, the roles and boundaries, particularly who is in power and how decisions get made, and their unspoken and explicit rules and expectations? Therefore, to begin, the observer will want to pay attention to who speaks to whom, about what, and who in the group is encouraged to or discouraged from participating. Furthermore, does there seem to be a shared emotional climate or tone to the group or do different members appear to be expressing different kinds of feeling? Tentative answers to these questions can emerge from a combination of informal observation and interviewing.

More formal procedures for observing couples and families have been developed but remain largely in the realm of research. In fact, a survey of practicing marriage and family therapists (Boughner, Hayes, Bubenzer, & West, 1994) found that only a small minority used any kind of standardized assessment instrument, and none reported using formal observation procedures. Several instruments for measuring couples and families on certain dimensions while engaged in some task have been developed. These include the *Marital and Family Interaction Coding System, Card Sort Procedure, Beavers-Timberlawn Family Evaluation Scale,* and *Family Task*

Interview/Family Health Scale (Fredman & Sherman, 1987). These formal observation systems differ in the type of task family members are directed to engage in—discussing a family vignette or desired change, solving a puzzle, or planning something together—but collectively assess family dimensions such as communication style, affect, family structure, and problem-solving style. These instruments, however, require significant training time to use properly and are weak in terms of their technical properties (Fredman & Sherman, 1987) (see Chapter 7 regarding technical properties).

Problem Identification and Analysis with Functional Behavior Assessment

A semistructured method for developing a contextual understanding of a problem that incorporates observation and information gathered from interviews is a **functional behavioral assessment (FBA)**. FBA is a process for identifying and analyzing factors that contribute to the onset and maintenance of problematic behaviors and has been used primarily in educational settings (Crone & Horner, 2003). An FBA is now required by the Individuals with Disabilities Educational Act (IDEA) in cases where a student with a disability is exhibiting behaviors that are impacting academic or social performance (Ravensberg & Tobin, 2008). It can, however, be used for a host of problems that typically present in mental health and other counseling settings. The goal of an FBA is to develop a tentative hypothesis about the function or motivation underlying a specific behavior. The hypothesis statement is the final step in a process that begins with an operational definition of the problem and then proceeds to the identification of possible antecedents and maintaining consequences. The data for an FBA typically comes from a variety of methods and sources: interviews with client or significant others, observations, and standardized ratings scales or questionnaires that may be completed by teachers, parents, or the client.

What are the components of the FBA and how does one identify them for a particular client? Once a behavior is operationally defined—throwing objects in a classroom, for example—the search for the antecedents to that behavior begins. Antecedents are situational, interpersonal, or psychological factors (emotional or cognitive states) that precede and theoretically trigger the onset of a specific behavior. That behavior could be anything from disruptive behavior in a classroom, such as throwing things, to excessive alcohol consumption before and after work. In some FBAs, antecedents are subdivided into setting events and proximate events. Setting events set the stage for problematic behaviors and occur with a high degree of regularity but are not as closely connected in time as proximate events. Examples of setting events could be day of the week, time of day, seasonal or anniversary date, visit with a family member, school tests, and so on. Proximate events are more closely related in time to the problematic behavior than setting events and tend to be more psychological and interpersonal. Examples of these kinds of antecedent events include mood state (anxious, fearful, sad, or angry), perceiving a task as too demanding or difficult, or fight with a family member, peer, or friend. Antecedents, theoretically, are associated with the onset of a behavior, and maintaining consequences keep it going.

Maintaining consequences are those things that occur after the problematic behavior and serve to reinforce its continued occurrence. Typically there are two broad categories of maintaining consequences: 1) escape and 2) attention or need. Behaviors that result in an escape from or avoidance of an aversive situation tend to recur because they enable the person to eliminate or lessen a distressing emotional or psychological state. Disruptive behavior in a classroom is likely to recur if that behavior enables a student, for example, to get out of an anxiety-provoking situation such as a difficult and overwhelming task. In this example, the function of the student's disruptive behavior is to avoid feeling overwhelmed and possibly frustrated, and this behavior will be maintained as long as it serves to accomplish the goal of task avoidance. Similarly, behaviors that bring social attention or a positive emotional state also tend to recur. If the child who disrupts the class by telling jokes or tossing paper airplanes receives laughter from his classmates, that behavior is likely to continue for as long as that positive attention persists.

The FBA process and how it becomes a pathway to intervention can be illustrated with two different case examples. Johnny, an 8-year-old second-grade boy, was repeatedly engaging in disruptive classroom behaviors. His teacher, after unsuccessful attempts at curtailing his disruptions, brought Johnny's problem to her school behavior support team in the hope that something could be done to help him. The school counselor was assigned the task of developing an FBA for Johnny. As an initial step in the process, Janice, the counselor, met with Johnny's teacher to develop an operational definition of disruptive behavior. An operational definition specifies what can be observed and counted. Janice asked Ms. A., Johnny's teacher, "What does he do when he's acting disruptive?" Ms. A. said, "It seems like every time I ask the class to get out paper for their spelling words, he leaves his desk, runs over to the pencil sharpener and is bumping into desks and talking to kids on the way back to his seat." Now Janice had a target behavior set that could be observed and counted: leaving his seat, bumping into desks, and/or talking to others when out of his seat. With that target behavior established, Janice, through a combination of further interviews with Ms. A. and Johnny's mother and classroom observations of Johnny, was able to gather antecedents and maintaining consequences. In this case, the antecedent events were returning home from weekend visits with his father and father's girlfriend, days following a night he stayed up until 11:00 p.m., and teacher directions to the class to take out paper or their reading book. Johnny's behaviors after leaving his classroom seat were interfering so much with the other students' ability to pay attention and learn, Ms. A. was sending him to the principal's office each time this happened. Consequently he was able to temporarily avoid spelling or reading tasks in the classroom, which maintained his problematic behavior. He was more likely to want to avoid those tasks on days he was tired from inadequate sleep, sad about a visit with his father, or anxious about being made fun of during spelling or reading time. This functional assessment enabled Janice, Ms. A., and Johnny to develop a behavior support plan for Johnny and minimize his disruptive behavior.

One illustration of an FBA in a counseling context comes from the case study at the opening of Chapters 3 and 4. After Brian's temper and sleep problems were clarified and defined, he revealed a pattern of excessive alcohol consumption that was connected to both of those problems. Brian's drinking a six-pack of beer or more in one night was the target behavior. Through a series of questions—"When do you drink?," How are you feeling before you start drinking?," "Where do you drink?," and "What's the difference between those times you have one or two beers and those times when you go through a six-pack or more?"—Melanie, the clinician, was able with Brian to identify antecedents to his excessive drinking: feeling awkward and uncomfortable when going out with a group of people, especially if women were part of the group, Wednesday nights (softball or ice-hockey league nights), phone calls from his father harassing him about his job, which left him feeling "pissed off," and nights after his boss "chewed him out." What helped to maintain his excessive alcohol consumption was his belief that it was a "social lubricant." He felt more at ease and more confident and talkative with groups of people when he drank. Drinking also helped him to calm down after getting angry with his father or boss. Melanie and Brian's mutual awareness of the antecedents and maintaining consequences for his excessive alcohol use allowed them to collaborate on replacement behaviors for his drinking: less risky methods for increasing his social comfort and confidence as well as managing his anger.

Summary and Conclusions

Together, interviewing and observing are typically the primary assessment procedures for gathering and organizing information about clients and their presenting problems in most counseling settings. Along with the information gathered from interviews, observations about a person's appearance, behaviors, speech, emotional and cognitive functioning, and interactions with the interviewer help the counselor in developing a case conceptualization or working hypothesis of what is going on, a preliminary diagnosis, and treatment plan. Observations are most often gathered in an unstructured informal way; however, certain aspects of cognitive processes—orientation, memory, verbal reasoning, attention, and visual–spatial skills—can be evaluated in a formal structured manner.

The mental status evaluation is the most common procedure that counselors and other helping professionals rely upon for collecting and integrating information about a client's behavioral, emotional, and psychological functioning at the time of the interview. In that sense, the mental status evaluation and the formal component of it, the *Mini-Mental State Examination,* provides a snapshot of a client's functioning. Although the MMSE is often used informally and incorporated into intake assessments in mental health settings, formal mental status tests exist that have standardized scoring systems. Those are used primarily when there is reason to suspect some kind of cognitive impairment such as in cases of schizophrenia, dementia, or severe and chronic substance abuse.

Formal observation systems exist for evaluating children's behavior and analyzing couples and families. The Student Observation System and the Direct Observation Form are two examples of child observation systems that have been used primarily in educational and institutional settings: residential treatment facilities, hospitals, or juvenile correctional facilities. Observation coding systems for couples and families are still primarily research tools.

One systematic assessment process that incorporates both interview and observation data is the functional behavior assessment, or FBA. The FBA is particularly helpful for case conceptualizing and intervention designing purposes. Although used primarily with children in educational and other institutional settings, an FBA can be applied to adults in a variety of counseling settings.

Reflection Questions and Experiential Exercises

1. Imagine you are interviewing someone who starts crying. What might that be like for you?
2. What are any other aspects to a client's presentation, appearance, or behavior you might have an emotional reaction to?
3. What are the informal parts of a mental status evaluation?
4. What aspects of cognitive functioning—thought processes and perception—are routinely covered in a mental status evaluation?
5. How are antecedents and maintaining consequences related and how are they different?
6. Watch a video or DVD of a counseling session. Watch first with the sound off, then watch with the sound on. Record your observations of the client's appearance, behavior, and affect each time you watch, and compare your observations.

6 PSYCHOLOGICAL TESTS AND MEASUREMENT CONCEPTS

Chapter Objectives

After reading this chapter, you should be able to:

■ Explain the concept of a psychological construct and how tests are designed to measure it.

■ Understand the difference between the two major categories of tests: norm referenced and criterion referenced.

■ Understand fundamental measurement concepts: frequency distributions and measures of central tendency and variability.

■ Explain the concept of a standardized score and understand different types of standardized scores.

Melanie Grenvue, a recently Licensed Mental Health Counselor, has just completed her intake interview with Tammy, a new client who presented concerns suggestive of depression and anxiety. With the information she has in hand, Melanie is considering administering a psychological test or questionnaire as a next step in order to be more confident and clear about her diagnostic impressions and case conceptualization. She recognizes that a questionnaire may help her sort out a diagnosis, but she has often been uncomfortable with using numbers and is hesitant to use a tool that may require a lot of complicated math. As she once told her adviser in graduate school, "If I was good with numbers I would have gone into accounting, not counseling." She says to herself, uncomfortable memories of an algebra class spinning in her head, "Maybe I don't really need to administer a test—perhaps several more interview questions will be enough to develop my case conceptualization and diagnosis." She also thinks, "If I do give Tammy a questionnaire, what kind of statistical knowledge will I need to use the test appropriately?" What are the measurement concepts Melanie will need to understand to make sense out of any set of test scores and results?

OVERVIEW

As discussed in Chapter 1, psychological testing is an umbrella term covering one type of assessment method: formal standardized. This assessment methodology is quite diverse, coming in many shapes and sizes. Psychological tests vary among a number of different dimensions: content, length, format, age range, psychometric properties, and cross-cultural applicability. Therefore, the selection of an appropriate test or a referral for psychological testing requires consideration of all of these factors as well as an understanding of what kind of information can be provided by the test's results. This may make it seem like the task ahead is a daunting one for Melanie or any other professional who wants or needs to use a test as part of the assessment process. This and the next chapter are designed, however, to make the process of selecting and using psychological tests a more manageable one. This chapter is devoted to the general nature of psychological tests and their underlying measurement concepts. Measurement concepts such as frequency distributions, measures of central tendency and variability, and standardized scores will be the focus. Consequently, this chapter will serve as the building block for the next chapter, which focuses on additional psychometric concepts (reliability and validity), and the remaining chapters will focus on specific kinds of psychological tests.

The decision to include a psychological test or measure in the assessment process involves multiple considerations for counselors and other helping professionals. When deciding whether or not to incorporate a test or standardized measure into the assessment process, clinicians will want to consider 1) the different purposes for using standardized measures, 2) what a particular test can reveal about a client, and 3) test user qualification guidelines (see Chapter 2). One aspect of being qualified to administer, score, and interpret psychological tests is having the requisite math and statistical knowledge. Having a solid understanding of certain statistical concepts and an ability to think quantitatively are necessary skills for using psychological tests. Having said that, most of the measurement concepts fundamental to psychological testing are typically covered prior to college. Therefore, what will be presented in this chapter is more likely to involve review rather than first-time learning. Furthermore, it is important to keep in mind that although a measure is standardized and can produce quantitative information, that does not necessarily make it a better, more accurate, or legitimate assessment tool—just a different kind of tool with its own benefits and limitations.

WHAT DO PSYCHOLOGICAL TESTS MEASURE?

As you may recall from Chapter 1, a psychological test can be defined as an objective and standardized procedure with items designed to measure characteristics of human beings that pertain to a *sample* of behavior (Anastasi & Urbina, 1997; Kaplan & Saccuzzo, 2005). The specific characteristic or trait being measured by a test can be a broad ability like intelligence, a more narrow aptitude like reading comprehension, a personality type, a vocational interest, psychiatric symptoms, or attitudes, beliefs, and feelings. These psychological traits are what are known as **psychological constructs**.

Psychological Constructs

Regardless of whether we call an assessment procedure a test, a measure, an inventory, or a standardized questionnaire, these assessment instruments all measure psychological constructs. Psychological constructs are abstract theoretical concepts. A psychological test, therefore, is a reflection of a particular operational definition of a specific construct (McIntire & Miller, 2007). Intelligence, personality, psychopathology, and self-esteem are just a few examples of psychological constructs. A good deal of hypothesizing and theorizing about the nature of these constructs often occurs, but nevertheless they remain abstract ideas until defined and studied to see if there is evidence to support a specific conceptualization. Furthermore, constructs are not readily observable behaviors. What does it mean, for example, to act intelligently, abnormally, or with a positive self-image? The degree to which an individual has an ability, trait, or characteristic is inferred by one's performance on a test designed to measure it. To illustrate this, let's look further at the construct of intelligence. One way to define intelligence is the depth of one's vocabulary. An equally plausible definition is one's social comprehension and reasoning skills. So, is intelligence equivalent to verbal reasoning, problem-solving skills, creativity, street smarts, or something else entirely? It depends on whom you ask and how that particular theoretician, scholar, or clinician defines it.

Definitions of constructs vary among experts in counseling and psychology including those who ultimately develop a test that purports to measure it. Therefore, the types of items that are found on a test represent a particular conceptualization of a construct. For example, if intelligence is defined as verbal reasoning ability, then the test is likely to be filled with items requiring word definitions, verbal analogies, or reading comprehension questions. Alternatively, if intelligence is defined as problem solving with unfamiliar visual–spatial material, the test items and procedures are likely to focus on stimuli related to visual–perceptual reasoning. The extent to which a test measures the construct it purports to measure is the concept of **construct validity**. Once the construct is defined and elaborated upon, then a test can be developed that in essence represents this particular operational definition *to some degree*. Establishing a test's construct validity is an ongoing process in which the test is compared to other tests and methods that are either similar or different in terms of the construct in question. Furthermore, the extent to which a test measures what it is intended to measure can be quantified statistically. The best test of construct validity is the degree to which behavior exhibited on a psychological test can be shown empirically to correspond to behavior beyond the testing situation. For example, if a child scores high on a test purported to measure intelligence, and if the test has good construct validity, that child should often act intelligently in a variety of situations—classroom, playground, and living room—compared to those students who did not perform as well. This process of establishing a test's construct validity and how to measure it will be taken up further in Chapter 7.

Building Tests to Measure Constructs

The process of creating, refining, and field testing questions and items for psychological tests is a long, arduous, and complicated process involving experts in the field: researchers, clinicians, and educators. Once the construct to be measured is operationally defined, the pilot phase of test construction begins. A group of test items or questions is generated and written, along with the response format (e.g., "never true," "true," "often true"). Then the items are reviewed by experts in the field and refined. At that point in the development process, a sample group is selected to take the test. Items can be evaluated, revised if necessary, and the final items, response format, and test length is decided upon. A general description of how test items were selected for a specific test is typically found in the test manual or research article if the manual does not provide that information.

Either through initial design or subsequent statistical analysis, many tests contain subtests or scales. Each scale is considered a factor of the overall psychological construct being measured. Depending upon the test, the items that are included on the sub-tests on any given test may be very similar in nature or widely divergent. Similarly, the manner in which the test taker responds to subtest items and questions may be relatively consistent, highly variable, or somewhere in between.

TEST RESPONSE FORMAT   All psychological tests have a standardized format so that anyone taking the test is given all the items or questions in the same sequence and every test taker has the same response format. What is meant by response format? As you may know from your own educational experience, some tests expect you to respond by selecting one answer from a group (i.e., multiple choice). Other tests pose a question and you are free to respond in an open-ended fashion, sometimes in writing, other times orally. And some tests combine formats. The same is true for psychological tests.

The types of items and questions found on psychological tests vary considerably and therefore response formats do so as well. Why one type of response format is chosen over another depends on the nature of the construct being measured and what is considered an effective procedure for getting someone to demonstrate a behavior indicative of the construct. On ability and achievement tests, for example, some items require the test taker to point to the correct response, others require an open-ended verbal response, and at times the test taker is asked to write down symbols. Some tests of personality require a story to be told, others a verbal description of what an inkblot looks like, and some have questions with multiple-choice answers. Therefore, how effective any one test is at measuring a particular psychological construct is in part a function of the items and response format. Someone may be very intelligent, for example, but not be able to demonstrate much of their intelligence on a particular test if the test requires mostly long verbal responses and the individual has a significant speech and language impairment. Or a client's primary language is Spanish but the test is in English. Requiring the client to respond in his or her secondary language may produce test results that reflect a language barrier rather than the degree to which a construct is present.

Many of the tests discussed in this text belong to the category of self-report, and have a variety of response formats. The response format of self-report questionnaires may include true–false, multiple-choice items, scaling, or a combined format. One example of a self-report test that combines formats is the *Self-Report of Personality* (SRP), from the *Behavior Assessment for Children, Second Edition* (see Chapter 10). The SRP has a mixture of true–false and scaling items.

Scaling items require the respondent to use typically a 3- or 5-point scale to rate the frequency or intensity of some type of personal experience. With frequency scales, respondents judge how often something occurs such as a behavior, an emotion, or a physical symptom. Like frequency scales, intensity scales ask the respondent to rate the intensity of a feeling, idea, or action generally using three or five levels. Therefore, scaling formats use a continuum, and the respondent decides where along the continuum to rate his or her experience. Although 3- to 5-point continuum scales are most common, some tests may utilize finer gradations such as a 7- or 10-point scale. In addition to the length of the scales varying among psychological tests, so will the words used to describe the ends of the continuum and the midpoints. How scale labels like "moderately" and "extremely" are interpreted will clearly vary from person to person, and some individuals may have difficulty with certain response formats.

One other common response format found on self-report tests is a Likert-type scale. Likert scales measure strength of belief or feeling, typically on a 5- or 7-point scale. You may have seen a scale like this and taken a test or survey that included this type of response format. One example is a scale that ranges from "disagree strongly" to "agree strongly."

TEST SIZE   The size or length of psychological tests also varies considerably. At the shorter end of the continuum, questionnaires and self-report inventories designed to assess a single construct such as anxiety or depression may have 20 items. On the other end, tests of cognitive ability and intelligence often consist of a dozen or more subtests, each containing 12 or more items. The CAGE, a commonly used, effective test for screening for alcohol abuse and dependence, contains just four items. The *Minnesota Multiphasic Personality Inventory* (MMPI), one of the oldest and most widely used personality and psychopathology tests, is at the other extreme with nearly 600 questions. The MMPI, however, is used to assess a much wider range of disorders than the CAGE.

For all intents and purposes, the size of the test does not matter. What matters is the ability of the test to provide information that is accurate and useful. To illustrate this point, imagine a 10-item test designed to assess shyness in teenagers. Ten items may seem woefully inadequate to identify all the ways in which a youth could display shy behavior or the lack thereof. If, however, individuals who score high on this imaginary shyness test are found to be displaying interpersonal behaviors that are thought to be representative of shyness and those who score low are discovered acting gregariously in social situations, then perhaps the test is a valid shyness test. On the other hand, another imaginary shyness test might have 100 items, but scores on the test are shown to have little relationship to interpersonal behavior in social situations. This much longer shyness test would have little validity in terms of being a shyness test.

Types of Psychological Tests

NORM-REFERENCED AND CRITERION-REFERENCED TESTS   Clinicians like Melanie, and all those who use psychological tests need to understand the distinction between norm- and criterion-referenced tests so that appropriate interpretations can be made. Once a test is built, it needs to be given to some group of people whose performance on the test will serve as the benchmark or reference point from which a future test taker's performance will be compared. This benchmark group is alternatively referred to as the **standardization** or **normative** group. Norm-referenced tests enable comparisons to be made between the test taker and the normative group. So if Melanie is going to give a test to her client Tammy, she might be curious about whom the normative group comprises for the test she will use and how the group was selected.

In order to gather a normative group, one has to figure out the population from which the group will be selected. A population consists of all the individuals residing within a certain geographical area or a community. Populations vary in size and could be as large as all elementary students in the United States or smaller, such as outpatients in community mental health clinics in the Northeast. It is very costly and time consuming, however, for a test developer to give a newly constructed test to the entire population of interest. Rather than the developer incurring the cost in terms of time and labor resources and the complex logistical problems in testing an entire population, a subset of the population or a **sample** is chosen to take the test one time. Their test performance provides the **norms** for a particular test (Kaplan & Saccuzzo, 2005). This is a critical point. Test norms are based on a *single* performance of *one* select group of people, not the average scores of repeated administrations of the test to multiple samples. The normative group's scores then becomes the benchmark on which future test scores and the interpretation of those scores are based. This is the comparison group that serves as the reference point so that a score from a client like Tammy can be evaluated and ranked. Is her score average, above, or below average? Average compared to what? Tammy's score is compared to the performance of the standardization group, otherwise known as the test's norms. Even more precisely, the norms enable the test user to rank the individual test taker and come up with a percentile score. A fuller discussion of percentiles and how they are calculated will take place in the following section.

Normative groups can vary widely in terms of their size; some are in the hundreds, others in the thousands. They also vary to the extent they are representative of different gender, ethnic, racial, and other groups within a population. So when norms have been established for a test, the test is considered norm-referenced.

How are individuals selected to be part of a standardization or normative sample? There are various sampling strategies that are used to obtain a group that is representative of specific cultural variables. One sampling method is convenience. The test authors and developers have access to a group from which they can recruit participants to take the test that has been developed. This was done recently with a questionnaire designed to screen for attention deficit–hyperactivity disorder. The normative group was relatively small—243 individuals—and they were the parents of children from one urban elementary school setting to which the authors had access (Wolraich et al., 2003). On the other hand, more intentional strategies can be used to create large representative samples. These include stratified and cluster sampling processes (Whiston, 2009). A stratified sampling process is one in which the test developer decides a priori which demographic or cultural variables should be represented in the standardization group and tries to obtain a certain proportion of individuals from various categories. The specific demographic factors that are typically identified for selection in standardization samples include gender, age, race or ethnicity, socioeconomic class, and geographic location. Other demographic variables such as religion and sexual orientation are rarely considered in test standardization samples. Once the demographic variables of interest are identified, the goal of the test developer is to have a group whose gender, racial–ethnic, and geographic proportions match some predetermined target such as United States Census data.

Imagine you have a client who is an African American female teenager living in an inner city, and you are considering giving her a self-report questionnaire like the one from the *Behavioral Assessment System for Children,* 2nd edition (BASC-2) (see Chapter 10) to clarify a diagnosis of depression. As the clinician, you want to know how the normative group was chosen and whether or not it is representative of the population you want to make comparisons with to determine statistical deviance. To answer this question you would typically consult the manual for the standardized measure (typically sold separately from the measure or test) or review articles about the measure. To illustrate the question of representativeness with some simple math, let's say the standardization sample contained 1,000 individuals and 15% were African Americans, and of that 15% (150), half were female (75). You may feel comfortable in knowing the percentage of African Americans in the standardization sample was very close to the percentage in the U.S. population, which in 2010 was 14% (Rastogi, Johnson, Hoeffel, & Drewery, 2011) and therefore is adequately represented in the normative group. (Test manuals will typically present census data to let the test user see how closely different demographic groups, represented in the standardization sample, match the U.S. census.) In fact, the standardization group for the BASC-2 *Self-Report of Personality* was unusually large (1,900) and representative of more demographic variables than many existing tests or measures: age, gender, race–ethnicity, socioeconomic status, and geographic region. The manual provides separate norms for different age ranges and genders, and therefore the BASC-2 user could compare this teenage female's score with others her same age range and gender to see how discrepant they are from the average scores of teenage females who took the self-report questionnaire during the standardization process.

Cluster sampling, on the other hand, selects groups rather than individuals for their representativeness. For example, outpatient clinics might be chosen randomly from a list of all clinics in the United States. Each test will vary on the number of variables upon which the sampling process is guided and the degree to which the normative sample matches proportionally a particular population.

A **criterion-referenced** test is one in which a particular score is established as indicating the benchmark by which an individual's score is compared. Rather than comparing the individual's score to the performance of the normative group, the score is evaluated with respect to some criterion. This benchmark or criterion may be used in various ways. One way in which a criterion-referenced test may be used is for the purpose of establishing a **cutoff score**. In mental health settings, for example, cutoff scores may be used for diagnostic screening purposes. Someone who scores at or above the cutoff score is considered to be at risk for a particular disorder and in need of additional assessment. Those scoring below the cutoff score are considered not to be at risk. In research settings, cutoff scores are often used for diagnostic purposes to determine inclusion or exclusion in the study. Although a test may function as a criterion-referenced test, it may also have norms that are used to establish the criterion. For example, self-report tests of depression such as the *Beck Depression Inventory* and the *Children's Depression Inventory* have norms and scores at certain levels are sometimes used as the criterion for deciding whether or not this is a case of depression.

Criterion-referenced tests are also utilized in educational and vocational settings. In those settings a test's benchmark or criterion indicates a level of performance such as mastery or proficiency in a particular area. For example, a score of 90 or above on a criterion-referenced test of third-grade reading comprehension would be the score needed to demonstrate mastery in that subject area. Likewise, in a vocational setting a criterion-referenced test would be used to determine whether an employee has demonstrated proficiency in a job or skill. One example of a criterion-based test that many helping professionals in their early careers are likely to encounter is a professional licensing exam. Different state licensing boards have established different benchmark scores, 75% correct for example, that theoretically indicate proficiency with an array of counseling competencies and knowledge.

Criterion-referenced tests have a couple of limitations that are important to recognize when used to assess for mastery (Whiston, 2009). The first problem is that defining mastery in a particular subject area can be very difficult. The main question to be addressed is, What criterion would constitute mastery? Is 75% correct a sufficient standard or should some higher benchmark be the indicator? Furthermore, how much below the benchmark might an individual score and still have significant competency in the particular subject matter even if not at the proficient or mastery level? Experts in the field often do not agree on the answers. Another area of disagreement among experts pertains to the test content. What aspects of math knowledge belong on a math-focused achievement test, for example? Similarly, there can be disagreement about which counseling skills and competencies belong on a licensing exam that would be valid indicators of mastery.

COMMONLY USED PSYCHOLOGICAL TESTS While reading about the two main types of tests, a few specific tests have been mentioned, but you may have been wondering about other commonly used psychological tests and measures. Surveys of professionals in the United States and Britain who represent different disciplines and specialties—clinical psychologists, vocational rehabilitation counselors, licensed mental health counselors, social workers, child and adolescent psychologists—have revealed that although certain tests are used more often in particular settings, there is a good deal of overlap among various professional groups in their use of norm-based tests (Camara, Nathan, & Puente, 2000; Donoso, Hernandez, & Horin, 2010; Frauenhoffer, Ross, Gfeller, Searight, & Piatrowski, 1998; Watkins, Campbell, Nierberding, & Hallmark, 1995). The most commonly used psychological tests and their purpose are listed in Table 6.1. It should be noted again, however, that when surveys of professionals have asked about informal and formal assessment practices, the most commonly used assessment method is an informal interview (Bekhit, Thomas, Lalonde, & Jolley, 2002; Piotrowski, 1999; Watkins et al., 1995). Furthermore, one of the more recent surveys (Camara et al., 2000) found that clinical psychologists who engage in assessment practice more than 5 hours per week, use on average 13 separate tests.

Where does one go to learn more about a specific test? Several excellent sources are available where independent reviews of tests and measures can be found. The *Mental Measurements Yearbook* (MMY), published by the Buros Institute, is *the* reference source of psychological

Table 6.1 24 Commonly Used Psychological Tests by Category

Category	Name	Ranking[1]	Publisher – Level[2]
Personality & Psychopathology	Beck Depression Inventory	7.25	Pearson – C, Q2
	Beck Anxiety Inventory	10[a]	Pearson – C, Q1
	Child Behavior Checklist (CBCL)	16.5	ASEBA – C
	Children's Apperception Test	15.5	Bellak & Bellak – C
	House-Tree-Person Drawing	8.25	WPS – No level
	Human Figures Drawing	9.75	WPS – No level
	Millon Clinical Multiaxial Inventory	12	Pearson – C
	Minnesota Multiphasic Personality Inventory-2 (MMPI-2)	2.25	University of Minn. Press – C
	Myers-Briggs Type Inventory	23[b]	CPP – Master's degree or equiv.
	Sentence Completion Test	8	
	Sixteen Personality Factors (16PF)	20	IPAT – B
	Symptom Checklist 90-Revised (SCL-90-R)	20	Leonard Derogatis – B, Q1
	Rorschach Inkblot	8.4	Verlag Hans Huber – C
	Thematic Apperception Test (TAT)	9.5	WPS – C
Cognitive Ability & Neurological Functioning	Bender Visual Motor Gestalt Test	6.25	American Orthopsychiatric Assn. – C
	Wechsler Adult Intelligence Scales (WAIS)*	1.5	Pearson – C
	Wechsler Intelligence Scales for Children (WISC)*	4.33	Pearson – C
	Wechsler Memory Scale-Revised	9.75	Pearson – C
Achievement	Peabody Picture Vocabulary Test	15	Wascana LPC – B, Q1
	Wide Range Achievement Test (WRAT)*	6.35	PAR – B
	Woodcock-Johnson Educational Battery*	15.5	Riverside, Medium
Career Interests – Vocational	Kuder Occupational Interest Survey	27[b]	Kuder Inc.
	Strong Interest Inventory**	14[b]	CPP – Master's degree or equiv.
	Self-Directed Search	27[b]	PAR – A

[1]The rankings are based on the average of four surveys from 1995 to 2010 of various professionals (Camara, Nathan, & Puente, 2000; Donoso, Hernandez, & Horin, 2010; Frauenhoffer, Ross, Gfeller, Searight, & Piotrowski, 1998; Watkins, Campbell, Nieberding, & Hallmark, 1995).

[2]Test levels are discussed in Chapter 2.

a = identified only on Donoso et al.; b = identified only on Watkins et al.

* = different editions of these tests were listed on various surveys

tests and measures. MMY is updated annually and contains two independent reviews for any new or revised test. The reviewers are independent in the sense that they are not the developers of the test nor do they have a financial stake in the sales of the instrument. These reviews can be accessed via the web at ***http://www.unl.edu/buros/bimm/index.html***, for a fee (see Appendix B: Additional Resources). Other independent review sources include peer-reviewed journals such as *Psychological Assessment* and handbooks of texts that offer a compendium of reviewed tests. Publishers' websites will provide basic information about a test's cost, age range, and administration time but are less likely to offer the kind of in-depth analyses found in MMY or journal articles.

REVISING TESTS   Psychological tests can be thought of as works in progress. Many of the current psychological tests are in their second, third, or even fourth editions. In fact, some of the tests you will read about may already have been replaced by a newer version. Once a test is published, its developers undertake the process of considering what changes may need to be made to correct possible flaws. Why are tests continually revised? Some reasons have to do with a desire to correct flaws in the test that subsequent research has identified, and others have to do with a need to improve and expand the use of it (Ranson, Nichols, Rouse, & Harrington, 2009). Ranson et al. describe three kinds of problems that have been identified in the assessment literature that drive the revision process. The first is a realization that items on the test have become outdated because they have little if any relevance to the current generation of test takers, or cultural trends have altered the meaning of a word and therefore the item. An example of that might be, "I enjoy going to parties that are lively and gay." This item appeared in the *Minnesota Multiphasic Personality Inventory* (MMPI), which was developed in the 1930s and revised in 1989 (see Chapter 9). The second problem that prompts test revision is a normative sample that is no longer valid for the purposes for which the test is being used. A test that was normed with a psychiatric population, for example, might be then used in organizational and employment settings, and therefore a more representative normative sample is required. Finally, in this era of the Internet, test items are easily made available to the public, and once that happens, the administration of the test is altered. That is, those who have familiarity with the test items take the test from a different vantage point than those who do not, and consequently scores on the test for the former group may in part reflect knowledge of the test items. Furthermore, tests may be revised because theory and statistical analyses may suggest that the construct the test items were designed to measure has changed, or the items on a scale within the test are actually measuring a construct that is somewhat different than what the scale was designed to measure.

HOW ARE PSYCHOLOGICAL CONSTRUCTS MEASURED?

Melanie, the counselor, was able to get past her hesitation and unease and gave a questionnaire to her client to measure the client's emotional functioning. Perhaps Melanie asked herself a number of questions to guide her incorporation of a psychological test into the assessment process (see Practice Suggestion: Identifying and Using the Proper Psychological Test). She is now faced with the task of making sense out of the scores. Scores on a psychological test take on meaning when they can be compared to some benchmark or reference point (e.g., the normative group). Without a reference point, a score on a test is meaningless. If Tammy earned a score of 15 on the questionnaire she filled out, what does that mean? That actual number or score on a test is considered the **raw score**. Raw scores on a test acquire meaning once they have been converted into some type of derived or standardized score. **Standardized scores** provide a context

PRACTICE SUGGESTION
Identifying and Using the Proper Psychological Test

TEN QUESTIONS TO CONSIDER

1. What construct am I trying to assess?
2. What tests or measures are available for the construct?
3. Do I need a norm- or criterion-referenced test?
4. Does the test or measure have a user level associated it with it? If so, do I meet the publisher's qualification criteria?
5. Do I have access to the most recent edition of the test? If not, what is its cost?
6. What age range do I need a test for?
7. Where can I learn more about the test I am interested in using or reviewing?
8. How much time is involved for administering, scoring, and interpreting the test I've identified?
9. What type of standard scores does the test use?
10. How well do I understand the relationship between various standard scores and the normal curve?

for interpreting test results. In order to interpret test scores, one needs to have an understanding of basic measurement concepts. These concepts include measurement scales, frequency and distribution, measures of central tendency (commonly known as averages), measures of variability, and raw scores versus standardized scores.

Measurement Scales

In order to measure any construct, be it psychological or physical, a measurement scale is needed. You are probably familiar with the scales found on instruments used to measure physical properties like size, weight, and temperature. A thermometer is one type of measuring device containing a scale—degrees in Fahrenheit or Celsius—and as such, properties and rules about its scale enable one to understand the difference between a temperature of 98.6 and 102, for example. Although thermometers come in different shapes and formats, they all are based on the same type of measurement scale. Psychological tests also exist in a wide variety of sizes and formats. When using psychological tests, it is essential to understand the type of scale the test is based on and the differences among these scales.

There are four different types of measurement scales: nominal, ordinal, interval, and ratio. Because each of these scales has different properties, the kinds of statements that can be made about a psychological trait or construct will vary depending upon the kind of scale used. Furthermore, the type of scale determines which kinds of mathematical and statistical calculations can be performed. Therefore, if a clinician is going to incorporate a psychological test into the assessment process, it is important to understand how the test's scale impacts what can and cannot be said about the person being measured.

NOMINAL SCALES A nominal scale is the most fundamental scale in that it simply categorizes people or objects. People can be classified, for example, as belonging to an ethnic–racial group, for example, and the numbers on the scale merely represent the different groups, not quantity: 1 = African American, 2 = Caucasian, 3 = Hispanic, 4 = Native American, 5 = Other. The sole purpose of a nominal scale is to place people and objects in categories, and therefore the only mathematical calculations that can be performed with it are counting and dividing to obtain percentages. First, the number count belonging to each category can be done. The number per group can then be divided by the total number of people measured with the nominal scale to calculate the percentage of people belonging to each group. Percentages can then be compared to determine the relative sizes of the particular categories being measured.

ORDINAL SCALES   An ordinal scale orders or ranks individuals or objects along some dimension. The dimension could be weight, and objects could be organized from lightest to heaviest. Similarly, using the earlier example of a hypothetical shyness test that is based on an ordinal scale, students in a classroom could be rated from least to most shy. The numbers on the ordinal scale would indicate only the relative ranking or standing with the characteristic being measured, in this case shyness. Therefore, ordinal scales provide more information than does a nominal scale, but again, the information is limited. What ordinal scales do not tell us is the degree of difference between the first and second person or the middle and last. This can be illustrated with another example, height. Imagine the students in this classroom are measured with an ordinal height scale. Because the scale arranges people from shortest to tallest only, we don't know from the ranking on the scale how many inches separate the first from the second and the next to last from the last. Without knowing anything about the space or intervals between the rankings on an ordinal scale, the types of statistical calculations that can be done are also limited. The scale that provides information about the degree of space between the numbers on the scale is the next type: the interval scale.

INTERVAL SCALES   An interval scale has the ranking feature of an ordinal scale, but the distance or interval between each number on the scale is the same. By having equal distance between each interval on the scale, certain kinds of mathematical calculations and comparisons can be made that are not possible with an ordinal scale. So, for example, a test that measures IQ is considered an interval scale because the distance between 85 and 90 is considered equivalent to that between 100 and 105. (Some clinicians and educational professionals might suggest, instead, that a 10-point difference between an IQ of 80 and 90 is not the same degree of different intellectual ability as between 10 points at the other end of the scale, 120 and 130. That, however, is a theoretical debate for another time.) Many psychological tests are based on an interval scale. Some, however, are really ordinal in nature but treated as if they are interval in order for statistical calculations to be performed with it. A clearer example of this is a Likert scale that measures strength of agreement but assigns numbers to the phrases "strongly disagree," "disagree," "agree," and so on, and then the scale is treated as if it is an interval scale. That is, the distance between those phrases is theoretically the same from one end of the scale to the other.

   Despite having numbers that represent equal distances along the scale, an interval scale does not have an absolute zero point. Psychological tests measure constructs that people have more or less of but not an absence of. There is no such thing, for example, as a zero IQ. Because an interval scale does not have a zero point, unlike physical scales, ratio comparisons cannot be made between scores. Therefore, it is not accurate to conclude, for example, that someone who has an IQ of 150 is twice as intelligent as someone with an IQ of 75.

RATIO SCALES   A ratio scale has all the features of interval scale—ranking and equal intervals—and contains a zero point. Instruments used to measure physical characteristics such as length, reaction time, and blood level utilize a ratio scale. One example of this type of scale is a decibel meter for determining the volume at a music concert. By virtue of having a zero point on the scale, ratio comparisons can be made between objects or people. For example, 100 decibels is considered twice as loud as 50 decibels. In general, psychological constructs are not, however, conceptualized along a spectrum that includes zero, and therefore psychological tests, unless they are purely speed or reaction-time tests, are not based on a ratio scale.

Measurement Concepts

RAW AND STANDARDIZED SCORES   Regardless of the type of scale used on a psychological test, a test score generally has no meaning until it is contextualized, that is, converted into a **standard score**. What would it mean if Tammy earns a raw score of 15 on a personality test? It would mean little unless you knew what the typical scores were of the normative group. The raw scores from the normative groups are used as the basis for establishing standard scores for the test. Therefore, standard scores enable comparisons to be made between the test taker and the normative group and as a result are the score from which interpretations about an individual can be drawn. When using a criterion-referenced test, however, a raw score may not be converted into a standard score; the raw score is viewed as being at, above, or below the established criterion.

Raw scores are a function of the test's scale type (ordinal or interval) and the scoring system used. The system for scoring a test and producing raw scores is based on the test's response format. A system is then devised for assigning points to answers (e.g., correct equals 1, and incorrect 0). The total raw score then represents the total correct. On the other hand, a test might utilize a frequency or intensity scale for each item and a value is associated with each interval on the scale. For example, an intensity scale can be found on the *Symptom Checklist-90-R*: "not at all," "a little bit," "moderately," "quite a bit," or "extremely," and those responses have corresponding scores: 0, 1, 2, 3, and 4. Some would suggest, however, that this is another example of an ordinal scale being treated like an interval scale because an assumption is made that the space between "not at all" and "a little bit" is the same as distance between "a little bit" and "moderately." Again, just because numbers are assigned to labels doesn't necessarily make it an interval scale.

FREQUENCY DISTRIBUTIONS   One way to organize and make sense of raw scores before they are converted into standard scores is by their frequency distribution. That is, how often does a particular score or range of scores occur? Some scores may be fairly common and others rare. To illustrate this, we could have 10 hypothetical test scores from the *Beck Depression Inventory* (BDI), which Melanie used in her evaluation of Tammy (see Table 6.2). The table indicates that 16 is the score that occurs most frequently, or what is known as the **modal score**. From this group of 10 scores, a BDI score of 16 occurs four times, or 40% of the time, and scores 10 and 20 occur 20% of the time. The remaining scores, the lowest and highest, each occur once, or 10% of the time. Frequency distributions, therefore, provide one piece of important information: the commonality or unusualness of a particular test score.

In addition to a tabular representation, frequency distributions can be portrayed visually with graphs (see Figure 6.1). There are two types of frequency distribution graphs: a **frequency polygon** or histogram. In either type of graph, the horizontal line, or x-axis, contains the test

Person	BDI Score	(Score—Mean) Squared
Betty	10	36
Charlie	6	100
Danielle	16	0
Evan	16	0
Fanny	20	16
George	10	36
Henrietta	20	16
Isaac	30	196
Jane	16	0
Tammy	16	0
Total	160	

Table 6.2 Distribution of Scores, Squared Scores, and Averages

Note: The mean, the mode, and the median are the same number (16) in this example, which illustrates that these numbers are approximately the same in a normal, or bell-shaped, curve.

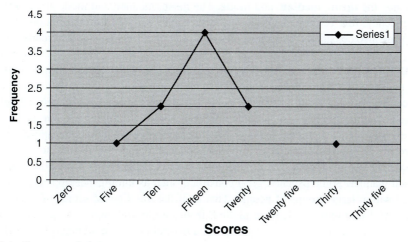

FIGURE 6.1 Frequency Polygon

scores and the vertical line, or y-axis, represents the number of times a score occurred (i.e., the frequency count). Sometimes when there are a large number of scores to count and graph, score intervals rather than individual scores will be displayed on the x-axis. The intervals used will depend upon the range of scores on the test and what makes most sense in terms of visually displaying a frequency distribution.

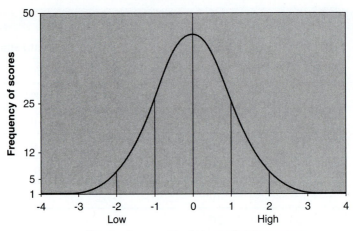

FIGURE 6.2 Normal Curve

If the frequency polygon in Figure 6.1 is smoothed out, it depicts a bell-shaped curve, or what is known as a normal distribution of scores. The normal curve has several important features and its relationship to standardized scores will be explored in detail in subsequent sections (see Figure 6.2). Perhaps the first feature to note is the symmetry of the distribution. The curve can be sliced into two equal halves and the midpoint of the curve is where there are three important numbers: the **mean**, **median**, and **mode**. The mean, median, and mode are all measures of central tendency; that is, they quantitatively express the middle of a distribution of scores. As such, they are also considered average scores, but each one is calculated differently.

DISTRIBUTION OF SCORES: NORMAL AND SKEWED DISTRIBUTIONS In a normal distribution, the majority of scores cluster around the middle or top of the curve with fewer and fewer scores occurring toward both tails in the curve. Another feature of a symmetrical bell-shaped distribution of scores, which will be explained further in the following section, is that the three types of averages (mean, mode and median) for any range of scores are approximately the same number. The normal curve is an important concept to understand because many statistical calculations used to interpret psychological tests are based on having scores distributed in this bell-shaped manner. Some psychological constructs such as intelligence appear to be normally distributed within large groups of people. That is, if the intelligence scores of a representative group of over 1,000 individuals were plotted, from low to high along the x-axis, and the frequency of each score on the y-axis (a polygon), a normal curve would emerge. Not all psychological constructs, and therefore test scores, are normally distributed, however.

On the other hand, a distribution of scores can be asymmetrical, or what is known as a skewed distribution. A distribution can be skewed in either a positive or negative direction (see Figure 6.3). In a positively skewed distribution, the majority of scores fall around the low end with fewer scores at the higher end or toward the tail. A test that has a positive skew has a floor effect in that there is little differentiation among scores at the low end of the scale. In other words, the majority of scores are bunched around a relatively narrow range at the lower end of the scale and the scores are more spread out toward the higher end of the scale, providing more

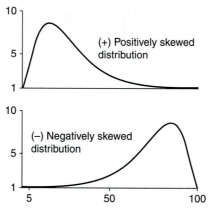

FIGURE 6.3 Skewed Distributions

differentiation. Those fewer high scores in the tail of the curve pull the mean to the right, or the high end of the scale, thereby raising it. *Why* will be illustrated in a moment when the relationship between frequency distributions and averages are discussed, but briefly, one or two atypically high numbers in a distribution will raise the mean. The reverse is true with a negatively skewed distribution; the tail goes toward the low end of the scale. As Figure 6.3 depicts, the majority of scores cluster around the high end of the scale and therefore a ceiling effect exists: little difference in scores at the high end of the scale. This time the lower scores in the tail reduce the mean. One way to remember the two and sometimes-confusing types of skewed distributions is with the alliterative phrase "the tail tells the tale." A tail that goes to the high end occurs in a positive distribution, and a tail that goes to the low end is a negative distribution.

MEASURES OF CENTRAL TENDENCY   Another way to describe a collection of test scores is by measures of central tendency. Measures of central tendency refer to average scores or the score around which the majority of scores cluster (see Figure 6.2). This is a concept you are probably already familiar with from a high school math class. These scores tell you how common a score is. By knowing the average score, one can then judge how far away from the average any given score falls.

   Mean   The mean is the arithmetic average of all the scores. As you may recall, the mean is calculated by adding the scores and dividing the total by the number of scores (see Table 6.3). Using the 10 BDI scores from Table 6.2 as an example, the mean is 16. The 10 scores total 160, and 160 divided by 10 equals 16. The mean is the one measure of central tendency that takes into account the magnitude of the scores, and it is most affected by outlier scores—ones that are very high or very low, even if they do not occur frequently. For example, if just one score from this group is altered, changing Isaac's score from 30 to 60, the mean would become 19.

   Median   The median is the score that divides a range of scores, from lowest to highest, in half. Half of the scores are below the median and half are above it. When there is an odd number of scores, then the middle score (e.g., the sixth in a range of 11 scores) would be the middle, or median, score. When there is an even number of scores, as in the example being used here, the median is the average of the two middle scores. In this case, the median is 16 ([16 + 16] / 2). The median, unlike the mean, is unaffected by atypically high or low scores, but it is affected by the overall distribution of scores.

Table 6.3 Formulas: Mean, Variance, and Standard Deviation

Mean (m) = Σx/n
Σ = sum the numbers (x), n = number of scores
Using the data from Table 6.2:
10 + 6 + 16 + 16 + 20 + 10 + 20 + 30 + 16 +16 = 160/n (10) = 16

Variance = Σ(x − m)^2/(n)*
Using the data from Table 6.2:
(10 − 16 = −6 and −6^2 = 36) + (6 − 16 = −10 and −10^2 = 100) . . . (16 − 16 = 0 and 0^2 = 0)
36 + 100 + 0 + 0 + 16 + 36 + 16 + 196 + 0 + 0 = 400/(10 − 1) = 44.4

Standard deviation = Square root of the variance
Using the data from Table 6.2: $\sqrt{44.4}$ = 6.7

*This formula is used when calculating the variance from a known sample of scores. When one is interested in estimating the variance for an entire population, based on that sample, and estimates the population variance in an unbiased fashion, the denominator in this equation becomes (N−1).

Mode   The mode, as mentioned previously, is the most frequently occurring score. In this example, the mode is also 16. That is, the score 16 occurs four times, more than any other score. It is possible that with a large distribution of scores there are two modes, that is, two scores that occur with the same frequency. In that case, the distribution of scores would be a bimodal one.

Now let's return to the normal and skewed curves to understand the relationship between the distribution of scores and measures of central tendency. When the frequency of test scores has that normal or bell-shaped distribution (see Figure 6.2), the mean, median, and mode are one and the same, or approximately the same in large groups of numbers. When the scores are normally distributed, it does not matter which measure of central tendency is used to describe the score because numerically they will be the same. As mentioned before, scores on many psychological tests are not normally distributed. When scores are positively skewed, relatively more scores occur at the lower end of the distribution. Therefore, the mode is less than the median, but the higher scores in the tail raise the average score so that the mean is greater than the median. The opposite is true when scores are negatively skewed (more scores at the higher end); the mean is less than the median and the mode is the highest (see Figure 6.4). As noted earlier with the example of the BDI scores, if just one score is much higher than the rest, the distribution becomes skewed and the mean becomes higher, or shifts to the right, along that x-axis.

MEASURES OF VARIABILITY   In addition to frequency counts and averages, a collection of numbers or test scores can be described by its variability. There are three concepts that describe test score variability: **range**, **variance**, and **standard deviation**. The range of scores can be wide or narrow, and is simply calculated by subtracting the lowest score from the highest. The range in Table 6.2 is 24 (30 − 6). Variance and standard deviation are more complicated to calculate and represent the average spread of the scores from the mean. This average spread is referred to as a standard deviation unit. A standard deviation unit is equivalent to the area under the curve in a distribution of scores and therefore represents the percentage of individuals with scores falling within a certain range.

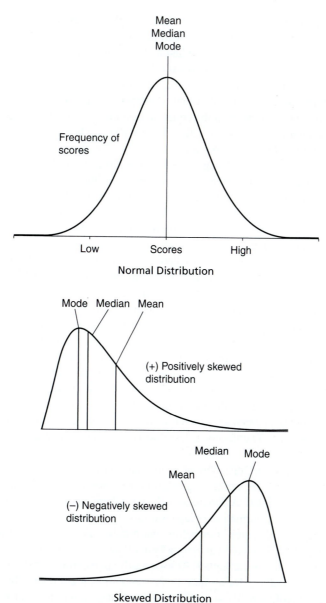

FIGURE 6.4 Mean, Median, and Mode of Normal Curves and Skewed Distributions

Variance and Standard Deviation   The variance for a distribution of scores is calculated by obtaining the average distance between the mean and each individual score. To understand the variance, conceptually, it helps to see the multistep process for calculating it using the 10 scores from Table 6.2. Once the mean for a set of scores is obtained, the difference between each score and the mean is obtained. For example, the mean from the table of BDI scores is 16. Betty's score is 10, and $10 - 16 = -6$. Her score is 6 points below the mean. This process is repeated for each score (see Table 6.3). The next step is to square each of these difference scores and sum these squared scores. The reason why the difference scores are squared is because of the symmetry of a normal curve: half the scores will be above the mean and half below. Therefore if the difference scores were not squared, when added up the resulting number would be zero. After the sum of the squared difference scores is calculated, that sum is divided by the number of scores (N). This is the formula when determining the variance from a group of scores obtained from a known sample. When one is interested in estimating the variance of a population in an unbiased way, then the denominator in the equation becomes N − 1 (Hays, 1981). Why the sum of the squares is being divided by N − 1, rather than by just N when estimating the variance of a population is a matter of more complex statistical theory. Calculated either way, the variance as shown in Table 6.3 represents the average spread of the scores from the mean. To put it another way, the variance quantifies the average distance between the mean and all the other scores along the frequency distribution curve. The variance, however, was computed by squaring the differences between the score and the mean, so to compensate for that, the squaring is undone by taking the square root of the variance. The resulting number is the standard deviation. The standard deviation is then the building block for understanding other types of standardized scores.

A standard deviation is another way to represent an individual's test score in comparison to the normative group. For example, knowing that Tammy has a raw score of 15 is meaningless, but knowing her score is at 1.5 standard deviations now has meaning. She performed better than average; in fact, her score deviated from the mean by 1.5 units. In that sense, a standard deviation (SD) score for an individual is a measure of statistical deviancy. Standard deviation unit scores are also related to other kinds of standard scores. Each standard deviation unit in a distribution of scores refers to the percentage of individuals with scores in the space under the curve (see Figure 6.5). When the frequency distribution of scores resembles the bell-shaped or normal curve, then approximately two-thirds of all the scores fall within plus or minus one standard deviation. The farther along the normal curve, or the more standard deviation units away from the center or mean, the more sharply the percentages of scores fall. In a normal distribution of scores, scores that are plus or minus three SD units occur less than 0.5% of the time; they are very atypical.

PERCENTILES   **Percentiles** are one type of score that you may be familiar with. A raw score that is at the 98th percentile, for example, is useful information. Percentiles are not the same as percentages, but they are related. A percentile indicates where a person stands relative to the distribution of test scores in the normative group (Anastasi & Urbina, 1997). The percentile number represents the percentage of scores at or below that number. For example, an individual whose score is at the 98th percentile scored equal to or better than 98% of the normative group, and 2% of that group had scores that were higher. Consequently, percentiles constitute an ordinal scale because they provide a ranking for an individual. Percentiles are a relatively easy measure for professionals and nonprofessionals to understand. Percentages, on the other hand, describe the number of items correct or the number of items endorsed as occurring as a fraction of the total number of test items. For example, if a client got 5 out of 10 items correct, the client's percentage would be 50%. In a normally distributed range of score, percentiles correspond to standardized scores, as Figure 6.5 illustrates.

The main disadvantage in using percentiles to express an individual's position on the test is the inequality of units along the percentile scale. To understand this problem we need to look at the typical distribution of a range of scores. Typically, test scores are distributed so that there are very few people who receive scores at the low and high ends of a test, and the majority of individuals, approximately two-thirds, have scores in the middle range. As Figure 6.5 illustrates, percentile scores in the middle range are close together, and at the two ends, or tails,

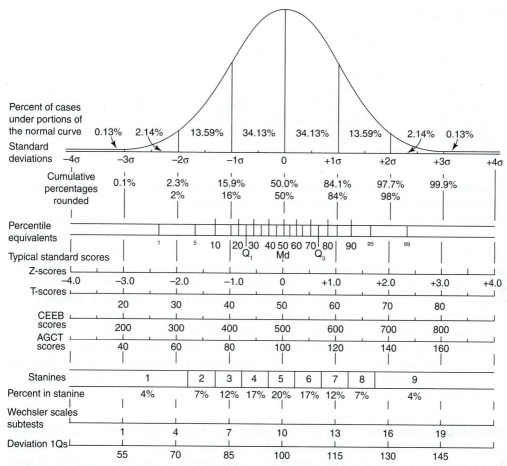

FIGURE 6.5 The Relationship Between the Normal Curve and Standard Scores*

*This figure is based on a chart that was placed in a Test Service Bulletin (48) from the Psychological Corporation in 1955. It was not copyrighted and was intended for reproduction.

of distribution are much farther apart. As a result, when raw scores are converted to percentile scores, the percentile differences in the middle range tend to exaggerate the raw score differences and minimize differences at the two ends. For example, the space between the 40th and 50th percentiles is much smaller than the space between the 90th and 99th percentiles so that the 10-point percentile difference between 40 and 50 contains raw scores that are much closer than the raw scores between the 9-point percentile difference between 90 and 99. These inequalities become even more striking when the distribution of test scores does not conform to a bell-shaped distribution and instead takes on a different shape. When it comes to measures of personality and psychopathology, however, the inequality of percentile units is less of an issue because generally the dividing line or cutoff between normal and abnormal is at the 95th percentile or greater. One more example may help to understand the inequality issue and the relevance for measures of psychopathology. On the Hyperactivity scale of the Teacher Rating Scale in the *Behavior Assessment System for Children* (see Chapter 10), there is only a 2-point raw score difference between the 58th and 69th percentiles, whereas there exists a 22-point difference between the 90th and 99th percentiles. But only scores at the 95th percentile or higher become a clinical concern.

Standardized Scores

Once a raw score is converted into a standardized score, the interpretation process begins. Standardized scores provide a way to evaluate the statistical typicality or unusualness of the score. They also provide a frame of reference from which diagnostic or treatment decisions can be made. For example, if a standard score is at or above a certain level, then it could be a positive indicator of a DSM-IV diagnosis and medication might be recommended. A standardized score provides information about where an individual score is in relationship to the normative group, and by being standardized, comparisons can be made between different tests. Two common standardized scores found on many psychological tests are the *z* scores and *t* scores.

Z SCORES   A *z* score is a fundamental standardized score on which other types of standardized scores are based. A *z* score represents the ratio of the distance between a raw score and the mean relative to the standard deviation for that group of scores. In other words, given the variability of a group of numbers, or in this case, test scores, a *z* score tells you how far from the mean the score is, given the variability of the scores. To calculate a *z* score, the mean is subtracted from the raw score and divided by the standard deviation (see Table 6.3). For example, using again the data from Table 6.2, Betty's *z* score is (10 – 16) / 6.7 = –0.9, or approximately 1 z score below the mean. This is known as a linear transformation of raw scores (Anastasi & Urbina, 1997). A linear transformation preserves the order and magnitude of the distribution of raw scores because constants are used to subtract from the raw score and then divide. In math, any time a constant is added, subtracted, or divided from a group of numbers, the new distribution matches the original one in terms of its shape and variability. To put it another way, when raw scores are transformed linearly into *z* scores, differences between the raw scores are maintained. Therefore, the problem of unequal units of scale found in percentiles does not occur.

T SCORES   Another type of commonly used standardized score is the **t score**. *T* scores are most commonly found on tests of personality and psychopathology, not tests of cognitive abilities and aptitudes. They are, in essence, a special kind of *z* score. *T* scores have a mean of 50 and a standard deviation of 10. A linear *t* score is one in which the *z* score is multiplied by this standard deviation (10) and the mean (50) is added. So, for example, Betty's *z* score of –0.9 can be converted to a *t* score like this: (–0.9 × 10) + 50 = 41. This conversion from *z* to *t* score does away with negative scores and decimals found in many *z* scores, thereby making the *t* score easier to use and perform calculations on. Standard scores such as *t* scores allow comparisons within measures containing multiple scales to be made. Knowing, for example, that a client had a score of 60 on an anxiety scale but a 40 on a depression scale allows for a more meaningful comparison to be made from those two scores. As mentioned earlier, standard scores have a relationship to one another when the scores are normally distributed. Figure 6.5 shows, for example, that *t* scores of 70 correspond typically to the 98th percentile.

When a group of raw scores has a nonnormal distribution, a nonlinear or "normalizing" process will be used to convert raw scores to *t* scores (Anastasi & Urbina, 1997). A nonlinear transformation involves using the percentage of scores falling at different standard deviation units from the mean in a normal curve and fitting the raw scores of the original distribution to the normal curve. That is why with some measures and scales you will find *t* scores of 70 equal to the 94th through 97th percentiles rather than the 98th percentile, which is the case with a linear *t* score. The precise percentile for any given *t* score for a test or scale within a test will be found in the test manual. These normalizing transformations to obtain *t* scores should be done only when the construct is believed to be normally distributed, *but* the normative group's test scores do not correspond to a normal curve and the normative group is relatively large and representative (Anastasi & Urbina, 1997). The closer the raw scores of the standardization group get to matching a normal curve, however, the more linear and nonlinear *t* scores will correspond.

OTHER STANDARDIZED SCORES   Other types of standardized scores include the **stanine**, **deviation IQ**, and **age** and **grade equivalent**. Stanine scores are normalized standard scores ranging between 1 and 9, with a mean of 5, and a standard deviation of approximately two. They are derived by arranging the raw scores in the normative group in order from lowest to highest. The percentage of cases at different intervals becomes the respective stanines. For example, the first 4% of the scores make up the first stanine, the next 7% the second, the next 12% the third, and so on until you reach stanine 9. These percentages are based on the percentile increments along the normal curve, so that stanine 1 includes percentiles 1 to 4, and stanine 9 includes percentiles 96 to 99. It is important to keep in mind that each stanine score represents an interval of percentile scores and therefore two individuals could be only one percentile apart but belong to different stanines. Stanines are used mostly with achievement and aptitude tests (see Chapter 13).

Deviation IQ scores are another type of standardized score that can be converted from a *z* score. They are used with intelligence and cognitive ability tests. They typically have a mean of 100 and a standard deviation of 15 (some cognitive ability tests, however, have slightly different standard deviations; see Chapter 13). Deviation IQs were developed in response to the statistical problem with the original IQ formula: mental age divided by chronological age multiplied by 100. The statistical problem with the original IQ was that different standard deviations existed at different ages. Therefore, it was possible to have two children, a 5- and a 6-year-old, for example, get two different scores, such as 80 and 90, but those two scores fell at the same standard deviation below the mean for the respective age groups. Therefore, what was needed was a standard score that was comparable across the lifespan, as is the case with a deviation IQ score. Now a deviation IQ score of 100 has the same meaning whether the individual is 6 or 60.

The other standard scores you may be familiar with are those found on tests that assess applicants' qualifications for college and graduate school programs. Tests such as the Scholastic Achievement Test (SAT), Graduate Record Examination (GRE), and the one distributed by ACT® use standardized scores. The SAT and GRE, for example, have a mean of 500 and a standard deviation of 100. These scores are produced by the College Entrance Examination Board (CEEB) and are sometimes referred to as CEEB scores. The relationship between CEEB scores and other standardized scores is illustrated in Figure 6.5.

DEVELOPMENTAL SCORES   Two other types of standardized scores represent developmental norms: age and grade equivalents. These types of scores are useful to describe a child's test performance but they lack the statistical sophistication of other standardized scores. Basically, these scores represent the level at which the majority of individuals from the normative group, at a certain age or grade level, performed successfully on a test. Age and grade equivalent scores are typically found on cognitive ability, achievement, and aptitude tests.

An age equivalent score is derived by determining the mean score on a test for a group of individuals at a specific age. For example, the mean score of the 10-year-olds who comprised the standardization sample of a hypothetical reading achievement test would become the 10-year-old age equivalent score. Mean scores for each age group would be established from the raw scores within each age level. Within each age, other age equivalent scores would be derived by determining how far above or below the mean the raw score is and estimating a corresponding age score. What that means, for example, is that a 10-year-old with a 9-year-old age equivalent performed below the mean of the 10-year-old group. That is not the same as saying this 10-year-old is at a 9-year-old level. In addition, development does not occur in equal intervals. As with height, a good deal of cognitive developmental change occurs during the first few years of a child's life, with the amount of change per year diminishing as a child gets older. Therefore, age equivalent scores represent how on target one's ability is compared to others of the *same* age group, not the age level of performance.

Grade level equivalent scores are based on a similar process and rationale and therefore have the same problem associated with them. For example, taking a hypothetical reading test where 15 was the mean score for the first graders in the normative group who took the test in September. A score of 15 then becomes a 1.0 grade score for first graders. The process is repeated for each grade level represented by the normative group. The decimal points (1.5) for example, represent the months along the school year. Therefore, like an age score, a grade equivalent score is comparing only how an individual in his or her grade performed relative to others in that grade. It does not provide a measure of the grade level an individual is at. For example, a first grader who has a 3.5 grade equivalent score on this hypothetical reading test is not necessarily reading at the mid-third-grade level, but rather is reading well above average compared to other first graders.

Despite their intuitive appeal, grade equivalent scores have several limitations. One is that, like with development, learning does not occur in a uniform equal-interval fashion within grades. Another limitation is that curriculum content and teaching methods vary considerably across schools, and therefore average scores in a standardization group are in part a reflection of this diversity in teaching methodology. Related to that is the lack of consensus about what content in particular subject areas should be mastered by the end of a grade. A final problem with grade equivalencies is that they reflect the scoring system of the test publisher (Whiston, 2009). For example, one publisher's reading test might result in the first grader in the previous example earning a 1.8 grade level score and a similar reading test from another publisher might yield a 2.2 grade score. The different scores probably reflect slight scoring differences with the respective tests rather than an almost half-year difference in ability level.

Converting Raw Test Scores to Standard Scores

Now it's time for Melanie to convert Tammy's raw score of 15 to a standardized score. How will she do that? Typically, the test's manual will include the necessary information and specific procedure for converting raw scores into standard scores. With many tests available today, the conversion from raw to standard scores can either be done by hand or with a computer software program. Hand scoring of most measures is a relatively quick and easy clerical task. The simplest process involves summing the score for each item to get the raw score and then using a table in the test manual to find the corresponding standardized score (*t* score, for example,) or percentile. When tests have multiple scales, this process is repeated for each scale. With certain tests, templates or other systems are available to facilitate the scoring process.

Computerized scoring is costlier but is advantageous when client volume is large and clinician time is better spent interpreting and integrating test scores with other assessment data. Once a raw score is converted into a standard score, those scores and percentiles can be displayed visually in graph form, or what is sometimes referred to as a profile form. That is a nice feature for clinicians and clients who are visual learners.

Summary and Conclusions

The purpose of this chapter was to expand the discussion of the nature of psychological tests. It presented the measurement and statistical concepts that are essential to understand if one is to use tests in a competent and ethical manner. Psychological tests vary in their format, length, and the underlying construct the test is purported to measure. The vast majority of tests that counselors and other professionals utilize are normative. That is, some representative group took the test, and their performance on the test serves as the benchmark to which future test takers' scores are compared. Some tests are criterion referenced in that a particular score or level serves as a benchmark for proficiency or mastery in a particular domain or is used as a cutoff point when screening for diagnoses. Psychological tests are based on a measurement scale, typically an ordinal or interval one. Ordinal scales have the property of ranking, but the distances between the rankings or points on the scale are uneven. Interval scales have both a ranking feature and equal distance between each segment on the scale. Interval scales are necessary for performing most of the statistical calculations required for interpreting test scores.

It is important to keep in mind that psychological tests, be they normative or criterion referenced or both, are descriptive, not explanatory. That is, tests provide quantitative data about an individual's characteristics, traits, abilities, attitudes, or symptoms. They do not, however, have the ability to explain why an individual's performance was such. That is the task of the counselor. Test results are one of several pieces of information that need to be synthesized in order for a counselor to further a case conceptualization, arrive at a diagnosis, establish a treatment plan, or monitor progress.

In order to understand and make sense of the numbers on tests, knowledge of some fundamental math and statistical concepts is necessary. Those essential concepts include normal and skewed distributions, measures of central tendency or averages, measures of variability, especially the standard deviation, and various standardized scores. The standard scores that counselors and other professionals will use and interpret include: z scores and t scores, deviation IQs, stanines, and age and grade equivalents. A z score is the basic standard score upon which the t score and other standard scores are based. Having gained an understanding of measurement concepts and standards scores, the stage is set for the next critical topic: reliability and validity.

Reflection Questions and Experiential Exercises

1. Psychological tests measure constructs like intelligence, personality, and psychopathology. What are examples of other constructs you could measure? What type of measurement scale would you use?
2. You've given a psychopathology measure to a client and the client's t score was 70. How would you explain the meaning of that score to your client?
3. Calculate the mean, standard deviation, and z scores from the following test raw scores: 100, 95, 105, 98, 114, 87, 101, 106, 99, and 102. (Hint: There will be one mean and one standard deviation but 10 z scores.)
4. Given what you know so far about psychopathology, in small groups of 3–5 students, design a 10-item test that would be a measure of psychopathology. Once you have created 10 items, decide whether the items will be rated for intensity or frequency, and what will those rating be (e.g., "not at all," "a little bit," "some," "a lot"). When your test is complete, share it with other groups.
5. How would you go about selecting a standardization group to create norms for your psychopathology test? What would be the advantages and limitations in selecting that particular group?

7 RELIABILITY AND VALIDITY

Chapter Objectives

After reading this chapter, you should be able to:

■ Understand the concept of reliability and the major types of reliability.

■ Understand the correlation coefficient statistic and how it is used to calculate reliability.

■ Explain the concept of standard measurement error.

■ Identify the factors that affect test reliability.

■ Understand the different types of validity.

■ Explain the concept of decision theory.

■ Identify factors that affect the selection and use of assessment tests and measures.

OVERVIEW

An understanding of the complementary concepts of reliability and validity is essential for evaluating the usefulness of any type of standardized assessment measure, and yet it is these two concepts students often want to avoid learning. The sight or sound of these two words can bring fear and loathing. Eyes tend to glaze over and hearts start to race. Even at the end of an assessment course, a clear understanding of these fundamental psychometric principles can remain a challenge. Upon completing this chapter, the author hopes you will feel comfortable accessing the technical section of a test manual or the results section of a journal article, where reliability and validity information can be found, and use that information to guide decisions when selecting appropriate measures for counseling assessments.

Reliability and validity are the pillars of psychological assessment. They are the foundation upon which all standardized tests and measures are evaluated. The essential difference between a standardized and nonstandardized assessment measure is that the former has been shown empirically to have adequate reliability and validity. The purpose of this chapter is to provide a conceptual examination of reliability and validity and to show how reliability and validity inform the selection of tests used as part of an assessment process that counselors and other helping professionals conduct. The chapter covers the multiple types of reliability and validity, their relationship to each other, and their statistical calculations. A more in-depth discussion of psychometric principles and statistics, however, is beyond the scope of this text and the reader is advised to consult Anne Anastasi's classic text, *Psychological Testing,* now in its seventh edition (1997) and co-authored by Susana Urbina, or *Psychological Testing: Principles, Applications, and Issues* (5th ed.) by Kaplan and Saccuzzo (2005) for more information.

RELIABILITY

Reliability refers to the consistency or stability of scores obtained by the same group of individuals when readministered the same test at two different times or when given equivalent forms of the same test (Anastasi & Urbina, 1997). This definition implies that there are different types of reliability, as will be explained. In general, the first step in determining a test's reliability is to identify a relatively large group of individuals, and each individual will receive two scores. The two sets of scores can come from one test given twice, or from two parallel versions of the same test where each individual in the group is given both versions A and B. The next step in calculating a test's reliability is to determine how much variation in scores there is from time 1 to time 2, or between form A and form B, and quantify that variation. In theory, one could take an infinite number of measurements of a group of individuals' behavior and a perfectly reliable test would produce the same result each time. But when it comes to psychological tests it would be impractical to measure someone's behavior thousands of times, and furthermore the thing we are reliably trying to measure—behaviors, feelings, attitudes, and beliefs—is a moving target. And sometimes what is being measured can change very quickly. Therefore, the second score obtained for each individual in the group may not be exactly the same as the first one, which is often the case. Another way to think about the concept of reliability is to consider the following question. How accurate is the score or result obtained for any given individual with a particular test? It is a given that no psychological test is perfectly accurate. Therefore, all psychological tests have some degree of measurement error associated with them. That error is referred to as the **standard error of measurement (SEM)** and the calculation of it will be discussed later in the chapter.

To make reliability and its calculation more understandable, let's take an example of a medical device you are probably familiar with, a thermometer. Now imagine someone has invented a new thermometer that measures body temperature by placing a strip around your index finger. In order for the strip thermometer to be perfectly reliable, the body temperature reading at time 1 would be the same as the temperature reading at time 2 and time 3 and so on. Body temperature, however, fluctuates over a 24-hour period by a couple of degrees. Therefore, the second and third measurements would need to be taken within a brief period of time, otherwise it would be hard to know if variation in temperature reading was due to an unreliable thermometer or to normal changes in body temperature. Furthermore, a number of factors can affect the result or score obtained from this new strip thermometer other than the "true" variability in temperature over the course of a day. Therefore, the new thermometer could produce two different temperature readings for the same person at two different times because body temperature actually changed, or because the temperature was really the same the second time it was measured but other factors accounted for the different temperature reading: placement on the finger, blood circulation, time between measurements, time of day, where the strip was stored, and so on. These other factors are considered "error variance." Therefore, the thermometer is not always measuring the "true" body temperature. The more reliable any instrument or test is, the closer it comes to measuring the true physical or psychological state and the less error is involved in the measure. Medical devices and psychological tests, unlike the instruments of physics, do not produce the same result each time because they are never perfect measuring tools and, unlike physical properties such as length and distance, psychological and physiological constructs are relatively unstable.

To illustrate the quantitative relationship between body temperature readings at time 1 and time 2, a **scatter plot** can be produced that depicts the relationship between those two temperature readings (see Figure 7.1). The horizontal or x-axis represents the range of body temperatures measured at time 1 and the vertical or y-axis represents the range of readings at time 2. Each dark

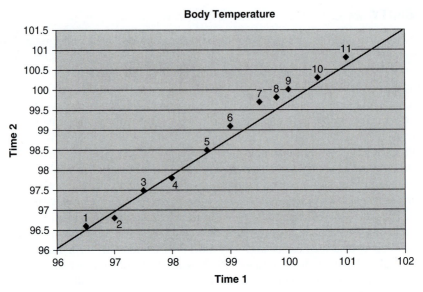

FIGURE 7.1 Scatter Plot

square on the scatter plot represents an individual whose body temperature was measured twice with the same strip. Since reliability is about the relationship or degree of correspondence between two variables or sets of scores, this relationship can be quantified. It is also important to keep in mind when examining this figure that sometimes the individual's temperature is exactly the same at time 1 and time 2, as is the case with the first individual represented by the square on the lower left side of the graph. On the other hand, as is the case with individual number 2, the temperatures are different (97° vs. 96.8°) at times 1 and 2, but the relative position of this individual is still unchanged at number 6. Therefore, the relationship between two sets of scores for a group of individuals is about the ranking, not the absolute score.

The Correlation Coefficient

Reliability is measured with the correlation coefficient statistic. Although there are various ways to calculate it, the more typical way is to use the **Pearson product–moment correlation**, or **Pearson** r, so named because the statistic was developed by Karl Pearson (see Chapter 1). Correlation coefficients range between –1.0 and 1.0. Figure 7.1 represents a perfect correlation of 1.0 because even if the absolute temperature readings for an individual changed from time 1 to time 2, the ranking of individuals on body temperature does not change. That is, the person with the lowest temperature at time 1 also had the lowest temperature at time 2, the person with the next lowest at time 1 also was the next lowest at time 2, the person with the highest temperature at time 1 also was the highest at time 2, and so on. A correlation of negative 1.0 is also a perfect correlation. The two scores, however, have an inverse relationship: as scores on the x-axis get higher, scores on the y-axis get lower (see Figure 7.2). If there is no relationship between how an individual scores on time 1 versus time 2, then the correlation is 0.0, which graphically resembles a rectangle or circle (see Figure 7.3).

Typically, standardized psychological tests and questionnaires have reliability coefficients ranging from 0.6 to 0.9, though correlation coefficients below 0.7 are deemed to be an inadequate measure of reliability (Hunsley & Mash, 2008).

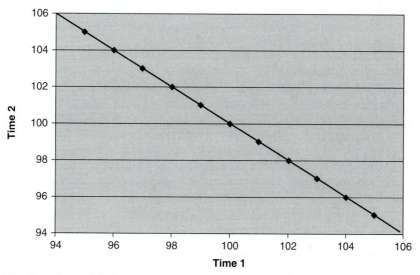

FIGURE 7.2   Negative Correlation

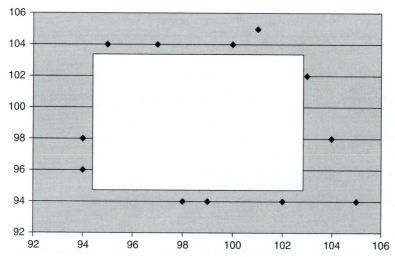

FIGURE 7.3   0.0 Correlation

The correlation coefficient can be calculated in a variety of ways, but the most common and easiest formula to understand is:

$$R_{xy} = \frac{\Sigma_{xy}}{(N)\,(SD_x)\,(SD_y)}$$

Let's take a closer look at this equation. To help you understand it, the scores from a hypothetical group of 10 students who took a test you may be familiar with, the Graduate Record Exam

Student	GRE1	GRE2	x	y
Table 7.1 Graduate Record Exam (GRE) Scores				
Ashley	620	600	21	−1
Bill	580	590	−19	−11
John	450	430	−149	−171
Susan	780	780	181	179
Henry	690	670	91	69
Nancy	600	610	1	9
David	590	610	−9	9
Joanne	650	650	51	49
Ben	550	550	−49	−51
Sarah	480	520	−119	−81
Total	5,990	6,010		
Means	599	601		

(GRE) two times, one week apart will be examined. Those scores are listed in Table 7.1. In this formula, x is the difference between an individual's obtained score on a test at time 1 (GRE1), and the mean for all the individuals taking the test, and y, likewise, is the difference between the individual score and the test mean for the second time (GRE2).

The mean scores are 599 for GRE1 and 601 for GRE2. In case you forgot what a mean means, it is the arithmetic average, the total, 5,990 divided by 10 for GRE1, and 6,010 divided by 10 for GRE2. Therefore, Ashley's difference score for GRE1 is 21, and −1 for GRE2, and Bill's difference scores are −19 and −11 respectively. N represents the number of individuals who took the test, and *SD* represents the standard deviation. The standard deviation, as you may recall from the previous chapter, is the square root of the sum of the difference scores, which are squared and then divided by the number of individuals ($SD_x = \sqrt{\Sigma x^2 / N}$). This hypothetical and unrealistic correlation between GRE1 and GRE2 is 0.98. You can take the author's word for that or do the math yourself (see Experiential Activity 5 at the end of the chapter). The correlation coefficient then is a measure of how two sets of scores co-vary.

The math underlying the correlation coefficient is key to understanding reliability and validity. As a statistic that quantifies the relationship between any two variables, it is also used to measure different types of validity, and slight modifications of the Pearson *r* formula are used to calculate other types of reliability.

STATISTICAL SIGNIFICANCE When two variables are found to correlate, it is possible that the relationship is due to chance or sampling error, rather than a true correlation between the two variables. In other words, what is the probability that in reality the relationship between two variables is of some magnitude greater than zero, and not a result of some type of error?

As you recall, a correlation coefficient is calculated based on two test scores from one group of individuals. It is possible that the correlation found was a function of how that particular group performed on the test rather than the actual stability or consistency of the test. Essentially, the correlation could be a fluke given the particular makeup of the group. Therefore, a statistical procedure is needed to quantify the likelihood that the correlation found between two variables, for example GRE scores at time 1 versus time 2, with one group can be replicated with other groups. The concept of statistical significance is a way of stating how confident one is that the relationship between two variables exists, i.e., is greater than zero. Statistical significance is expressed mathematically with the notation *"p"* and the symbol for less than ($<$), for example $p < 0.05$. The expression $r = 0.45$ ($p < 0.05$) means that there is less than a 5 in 100 probability that the correlation of 0.45 is due to some sampling error or idiosyncrasies about the first group with which the correlation coefficient for a particular test was calculated. The 5% probability that a correlation is due to sampling error is a generally accepted minimum professional standard. More stringent benchmarks for calling a correlation a true correlation would be either the 0.01 or 0.001 levels of statistical significance. That is, a less than 1 in 100 chance in the first case, 1 in 1,000 in the second, that measured correlation is an error.

Types of Reliability

TEST–RETEST RELIABILITY   In the previous example, test–retest reliability is being illustrated. The same group of individuals is given the exact same test twice, and there is some specified time interval between the two testtaking events. Depending upon the construct being measured, the interval between time 1 and time 2 may be as short as a day and as long as several months. A correlation coefficient is determined using time 1 and time 2 as the two variables on which a group of individuals will obtain scores. Theoretically, as noted previously, a test that was completely reliable would produce the same rank order scores for all individuals the second time around even if their exact scores fluctuate. When the ability, trait, or construct being assessed is unlikely to change over a short period of time, let's say two weeks, then giving the individual the same test again to determine reliability of the test makes sense. Adult intelligence and personality are considered relatively stable abilities and traits, over a six- to 12-month period or perhaps even longer depending upon which aspects of those constructs are being measured. Even though those constructs are thought to be stable, a number of factors could influence someone's performance or responses on a test: knowledge of the test, practice, fatigue, mood, the testing environment, and so on. And this is why repeated measures of human behavior or performance will not yield the same results. Test–retest reliability becomes an even more problematic concept at the toddler level, where changes in intelligence and personality can occur in a matter of weeks. Many of the measures counselors are likely to use are designed to assess moods, behaviors, perceptions, and attitudes. Those aspects of human beings are likely to change from time 1 to time 2 even when the time interval is relatively short, such as two weeks. One might expect, for example, that a measure of depression symptoms would produce different scores between times 1 and 2, not necessarily because the measure is unreliable, but because depression symptoms by their nature fluctuate during the course of a day, let alone two weeks. Consequently, for most of the standardized questionnaires and inventories that counselors are likely to encounter, test–retest reliability is a somewhat illogical measure. If, however, a test's test–retest reliability is determined, knowing the time interval between testing and that information, which is usually provided in the test manual, is important. Test–retest reliability for intervals of several days to several weeks should be at least 0.70 to be considered adequate (Hunsley & Mash, 2008).

Fortunately, there are alternative ways to calculate a test's reliability when test–retest reliability is not feasible or logical.

ALTERNATE-FORM RELIABILITY   As the name implies, alternate-form reliability is determined by creating two equivalent or parallel forms of the same test or questionnaire. Again a group of individuals will obtain two scores, but this time one will come from version A, the other from version B, and a correlation coefficient is calculated in the same way as illustrated above. Alternate forms of the same test are typically administered in immediate succession, which solves the time interval problem with test–retest reliability but does not necessarily resolve other problems associated with retaking a test such as practice or fatigue, especially if the test in question is lengthy.

   Creating alternate versions of a test creates some other problems. First, the time and cost involved in developing one form of a test or questionnaire is large and therefore for many test developers, the costs associated with an alternate version can be prohibitive. Second, equivalency is nice in theory but is challenging to achieve (Anastasi & Urbina, 1997). Even though the two forms may contain an equal number of items, the same instructions, and the same overall content, they may differ at the level of item interpretation. For example, form A of a depression questionnaire might have an item such as, "How often do you feel sad?" and form B might ask, "How often do you feel down?" For some, the words *down* and *sad* connote the same feeling; for others, something very different. If the two versions of the same questionnaire contained these types of item differences, would they really be equivalent? Given these limitations with alternate forms of a test, a third method for determining reliability was developed.

SPLIT-HALF RELIABILITY   Rather than relying on two administrations of the same test or developing parallel forms, reliability can be calculated by using one test and splitting it in half. This approach is not used frequently, but it is covered here because you might hear the term used at some time, so you should be familiar with it. This time the two variables being correlated are scores on part 1 and scores on part 2 for a group of individuals. If you recall, the definition of reliability includes the concepts of stability over time and consistency. By using one test and one administration of the test, the issue of temporal stability is resolved. A very common way to split a test in half is odd versus even items. This procedure works well with lengthy tests that assess an ability or aptitude such as math skills. However, it is not well suited for many of the assessment measures covered in this text because there may only be one item covering a particular symptom, attitude, or behavior, and therefore the content of the even items may be appreciably different than the odd items. Another way to split the test might be randomly. That is, all the items are placed, randomly, into one half or the other. Regardless of how the test is split in half, two parallel tests have been created and the calculation of reliability is the same as described earlier with the Pearson formula. A problem that arises with the split-half method is that reliability is affected by test length, and therefore a split-half reliability would be a much lower estimate of reliability than a method that calculated reliability with twice as many items. The Spearman–Brown formula, discussed later in this chapter, was developed to mathematically account for the reliability reduction when splitting a test in half.

INTERNAL CONSISTENCY—RELIABILITY   Another way to measure the consistency of a test is to calculate the inter-item correlations. Like with split-half reliability, one test is given to a group, but rather than comparing scores from one half versus another half, the individuals' consistency in responses to all the items is calculated (Anastasi & Urbina, 1997). Two formulas have been developed for calculating a test's internal consistency reliability. One formula for calculating internal consistency reliability was developed by Cronbach (1951). Cronbach's method, or **alpha coefficient**, applies to tests where the items have multiple possible responses. Most of the personality and diagnostic questionnaires counselors work with do not have right or wrong or pass–fail items. Instead they contain items where the person taking the questionnaire rates the frequency of the item (e.g., "rarely" to "always") or contains a Likert scale indicating degree of agreement with the item (e.g., "strongly disagree" to "strongly agree"). Cronbach's alpha coefficient is the most common form of internal consistency reliability counselors and other helping professionals are likely to see in test manuals or reported in research studies. This statistic is a ratio of the variance of all the test items to the average variance or standard deviation for the test. One way to judge a test's or measure's reliability is by its alpha coefficient. Alpha coefficients should be 0.70 at a minimum, and 0.90 or higher is now considered excellent (Hunsley & Mash, 2008). Many of the standardized measures available meet this benchmark. Cronbach demonstrated mathematically that the coefficient alpha is equal to the mean of all the possible ways to split a test in half. Another internal consistency reliability formula is the Kuder and Richardson (1937), which applies only to tests whose items have a right or wrong answer, like an intelligence test or a personality test like the *Minnesota Multiphasic Personality Inventory* (MMPI), where items are responded to as true or false. When the items on the test are relatively homogeneous (e.g., all items have to do with depression symptoms), then the test's reliability will be higher than tests that have fairly heterogeneous items. That is because people are more likely to respond in a consistent fashion when being asked questions about similar things, for example depression symptoms, than when being asked about different concepts on the same test, for example depression, psychotic thinking, and phobias. When tests have multiple dimensions or factors it is common that both overall test internal consistency (alpha coefficient) is documented, as well as the alpha coefficients for each separate factor.

Standard Error of Measurement

Classical test theory, the model upon which most traditional psychological tests are built, postulates that an individual's test score is equal to the true score plus or minus test error (Anastasi & Urbina, 1997). The true score is theoretically how much of an ability, trait, or characteristic the person is believed to possess. Tests that have small error variance or standard error of measurement associated with them are considered to be more stable, consistent, and reliable. Classical test theory is one of two models for building tests; the other is item response theory (IRT). The nature of IRT and its practical applications with relatively new tests will be taken up in the final chapter.

The standard error of measurement (SEM) provides a way of interpreting an individual's score on a test given the reliability of a test. The standard error of measurement and reliability are inversely related—the higher the reliability, the lower the standard error. This relationship can be seen with the formula for the SEM:

$$SEM = SD\sqrt{1 - r}$$

In this formula *SD* again stands for the standard deviation, and *r* the reliability of a test for the group of individuals those two statistics are based on. Since no test is perfectly reliable (i.e., *r* is always some value less than one), there will always be some error in an individual's score, as was pointed out earlier. If we could have an individual take the test many times, we would have a range of scores surrounding the "true" score and therefore the SEM could be thought of as the theoretical average score for an individual if we had the ability to test that person over and over. Since that is not feasible, the SEM provides an upper and lower limit for an individual's score. For example, if Bill's test score is 100 and the SEM is 5, then Bill's "true" score is *likely* to be between 95 and 105. How likely depends on how confident you want to be about what Bill's true score is. If we assume we test Bill hundreds of time, then his scores are likely to be distributed along a normal curve. As Figure 6.1 from Chapter 6 illustrated, 68% of a range of normally distributed scores fall within one standard deviation. Therefore, we can say that there is a 68% likelihood that Bill's score is somewhere between 100 plus or minus one SEM. That same figure tells us there is a 99.7% probability that his score is somewhere between 100 plus or minus 3 SEM.

In summary, the reliability coefficient is a statistic that allows us to compare tests in terms of their internal consistency or stability, and the SEM associated with a given test provides a range in which the individual's true score falls. The magnitude of the SEM for any particular test will be dictated by the size of the reliability coefficient, which is based on one sample of scores.

Factors Affecting Reliability

The magnitude of a reliability coefficient can be affected primarily by the variability or range of scores and the number of items on a test. When the range of scores is restricted or is narrow, correlation coefficients tend to be very low. If you go back and look at Figure 7.1, you perhaps can understand why that is. If all the scores on at least one of the two variables is clustering around one score, then a horizontal line, rather than an ellipse, is formed—and as noted earlier, the correlation will be closer to zero. In general, a wide range of scores is more likely to occur on any given test the more heterogeneous the group is in terms of ability, personality, or psychiatric symptoms. When reliability coefficients are calculated from a sample that is fairly homogenous (e.g., middle class Caucasian females ages 40–50), the correlation in general will be smaller because similar people are more apt to give similar responses and obtain similar scores, thus reducing the range of scores. Therefore, if a counselor wants to use a test with a group that is more homogenous than the group from which reliability was determined, the reliability of the test for the more homogenous group may be smaller (Anastasi & Urbina, 1997).

In general, as the number of test items increases, the reliability coefficient increases up to a certain limit. As noted earlier, the Spearman–Brown statistical formula was developed for estimating how much larger or smaller a reliability coefficient would become when the number of items on a test is lengthened or reduced. For example, if a new 10-item test to assess obsessive–compulsive disorder was developed and found to have a Cronbach's alpha coefficient of 0.30, the Spearman–Brown formula would estimate the new reliability coefficient to be 0.46 if the number of items on the test was doubled. Therefore, a test's internal consistency reliability can be artificially inflated by asking redundant questions or presenting similar items multiple times.

Although a test developer can establish that a test's reliability—its internal consistency or stability over time—is at an acceptable level, that does not mean that the test is measuring the construct the developer claims it is measuring. That claim will also need to be established empirically.

VALIDITY

Validity refers to "*what* a test purports to measure and *how well* it does it" (Anastasi & Urbina, 1997). Validity is not something inherent in a test, but rather, like reliability, is established by gathering data that compares a group of individuals' performance or responses on a test with some other measure of the behavior, trait, or ability in question. Remember that reliability is concerned with a test's *internal consistency*—how well the test items correlate with one another—or temporal *stability*—how well a group of individuals' performance on the same test administered twice is correlated. Validity, on the other hand, is concerned with looking beyond the test to compare the performance or responses of individuals using two different methods—the test you are trying to validate and a different test or methodology—and compare how much agreement there is between the scores on the two measures. Validity, therefore, can be thought of as a measure of *external consistency*. For example, if a test supposedly measures personality, then it should correlate well with other methods (external to or different from the personality test) for determining one's personality but less so with a theoretically unrelated construct, like intelligence. There is no reason, for example, to suggest that shy people as a group have more or less intelligence than extroverted people. Later in this chapter we will examine the process for evaluating whether or not two methods for assessing the same construct correlate more highly with each other than two measures involving two different constructs, and what those similarities and differences can tell us.

Although there are several methods for determining test validity, the question of a test's validity is typically determined by the strength of a correlation between the test in question and some other measure. In general, a test can have high reliability but low validity; however, the opposite is not true. If a test has "adequate" validity, then high reliability must have been established. Once a particular type of validity has been established, then a clinician, researcher, or test user can make legitimate inferences from the test. Any professional who uses a psychological test or assessment measure has an ethical obligation to know what type of validity has been established for it in order to understand the kinds of reasonable interpretations that can be drawn from the measure. Like reliability, there are various methods for determining validity. The following sections will discuss the three principal types of validity: *content, criterion,* and *construct,* and the chapter will conclude with a discussion of evaluating a test's utility or usefulness in the assessment process.

Content Validity

A question to determine whether a test has **content validity** is, "How representative of the construct are the items on the test?" This type of validity is one that students are routinely concerned about when they take exams. A student may complain that a five-question Theories of Counseling final exam is "not fair" (and perhaps invalid) if the test questions do not appear to represent all the course material and instead cover only the instructor's favorite theories. For the exam to be a legitimate or valid indication of what a student has learned in this hypothetical theories course, the exam should contain questions that would enable the instructor to assess how much knowledge was gained. A psychological test's representativeness is determined by a group of judges with expertise in the test construct, not by a statistical calculation. This is the only method of determining validity that does not involve a correlation coefficient or some other statistical calculation. Experts might be clinicians, teachers, researchers, or anyone else who has considerable knowledge about the subject matter.

Let's consider a questionnaire designed to assess emotional and behavioral disorders in elementary school age children. For the questionnaire to have content validity, the items on the test, as in the previous hypothetical exam, should be both comprehensive and representative of the subject or topic, in this case emotional and behavioral problems in children. The experts who have the task of determining the item or question content on this questionnaire might be child therapists, child development specialists and researchers, or education professionals. They will select items based on a review of the research literature, their clinical or practical experience, or their accumulated knowledge base. Their task would be to evaluate how well the questionnaire items—based on their knowledge of what are considered normal and abnormal behaviors, thoughts, feelings, and characteristics of school-age children—assess emotional and behavioral disorders. For example, items such as "complains of stomachaches," "refuses to go to school," and "has temper tantrums" might be considered valid content for this questionnaire, whereas items involving long division problems, vocabulary definitions, and copying geometric figures might not. The creation and selection of test items is the first in a series of steps aimed at establishing a test's content validity.

The additional steps needed for determining content validity can be illustrated with a group of counselors and mental health experts who want to develop a questionnaire for measuring the therapeutic alliance (see Chapter 14). This group is likely to go through stages of test development in order to come up with the final content for their alliance questionnaire. Once the experts have put together a pool of items or questions, the item pool may be judged by an independent group of experts who decide if the items are relevant to the construct being measured. Items will then be refined, added, or deleted based on the opinions of this other group of experts. The next stage of development and establishing content validity would consist of piloting the questionnaire. The pilot questionnaire would be administered to different groups of people, therapy clients in this case, and further content revision would occur based on the responses from this initial group. These are the broad steps typically taken to establish that a test has content validity.

A related but different concept is face validity. **Face validity** refers to whether or not the items on a test appear to be the types of items that common sense would suggest belong on the test. For example, a questionnaire used in the screening of depression would be considered to have face validity if the items on the questionnaire represented symptoms of depression rather than a personality trait like extraversion. A test, however, does not need to have face validity in order for it to be useful. One of the most widely researched and commonly used personality tests, the MMPI, lacks face validity but is still considered an excellent tool for assessing both psychopathology and personality. Face validity is a desirable feature of tests but not a necessary one. Test publishers and consumers of tests are probably more concerned with face validity than test users because the former are likely to have an easier time accepting a test's legitimacy and purpose if it appears, at least on the surface, like it is measuring what it claims to.

Once the content for a test or questionnaire has been established, the instrument will be administered to groups of people in the hope that it can be a useful diagnostic or predictive tool. A predictive tool is designed to identify those who are likely to develop a disorder, problem, or condition at some later time. The validation procedures for determining whether a test is a useful diagnostic or predictive tool are referred to as *criterion-related* and *construct validity*.

Criterion-Related Validity

As the name implies, the process of establishing **criterion-related validity** involves selecting a criterion by which the test one wants to validate is compared. The criterion could be any type of benchmark: another test, performance of a set of skills, a diagnostic classification, or a set of behavioral observations. When a group of individuals is given the test in need of validation and a criterion measurement is obtained at the same time or shortly thereafter, that process is termed **concurrent validity**. When a group is given the test and at some future date is measured with the criterion, the process is referred to as **predictive validity**. The difference in time between when the two measures are obtained (approximately at the same time or much later) is one way to think of these two types of criterion validity. Another way to think about the distinction between concurrent and prediction validation processes is the difference in objectives. The purpose of establishing concurrent validity for a test is to answer a diagnostic or classification question, for example, "Does John have attention deficit–hyperactivity disorder (ADHD)?" Predictive validity, on the other hand, is concerned with the question "Will John develop ADHD?" A test that has criterion validity does an effective job of *estimating* an individual's performance or status currently, or at some future point, and addresses those two questions that the content validation process does not.

To illustrate the process of establishing concurrent validity for a test, let's look again at the question "Does John have ADHD?" The first step in the validation process would be to develop the content for a new ADHD diagnostic test, using the methodology discussed in the content validity section. Once the content for the new ADHD diagnostic test is established, a criterion against which the ADHD test will be compared is selected. Remember that the criterion could be another questionnaire for assessing ADHD, performance of skills known to be affected by ADHD such as working memory, a set of observations, or any other way of measuring the construct at hand. In this example, the criterion will be the amount of time spent off task during an academic activity such as reading, as observed and measured by the school counselor. The next step would be the data collection process for a large group of individuals. Each individual would have two scores collected on the same day: ADHD test score and time off task. This hypothetical ADHD test contains 30 items and is given to teachers in order to rate a particular student. The total ADHD test score is obtained from the 30 test items classroom teachers were asked to rate students on, averaged over hundreds of students from around the country. Later that day the school counselor observes the same individual whom a teacher had rated and measures the time spent in off-task behavior during reading time. Similarly, this process would be repeated for all of the individual students taking part in this validation project. The final step would involve the calculation of the now familiar Pearson *r*. The formula for calculating the correlation coefficient would be same as the one used for measuring test–retest reliability but now it would be called a **validity coefficient**. In this case, the two variables we would plug into the correlation equation are ADHD test score and time off task. If the test designed to screen for ADHD in elementary school children has concurrent validity, then for the most part children who score high on the test will be the ones who spent a lot of time off task, and the ones who score low on the test (i.e., who are not ADHD) would have had little time off task (see Figure 7.4). The correlation between the hypothetical ADHD test score and time off task is 0.72, a very high validity coefficient.

A similar process would occur for determining the predictive validity of our hypothetical ADHD test. This time, imagine a group of preschool children's parents completing the parent version of the ADHD test for the purpose of determining which of those children is likely to receive a diagnosis of ADHD at some later time. If the test has predictive validity, then it should be reasonably effective at making this judgment or, to put it another way, reasonably effective in estimating who will meet the criterion (i.e., diagnosed with ADHD by some expert). Again, the expert would be someone deemed highly qualified to make diagnoses of ADHD. At some point in the future, the test scores would be compared with diagnostic status: has ADHD, has another disorder, or no disorder present. If this hypothetical ADHD test has predictive validity, then a significant number of the preschool children whose parents rated them as having a number of symptoms and features of ADHD should have received this diagnosis when evaluated by the ADHD diagnostician.

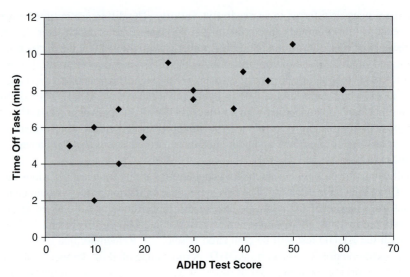

FIGURE 7.4 Criterion Validity

MAGNITUDE OF VALIDITY COEFFICIENTS Validity coefficients are much lower than reliability coefficients and typically range between 0.30 and 0.60 for most psychological tests and measures (Kaplan & Saccuzzo, 2005). Why is it that validity coefficients, despite being calculated using the same correlation statistic as is done with test re–test reliability, tend to be considerably lower in magnitude? Remember that with reliability, the quantitative relationship is between the same test administered twice or two parallel versions of the same test. Therefore, if the test is stable, the test takers' relative rank on both testing times or versions—lowest, highest, middle, and so on—should not change too much. On the other hand, when the relationship between a test and a criterion measure is evaluated, the coefficient will necessarily be lower because the measures are different: teacher rating scale versus observation of time off task. And the difference in measurement methods may mean that factors somewhat different than the construct in question are affecting the obtained scores. In this case, a teacher's rating of a student on ADHD items could be affected by the teacher's response bias (e.g., tends to give all students positive ratings), prior experience with students who tend to get off task, or attitude toward questionnaires in general. In addition, the time spent off task during reading could be due to a number of non-ADHD factors: reading ability, interest level, motivation, time of day, fatigue, and attitude toward reading. Therefore, these non–construct factors will affect one's rank—1st, 2nd, 3rd, and so on—on the two different measures, thereby lowering the magnitude of the coefficient.

There is not a general answer to the question of how high the validity coefficient should be, but the correlation obtained should be statistically significant in the sense that there is a high probability that the correlation is greater than zero. Test manuals and journal articles will typically provide information about the sample and criteria used for establishing a validity coefficient. The magnitude of the validity coefficient will be influenced by several factors, including the reliabilities of both the test and the criterion and the range of scores in both variables. As mentioned earlier with reliability, the more heterogeneous the group is, the wider the range of scores. So, the more heterogeneous the validation group is, the greater the likelihood of obtaining a higher validity coefficient (Kaplan & Saccuzzo, 2005).

To conclude, however, that a test has a high or low degree of validity is misleading (Gay & Airasian, 2003). Rather, a test is valid for a particular kind of interpretation (e.g., who will benefit from psychotherapy?) and is specific to the group tested (e.g., community mental health center clients). Even tests having relatively low validity coefficients may have a useful, practical purpose in clarifying a diagnosis. The decision to use a psychological test depends upon consideration of several factors, but primarily is based on what additional information can be gained from it, and at what cost to the client and counselor. A cost–benefit decision analysis for test selection will be discussed shortly.

CRITERION SELECTION AND BIAS   Selecting a criterion variable from which one will compare a score on a psychological test is a challenge. In the previous example, time on task seems like an appropriate criterion to compare our hypothetical ADHD test given that individuals with ADHD have difficulty sustaining their attention. But which task *should* we use as our criterion measure: reading, solving math problems, participating in class discussion, playing at recess? And who will observe the child and how will time on task be determined? The amount of time spent on the task might be very different if it involves completing math problems at a desk versus completing a math game on the computer. Furthermore, the person observing and measuring time on task needs to do so in an objective, unbiased fashion. Different factors could unwittingly impact the observer's ability to measure time off task. One biasing factor would be prior knowledge of the child being observed. Knowledge of the student's test results (i.e., is or is not ADHD), could certainly influence the observer's measurement. As was discussed in Chapters 1 and 5, a substantial body of social psychological research has demonstrated that both laypersons and trained professionals, when judging or evaluating someone else's behavior, unconsciously employ specific types of biased strategies. One such bias that was previously discussed is a confirmatory bias, otherwise known as a self-fulfilling prophecy. When an individual has a hypothesis, in this case child A has ADHD, the unconscious tendency is to look for data that support or confirm that hypothesis and not assimilate data that would support a counter idea: child A is normal. In addition, the observer's measurement of off-task behavior could be flawed or error laden if he or she lacks an understanding as to what constitutes off-task behavior. Is off-task behavior limited to eye movements away from the task, motor movement irrelevant to the task, or something else entirely? Needless to say, systematically measuring some criterion against which a test will be validated can be an endeavor as equally challenging as test development.

As the above example suggests, criterion validation is a complex process. It can also be a synergistic process. The correlation between a criterion and a test can reveal something about the criterion, the test, or both, and the information gained, the validation coefficient, can be the impetus for further refinement of the test and construct. The refined test can then be correlated once again with the original or another criterion measure, creating an ongoing feedback loop of test refinement, leading to more validation studies and back again to test refinement. Common criterion measures in the field of counseling can include expert's or clinician's judgment, another test measuring the same construct but in a slightly different way, job or task performance (e.g., supervisor ratings of basic counseling skills), and contrasted groups. Using contrasted groups as the criterion measure has been typical in the development of personality and vocational tests. The contrasted group's validation process consists of comparing scores of two select groups: one that theoretically should possess more of the aptitude, skill set, or trait that the test is supposedly measuring, and an alternative group that is likely to have less of the trait or aptitude. For example, a new test designed to measure introversion and extraversion might be examined by giving it to two different groups. The first would consist of college students that common sense might suggest would be high in extraversion, given their jobs or roles: sorority and fraternity leaders. Their scores on the extraversion test should be higher than scores of the contrasting group—students who elected to live in a single room dorm and are probably more introverted. If that is the case, then a study like that would lend support to the test's validity as a measure of introversion and extraversion. The test gains credibility or criterion validity if the contrasting groups do indeed score differently and in the direction the theory would predict: people who affiliate with social organizations and take on a leadership role are more extraverted than those who prefer solitary living arrangements. If that is not the case, then perhaps the test is not a valid measure of this particular personality trait, or maybe it is but the study was flawed in some way. Perhaps students who elect to live in single dorm rooms at the college selected for this fictional study turn out, contrary to the theory, to be very gregarious.

Construct Validity

The third type of validity that can characterize a test or assessment measure is **construct validity**. As discussed in Chapter 6, a construct is a theoretical or hypothetical trait, ability, or condition such as intelligence or depression. Construct validity addresses the following questions: 1) Does this test or questionnaire measure the construct of interest? 2) How well does it measure the construct? 3) What can the scores on the test tell us about an individual? Now you might be thinking those questions are similar to the ones posed when content and criterion validity were examined, and that the previous example regarding personality and living arrangement was also about construct validity. If those thoughts did pop into your head, then you have followed this discussion and you are onto something. At the end of this chapter, we will return to the discussion of whether *construct* validity is a distinct type of validity or an overarching unifying concept.

CONVERGENT AND DISCRIMINANT VALIDITY   For almost 50 years, the gold standard for establishing construct validity for any assessment measure has been the "multitrait–multimethod" process described in a groundbreaking article by Donald Campbell and Donald Fiske (1959) and influenced the multimethod, multisource assessment process described in Chapter 1. Campbell and Fiske argued that test developers should provide evidence for both *convergent* and *discriminant* validity. **Convergent validity** occurs when one method, such as self-report questionnaires, for measuring the same construct (e.g., depression) are highly correlated. **Discriminant validity** occurs when two theoretically unrelated constructs (e.g., depression and intelligence) have little or no correlation. Individuals with a high level of intelligence as measured with a traditional standardized intelligence test (see Chapter 13) should be both depressed and not depressed since there is no theoretical or empirical evidence that those two constructs are related. This might not be the case if we were correlating emotional intelligence and depression, however. According to the multitrait–multimethod approach, a minimum of two correlations would be needed before a test developer could claim evidence of construct validity. Better yet, Campbell and Fiske argued, was the collection of a group of correlations for the establishment of construct validity for a given test.

To illustrate this process, let's imagine that clinicians and researchers are dissatisfied with existing depression measures because they believe they don't adequately measure depression in the way it presents in clinical settings. To remedy this problem, a research group develops a new depression questionnaire, NDQ for short. In order for them to assert that the NDQ actually measures depression, they need to obtain a series of correlations between the NDQ and other methods for measuring depression. Table 7.2 illustrates the multitrait–multimethod approach

Table 7.2 Multitrait–Multimethod Matrix Example						
Traits	**Method 1 (Self-Report 1)**		**Method 2 (Self-Report 2)**		**Method 3 (Inkblot Test)**	
	A_1	B_1	A_2	B_2	A_3	B_3
A_1 (Dep.)	(0.85)					
B_1 (Psy.)	0.23	(0.81)				
A_2	**0.58**	0.18	(0.71)			
B_2	0.20	**0.31**	0.18	(0.71)		
A_3	**0.40**	0.10	**0.35**	0.15	(0.75)	
B_3	0.11	**0.45**	0.11	**0.38**	0.12	(0.78)

In this example, Trait A is depression (dep.) and Trait B is psychosis (psy.). The numbers in parentheses along the main diagonal are reliability coefficients. The boldfaced numbers are convergent validity coefficients (same trait, different method) and the remaining numbers are the discriminant validity coefficients (different traits measured with different methods).

Campbell and Fiske developed for demonstrating a test's construct validity. As Table 7.2 illustrates, the highest correlations obtained are those that are in parentheses because they are the reliability coefficients. They represent reliability coefficients because the correlation is about the measure itself (i.e., internal consistency), not a correlation between one test and another method for measuring the construct. The next highest correlation should be between the NDQ and some other validated method for measuring depression (e.g., the *Beck Depression Inventory–II*). Since these two methods are similar, the correlation between the NDQ and the BDI should be even higher than the correlation between the NDQ and a very different methodology for assessing depression (e.g., responses to an ink-blot test such as the Rorschach). In Table 7.2 these are the boldface numbers, which represent convergent validity coefficients. Other methods for assessing depression not included in Table 7.2 might be behavioral data (e.g., people spoken to at a party) or a counselor rating method such as the *Hamilton Rating Scale*. The remaining task would be to correlate the NDQ with an unrelated construct such as psychosis. If the different trait and different method correlations are lower than the boldface correlations, then there would be evidence of discriminant validity since, theoretically, different traits should be less correlated than the measures of the same trait. Inspection of Table 7.2 finds this to be the case. Now the research team would have both convergent and discriminant validity for the NDQ and therefore adequate construct validity. That is, this group of correlations provides evidence that the NDQ is a measure of depression and not some other psychiatric condition.

This discussion of construct validity brings us back to reliability. Another way to think about the relationship between reliability and construct validity is to think of the NDQ and the BDI as being analogous to parallel or alternative forms of the same test since they are both depression measures using the same method, client self-report. Correlation coefficients, whether we call them validity or reliability coefficients, are mathematically the same. Therefore, two different depression tests are like equivalent forms of the same test, so in this sense the process for establishing reliability and convergent validity are the same. So, rather than being distinct measurement processes we can think of them as being on a continuum with reliability at one end and discriminant validity at the other end (Anastasi & Urbina, 1997).

CONSTRUCT VALIDITY WITH TREATMENT GROUPS   Another method for gathering evidence of a test's construct validity is through some type of intervention or treatment. A group of individuals could show changes in test scores if they have undergone a treatment that is known to impact the construct of interest. This can be illustrated with our hypothetical depression questionnaire and an intervention such as cognitive–behavioral therapy (CBT), which has been shown to be an effective treatment for depression (Beck, 1995). A group of individuals screened for signs of depression would randomly be assigned to either receive CBT or a wait-list condition. Both groups would be given the NDQ before treatment or wait-listing begins, and assessed with the NDQ and an already-validated depression screening tool, like the BDI, when treatment ends. For purposes of illustration, let us assume that the NDQ is really measuring only depressive thinking, not the biological symptoms of depression. The scores from the screening tool and the NDQ could then be correlated. Even though the individuals assigned to the wait-list condition might report fewer physiological depression symptoms after a period of time, they are less likely than the CBT group to report changes in depressive cognitions with simply the passage of time. Therefore, if the NDQ was conceptualized as a measure of only depressive cognitions, the CBT group should report lower scores on the questionnaire following treatment than the wait-list individuals do. If the NDQ and BDI scores are correlated and the group receiving CBT shows significantly lower scores than the wait-list group on the NDQ following treatment, further evidence that the NDQ is indeed measuring depression, or at least the cognitive component of it, has been obtained.

Factor Analysis

Some developers of psychological tests establish construct validity through a sophisticated statistical procedure called factor analysis. A psychological construct could conceivably have multiple dimensions or factors to it or could have just a unitary dimension. Factors are more specific aspects of the overall construct. For example, we might think of the overall construct, depression, as consisting of multiple subfactors: negative moods, negative thoughts, and physiological symptoms. Factor analysis is a complex process by which a correlation matrix is developed from either a group of tests or all of the items on a test. In the first case, a group of tests is correlated and those items from the different tests that are shown to correlate relatively highly with one another are grouped together as a factor. This can be illustrated with four depression measures (see Chapter 9): *Beck Depression Inventory-II, Hamilton Depression Rating Scale, Reynolds Depression Screening Inventory, Quick Inventory of Depressive Symptomatology–Self-Rated.* Those four depression measures could be given to a group of 100 individuals and each test would then be correlated with one another. Since each test is measuring slightly different aspects of depression, the inter-test correlations might reveal the factors suggested above.

More technical forms of factor analysis have been developed for mathematically analyzing the relationship between each item on a test and an item's relationship to a subtest or the overall test score. Using a statistical software program, correlation tables are generated from all possible inter-item correlations and the item–scale correlation. Rather than computing a correlation between two tests, a correlation between individual items or between an item and a scale or subtest is calculated. Those items that correlate relatively highly with one another are grouped together as a factor or subcategory of the overarching trait the test claims to measure. The factor is then given a label based on the correlated items comprising it. Factor analytic research was done multiple times with the *Children's Depression Inventory* (CDI) using different statistical procedures (Kovacs, 1992). Those studies reveal that the CDI consists of five factors: Negative Mood,

Interpersonal Problems, Ineffectiveness, Anhedonia, and Negative Self-esteem (Kovacs). Keep in mind that the items chosen for the factors are based on statistical analysis: they are shown to correlate relatively highly with one another and not as much with items on the other factors. But ultimately the choice of factor label is up to the discretion of the test developer. Someone else looking at the items that clustered together on the scale labeled Negative Mood might have called it, for example, Sadness.

To put it another way, factor analysis is a fancy statistical technique for demonstrating convergent and discriminant validity. An excellent example of the use of factor analysis to establish construct validity was conducted with the development of the *Child Behavior Checklist* (CBCL) (Achenbach & Rescorla, 2001). (See Chapter 10 for a fuller discussion of the CBCL and its construction.) The CBCL consists of two large constructs (i.e., factors): internalizing and externalizing. Within each of the two main factors are several subfactors or scales. The items that comprise the CBCL internalizing scale have a relatively high correlation with each other, convergent validity, but the internalizing items show significantly lower correlations with the externalizing items, discriminant validity.

TEST UTILITY AND SELECTION

Another way to think about what a validity coefficient can tell us is the degree to which a test can account for, or predict, the variance or a range of scores in some criterion measure. The amount of shared variance between two variables—the predictor and the criterion—is determined by squaring the correlation coefficient. A squared correlation coefficient is referred to as the **coefficient of determination**. This concept can be illustrated with two variables such as client's therapeutic alliance rating and counselor's therapy outcome rating. The client rating of the therapeutic alliance (on a scale from 1 to 36 with 1 meaning an extremely weak alliance and 36 indicating a very strong alliance) is the predictor variable in this example. Counselor rating of therapy outcome (1 = no improvement, 2 = little improvement, 3 = some improvement, 4 = improvement, and 5 = much improvement) is the criterion variable. Imagine, based on a number of research studies, if this hypothetical therapeutic alliance questionnaire was found to have a construct validity coefficient of 0.60, which is at the high end of most validity coefficients, then we could say that 36% (0.6 squared) of the range of therapy outcome scores is based on the range of therapeutic alliance scores What other factors besides a client's rating of the therapeutic alliance could account for the degree of improvement in therapy? There could be any number of client factors—chronicity and severity of the presenting problem, client support system, previous therapy experience, to name just a few—and treatment factors—length of treatment, type of therapy, counselor experience. All of these factors could contribute to a particular client's outcome in therapy, to lesser or greater degrees. In this example, 64% (100 minus 36) of the range of outcome scores is related to these other factors.

Ultimately, as counseling professionals we want to know how useful a test is in making predictions about whether someone has a status or diagnosis, such as successful, depressed, learning disabled, and so on, or will achieve a certain outcome, such as symptom improvement, pass a course, or develop a diagnosis. To put it another way, how much error will result when trying to predict a criterion score from a test score? Another example illustrating test utility that might be familiar to you is a test that predicts graduate school grade point average when applying for candidacy. The hypothetical test we will call the GSE (Graduate-school Success Exam) measures things like critical thinking skills, interpersonal skills, and quantitative reasoning and is given to students prior to entering graduate school. The relationship between the predictor score (GSE) and the criterion (GPA at candidacy) can be defined mathematically and is called the **standard error of estimate** (σ_{est}). The formula for the standard error of estimate is:

$$\sigma_{est} = SD_y \sqrt{1 - (r_{xy})^2}$$

In order to decipher this formula, let's look closely at the part involving the square root. The predictor test is symbolized by x and the criterion is symbolized by y. If there was a perfect correlation between x and y (GSE and GPA when applying for candidacy), then r equals 1.0, and 1 minus 1 is zero. Therefore, the σ_{est} = zero—that is, there is no error associated with predicting candidacy GPA from the GSE. But when it comes to psychological variables, perfect relationships do not exist. No matter how good our GSE is, it would never predict with 100% accuracy who will be selected for candidacy and who will not. So let's look at the standard error of estimate using a more realistic but relatively high validity coefficient, 0.6. With a correlation of 0.6, $1 - 0.6^2 =$ 0.64, and the square root of 0.64 = 0.8. This means that our standard error or estimate is now 80% as large as it would be by randomly guessing GPA scores. That means that if we wanted our test to predict who would be successful in graduate school in terms of future GPA, the GSE would only be 20% better than a prediction of which entering students will be successful in graduate school at the time of candidacy and which will not. Furthermore, this hypothetical test may not tell us anything about final grade point status let alone what you might think of as other more valid success criteria. Now having seen the math, one might wonder, why bother? That really depends upon the reason you are choosing to use a test—to aid in diagnosis or selection or facilitating a prediction—and whether the benefit (i.e., improvement in diagnostic or predictive accuracy) is worth the cost in terms of time, money, and other resources. It also depends upon whether the test is going to be used as a single predictor of future status or outcome or whether it will be combined with other tests or assessment measures in order to make more accurate predictions.

Sensitivity and Specificity

Two complementary terms that also reveal a test's utility are **sensitivity** and **specificity**. Both terms are expressed as percentages. Sensitivity refers to a test's ability to accurately predict whether or not an individual has a condition or disorder (e.g., high blood pressure or depression). A test wrongly identifying someone as having the condition is called a **false positive**. Specificity, on the other hand, refers to a test's ability to correctly identify an individual as not having the condition. A test inaccurately identifying someone as not having the condition or disorder, who indeed has it, is called a **false negative**. Determining a test's sensitivity and specificity is necessary if a test is going to be used for screening purposes. If a test is going to be used to screen for the presence of disorder, such as depression, then cutoff scores will be used to determine whether the disorder is present. A cutoff score is the score that differentiates disorder from nondisorder. Cutoff scores will affect sensitivity and specificity ratios simultaneously because they are complementary concepts. As the cutoff score is lowered, the test has greater sensitivity because more people will be identified as positive, or having the condition, but so will the false positive rate. Conversely, raising the cutoff score has the opposite effect, increasing specificity but increasing the likelihood of false negatives. Therefore, depending upon the researcher's or practitioner's goal, cutoff scores can be adjusted in order to make the test more or less sensitive and specific. If having more false positives is less of a concern than having false negatives, then the cutoff score will be set in a way to minimize false negatives. In the case of a test predicting postpartum depression, for example, it may be more problematic to have the test miss those who are depressed (false negatives) than it would be to wrongly label a nondepressed person as depressed (false positive) because the consequence of missing depression and not treating it might be greater than calling someone depressed who really isn't. If, on the other hand, a test is being used to screen applicants for a job, then minimizing false positives might be of more value from the employer's perspective. The employer is probably less concerned about false negatives, screening out people who might later prove to have the condition, job success, than false positives—identifying too many people as job successes who turn out to be poor employees. Test manuals of psychological tests used for diagnostic purposes will sometimes include sensitivity and specificity percentages for different cutoff scores. Those scores are another way to judge the validity of the test. A test that is very sensitive and specific is one that also possesses a high degree of validity.

Decision Theory

The final decision to use or not use a test or questionnaire as part of the assessment process depends not only on our purpose but on two other psychometric concepts—*base rates* and *incremental validity*. **Base rates** refer to the percentage of individuals in a population who have a characteristic, or condition, such as high blood pressure or suicide attempts. When base rates are below 50%, then the predictive power of a test is greatly diminished (Wiggins, 1973). **Incremental validity** refers to the increase in accuracy of a prediction when two or more tests or other assessment methods are used in combination.

The decision to use a particular test can be illustrated with the serious and often anxiety-provoking challenge of predicting who is at risk for suicide. One factor that should influence the decision to use a test is the concept of base rates. Most of the disorders that counselors treat have base rates well below 50%, and the base rate for suicide completers can be less than 1%, depending on the population demographic. Therefore, if we have a test of suicide risk (see Chapter 11) and are trying to classify people in the general population as high or low risk, our test is not likely to be particularly helpful. That is because 99% of the general population will not attempt suicide and therefore if we were to predict that an individual is not going to attempt suicide, we would be correct almost every time, even without a test. If, however, we want to assess the risk for a group of clients found to have a base rate of suicide attempts close to 50%, as is the case with childhood victims of sexual abuse (Linehan, 1993), a suicide attempter prediction test will potentially be a more helpful tool than relying solely on clinical judgment.

CASE EXAMPLE USING DECISION THEORY

Juanita, a 27-year-old mother of two children, ages 2 and 4, comes to a mental health clinic upon her primary care doctor's referral after he prescribed an antidepressant to her. Juanita tells the counselor she is feeling lousy, down, and bored. She has been having trouble sleeping and difficulty enjoying playtime with her children.

Juanita and the children's father, Mark, separated two months ago. The separation followed Mark's arrest for assault and driving under the influence of alcohol. Juanita is enrolled in an associate's degree program. Her mother and stepfather live in Puerto Rico. An older sister lives in the same town as Juanita.

The mental health counselor assessing Juanita was concerned about her suicide risk given her presenting problems and background information. She wanted to assess Juanita's level of risk (see Chapter 11) by asking her a series of questions: "Are you having thoughts of wanting to kill yourself today?" "Have you ever had thoughts of wanting to kill yourself?" "Have you ever attempted to kill yourself?" Based on Juanita's answers of no current suicidal thoughts but a history of suicidal ideation and an overdose attempt one year ago, the interviewer remained uncertain as to Juanita's level of risk and wanted to further assess her risk. She chose the *Beck Scale for Suicide Ideation* (BSSI) because of its high reliability and adequate validity for assessing suicide risk particularly among community mental health clients diagnosed with depression (Knock, Wedig, Belle Janis, & Deliberto, 2008). Furthermore, the counselor understood that the base rate for suicide attempts is much greater among a group of psychiatric clients than among the general population. Although the BSSI cannot conclusively predict who will attempt suicide (nor can any test for that matter), the counselor was able to use both the information gained from the interview questions along with the BSSI responses and score to develop a helpful risk management plan. Because the test, the BSSI, was not being used to predict future status (i.e., will or will not attempt suicide), but rather for treatment planning purposes, its use in the assessment process had some degree of benefit beyond what interview alone could provide. That was because the BSSI provided information about risk factors that the interview did not, and those factors were worked on in subsequent counseling sessions.

Incremental Validity

As noted earlier, *incremental validity* refers to the increase in accuracy of a prediction when two or more tests or other methods are used in combination to make a decision: hire or not hire a job applicant, accept or reject a school candidate, diagnosis with a disorder or not. It is perhaps the most important validity concept for counselors conducting assessments. When multiple tests or methods (e.g., an interview and a questionnaire) are used together to predict a criterion (e.g., a clinical diagnosis), they are referred to as a test or **assessment battery**. For example, imagine being faced with the basic task of determining a diagnosis for a client you are assessing for an initial counseling interview. At the end of the interview you remain uncertain about your client's diagnosis. Now what? Will you conduct another interview? Whom will you interview: the client, a family member, or someone else? Will you administer a questionnaire? Or will you consider referring the client for a personality test? You want to be both efficient and accurate in your diagnosis in order to arrive at a treatment plan. Therefore, you need to consider how much more information will be gained and how much more certainty will be achieved with additional assessments procedure: testing, interviewing, or observing.

In theory, having multiple information-gathering procedures should increase a counselor's predictive ability, especially if each procedure provides a unique data set. This premise rests on two basic assumptions. The two assumptions underlying a multimethod process are 1) the clinician can integrate large amounts of information, and 2) reliability and accuracy are gained as more and more pieces of information become available (Wiggins, 1973). These rationales for using multiple assessment procedures, whether it's for the purpose of increased diagnostic or predictive accuracy, have at times not been supported by research. Wiggins reviewed three studies that demonstrated that these two basic assumptions are not always supported and, in fact, sometimes diagnostic accuracy will be reduced, not improved, when multiple methods are used. He went on to conclude, "…the relationship between amount of input data and accuracy of clinical judgments does not always hold…" and that "individual differences will be found among clinicians, both in their accuracy and in the manner in which they utilize specific input variables [i.e., assessment methods] for specific patients" (Wiggins, p. 142).

A sophisticated statistical procedure, **multiple regression**, has been used for making clinical predictions based on multiple "input" variables or data. Multiple regression is a kind of correlational analysis where the input variables are assigned numerical weights based on research and a criterion score for an individual is produced. Essentially, the weights for each test are determined by two factors: the correlation between the variable and the criterion, and the correlation between the variables. A test that correlates most highly with the criterion and very little with other tests is given a higher weight because it is in theory providing unique information and is related to the criterion or outcome variable. For example, the input data for a regression equation could be demographic information, such as gender and age; a score from a questionnaire, like the BSSI; and a DSM diagnosis based on a clinical interview. The output for the equation would be some criterion, such as level of suicide risk. If a multiple regression analysis produced a strong correlation between this combination of input variables and the criterion, then those would be the variables a counselor would want to consider in making assessment decisions, in this case about suicide risk. The statistical calculations in multiple regression analyses are complex and the interested reader can consult a statistics text for more information. Although the math is complex, this type of statistical analysis provides a quantitative method for combining different pieces of information about an individual in order to make a prediction.

Controversy and debate over who is better at combining data and making predictions, the clinician or the statistician, has riven the assessment field (Dawes, 1994) ever since psychologist Paul Meehl (1954) first raised the provocative question. Either/or arguments and questions are not particularly helpful in counseling, in general, and in assessment in particular. A more useful series of questions can be considered: Under what circumstances might clinical judgment alone be more beneficial than statistical judgment? Under what circumstances might statistical judgment be more beneficial? And when would the combination of approaches best serve the client?

In essence, incremental validity involves a cost–benefit analysis. What is the cost, not just in monetary terms, but in time and psychological impact on the client, each time another method is added to the assessment process? A guiding ethical principal of the American Counseling Association and American Psychological Associations codes of ethics is beneficence—the acknowledgment that our actions and words contribute to the positive welfare of our clients. Therefore, we do not want to unnecessarily burden our clients because doing so would be antithetical to the spirit of beneficence. Furthermore, Section E of the ACA Code of Ethics states, "The primary purpose of educational, psychological, and career assessment is to provide measurements that are valid and reliable in either comparative or absolute terms." This guideline pertains both to specific tests and the validity of the overall assessment process when multiple measures are combined. If, however, the consequence of a diagnosis is restraint of freedom, a client is hospitalized, or a powerful psychotropic medication is started, then having a multi-method assessment process whereby diagnostic accuracy can be improved is critical.

Summary and Conclusions

Reliability and validity are two complementary foundational measurement concepts that guide the development and use of psychological tests, questionnaires, or rating scales. Reliability is a measure of the stability of a set of scores a group of individuals obtains on the same test given twice over some specified interval, or the consistency of their scores when given equivalent forms of the test, or the inter-item correlations within the test. Validity refers to what a test claims to measure and how well it does

that. By definition, a test that has adequate validity must have high reliability, but a test can be found to be very reliable but not valid.

The different types of reliability and validity and the procedures for establishing them were examined in this chapter. An understanding of the correlation coefficient statistical formula is essential for understanding all forms of reliability and almost all forms of validity. A correlation coefficient quantifies the degree to which two variables (e.g., test scores) are related, and reliability and validity are expressed as correlation coefficients. Although different types of validity were discussed—content, criterion, and construct—Anastasi (1988) made the case that construct validity can be thought of as an umbrella term encompassing the other forms of validity since at its core, validation procedures are always about establishing evidence for a particular theoretical construct like intelligence, personality, or deviance. Because construct validity is concerned with whether or not a test is measuring the construct it claims to measure, evidence in support of a test's validity is an ongoing, multistep process, with each step providing more or less empirical support for the construct.

In order for a psychological test to be accepted, a test developer needs to demonstrate the test's reliability and validity. In addition, test users have an ethical obligation to use only those tests and procedures that have been shown to have adequate levels of both reliability and validity. Simultaneously, as assessors we need to not place undue importance on standardized tests. Just because a theoretical construct can be reliably measured and validated does not make the test measuring the construct a more accurate or useful assessment method than a nonstandardized method like a clinical interview. A standardized test is another assessment tool, albeit a potentially very beneficial one, to be included in the mix of methods.

Reflection Questions and Experiential Exercises

1. What do you think might be examples of counseling tests that are positively correlated?
2. What might be different criteria against which a questionnaire to assess one or multiple psychiatric conditions could be validated?
3. Why are reliability coefficients always higher than validity coefficients?
4. Given that any test is a measure of a sample of behavior, what factors might affect a client's behavior when responding to a questionnaire about one's feelings, thoughts, behaviors, or symptoms?
5. Why is internal consistency reliability a more common procedure for estimating a test's reliability than the test–retest method in the counseling field?
6. Select a construct you are interested in learning more about such as self-esteem, anxiety, introversion/extraversion, or anything else. Now find a test or questionnaire that measures that construct and find out a) what type of reliability was measured, b) the size of the reliability coefficient, c) and how validity was determined.
7. In small groups of three to five students, come up with items for a test to screen for readiness for counseling. Once you have the readiness for counseling items, discuss in your group how you would go about establishing reliability and validity for your questionnaire.
8. Select a test or questionnaire you are interested in learning about. What was the demographic and/or cultural makeup of the sample(s) from which the test scores were obtained to calculate the reliability of the test? This information can be found in the test manual or a journal article.
9. Compute a correlation coefficient based on the data in Table 7.1 in the reliability section.

8 PERSONALITY AND INTEREST MEASURES

Chapter Objectives

After reading this chapter, you should be able to:

■ Understand personality theory and methods for constructing personality tests.

■ Identify common objective self-report and projective measures used for personality assessment and understand their advantages and limitations.

■ Understand how the results of a personality test are used for case conceptualization and treatment planning and monitoring purposes.

■ Understand how self-report interest measures are related to personality measures and how they are used in counseling.

Presenting Problem

Nancy, a 35-year-old biracial female, contacted her insurance company in search of clinics in her community. She was experiencing "a lot of stress" and her "old ways of coping" were not working. During an intake interview at a local United Way agency Nancy told the intake clinician that she had lost her "ambition," was feeling "a whole bunch of built-up anger," and had "trouble waking up a lot." She quickly added, "My belief in God keeps me going." She also reported "issues" with her husband who had recently returned from Iraq. Nancy's concerns and problems had been going on for "several months." After exploring Nancy's presenting concerns, Melanie, the intake clinician, obtained the following background information.

Background Information

Nancy is currently in an associate's degree program to become a nurse. In addition to caring for her 2-year-old son, she spends her days studying, reading the Bible, and working with crystals. She has had various jobs over the past two years but has had trouble keeping them due to taking repeated time off to care for her son, who gets sick frequently. Nancy has been married for six years but is socially isolated. She reported having "just" one friend whom she seldom sees. She reported that her husband is drinking more since he got back and has been verbally abusive to her.

Prior to her marriage, Nancy was involved in several relationships, one of which was "abusive." She reported being "raped" at 18 when she was with a group of people who tried to "get me to party." Raised in New Jersey, her parents divorced when she was 6 and she lived mostly with her father and stepmother. She reports that her stepmother was "verbally abusive." Her childhood was also difficult because of being "teased a lot." Nancy has been experiencing flashbacks about the rape and the teasing.

Nancy completed high school and dropped out of college after one semester. She moved to Vermont when she was 24. She has held various jobs, including one as a secretary and another as an assembly worker in a manufacturing plant.

Nancy has a prior mental health history. She was seen in outpatient therapy for two years about four years ago because of feeling "nervous a lot and down." She reports that in high school, "I was anorexic, but got over it on my own." She denies any history of substance usage and does not like taking any kind of medication, preferring "natural treatments."

Mental Status

Client presents as a tall, large-framed female who is wearing no makeup. She displays some restlessness and muscle tension. Her speech is unremarkable. She appears sad and teary when talking about her husband's decision to enlist and is angry that they have not gotten help from the VA. She was well oriented and denied auditory hallucinations but reported seeing "odd shapes" in her home that she thought bothered her. She also reported other unusual beliefs such as having a "sixth sense" and being clairvoyant about her nursing school patients. She reports having special healing powers such as helping a man recover from diabetes by her "touch." She is troubled by "dreams that predict the future" but is "not sure if it is God or my subconscious trying to send me a message."

Psychological Testing

Nancy completed the *Minnesota Multiphasic Personality Inventory-2* (MMPI-2) and was found to have a 6–8 code type. Following two months of individual counseling, she also completed the *NEO-Personality Inventory-R* (NEO-PI-R).

OVERVIEW

Although Nancy's story includes a description of the problems that led her to seek mental health counseling, as well as descriptions of her family, work, and interpersonal history, it does not include discussion of her personality. How would a clinician go about assessing Nancy's personality and how might that personality assessment inform her counseling? Even more fundamentally, what is meant by *personality*? And how are personality and psychopathology related? One way to assess Nancy's personality would be to follow her around and make detailed observations about her behavior in a number of different settings over the course of several weeks. Although this method is comprehensive and perhaps would produce a more accurate picture of her personality than other methods, it is neither practical nor feasible, not to mention that it would be ethically questionable without Nancy's consent. Alternatively, Nancy could complete a personality test, inventory, or rating scale. This methodology for assessing personality contains two categories: objective self-report and projective. Objective self-report tests or measures contain a list of questions or items related to one's behaviors, attitudes, beliefs, feelings, and self-concept, which an individual agrees or disagrees with in some fashion. Projective tests present an individual with some type of ambiguous visual stimulus about which the individual creates a perception. For example, in the Rorschach test, an individual is shown a series of inkblot patterns and is asked what they are meant to be. Both methods have been used by professional counselors and psychologists to understand different aspects of a client's personality.

This chapter introduces the concept of personality assessment. Theories of personality are introduced along with an overview of personality disorders and their relationship to models of "normal" personality. The two main approaches to personality assessment—objective and projective tests—are described but the emphasis is on objective self-report measures. The standardized personality and multidimensional psychopathology measures that will be discussed in-depth include the *Minnesota Multiphasic Personality Inventory-2* (MMPI-2), *Millon Clinical Multiaxial Inventory-III* (MCMI-III), *NEO-Personality Inventory–Revised* (NEO-PI-R), and *Myers-Briggs Type Indicator* (MBTI). This chapter also discusses several commonly used career or vocational interest measures—*Strong Interest Inventory (SII), Self-Directed Search,* and *Kuder Surveys*—and their relationship to personality tests.

A comprehensive discussion of all the existing standardized measures for assessing personality, personality disorders, and multiple dimensions of psychopathology could fill volumes, let alone one chapter. Necessity dictated a limit to the number of measures included in this and subsequent chapters. This primarily examines independently reviewed measures. Independent review means that a researcher or team of researchers other than the original test developer has critically examined the measure. Measures included are those that were found to have acceptable levels of reliability and validity for at least one of the following assessment purposes: diagnostic clarification, case conceptualization, treatment planning, or treatment monitoring.

THE NATURE OF PERSONALITY

How Nancy, the client in the opening case study, experiences emotions and copes with her psychological problems is, in part, a function of her underlying personality traits. Some people are generally optimistic, resilient, assertive, and emotionally stable. Others are emotionally sensitive, pessimistic, and vulnerable. One way to conceptualize personality is that of an underlying psychological structure that disposes an individual to express a pattern of behaviors, thoughts, and emotions (Harkness, 2009). These enduring patterns of behaving and emoting, or traits, get displayed in a variety of settings: home, work or school, community, and social. Furthermore, broad personality types appear to be connected to primary emotional responses according to current personality theory. For example someone like Nancy, who has a "negative emotionality" personality trait, is more prone to experiencing fear, anger, and sadness than one who has a positive emotional trait. There appears to be consensus among psychologists and counselors that individuals indeed have personalities and that the concept of personality is related to but distinct from clinical disorders such as anxiety, depression, or schizophrenia. On the other hand, there is ongoing debate regarding several fundamental aspects of personality: how it is formed, to what extent it causes behavior, its malleability as one ages, the number of traits humans possess, and the names or labels that should be given to these traits (Harkness, 2009; McCrae & Costa, 1997).

The topic of human behavior and personality has been a fascination and focus for philosophers, writers, theologians, doctors, and scientists long before modern assessment tests came into being. Well-developed theories and research into personality within the fields of psychology and counseling are, however, relatively recent endeavors. Many of the major influential counseling theories—psychoanalytic, humanistic, gestalt, and behavioral—have offered descriptions and explanations about the nature of personality. Freud and his followers focused on behavior styles that were characteristic ways of defending against threatening impulses, drives, and thoughts. In his model, different personality styles were a function of the interplay between the ego, superego, and the id. Adler conceived of personality as a lifestyle or plan of life that motivates people to achieve goals. Fritz Pearls, in his gestalt model, conceptualized personality in layers, each of which shaped how emotional experience was expressed. Humanistic theorists such as Carl Rogers were less concerned with personality types and more with how individuals search for meaning in their lives, balance freedom and responsibility, and how one's self-concept is related to an actualizing tendency to achieve psychological growth. Collectively, theories of counseling and psychotherapy have offered general ideas about the nature of the self—how we behave and what motivates us to do what we do—but not specific personality typologies that may be used to describe and predict styles of behaving, functioning, and coping.

Modern Personality Theory: Traits versus States

Current personality assessment is based on the distinction between traits and states. Personality traits are considered enduring and predictable patterns of behavior, emotional experience, and attitudes and values that are exhibited across different situations and settings. Someone who is introverted for example, is likely to behave in a shy reserved, and reflective manner most of the time in many different places. States, on the other hand, are temporary or transient ways of behaving and experiencing emotion that are related to specific situations. Nancy, for example, experiences discrete episodes or states of irritability, anger, and stress. At the same time she might be described as having a neurotic or emotionally unstable trait or, more specifically, an angry hostile personality trait, which suggests she has a tendency to display angry hostile behavior in various situations. Nancy's traits, however, do not guarantee that she will act in an angry hostile way all the time. Someone else who typically acts introverted may, on certain occasions, appear very gregarious, sociable, and outgoing and be in a different state of mind so to speak. Why is that? As best we know, personality traits are somewhat flexible, and traits may represent an end of a continuum that suggests the likelihood of acting, thinking, and emoting with a particular style most but not all of the time. Some researchers, however, particularly those with a behavioral orientation, have taken a radical position and questioned the validity of personality traits as a construct. Their critiques of the concept of personality traits have centered on several fundamental premises of personality theory (Smith & Zapolski, 2009; Wiggins, 1973). One is that trait types are an artifact of the methods for assessing traits and reflect more about the observer or recall biases of the person taking the personality test, than the internal dispositions of that person. Another criticism is the lack of research evidence for trait consistency: little empirical evidence is available regarding the relationship between traits as measured by personality tests and a person's subsequent behavior. A third area of concern is the failure of many traits theorists to consider the impact of environmental factors on behavioral styles. Among those who do accept the idea of personality traits, no consensus exists about how many traits human beings possess and how to characterize and label them. Some models have suggested that humans are comprised of only three, whereas others have suggested as many as 30 fundamental traits. In addition, some personality trait labels, like extraversion, mean different things to different theorists.

Notwithstanding those criticisms and debates, trait models of personality have had a long, rich history since World War I and have shaped the development of current personality tests. The study of personality traits has been linked to two movements in psychology: the study of individual differences and correlational analysis. Like many fields of psychology and counseling, personality assessment has had many important scholars and contributors, but several were key figures. Allport and Odbert (1936) were the first to create a list of trait-like adjectives gathered from *Webster's New International Dictionary* and came up with almost 18,000 words. Theirs was the first attempt to come up with a meaningful but perhaps unmanageable scientific description of personality. That list was later reduced to 4,500 words that could refer to consistent and stable tendencies in people. Various researchers—Cattell (1947), Fiske (1949), Tupes & Christal (1961), and Norman (1963)—attempted to come up with a more manageable and specific personality classification scheme.

Cattell (1947) was the first personality researcher to observe that the same personality factors kept reemerging through different assessment means: laboratory tests, self-report, or rating one's peers. With the Allport and Odert list in hand, Cattell embarked on a series of studies to determine if the number of personality descriptors could be reduced and whether there was evidence of some kind of relationship among the many descriptors. His research was also guided by the work of Robert Woodworth, who developed the Woodworth Personal Data Sheet (see Chapter 1), a tool for screening out "disturbed" men from military service. The list of items on the Woodworth inventory focused on psychiatric symptoms such as fears and phobias, and the individual filling it out would respond either yes or no. Woodworth's inventory, however, was lacking in reliability and statistical techniques for selecting and constructing the items. Cattell in his research applied the newly developed statistical technique of cluster analysis, similar to factor analysis (see Chapter 7), to the list of traits.

Factor analysis became both a procedure for selecting items on personality trait inventories and a method for refining the items (Wiggins, 1973). As you may recall from Chapter 7, the factor analytic approach is a complex statistical process in which a correlation matrix is developed from a group of potential test items. Using a statistical software program, correlation tables are generated from all possible inter-item correlations. The items that tend to correlate and go together with one another comprise a factor or scale for the test. The factor is then given a label based on the correlated items comprising it.

Cattell's analyses resulted in the identification of 36 dimensions of personality that were used to construct 35 rating scales. Each scale measured a bipolar trait along a continuum (Cattell, 1947). One example of a factor was the dimension ranging from "Emotionally Stable" to "Changeable." Emotionally stable individuals were defined as being realistic, dependable, and "without emotional prejudice," whereas changeable individuals were considered "undependable, and sees things in terms of the emotion of the moment" (Cattell, p. 201). Another factor was "Depressed, Solemn" versus "Cheerful," and a third example was "Forthright" versus "Shrewd." His scales were then given to different college, military, and clinical groups and the study participants would then rate a peer whom they knew well in terms of these bipolar traits. Cattell also conceptualized different types of traits: dynamic, ability, and temperament. Ultimately this and other research resulted in the publication of the *Sixteen Personality Factor Questionnaire* (16PF) in 1949, one of the first self-report trait measures (Cattell & Eber, 1972). The 16PF is now in its fifth edition but aside from research purposes is used mostly for vocational and career counseling purposes (see below).

The current trait theory that has received substantial research support for conceptualizing normal personality (McCrae & Costa, 1997) is the current five factor model (FFM). The FFM is the culmination of over 50 years of research and theorizing about normal personality traits (Costa & McCrae,1985; Digman & Takemoto-Chock, 1981; McCrae & Costa, 1997; Norman 1963; Tupes & Christal, 1961). Researchers such as Costa and McCrae (1985) believed that personality theories based solely on analyzing the English language, as was Cattell's, were incomplete. What was needed was a theory that linked traits with behaviors. Their goal was to analyze all of the existing personality assessment measures, looking for common traits and the behavioral correlates of those traits. Initially, they developed a three-dimensional model consisting of three broad traits: Neuroticism, Extraversion, and Openness. *Neuroticism* was considered one end of a dimension, with *emotional stability* at the other end. *Introversion* was thought of as the polar opposite of *extraversion,* and *uncurious or close-minded* as opposed to *openness to experience* was the third factor. Like Cattell's model, these traits were bipolar in nature with the trait labels representing two end points of a personality dimension. Furthermore, each broad dimension contained subdimensions that also were bipolar in nature. The three broad dimensions were also conceptually similar to Norman's view of personality factors, another prolific personality trait researcher. This became the NEO model of personality theory and led to the construction of the *NEO Personality Inventory.* Costa and McCrae (1985), through a longitudinal study that used their NEO inventory and another personality test, identified two other independent dimensions—*Agreeableness* and *Conscientiousness*. They concluded that a five-dimensional or factor model was sufficiently broad in scope, albeit lacking in depth, for classifying human personality. The NEO-PI was later revised to incorporate these two additional factors. The FFM, however, is based on the factor analytic model, which has its own limitations. Detractors argue that the FFM is lacking a coherent theory and testable set of hypotheses (Block, 1995).

Despite that criticism, the five factor model of personality has been shown to have substantial cross-cultural validity (McCrae & Costa, 1997) and is being used as a way to potentially reconceptualize personality disorders in the DSM-5 (Lowe & Widiger, 2008; Miller et al., 2010; Mullins-Sweatt & Widiger, 2006). Its emergence as a generally accepted model of human personality has meant it is influencing the development of new personality measures as well as the revisions of some classics like the MMPI, one of the oldest tests for assessing both personality and psychopathology.

An important unresolved debate in counseling and psychiatry is whether psychopathology represents an extreme personality trait (i.e., a dimensional model of psychopathology) or a separate state (i.e., a categorical model). Psychopathology as an extreme form of a personality trait as contrasted with the concept of pathology belonging to a related but separate category can be illustrated with the following example. Nancy, the client in the case study, scores high on a personality test's measure of "neuroticism." Individuals scoring high on the trait neuroticism tend to experience worrisome thoughts, nervous feelings, and react with strong emotionality in most of their environments: home, work or school, and community. Since the trait neuroticism includes worry and nervous feelings, it might be considered a form of anxiety. Therefore, certain anxiety conditions like generalized anxiety and panic could be conceptualized as a dimension of the trait neuroticism, which ranges from emotional stability at one end of the continuum to high anxiety or panic at the other end. On the other hand, anxiety or panic attacks can be thought of as discrete events or states that can occur regardless of whether individuals are typically emotionally stable or neurotic in their personality. Recent research supports a dimensional model of personality, and suggests that individuals having certain personality traits such as neuroticism are more prone to categories of psychiatric disorders (Lowe & Widiger, 2008; Maddux, Gosselin, & Winstead, 2008). The debate over dimensional versus categorical models of personality traits was not resolved by the time the DSM-IV was published; but for the first time in the DSM system, a brief mention of the dimensional model was presented in the personality disorders section as a topic that "remains under active investigation" (American Psychiatric Association, 1994, p. 634).

Personality Disorders

The *Diagnostic and Statistical Manual of Mental Disorders,* Fourth Edition, Text Revision (DSM-IV-TR) defines personality disorders as traits that are "inflexible and maladaptive and cause significant functional impairment or subjective distress … across a broad range of personal and social situations," and are of "stable and of long duration, and its onset can be traced back at least to adolescence or early adulthood" (American Psychiatric Association, 2000, p. 686). Since the introduction of a multiaxial diagnostic system in the third (1980) revision of the DSM, personality disorders have been conceptualized as separate from Axis I disorders, such as depression or anxiety. They may impact Axis I clinical problems, but are conceptualized as a discrete set of disorders and therefore are diagnosed separately on Axis II. The DSM-5 workgroups, however, are proposing doing away with the distinction between Axis I and Axis II disorders (APA, 2010).

Currently, the DSM-IV-TR groups 10 personality disorders into three clusters: odd/eccentric (Paranoid, Schizoid, and Schizotypal Personality Disorders), dramatic/emotional (Histrionic, Anti-social, Borderline, and Narcissistic), and anxious-dependent (Avoidant, Dependent, and Obsessive–Compulsive). Shea (1998) has proposed a slightly different naming of the clusters and grouping of disorders within those clusters based on how patients typically experience the disorders: Anxiety Prone (same three disorders as "anxious dependent"), Poorly Empathic (Schizoid, Anti-social, Histrionic, and Narcissistic), and Psychotic Prone (Borderline Schizotypal, and Paranoid).

The prevalence of personality disorders in the United States is estimated to be approximately 10% to 15% based on DSM-IV-TR criteria (Mattia & Zimmerman, 2001). The accurate assessment of a personality disorder in a client is of significant concern not only because of its prevalence but also the associated costs and needed resources. Borderline and antisocial personality disorders, in particular, are often associated with increased cost and difficulties in treatment because of higher rates of hospitalizations, the need for longer-term outpatient treatment, greater usage of overall mental health services, and greater risk of harm to self and others (Linehan, 1993; Lowe & Widiger, 2008).

Until very recently, the research regarding normal personality traits described above has been disconnected from the conceptualizations, research, and treatment of personality disorders. Those theorizing and researching personality in nonclinical populations have tended to investigate different concepts and represent different theoretical perspectives and disciplines (e.g., psychology vs. psychiatry) than those studying and treating personality and other DSM disorders (Linehan, 1993; Lowe & Widiger, 2008). As a result, the research and descriptions of personality traits, their facets and essential attributes, and the treatment of personality disorders has occurred in separate spheres. The application of normal personality theory to personality disorders and psychopathology has begun just within the past decade and is likely, for the first time, to have an influence on the revision of DSM personality disorders and how they are conceptualized (American Psychiatric Association, 2010). Some personality disorders experts have argued, however, that a reconceptualization of DSM personality disorders based on the five factor model is premature and lacking sufficient scientific evidence (Black, 2011; Davidson, 2011; Skodol, 2011).

PERSONALITY ASSESSMENT METHODS

Current Personality Assessment Methods

Personality tests can be subdivided into two broad categories, objective self-report measures and projective measures. Objective self-report measures, such as the MMPI-2, have a set number of items or questions that an individual responds to as being either true or false; or the items are answered using a Likert scale of agreement (e.g., "strongly agree" to "strongly disagree"). The projective category includes tests like the Rorschach inkblot test, the *Thematic Apperception Test* (TAT)—a test where an individual produces a story in response to a series of black and white drawings involving people in different situations—and other picture-story tests, and human figure drawings. Personality tests, both objective and projective types, when used by clinicians in mental health settings, have been relied on for diagnostic and case conceptualization purposes; less so for describing underlying personality traits. In other counseling settings—career and organizational—tests of normal personality traits are used to help individuals gain an understanding of themselves and how their traits may affect interpersonal relationships and behavior in particular environments. How much of a personality description is provided by a specific test depends upon the test developers' theory of personality or psychopathology. The information provided by personality tests that can have a bearing on understanding clinical problems and guiding the course of counseling include typical defenses, coping styles, interpersonal relationship styles, perceptions of self and the interpersonal environment, and typical emotional and behavioral responses.

Developing Objective Self-Report Personality Measures

Several test construction models have been used to develop self-report personality measures. One construction methodology is the theoretical, which utilizes a rational and content-related approach. Another is the empirical approach, which relies on criterion keying or factor analysis (Kaplan & Saccuzzo, 2005). Some tests can be considered hybrids in that they combine a theoretical and an empirical methodology. The content-related approach is intuitive and the easiest to understand. Using a logical deductive reasoning process, test items are identified usually in consultation with researchers and clinicians who are considered experts regarding the construct the test is intended to measure. A list of items is generated that are thought to theoretically represent a particular aspect of personality or psychopathology, introversion for example. Second, the item response format is decided upon, such as true or false, or Likert scale measuring agreement or disagreement with the question. This method assumes the individual will respond to test items such as "I get headaches often" in an open and honest fashion (Kaplan & Saccuzzo). Most of the questionnaires discussed in subsequent chapters were developed from a theoretical content-related perspective, as was the *Millon Clinical Multiaxial Inventory,* which is discussed in depth later in this chapter. Millon developed a theory of personality and from that theory he and his colleagues (Millon, Davis, & Millon, 1997) logically deduced items that would reflect his particular conceptualization of personality.

The most well-known, well-researched, and widely used example of an empirical criterion measure is the MMPI, now in its second edition. The MMPI was developed using an empirical criterion method of test construction and was modeled on the *Strong Vocational Interest Inventory* (Dahlstrom & Dahlstrom, 1980). Empirical criterion test construction is a multistep process of administering a test to groups of people meeting a criterion (in this case, a diagnostic status) and comparing the average responses of the criterion group to those of a "normal" comparison group. Items are then assigned a score based on whether the item differentiated the normal control group from the diagnostic group.

The construction of the original MMPI produced 1,000 items created from the developers' clinical experience, psychiatric examination forms and textbooks, medicine and neurology directions for obtaining case histories, and attitudinal surveys (Hathaway & McKinley, 1980). Its construction was influenced by tests considered empirical at the time, such as Binet's intelligence tests and the *Strong Vocational Interest Blank*, and was intended to make up for the transparency and deficiencies in the existing personality tests (Dahlstrom, Welsh, & Dalstrom, 1972). From the original 1,000 items created for the MMPI, 567 were retained because they statistically differentiated the control and criterion groups, even though a number of the items, such as "I like mechanics magazines," did not appear to have face validity. Despite the lack of face validity, those items were retained because at least one of the diagnostic groups responded to them in either the true or false direction significantly more so than did the control group. For example, if 60% of the patients in a diagnostic or criterion group responded to an item in one direction (false) but only 30% of the normal group responded false, the item would be retained because there was enough of a difference, on average, between the two groups' response to the item.

Bear in mind that criterion groups who were given the pilot MMPI were psychiatric patients at University of Minnesota (UM) Hospitals in the 1930s and their diagnoses were based on conceptualizations of psychopathology at that time, not on the modern DSM system published in 1980. Those diagnoses included psychosis, manic–depressive psychosis, psychoneurosis (hypochondriacal), psychathenia (a combination of phobic, anxious, and obsessive–compulsive patients), schizophrenia, and anti-social personality disorder (Hathaway & McKinley, 1940). There were four unrepresentative control groups selected as the comparison groups. The first was a group of friends and relatives of the psychiatric patients and were found in the waiting rooms at the UM Hospital. The second was a group of high school graduates who came to the University of Minnesota Testing Bureau for college advice. The third comprised "skilled workers" identified from a local Works Project Administration. The fourth group consisted of general medical patients not diagnosed with a psychiatric disorder (Hathaway & McKinley, 1980). This unrepresentative group serving as the normative group was a problem that MMPI restandardization committee addressed when looking to revise the test. Despite the lack of a representative comparison group, the original MMPI turned out to be a very valuable tool in many diverse settings: counseling, medical, forensic, and organizational. Furthermore, the empirical-criterion process used in the development of the MMPI became the standard that future test developers would draw upon if wanting to use this type of approach.

OBJECTIVE SELF-REPORT PERSONALITY TESTS: ASSESSMENT OF PERSONALITY DISORDERS AND PSYCHOPATHOLOGY

Minnesota Multiphasic Personality Inventory-2 (MMPI-2)

The MMPI-2 is a self-report measure consisting of 567 items answered as true or false. It is designed to assess general psychopathology in adults, with an emphasis on maladaptive interpersonal styles (Butcher et al., 2001). The MMPI-2 was the culmination of a seven-year restandardization project that began in 1982 and was completed in 1989. The decision to revise the original MMPI was based on several factors, but the primary reason was the need to revise the norms of the original version because they were unrepresentative and outdated (Archer, 2006). Another consideration was the need to revise the language with some of the items that no longer had meaning for most test takers. For example, there are items on the original MMPI that made reference to games no longer played, such as "drop the handkerchief," or behavior whose meaning has altered because of cultural changes, such as "cutting up in school." Surveys of mental health professionals indicate that the MMPI-2 is one of the most frequently used psychological tests (Camara, Nathan, & Puente, 2000; Frauenhoffer, Ross, Gfeller, Searight, & Piotrowski, 1998) and since its inception and revision has been the most widely used self-report personality assessment test (Archer, 2006). The MMPI-2 is primarily used in clinical settings—outpatient mental health, inpatient, and substance abuse clinics—but its ability to detect the presence of psychiatric disorders, psychological problems, and interpersonal styles has resulted in its use in nonclinical settings including military, workplace, medical, and forensic (Butcher, 2006). When used in clinical settings, it is a helpful tool for counselors and other mental health practitioners for treatment planning and case conceptualization purposes, and to a lesser extent, assessing treatment outcomes (Greene & Clopton, 1999; Perry, Miller, & Klump, 2006). The University of Minnesota Press publishes the MMPI-2 and it is available from Pearson Assessments as a Level C Test (***PearsonAssessments.com***). An adolescent version, for youth ages 14–18, was created in 1992, and in 2008 the *MMPI-2 Restructured Form* was produced.

Like its predecessor, the MMPI-2 is a complex instrument. It consists of 10 Clinical scales (shown in Table 8.1), 7 Validity scales, and 25 Content and "Supplemental scales. All of the items are responded to as either true or false. The items range from somatic concerns such as stomach ailments and energy level to emotional (e.g., crying), behavioral (e.g., breaking things), and perceptual ones (e.g., someone is out to get me).

Table 8.1 MMPI-2 Clinical Scales and Associated Personality Characteristics

Number	Name (Abbreviation)	High Score Interpretations
1	Hypochondrias (Hs)	Many vague physical and somatic complaints including weakness and low energy; ego-centric and generally dissatisfied and unhappy
2	Depression (D)	Depression symptoms including: Depressed mood, pessimism, low self-esteem and feeling of inadequacy
3	Hysteria (Hy)	Lacking psychological mindedness; and develop somatic problems instead; other defenses include denial and repression; dependent and naive
4	Psychopathic Deviate (Pd)	Antisocial behavior such as deceitful, manipulative, rebellious, aggressive, and immature; and sociable and outgoing
5	Masculinity–Femininity (M/F)	Males tend to be sensitive, passive, and aesthetic; may have sexual identify conflict; females tend to be rough, aggressive, and insensitive
6	Paranoia (Pa)	Psychotic thinking and behavior: suspicious, guarded; ideas of reference, delusions of grandeur; externalize blame and use projection
7	Psychasthenia (Pt)	Introspective, ruminating, and obsessive thinking; feelings of insecurity, worry, nervousness and tension; experience psychological distress and fears
8	Schizophrenia (Sc)	Unusual and strange thinking; poor reality testing & schizoid-like behavior, unusual sensory experiences & hallucinations; feel isolated and alienated
9	Mania (Ma) Hypomania	High energy and talkative with rapid speech; unrealistically high self-evaluation; fail to complete projects; impulsive and gregarious
0	Social Introversion (Si)	Insecure and uncomfortable socially; timid, shy, and prefer solitary activities

Source: Excerpted from the MMPI®-2 (Minnesota Multiphasic Personality Inventory®-2) Manual for Administration, Scoring, and Interpretation, Revised Edition. Copyright © 2001 by the Regents of the University of Minnesota. Used by permission of the University of Minnesota Press. All rights reserved. "MMPI" and "Minnesota Multiphasic Personality Inventory" are trademarks owned by the Regents of the University of Minnesota.

Two points need to be made about the clinical scales. First, they represent syndromes that reflect both pathological conditions (e.g., depression, mania, paranoia) and personality traits (e.g., introversion, gender identity). Second, the labels that were chosen for the 10 clinical scales (e.g., Hysteria and Psychasthenia) were a reflection of the diagnostic terminology and conceptualizations of an earlier era, not the current DSM system. Although the original clinical scale labels have been retained in the MMPI-2, the test continues to be a useful one to augment the assessment of some DSM-IV disorders such as personality disorders (Derksen, 2006), post-traumatic stress disorder (Penk, Rierdan, Losardo, & Robinowitz, 2006), schizophrenia, and mood disorders: both major depression and to a lesser extent mania (Nichols & Crowhurst, 2006). Unlike the content scales, the items on the clinical scales are heterogeneous and were included on the scale because they were responded to differently by the criterion and normal groups. That is, the clinical scales were empirically derived: a set of items were found to cluster together not necessarily because of measuring the same construct, for example, depression, but rather because of the ability of a cluster of items to be responded to, on average, one way by a criterion group and another way by the normal group.

TECHNICAL INFORMATION   The normative group for the MMPI-2 consisted of 2,600 United States residents and was much more representative of the country's population in terms of age, gender, ethnicity, marital status, educational level, and occupation than the original group (Greene & Clopton, 1999). The normative group matched U.S. census data at the time on all these variables with the exception of educational level and occupation, where the normative group had a level higher than average. Separate norms were developed for males and females. To date, little systematic research exists investigating the impact of demographic variables on patterns of response to the MMPI-2, but from the existing evidence one review has speculated that demographic variables will have little impact on the MMPI-2 scores for most clients (Greene & Clopton, 1999).

Reliability estimates for specific MMPI-2 scales are in the adequate to excellent range. Test–retest reliability for the 10 clinical and 5 validity scales ranged from 0.68 to 0.92 with a two-week interval (Butcher et al., 2001). Test–retest reliabilities have a similar range for the content scales (0.78 to 0.91) (Butcher et al.). Thousands of validity studies have been conducted using the original MMPI, but given the new norms and changes in calculating t scores for all of the scales, the extent to which those studies are applicable to the MMPI-2 remains a focus of ongoing research and debate (Greene & Clopton, 1999).

ADMINISTRATION   Because the MMPI-2 is a self-report inventory, the presence of a clinician is not required during administration. The clinician will want to ensure, however, that the test taker understands the directions, has a minimum of a sixth-grade reading level, and is in a setting that is comfortable and free of distractions (Butcher et al., 2001). The author's experience is that the inventory can be completed within 60 to 90 minutes (the test manual does not provide a time length). Some individuals may require more time, and it is permissible to break up the administration of the MMPI-2 into shorter sessions (Butcher et al.). A digital audio version of the test is also available from Pearson/NCS and can be used with clients with reading difficulties or other problems necessitating the need for the test to be read aloud. The instructions on the test booklet simply state, "Read each statement and decide whether it is *true as applied to you* or *false as applied to you*." Additionally, respondents are told to "give **your own** opinion of yourself" and "try to respond to every statement."

SCORING   Both hand scoring and computer software scoring is available. Computer-generated scoring can be purchased through NCS/Pearson. Scoring is somewhat complex if done by hand but templates are available to facilitate the process. Raw scores are plotted on a gender-specific profile sheet, where those raw scores are converted to *t* scores (see Figures 8.1–8.2) (Butcher et al., 2001). In the original MMPI, *t* score values of each scale did not correspond to the same percentile equivalent (see Chapter 6). This was changed so that the MMPI-2 has uniform *t* scales. This means, for example, that a *t* score of 70 is at the 98th percentile on all scales.

INTERPRETATION   Interpretation of MMPI-2 scores is a multistep process and involves integrating scores from all of the scales: Validity, Clinical, Content, and Supplementary (Friedman, Lewak, Nichols, & Webb, 2000; Graham, 1993). The validity scales are examined first to ensure that the other scales can be appropriately interpreted. The test taker's answers could indicate a pattern of responding to the test that would call into question how open and honest or random he or she had been and how much caution needs to be exercised when evaluating the remainder of the scales. Sometimes the validity scales will indicate that the MMPI-2 is invalid and no further interpretation is warranted. If the validity scales indicate that the person responded in a forthright and open manner, without a serious response bias or tendency to fake answers, then clinical, content, and supplementary scales can be interpreted. The validity scales have also been shown to be related to certain personality styles.

Validity Scales   Each of the validity scales is interpreted individually and in combination with other validity scales to determine if the profile is a valid one, meaning did the client respond in an open and unbiased fashion. The inclusion of scales designed to assess for different types of test-taker response bias was a novel idea in the 1940s but is no longer unique to the MMPI-2. High scores (*t* > 65) on any of these scales is more common in noncounseling settings such as employment, where test takers have more reason to distort or "fake" their responses (Butcher et al., 2001).

Although technically not a scale, the first step in examining the validity of an MMPI-2 is to count the number of unanswered or unusable items (marked both true and false). This is also known as the "Cannot Say" score (Graham, 1993). Cannot Say scores of 30 or more means the remainder of the test is highly suspect or should not be considered valid (Graham).

The L, or, Lie scale is analyzed next. High scores (*t* > 65) on the L scale indicates that the respondent might have answered many items in a defensive fashion, concealing the presence of symptoms and minor personality flaws (Butcher et al., 2001). A high score could also be the result of a false response bias—in other words, a tendency to respond to most items as false. Conversely, low scores on the L scale suggest the person responded to the items in an open and honest way.

After the L scale is scored and interpreted, the F (Frequency) scale is examined. Originally designed as a measure of infrequent or atypical responses, the F scale is now used to detect another kind of distorted responding: "faking bad." Several possibilities can account for unusually high scores on the F scale (*t* scores > 100). One possibility is that the individual responded randomly to the test or the reading level of the test was too high for that person. Another possibility is that the respondent endorsed an elevated number of items correlating to pathology, suggesting a distorted more pathological view of self than is present. A third possibility is the presence of psychosis. Very high F scales are not uncommon with inpatients (Graham, 1993).

The K (Correction) scale was created after the original MMPI was published and is used to adjust the scores on some of the clinical scales (see Figure 8.1). The K scale also represents defensiveness and the tendency to respond to the test in a socially desirable fashion. For example, an individual who has an elevated K scale would respond *true* to an item such as "I rarely argue with my family." Both demographic variables such as education level and social class and some personality characteristics, for example, self-esteem, have been shown to be related to high K scores (Butcher, 1990).

The three validity scales that were added to the MMPI-2—Back Side (Fb) scale, variable response inconsistency (VRIN), and true response inconsistency (TRIN) are meant to complement the L, F, and K scales, and are a measure of test taker responding inconsistently and contradictorily (Butcher et al., 2001). The Fb scale is designed to detect random or deviant responding after the 370th item. The original F scale was made up of items from earlier on in the test and this new scale can identify individuals who for some reason had an unusual response pattern toward the end of the test.

The TRIN scale is designed to detect a true or false response bias. That is a tendency to answer questions as true most of the time, or false, regardless of the content of the item. Individuals with this tendency are referred to acquiescers or nonacquiescers, or more colloquially as "yea or nay sayers." High TRIN scores indicate a "true," or acquiescence, response bias and low scores reflect a "false," or nonacquiescence, bias.

Similarly, the VRIN scale is designed to detect inconsistent responding. The scale is made up of 67 item pairs that reflect inconsistent or contradictory responses. For example, an item about feeling rested in the morning would be paired with an item about disturbed sleep. Answering *true* to both items would, for example, produce one point for the VRIN scale because of that inconsistency (rested in the morning but a fitful sleep).

Clinical Scales   Once the validity scales are interpreted and there is no evidence of serious response bias, the clinical scales are analyzed. High scores (generally those above a t score of 65) on the clinical scales are a starting point for determining if psychological problems are present and are interpreted along with content scales that are similar in nature (Greene, 2006); for example, Clinical scale 2 (Depression) and the Depression content scale. The meaning of high t scores on the clinical scale can be found in Table 8.1. Furthermore, clinical scales, when interpreted along with validity and some content scales, can provide information about client readiness for change and attitude toward psychological help and counseling (Perry et al., 2006). A second way in which clinical scales are interpreted is based on the concept of **code types**. Typically a code type is based not on the score of a single clinical scale, but rather on the two or three highest scales with t scores at or above 65.

The second part of clinical scale interpretation involves looking for and examining **code types**. Code types were developed from the original MMPI and continue to be part of the interpretation process with MMPI-2. Several groups of investigators developed these code types during the late 1950s and early 1960s. A set of rules pertaining to the elevation of the clinical scales and the K scale ($t \geq 70$), as well as the t score difference between clinical scales were applied to hundreds of original MMPI profiles obtained from patients in various mental health facilities. A number of 2- and 3-point code types were developed based on the results (Marks, Seeman, & Haller, 1974). One example is the Marks-Seeman system, which identified 16 code types based on the frequency of their occurrence in several inpatient and outpatient samples obtained between 1960 and 1962. A "2-3-1" is one of these 16 empirically derived code types on which MMPI and MMPI-2 clinical scale interpretations are based. The personality descriptors for each of the Marks-Seeman code types were obtained through a combination of case history data common to the patients with that specific code type and a Q-sort technique (Marks et al.). The interpretation of the clinical scales is still based on code-type interpretation, that is, the two highest clinical scales with *t* scores ≥ 65 (Greene & Clopton, 1999). Using *t* scores of 65 as the cutoff point for judging clinical significance is a change from the original MMPI, in which a *t* score of 70 was the cutoff. Computer-generated interpretative reports can be obtained from Pearson NCS, or a clinician can consult one of the MMPI-2 interpretation guides (*MMPI-2: Assessing Personality and Psychopathology* [Graham, 1993] or *MMPI-2 Adult Interpretive System*, 2nd ed. [Greene & Brown, 1998]). Clinicians are urged to not view a computer-generated interpretation in isolation nor view it as personality and psychopathology descriptions that can be reproduced verbatim in a psychological report. Clinical skill and care is needed to integrate the computer-generated report with other information the clinician has about the client in order to produce a more meaningful portrayal.

Content and Supplementary Scales   The 15 content scales cover a wide array of problem areas, including anxiety, fears, depression and low self-esteem, health concerns, alcohol abuse, bizarre thinking, anger and cynicism, antisocial behavior. Family, work, and treatment problems can also be interpreted (see Table 8.2). Unlike the empirical criterion approach used to develop the clinical scales, the content and supplementary scales were constructed using rationale and statistical methods such as factor analysis. The content scales provide an additional window into the client's current concerns, symptoms, and interpersonal functioning. In this sense, interpretation of clinically significant content and supplemental scale scores is relatively more straightforward and more similar to the interpretation of other uni- and multidimensional measures discussed both later in this chapter and in Chapter 9. That is, *t* scores at 65 or above on these scales indicate the client is experiencing unusually high levels of what the scale is intended to measure: anxiety, fear, depression, low self-esteem, anger, and so on. In addition, these scales are used for the purpose of filling in and focusing the interpretations gleaned from the clinical scale code types.

The supplementary scales are similar to the content scales and typically the last set of scales to be analyzed when using the MMPI-2. Over the course of the history of the MMPI, hundreds of supplementary scales were developed but only a small subset was retained with its second edition (Graham, 1993). The supplementary scales for the MMPI-2 include Factor scales A and R, Ego Strength scale, Overcontrolled-Hostility scale, Dominance scale, Social Responsibility scale, College Maladjustment scale, two different Post-Traumatic Stress Disorder scales, Gender Role scales, Marital Distress scale, and three Substance Abuse scales (MacAndrew Alcoholism scale, the Addiction Potential scale, and the Addiction Acknowledgment scale). Most of these scales were chosen for inclusion in the MMPI-2 because of research supporting their validity (Friedman et al., 2000). Factor scales A and R are based on factor analyses of the clinical and validity scales and represent two primary traits and states underlying an individual's response pattern. Individuals who score high on Factor A are generally acknowledging significant distress, maladjustment, and personal inadequacy. Individuals with a high Factor R score are often emotionally constricted, use suppression as a coping strategy, and prefer familiar, predictable, and conventional situations (Friedman et al., 2000). Overall, the other scales, particularly the Ego Strength, Overcontrolled-Hostility, and MacAndrew scales are somewhat limited in their cross-cultural validity, usefulness for treatment planning, and predicting how a client may respond to counseling when used as separate assessment measures (Friedman et al., 2000; Graham, 1993).

ADVANTAGES AND LIMITATIONS   Despite the title "multiphasic *personality* inventory," the MMPI-2 is a much more useful assessment tool for clarifying DSM Axis I disorders than personality disorders. This is because the original MMPI was conceptualized and developed long

Table 8.2 MMPI-2 Content Scales

Name	High Score Interpretations
Anxiety (ANX)	Anxious, nervous, tense, worried, indecisive, sleep and somatic complaints
Fears (FRS)	Many phobias and fears and often feeling uneasy
Obsessiveness (OBS)	Worry and ruminate, indecisive, and compulsive behavior
Depression (DEP)	Depression symptoms: feeling depressed, hopeless, and guilty, pessimistic and suicidal thinking, crying easily, and low self-esteem
Health Concerns (HEA)	Health worries, somatic complaints, and feelings of fatigue
Bizarre Mentation (BIZ)	Psychotic thinking including hallucinations, and suspicious and paranoid thinking
Anger (ANG)	Frequent feelings of hostility and anger, self-control problems including swearing, breaking objects, and throwing tantrums; easily annoyed and irritated
Cynicism (CYN)	View people as users, self-centered, and dishonest; interpersonally lack trust and tend to be guarded
Antisocial Practices (ASP)	Often display antisocial behaviors, acting-out, and low frustration tolerance
Type A (TPA)	Impatient, driven, fast-paced individuals and are easily annoyed
Low Self-Esteem (LSE)	Feelings of inadequacy, inferiority, and incompetency are common along with general negative attitudes about self
Social Discomfort (SOD)	Tend to be shy and prefer solitary to group activities; experience social awkwardness
Family Problems (FAM)	Individuals who report significant family conflict, emotional neglect, and alienation from family members
Work Interference (WRK)	Behaviors and thoughts affecting workplace effectiveness
Negative Treatment Indicators (TRT)	Feelings of helplessness, apathy, and difficulties with Motivation and self-disclosure

Source: Excerpted from the MMPI®-2 (Minnesota Multiphasic Personality Inventory®-2) Manual for Administration, Scoring, and Interpretation, Revised Edition. Copyright © 2001 by the Regents of the University of Minnesota. Used by permission of the University of Minnesota Press. All rights reserved. "MMPI" and "Minnesota Multiphasic Personality Inventory" are trademarks owned by the Regents of the University of Minnesota.

before current understandings of Axis II disorders (Green & Clopton, 1999). In this regard it is a very helpful instrument for case conceptualization and treatment planning purposes for a wide range of clients in a variety of settings—college counseling centers, outpatient clinics and community mental health centers, inpatient and residential facilities, substance abuse treatment

BOX 8.1
Case Illustration with the MMPI-2

Nancy, the client in the chapter's opening case study, was given the MMPI-2 following an intake interview at a local United Way agency. She reported a wide range of symptoms, problems, and unusual perceptual experiences—seeing "ghost-like shapes," a history of trauma and flashbacks, loss of ambition, heightened anger, and difficulty coping with stress—that did not fit with a particular syndrome or pattern, making the diagnostic and treatment planning process complicated. Nancy had reported a prior outpatient mental health history several years ago that may have been related to anxiety and depression. In an attempt to better understand her personality traits that may be impacting the experience of and resolution to her presenting problems, to clarify her diagnosis, and to address which kind of counseling approach she might be better suited for, she was administered the MMPI-2. Her scores on the Validity, Clinical, and Content scales were graphed using the MMPI-2 profile forms and are shown in Figures 8.1 and 8.2. The interpretation of Nancy's MMPI-2 and recommendations that follow from this interpretation might read such as:

Nancy's MMPI-2 is a valid and interpretable one. Her scores on scales L, F, K, VRIN, and TRIN suggest she responded to the test in an honest, open, and forthright manner. With the exception of the F scale, these scale scores were in the average range. There was not evidence of her responding randomly, inconsistently, or in a highly defensive way. Her F scale was higher than average (t = 75), indicating that she acknowledges beliefs and attitudes that are highly atypical and may be experiencing severe psychopathology.

Nancy's high F score, code type 6–8, and her high score on the Bizarre Mentation Scale are suggestive of an individual who is experiencing serious psychopathology, possibly psychotic symptoms. Individuals with this code type often demonstrate loose, tangential, and very idiosyncratic ways of thinking. These individuals will also report persecutory and paranoid delusions. They are likely to experience problems with attention, poor judgment, memory lapses, and many fears that are often unusual. Nancy's high score on the Fear scale provides further support for her significant and unusual fears. This suggests someone who is often fearful of being harmed and as result has an avoidant style in many circumstances.

Interpersonally, Nancy is likely to be mistrustful of others' motives and tends to avoid close emotional involvement with others. She sees her world as

a dangerous and threatening place. She may be described by others as being aloof and odd. Her interpersonal difficulties are apt to be related to feelings of inferiority, a negative self-image, and a tendency to misperceive others' intentions. Individuals with a 6–8 profile tend to have very few close friends but despite their interpersonal difficulties tend to function adequately in work environments

Nancy has few psychological coping strategies available to her and at times will have poor control over her emotions. When under stress she is likely to withdraw into her own inner fantasy world. Nancy may also be prone to anger, hostility, and at times inappropriate emotional responses. This is characteristic of both individuals with a 6–8 code type and high scores on the Anger scale.

Individuals with a 6–8 code type and high scores on the Bizarre Mentation and Fears content scales often are diagnosed with schizophrenia, schizoaffective disorder, or schizoid personality disorder. This code type, however, can be a result of traumatic developmental experiences. Nancy did report a history of sexual abuse and that her husband is verbally abusive to her. Furthermore, she did have elevated scores on both Post-Traumatic Stress Disorder scales. A secondary diagnosis of PTSD may be indicated.

Nancy's MMPI-2 results suggest that she would benefit from a long-term therapeutic approach that is less insight oriented and more supportive and educational. She is likely going to have difficulty developing a trusting therapeutic alliance with a therapist and this process will likely take months. She would benefit from a focus on teaching skills such as anger and stress management. With an insight-oriented approach she is more apt to become confused and easily disorganized. She may have a tendency to focus more on others than herself.

Nancy's MMPI-2 results were integrated with the background information obtained from her intake interview and a subsequent interview. Collectively, the assessment information suggested that an Axis I diagnosis of PTSD, not schizophrenia, was more appropriate, but there was ample evidence that she met an Axis II diagnosis of schizotypal personality disorder. She was seen for 14 months of individual therapy and decided to end her treatment when she felt she was managing her anxiety better and had decided to quit nursing school and pursue a career as a Reiki therapist.

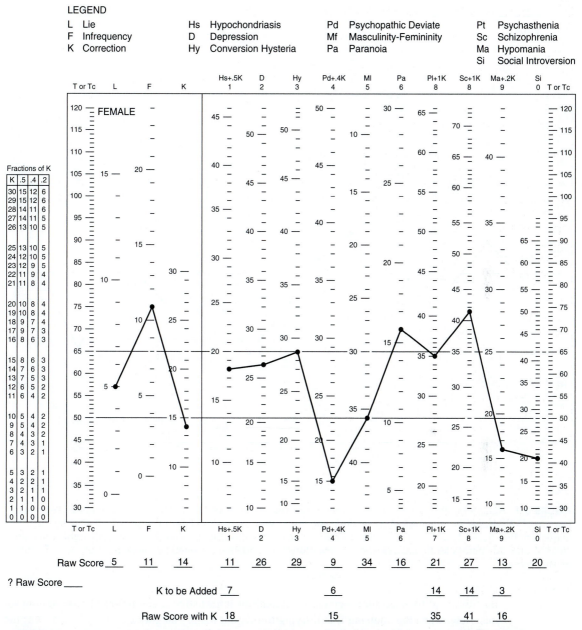

FIGURE 8.1 Nancy's MMPI-2 Validity and Clinical Scales Profile *From:* Excerpted from the *MMPI®-2 (Minnesota Multiphasic Personality Inventory®-2) Manual for Administration, Scoring, and Interpretation*, Revised Edition. Copyright © 2001 by the Regents of the University of Minnesota. Used by permission of the University of Minnesota Press. All Rights reserved. "MMPI" and "Minnesota Multiphasic Personality Inventory" are trademarks owned by the Regents of the University of Minnesota.

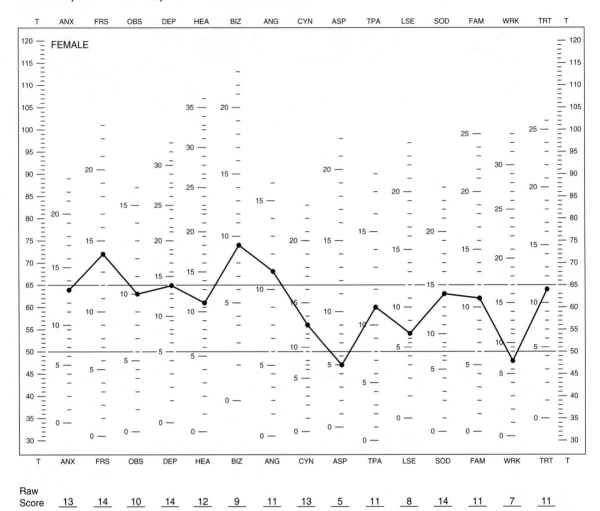

Raw Score	ANX	FRS	OBS	DEP	HEA	BIZ	ANG	CYN	ASP	TPA	LSE	SOD	FAM	WRK	TRT
	13	14	10	14	12	9	11	13	5	11	8	14	11	7	11

FIGURE 8.2 Nancy's MMPI-2 Content Scale *From:* Excerpted from the *MMPI®-2 (Minnesota Multiphasic Personality Inventory®-2) Manual for Administration, Scoring, and Interpretation*, Revised Edition. Copyright © 2001 by the Regents of the University of Minnesota. Used by permission of the University of Minnesota Press. All Rights reserved. "MMPI" and "Minnesota Multiphasic Personality Inventory" are trademarks owned by the Regents of the University of Minnesota.

facilities, and forensic sites—given the breadth of information it can produce. After the intake interview, when the clinician is still trying to rule out major categories of disorders, as was the case with Nancy, the MMPI-2 is a particularly helpful diagnostic tool. In addition, the validity scales are valuable tools in cases where malingering, a distorted self-report, or secondary gain is suspected. On the other hand, many have found the discriminant validity of the MMPI-2 to be lacking (Archer, 2006; Finn & Kamphuis, 2006; Ranson, Nichols, Rouse, & Harrington, 2009; Tellegen et al., 2006). That is, it may be sensitive to detecting general emotional distress or maladjustment but less able to distinguish among specific type of pathology or disorder. That was part of the rationale for the construction of the *Restructured Clinical Scales,* which will be discussed shortly.

The MMPI-2 was not designed to be a treatment outcome or treatment monitoring measure, and indeed is less useful when used as such. Relative to other briefer multidimensional measures like the ones described in subsequent chapters, the MMPI-2 is not as sensitive to client changes that occur during counseling, nor is it as efficient as other treatment monitoring measures. The nature and wording of many of the items reflect past behavior rather than current symptoms or problems, making it difficult for the MMPI-2 to detect changes in client mood and behavior over short periods (Green & Clopton, 1999). Furthermore, given the length of time needed to complete and interpret it, a clinician who wants quantitative information regarding client changes is likely to use a shorter, less costly, and more useful measure.

CULTURAL CONSIDERATIONS   The breadth and sheer quantity of cross-cultural research studies and clinical applications of the original MMPI and the MMPI-2 is striking. Notwithstanding translation problems and the need for linguistic equivalents for particular items, a review of the cross-cultural MMPI research by Butcher and Clark (1979) found it was being used for practical clinical applications in many countries throughout Europe, Asia, South America, and the Middle East. In their review they noted the diverse countries where the MMPI had been translated: Chile, Greece, Hong Kong, Kuwait, Lithuania, and Turkey. They concluded their review by stating, "It can be used effectively in other cultures with the same level of accuracy as it is in the United States" (p. 109).

A generation later, Butcher (2004) also noted that additional research on the MMPI-2 suggests that it is as effective with minority populations as it is with the majority population within the United States. By the end of the 20th century, the MMPI-2 was translated into 32 different languages, used in over 40 countries, and valued as a very useful diagnostic tool (Butcher, 2004). Its international acceptance and usage appears to be growing. The MMPI-2 was adopted in countries including Holland, where it was previously resisted due to translation problems. In the United States, alternative language versions such as Hmong (Laotian) and Vietnamese have been used successfully with their respective refugee populations. Cross-cultural research has demonstrated the generalizability of the 8–6/6–8 MMPI code type as it applies to the construct paranoid schizophrenia and similar research is ongoing (Butcher, 2004).

RESTRUCTURED CLINICAL SCALES AND *MMPI-2 RESTRUCTURED FORM*   The MMPI continues to be a work in progress. The latest version, the *MMPI-2 Restructured Form* (RF) is different theoretically and developmentally from the original and second editions. The MMPI-2 RF grew out of the restructuring of the clinical scales. The impetus for changing the clinical scales from the original MMPI stemmed from concerns about the interpretations drawn from these 60-year-old scales based on subsequent factor analytic research (Tellegren et al., 2003). One concern about the original clinical scales is that they all contain items that reflect a general maladjustment and distress, or what Tellegren et al. (2003) labeled "demoralization." Consequently, the original clinical scales may be less useful in clarifying specific aspects of psychopathology and indirectly certain diagnoses if they all measure the overarching phenomenon of demoralization (Sellbom, Ben-Porath, & Bagby, 2008). Demoralization is similar in nature to dysphoria but also includes feelings of helplessness, perceived difficulty in coping with life events and "general dissatisfaction with one's condition" (Tellegen et al., 2006, p. 157). Furthermore, the restructured clinical scales are based on contemporary models of emotions and psychopathology and therefore are more theoretically driven than the original MMPI's strict empirical approach. To what extent these newer scales accomplish the goal of providing more useful clinical information about psychopathology syndromes than the MMPI-2 clinical scales has been the subject of numerous research articles and debate (Meyer, 2006; Nichols, 2006; Tellegen et al., 2006). Some have suggested that the restructured clinical scales better reflect current conceptualizations of psychopathology and personality than the clinical scales and may be more valid for making diagnostic predictions (Hoelzle & Meyer, 2008; Sellbom et al., 2008). On the other hand, Rouse, Greene, Butcher, Nichols, and Williams (2008) concluded based on their analyses of 25 clinical samples of over 75,000 MMPI-2 profiles that the restructured clinical scales provided little new information beyond what is contained in the existing content and supplemental scales.

The restructured clinical scales paved the way for a major overhaul in the MMPI-2 and led to the publication in 2008 of the *MMPI-2—Restructured Form* (RF), a 338 item version of the MMPI-2 for adults 18 to 80 (Ben-Porath & Tellegen, 2008). The MMPI-2-RF contains 50 new scales: several additional Validity scales, Somatic/Cognitive and Internalizing scales, and Externalizing, Interpersonal, and Interest scales (see Table 8.3). Due to the recency of this latest and radical revision of the MMPI-2, few independent research or reviews have been published regarding its use in clinical, medical, and forensic settings but that research is quickly growing (see, for example, Thomas & Locke, 2010; Sellbom et al., 2008).

MINNESOTA MULTIPHASIC PERSONALITY INVENTORY—ADOLESCENT The *Minnesota Multiphasic Personality Inventory-Adolescent* (MMPI-A) is the adolescent version of the MMPI-2 and is designed to assess psychopathology and the broad construct of personality in adolescents ages 14 to 18 (Butcher et al., 1992). It is shorter in length than the MMPI-2, consisting of 478 items requiring 60 to 90 minutes to complete. The clinical and validity scales are the same ones as the MMPI-2 and the content scales are similar except for the exclusion of the Type A scale and the addition of three adolescent-specific scales: Alienation, Low Aspirations, and School Problems. The MMPI-A, like its adult counterpart, provides a comprehensive personality description, including interpersonal and coping styles, that goes beyond what can be gleaned from other multidimensional self-report measures. In addition, because it is so comprehensive in scope with its clinical, content, and supplemental scales, it can provide information about certain aspects of psychopathology either not covered or minimally addressed with other measures such as psychotic and manic symptoms. Its main drawback, however, is its length and time to administer, particularly with adolescents who are less likely than adults to finish it, and added time to score and interpret it relative to other measures. These limitations have resulted in several unsuccessful attempts to come up with valid shorter versions (Archer, Tirrell, & Elkins, 2001).

When then might it be useful to incorporate a more complex and time-consuming measure into the assessment of an adolescent with emotional and behavioral problems? The MMPI-A can be a valuable assessment tool when other sources of information typically relied upon for evaluating troubled youth such as parents, guardians, and teachers, are not available or are difficult to access. Difficulties accessing parent and teacher information in a timely manner can arise when youth are placed in certain settings such as foster care, residential, or juvenile correctional facilities. Diagnostic and treatment planning and service delivery decisions need to be made quickly as youth enter those settings, and the MMPI-A can generate a good deal of comprehensive information quickly. Furthermore, having information about personality style and functioning can be especially helpful for case conceptualization and treatment planning purposes in a variety of settings including outpatient, community, and educational; especially when after interviews with the youth and knowledgeable adults have been conducted, the youth's diagnosis remains an enigma. The MMPI-A can be useful in sorting out a complex and

Table 8.3 MMPI-2 Restructured Scales

Scales

Validity:

?	Cannot Say (reported as a raw score only, not plotted)
VRIN-r	Variable Response Inconsistency
TRIN-r	True Response Inconsistency
F-r	Infrequent Responses
Fp-r	Infrequent Psychopathology Responses
Fs	Infrequent Somatic Responses
FBS-r	Symptom Validity
L-r	Uncommon Virtues
K-r	Adjustment Validity

Higher-Order (H-O) and Restructured Clinical (RC):

Higher-Order (H-O):

EID	Emotional/Internalizing Dysfunction
THD	Thought Dysfunction
BXD	Behavioral/Externalizing Dysfunction

RC (Restructured Clinical):

RCd	Demoralization
RC1	Somatic Complaints
RC2	Low Positive Emotions
RC3	Cynicism
RC4	Antisocial Behavior
RC6	Ideas of Persecution
RC7	Dysfunctional Negative Emotions
RC8	Aberrant Experiences
RC9	Hypomanic Activation

Somatic/Cognitive and Internalizing:

Somatic/Cognitive:

MLS	Malaise
GIC	Gastrointestinal Complaints
HPC	Head Pain Complaints
NUC	Neurological Complaints
COG	Cognitive Complaints

Internalizing Scales:

SUI	Suicidal/Death Ideation
HLP	Helplessness/Hopelessness
SFD	Self-Doubt
NFC	Inefficacy
STW	Stress/Worry
AXY	Anxiety

(continued)

Table 8.3 MMPI-2 Restructured Scales (*continued*)	
	Scales
ANP	Anger Proneness
BRF	Behavior-Restricting Fears
MSF	Multiple Specific Fears

Externalizing, Interpersonal, and Interest:

Externalizing:

JCP	Juvenile Conduct Problems
SUB	Substance Abuse
AGG	Aggression
ACT	Activation

Interpersonal Scales:

FML	Family Problems
IPP	Interpersonal Passivity
SAV	Social Avoidance
SHY	Shyness
DSF	Disaffiliativeness

Interest Scales:

AES	Aesthetic-Literary Interests
MEC	Mechanical-Physical Interests

Personality Psychopathology Five (PSY-5) Scales:

AGGR-r	Aggressiveness-Revised
PSYC-r	Psychoticism-Revised
DISC-r	Disconstraint-Revised
NEGE-r	Negative Emotionality/Neuroticism-Revised
INTR-r	Introversion/Low Positive Emotionality-Revised

From: Excerpted from the *MMPI-2-RF Manual for Administration, Scoring, and Interpretation*, by Yossef S. Ben-Porath and Auke Tellegen. Copyright © 2008, 2011 by the Regents of the University of Minnesota. Reproduced by permission of the University of Minnesota Press. All Rights reserved. "Minnesota Multiphasic Personality Inventory-2-RF®" and "MMPI-2-RF® are trademarks owned by the Regents of the University of Minnesota.

unclear diagnostic picture especially in cases where bipolar disorder, schizophrenia, conduct disorder, and some personality disorders are still being ruled out. On the other hand, it has been faulted for its inability to detect psychopathology in those adolescents who by virtue of the setting they are in—juvenile justice, inpatient, or residential—clearly have significant emotional and behavioral disorders. That is, many research studies have shown that a significant number of youth in restricted settings score in the normal range on MMPI-A clinical scales, which may be due to the normative sample endorsing a significant number of clinical significant items on each scale (Archer, 2005; Archer, Handel, & Lynch, 2001). The problem with false negatives (identifying an individual as normal when that person has a psychiatric disorder) associated with the MMPI-A may reflect a larger reality that in adolescence it is much harder to distinguish normal from abnormal functioning than it is in adults, given that adolescence is a transitional period marked by emotional swings, acting-out behaviors, excessive self-consciousness, and struggles with independence and dependence (Archer, 2005). Despite the changes that were made to some of the original MMPI items in order to make them more adolescent friendly, the test is not grounded in theories of adolescent development and psychopathology and the internal consistency reliabilities for some of the clinical and content scales are less than adequate (Kamphaus & Frick, 2005).

Millon Clinical Multiaxial Inventory-III (MCMI-III)

The *Millon Clinical Multiaxial Inventory-III* (MCMI-III) is similar to the MMPI-2 in structure, though significantly shorter in length, and is designed primarily for the assessment of DSM personality disorders and some Axis I disorders. The MCMI-III consists of 175 true–false items and is intended for use in adults ages 18 and older who are referred for or obtaining mental health treatment (Millon, Millon, Davis, & Grossman, 2009). There is, however, a separate inventory, the *Millon Index of Personality Styles,* which is intended for use with nonclinical adult populations for describing personality types rather than as a diagnostic tool (Millon, 1994). In addition, an adolescent version, the *Millon Adolescent Clinical Inventory,* for youth ages 13 to 19 is available as well. The MCMI-III can typically be completed within 20 to 30 minutes and requires a minimum of an eighth-grade reading level. Like the MMPI-2, the MCMI-III is a level C test and is not designed to assess normal personality traits.

The MCMI was developed during the early 1980s for the purpose of assessing Millon's conceptualization of personality disorders. His premise, which evolved through research with colleagues, postulates that all individuals are attempting to adapt to their environment through seeking pleasure and avoiding pain and that adaptation can be an active or passive process with a primary orientation to self or other (Millon et al., 2009). Unlike the categorical approach of the DSM, Millon views personality disorders as a dimensional combination of traits and behavioral styles. These dimensions, or polarities, are pleasure–pain, self–other orientation, and active–passive accommodation style. It is the specific combination of polarities from which personality disturbances are derived (Davis, Meagher, Goncalves, Woodward, & Millon, 1999). For example, someone with a narcissistic personality disorder is high in self orientation and low in other orientation, and has a passive style of adapting or accommodating to his or her interpersonal environment.

Not only is the MCMI-III the personality test most closely aligned with the DSM's personality disorders, but it is also based on a multiaxial diagnostic format like that of the DSM (Davis et al., 1999). According to Millon and his colleagues, the three polarities described above are manifested through four domains—behavioral, phenomenological, intrapsychic, and biophysical—that form the foundation for MCMI-III interpretations. Fourteen personality scales, 10 clinical syndrome scales, and 5 corrections scales (modifying indices and response-style indicators) comprise the MCMI-III (Millon et al., 2009 p. 2).

Correction Scales

- *Modifying Indices:* Disclosure, Desirability, and Debasement and **Random Response Indicators:** Invalidity and Inconsistency

Clinical Scales

- *Clinical Personality Patterns (Axis II):*
  - Schizoid
  - Avoidant
  - Depressive
  - Dependent
  - Histrionic
  - Narcissistic
  - Antisocial
  - Aggressive (Sadistic)
  - Compulsive
  - Negativistic (Passive–Aggressive)
  - Masochistic (Self-defeating)
- *Severe Personality Pathology:* Schizotypal, Borderline, and Paranoid
- *Clinical Syndromes (Axis I):*
  - Anxiety
  - Somatoform
  - Bipolar: Manic
  - Dysthymia
  - Alcohol Dependence
  - Drug Dependence
  - Post-Traumatic Stress Disorder
- *Severe Clinical Syndromes:* Disorder, Major Depression, and Delusional Disorder

The changes incorporated into the third version of the Millon inventory include a more comprehensive theoretical model based on evolution theory and the principle of adaptation to one's environment; 95 new items able to distinguish between different personality disorders; the weighting of certain items for the scoring system; and the addition of a personality scale (Depressive Personality) and an Axis I scale (Post-Traumatic Stress Disorder) (Millon et al., 2009). The specific items focus on traits and abilities such as sociability and making friends, having a changeable and erratic personality, fears and inhibitions, and maladaptive coping strategies.

TECHNICAL INFORMATION   The MCMI-III normative sample consisted of 998 adults ages 18–88 drawn from two separate groups—a standardization sample and a cross-validation sample (Millon et al., 2009). The two samples were made up of males and females selected from 26 states and parts of Canada. These samples, however, overrepresented Whites and underrepresented other racial/ethnic groups (Kwan & Maestas, 2008).

The reliability of the MCMI-III is in the adequate to excellent range both for the internal reliabilities of the majority of the scales and test–retest reliabilities (5- to 14-day retest intervals) (Millon et al., 2009). However, much lower test–retest correlations were found (ranging from 0.01 to 0.27) for four of the scales (Borderline, Compulsive, Negativistic, and Schizotypal) in a group of psychiatric inpatients (Widiger, 2008). Its predictive validity (i.e., the degree to which a respondent's highest scale score correlates with a clinician's diagnosis) is in the moderate to excellent range depending upon the personality disorder. For example, 81% of individuals scoring high on the Dependent Personality scale were also diagnosed with dependent personality disorder by a clinician who had significant experience with the individual, whereas only 50% of those scoring highest on the Antisocial scale received that diagnosis from a clinician (Davis et al., 1999).

ADMINISTRATION, SCORING, AND INTERPRETATION   Both hand- and computer-scoring systems are available, but the hand-scoring system is complex and relatively long, taking up to 40 minutes to complete (Millon et al., 2009). Unlike other measures reviewed in this chapter, the MCMI-III interpretations are derived from base rates rather than t scores (see Chapter 7). Base rates for each scale were calculated using an estimate of the prevalence of specific disorders across various clinical mental health settings. Then cutoff points for each scale were generated from the base rate information. As was discussed in Chapter 7, a cutoff score on a scale represents the border between normal and clinical; in this case a personality disorder or clinical syndrome. Cutoff scores derived from base rates are different than t scores because a t score represents the percentage of the standardization sample that scored at or below the score (equivalent to a percentile). As you may recall, if base rates are high, then the predictive power of a test is good. Conversely, if the base rate for a specific personality disorder is low, then the predictive accuracy of the scale will be poor and can produce a number of false positives.

As with the MMPI-2, the process of MCMI-III interpretation begins with an examination of the correction or validity scales and the response set scales (Millon et al., 2009). The four-item validity scale is designed to detect random responding or an inability to read and understand the test. A score of 1 or more indicates that the test is probably not valid, and is interpreted cautiously or not at all. The Disclosure index is a measure of "faking bad," the Desirability index indicates whether a client was trying to portray him or herself in a positive manner, whereas the Debasement index is another measure of trying to paint a negative picture of one's self.

One recommended approach to MCMI-III interpretation is to consider the scores on the eight personality style scales (nonsevere personality scales) as measures of stylistic ways of interacting and fundamental beliefs and assumptions (Choca, 2004). A narrative of the client's personality style can then be generated through the use of a computerized report or an interpretation guidebook. The remaining personality and clinical scales are interpreted as indices of personality and clinical syndromes similar in conceptualization to DSM-IV disorders.

ADVANTAGES AND LIMITATIONS   The MCMI-III, like the MMPI-2, is extensively researched and widely used throughout the world, having been translated into other languages (Choca, 2004). It is an appealing instrument for clinicians because it assesses personality disorders that are recognized in the DSM system, unlike the MMPI or measures of normal personality. Furthermore, it is significantly shorter in length than the MMPI-2 but has similarly high levels of reliability and validity. Both the MMPI-2 and the MCMI-III, however, were judged to be less useful clinical tools for diagnostic purposes as compared to structured interview schedules for personality disorders (Widiger, 2008). The scoring system creates two limitations with the MCMI-III. First, the hand-scoring system is complex and long. Second, because the cutoff scores are based on base rates, the test is likely to produce a number of false positives in counseling settings where the prevalence of personality disorders is low, such as in college counseling centers (Widiger, 2008).

CULTURAL CONSIDERATIONS   The cross-cultural utility of the MCMI-III is mixed. On the one hand, it has been translated into several different languages and a Spanish version is available from Pearson. On the other hand, clinicians have been advised to be cautious in their use of the MCMI-III with non-White individuals because, with the exception of Native Americans, racial/ethnic groups were underrepresented in the normative sample and little cross-cultural research has been done on the MCMI-III since its publication (Kwan & Maestas, 2008). In that regard it is a more valid tool when used with non-Whites for the purpose of confirming a suspected diagnosis rather than predicting one. The studies involving non-White populations in the

United States pale in comparison to the MMPI-2, and five out of six of them have involved only males (Kwan & Maestas). Studies that have compared MCMI-III scores for Whites and non-Whites—African Americans, American Indians, Asian Americans, and Latino/as—have typically found non-Whites to score higher on select personality disorder and alcohol dependence scales (Kwan & Maestas). Why those differences exist is unclear. Further research is needed to untangle whether higher scores are a reflection of greater psychopathology in certain groups or specific cultural factors unrelated to what the scale purports to measure.

MILLON CLINICAL ADOLESCENT INVENTORY The *Millon Clinical Adolescent Inventory* (MCAI) (Millon & Davis, 1993) is the adolescent version of the MCMI-III and is designed for youth ages 13 to 19 with a sixth-grade reading level or higher. There are 160 true–false items, which can be completed in 25 to 30 minutes. The MCAI is a level C test and was normed on over 1,000 adolescent clients in residential, outpatient, and inpatient settings in the United States and Canada. The MCAI was developed prior to the DSM-IV and like the MMCI-III assesses traits based on Theodore Millon's biosocial conceptualization of personality and personality disorders (Davis, 1999). The MCAI's nine personality scales include Introversive, Inhibited, Doleful, Submissive, Dramatizing, Egotistic, Unruly, Forceful, Conforming, Oppositional, Self-Demeaning, and Borderline Tendency. There are also Clinical Syndrome and Expressed Concerns scales. Each of the nine personality scales includes three subscales. For example, the Introversive scale contains the following subscales: Expressively Impassive, Temperamentally Apathetic, and Interpersonally Unengaged. All of the personality scales and subscales assess negative maladaptive traits. There is not a scale, however, designed to assess interpersonal competencies or adaptive skills like other adolescent self-report measures contain (see Chapter 10). However, Millon did create a complementary measure, the *Millon Adolescent Personality Inventory* (MAPI), which was normed on both clinical and nonclinical adolescents and assesses adaptive personality styles such as Sociable, Cooperative, Respectful, and Confident.

Additional Personality Disorders Measures

Several other measures with adequate reliability are available to assist in the diagnosis and case conceptualization of personality disorders. These include the *Personality Assessment Inventory* (PAI), the *Personality Diagnostic Questionnaire-4* (PDQ-4), the *Wisconsin Personality Disorders Inventory* (WISPI), and the *Coolidge Axis II Inventory* (CATI) (McClough & Clarkin, 2004; Widiger, 2008). These measures vary in their theoretical foundation, which shapes item content as well as their correspondence to DSM-IV criteria for the various personality disorders. For example, the PAI is based on an interpersonal model, whereas the PDQ-4 items are based on DSM-IV criteria (Widiger). With the exception of the test manual of the PAI, these personality measures lack sufficient normative information that is found with the MMPI-2 and the MCMI-III (Widiger).

ASSESSING NORMAL PERSONALITY TRAITS

NEO INVENTORIES All of the aforementioned personality measures were designed to assess personality disorders in particular and psychopathology in general. The NEO inventories are based on the five factor model of normal personality discussed earlier, which is now considered the major theoretical model of normal personality structure (Costa & McCrae, 1992; McCrae & Costa, 1997; Widiger, 2008). The original NEO-PI was developed in 1985 and was designed to measure the following five personality dimensions: Neuroticism, Extraversion, Openness, Agreeableness, and Conscientiousness. Each of those dimensions has six subfactors and is considered the end point of a continuum of personality structure (see Table 8.4). For example, an individual who scores high on Neuroticism tends to worry often, get anxious easily, and is typically self-conscious; whereas someone at the other end of this continuum would characteristically be unconcerned, dispassionate, and shameless.

Because the NEO-PI- is based on a dimensional model of personality, it does not utilize cutoff scores to diagnosis or categorize respondents. For example, rather than labeling an individual as an introvert or extravert, the test indicates where along this personality dimension an individual is in terms of percentiles with most people on this dimension being "ambiverts"—a mixture of the six extraversion subtraits (Costa & McCrae, 1992).

The NEO-PI-R is a 240-item inventory that can be used in nonclinical and clinical settings for the multiple purposes of assessing client interests, psychological well-being, coping styles, behavior, and health (Costa & McCrae, 1992). It also can be used to help an individual gain an understanding of his or her personality traits and the behavioral implications of those characteristic styles of relating. The items are answered with a 5-point Likert scale from "strongly disagree" to "strongly agree." It is for individuals ages 17 and older and requires a sixth-grade reading level. There is also a short version of the NEO-PI-R, the *NEO Five-Factor Inventory,* consisting of 60 items and 30 scales corresponding to the 30 subfactors (or facets) in the five factor model. There are self-report, observer rating, and abbreviated versions of the NEO-PI-R. All are available from *Psychological Assessment Resources* and are level B tests. The second revision of the NEO, the NEO-PI-3, is now available and has been extended for youth 12 and older (McCrae & Costa, 2010). The NEO-PI-3 has separate norms for adolescents and adults and some items were revised to make them more appropriate for adolescents and easier for them to read.

Technical Information   The NEO-PI-R norms are based on a sample of 500 men and 500 women drawn from three different groups that included 1,539 men and women taking part in a job-performance study and two smaller groups taking part in a longitudinal study on aging (Costa & McCrae, 1992). Inspection of the normative sample reveals it closely matched the 1985 U.S. Census projections for age and race. However, race consisted of only three categories: "White," "Black," and "Other," and no information regarding the geographical representativeness of the normative sample is provided in the test manual.

Internal consistency coefficients (alpha) were in the good to excellent range for the five domains. Alpha coefficients ranged from 0.86 to 0.92 for the domains on both the self-report and observer rating versions (Costa & McCrae, 1992). The alpha coefficients for the 30 individual facets were lower than the domains, as would be expected based on statistical principles, but for the most part were within acceptable ranges (0.56 to 0.81 for the self-report).

Administration, Scoring, and Interpretation   Like the previously described measures, the NEO-PI-R and NEO-PI-3 are self-report inventories that simply require the clinician using it to ensure that the respondent has the required reading level (sixth grade) and understands the directions. Typically they can be completed in 30 to 40 minutes (McCrae & Costa, 2010). The test can be either hand or machine scored, and profile forms are used when hand scoring to convert raw scores to standard *t* scores. There are separate profile forms for adults, college-age clients, and adolescents, with one side of the profile form for males and the other side for females. The profile forms visually display the percentile and *t* scores for the five dimensional factors.

A global personality description based on where the individual fell, either low, average, or high on each of the five factors or dimensions can be obtained from the publisher

Table 8.4 NEO-PI-R Major Domains and Subtraits	
Domains and Subtraits	**Words Used to Describe Individuals with High Scores on Domains and Facet Scales[1]**
Neuroticism:	an individual who is prone to negative emotional lability and psychological distress
Anxiety	nervous, tense, fearful, high-strung
Angry Hostility	angry, irritable, demanding, edgy, moody
Depression	discontented, worrisome, self-effacing
Self-Consciousness	defensive, shy, timid, inhibited
Impulsiveness	excitable, hasty, self-centered, loud
Vulnerability	lacking self-confidence, fuzzy thinking, careless
Extraversion:	someone who puts energy into social activities
Warmth	friendly, warm, kind, affectionate
Gregariousness	sociable, outgoing, chatty, spontaneous
Assertiveness	assertive, self-confident, bold passionate
Activity	active, energetic, hurried, fast
Excitement Seeking	adventurous, daring, pleasure-seeking, charismatic, spunky
Positive Emotions	enthusiastic, humorous, complimentary, care-free
Openness to Experience:	a person who seeks out and prefers activities for their own sake
Fantasy	unconventional, imaginative, creative, complex
Aesthetics	artistic, cultured, innovative, original
Feelings	deep, sophisticated, spontaneous, excitable
Actions	daring, adventuresome, prefers variety, versatile
Ideas	curious, analytical, nonconforming, perceptive
Values	liberal, untraditional, independent, flirtatious
Agreeableness:	an individual who prefers compassionate interpersonal interaction
Trust	trusting, fair, selfless, soft hearted
Straightforwardness	simple, patient, democratic, straightforward
Altruism	generous, kind, selfless, good natured
Compliance	agreeable, flexible, courteous, tolerant
Modesty	humble, acquiescent, sympathetic, agreeable
Tender-Mindedness	kind, warm, soft hearted, gullible, gentle
Conscientiousness:	a person who tends to be organized, persistent, and motivated to achieve goals
Competence	efficient, confident, intelligent, economical, resourceful
Order	organized, practical, careful, neat
Dutifulness	scrupulous, conscientious, thrifty, steady, dependable
Achievement Striving	ambitious, hardworking, self-disciplined, persistent
Self-Discipline	disciplined, economical, organized, practical, self-reliant
Deliberation	deliberate, methodical, patient, careful

[1]The terms used to describe the NEO-PI-R facets are based on Five Factor Model research (McCrae & Costa, 1985; Goldberg, 1992; Saucier, 1994; McCrae & Costa, 2010).

(PAR Inc.—*www.parinc.com*). This interpretive report includes more detailed personality descriptions based on the six facets of each dimension and a third section, "Personality Correlates." The "Personality Correlates" section provides information about Coping and Defenses, Somatic Complaints, Psychological Well-Being, Cognitive Processes, Interpersonal Characteristics, and Needs and Motives (Costa & McCrae, 1992). The main part of the personality interpretation report for a client like Nancy, in the case study at the beginning of the chapter, might read as follows: "The most distinctive aspect of this woman's personality is the Neuroticism factor." Individuals who score high on this factor are prone to experience a good deal of negative emotions including anger, worry, and embarrassment when meeting new people. Her extraversion scores suggest this is an individual who has "an average degree of interpersonal warmth," but rarely enjoys going to "large, crowded, noisy parties." She has trouble asserting herself and tends to stay in the background during discussions. She is unlikely to seek out activities that are very stimulating and thrilling (Costa & McCrae, 1992).

Advantages and Limitations   As a measure of "normal" personality, the NEO-PI and its revisions have been used primarily in research settings, although it is also a very useful and recommended tool for facilitating case conceptualization (Bagby, Wild, & Turner, 2003; Widiger, 2008). More specifically, it can help identify a client's emotional and coping styles, interpersonal patterns, and self-concept, all of which have direct bearing on many types of therapies and treatments.

The NEO-PI-R and the other NEO inventories have a remarkable research base, especially the cross-cultural studies conducted with it. Furthermore, the five factor model (FFM) upon which it is based has been used to reconceptualize the DSM-IV personality disorders (see Table 8.5). One study in particular (Lynam & Widiger, 2001) illustrated how the FFM can be applied to the 10 DSM-IV personality disorders. Experts in the field were asked to describe a case representative of a particular personality disorder, such as borderline personality, and then use the model's 30 facets to rate whether that prototypic case was either low or high in those personality traits. This rethinking of the DSM-IV personality disorders as extreme versions of these five normal personality dimensions suggests a usefulness of the NEO-PI-R in ruling out personality disorders as well as an instrument for identifying and describing an individual's less extreme traits and styles.

As a measure of "normal" personality, the NEO-PI-R and the model it is based on lack sufficient research for its use in treatment planning, however (Widiger, 2008). Knowledge of a client's underlying personality, high in neuroticism for example, does not necessarily help a clinician in selecting among different interventions, such as medication, individual therapy, group therapy, and so on, but it can certainly aid in understanding personality dynamics that can affect the course of those treatments.

Cultural Considerations   The five factor model and the NEO-PI have been cross-culturally validated in a number of European, Asian, Latin American, and African cultures. Like the other measures described in this chapter, validated translations of the NEO-PI-R into numerous languages and dialects continues to accelerate (there are so far 24 versions) (McCrae & Costa, 2010). Together, the existing studies have demonstrated support for the five factor model of personality across many diverse cultures including those viewed as more "collectivistic" than the individualistic American culture. Because the NEO-PI-R was designed as a measure of normal personality, the cross-cultural research has typically involved nonclinical samples and nonclinical purposes. Two recent exceptions include a study that examined the ability of the Neuroticism factor to predict level of acculturation stress in Mexican-American college students

Table 8.5 Applying the Five Factor Model to Common DSM-IV Personality Disorders

FFM Factors & Facets:	Antisocial	Borderline	Compulsive	Dependent	Narcissistic	Schizotypal
Neuroticism:						
Anxiousness	2	4	4	4	—	4
Angry Hostility	4	4	—	—	4	—
Depressiveness	—	4	—	—	—	—
Self-Consciousness	2	—	—	4	2	4
Impulsiveness	4	4	2	—	—	—
Vulnerability	—	4	—	4	—	—
Extraversion:						
Warmth	—	—	2	—	2	2
Gregariousness	—	—	—	—	—	2
Assertiveness	4	—	—	2	4	—
Activity	4	—	—	—	—	—
Excitement Seeking	4	—	2	—	4	—
Positive Emotions	—	—	—	—	—	2
Openness:						
Fantasy	—	—	—	—	—	—
Aesthetics	—	—	—	—	—	—
Feelings	—	4	2	—	2	—
Actions	4	4	2	—	4	—
Ideas	—	—	2	—	—	4
Values	—	—	2	—	—	—
Agreeableness:						
Trust	2	—	—	4	2	—
Straightforwardness	2	—	—	—	2	—
Altruism	2	—	—	—	2	—
Compliance	2	—	—	4	2	—
Modesty	2	—	—	4	2	—
Tendermindedness	2	—	—	—	2	—
Conscientiousness:						
Competence	—	—	4	—	—	—
Order	—	—	4	—	—	2
Dutifulness	2	—	4	—	—	—
Achievement Striving	—	—	4	—	—	—
Self-Discipline	2	—	4	—	—	—
Deliberation	2	2	4	—	—	—

Note: Experts in personality disorders rated prototypical cases of one to three personality disorders as being low (1) to high (5) on each of the 30 facets of the five factor model. The table represents average ratings across experts (2 = 2 or less, 4 = 4 or more, — = 2 to 4).

From: "Using the Five Factor Model to Represent DSM-IV Personality Disorders: An Expert Consensus Approach," by D. R Lynam and T. A Widiger, 2001, *Journal of Abnormal Psychology.* 110, p. 404. Copyright 2001 by the American Psychological Association. Adapted with permission.

(Mangold, Veraza, Kinkler, & Kinney, 2007), and a study of Chinese psychiatric patients that found that the NEO-PI-R traits correlated highly with personality disorders in that sample (Yang et al., 2002).

***MYERS–BRIGGS TYPE INDICATOR* (MBTI)**   Another measure of normal personality that is widely used in the counseling profession is the *Meyers–Briggs Type Indicator* (MBTI). The MBTI is a self-report measure for individuals 14 years and older and comes in several forms: M (93 items), Step-II (144 items), and an online version (Center for Applications of Psychological Type [CAPT], 2010). Form M is designed at a seventh-grade reading level and can be completed within 25 minutes. It was revised in 1998 and incorporated a more sophisticated test construction methodology to compensate for criticisms of the scoring system in the original version (Fleenor, 2001). There is also the *Murphy–Meisgeier Type Indicator* for children (MMTIC) a 43-item inventory for youth grades 2 through 12, which incorporates MBTI typologies (CAPT, 2010). The MBTI is designed to measure personality preferences rather than traits or abilities. It is rarely used in mental health service settings, with the exception of some family counseling, but it has become a common assessment tool for career and organizational purposes such as team building (Whiston, 2009).

The MBTI is based on Carl Jung's theory of psychological types and was designed to be a practical way to apply his theory to adolescents and adults in various settings (Myers & McCaulley, 1985). Jung theorized that human beings differ along dichotomous dimensions that reflect how they use mental processes he called sensing, intuition, thinking, feeling, and judgment. Jung also believed an individual's personality was based on two polar opposite and complementary attitudes toward life: extraversion–introversion and judgment–perception. The Jungian concept of introversion–extraversion does not, however, fully match other conceptualizations of this personality type such as in the five factor model described earlier. According to Jung's theory, extraverts are drawn to and get stimulation from the people and objects in their environment; whereas introverts take their energy from the environment and prefer ideas and concepts and gain enjoyment through quiet reflection (Myers & McCaulley, 1985). This model posits individuals as having four main preference styles and attitudes: Extraversion or Introversion (EI), Sensing or Intuitive Perception (SN), Thinking or Feeling Judgment (TF), and Judgment Perception (JP). These processes and attitudes can be combined to produce 16 psychological types. Each type represents a dominant process and an auxiliary one (Myers & McCaulley, 1985). MBTI interpretation is based on the characteristics each type is theorized to represent. For example, one type is ISTJ, the "the thoughtful realists," who tend to be "serious, quiet, earn success by concentration and thoroughness. Practical, orderly, matter-of-fact, logical, realistic, and dependable" (Myers & McCaulley, 1985, p. 20).

Despite the MBTI's widespread popularity amongst counseling professionals, it has not gone without criticism, both on theoretical and psychometric grounds, as well as recommendations for limiting its use. Although internal consistency reliabilities have ranged from 0.80 to 0.90 and higher, test–retest reliabilities have been less impressive with over one-third of individuals, on average, obtaining a different dichotomy score within a month (Fleenor, 2001; Mastrangelo, 2001). That is, depending upon the study, anywhere from 20% to 45 % of individuals had a different preference (e.g., introversion vs. extraversion or sensing vs. intuition) between test time 1 and 2. Even if the test is measuring personality preferences rather than traits, the significant number of individuals who are found to switch preferences within a relatively short period of time calls into question the test's construct validity. Furthermore, Mastrangelo (2001) and Boyle (1995) have reviewed the studies that were attempts to demonstrate evidence of the MBTI's construct validity or theoretical rationale and found them to be lacking support. These reviewers have cautioned against using it as a tool for employment selection but that it can be valuable for promoting self-understanding of one's personality styles.

SIXTEEN PERSONALITY FACTOR QUESTIONNAIRE—FIFTH EDITION (16PF FIFTH EDITION) One other measure of normal personality functioning commonly used by counselors and to a lesser extent, psychologists, is the *Sixteen Personality Factor Questionnaire* (16 PF) developed by Raymond Cattell in 1949 and designed to measure two-dimensional personality traits that all adults were considered to have to some degree (Cattell & Eber, 1972). Some of the bipolar traits Cattell identified through 10 years of factor analytic research as comprising normal adult personality included: Factor A—Reserved vs. Outgoing; Factor B—Less Intelligent vs. More Intelligent; Factor C—Affected by Feelings vs. Emotionally Stable; Factor E—Humble vs. Assertive; and Factor H—Shy vs. Venturesome. The 16 PF, now in its fifth edition, consists of 185 multiple-choice questions, and measures 16 primary bipolar traits (some of the trait labels have been changed from the first three editions) and five global ones: Extraversion, Anxiety, Tough Mindedness, Independence, and Self-Control (Cattell, Cattell, & Cattell, 1993). Like the aforementioned normal personality measures, it has been used in different contexts—business, organizational, and mental health—and for a variety of reasons. In 2000 its norms were updated on a sample of over 10,000 individuals to reflect the U.S. Census. There are also adolescent and Spanish-American versions of the 16 PF.

INTEREST MEASURES

Related to the concept of personality and perhaps another aspect of it, is the notion that as human beings we have values, interests, and preferences. We also have a need to be involved in work and leisure activities that provide fulfillment and meaning in our lives. Individuals who are engaged in and committed to purposeful, meaningful, and fulfilling work have been found to have greater resilience or stress "hardiness," and for those who don't, this lack of fulfillment is a significant stressor (Brooks & Goldstein, 2004). Often, older adolescent and adult clients entering counseling because of problems with psychiatric disorders and interpersonal relationships discover that major sources of their unhappiness and dissatisfaction is a lack of purpose and meaning in their jobs and career.

Nancy, for example, struggled both with her dissatisfaction in her role as a stay-at-home mother and with her uncertainty about what else she wanted to do and might have a talent for. Ultimately she made a decision to go back to school to become a nurse. A mental health professional working with Nancy could refer her for a career counseling assessment to help her ease her struggle and confusion. A career counselor, in addition to interviewing Nancy, would likely administer one or more career counseling interest measures in order to assist her in identifying an occupation that fits her abilities, interests, and values, and the demands of a particular occupation.

Interest measures help individuals to identify vocational and avocational pursuits that are constant with who they are, including their skills and their passions. An assessment of interests and values is typically conducted in the context of career counseling that often takes place in educational, workplace, or private practice settings. Interest measures are considered one of three separate but related categories of career counseling assessment measures, which also include values, abilities, and career planning or process (Whiston, 2009). Regardless of the type of measure, all of them share the common goal of promoting greater self-understanding for the purpose of facilitating vocational and career planning (Savickas, 2000). Collectively, these measures are based on models of lifespan development, personality theory, and career counseling, and are typically covered in greater detail in career counseling courses. The interest measures, however, share a relationship to traditional personality measures discussed previously, and therefore, several of the more prominent interest measures will be discussed.

Like other personality measures, the underlying theoretical foundation and test construction methods vary among these interest measures. Several counseling psychologists (Armstrong, Day, McVay, & Rounds, 2008; Blake & Sackett, 1999; Holland, 1999; Savickas, 1999) have made the point that interests and personality are interrelated constructs, although interests may reflect a more circumscribed aspect of personality that is expressed in work, hobbies, and leisure. Among them, Holland (1997, 1999) has been one of the strongest and clearest advocates of the interrelationship and equivalence of interests and personality measures. Applying his own experiences as a vocational counselor and reviews of the vocational literature, Holland developed his own personality typology theory.

Holland's Theory of Vocational Personalities and Environments

According to Holland's model, originally formulated in 1959, there are six types or traits that are related to a pattern of interests, vocational preferences, life goals and values, and beliefs about one's self (Holland, 1997). Those traits are Realistic, Investigative, Artistic, Social, Enterprising, and Conventional. Collectively those traits have been referred to as the RIASEC model and descriptions of each trait are shown in Table 8.6. His typology model was developed from his own experience as vocational counselor but has its roots in other typologies such as Jung's and Murray's hierarchy of needs and environmental presses as well as the vocational literature and assessments (Holland, 1997). He further conceived of the types in terms of their degree of resemblance or lack of congruence and visually represented this with a hexagonal model. The closer two types are along the hexagon, the more closely related they are, and the further apart, the more they are different (see Figure 8.3). Like other typology models, Holland's included patterns of types as a way to categorize people or environments, for example the RIS type.

Holland also proposed that that there are six parallel interpersonal model environments where the majority of individuals in that setting represent a particular type, for example, realistic. The environment's interpersonal climate is a reflection of their shared values, interests, and beliefs. He further believed that individuals have a tendency to seek out environments that will be a good fit for their personality and allow them to make the most of their abilities and values. The interaction of the individual's personality type with the interpersonal environment typology will, according to the model, predict to some degree vocational choice, stability, and accomplishment and personal competencies and behavior (Holland, 1997).

Much research since the 1950s has examined the validity of different aspects of Holland's model. Some of the more recent studies have found evidence in support of his original theories, particularly the notion of interest measures as personality measures. An empirical relationship between Holland's six traits and four of the five factor model dimensions—Extraversion, Openness, Conscientiousness, and Agreeableness—was found in a heterogeneous group of individuals participating in vocational assessment study (Blake & Sackett, 1999). Other research examining the correlations between the RIASEC types and personality measures—NEO-PI-R, MBTI, and 16PF—has supported an integrative and synergistic model of interests and personality traits consistent with Holland's premises (Armstrong et al., 2008). For example, the model purports that extraverts prefer work settings that provide more social connection, whereas introverts prefer less social environments, and that personality–environment fit will affect the

Table 8.6 Holland Personality Types

The realistic type:

Possesses traditional values including self-control, freedom of choice, and practicality; prefers work environments that have little flexibility with people of similar values, interests, and beliefs. Is apt to be described as conforming, inflexible, hard-headed, persistent, practical, realistic, materialistic, and self-effacing.

The investigative type:

Values scholarship and scientific achievements and traits such as intellectual, logical, and ambitious; prefers work environments that involve investigative work. Is commonly portrayed as analytical, cautious, curious, intellectual, introspective, precise, rational, reserved, and unassuming.

The artistic type:

Values aesthetic expression and experience and traits such as imaginative and courageous, but not obedient and openness to feelings, ideas, and people. Prefers work environments that are artistic and promote use of artistic ideas and beliefs to solve problems. Is apt to be viewed as complicated, disorderly, emotional, expressive, idealistic, imaginative, impulsive, nonconforming, open, and sensitive.

The social type:

Values service to others and equality; prefers work environments that are highly interpersonal and interact with others of similar beliefs and values and promote social skills and traits when solving problems. Is apt to be described as agreeable, cooperative, empathic, friendly, helpful, idealistic, warm, patient, and sociable.

The enterprising type:

Values controlling others, freedom of choices and actions, and ambition and using social influence to solve problems; prefers entrepreneurial and enterprising settings. Is often described as adventurous, ambitious, energetic, enthusiastic, extroverted, forceful, optimistic, self-confident, and sociable.

The conventional type:

Values social convention—obedience, politeness—and tends to be close-minded. Prefers working within organizational structure and rules and relies on authority for advice about problems, and likes methodical planning and problems-solving approaches. Is typically seen as careful, conforming, conscientious, dogmatic, efficient, inflexible, methodical, orderly, practical, and unimaginative.

Source: Making Vocational Choices: A Theory of Vocational Personalities and Work Environments, 3rd ed., by J. Holland, 1997 (Odessa, FL: Psychological Assessment Resources).

development and use of skills necessary for effective workplace functioning. Although other individual differences such as decision-making readiness, development maturity, and decidedness or certainty have guided the development of other types of career counseling scales (Savickas, 2000), Holland's model has had the greater influence on two prominent and widely used interest tests: *Strong Interest Inventory* and *Self-Directed Search*.

STRONG INTEREST INVENTORY (SII) The *Strong Interest Inventory* (SII) is the most frequently used and researched career and vocational measure (Hood & Johnson, 2007). It has been

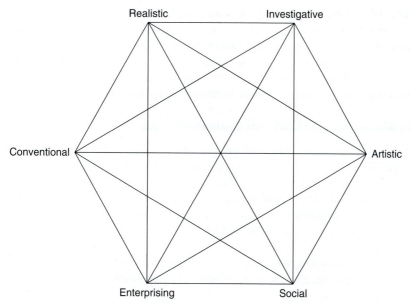

FIGURE 8.3   Holland's Model   Reproduced by special permission of the Publisher, Psychological Assessment Resources, Inc., 16204 North Florida Avenue, Lutz, FL 33549, from Making Vocational Choices, Third Edition, Copyright 1973, 1985, 1992, 1997 by Psychological Assessment Resources, Inc. All rights reserved.

revised five times since its original publication as the *Strong Vocational Interest Blank* in 1927. The newly revised Strong, published in 2004, is based on Holland's theory of personality.

The SII is a 291-item inventory that measures "likes" and "dislikes" on a 5-point Likert scale relative to specific occupations, academic subjects, leisure activities, and types of people. Its psychometric properties (including test–retest and internal reliability coefficients) are in the adequate to excellent range and validation studies of the 1994 version demonstrated the predictive ability of the occupational scales (Donnay, Thompson, Morris, & Schaubhut, 2004; Hood & Johnson, 2007). Four scales comprise the SII: General Occupational Themes, Basic Interest, Occupational, and Personal Style. Changes made to the 1994 version include 1) adopting a 5-point Likert response scale (versus a 3-point); 2) 99 new or modified items; 3) a more representative normative sample in terms of matching the race and ethnicity of the 2000 U.S. Census; and 4) updating the occupations.

Similar to the MMPI-2 and MCMI-III, the SSI produces code types, although these represent themes of strong or preferred interest rather than a personality type. For example, a client whose strongest interests are represented by the artistic, conventional, and social themes might be highly interested in activities comprising those themes. These may include the visual arts, writing, and culinary arts (Artistic); religious activities (Social); and computer activities (Conventional). The Occupational scale measures the degree to which the client's responses are similar to the interests of individuals working in 244 specific occupations, ranging from accountant to veterinarian (the 1994 Strong contained 211 occupations). The Personal Style scale measures five areas: Work Style (preferences for working with things and data vs. people), Learning Environment (practical vs. academic), Leadership Style (comfort with taking charge of others vs. not taking charge), and Risk Taking/Adventure ("like" vs. "dislike" of risk and adventure), and, new to the 2004 version, Team Orientation (can work autonomously vs. as part of a team).

SELF-DIRECTED SEARCH   The *Self-Directed Search* (SDS) developed by John Holland is both an interests and abilities measure (Holland, 1997). The SDS can be both self-administered and self-interpreted and is available online at ***http://www.self-directed-search.com***. Respondents rate their degree of liking activities and occupations and estimate their competencies and abilities. Like the SII, the SDS produces a code type based on Holland's typology, which is then mapped to occupations and college majors that are similar or identical to the individual's code type.

Interest Measures and Cultural Considerations

As with personality measures, cross-cultural uses and research with interest measures has been ongoing. The SII's standardization group is representative of the U.S. population in terms of racial–ethnic proportions, and the SDS has been translated into 25 different languages. Concerns, however, have been raised about the cultural limitations of the interest surveys described in this section, for women and ethnic minorities, because answers to items may reflect more the opportunities one has had to participate in certain activities, which are often socially constrained, rather than one's interest level (Whiston, 2009). In addition, some research has called into question Holland's premise and shown that interest inventories may have only a minimal relationship to job satisfaction and success, and might be better thought of as measures of potential interest (Erford, 2006).

PROJECTIVE TESTS

The use of projective tests for the purposes of diagnosis and treatment monitoring has become highly controversial, less so for case conceptualization and treatment planning purposes. Many clinicians have found projective instruments useful because they provide a window into a client's unconscious and underlying personality traits and are less subject to faking compared to self-report measures. Furthermore, they can reveal themes, concerns, and problems that may not have been identified through clinical interviews or objective tests. These tests are based upon the projective hypothesis. In essence, this theory states that when confronted with ambiguous stimuli like inkblots, individuals will resolve the ambiguity of the stimulus by giving it definition. How one creates structure out of vague and undefined stimuli, like inkblots or ambiguous drawings of people, is supposedly an expression of underlying perceptions, beliefs, and feelings and ultimately psychopathology. Clinicians who rely on projective tools argue that they can reveal aspects of a person that objective personality tests cannot, but that viewpoint has galvanized extensive controversy and debate regarding the use of these tests (Lilienfeld, Wood, & Garb, 2000).

Rorschach Inkblot Test

The best known example of a projective test is the inkblot test developed by a Swiss psychiatrist, Herman Rorschach. The Rorschach inkblot test has remained one of the most commonly used psychological tests for over 40 years (Camara et al., 2000), despite strong criticisms from professionals within the fields of psychology and counseling. The Rorschach consists of 10 symmetrical inkblot cards, 5 of which are black and gray, 2 are mostly black and gray with some red coloring, and 3 have a variety of colors. The cards are handed to the client and he or she is asked to respond to the question, "What might this be?" The individual is allowed to rotate the card and look at it in any position to come up with a perception. Once all 10 cards have been responded to, the evaluator reviews client responses to determine which aspects of the blot—form, color, shading, texture, and location—were used in creating a perception.

Following Herman Rorschach's death in 1922 a number of systems have been developed for scoring and interpreting client perceptions and responses. The interpretation system that has had the widest usage but received the greatest criticism is the one developed by John Exner (1974). The Exner system is very elaborate, with over 25 different scores and indexes that have been used primarily for diagnosing psychopathology, and describing interpersonal and coping styles, but not as a tool for measuring normal personality traits. The Exner system integrates both the content of the perception and the elements of the inkblot that were used in putting together a percept. The types of content responses that are analyzed include animal or human figures, whether or not the percept included movement (e.g., two bears dancing), and the commonality or popularity of the response. Scores are also derived based on the use of color, shading, texture, and other aspects of the blot that may be used to form a response. These scores are then used to assess for the presence of pathological states such as depression, thought disorder, suicidal thinking, and interpersonal styles of relating to and perceiving others, as well as typical coping styles.

From a practical perspective, the Rorschach has some limitations and advantages. It is a level C instrument and can take hours to administer, score, and interpret. Because there is no way of knowing ahead of time how many responses in total a client may give—some respond with only one perception per card, others may see three or four—the time involved is highly variable and unpredictable. Although a survey of clinical psychologists found that, on average, 45 minutes is spent administering it, and another 95 minutes for scoring and interpretation (Camara et al., 2000). Many studies have shown that when used with the Exner scoring system, the Rorschach can be a clinically useful and valid tool on par with other instruments such as the MMPI (Viglione & Hilsenroth, 2001).

Picture-Story Tests

Another type of projective test involving a series of cards is the picture-story test. Picture-story tests vary in terms of how realistic versus impressionistic are the pictures on the cards. Like the Rorschach, the individual taking the test is handed the card but in this case is asked to tell a story based on the images on the card. The story that's told is seen as a reflection of underlying emotional concerns, perceptions, themes, and beliefs that might not be revealed through more direct methods like a counseling session or interview. The oldest and most widely used of this type of test is the *Thematic Apperception Test* (TAT). Like the Rorschach, the TAT has remained a very popular and widely used test despite even greater concerns about its reliability and validity than that of the Rorschach. There is also a child version, the *Children's Apperception Test,* which has pictures that young children are more apt to relate to. Examples of picture-story tests that involve more realistic drawings and situations are the *Roberts Apperception Test for Children*–Second Edition and the *Tasks of Emotional Development* (TED). Both the Roberts and the TED are designed exclusively for children and adolescents.

Picture-story tests can be a useful supplement to counseling sessions for those clients who need more structure but are less apt to open up to direct questions. In that regard they can be a useful clinical tool and used informally for developing hypotheses about a client that become part of a case conceptualization. Scoring systems exist for the TAT, the Roberts, and other picture-story tests for the purpose of identifying underlying themes, concerns, and needs rather than generating elaborate personality trait descriptions. Furthermore, these tests are unlikely to be used outside of clinical settings.

Drawings

One remaining category of projective techniques, which is still widely used, are drawings. The three most common types of drawings are Draw-A-Person, Kinetic Family Drawing, and the House-Tree-Person. These techniques involve giving a client a blank piece of paper and asking them to draw either a person, house, or tree or their family with everyone in the family doing something. Generally, there is some discussion afterwards about the drawing, and depending upon the technique, specific probe questions may be used. Although scoring systems have been developed for these kinds of drawings, like for picture-story tests, they are more typically used as tools to gain a better understanding of a client, especially a child, and as a vehicle for promoting more counseling conversation, not a method of personality assessment. A good deal of controversy has surrounded the use of scoring drawings and interpreting those scores as indices of emotional disturbance (Lilienfeld et al., 2000; Merrill, 2008) but the one system that has demonstrated some validity in this regard is the DAP screening procedure for emotional disturbance (DAP:SPED) (Naglieri, McNeish, & Bardos, 1991).

PRACTICE SUGGESTION
Guidelines for Using Personality Tests

1. Determine the purpose in using a personality test:
   a. Enhance client's understanding of self and the interrelationship between one's personality traits and interpersonal or work environments.
   b. Enhance client's understanding of how one's personality traits may affect emotions, behaviors, and thoughts.
   c. Promote client understanding of self to facilitate career and vocational planning.
   d. Clarify diagnosis of personality disorders.
   e. Identify pathological traits and states or maladaptive defenses or coping styles.
   f. Enhance case conceptualization to inform treatment planning.
2. Select a test that matches the intended purpose (e.g., a test of normal personality traits such as the NEO-PI-R [for 1a] or the MMPI-2 [for 1e]).
3. If the diagnosis of a personality disorder is being considered, only the MCMI-III or certain structured interviews are aligned with current DSM criteria for personality disorders; but some research has been done on using the NEO-PI-R to assess personality disorders.
4. A test that has norms that are pertinent for the client should be selected.
5. If a client is to be referred to another clinician for personality testing, clarify during the referral process how the results of the test will be communicated to the client and to you.
6. Although reliable standardized scoring systems have been developed for projective techniques, they require much more clinician time to score and interpret than self-report questionnaires and the diagnostic validity is questionable.
7. Projective techniques can help, however, with case conceptualization and identifying themes or concerns that may not have been revealed through clinical interviews.

Limitations of Projective Tests

Experts in the field of personality assessment have hotly debated the merits of tests like the Rorschach and the TAT, and proponents of those tests have argued that they provide clinicians with valuable information other tests do not. Others have strongly criticized those measures on psychometric grounds (i.e., poor reliability and limited evidence of validity) (Anastasi & Urbina, 1997; Dawes, 1994; Hunsley & Bailey, 2001; Kaplan & Saccuzzo, 2005; Lillenfeld et al., 2000; Merrell, 2008). The Rorschach in particular has been the subject of contentious debate in scholarly journals with some questioning whether it has any clinical utility and even calling for a moratorium on its use in clinical settings (Dawes, 1994; Garb, 1999; Garb, Wood, Nezworski, Grove, & Stejskal, 2001; Hunsley & Bailey, 2001). This debate has continued even with the development of John Exner's comprehensive system for scoring and interpreting the Rorschach, a system that did bring greater interrater reliability than previous scoring systems had, but did not provide adequate support for its validity according to a number of researchers in the assessment field. On a practical level—the amount of clinician time and cost required to administer and interpret the Rorschach and other projective measures relative to the amount of new clinical information these measures reveal compared to objective self-report measures, can make them of questionable utility in some cases. In managed care settings, for example, they are less practical tools than they potentially are in nonmanaged settings. Managed care and commercial insurance companies have significantly reduced the amount of psychological testing they will reimburse for, and therefore it is very difficult for clinicians to be compensated for the time needed to administer, score, and interpret projective techniques.

Summary and Conclusions

Faced with a client like Nancy—who presents a case conceptualization enigma—the inclusion of a personality or a multidimensional psychopathology measure can be a valuable component of the overall assessment process. The decision to incorporate one or more of these measures into one's own assessment, or refer a client elsewhere for psychological testing, is based on several factors. The primary consideration is the kind of information that can be gained from having a client complete a standardized multi-dimensional measure (see Practice Suggestion: Guidelines for Using Personality Tests). The measure ought to yield information that additional interviews alone may not produce. If, for example, in the case of Nancy, the clinician is deciding upon several different diagnoses, including a possible diagnosis of a personality disorder, then a test like the MMPI-2 or MCMI-III can potentially facilitate that process by efficiently identifying clinical problems and personality traits not readily gleaned from one or two intake interviews. Additional factors for considering using standardized self-report measures as part of the assessment process

include 1) needing a baseline or ongoing measure of client distress, symptom severity, and interpersonal functioning; 2) needing information to enhance clinical case conceptualization; and 3) wanting additional information for treatment planning.

This chapter focused on the concept of personality theory and reviewed specific objective self-report measures that clinicians commonly use in the overall assessment process in order to gain a more comprehensive understanding of a client's personality and interpersonal dynamics. Objective measures constitute one of two broad categories of personality assessment, the other being projective tests.

Some objective self-report measures, like the MMPI-2 and MCMI-III, are designed for assessing pathological personality traits, disorders, and styles. These measures are routinely used in some mental health settings for the purposes of diagnostic formulation, case conceptualization, treatment planning, or treatment monitoring purposes. They are also used for nonclinical purposes such as forensic and employment screening. On the other hand, self-report tests, like the NEO-PI-R and MBTI, are to be used for measuring normal personality traits based on a specific personality theory. Assessment of normal personality traits is more often done outside of clinical settings for either research purposes or for helping a client gain a greater understanding of self and how one's traits affect interpersonal functioning. Most of these self-report measures are at the highest user qualification level (see Chapter 2).

Related to the concept of personality are one's interests, preferences, and values. An understanding of client interests and values can promote greater understanding of self and is often an area that career

counselors have focused on. Two common and widely used career and vocational interest measures—the *Strong Interest Inventory* and the *Self-Directed Search*—were also reviewed, albeit more briefly.

Projective tests and techniques is the third category of personality assessment. Two of the most widely used projective tests—the Rorschach inkblot and the *Thematic Apperception Test* (TAT)—were discussed with a focus on the limitations and controversies surrounding these tests. How these tests and projective techniques, like drawings, can be used informally for case conceptualization purposes was briefly discussed.

Reflection Questions and Experiential Exercises

1. Think of words and phrases that describe someone you know well. How do those descriptions fit with the five factor model of personality?
2. What is your view of the relationship between personality and psychiatric disorders? Which do you find more helpful, a categorical or dimensional approach to psychopathology?
3. In small groups, design your own personality test. Brainstorm a list of potential items/questions you would want on the test. What type of response format would you want for the items (e.g., true–false, Likert scale, or combination)?
4. Interview clinicians at your practicum or internship site about their use of personality tests. Address the following questions: 1) Why or why not are these

measures used? 2) Who is using those measures? and 3) For what purposes are they being used?
5. It is more commonplace for tests of "normal" personality like the NEO-PI-R to be used in nonclinical settings, and tests like the MMPI-2 and MCMI-III to be used in clinical ones. What do you think about that practice and what advantages might there be in using tests of "normal" personality for assessment in mental health settings?
6. When would you consider having a client complete an interest measure?
7. Tests like the MMPI-2 and MCMI-III have validity scales to assess biased and distorted responding. With measures that do not have built-in validity scales, what kind of pattern of responding might you look for to detect distorted responding?

9 ASSESSING PSYCHOPATHOLOGY: MOOD AND ANXIETY DISORDERS

Chapter Objectives

After reading this chapter, you should be able to:

- Identify specific assessment measures for depression, anxiety, and other problems.
- Explain how and when these measures can be used.
- Identify the advantages and limitations of specific psychopathology questionnaires and rating scales.

The Case of Susan

Susan, a 28-year-old recently divorced female, was referred to a mental health counselor by her primary care physician who had prescribed her Paxil, an antidepressant medication. Susan told the intake counselor she had been on Paxil for a month and was "feeling all stressed out," waking up a lot during the night, and getting "annoyed" quickly. At times she lost her temper and threw things in her room.

Susan's parents divorced when she was in seventh grade, at which point she lived with her mother, who remarried when Susan went to college. Susan has one younger sister, age 27. Susan experienced some recent stressors in addition to her divorce: she lost her dog and was laid off one month ago from her sales job.

Susan reported that her symptoms of stress and feeling "annoyed" and "down" had grown progressively worse over the past month. Some days she is eating only one meal. She has trouble finding the energy to job hunt, and when friends have called she doesn't answer her phone. When venturing out to see a friend or obtain a job application she experiences "nervousness, heart racing, and feeling like I am going to faint." She recalled similar feelings when her parents divorced, at which time her mother had her see the school counselor. She added that her father was "a drinker" and not around much, and that her mother made "lots of excuses" for him.

During the past month her intake of wine increased from an "occasional" glass when "out with friends" to two to three glasses a night. She denied other substance usage, and reported quitting smoking five years ago. When asked about her former marriage, Susan started to tear up and said "I miss him." She added, however, that he had been cheating on her and that she thinks it was her fault.

Susan presented as an attractive petite female who was not wearing any makeup. She was dressed in jeans and a blouse. She appeared oriented X3 and there was no evidence of loose or delusional thinking. She did acknowledge thinking about suicide from time to time.

Susan was asked to complete the SCL-90-R and BDI-II following the intake interview. The clinician explained to her that these questionnaires "would help us see if you are having any other problems that we could focus on in the counseling and give us another way to see how you are doing as counseling progresses."

OVERVIEW

Susan's story is representative of the majority of clients who seek outpatient mental health services. Like many others, Susan is experiencing a combination of depression and anxiety symptoms and is likely to meet the DSM-IV-TR diagnostic criteria for depression. Her symptom picture is also suggestive of mixed anxiety and depression, a disorder that is listed in the DSM-IV-TR appendix but is being proposed for inclusion with Axis I Mood Disorders in the DSM-5 (American Psychiatric Association, 2010). Susan is also experiencing problems that a measure designed exclusively for assessing depression or anxiety would not identify. Her problems with temper outbursts, substance usage, and interpersonal difficulties are also in need of further clarification.

The assessment of mood and anxiety disorders and related problems can be conducted through interviews, either semistructured or structured, and observations, as discussed in Chapters 3 through 5. In addition, numerous psychometrically sound questionnaires and rating scales are available that can be used for the assessment of these disorders and other types of problems and symptoms. The purpose of this chapter is to describe the most commonly used clinical measures and discuss their application, including cross-cultural uses, as well as their advantages and limitations. The measures discussed in this chapter are most typically used for case conceptualization and treatment planning and monitoring purposes. In clinical settings, the self-report measures discussed here are not intended, on their own, to be used for diagnostic purposes. In other words, a score on a questionnaire or rating scale should not be construed as the criterion for the presence or absence of a disorder in the way that a blood test can sometimes indicate disease or pathology.

MULTIDIMENSIONAL SYMPTOM AND PROBLEM MEASURES

The measures that were discussed in the previous chapter are considered multidimensional in that they assess different aspects of personality or various dimensions of psychopathology: Axis I versus Axis II disorders in the DSM system, for example. Multiple personality traits or disorders can be evaluated with one instrument. Similarly, other types of multidimensional questionnaires exist that are not designed to assess personality, but instead measure different dimensions of psychiatric symptoms and problems related to various disorders.

These other multidimensional measures are much briefer than the personality measures and are therefore more client and clinician friendly. They are friendlier in the sense that they take less time to complete, the questions and items are more straightforward, and feedback to clients can occur relatively quickly because of the ease in scoring and interpretation. As briefer measures, they are useful for both gaining an understanding of symptom or problem severity or frequency, and as a tool for engaging clients in the counseling process. The process of giving a client a self-report measure sends the message that counseling will require self-reflection and self-assessment beyond what can be accomplished within a single session. How the client responds to that message is further data, particularly about readiness for change. Does the client readily agree to complete a questionnaire and understand what can be gained from doing so or does she question the necessity of it?

Two multidimensional measures, the *Symptom Checklist-90-Revised* (SCL-90-R) and the *Outcome Questionnaire-45.2* (OQ-45.2) are commonly used, beneficial self-report questionnaires that can be incorporated into the assessment and ongoing counseling process. With clients like Susan, who are experiencing multiple problems and symptoms that don't fit neatly into a clinical category, beginning the assessment process with a multidimensional measure can be advantageous. This enables the clinician to cast a wide assessment net and gather a comprehensive picture of what it is going on before narrowing the scope of the assessment with a unidimensional anxiety or depression measure.

Assessing Psychopathology Symptoms and Level of Functioning

SYMPTOM CHECKLIST-90-REVISED **(SCL-90-R)**   The *Symptom Checklist-90-Revised* (SCL-90-R) is a 90-item self-report rating scale that can be used as part of an initial assessment process as well as for monitoring treatment progress and outcome (Derogatis, 1994). There is also a brief version of the SCL-90-R, the *Brief Symptom Inventory* (BSI), consisting of the same scales but only 53 items. The SCL-90-R assesses for the presence of psychopathology symptoms and problems, predominantly anxiety and depression, in adolescents and adults ages 13 and older. Clients are asked to rate "How much that problem has distressed or bothered you during the past 7 days including today," with a 5-point scale from "not at all" to "extremely." It can typically be completed within 20 minutes and requires a minimum of a sixth-grade reading level. The items cover a wide array of concerns and symptoms such as somatic aches and pains, memory and other thinking problems, crying and other depression symptoms, fears and phobias, violent urges, and interpersonal sensitivity.

The development of the SCL-90-R can be traced back to the first self-report type symptom inventory in 1918, the *Woodworth Personal Data Sheet* (Derogatis & Savitz, 1999). Both the SCL-90-R and the BSI are routinely used for screening and diagnostic purposes in many inpatient and outpatient mental health settings because of the range of symptoms covered, the brief time requirements to complete and score them, and their clinical utility. Consistent with the multimodal assessment process advocated in this text and elsewhere, an observer rating version of the SCL-90-R also exists, the *Derogatis Psychiatric Rating Scale* (DPRS). This scale is designed for experienced clinicians to rate clients on symptoms that comprise the same nine scales of the SCL-90-R as well as eight additional dimensions (Derogatis & Savitz).

Administration, Scoring, and Interpretation   The SCL-90-R can be hand or computer scored, though hand scoring is relatively easy. There are male and female adult outpatient and inpatient norms, adult community nonpatient norms, and nonpatient community adolescent norms from which t scores are derived. T scores are obtained for each of the nine scales as well as for three global distress indices: Global Severity index, Positive Symptom Distress index, and Positive Symptom Total. The nine scales include Somatization, Anxiety, Phobic anxiety, Depression, Interpersonal sensitivity, Paranoid ideation, Psychoticism, Hostility, and Obsessive–Compulsive. The Global index includes a total number of symptoms endorsed as occurring a "little bit" or more, and the mean problem severity is the average severity rating across the 90 items (or items with a score of 1 or greater).

Technical Information   The SCL-90-R and BSI norms are based on four separate samples: 1,002 psychiatric outpatients, 974 community nonpatients, 423 psychiatric inpatients, and 806 community adolescents (Derogatis, 1994). The psychiatric outpatient sample was drawn from three clinics in the East and one in the Midwest and was disproportionately female (58%). Further review of the manual's normative information indicates that Blacks are overrepresented in the psychiatric outpatient sample (33%) and non-Whites are underrepresented in the community sample (14%). The nonpatient community sample was obtained from one county in an eastern state. Only gender and racial demographics are found in the manual.

Studies indicate that the reliability of the SCL-90-R is adequate or better (Derogatis & Savitz, 1999). Both measures of internal consistency and test–retest reliabilities for the nine scales are in the adequate to excellent range. Furthermore, numerous research studies have provided evidence that the SCL-90-R and the BSI are valid tools for assessing response to counseling and pharmacologic treatments, overall distress level, variations in psychopathology, and treatment outcomes (Derogatis & Savitz; Pauker, 1985; Payne, 1985).

Advantages and Limitations The main advantage of the SCL-90-R is its combination of comprehensiveness and short completion time. It is a valuable tool for supplementing unstructured and semistructured intake interviews because of its ability to detect symptoms and problem areas not identified during an interview. Both the SCL-90-R and the briefer BSI can be used in almost all counseling settings. Furthermore, a significant amount of psychotherapy research with diverse diagnostic groups has shown the SCL-90-R and the BSI to be effective self-report measures for assessing changes in overall distress and specific diagnostic symptoms such as anxiety and depression (Derogatis & Savitz, 1999). Clinicians who want a reliable and valid measure of whether clients are experiencing changes in symptoms and overall distress over a relatively brief period of time (weeks vs. months) are more apt to detect those changes with measures like the SCL-90-R than they are with the more trait-oriented personality measures described in Chapter 8. Conversely, the usefulness of the SCL-90-R and BSI for diagnostic purposes is limited because the symptoms covered don't necessarily correspond with the DSM-IV-TR symptom criteria for a number of disorders.

Cultural Considerations As of 2004, the SCL-90-R and the BSI had been translated into 26 languages. Racial and ethnic information about the standardization samples suggest, however, that it was a fairly homogenous group. Derogatis reported that the outpatient sample was approximately two-thirds White and was drawn from four teaching hospitals in the Midwest and East (Derogatis & Savitz, 1999). The adult community norms were based on a sample that was 85% White and 12% Black with the remaining 2% consisting of other racial groups. Additionally, the adolescent community sample is almost entirely White. Recent research, however, with a few relatively small samples has demonstrated its validity with specific ethnic groups: African American and Hispanic college students (Ayalon & Young, 2009; Martinez, Stillerman, & Waldo, 2005) and Central American immigrants (Asner-Self, Schreiber, & Marotta, 2006).

OUTCOME QUESTIONNAIRE-45 (OQ-45.2) The *Outcome Questionnaire-45,* version two (OQ-45.2) is a self-report measure designed to assess psychiatric and stress-related symptoms, interpersonal satisfaction and problems, and degree of dissatisfaction and conflict related to family life, work tasks, and leisure activities (Lambert & Finch, 1999). It is intended to be strictly a treatment monitoring and outcome measure, not a diagnostic tool. However, the symptom distress and interpersonal difficulty items on the OQ-45.2 could be targeted for counseling interventions. The 45 items are rated on a 5-point Likert scale from "never" to "almost always," and are phrased at a sixth-grade reading level. The items belong to one of three subscales—Symptom Distress (25 items), Interpersonal Relationships (11 items), and Social Role (9 items)—and there are five "critical items" regarding suicide, substance abuse, and workplace violence. A total score is also calculated. There are various versions of the OQ-45.2 including adult (age 18 and above, 45 items), youth self-report (ages 12–17, 64 items), parent rating (ages 4–17, 64 items), and abbreviated adult and youth (30 items). The shorter OQ-30 has been shown to be comparable to the 45-item version in terms of identifying a client's level of functioning and evaluating treatment outcome (Ellsworth, Lambert, & Johnson, 2006). All of these versions and the respective manual can be obtained from the website of the American Professional Credentialing Services LLC at *http://www.oqmeasures.com*.

Technical Information Several geographically diverse samples form the normative data base: three undergraduate groups, a community sample, an employee assistance program, two outpatient samples, and one inpatient sample (Lambert & Finch, 1999). More than 2,500 individuals completed the OQ-45.2 for the normative data with the largest sample being the community one (815). When the OQ-45.2 was administered to African American and Hispanic groups, there were no significant differences on the total score and the three subscale scores between these groups and a Caucasian group, though differences between Caucasians and African Americans were found on several items (Lambert & Finch).

Studies of the OQ-45.2's reliability and validity have demonstrated adequate or better psychometric quality as a counseling monitoring and outcome measure. Internal consistency reliability is excellent for the total score and the Symptom Distress subscale (alpha > 0.90) and in the adequate range (0.70 to 0.74) for the Interpersonal Relations and Social Role subscales (Lambert & Finch, 1999). Test–retest reliability, however, has been assessed in only undergraduate samples, not clinical samples, and they ranged from 0.78 to 0.84 (Pfeiffer, 2005). The concurrent validity of the OQ-45.2's total and subscale scores correlates highly with measures of similar constructs, such as the Global Severity index of the SCL-90-R. Furthermore, the construct validity, sensitivity, and specificity of the total scale score and subscale scores effectively discriminates between community and clinical samples, as well as between clients with any type of DSM disorder and those with only a V-code diagnosis (Lambert & Finch). A V-code diagnosis is reserved for problems and conflicts that may be a focus in counseling but do not meet the criteria for an Axis I or II diagnosis (American Psychiatric Association, 2000).

Administration, Scoring, and Interpretation The OQ-45.2 can typically be completed within five minutes, though some individuals may need 20 minutes (Lambert & Finch, 1999). If necessary, the measure can be administered orally. Respondents are asked to rate the frequency of symptoms and problems on a 5-point scale from "never" to "almost always."

Scoring is simple and straightforward. Raw scores do not need to be converted to a standardized score (such as a *t* score). A cutoff score approach is used for interpretation (i.e., scores above the cutoff are considered clinically significant and scores below suggest an absence or denial of symptoms and interpersonal problems). The cutoff score for the total score is 63. The cutoff scores for the three main scales are as follows: Symptom Distress – 30, Interpersonal Relations – 15, and Social Role – 12. Although the OQ-45.2 is not intended as a diagnostic measure, individuals scoring above the total or Symptom Distress cutoff scores are very likely to be experiencing anxiety, depression, adjustment, or stress-related disorders. Changes of 14 or greater on the total score are considered reliable changes (i.e., changes that are real and not an artifact of error associated with the measure) (Lambert & Finch, 1999).

Advantages and Limitations Designed for clinical use in outpatient settings, particularly managed care ones, the greatest strength of the OQ-45.2 is that it is a simple, economical, and psychometrically sound tool for measuring client progress and status at the end of treatment. It is a valuable tool because it can effectively track client changes in symptomatology and interpersonal and social-role functioning, and meaningful feedback regarding those changes can be given to clients, organizations, and third-party payers. Counselors and clients can collaboratively use the OQ-45.2 to assess progress or the lack thereof and, if necessary, modify the counseling accordingly. For example, Susan, the client from the chapter case study may transition from attending sessions weekly to every other week once her scores fall below the established cutoff points. Conversely, a repeated administration of the OQ-45.2 revealing either no change or a worsening in Susan's distress or functioning could indicate the need for additional treatment such as medication, more intensive counseling, or another counseling modality such as group therapy.

Despite its brevity and simplicity, the OQ-45.2 may be a valid measure only of general distress, not interpersonal functioning. Factor analysis and other research suggest that client interpersonal and social role subscale scores may have limited usefulness for clinicians beyond what the Symptom Distress scale provides (Lambert & Finch, 1999). This research revealed, not surprisingly, that the more symptomatic distress one is experiencing, the more likely interpersonal relationships and social role functioning suffer, and vice versa. Therefore, rather than measuring three factors or constructs as it purports to do, the questionnaire may be measuring one factor, either symptom distress or overall emotional well-being. Another limitation is the extent to which it can be applied cross-culturally because of a lack of information about the standardization groups (Hanson, 2005; Pfeiffer, 2005).

Cultural Considerations   The OQ-45.2.2 has been translated into eight different languages, including German and Spanish. Despite the multiple language versions, some cautions have been raised by the authors themselves regarding its cross-cultural usage. Lambert and Finch (1999) caution about the generalizability of the OQ-45.2 norms to Asian and Polynesian populations. They suggest that clinicians keep in mind that for individuals of Asian descent, especially recent immigrants and family members, high scores may represent linguistic and cultural factors rather than psychopathology. The data from the normative samples suggest, however, that it does not over- or under-pathologize African American and Hispanic groups (Okiishi et al., 2006; Pfeiffer, 2005). Even though important demographic information for the normative samples such as race, ethnicity, age, and SES is either incomplete or missing from the manual, it still provides useful counseling progress information for a diverse range of clients.

ASSESSING DEPRESSION

The Nature of Depression

Our current understanding of depression as a psychosocial disorder is based on the groundbreaking work of Aaron Beck (1967), though as Beck and others have observed, the concept of depression or what alternatively has been called *melancholia* has been around for over 2,000 years (Ingram & Smith, 2008). Beck recognized that depression manifests itself somatically, psychologically, and socially in human beings and its causes are multiple and complex. Trained as a physician and psychoanalyst, Beck's most influential contribution to contemporary views of depression was his cognitive theory. The cognitive theory of depression is a triadic model that posits depressed people develop negative views about the self, the future, and the world, and that these views are maintained through perceptual distortions (Beck, 1967). Beck theorized that negative beliefs or schemas are formed during childhood, creating a vulnerability or sensitivity, what he termed "depressogenic" thinking. This vulnerability is triggered by specific psychological stressors, especially loss, and result in depression. Although there is neither consensus regarding the definition of depression nor what causes it, there is a commonly held view in the fields of counseling, psychology, and psychiatry that depression is part biological, part psychological, and part interpersonal in nature. The degree to which each part is cause and effect remains a matter of ongoing debate and research.

Depression, as it has been defined in the DSM system since the current multiaxial system emerged in 1980 with DSM-III, is a prevalent and costly disorder. Household interview surveys have found the incidence of depression has been increasing in the United States and elsewhere over the past 30 years. It is estimated that 21% of adults in the United States will experience some type of depressive or other mood disorder at some point during their lifetime (Kessler, Berglund, Demler, Jin, & Walters, 2005). It has even been suggested that the prevalence of depression worldwide has reached epidemic proportions (Ingram & Smith, 2008). The likelihood of being diagnosed with a mood disorder varies by gender, ethnicity, and marital status. Women are 1.5 times more likely than men to have some type of mood disorder. On the other hand, Hispanic and non-Hispanic Blacks are at significantly less risk than Whites for developing a mood disorder at some point in their lifetime. Regardless of one's race, having been previously married poses a significantly higher risk for depressive disorders (Kessler et al.).

The cost to societies and families is enormous. American and Australian workers with depression report losing significantly more performance time than nondepressed workers. Employer costs for lost productivity is significantly more with depression than other health-related problems, with losses in productivity ranging from 17 to 31 billion dollars (Lim, Sanderson, & Andrews, 2000; Stewart, Ricci, Chee, Hahn, & Morganstein, 2003). Living with a depressed family member can create serious strain and stress, especially given that depression often co-occurs with other mental health problems, especially anxiety and substance abuse. Depression also poses a significant risk for increased somatic complaints and poorer overall health status (Price, Choi, & Vinokur, 2002). Individuals with a major depressive disorder and those experiencing depression as part of another disorder (such as schizophrenia) are at significant risk for suicide completions (Shea, 1998). Given these significant personal, familial, and societal costs, accurate assessment and treatment of depression is critical.

Depression is not a unitary construct. The DSM classification scheme recognizes several disorders relating to depression, including major depression, dysthymia (a milder but chronic form of depression), and bipolar disorder (a disorder consisting of both depressive and manic episodes). According to the DSM-IV-TR, major depression consists of a depressive episode, which is defined as "a period of at least 2 weeks during which there is either depressed mood or the loss of interest or pleasure in nearly all activities and represents a change from the previous functioning" (American Psychiatric Association [APA], 2000, p. 327). In order to meet the DSM-IV-TR criteria for a depressive episode, an individual must also have five out of nine symptoms present, almost daily, during that the same two-week period. Those additional symptoms are the following:

1. Significant weight loss when not dieting or weight gain or decrease or increase in appetite nearly every day
2. Insomnia or hypersomnia nearly every day
3. Psychomotor agitation or retardation
4. Fatigue or loss of energy
5. Feelings of worthlessness or excessive or inappropriate guilt
6. Diminished ability to think or concentrate or indecisiveness
7. Recurrent thought of death (not just fear of dying), recurrent suicidal ideation without a specific plan, or a suicide attempt or a specific plan for committing suicide.

To qualify as a depressive episode, those symptoms are not the result of the physiological effects of a substance, a medical condition, or bereavement (APA, 2000). An additional diagnostic criterion for major depression is impairment in functioning, either socially or in daily living.

Susan's self-report at the intake interview suggests she is experiencing some of these major depression symptoms. Her report of feeling "annoyed" is often a sign of irritability, and "down" typically connotes a sad mood. She also indicated frequent sleep disturbance and a reduction in meals, which suggests a loss of appetite. Although her response to intake questions indicates that some of the DSM-IV-TR criteria are present, it remains unclear whether indeed she is experiencing major depression. Her loss of temper, for example, might be a symptom of a manic, not depressive, episode, which would suggest she is experiencing a bipolar disorder. She is also reporting symptoms suggestive of anxiety—sleep disturbance, nervousness, heart racing, and feeling faint when she leaves her home. One of the very common client presentations in outpatient mental health settings is a mixed anxiety and depression picture (Westen & Morrison, 2001). To qualify for the diagnosis of mixed anxiety and depression, an individual would not need to be experiencing as many symptoms as are necessary for either a diagnosis of major depressive disorder or generalized anxiety disorder. Mixed anxiety and depression, as a new mood disorder, has been proposed by the DSM-5 Mood Disorders Work Group because of the frequency in which anxiety and depression co-occur as well as the common genetic and temperament factors that place individuals at risk for developing depression and anxiety (APA, 2010). Further assessment via standardized self-report measures as well as further interviewing could help clarify Susan's diagnosis and the severity of her symptoms. The information obtained from standardized self-report measures can also serve as a guide to focus subsequent counseling and provide a baseline of symptom severity from which treatment progress can be measured.

Depression Questionnaires and Rating Scales

BECK DEPRESSION INVENTORY-II (BDI-II)   The *Beck Depression Inventory* (BDI) is the oldest and most widely used measure of depression. Dissatisfied with the heterogeneity of items on the MMPI depression scale, Beck and his colleagues developed the inventory in 1961 (Beck, 1967). The current version of the inventory (BDI-II) represents only a slight change from the original inventory in format, and is intended for individuals aged 13 and older (Beck, Steer, & Brown, 1996). Like other self-report depression measures, the BDI-II is designed to measure only depression, not the manic symptoms found in bipolar disorders. Part of the impetus for the BDI revision was a desire to align the measure with the DSM-IV symptom criteria for depression (Beck et al., 1996). The BDI-II, like the original, consists of 21 items, each with four response options that range in score from 0 to 3. The items cover the somatic or physiological symptoms of depression (sleep, appetite, energy level, and libido), cognitive symptoms (negative views about self, future, and suicide), and emotional symptoms (sadness, guilt, anhedonia, and irritability). The changes to the original BDI included dropping four items regarding weight, body image, work, and somatic pre-occupation, and adding four items regarding agitation, worthlessness, concentration difficulty, and energy (Beck et al., 1996).

Technical Information   Four outpatient samples were combined for a total of 500 individuals in the normative sample (Beck et al., 1996). The sample was predominantly White females, with African American, Hispanics, and Asians making up only 4%, 1%, and 4% respectively, of the normative group. Reliabilities are in the excellent range. The internal consistency reliability for the combined outpatient sample is 0.92; a comparison group of college students is 0.93. Test–retest reliability with approximately a one-week interval is 0.93 for a subsample of 26 clients (Beck et al., 1996).

Scoring and Interpretation   To score the BDI-II the clinician simply adds the scores on the front and the back of the inventory to get a total raw score. Raw scores are not converted to a standardized score (such as a *t* score). The manual suggests the following guidelines for interpreting depression severity:

0–13 minimal

14–19 mild

20–28 moderate

29–63 severe

Advantages and Limitations   The BDI-II is the most popular unidimensional measure for the assessment of depression severity and monitoring of treatment of depression. Furthermore, the BDI-II and the QIDS (covered later in the chapter) were the only two self-report measures that were "highly" recommended for diagnostic purposes based on criteria developed for judging psychological tests (see Chapters 6 and 7) (Persons & Fresco, 2008). In the multitude of studies examining the effectiveness of cognitive–behavioral therapy and other interventions for the treatment of depression, the BDI-II is typically used both to determine eligibility for inclusion in the study and as a measure of treatment outcome (Westen & Morrison, 2001). Beck and his colleagues as well as other researchers have found that the BDI and BDI-II are sensitive measures for discriminating between those with depressive disorders and those with other DSM disorders (Persons & Fresco). That is, clients with some type of mood disorder score, on average, significantly higher on the BDI-II than those with anxiety, adjustment, and other disorders.

Its sensitivity, however, may be reduced when used with adults over age 60. Studies of the BDI with older adult clinical samples had mixed results. Some suggest good reliability and validity while others indicate poor sensitivity; that is, the ability to accurately detect depression in a particular population (Fiske & O'Riley, 2008). Given that the normative sample is predominantly White and female, the BDI-II should be used cautiously as a diagnostic tool with clients of other demographics, especially geriatric clients.

CHILDREN'S DEPRESSION INVENTORY   The *Children's Depression Inventory* (CDI) is a child-friendly version of the *Beck Depression Inventory* that assesses for the presence of depression symptoms—mood, negative thinking about self and the future, interpersonal problems, anhedonia, and physiological changes over the past two weeks in children ages 7 to 17 (Kovacs, 1992). It is somewhat longer than the *Beck Depression Inventory* (27 vs. 21 items) and the response format is a 3- rather than a 4-point scale. In addition to being written at an elementary school level, it differs from the Beck in that some of the items focus on school and friendships. Of all the existing child self-report measures this is the one most often used clinically and in research studies (Merrell, 2008). Hand scoring and computer-assisted scoring is available, though the brevity of the inventory and the relative ease in scoring obviates the need for the more expensive computer scoring. There is also a 10-item short form available. In 2003 shorter parent (17 items) and teacher (12 items) versions were published by Multi-Health Systems. That is, a parent or teacher rates a child on a subset of the CDI items. The full CDI is available from Multi-Health Systems, Pearson Assessments, or Western Psychological Services.

Administration, Scoring, and Interpretation   Items can be read aloud to children with reading problems or younger children, while the child reads along on his or her form. The CDI can typically be completed in 10 to 15 minutes and can be scored in less than five minutes. A total score and five scale scores can be obtained: Negative Mood, Interpersonal Problems,

Ineffectiveness, Anhedonia, and Negative Self-Esteem (Kovacs, 1992). The total raw score for the CDI and the raw scores for the individual scales are easily converted to *t* scores and percentiles using double-sided questionnaire forms where the scoring and raw score conversion is done on the backside of the questionnaire. Percentiles and *t* scores are based on gender and age (7–12 and 13–17). It is unclear, however, why separate gender norms are provided given the lack of differences between boys and girls in these two age ranges found in two separate analyses (Kovacs; Finch, Saylor, & Edwards, 1985). The manual suggests *t* scores 65 or greater in clinical populations are clinically significant whereas *t* scores of 70 or 75 should be used in nonclinical settings for inferring depression problems (Kovacs). When using the CDI for screening purposes in a general population, a cutoff score of 20 is recommended. This means that children scoring 20 or above are likely to have depression and further assessment is warranted. In settings where depression is more prevalent, such as mental health settings a cutoff score of 13 is recommended.

Technical Information   The CDI was normed on a large but narrow group of over 1,200 Florida public school students, grades 2 through 8 (Kovacs, 1992). Unfortunately the standardization group was not selected for race–ethnicity or socioeconomic status and only estimates of the white, non-white percentages are provided. Kovacs indicates that her norms were based on the Florida sample (Finch et al., 1985), which included 1,463 students, but it is not clear from the manual or this 1985 study why the CDI norm sample in the manual is shown as 1,266, rather than 1,463. The reliabilities for the CDI are all within the adequate or better range for standardized measures. The internal reliability coefficient (alpha) for the overall CDI is 0.86 and internal reliabilities range from 0.59 to 0.68 on the five scales. Ample evidence for the CDI's concurrent validity—it correlates highly with other child self-report measures of depression—has also been found. Some studies have shown the CDI can discriminate well between "normal" youth and depressed youth but not as well differentiating between different psychiatric conditions (e.g., major depression versus adjustment disorder with depressed mood). The CDI manual provides an excellent annotated bibliography summarizing the research with the CDI through December 1991.

Advantages and Limitations   The CDI is an easy, quick, and very useful measure to administer, score, and interpret when a clinician is concerned about either the presence of depression or obtaining a baseline measure of depression symptom severity for assessing treatment progress. It can also aid in identifying depression symptoms and problems that may not have been revealed during clinical interviews. The main drawback of the CDI is that its norms are based on a narrow, nonrepresentative sample. Therefore, its use with various racial and ethnic groups, given the lack of information provided in the manual, should be done cautiously. Unlike some of the newer self-report inventories for children, the CDI lacks any kind of scale for detecting invalid responses or faking. The overall pattern of responding, however, may provide a clue. For example, a child who endorses every item with the "zero" response or conversely the "two" response may be exhibiting a response bias: either a tendency to deny problems or the opposite pattern, acknowledging symptoms but exaggerating their severity. Given the mixed findings about its ability to differentiate between psychiatric groups, it is possible that the CDI is measuring general distress in a child rather than depression. Therefore, clinicians should never rely exclusively on the CDI for the assessment of depression when a child is experiencing anxiety or other emotional problems (Comer & Kendall, 2005).

HAMILTON RATING SCALE FOR DEPRESSION (HRSD)   The *Hamilton Rating Scale for Depression* (HRSD) is a clinician-rated measure designed for use in conjunction with an unstructured or semistructured interview (Hamilton, 1967). Clinicians can record and quantify their impressions and observations gleaned from an interview with the scale's structured format. The original HRSD consists of 21 items, 17 of which are scored, and is intended to measure depression severity and client functioning (Hopko, Lejuez, Armento, & Bare, 2004). Clinicians are expected to make their ratings within 30 minutes of an interview and it can be completed within five to 10 minutes. Along with the BDI-II, the HRSD is the most frequently used measure in studies evaluating the effectiveness of treatments for depression (Hopko et al.). Like the BDI-II, it focuses on a range of depression symptoms including depressed mood, guilt, suicidal ideation, insomnia, and loss of libido. However, it has a higher concentration of somatic symptoms more commonly associated with anxiety, such as gastrointestinal symptoms, autonomic nervous system reactivity, general somatic symptoms, and hypochondriasis. It was recently revised and is available for purchase from WPS.com, though the original can be obtained online free of charge at ***http://healthnet.umassmed.edu/mhealth/HAMD.pdf***. In addition to the HRSD, there is both a 17- and a 23-item self-report version (Reynolds & Kobak, 1995). The 17-item version was designed as a companion for the HRSD and also has strong psychometric properties.

Technical Information   A large-scale review of numerous studies using and evaluating the psychometric properties of the 17-item HRSD concluded that overall internal and interrater reliability is adequate, but the interrater reliability for some individual items was less than adequate (Bagby, Ryder, Schuller, & Marshall, 2004). Ten of the 12 studies of its psychometric properties found internal reliability estimates ranging from 0.70 to 0.90 or better, and inter-rater reliabilities from 0.82 to 0.98 (Bagby et al.). Their review also included a number of studies that established the HRSD's convergent and discriminant validity. Not only does the HRSD correlate highly with the BDI and other measures of depression, it also discriminates between depressed and nondepressed clients, as well as between depressed clients and those with other psychiatric disorders.

Scoring and Interpretation   About half the items are scored on a 5-point scale (0–4), and the other items on a 3-point scale (0–2), with zero indicating the symptom is absent. The higher the score, the more severe are the symptoms of depression.

Advantages and Limitations   The HRSD is an efficient standardized measure for a clinician to use to help make the diagnosis of major depression and rate the severity of a client's depression. Despite the fact that concerns have been raised about individual items measuring constructs other than depression and unclear scoring procedures for particular items, it is one of the few observer-rated tools available for the diagnosis of depression with reasonable psychometric properties (Bagby et al., 2004). Studies also suggest it is an effective instrument for measuring client response to therapy because it is sensitive to symptom changes occurring within a relatively short period, weeks not months (Lambert, Masters, & Astle, 1988). One recent study determined it is a useful diagnostic and treatment progress tool in primary care settings when used in conjunction with a clinical interview and a more comprehensive system for scoring than is typically utilized (Morriss, Leese, Chatwin, & Baldwin, 2008).

REYNOLDS DEPRESSION INVENTORIES   The *Reynolds Depression Screening Inventory* (RDSI) is a 19-item self-report measure aligned with the DSM-IV criteria for major depression for adults ages 18 through 89 (Reynolds & Kobak, 1998). Versions for children and adolescents also exist, the *Reynolds Child Depression Scale* and the *Reynolds Adolescent Depression Scale* (now in its second edition), respectively. The RDSI is designed to assess for symptom severity and, like the BDI-II, uses a cutoff score approach. It is based on the *Hamilton Rating Scale,* and its content is similar: each item has a three- or five-item response set along a continuum like the BDI-II (Campbell, 2001). The content includes mood, cognitive, vegetative, psychomotor, and somatic symptoms, and interpersonal problems. Raw scores above 16 indicate that further evaluation for a diagnosis of major depression is needed (Hopko et al., 2004).

Although the Reynolds is based on a normative sample that is disproportionately Caucasian (89%) and geographically narrow, its psychometric properties are more than adequate (Flanagan, 2001). Both internal reliability and test–retest reliability estimates are in the excellent range (Hopko et al., 2004). Internal reliability coefficients range from 0.89 for a psychiatric outpatient sample to 0.93 for the total normative group. Test–retest reliability using a smaller subset of individuals is 0.94 with a one-week interval (Flanagan). Although reviewers of the Reynolds (Campbell, 2001; Flanagan) have praised it for its reliability and validity, they have also questioned whether it adds information beyond what the BDI-II or HRSD can provide.

REYNOLDS CHILD AND ADOLESCENT DEPRESSION SCALES (RCDS) The *Reynolds Child Depression Scale* (RCDS) consists of 30 items, each with a 4-point scale, designed to measure depression symptoms in children ages 8 to 12. The items were based on several diagnostic systems including the DSM-III-R and Research Diagnostic criteria for depression (Carlson, 1992) and it is the child version of the *Reynolds Adolescent Depression Scale*. The RCDS is written at a second-grade level but it is administered orally to children in grades 3 and 4. Item content includes mood, loneliness, feeling loved, worries about school, self-worth, and somatic complaints. It is published by Psychological Assessment Resources Inc.

Administration, Scoring, and Interpretation Children are instructed to rate their symptoms over the past two weeks with the following frequency rating: "almost never," "hardly ever," "sometimes," and "all the time." Typically it can be completed in 10 to 15 minutes. The scoring of the RCDS, like the CDI, is straightforward and can be done by hand with a scoring key. Higher scores reflect a greater level of depression symptomatology. Raw scores are converted to percentile scores, and a raw score of 74 or above is considered to be in the clinical range and highly suggestive of a diagnosis of depression.

Technical Information The RCDS was standardized on a group of over 1,600 children from the midwestern and western United States. Unfortunately, how representative the standardized sample is for the U.S. population is not documented, but gender and ethnic demographics are provided (Kamphaus & Frick, 2005). Reliability coefficients are in the adequate to excellent range. The internal consistency coefficient for the entire normative sample is 0.90. Test–retest reliability coefficients range from 0.81 to 0.92 at a four-week interval, which are relatively high values for test–retest reliability on a self-report rating scale (Merrell, 2008). Both the RCDS manual and independent studies have provided evidence for its construct validity, both convergent and discriminant validity. Moderately high convergence was found in five studies using measures of self-esteem and three studies of anxiety. Low convergence (i.e., divergence) was found in six studies using measures of academic achievement (Merrell).

The *Reynolds Adolescent Depression Scale, Second Edition* (RADS-2) is designed for youth ages 11 to 20 and is similar in length, format, and content to the RCDS. Like the RCDS, there are 30 items on the same 4-point scale ("almost never" to "all the time"). Its psychometric properties are similar to its companion scale, the RCDS (Dougherty, Klein, Olino, & Laptook, 2008).

Advantages and Limitations Both the RADS and RCDS are very useful assessment tools when considering the possibility that a child or adolescent is experiencing or at risk for depression. The RCDS and RADS have been used primarily in community and educational settings, less often in clinical settings. The RADS is very useful for clarifying diagnosis, conceptualizing cases, planning treatment, and measuring treatment outcome (Dougherty et al., 2008). Like the CDI, it is brief and easy to administer and score. One potential drawback in using the RCDS is its limited generalizability relative to the RADS.

ADDITIONAL SELF-REPORT MEASURES   The *Quick Inventory of Depressive Symptomatology–Self-Rated* (QIDS-SR) is a newer brief self-report measure that also assesses for the presence and severity of DSM-IV symptoms of major depression (Rush et al., 2003). This 16-item inventory is used for case conceptualization and diagnostic purposes. It is an abbreviated version of the *Inventory of Depressive Symptomatology,* which measures both depression and anxiety symptoms. The QIDS-SR has been translated into a dozen languages and is highly recommended for use in diagnosing depression given its psychometric properties and clinical utility (Persons & Fresco, 2008).

Several other self-report measures exist for assessing more specific aspects of depression. These measures are designed for case conceptualization and treatment planning purposes, not for diagnostic evaluation, and are based on a cognitive–behavioral conceptualization of depression. They include the *Pleasant Events Schedule, Dysfunctional Attitude Scale, Experiences Questionnaire,* and *Emotion Regulation Questionnaire* (Persons & Fresco, 2008). The *Pleasant Events Schedule* asks clients to rate how often they engage in a specific activity. The *Dysfunctional Attitude Scale* is based on Beck's model of depression, and measures distorted and illogical beliefs about one's self, the future, and the world. And the *Emotional Regulation Questionnaire* is a brief inventory to assess how one controls emotions (Persons & Fresco). The *Pleasants Events Schedule* and its manual are available for free online at ***http://www.ori.org/Research/scientists/lewinsohnP.html***, as is the *Emotional Regulation Questionnaire* at ***http://www-psych.stanford.edu/~psyphy/resources.html***.

There are also measures for assessing depression in older adult populations. Specific measures are increasingly being used for older adults (ages 60 and older) because of a realization that depression is experienced differently in late adulthood (Fiske & O'Riley, 2008). When depression occurs in later life, sadness or depressed mood may be masked by greater somatic concerns, which can be affected by greater physical ailments, and an absence of cognitive symptoms, such as suicide ideation, negative self-worth, and beliefs about punishment and guilt. Clinician and self-report measures that are used to assess depression in geriatric populations include the *Geriatric Depression Rating Scale* (an interviewer-rated scale like the HRSD), the *Zung Self-Rating Depression Scale,* the *Center for Epidemiologic Studies Depression Scale* (self-report), and the *Geriatric Depression Scale* (self-report) and structured interview schedules (Fiske & O'Riley).

Structured Interview Schedules for Mood Disorders

A diagnostic evaluation for depression can be accomplished using a structured interview schedule, but this type of interview is rarely used outside of research studies. The ones that have been developed for evaluating mood disorders are based on and aligned with the DSM-IV-TR criteria. These interviews can take from one to three hours to complete and therefore their use in managed care and other short-term counseling settings is limited. On certain occasions clinicians may find structured interviews, despite their length, to be a valuable tool. When referral information suggests that a differential diagnosis may be difficult to make (e.g., major depressive disorder versus bipolar disorder), a structured interview approach could be used. The following is an example of a client for whom a clinician might select a structured approach over the more typical unstructured intake interview.

Fred, a 22-year-old Hispanic male, was brought to a local psychiatric hospital following an arrest for a domestic violence incident with his live-in girlfriend. Fred punched his girlfriend and threatened to steal her
car and take her children. Fred told the arresting officer, "She dresses like a whore from the islands, I need
to do God's work and punish her for her sins, peace my friendly man, save you." He then told the police
officer, "We all need to be gone." The arresting officer believed Fred was intoxicated when he arrested him.

Fred's parents divorced when he was 6 years old. Fred's father used to "beat me with a strap." Fred
has a GED and an erratic work history. This is his first time receiving mental health services.

Using a structured interview with Fred might be beneficial for several reasons. His
presentation and history suggest a number of diagnostic possibilities—mood disorders, substance abuse, and psychosis—and potential treatments, both pharmacological and psychosocial.
Because of the different major diagnostic categories that are possible, it would be important to be
as accurate as possible in arriving at the correct diagnosis(es). Diagnostic accuracy is particularly
important in this case because of the heightened risk of harm to self and others. Furthermore,
given Fred's school history he might be put off by reading and taking a "test," and therefore he
might have more difficulty completing a self-report measure than he might a structured interview. Recommended structured interviews for depression and other DSM disorders include the
Schedule for Affective Disorders and Schizophrenia (SADS), *Structured Clinical Interview for
DSM-IV—Patient Version* (SCID-I/P), and the *Anxiety Disorders Interview Schedule* (ADIS-IV)
(Hopko et al., 2004; Persons & Fresco, 2008). The ADIS-IV (available at *www.oup.com*) is particularly helpful given the overlap between anxiety and depression and because it also screens
for mania, psychosis, and substance abuse. An abbreviated version of the SCID-I/P designed for
clinicians can be downloaded from American Psychiatric Publishing (*www.appi.org*). Although
these structured interview schedules have high interrater reliability, a disadvantage is the extensive
training needed to use them (Hopko et al.).

ASSESSING BIPOLAR DISORDER

Bipolar disorder is a much less common form of a mood disorder consisting of both depressive
and manic episodes. A manic episode, according to the DSM-IV-TR, is a period of at least one
week during which an individual experiences an "elevated," an "expansive," or an "irritable"
mood (American Psychiatric Association, 2000, p. 357). Additional core symptoms include
inflated self-esteem or grandiosity, decreased need for sleep, pressured speech, flight of ideas,
distractibility, increased involvement in goal-directed activities such as work or school projects,
agitation, and excessive involvement in pleasurable activities that are likely to have negative consequences for the person, such as sexual promiscuity, lavish shopping sprees, or business purchases
(APA, 2000). If the person's mood is elevated, only three additional symptoms are required to
meet the symptom criterion for bipolar I; if the mood is irritability, then four are required.

The DSM now recognizes a second type of bipolar disorder. Prior to DSM-IV, the DSM
classification system defined only bipolar disorder as previously described. Bipolar II is characterized by "one or more major depressive episodes" and "at least one hypomanic episode" (APA,
2000, p. 392). A hypomanic episode is essentially a less severe form of a manic episode. The
list of symptoms is the same, though only four days of symptoms rather than seven are required,
as it is the level of functional impairment that distinguishes the two. The criterion for type I is
"marked impairment . . . in functioning" or the need for hospitalization to prevent harm to self
or others (p. 362). Type II requires only "a change in functioning . . . observable by others"
(p. 368). Assessing the difference between a "change" in functioning and a "marked impairment" in functioning can be difficult with some clients.

The diagnosis of bipolar disorder of either type is typically made after conducting clinical interviews, either semistructured or structured. These interviews typically involve significant others (family members or friends) who are more likely than the client to observe and report changes in mood and functioning. Self-report measures to aid in the diagnostic evaluation of bipolar disorder have only recently been developed, and overall are still lacking acceptable reliability and validity (Johnson, Miller, & Eisner, 2008). However, recent studies have shown the *General Behavior Inventory* (GBI) to be a sensitive and specific measure for identifying bipolar disorder (Johnson et al.). There are several versions and each of them assesses symptom frequency, duration, and intensity. In addition, several self-report measures have been developed for the purpose of tracking mania symptoms while a client is in treatment. These include the *Young Mania Rating Scale,* the *Bech-Rafaelsen Mania Scale,* the *Schedule for Affective Disorders and Schizophrenia-Change Mania Scale,* and the *Altman Self-Rating Mania Inventory* (Johnson et al.).

ASSESSING ANXIETY

The Nature of Anxiety

Like depression, anxiety is a common, multifaceted, and serious clinical problem. As previously noted, one of the more frequent occurrences among individuals like Susan is the presence of depression and anxiety symptoms that do not meet the full DSM-IV-TR criteria for a mood or anxiety disorder but would probably qualify for a "mixed anxiety and depression disorder" if adopted in the DSM-5.

The DSM-IV-TR recognizes nine anxiety disorders: generalized anxiety disorder (GAD), agoraphobia (with and without panic attack), panic disorder without agoraphobia, obsessive–compulsive disorder (OCD), post-traumatic stress disorder (PTSD, acute and chronic), specific phobias, and social phobia (also referred to as social anxiety disorder) (American Psychiatric Association, 2000). Collectively, anxiety disorders are the most common DSM disorder with an estimated lifetime prevalence rate of 29% in adults (Kessler et al., 2005). Among the anxiety disorders, specific and social phobias are the most prevalent (12.5% and 12.1% lifetime prevalence, respectively), followed by PTSD (7%), GAD (6%), panic disorder (5%), OCD (2%), and agoraphobia without panic (1.5%) (Kessler et al.).

All anxiety disorders consist of similar physiological reactions: increased autonomic nervous system activity. This includes accelerated heart rate, rapid and shallow breathing, increased perspiration and tightening of muscle groups. An extreme form of this nervous system response is panic. Panic symptoms include not only the previously listed physiological symptoms, but also a feeling of choking, stomach distress or nausea, dizziness, chills or hot flashes, chest pain, trembling, and shaking (American Psychiatric Association, 2000). A panic attack commonly occurs without an obvious trigger and the person experiencing the attack feels intense fear or dread. The physiological symptoms of a heightened nervous system response are not, however, unique to anxiety. The same pattern of autonomic nervous system activity occurs when one experiences any strong emotion, including anger and sexual arousal. Furthermore, heightened arousal patterns typically associated with anxiety occur when people are not scared or nervous, such as when exercising. To complicate the picture, research indicates that some people report feeling scared, fearful, or panicky without any physiological arousal (Williams, 2008). This has led, in part, to some researchers and theorists dismissing the existence of DSM-defined anxiety disorders, and instead advocating for a dimensional approach to the different aspects of anxiety (Bandura, 1997; Persons, Roberts, & Zalecki, 2003; Williams).

On a cognitive and emotional level, anxiety involves the perception of danger and the feeling of fear. When our brains perceive a physical or psychological threat, a fight, flight, or freeze behavioral response is triggered in much the same way that an animal feeling threatened responds. The focus of the fear, the content and style of the thinking accompanying the fear, and the behavioral responses to the perceived threat are what distinguish the different anxiety disorders. In GAD, for example, the cognitive component is typically experienced as worry about future events, usually taking the form of "what if" thinking. In PTSD, the mind can produce flashbacks. In OCD, thinking is perseverative or obsessional in nature, and the content of thoughts surround the emotion of fear, such as fear of contamination or becoming sick, or fear of harm befalling self or others should the individual not lock doors or turn off a stove.

When a danger truly exists, ramping up the nervous system is adaptive, as the threat is then better avoided because of increased alertness and bodily responses that prepare the individual to flee or fight. If an individual continues to perceive threats that are more illusory than real, his or her immune system will be compromised and daily functioning and interpersonal relationships will suffer. Left untreated, anxiety can be debilitating.

GAD, as defined in the DSM-IV-TR, consists of somatic, physiological, and cognitive symptoms. The somatic and physiological symptoms include fatigue, muscle tension, insomnia, and restlessness. The cognitive symptoms involve excessive worry that is difficult to control and difficulty concentrating (American Psychiatric Association, 2000). Worries have been conceptualized as thoughts about future events that are expected to involve a psychological or physical threat and are more difficult to control than other types of thinking (Meyer, Miller, Metzger, & Borkovec, 1990). For example, in the chapter case study, Susan worries about losing control when she shows her feelings, getting into a car accident, and "messing up" during job interviews.

In general, current anxiety measures are disorder specific. Dozens of self-report measures exist for GAD, panic disorder with and without agoraphobia, OCD, PTSD, and specific and social phobia. They differ widely in their psychometric properties, clinical usefulness, function, and research base. Clinicians are likely to begin with measures that assess general anxiety symptoms to supplement intake interviews in which client symptoms are suggestive of anxiety problems, and then move to more specific disorder measures depending upon the information obtained.

Anxiety Measures

BECK ANXIETY INVENTORY (BAI)   The *Beck Anxiety Inventory* (BAI) is a 21-item self-report measure designed for assessing the severity of the somatic and physiological aspects of generalized anxiety and to a lesser extent fears and panic symptoms in adults ages 18 to 65 (Beck, Epstein, Brown, & Steer, 1988). Clients are asked about how "bothered" they have been by symptoms during the past week using a 4-point scale ranging from 0 – "Not at All" to 3 – "Severely—I could barely stand it." Items on the BAI are similar to:

- "feeling numb or tingly"
- "rapid heart beat"
- "hands shaking"
- "fearing bad things happening"
- "other fears"

It can be completed in fewer than 10 minutes, and clinicians have the option of administering it orally.

Technical Information   The BAI was initially validated with a small outpatient sample of 160 clients who were diagnosed with mood or anxiety disorders (Beck, Epstein et al., 1988). A subsequent community study of nondiagnosed individuals ages 18–65 was conducted by Gillis, Haaga, and Ford (1995) for the purpose of establishing norms for the BAI and other anxiety measures. The study's normative sample of 267 adults closely matched the demographic variables of the 1990 U.S. Census data, with the exception that the Hispanic participants were recruited differently than other participants, and in some cases were administered the BAI orally. Studies evaluating the BAI determined that it has adequate construct validity, with internal reliability estimates in the excellent range and test–retest reliability in the adequate range (Gervais & Dugas, 2008).

Scoring and Interpretation   In addition to measuring the severity of anxiety symptoms, the BAI is useful for differentiating between anxiety and depression symptoms. Hand scoring is simple and straightforward: scores for each item are summed to get a total score between 0 and 63. Using the norms established by Gillis et al. (1995), scores above 17 are considered above the 90th percentile. That is, in their community sample, only 10% of the group received scores of 18 or greater and therefore scores at the level could suggest the presence of a generalized anxiety disorder.

Advantages and Limitations   The BAI can aid in case conceptualization and treatment planning because it has both clinical and nonclinical norms. Therefore, it can be useful both with those clients who meet the DSM-IV-TR criteria for GAD and clients who are experiencing some anxiety symptoms but not at the level that would qualify for a diagnosis of GAD. Since it is brief and clients can complete it quickly, symptoms and concerns that may not be uncovered during a clinical interview but that are a needed focus in counseling can be readily identified. Its overall usefulness is limited by the fact that it is primarily a measure of somatic or physiological arousal, with only a few items related to fears and worries. In that regard, other self-report measures, which assess more comprehensively the cognitive, emotional, and behavioral aspects of anxiety, have been recommended for use in diagnostic evaluation, case conceptualization, treatment planning, and measuring counseling progress in clients (Gervais & Dugas, 2008).

PENN STATE WORRY QUESTIONNAIRE   The *Penn State Worry Questionnaire* (PSWQ) is designed to assess the cognitive or worry component of GAD (Meyer et al., 1990) and has become the standard measure for worry assessment (Gervais & Dugas, 2008). It can be obtained from the original journal article (Meyer et al., pp. 487–495).The questionnaire consists of 16 items, each rated on a 5-point Likert scale from 1 – "Not at all typical of me" to 5 – "Very typical of me" (Meyer et al.). The items cover one's perception of control over worries, the impact of worries, and the generality and excessiveness of worry. Sample items include:

- "I know I shouldn't worry about things but I just can't help it."
- "I find it easy to dismiss worrisome thoughts."
- "When I am under pressure I worry a lot."
- "I have been a worrier all my life."

There is also a 14-item PSWQ for children ages 8 through 12 with very similar items on a 4-point Likert scale (Chorpita, Tracey, Brown, Collica, & Barlow, 1997).

Technical Information   The initial reliability and validity sample consisted of 436 anxiety patients and 32 "normal" controls (Brown, Antony, & Barlow, 1992). Community norms were established with a sample of 267 U.S. adults ages 18–65 that closely matched the 1990 census data for race and ethnicity, educational level, and marital status (Gillis et al., 1995). Subsequent research has included samples of African American and Asian American college students (Scott, Eng, & Heimburg, 2002); children (Chorpita et al., 1997), and older adults (Crittendon & Hopko, 2006). Mean scores for various demographic groups have also been established (Startup & Erickson, 2006). The PSWQ has reliabilities in the adequate to excellent range and good construct and discriminant validity (Molina & Borkovec, 1994). Individuals with GAD scored higher on the PSWQ than did individuals with other anxiety disorders (Brown et al.; Gervais & Dugas, 2008).

Scoring and Interpretation   A total score for the PSWQ is calculated by adding the numbers to get a total between 16 and 80, with high scores reflecting more severe worry. Five of the items—1, 3, 8, 10, and 11—are worded in a positive manner and therefore are reverse scored. A score of 65 has been used as the cutoff point for identifying GAD in some studies (Fresco, Mennin, Heimberg, & Turk, 2003).

Advantages and Limitations   Because worry is the central cognitive component in anxiety, the PSWQ is an excellent tool for assessing the extent to which worry is impacting a client. Along with interview information, it can help to differentiate between diagnoses of GAD and other anxiety disorders. Nonetheless, its primary purpose is to measure the severity of a client's worry; it is not meant by itself to be a diagnostic test. It is also helpful in measuring treatment progress. Scores on the PSWQ-Past Week (a modified version of the PSWQ) are sensitive to changes occurring over a short period of time (Gervais & Dugas, 2008). As a worry measure it does not, however, enable the clinician to assess somatic or physiological aspects of anxiety, nor does it assess the cognitive aspects of anxiety disorders such as OCD and PTSD.

REVISED CHILDREN'S MANIFEST ANXIETY SCALE: SECOND EDITION   The *Revised Children's Manifest Anxiety Scale: Second Edition* (RCMAS-2) is a 49-item inventory for youth and young adults ages 6–19 and is designed for assessing the presence of anxiety symptoms and related concerns including worry, concentration difficulties, physiological arousal, oversensitivity, and fear, and social and performance concerns (Reynolds & Richmond, 2008). The RCMAS is a revision of the original *Children's Manifest Anxiety Scale,* which was developed in 1978 and titled "What I Think and Feel" (Reynolds & Richmond, 1979). For the second edition the norms were updated and the standardization sample is more ethnically diverse than the first edition sample (Reynolds & Richmond, 2008). The RCMAS-2 is published by Western Psychological Services. In addition, Western Psychological Services sells a short form that is made up of items 1 to 10.

The RCMAS-2 includes two validity scales, a very rare feature in unidimensional self-report inventories for youth. The items that made up the original version "L" scale, now called Defensiveness, are designed to detect children who respond in a highly positive fashion or attempt to "fake good." When the Defensiveness scale standard score is 13 or greater, the clinician is advised to interpret the self-report with caution. In addition, there is a validity scale to detect inconsistent responding (i.e., answering two very similar items in the opposite way).

Administration, Scoring, and Interpretation   Children can complete the RCMAS-2 in approximately 10–15 minutes. The child is asked to decide if the item describes him or her and circle either yes or no. It requires a third-grade reading level and the directions are read aloud to children in grades K to 3. For children 9 years 6 months and older it can be administered in a group setting. Scoring is simple: sum the yes responses for each of the three subscales (Physiological Anxiety, Worry/Oversensitivity, and Social Anxiety) and the Defensiveness scale. A total score is also calculated. The raw scale scores are converted to standard scores with a mean of 10 and a standard deviation of 3 and the total score is converted to a t score. Interpretation of the RCMAS is also straightforward; the higher the score, the more anxiety symptoms are present. When the Defensiveness scale standard score is high, the clinician is advised to interpret the self-report with caution but the manual does not specify a value for high scores (Denzine, 2008).

Technical Information   The standardization group comprised over 2,300 children ages 6 to 19, which was fairly representative of the U.S. population in terms of race–ethnicity (Stein, 2008). The sample was an approximately equal mix of males and females and was also representative of geographic regions and socioeconomic status, unlike the original version. Because the RCMAS-2 was published fairly recently, little research has been done on it compared to its predecessor. The reliability and validity of the RCMAS, the prior version of the RCMAS-2, was found to be within the acceptable range for standardized tests. Results from various studies suggest that the Total Anxiety scores are typically reliable (median across 48 samples = 0.81). Subscale scores, however, are less reliable; median alpha coefficients are 0.61 for the Physiological subscale, 0.63 for the Concentration subscale, 0.77 for the Worry & Oversensitivity subscale, and 0.72 for the Lie subscale (Ryngala, Shields, & Caruso, 2005). A meta-analysis of 15 studies using the earlier RCMAS found support for its construct and criterion validity in that it was very effective in distinguishing children with anxiety from youth without any psychiatric disorders, and was moderately effective in distinguishing youth with anxiety from those with some type of externalizing disorder (Seligman, Ollendick, Langley, & Baldacci, 2004). The reliabilities for the RCMAS-2 are similar in range. The internal reliability for the Total Anxiety score is 0.92 and test re–test reliability after a one-week interval is 0.76 for a smaller clinical sample of 100 children (Denzine, 2008).

The RCMAS-2 is a beneficial child and adolescent self-report anxiety measure with a particular focus on performance and social anxiety. Its two validity scales make it a particularly useful clinical tool for facilitating case conceptualization and diagnostic decision making. On the other hand, it may be a better tool for assessing overall level of anxiety than for assessing specific aspects of it given the somewhat weak internal reliabilities of the three subscales (Stein, 2008).

STATE–TRAIT ANXIETY INVENTORY   An older and once commonly used measure to assess generalized anxiety in adults is the *State–Trait Anxiety Inventory* (STAI). Based on a state–trait conceptualization of personality (see Chapter 8) applied specifically to anxiety, Spielberger, Gorsuch, and Lushene (1970) created a 40-item inventory. Half of the items are designed to assess whether an individual is experiencing acute or state anxiety by asking how he or she "feels at the moment." The remaining 20 items assess an enduring pattern of anxiety (trait) and ask how one "generally feels." Both the state and trait inventory use a 4-point scale. Like other unidimensional measures, it is easy to score, and high scores reflect greater levels of state or trait anxiety.

The STAI has sound psychometric properties (Dreger, 1978; Katkin, 1978). Test–retest and internal reliability coefficients are presented separately for males and females. Test–retest reliabilities provide evidence of a state–trait distinction in that the coefficients are much lower for the state items than for the trait items, as would be expected. After a one-hour interval, test re–test reliability for the state questionnaire ranged from 0.16 (females) to 0.33 (males) and 0.76 to 0.84, respectively for the trait questionnaire (Dreger). Internal reliability coefficients ranged from 0.83 to 0.92 for the state questionnaire and 0.86 to 0.92 for the trait. Similar state-versus-trait differences in test–retest and internal reliabilities were found after longer intervals and with many more samples (Barnes, Harp, & Jung, 2002). There are also a number of studies supporting its construct validity (Dreger; Katkin). Over the past 30 years it has become the standard anxiety measure against which newer anxiety measures are validated (Okun, Stein, Bauman, & Silver, 1996; Shedler, Beck, & Benson, 2000; Sulkowski et al., 2008). It continues to be a useful clinical tool for assessing generalized anxiety. Extensive research and clinical use of different language versions of the STAI have been done in several East Asian countries (see chapter section "Cultural Considerations"). The children's version, however, is currently more widely used than the adult version in counseling settings.

STATE–TRAIT ANXIETY INVENTORY FOR CHILDREN (STAIC)   The *State–Trait Anxiety Inventory for Children* (STAIC), or "How-I-Feel Questionnaire," consists of two 20-item inventories designed to assess state and trait anxiety in children ages 9–12 (Papay & Spielberger, 1986). The STAIC was modeled on the *State–Trait Anxiety Inventory* for adolescents and adults. A recent meta-analysis review of 26 studies evaluating the STAIC and the *Revised Children's Manifest Anxiety Scale* found that it is useful for discriminating between children with anxiety disorders and those without anxiety, and is a beneficial tool for measuring treatment response (Seligman et al., 2004).

Although the STAIC is designed to be a measure of anxiety, both the state and trait inventories include items that assess general distress, or what might be thought of as measuring negative mood or depression (e.g., "I feel like crying"). Seligman et al. noted that 25% of the trait items overlap with the CDI and 10% of the state items overlap. This overlap may reflect something about these two constructs—anxiety and depression—rather than a limitation of the STAIC. Considerable evidence suggests that many children, and adults for that matter, experience a mixed anxiety–depression disorder, as was noted earlier (Seligman et al.).

ADDITIONAL SELF-REPORT MEASURES   The *Worry and Anxiety Questionnaire* (WAQ) is a relatively new brief self-report measure aligned with the DSM-IV criteria for GAD, and is used to assess both worries and somatic anxiety symptoms (Dugas et al., 2001). Unlike other common self-report measures, the first item is open-ended, asking clients to list the content of their worries. The remaining 10 items are rated on a 9-point Likert scale. It appears to be an effective tool for identifying clients with GAD (Buhr & Dugas, 2002). Like the PSWQ, it has been normed on both clinical and nonclinical samples (university students), but those normative samples are primarily French Canadians. The WAQ has good test–retest reliability over a four-week interval. In nonclinical samples, the measure was able to discriminate between participants with high, moderate, and low levels of worry (Dugas et al.).

In addition, there are measures derived from a cognitive–behavioral conceptualization of anxiety that focus on the cognitive components of anxiety, such as worry, beliefs about worry and uncertainty, and cognitive avoidance (e.g., suppressing thoughts). Examples include the *Intolerance of Uncertainty Scale,* the *Why-Worry II,* and the *Cognitive Avoidance Questionnaire.* These three measures are approximately the same length (27, 25, and 25 items, respectively) and each uses a Likert scale response format (Gervais & Dugas, 2008). They have all been developed within the past decade.

Assessing Post-Traumatic Stress Disorder (PTSD)

A number of well-designed, psychometrically sound self-report measures are available to facilitate the diagnosis and case conceptualization of post-traumatic stress disorder (PTSD) (Keane,

Silberbogen, & Weierich, 2008; Mozley, Buckley, & Kaloupek, 2004). A diagnosis of PTSD should be considered when a person has experienced a trauma or stressor that is outside the bounds of ordinary human experience. The DSM-IV-TR defines a trauma as an event involving "actual or threatened death or serious injury, or other threat to one's physical integrity" either directly or indirectly (witnessing the event)" (American Psychiatric Association, 2000, p. 463). Examples of traumatic events include sexual or violent assault, witnessing domestic violence or other forms of violence, and natural disasters. A diagnosis of PTSD involves establishing both the experience of a trauma and three other broad criteria: 1) reexperiencing or reliving parts or all of the trauma in some fashion, such as flashbacks or nightmares and experiencing the same unpleasant feelings as when the trauma was originally experienced; 2) avoiding stimuli associated with the trauma and experiencing emotional numbness; and 3) experiencing heightened physiological arousal such as an exaggerated startle response (p. 436). When a sufficient number of symptoms from these three categories have been present for at least one month, and significant distress or functional impairment exists, the DSM diagnostic criteria for PTSD is met. The diagnosis is usually arrived at after either an unstructured or structured clinical interview is completed. Self-report measures that assess the severity and frequency of specific symptoms can help to confirm or differentiate the diagnosis and provide quantitative information about treatment progress and outcome. Examples of self-report measures that are being used in research and clinical settings for diagnostic purposes include the *PTSD Checklist*, the *Posttraumatic Diagnostic Scale*, the *Mississippi Scale for Combat-Related PTSD*, the *Keane PTSD Scale of the MMPI-2* (PK), and *the Los Angeles Symptom Checklist* (Keane et al.). These measures vary in terms of length, response format (true–false vs. Likert scale), and targeted population (military vs. civilian) but are all relatively brief, ranging from 17 to 49 items, and typically can be completed within 15 minutes.

Several self-report measures focus only on whether an individual has experienced a specific type of trauma (e.g., a natural disaster), not on the specific PTSD symptoms. Because these measures assess only the experience of traumatic events and not PTSD symptoms, they are not used as part of a diagnostic evaluation. These measures include the *Life Events Checklist*, the *Life Stressor Checklist-Revised*, the *Traumatic Events Questionnaire*, and the *Traumatic Life Events Questionnaire* (Keane et al., 2008). In addition to identifying the specific types of trauma an individual has experienced, these questionnaires may also assess age at the time of the trauma, level of exposure (e.g., happened to me vs. witnessed an event), perception of danger, and injury from the event. They are often used both as part of an initial screening process and for case conceptualization.

Assessing Obsessive–Compulsive Disorder (OCD)

Although less prevalent than the other anxiety disorders, obsessive–compulsive disorder (OCD) is just as debilitating, if not more, because of its impact on work, school, and interpersonal functioning. The DSM-IV-TR defines OCD as a condition involving either obsessions or compulsions or the combination of the two. Obsessions are repeated intrusive and distressing thoughts, images, or impulses that are experienced by the individual as senseless, repugnant, or bizarre. The thematic content of obsessions will vary among individuals, but typically involves concerns regarding harm, contamination, sex, religion, or morals. Compulsions, on the other hand, are behavioral rituals or routines that can involve repeated checking, counting, washing, or touching, and require one hour or more to complete (American Psychiatric Association, 2000). These rituals are performed to allay an underlying fear. Typically the fear involves harm to self or others (e.g., becoming contaminated with germs and becoming seriously ill by not washing multiple times in an elaborate fashion, or repeated checking of doors out of fear that someone will come in and harm the person and family members if the doors are not adequately locked). An individual with OCD may have both obsessions and compulsions or just one of the two. About one-third of the people who have OCD also experience major depression, and approximately one-fourth abuse alcohol (Steketee, 1998). The considerable amount of time spent on elaborate rituals or experiencing distressing obsessions and the lengths people will go through to avoid feared situations make it a particularly severe and debilitating disorder.

YALE–BROWN OBSESSIVE COMPULSIVE SCALE SYMPTOM CHECKLIST (YBOCS)   The *Yale–Brown Obsessive Compulsive Scale Symptom Checklist* (YBOCS-SC) is considered by some to be the best instrument for an initial assessment of obsession and compulsion symptoms despite the fact that to date its reliability and validity are not established (Abramowitz, 2008; Goodman et al., 1989a; Steketee, 1998). The YBOCS-SC consists of 58 items, 37 of which pertain to obsessions and the remaining 21 items to compulsive behaviors. The checklist helps to identify obsessions and compulsions that are common in OCD that may not have been reported during an intake interview. Clients are first given a definition of obsessions and how they differ from worries ("possible negative things related to life problems that you are afraid might happen"; for example, "you may worry about failing an exam, finances, health or personal relationships") and then are given a definition of compulsions and how they differ from compulsive or "addictive" behaviors such as gambling, drinking alcohol, and overeating. Next the clinician reviews the 58 items with the client, noting whether the person "has ever," or is "currently experiencing" the symptom. Symptoms that are endorsed can be probed further by a clinician and may become the focus of treatment. Alternatively, OCD symptoms can be identified through a structured interview schedule such as the ADIS-IV, OCD module (Abramowitz).

A companion measure is the YBOCS-Severity Scale, a semi-structured interview tool for assessing the severity of OCD symptoms and functional impairment in clients already diagnosed with OCD (Goodman et al., 1989b). The Severity Scale consists of 10 items, which the clinician rates on a 5-point scale. Five items pertain to obsessions and five to compulsions. There are items that assess 1) how much of the client's life is taken up with obsessions and compulsions; 2) how much they interfere with social or work functioning; 3) the ability to exercise control over thoughts and rituals; and 4) how distressing they are. Those items are rated from "none" to "extreme." Four additional items are related to the client's control over obsessions and compulsions and ability to resist them. These items are also rated on a 5-point scale: "complete control to no control and definitely resists to completely yields" (Goodman et al., 1989b).

Unlike the checklist, the Severity Scale has clinical and nonclinical norms (Abramowitz, 2008). In addition, its psychometric properties are very good. Interrater reliability coefficients for the 10 items ranges from 0.80 to 0.95. The internal consistency reliabilities are also good, with alpha coefficients ranging from 0.88 to 0.91. Furthermore, its convergent validity has been established with moderately strong correlations between the YBOCS and two other separate measures of OCD (Goodman et al., 1989a).

A scoring system exists for measuring the severity of OCD symptoms independent of the number of obsessions or compulsions identified by the *YBOCS Symptom Checklist*. Scores in the 0–7 range are considered "subclinical"; 8–15 mild, 16–23 moderate, 24–31 severe, and 32–40 extreme. YBOCS scores have been used in dozens of studies as a measure of treatment effectiveness.

BROWN ASSESSMENT OF BELIEFS SCALE AND OTHER OCD MEASURES   Because individuals with OCD vary in their insight about the irrationality of their fears, level of insight and rigidity about an obsession can also be assessed. The *Brown Assessment of Beliefs Scale* (BABS) was developed to measure attitudes toward one or two specific beliefs—delusions, obsessions, concerns, or worries—that would be found in various psychiatric disorders, including OCD (Eisen et al., 1998; Eisen, Phillips, Cole, & Rasmussen, 2004). The belief or obsession in OCD might be, for example, "If I don't place my backpack down in the same spot in my living room after school every day, I will get contaminated with germs." The BABS is a 7-item clinician administered semistructured interview, which can be completed in less than 15 minutes. The respondent or client indicates for the past week his or her understanding or the validity, accuracy, and psychological nature of the belief along with a desire to confront and disprove the belief. There is an additional item related to ideas of reference because the BABS was originally designed to assess delusional beliefs in various disorders. Each item is scored on a 5-point scale from 0 to 4, where a 4 indicates no insight. A total score of 18 or greater and a 4 on item 1 indicates the belief is delusional. The BABS appears to have good psychometric properties including internal consistency, test–retest reliability, and discriminant validity (Eisen et al., 2004).

Several other psychometrically sound OCD self-report measures, useful for treatment planning and monitoring purposes, have been developed in the past decade. These include the *Obsessive Beliefs Questionnaire,* the *Interpretation of Intrusion Inventory,* the *Revised Obsessive Compulsive Inventory*, the *Vancouver Obsessive Compulsive Inventory* (which is a revision of the *Maudsley Obsessional Compulsive Inventory*), and the *Schedule of Compulsions, Obsessions and Pathological Impulses* (Abramowitz, 2008). These are all relatively brief measures.

Assessing Phobias

In addition to using an unstructured or semistructured clinical interview, assessment of excessive fears related to a specific object (e.g., spiders), a situation (e.g., driving), or social performance can be done with various self-report measures. Like the measures for other anxiety disorders, these are used more for case conceptualization (identifying specific symptoms and symptom severity) and treatment monitoring purposes—much less for diagnostic needs. The measures with the best psychometric properties and clinical usefulness include the *Social Phobia and Anxiety Inventory,* the *Social Phobia Inventory,* and *Anxiety Sensitivity Index* (Rowa, McCabe, & Antony, 2008).

CULTURAL CONSIDERATIONS

Cross-cultural research of depression and anxiety self-report measures is not yet on a par with older personality measures such as the MMPI. However, the translation and application of self-report measures for clinical use in various cultures is accelerating. Two excellent websites for finding research on non-English language versions of anxiety, depression, and other self-report measures are those of the Victorian Transcultural Psychiatry Unit, a governmental agency in Victoria, Australia (***http://www.vtpu.org.au/resources/translated_instruments/ researchliterature.html***) and the Psychosocial Measures for Asian American Populations: Tools for Direct Practice and Research at Columbia University (***http://www.columbia.edu/cu/ ssw/projects/pmap***). Different language versions—Spanish, French, Japanese, and Chinese, to name just a few—of measures including the BDI-II, BAI, STAI and STAI-C, PSWQ, and WAQ are now in use. These non-English versions have been incorporated into studies to determine if constructs such as depression and anxiety are generalizable to non-English speaking cultures (Novy, Stanley, Averill, & Daza, 2001). Studies utilizing a translated non-English language version of a measure can provide a preliminary understanding of its cross-cultural applicability. Often, however, studies in countries outside the United States have relied on nonclinical college students for their participants, thus limiting their generalizability to clinical groups (Ghassemzadeh, Mojtabai, Karamghadiri, & Ebrahimkhani, 2005; Scott et al., 2002; Wiebe & Penley, 2005). Two such examples were studies examining the psychometric properties of the Spanish and Persian versions of the BDI. Although both non-English versions were found to have reliabilities (internal consistency and test–retest) in the adequate to excellent range, both studies involved only college students, some of whom were bilingual (Ghassemzadeh et al.; Wiebe & Penley). On the other hand, a recent literature review of studies designed to assess the use of Chinese, Korean, and Japanese language versions of the BDI and STAI with clinical populations in their respective countries concluded that those two measures are valid predictors of depression and anxiety in those cultures (Leong, Okazaki, & Tak, 2003). Cross-language reliability studies, though necessary and important, do not address another important question: Are self-report measures, which are good predictors of depression and anxiety risk in White Americans, similarly predictive when translated into other languages and used with other populations?

For the most part, the measures described in this chapter have not been adequately validated in minority cultures (Okazaki & Tanaka-Matsumi, 2006). The normative samples of the measures described in this chapter, with few exceptions, tend to be relatively homogenous with respect to race, and demographic factors beyond gender and socioeconomic status (e.g., religious affiliation or acculturation status) are not mentioned. Based on their review of cross-cultural research, Okazaki and Tanaka-Matsumi have advised clinicians to recognize that acculturation status can affect client responses to self-report measures. As a result, they recommended caution when using scores to make conclusions about clients' affective states. Their review noted that people from collectivistic countries are more likely than people from individualistic cultures to respond to self-report measures based on cultural norms regarding happiness and distress rather than using subjective emotional experiences. These cultural differences can also impact retrospective judgments about how one is feeling (in order to respond to a self-report measure) and the perceived social desirability of demonstrating to the assessor that one's emotions are consistent across situations.

Case of Susan: Treatment Planning and Monitoring with the BDI-II and BAI

The intake interview and observations of Susan indicated that she met the DSM-IV-TR criteria for a major depressive episode, but did not meet the criteria for generalized anxiety. Susan was asked to complete the BDI-II and the BAI following the intake interview. The clinician explained to her that "these questionnaires would help us see if you are having any other problems that we could focus on in the counseling and give us another way to see how you are doing as counseling progresses." Susan was shown the two measures, the instructions for each were reviewed with her, and she was asked to return them the following week. She seemed willing to follow through with this task.

Susan's initial overall BDI-II score was 21, suggestive of a moderate level of depression symptoms typically found in clients with a diagnosis of major depression; her BAI score was 15, suggestive of some anxiety symptoms of moderate severity but not of sufficient number and magnitude to qualify for a diagnosis of generalized anxiety disorder. Of particular note were symptoms listed in the measures that were not identified during the intake interview, which later became a focus of her counseling. These included BDI-II items related to self-concept and guilt, such as "I feel I am being punished," "I am disgusted with myself," and "I blame myself for all my faults," as well as the BAI items "fear of the worst happening," and "fear of losing control," both of which she indicated were "severe." In reviewing the BDI-II and BAI with Susan, the counselor was able to explore with her those feelings and beliefs she had indicated on the two measures. For example, the item on the BAI she endorsed as severe, "fear of losing control," was related to her recent temper outbursts and belief that she had no control over these. The review of the BDI and BAI helped the clinician and Susan conceptualize her depression as not merely a biological "illness" but as a problem that had physical, psychological, and interpersonal components to it, and the maintenance of which was related to Susan's perceptions and beliefs. Collaboratively they decided that her counseling would focus on how she came to those views about herself and her fears. Additionally, the counseling addressed her overall distress, sleep difficulty, loss of temper, increased alcohol consumption, and relationships with males. After eight weeks of weekly outpatient counseling, Susan again completed both the BDI-II and the BAI: her BDI-II score dropped to 15, but her BAI score rose. It is common in the beginning of counseling for scores on self-report depression and anxiety measures to rise as clients begin to explore difficult feelings and beliefs about self. At the 24th and final session eight months later, her BDI-II score was 5 and her BAI was 6.

It has been the author's experience, as well as others (Allen, Montgomery, Tubman, Frazier, & Escovar, 2003; Finn & Tonsager, 1997) that providing feedback to clients based on

PRACTICE SUGGESTION
Assessing Psychopathology with Self-Report Questionnaires

1. When a client presents with a variety of problems and symptoms, a multi-dimensional questionnaire such as the SCL-90-R or OQ-45.2 can help clarify diagnosis and enhance case conceptualization.
2. Use a unidimensional self-report measure or brief version of a multidimensional measure when severity of diagnosis, client status at the beginning of counseling or other intervention, or client progress needs to be evaluated in a standardized manner.
3. Determine if the client has the necessary reading level, and if English is not the primary language, whether a language version of the questionnaire exists in the client's primary language.
4. Determine where the questionnaire will be completed, and verify that the client understands the directions.
5. After the questionnaire has been completed, explore with the client answers to critical items such as suicidal thinking, hearing voices, or trouble sleeping.
6. Consider cultural factors such as acculturation status that may have affected client responding.
7. Since almost all psychopathology self-report measures do not have validity scales, as the MMPI-2 does, consider whether the overall pattern of responding suggests a defensive style (denial or minimization) or, conversely, exaggerates distress.
8. Make sure the interpretation of the questionnaire's score(s) is understood.
9. Consider how and when feedback to the client will be given.
10. Collaborate with the client about whether problems or symptoms identified through responses to a questionnaire need to be a focus of subsequent counseling.

self-report measures has a number of therapeutic benefits. Both anecdotal and research evidence has shown that clients find it helpful and relieving to see that what they are experiencing can be verified and validated quantitatively. It is often reassuring for clients to see that a standardized measure confirms what they are experiencing, a lessening in symptoms over time. In addition, assessment feedback can enhance the therapeutic alliance and promote self-esteem and self-efficacy, psychological insight, and comfort (Finn & Tonasger). A brief summary of the practical steps to follow when using self-report questionnaires is provided in the Practice Suggestion: Assessing Psychopathology with Self-Report Questionnaires.

Summary and Conclusions

Depressive and anxiety disorders together represent the most prevalent psychiatric disorders, and therefore they are the conditions that clinicians most often assess and treat. Fortunately, clinicians have at their disposal a number of well-designed psychometrically sound tools to assist them in the assessment and counseling process. Typically self-report depression and anxiety measures are used to supplement an unstructured or semistructured clinical interview. They are used for the purposes of case conceptualization, treatment planning, and monitoring progress. In and of themselves, these measures are not designed as definitive diagnostic tools in that a particular score is not considered conclusive evidence of a disorder; but rather one piece of the assessment puzzle. Generally, high scores indicate a client is at risk for the disorder in question, and these measures can facilitate the

process of formulating a diagnosis by identifying particular symptoms, symptom intensity, and frequency that are part of the diagnostic criteria.

It is important to keep in mind that it is possible for a client to score above a cutoff score on a self-report measure for reasons other than having the disorder. These factors include idiosyncratic understanding of the instructions or particular items; a desire to appear more symptomatic; and a tendency to respond to psychological measures with the extreme ends of a rating scale, otherwise known as response bias. Most of the assessment instruments that were reviewed have been translated into multiple languages. Cross-cultural research of these measures, though not yet at the level of personality tests, is accelerating rapidly to meet the mental health needs of individuals throughout the world.

Reflection Questions and Experiential Exercises

1. What are the advantages and limitations of using the SCL-90-R versus the OQ-45.2 for a baseline measure of client distress and functioning? What are the relative advantages and limitations of each checklist for measuring ongoing client changes during counseling?
2. What are the advantages and limitations of the *Beck Depression Inventory* and *Beck Anxiety Inventory*?
3. When might you use an anxiety or depression measure?
4. How might different time frames (one week, two weeks, or one month) in the instructions for an anxiety or depression measure affect client responses?
5. How might you go about sharing the results of a self-report measure with a client like Susan from the case

study? How might you share results with a client with whom you are currently working?
6. Even though many anxiety and depression measures have been translated into different languages, why might the English and non-English versions of a test not be equivalent? For example, you could compare the English and Spanish versions of the BDI-II.
7. Complete one of the standardized questionnaires described in this chapter. What was your reaction to filling out the questionnaire? How easy or difficult was it for you overall? Were there any particular questions to which you had a strong reaction?

10 | ASSESSING CHILDREN AND ADOLESCENTS: SELF-REPORT AND ADULT PERSPECTIVES

Chapter Objectives

After reading this chapter, you should be able to:

■ Identify commonly used child self-report questionnaires.

■ Identify commonly used parent and teacher rating scales.

■ Explain the advantages and limitations of commonly used child self-report, parent, and teaching rating scales.

■ Understand the cultural considerations when using standardized child assessment measures.

Samantha, a tall, cherubic looking 9-year-old girl, was referred for evaluation and counseling by her pediatrician because of concerns regarding "focusing difficulties," which Sam's fourth-grade teacher had raised. Sam's mother had noticed that her daughter was having trouble paying attention during homework and was "spacey" at times but she was more worried about her self-esteem. "She puts herself down a lot and just kinda gives up," her mother said. Present during this initial interview session were Sam, her mother, and her mother's boyfriend of one year.

Through a semistructured intake interview, the school counselor, Ms. White, obtained further information about the presenting problems and Sam's history. Sam's parents divorced when she was 7 years old, and the year prior to the divorce was marked with significant tension, conflict, and volatility, according to her mother. Her father remarried shortly after the divorce to a woman who had two children from a previous relationship. Sam's week is divided between the two households and she experiences discomfort around her stepmother. Her parents are conflicted about how to get Sam to do her homework. Sam has a 7-year-old sister. Sam is half-way through the school year, and her grades have slipped from "mostly A's and Bs to mostly B's and C's."

During the intake, Sam oscillated between making drawings in a play area off to the side and joining the conversation to interject when she disagreed with her mother. In the allotted time, Ms. White, using a risk and resources framework, collected information about Sam's school functioning since kindergarten, her sleep and exercise patterns, her health history, and her view about transitioning between the two homes. By the end of the intake interview, a number of questions had been raised for Ms. White, which would require further assessment to answer.

Sam's school performance had been erratic the past two years and her current teacher's reports suggested that Sam might have some type of attention deficit–hyperactivity disorder. At the same time, she had been exposed to a traumatic event, witnessing the death of her grandfather, and her parent's ongoing battles and subsequent divorce. Her concentration problems, negative remarks about herself, and withdrawal from friends suggested she might be experiencing some kind of adjustment reaction, anxiety, or depression. Ms. White was trying to sort out what, if any, disorder or combination of disorders Sam might have, where to focus the counseling sessions given the complex and multiple presenting problems, and how to go about conducting further assessment. One assessment option was to continue gathering information through unstructured interviews with Sam and the various adults in her life: parents, stepmother, mother's boyfriend, teacher, and pediatrician. Another option was to use standardized assessment measures in order to clarify a diagnosis, help identify symptoms, behaviors, feelings, and beliefs that may not have been revealed during interviews but might indeed be a treatment focus, and have a baseline measure from which counseling progress could be evaluated. And if standardized measures were going to be incorporated into the assessment process, which ones would she choose? Ms. White was aware of a number of possibilities. Some she knew she was qualified to use, others she was not sure. She elected to pursue both options and decided on the *Behavioral Assessment System for Children,* 2nd edition (BASC-2) for the standardized assessment tool.

Sam, her mother and father, and her fourth-grade teacher completed different versions of the *BASC-2: Self-Report of Personality* (SRP), Parent Rating Scale (PRS), and Teacher Rating Scale (TRS).

OVERVIEW

Sam's story is illustrative of the multifaceted nature of child assessment. Various adults and the child are relied upon to provide information about the child's history, present functioning, and current concerns. As is the case with adult assessment, standardized assessment tools are valuable components of a comprehensive assessment process. The difference is that where children are concerned, individuals other than the client and therapist—parents, teachers, and other caregivers—will inevitably be additional sources of information about a child's emotional, behavioral, social, and academic functioning. A child's perception of self and his or her environments is a necessary but not sufficient piece of the overall assessment process.

The use of standardized measures for the identification and treatment of emotional, behavioral, and social problems in children, preschool through adolescence, has grown significantly since the 1960s. The increased development, research, and clinical use of standardized child rating scales, both child self-report and adult rating scales of children's behavior, has been especially dramatic in educational and mental health settings since the mid 1980s (Merrell, 2008). This growth has stemmed from several factors: the Individuals with Disabilities Education Act (IDEA); the prevalence and treatment of childhood psychiatric disorders in community settings; the revisions to the DSM, specifically the recognition of disorders with a childhood onset; an empirically based alternative classification system for children; and a public health model for identifying youth at risk in need of intervention (Kamphaus & Frick, 2005; Merrell). Despite the ability of children, elementary school age and older, to reliably rate the degree to which they are experiencing something such as an emotional concern or problematic behavior, counselors do not rely exclusively on a child's self-reports when conducting assessments of emotional and behavioral functioning.

In order to gain a comprehensive understanding of a child's emotional and behavioral problems, counselors rely on adults for providing contextual information in the areas of development, psychosocial history and functioning, educational history and performance, and health status. Parents and teachers are viewed as having special knowledge of a child's behavior and have been found to reliably report the degree to which behaviors exist in their children and students (Edelbrock & Achenbach, 1984). Furthermore, children typically do not refer themselves for mental health treatment or special education services. This means it is essential to gather the concerned adults' view of the problem because often adult and child perceptions differ significantly. Another layer of complexity stems from the fact that adults themselves can disagree about the nature and severity of a child's problems, particularly when those adults belong to different environments, such as home versus school (McConaughy, 1993). Therefore, a child may be rated in the "clinically significant range" on a teacher rater behavior scale but not on a parent version, or vice versa—not because one adult has a more accurate perception of the child, but rather because different environments are likely to influence different behavioral and emotional styles.

Information about the child referred for school counseling or community-based mental health services can be gleaned from both standardized and nonstandardized methods, including parent and teacher interviews, interviews with other knowledgeable adults (e.g., a child protective services worker), interviews with the child, projective assessments, and child and adult inventories or rating scales. In addition to child self-report measures, several well-researched parent and teacher questionnaires where adults rate the degree of behaviors in a child are considered by some to be necessary components of any comprehensive child psychological assessment (Schroeder & Gordon, 2002). Their use among mental health professionals has risen over the past two decades and supplanted the use of projective techniques, according to surveys of psychologists and child clinicians (Kamphaus, Petoskey, & Rowe, 2000).

The purpose of this chapter is to provide practical clinical and technical information about well-researched, psychometrically sound, and widely used multidimensional measures for the initial and ongoing assessments of children (ages 2½ to 18). The measures discussed in this chapter are meant to be illustrative of the range of standardized inventories and rating scales currently available for assessing the emotional and behavioral functioning of children. The chapter will describe **multidimensional** or **broadband questionnaires** that cover a broad array of childhood behaviors, symptoms, feelings, and thoughts. In addition, they typically have parallel parent, teacher, and child self-report versions. The chapter will also discuss multicultural issues that arise from the use of specific standardized measures for the assessment of childhood problems.

CHILD SELF-REPORT MEASURES

As any reader of the cartoon strip *Peanuts* knows, Charlie Brown, Lucy, and the rest of the Peanuts crew are keenly aware of and able to describe their moods, feelings, thoughts, aches, and pains. What happens when real children, like Samantha, are given questionnaires as part of an assessment process and asked to rate the intensity or frequency of their inner and outer experiences? The answer is, like adults, they can provide useful and unique ratings of their behaviors, thoughts, feelings, or symptoms (Kline, 1995). Consequently, a number of highly reliable and valid child self-report questionnaires have been developed and are now used routinely in the assessment of children as young as 6 years old.

The first generation of child self-report questionnaires were developed for what are called "internalizing problems" (Achenbach, 1982): anxieties, phobias, fears, and depression (see Chapter 9). In addition to internalizing problem questionnaires, children can complete rating scales that assess concepts such as trauma experiences, self-concept, school learning, and social skills. The applicable age range varies depending upon the particular questionnaire, but in general have been designed for children ages 6 to 18. A number of current child self-report questionnaires cover a wide range of internalizing and externalizing problems such as disruptive disorders like attention deficit–hyperactivity disorder (ADHD) and oppositional defiant disorder (ODD). Multidimensional measures are often used first in an assessment process because they cover a wider scope of symptoms and concerns than unidimensional measures. Depending upon the results obtained from multidimensional measures, more focused unidimensional measures may be needed later in the assessment process.

A quick note about engaging young children in standardized assessment is needed before reviewing specific measures. Elementary school age children need a short and child-friendly explanation about why they are being given a form to fill out. Terms like "test" or "question-naire" are best avoided because of their negative connotations and triggering of anxiety with some children. Instead, a girl like Samantha in the opening case story might be told, "One of the ways I can get to know more about what's bothering you, so I can help you as much I would like to, is for you to fill out this paper. How does that sound?" Generally an explanation like that will suffice. In this author's experience, children rarely have questions about this type of approach, especially if some relationship building has already occurred. Clinical experience would suggest, therefore, giving measures to children after rather than prior to an initial session, though that sequence is not a requirement of any of the measures discussed in this chapter. If the child is going to complete the inventory or rating scale while away from your presence, which is a typical practice when conducting individual assessments, it is important that you go over the instructions while the child is still with you.

Multidimensional Self-Report Measures

The two most extensively researched and most commonly used multidimensional child self-report measures are the *Youth Self-Report* (YSR) and the *Self-Report of Personality* (SRP). Both the YSR and the SRP are part of comprehensive child assessment systems that include parent and teacher ratings scales and direct observation forms. The YSR is part of the *Achenbach System of Empirically Based Assessment* (ASEBA) and can be administered to youth separately or as part of a more comprehensive assessment that could include the parent and teacher rating scales. The SRP is part of the *Behavior Assessment System for Children-2* (BASC-2) and likewise can be administered on its own or in combination with the adult rating scales. Rescorla (2009) has provided an informative, comprehensive summary of the similarities and differences between the ASEBA and BASC assessment systems. Those differences include how adaptive competencies are assessed, cutoff points for determining at-risk and clinically significant problem levels, assessing rater bias, response formats and scale composition, and multicultural applications. The most important similarity between the ASEBA and the BASC systems is that they both have parallel adult versions—parent and teacher—and both child and adolescent self-report scales (though the YSR has a narrower age range than the SRP). This allows for easier and more meaningful comparisons among the sources of information—child, parent, and teacher—because many items are similar, as are the response formats. As noted earlier, information from multiple perspectives is essential to comprehensive and effective child mental health and educational assessments. Parent, child, and teacher response may be congruent at times and at other times vastly different. Those similarities can help to clarify a diagnosis and suggest a path for intervention. The differences among the "informants" can help elucidate diagnostic enigmas and treatment planning uncertainties that need to be resolved, and can raise additional areas for exploration.

YOUTH SELF-REPORT (YSR)

Overview   The *Youth Self-Report* (YSR), for children ages 11 to 18, was the third rating scale developed for the ASEBA following the completion of the *Child Behavior Checklist* (CBCL) parent version and the *Teacher Rating form* (TRF). The YSR, developed by Achenbach and Edelrock, was initially published in 1991 and revised in 2001 (Achenbach & Rescorla, 2001). The 2001 revision retained the same format and all but six of the items from the 1991 version in order to better discriminate between children referred for mental health problems and nonreferred ones. In addition, some of the syndrome labels (to be discussed shortly) were changed. As mentioned previously, the YSR can be administered as a separate assessment measure or as part of a more comprehensive assessment that could include the CBCL and TRF. Youths with a fifth-grade reading level can complete the YSR, and a Spanish version is available at ***www.aseba .org***. In addition, the YSR was recently translated into French and a number of other languages (Achenbach et al., 2008; Wyss, Voelker, Cornock, & Hakim-Larson, 2003). The YSR is based on the ASEBA classification system, which includes two broad categories—internalizing and externalizing—and eight narrow ones: anxious/depressed, withdrawn/depressed, somatic complaints, social problems, thought problems, attention problems, rule-breaking, and aggressive behavior (see Table 10.1).

The YSR consists of two sections. The first section has four parts that ask the youth to rate their academic and social functioning and describe their interests. There is also space for answering an open-ended question regarding current concerns. The second section has a total of 112 items pertaining to emotional, behavioral, and social problems and social competence. Out of the total 112 items, one item asks about seven somatic complaints such as head- and stomachaches, and 11 ask about socially desirable items such as "I can be pretty friendly" or "I am pretty honest." Respondents are asked to rate each of the items in the second section on a 3-point scale: "not true," "somewhat or sometimes true" or "very true or often true." Sample items include:

- "I can't get my mind off certain thoughts (describe)."
- "I don't get along with other kids."
- "I feel that I have to be perfect."
- "I act without stopping to think."
- "I am shy."
- "I have a hot temper."

Administration, Scoring, and Interpretation   The amount of time typically required to complete the YSR is more variable than for other multidimensional inventories because of the open-ended questions but on average it can be finished within 30 to 45 minutes. On the second section of the YSR (the 112 emotional, behavioral, and social competence items) the instruction set is: "Below is a list of items that describes kids. For each item that describes you **now** or **within the past 6 months,** please circle the 2 if it is **very true** or **often true** of you. Circle the 1 if the item is **somewhat** or **sometimes true** of you. If the item is **not true** of you circle 0." The scoring of the YSR is relatively straightforward and user friendly and can be done by hand using a template and a hand-scoring profile or a computer software program. Separate male and female profiles exist since interpretation is based on gender norms. Raw scores are summed for each of the eight syndromes (see Table 10.1). Those raw score totals are converted to *t* scores and can be plotted on a profile form for quick visual inspection. *T* scores and percentiles for the overall internalizing, externalizing, and total problem scores can be obtained as well. The 2001 YSR includes DSM-oriented problem scales: Affective, Anxiety, Somatic, ADH, Oppositional defiant, and Conduct. Those scales are scored on separate profile forms.

The YSR, like the other ASEBA scales, is based on a cutoff score approach to interpretation. *T* scores above 65 (95th percentile) suggest a youth who is at risk for a particular syndrome or problem area, and 70 and above (98th percentile or greater) is considered the clinical range.

Table 10.1 ASEBA Scales

Scales	CBCL (6–18)	TRF	YSR
Competence & adaptive:			
Activities (Academic)	•	•	•
Social (Working)	•	•	•
School (Behaving)	•	•	•
Total Competence	•	•	•
Empirically based:			
Anxious/Depressed	•	•	•
Withdrawn/Depressed	•	•	•
Somatic Complaints	•	•	•
Social Problems	•	•	•
Thought Problems	•	•	•
Attention Problems	•	•	•
Rule-Breaking Behavior	•	•	•
Aggressive Behavior	•	•	•
Composite scales Internalizing	•	•	•
Externalizing	•	•	•
Total Problems	•	•	•
DSM-oriented:			
Affective Problems	•	•	•
Anxiety Problems	•	•	•
Somatic Problems	•	•	•
ADH Problems (Inattention) (Hyperactivity–Impulsivity)	•	•	•
Oppositional Defiant Problems	•	•	•
Conduct Problems	•	•	•

T scores below 65 are considered to be in the normal range. Scores in the clinical range are not meant to be indicative, by themselves, of the presence of a psychiatric disorder but rather indicate that the youth is reporting emotional, social, and or behavioral problems at a level that is greater than 97 out of 100 youth between the ages of 11 to 18. Therefore, a score at the 98th percentile indicates a high probability that the youth has some type of disorder. To determine why the scores fall into the clinical range and which DSM disorder might be present requires further assessment.

Technical Information   Each revision of the YSR has been shown to have excellent reliability and validity (Achenbach & Rescorla, 2001). Norms for the 2001 version were obtained from a multinational sample of 2,581 clinical and 1,057 nonreferred youths ages 11–18. The sample is representative of the U.S. population in terms of race, socioeconomic status, and setting (urban vs. rural).

Reliability coefficients range from adequate to excellent. Alpha coefficients range from 0.71 to 0.95 on the empirically based problem scales, 0.67 to 0.83 on the DSM-oriented scales, and 0.55 to 0.75 on the competence scales. Test–retest correlations range from 0.67 to 0.89 on the empirically based scales, 0.68 to 0.86 on the DSM-oriented scales, and 0.83 to 0.91 on the competence scales, with a mean interval of eight days (Achenbach & Rescorla, 2001). The manual also provides cross-informant correlations for every scale found on the YSR and the parent and teacher forms. This information allows the YSR user to gauge how much agreement is typically found between a youth and parent or youth and teacher on a particular scale.

Advantages and Limitations   The YSR is the most extensively researched multi-dimensional self-report questionnaire for children ages 11–18 (Merrell, 2008). Extensive research by Achenbach and his colleagues (Achenbach, Dumenci, & Rescorla, 2002; Achenbach & Rescorla, 2006) and other researchers (Ivanova et al., 2007) has found much support for the content, criterion-related, and construct validity of the YSR. It is an excellent tool for determining whether a youth is likely experiencing some type of emotional and/or behavioral disorder. A recent factor analytic study of over 30,000 youth representing 23 different countries (Achenbach et al., 2008) demonstrated its generalizability to diverse cultures including European, Asian, and Middle Eastern. This study provided preliminary cross-cultural support for the idea that these eight syndromes are valid constructs, though the degree to which cross-cultural validity exists depends upon the particular country studied. Although different cultures may conceptualize psychopathology somewhat differently than the DSM-IV, the syndromes established from the YSR data appear to have as much, if not greater, cross-cultural support than DSM-IV diagnoses do for children and adolescents. In countries as diverse as Sweden, Iran, and Japan, the YSR is a very good tool for identifying youth with some type of serious emotional or behavioral disorder. In addition to its vast research background, its open-ended format regarding social functioning, activities, and concerns is a unique feature among child self-report questionnaires. The inclusion of 11 social competencies items helps to balance the focus on problematic feelings, thoughts, and behaviors and can facilitate honest responding. Last, it is easy to administer, score, and interpret. In fact, the scoring and converting of raw scores to *t* scores is a straightforward clerical task that a non–mental health professional could be quickly trained to do, freeing up a clinician's time for other tasks.

There are a couple disadvantages to using the YSR in mental health settings. Its primary drawback is that it cannot be used with children younger than 11. A secondary weakness is its lack of validity scales. Unlike the SRP (see later in this chapter), there are no scales for detecting inconsistent, socially desirable, or negative patterns on responding. Inspection of the YSR may, however, reveal these patterns. For example if all but the socially desirable items are circled as "not true," that in and of itself should raise a red flag for the clinician that the youth was likely responding in a socially desirable and distorted way. Another issue to consider when using the YSR in mental health settings is that the ASEBA classification system is not accepted by third-party payers. Even though the syndrome label "aggressive behavior," for example, might better reflect a child's behavior problems, third-party payers—commercial insurers, managed care companies, and the government—continue to reimburse only for the treatment of DSM-defined disorders and as yet aggressive behavior syndrome does not exist in the DSM. The current YSR version (2001) does contain, however, DSM-IV-oriented scales and so there is less of an issue when using the YSR for clarifying and assigning a diagnosis. And keep in mind, as has been stressed throughout this text, one assessment tool alone is not sufficient for making diagnoses.

SELF-REPORT OF PERSONALITY (SRP)

Overview   The goal of the *Self-Report of Personality* (SRP) is to assess a child's or adolescent's perception of his or her feelings and thoughts about self, school, peers, and parents, and behavior problems (Reynolds & Kamphaus, 2004). The SRP is in its second edition and can be used with children between the ages of 6 and 18 and young adults. The SRP was included in the original BASC, published in 1992 and revised in 2004 (Reynolds & Kamphaus). Two separate questionnaires exist for children ages 8–11 (SRP-C) and 12–18 (SRP-A); the second edition also includes a young adult version (ages 18–25) of the SRP. In addition, an interview version of the SRP (SRP-I) was created for children ages 6 and 7 in 2005 and contains about a third of the SRP child items. Changes to the second edition of the SRP included a 4-point response scale for many items (the original SRP had only a true–false response scale for all items), two new primary scales (Attention Problems and Hyperactivity) and four content scales on the adolescent version, additional validity scales (for detecting overly biased responding, like with the MMPI-2) (see Chapter 8), and a small reduction in total items on both the child and adolescent versions (Reynolds & Kamphaus). The SRP typically can be completed in 30 minutes or less and is written at a third-grade reading level. The SRP could be administered orally through an audio recording for those youth with limited reading abilities. Using the audio recording, rather than a counselor dictating the items, is recommended because of the greater standardization with a recording (Reynolds & Kamphaus). Scoring can be done by hand, computer entry, or via scan forms. The SRP is published by Pearson Assessments and is a level C instrument. There is also a Spanish edition available.

The SRP-C includes 139 items and the SRP-A has 176 items covering a wide range of beliefs, feelings, behaviors, and concerns similar in nature to the YSR. What is unique about the SRP, however, is that it contains two different item response formats. Items 1–51 are rated as "true" or "false" and the remaining items are rated on a 4-point scale from "never" to "almost always." The BASC-2 manual indicates that one study demonstrated greater reliability for the mixed-response format over a single-type format. Unlike the YSR directions, there is no specified time interval (e.g., the past six months) for the SRP items. The SRP (Child and Adolescent versions) consists of the following clinical and adaptive scales: Anxiety, Attention Problems, Attitude to School, Attitude to Teachers, Atypicality, Depression, Hyperactivity, Interpersonal Relations, Locus of Control, Relations with Parents, Self-Esteem, Self-Reliance, Sense of Inadequacy, and Social Stress. The interview version for children ages 6 and 7 contains only seven of these scales. The SRP-A also includes a Sensation Seeking and Somatization scale, and the college version parallels the adolescent one with the addition of an Alcohol Abuse scale. The items on these scales focus on a wide array of concerns, symptoms, feelings, behaviors, and attitudes such as loneliness, sleep problems, pessimistic view of self, relationship with classmates, rule breaking, and hearing voices.

Administration, Scoring, and Interpretation   In addition to following the instructions printed on the booklet, clinicians are advised to tell children and adolescents, "The sentences in this booklet may or may not describe things about you. Please answer all of the sentences as truthfully as you can. You may think some sentences do not apply to you, but answer them anyway" (Reynolds & Kamphaus, 2004). Scoring of the SRP (child and adolescent) can be done by hand or via computer software, though the paper forms enable hand scoring to be easy and relatively quick. The scoring and profile sheets lie beneath the inventory and are separated from the inventory to allow for convenient scoring. The first step in scoring and interpreting the SRP is to obtain scores on the three validity indexes: F, V, and L. The F index is a measure of "excessively negative responses"; V is a measure of how many "nonsensical" items were endorsed; and L assesses for "denial of problems" (Reynolds & Kamphaus). In general, the higher the score on any one of the three validity indexes, the greater the likelihood that the child responded in a highly distorted fashion and the results of the SRP should be viewed with caution. A distorted pattern of responding, however, could be due to poor reading comprehension rather than excessive denial of problems or negativity. The second scoring step involves calculating the total raw scores on each of the clinical and adaptive scales and then, using the manual's normative tables, converting those raw scores to t scores. T scores in the 60–69 range suggest a youth who is at risk for the problem identified by the scale, and scores 70 and above are considered to be in the clinically significant range. A clinically significant score occurs in less than 2% of the normative population and suggests that the presence of a psychiatric disorder is very likely. The BASC-2 manual contains norms for males and females, clinical and general populations, and two specific clinical populations: ADHD and learning disability. Last, a user of the SRP can obtain five composite scores: Emotional Symptoms Index, Inattention/Hyperactivity, Internalizing Problems, Personal Adjustment, and School Problems. The clinical, adaptive, and composite t scores can be visually displayed on a profile graph similar to the YSR.

Technical Information   The standardization samples for the SRP-C (N = 1,500) and SRP-A (N = 1,900) were very diverse and matched very closely the U.S. population data from the March 2001 *Current Population Survey* for gender, age, ethnicity/race, and socioeconomic status, and geographic region (Reynolds & Kamphaus, 2004). Additionally, clinical norm samples were obtained from children whose parents indicated they had been labeled with an emotional, behavioral, or physical problem. The BASC-2 manual provides more detailed information about the standardization process and the normative groups.

The reliability coefficients for the SRP-C, SRP-A, and the SRP-I are in the adequate to excellent range. Internal consistency reliabilities for the combined male and female general norms sample range from 0.71 to 0.86 on the adaptive and clinical scales (median = 0.80) for the SRP-C, and from 0.68 to 0.88 (median = 0.82) for the SRP-A. The internal consistency coefficients for the clinical samples are also in the adequate to excellent range. The range of SRP-I coefficients is somewhat lower (0.72–0.82) but still in the adequate to good range. Test–retest reliability, measured somewhere between 13- to 66-day intervals, for the adaptive and clinical scales ranged from 0.63 to 0.82 (median = 0.71) on the SRP-C, 0.61 to 0.84 (median = 0.75) on the SRP-A, and again somewhat lower on the SRP-I: 0.56–0.79 (median = 0.70) (Reynolds & Kamphaus, 2004).

The BASC-2 manual documents three processes for establishing the validity of both the child and adolescent versions of the SRP: factor analysis, correlation with other self-report measures, and mean scale scores for different diagnostic groups. The manual presents evidence for the content, and construct (both convergent and discriminant) validity of the SRP and how those validity coefficients were determined. Criterion validity, however, is lacking, as Kline (1995) noted in his review of the original SRP. There is little distinction between the mean profile scores and specific mean scale scores of the two clinical populations (attention deficit–hyperactivity disorder and conduct disorder), and the scores of the nonclinical standardization sample, including those scales where you would expect a difference, such as Attitude to School. The BASC-2 includes additional clinical groups, but like the BASC, the ADHD and a combined emotional/behavioral disturbance (EBD) group are overrepresented. Also, the problem Kline identified in the original BASC remains for the BASC-2 SRP child version. For example, the mean *t* score for the ADHD group is higher than the EBD group on the depression scale and the *t* scores are equal on the anxiety scale. Conversely, there is a less-than-1-point difference on the Hyperactivity scale between these two groups, albeit in the expected direction (ADHD > EBD). Very similar mean profiles between the two groups exist at the adolescent level as well. Collectively, the technical evidence in the manual indicates that the SRP, both child and adolescent versions, is better at differentiating between youth with and without psychiatric disorders than between different disorders.

Advantages and Limitations   The SRP-C and SRP-A have a number of features that merit their use in the assessment of emotional and behavioral problems in youth. Although the interview version for children ages 6 and 7 is only a few years old and has not been evaluated as extensively, it is a welcome addition to the self-report measures for young children. The BASC-2 child and adolescent self-report inventories are very practical clinician-friendly measures that can be used with minimal training and supervision. Like the YSR, their advantages clearly outweigh any disadvantages. They are brief, efficient, and normative methods for obtaining a youth's perceptions about a broad range of problems, concerns, symptoms, and attitudes toward self and others. Furthermore, these perceptions can be evaluated along with a parent or teacher perspective from the other BASC-2 rating scales. Its major benefit is that it is an excellent tool for aiding in diagnosis, case conceptualization, and treatment planning. As noted earlier, it has been criticized for a lack of predictive validity, limited validity for the validity scales, and too many self-esteem scale items that focus only on personal appearance (Kamphaus & Frick, 2005).

PERSONALITY INVENTORY FOR YOUTH (PIY)

Overview   The *Personality Inventory for Youth* (PIY) is a 270-item child self-report rating scale modeled on the *Personality Inventory for Children,* a parent rating scale (Lachar & Gruber, 1995). The goal of the PIY, like the SRP and YSR, is to assess the emotional and behavioral adjustment, school adjustment, family characteristics, and interactions, and academic abilities in children ages 9 to 19 (Lachar & Gruber). Items are responded to as either true or false. There is also an 80-item abbreviated version that is designed for screening purposes in educational settings. In addition to generating normative information about a child's perceptions, elevated PIY scale scores produce a detailed personality description of the child. The PIY requires a mid-third-grade reading level or above and there is an audio version for youth with reading problems.

The PIY has nine clinical scales: Cognitive Impairment, Impulsivity and Distractibility, Delinquency, Family Dysfunction, Reality Distortion, Somatic Concern, Psychological Discomfort, Social Withdrawal, and Social Skill Deficits. There are four validity scales: Inconsistency (inattentiveness, oppositional or provocative responses), Dissimulation (malingering or exaggerated responses), Defensiveness (social desirability), and Validity (Lachar & Gruber, 1995).

A Spanish Language edition is available. The items cover a wide range of feelings, behaviors, thoughts, and symptoms and include such things as skipping school, moving quickly between activities, disobeying parents, unusual behavior, mood, and sleep problems. The PIY is published by Western Psychological Services (*www.wpspublish.com*).

Administration, Scoring, and Interpretation Youth can complete the PIY in about 45 minutes. There is an audiocassette available for children with less than a third-grade reading level. Both hand-scoring and computer-assisted-scoring programs are available. Raw scores are converted to *t* scores using gender and age norms.

Interpretation of the PIY involves several steps and like the YSR and SRP is empirically based (Lachar & Gruber, 1995). The first step is examining the validity scales to determine the usefulness of the scores on the clinical scales. Different cutoff scores have been established for the validity scales depending upon gender. If the PIY is deemed "valid," the second step involves identifying clinical scales with a *t* score 60 or greater and subscales with a *t* score 65 or greater (70 for the Hallucinations and Delusions subscale). *T* scores at or above those cutoff scores indicate the presence of clinical problems. A third interpretative step identifies clinical scales at 60 or greater that do not have a subscale in the significant range and, conversely, subscales at 65 or greater without their respective clinical scale falling in the significant range. An examination of the list of critical items is the last step. Unlike the SRP and YSR, there are no composite scales (e.g., "internalizing/externalizing") to score and interpret.

Technical Information The PIY was standardized with a normative group of 2,327 children and adolescents representing 13 public school districts in five U.S. states and is representative of the U.S. population in terms of race/ethnicity and parents' education level (Lachar & Gruber, 1995). The internal reliability coefficients (alpha) for the clinical scales are generally in the adequate to excellent range with a median of 0.85, as are the test–retest reliability coefficients (median = 0.82 for the clinical scales) (Kamphaus & Frick, 2005). The alpha and test–retest reliability coefficients for seven of the clinical subscales fall below what is considered an adequate measure of reliability (0.70 or above). The manual presents evidence of discriminant validity (i.e., the ability of the PIY to discriminate between regular education students and clinical cases). There is also evidence for convergent and construct validity (Kline, 1995).

Advantages and Limitations Like the other two multidimensional self-report rating scales presented in this chapter, the PIY is a very useful screening and diagnostic tool for a wide range of problems encountered in clinical settings. And relative to the SRP and YSR, the PIY manual provides the most interpretative guidelines and details regarding interpreting scores from each scale (Kline, 1995). The Cognitive Impairment scale enables the clinician to examine perceptions of learning and achievement problems in addition to emotional and behavioral ones. On the other hand, the PIY has seven subscales, almost a third of the total, with internal consistency coefficients that fall below what is now considered to be a minimum level of acceptable reliability. These low coefficients result, in part, from a small number of items on those subscales, which means *t* scores on those scales should be interpreted with caution.

THE MULTIDIMENSIONAL ANXIETY SCALE FOR CHILDREN (MASC) Although more limited in scope than the other multidimensional youth measures, the *Multidimensional Anxiety Scale for Children* (MASC), is an innovative addition to child self-report questionnaires that have an analogous parent version. The MASC, published in 1997, is both a self-report measure and parent rating scale designed to assess the emotional, behavioral, cognitive, and physical aspects of anxiety in children and adolescents ranging in age from 8 to 19 years (Schroeder & Gordon, 2002). It is a relatively brief and quick rating scale consisting of 39 items on a 4-point scale ranging from "never true about me" to "often true about me" and requires a fourth-grade reading level. What distinguishes the MASC from existing measures is its focus on child-specific anxiety symptoms such as separation anxiety and a multidimensional conceptualization of anxiety consistent with current views of anxiety as having cognitive, physiological, emotional, and behavioral components. Furthermore, it is a purer measure of anxiety in that it does not contain general distress and/or depression symptoms as is the case with some of the child self-report anxiety measures reviewed in the previous chapter. The MASC has four basic scales: Physical Symptoms, Harm Avoidance, Social Anxiety, and Separation/Panic. The first three scales also contain the following subscales: Tense Symptoms and Somatic Symptoms, Perfectionism and Anxious Coping, and Humiliation Fears and Performance Fears. The MASC also includes an Inconsistency scale to detect random or careless responding. Studies have shown it has adequate internal and test–retest reliability and discriminant validity and has recently been translated into Swedish (Ivarsson, 2006). In a recent review, the MASC received a "highly recommended" rating for three categories of assessment purposes: diagnosis, treatment planning, and monitoring progress. Among all the child and adolescent self-report anxiety measures reviewed, it was the only one to receive that rating in all three categories (Silverman & Ollendick, 2008).

Using Multidimensional Self-Report Scales in Counseling

There are several important reasons for including a multidimensional self-report measure in the assessment process. When Ms. White, the school counselor in the case study, used the SRP-C with Samantha, she wanted to clarify Samantha's diagnosis and elicit from her symptoms and problem areas that were not revealed during the intake. As noted previously, scale *t* scores of 70 or greater and percentiles at or above 98 are not in and of themselves indicative of the presence of a psychiatric disorder but suggest that the child is at high risk for having the disorder and further assessment is clearly warranted. Scores on the YSR, SRP, or PIY can also serve as a baseline or an initial counseling measure of emotional, behavioral, and or social problems. Readministration of these instruments can provide quantifiable information about whether the child perceives a change in his or her problems during the course of treatment. However, due to the nature of these rating scales, they will be more sensitive to change over the course of several months, not weeks. Because they cover such a wide range of behaviors and feelings, the clinician is likely to uncover concerns not reported during the clinical interview that may likely become a treatment focus. Furthermore, children, adolescents in particular, are sometimes more comfortable identifying problem areas via questionnaires than through an initial clinical interview when trust is still being established. Last, child and adolescent self-report measures, like adult ones, can be used as a way to promote self-reflection on the part of a client. In order to rate the frequency of one's feelings and behaviors over a specified time interval, one must reflect on his or her experience, which can potentially provide perspective about the degree to which a problematic feeling, behavior, or attitude exists, and what factors may affect their severity or frequency. Clients, including children and adolescents, benefit from counseling when they take an active role in the process, and any method that can facilitate engagement in the process is helpful. The features of the three most commonly used multidimensional self-report questionnaires for youth (PIY, SRP, and YSR) are compared in Table 10.2.

Table 10.2 Comparison of SRP, YSR, and PIY			
	PIY	**SRP**	**YSR**
Age range	8–18	8–18	11–18
Number of items	270	139(c) 176(A)	118
Time to complete (min.)	45	30	30–45
Validity scales	yes	yes	no
Prosocial/Competency scales	no	yes	yes
Non-English language versions	yes	yes	yes
Computer scoring	yes	yes	yes

PARENT, TEACHER, AND CAREGIVER RATING SCALES

Psychologists, counselors, and other mental health professionals have traditionally relied upon adults—parents, teachers, and other caregivers—for information about a child's history and emotional, behavioral, and social functioning. The tradition goes all the way back to one of Freud's famous case studies, "Little Hans," when Freud interviewed Hans's father. Like child self-report inventories, the development of standardized measures for which an adult provides his or her perceptions of a child's behavior came long after Freud's interview. The development of behavior rating scales for which adults provide their perspective on a child's emotional and behavioral functioning began independently with the work of Thomas Achenbach and Keith Conners and their respective colleagues, and predated child self-report inventories.

Adults who complete a behavior rating scale are deemed informants in that they are supplying information about a child from their unique perspective. Consequently, behavior rating scales, despite being considered "objective" assessment measures, are qualitatively different than direct observation measures (see Chapter 5), because they are ultimately measures of perception. As measures of perception they are subject to rater biases just as self-report measures are. Specifically, those biases can include the tendency to rate a child in a lenient fashion—that is, tending to rate a deviant behavior as occurring rarely (a negative bias); rating deviant behaviors as occurring almost always (a "halo" effect, or positive bias); or tending to provide overall positive or negative ratings because the rater was overly influenced by one positive or negative characteristic of the child, which clouds their judgment (Anastasi & Urbina, 1997).

The three adult-rater, child behavior scales that have been the most extensively researched and used in clinical practice are ASEBA, BASC-2, and the Conners' Rating Scales. All three have parallel parent and teacher versions with a high degree of correspondence between the items on both versions. The Conners' does not have a parallel child self-report version, as the AESBA and BASC-2 have, but it does have an adolescent self-report version (for ages 12–17). One commonality found in all three of these child behavior rating scales is that behaviors that might occur only in the home setting are found on the parent version and, similarly, those behaviors unique to a school environment are found only on the teacher versions. Furthermore, any adult who knows the child well and is a primary caregiver could complete the parent version. Likewise, any educational professional with a good working knowledge of the child could complete a teacher version. Even though the potential for rater bias exists, behavior rating scales have advantages over projective assessments and direct observations in terms of standardization, reliability, validity, and efficiency that outweigh this one drawback.

ACHENBACH SYSTEM OF EMPIRICALLY BASED ASSESSMENT (ASEBA)

Overview   The ASEBA *Child Behavior Checklist* (CBCL) parent version and the Teacher Report Form (TRF) rating scales are designed to assess a wide range of emotional and behavioral problems and academic and social competencies for children ages 1½–18 (Achenbach & Rescorla, 2007). The ASEBA also includes a direct observation recording form and manual for children ages 5–14 (see Chapter 5). The ASEBA system has the most extensive cross-cultural research base among the existing behavior ratings scales for children and adolescents. Published studies of the ASEBA now exceed 7,000, with over 80 cultures represented in that research body (Achenbach, 2011). In addition to its extensive multi-cultural research base, the parent and teacher rating scales have been translated into over 80 languages as of 2008.

The CBCL is designed for children ages 6–18 with separate gender and age norms (6–11- and 12–18-year-olds). There is a parallel version of the CBCL for children ages 1½–5. The CBCL for ages 6–18 is divided into two sections. The first section has a series of questions about social functioning, academic functioning, and two open-ended question regarding concerns and "the best things about your child." The format and content of this section is unique among the behavior rating scales for children. The second section contains a total of 113 items rated on a 3-point scale: 111 items covering a wide range of emotional and behavioral problems, one item regarding somatic or physical problems, and one item where the rater can describe any problem not included in the 111 items and also rate its frequency. The item content is similar to that of the YSR, enabling more systematic cross-informant comparisons. The CBCL for children ages 1½–5 includes a language development survey for ages 18–35 months and the problem list is shorter in length, having 99 items and 1 open-ended item. Item development for the prob-lem list for both scales began in the 1960s, the competency items were selected and refined in the following decade, and the original CBCL and TRF were published in the early 1980s. Since then the normative sample has been updated but only minor content changes have been made to the CBCL and TRF (Achenbach & Rescorla, 2001). The 2001 revision (third edition) of the CBCL/6–18 contains the same format and questions in the first section as the original version, and the length of the second section remains unchanged. Six items were removed from the problem list and six new ones were added: two regarding alcohol and tobacco use, two attention-deficit items, one item regarding enjoyment, and one regarding rule violations to main-tain the same 113-item length. One other substantive change was the inclusion of six DSM-oriented scales that were developed by psychologists and psychiatrists representing 16 different cultures (Achenbach & Rescorla, 2001).

The TRF is designed for children ages 6–18 and is similar in format and content to the CBCL. There is also a caregiver–teacher report form (C-TRF) for children ages 2–5. The TRF, like the CBCL, has two sections. The first is similar in format to the CBCL but the content pertains only to academic functioning. The second section is the same length and format as the CBCL and there is considerable overlap with item content. Only three items were changed from previous versions on the 2001 revision. Sample copies of the entire CBCL and TRF and the preschool versions of each can be viewed at the ASEBA website (*www.aseba.org*).

Administration, Scoring, and Interpretation   The CBCL and TRF are meant to be self-administered. That is, the clinician can simply give the forms to the adult and have them read the instructions. In the first section the rater is instructed, "Fill out this form to reflect your view of the child's behavior even if other people do not agree." For the problem list, the rater is told to describe your child/student "now or within the past 6 months" and then rate the behavior on a 3-point scale from "not true (as far as you know)" to "very true or often true." The scoring of the CBCL and TRF is rather straightforward and can be done by hand using a scoring template or computer software program. Hand scoring can be done in less than 30 minutes. Each item on the problem list is scored 0, 1, or 2.

The ASEBA system comprises eight narrowband "cross-informant" scales (the CBCL, TRF, and YSR contain the same eight scales) and three broadband scales (see Table10.1) (Achenbach & Rescorla, 2001). The first three narrowband scales make up the internalizing scale, the second three are independent scales, and the last two make up the externalizing scales. There are also three competence and adaptive subscales: Activities, School, and Social. In 2007, three additional scales were added to the CBCL and TRF: Sluggish Cognitive Tempo, Obsessive–Compulsive Problems, and Post-Traumatic Stress Problems (Achenbach & Rescorla, 2007).

Just about all of the items correspond to only one of the eight narrow scales. The raw scale score is obtained by summing the item scores for that scale. Raw scale scores are converted to t scores and percentiles with scale scores between the 95th and 97th percentiles falling into an "at risk" range. Scores at the 98th percentile and above are considered to be in the "clinically significant" range and are highly suggestive of clinical problems and possible DSM disorders. T scores are based on gender and age range (1½–5, 6–11, and 12–18). In essence, a t score of 70 means that the child is functioning at a level that is worse than 98% of his or her peers *according to the adult* who completed the scale. Why the adult has that perception and the "accuracy" of the perception is another matter.

Technical Information   The ASEBA's 2001 standardization group was representative of the 48 contiguous U.S. states, ethnic and racial diversity, socioeconomic status, and urban versus rural residence patterns (Achenbach & Rescorla, 2001). The CBCL sample included approximately 3,500 nonreferred children and adolescents (CBCL ages 1½–5 and 6–18 samples combined) and 4,994 additional clinically referred youth for the 6–18 range. The TRF sample consisted of approximately 3,300 nonreferred students (C-TRF and TRF samples combined) with 4,447 additional referred students. The ASEBA has a very long history of established reliability and validity and given that the content of the 2001 edition involves few item content changes, reliability and validity studies conducted with earlier versions would apply to the 2001 edition (Achenbach & Rescorla, 2007). On the eight narrowband scales and three broadband scales, test–retest reliability coefficients on the CBCL range from 0.82 to 0.94 with a mean interval of eight days. Alpha coefficients on those same scales on the CBCL range from 0.78 to 0.97. The TRF data are comparable with test–retest reliabilities in the 0.60 to 0.95 range (mean interval 16 days) and alpha coefficients in the 0.72 to 0.97 range (Achenbach & Rescorla, 2001).

Advantages and Limitations   The ASEBA is considered by some to be the gold standard for multidimensional child behavior rating scales and several independent reviews have praised it for its clinical usefulness (Merrell, 2008). It has by far the largest research base of all existing adult behavior rating scales of children (preschool children through adolescence) supporting its use in various mental health and educational settings. It applicability in many diverse cultures and populations is its greatest strength (Achenbach & Rescorla, 2007). It is easy to score and interpret and is excellent at discriminating between youth with and without emotional, behavioral, and/or social problems and disorders. It is also an excellent measure for identifying children and adolescents who are at risk for developing psychological disorders. The primary disadvantage in using the ASEBA for brief counseling is that respondents are asked about behavior over a six-month period. Changes in client behavior over a shorter period of time might not be detected and therefore it is less sensitive to change in short-term counseling. Another drawback is that it minimally assesses social competence and the reliability of the competence, and adaptive scales are relatively weak compared to the problem scales. Those drawbacks are outweighed by its clinical usefulness and it has received a "highly recommended" endorsement for the assessment of the major externalizing childhood disorders (Frick & McMahon, 2008; Johnston & Mah, 2008) such as ADHD, and other disruptive disorders (oppositional defiant and conduct disorder).

BEHAVIORAL ASSESSMENT SYSTEM FOR CHILDREN (BASC-2)   The second edition of the BASC includes the Parent Rating Scales (PRS) and Teacher Rating Scales (TRS) for children and young adults ages 2–21 (Reynolds & Kamphaus, 2004). In addition to the *Youth Self-Report of Personality* described earlier, the BASC-2 includes a structured developmental history form and a classroom observation form (see Chapter 5). Originally published in 1992, the BASC-2 contains 10 primary clinical and several adaptive skills scales designed to assess the emotional, behavioral, and adaptive functioning of a child or adolescent from the perspective of an adult rater. Although the clinical scales are the same between the teacher and parent versions, the adaptive skills scales vary depending upon rater (parent or teacher) and the age of the child. Like with the SRP, the PRS and TRS contain three validity scales (only one of which is available through the hand-scoring system) and a list of "critical" items such as "eats things that are not food" and "says, 'I want to die' or 'I wish I were dead'." The teacher rating scale can be completed by an adult—teacher, aide, day-care worker, or other professional—who has observed the child daily for at least one month, preferably in an organized structured setting like a classroom (Reynolds & Kamphaus). The parent rater can be any adult caregiver who has observed the child often. As the case study of Samantha illustrated, obtaining ratings from multiple parents can be very helpful because each perspective can add a different piece to the diagnostic and case conceptualization puzzle. There are separate parent and teacher forms for three different developmental groups: preschool (ages 2–5), child (ages 6–11), and adolescent (ages 12–21) and three formats: paper and hand scoring, computer administration and scoring, and scannable. The total number of items varies from 100 on the TRS-preschool to 160 on the PRS-child.

One of the unique features of the BASC-2 is the Spanish-language edition of the Parent Rating Scales, which was developed simultaneously with the revised parent scale (Reynolds & Kamphaus, 2004). Where other non-English versions of a measure exist, they typically are developed and standardized separately at some later point. Other changes to the revised BASC parent and teacher rating scales include updated norms, improved psychometric properties, new item content, new adaptability scales (Functional Communication, Activities of Daily Living, and Adaptability), and several new content scales.

Administration, Scoring, and Interpretation   Both the parent and teacher rating scales are designed to be self-administered and can be completed in less than 20 minutes. The instruction set is the same for both the TRS and PRS: ". . . mark the response that describes how this child has behaved recently (in the last several months)." Each item on the parent and teacher forms has a 4-point scale ranging from "never" to "almost always." The paper and pen hand-scoring form is two parts—the rating scale on the front and the scoring form underneath, making for a relatively quick and easy procedure. First the validity scale is scored to determine if the respondent displayed a very negative or extreme attitude when completing the inventory and, if so, the score on the BASC-2 should be interpreted with much caution. Next, raw scores are obtained for each of the clinical and adaptive functioning scales. The clinical scales include Aggression, Anxiety, Attention Problems, Atypicality, Conduct Problems, Depression, Hyperactivity, Learning Problems (teacher version only), Somatization, and Withdrawal. Raw scores are then converted to *t* scores using the norm tables in the manual when hand scoring; otherwise this is done by computer software. There are separate gender and age norms as well as three clinical population norms: a combined diagnostic population, a learning disability population, and an ADHD population. In addition to scale scores, like the ASEBA, composite scores can be calculated. These include externalizing, internalizing, and school problems, behavioral symptoms index, and adaptive skills. *T* scores in the 60–69 range are suggestive of a youth who is at risk for the problem indicated by an individual or composite scale. Scores 70 and above are considered to be "clinically significant." The interpretation of the adaptive scales is the reverse. High scores indicate adaptive functioning, and *t* scores at or below 30 are considered clinically significant. Again, the term *clinically significant* is not meant to indicate that a child has a particular diagnosis but rather that there is a greater likelihood that a disorder is present and further assessment to establish the diagnosis is warranted.

Technical Information   The BASC-2 was standardized with a large national sample (over 4,500 cases) matched to the 2001 U.S. population survey in terms of age, gender, race/ethnicity, geographic region, and socioeconomic status as measured by the highest school grade completed by the child's mother or female guardian (Reynolds & Kamphaus, 2004). The manual contains comparison tables between the percentages found in the U.S. population for a particular group (e.g., preschool African-Americans) and the BASC-2 samples, and inspection of those tables shows that Reynolds and Kamphaus's goals were met: the percentages match very closely.

Reliability and validity coefficients for the BASC-2 parent and teacher rating scale are in the adequate or better-than-adequate range. Median alpha coefficients range from 0.80 to 0.86 on the individual PRS scales and a slightly higher range, 0.84 to 0.88 on the TRS scales. Test–retest reliability coefficients based on intervals of 15 to 65 days range from 0.81 to 0.86 on the individual scales of the TRS and from 0.76 to 0.84 on the PRS scales. Interrater reliability coefficients were also obtained for the PRS and TRS and vary much more than the two other reliability coefficients. Given that two individuals are likely to have different perceptions of a child's behavior, it is not surprising that these coefficients are the lowest of the three types. Several inter-rater reliabilities are especially lower (less than 0.30) for some of the internalizing scales: anxiety (child TRS), somatization, and withdrawal (adolescent TRS). This too is not surprising, given that it is harder to observe and therefore agree on internalizing problems, especially in adolescents, than it is with externalizing problems.

The BASC-2 manual provides ample evidence of the construct validity of the PRS and TRS obtained through factor analyses and correlations with other rating scales including the ASEBA and Conners'. The predictive or criterion validity of the PRS and TRS, however, is poor or lacking. BASC-2 scores on the PRS and TRS do discriminate well between "normal" children and those with some kind of emotional and/or behavioral disorder. However, the profile scores of different diagnostic groups (e.g., ADHD, bipolar, and depression) show little difference and sometimes not in the expected direction. For example, the mean score on the hyperactivity scale of the child PRS is less for the ADHD group than it is for the depression group.

ADVANTAGES AND LIMITATIONS   The BASC-2 is an excellent comprehensive assessment tool that can assist in determining whether or not a child has some type of psychiatric or developmental disorder and facilitate the treatment planning process for youth from preschool age through adolescence. Furthermore, its three adaptive skills scales are unique among adult rater child behavior questionnaires. The PRS and TRS can provide standardized measures of adaptive functioning, which is equally important for diagnosing, case conceptualizing, and treatment planning. The large number of items on the parent and teacher scales supplements the process of a clinician identifying symptoms, problems, or areas of concern that may not have been revealed during clinical interviews. Its length can also be a disadvantage if a clinician or organization wants to use the TRS or PRS as a screening or treatment monitoring measure. The author's experience with this measure is that parents or teachers rarely, if ever, complain about its length when used as part of an initial assessment. Rather, concerns from those completing it have focused on trouble discerning either the frequency of an item or its meaning. The two-sided hand-scoring forms make it a particularly easy and efficient tool for clinicians to score and interpret.

CONNERS' RATINGS SCALES—REVISED   Traditionally the Conners' Rating Scales have been used primarily for evaluating the presence of ADHD and the effectiveness of medications for treating ADHD (Kamphaus & Frick, 2005). This changed in 1997 when the Conners' was not only revised but significantly expanded to include anxiety, family, and anger-control–related problems (Merrell, 2008). In 2008 the Conners Third Edition was released but as of this writing it had not been independently researched or reviewed. Despite the revisions and updated norms, the *Conners' Rating Scales—Revised* (CRS-R) still remains primarily a tool for the assessment of ADHD, Oppositional Defiant Disorder, and Conduct Disorder. There are both long and short versions of the parent (80 items long and 27 short) and teacher (59 and 28 items respectively) rating scales designed for youth ages 3–17 (Conners, 1997). In addition to scales measuring attention, hyperactivity, and oppositional problems, there are scales for anxious–shy, perfectionism, and social and psychosomatic problems on the long form for the parent rating scale. (The teacher rating scale contains all these subscales with the exception of the psychosomatic.) The short parent and teacher rating scales contain only ADHD and oppositional symptoms and behaviors. Spanish and French language versions of the CRS-R are available.

Administration, Scoring, and Interpretation   The long form of the CRS-R can be completed within 20 minutes and scoring can be done within 15 minutes. Parents and teachers are asked to rate the child's behavior based on the past month. All items on the parent and teacher scales (both long and short forms) have a 4-point scale ranging from "not at all" to "very much." Raw scores are changed to *t* scores and percentiles for all the scales. There are separate norm tables for boys and girls in three-year intervals. There is an ADHD index on both the long and short forms and a Conners' global index on the long forms. The global index is considered a brief screening measure of psychopathology.

Technical Information   The CRS-R (Second Edition) was standardized on a very large (over 8,000 total cases) U.S. and Canadian sample that includes gender and racial/ethnic subgroups. Reviewers of the CRS-R (Hess, 2001; Knoff, 2001) have noted some concerns with the standardization sample such as disproportional racial groups and a lack of information about the gender percentages of the parents and the selection of participants. The internal reliability coefficients are in the adequate to better-than-adequate range on the long form of the Parent Rating subscales (0.73 to 0.94). Test–retest reliabilities for the parent and teacher scales range from 0.47 to 0.92 based on six- to eight-week intervals.

ADVANTAGES AND LIMITATIONS   The Conners' has a long research and clinical history for the assessment of ADHD and other disruptive externalizing disorders. The revised parent and teacher scales have been endorsed as "highly recommended" for the diagnosis, case conceptualization, and treatment planning for children and adolescents for whom ADHD is suspected (Johnston & Mah, 2008). The abbreviated parent and teacher forms are particularly useful tools for monitoring a child's response to pharmacological and behavioral treatments. The short forms are sensitive to change and teachers and parents are more likely to complete those versus 100-plus-item questionnaires like the BASC or ASEBA when weekly assessments are needed. In addition, the multiple language versions of the CRS-R enhances its cross-cultural utility.

As a broadband behavior rating scale system, the CRS-R is limited with respect to internalizing disorders. Somatic problems are addressed only on the long parent scale, and depression and atypical behaviors and symptoms are not assessed at all. Although the CRS-R is intended for a wide age range, 3–17, a separate preschool version does not exist as it does for the ASEBA and BASC-2 rating scales. Two other drawbacks that have been noted are, one, a manual lacking sufficient detail, and two, a limited number of independent validation studies (Merrell, 2008).

CLINICAL ASSESSMENT OF BEHAVIOR (CAB)   The *Clinical Assessment of Behavior* (CAB) is a newer and more developmentally grounded comprehensive behavior rating scale system designed to aid in the evaluation and diagnosis of emotional and behavioral disorders and adaptive competencies and strengths in children and adolescents ages 2–18 (Bracken & Keith, 2004). An innovative feature of the CAB is its grounding in a developmental model of child psychosocial adjustment. Consequently, its scales reflect that model: Social Skills, Anger Regulation, Executive Functioning, and Autism Spectrum Behaviors. Critical items reflect important problem areas either not found or marginally assessed in other parent and teacher rating scales: psychotic behaviors, bullying and gang-related behaviors, and behaviors associated with learning disabilities. In addition, some of the CAB items are aligned with IDEA and DSM-IV criteria for educational conditions or exceptionalities such as learning disability, mental retardation, and gifted and talented.

The CAB consists of three rating scale versions: parent, teacher (70 items each), and extended parent form (170 items). It is the only comprehensive parent and teacher rating system with a response format containing a 5-point scale. The final pool of items that were selected for the parent version was, in part, based on that fact that those items demonstrated high inter-parent agreement, whereas those items in the initial pool with low parental agreement were eliminated. A comprehensive computer software program provides a very comprehensive scoring and interpretative report. In addition to clinical scales that are similar to those found on the ASEBA and BASC systems, such as anxiety and aggression, there are Anger, Bullying, and Autism Spectrum Behaviors scales. There is also an Adaptive scale, which includes a "Gifted and Talented" subscale.

The psychometric properties of the CAB compare very favorably to the BASC-2 Parent and Teacher Rating Scales. Both internal and test–retest reliability coefficients for the CAB were found to be very high, and there are high correlations with the comparable BASC-2 scales, though more validation studies are needed. The CAB has already received a very enthusiastic endorsement: "one of the very best additions to the pool of child behavior rating scales during the past decade or two and it appears to hold a great deal of promise for becoming a highly useful clinical and research tool" (Merrell, 2008, pp. 118–119).

Case Example Using Child Self-Report and Parent and Teacher Rating Scales

SELECTING THE APPROPRIATE MEASURES   Let's return to the case of Samantha in the opening of the chapter. Ms. White, the school counselor, decided to incorporate standardized child measures into the assessment process for several reasons: to clarify Samantha's diagnosis, develop a richer case conceptualization, and establish a focus for counseling. In the case of Samantha, the parents and teacher completed the respective parent and teacher rating scales from the BASC-2, and Samantha filled out the *Self-Report of Personality*. Ms. White chose the BASC-2 because of Samantha's age and the need to obtain multiple perspectives about Samantha, given that there were major differential diagnostic questions: Does she have ADHD, anxiety and depression, or is she experiencing an adjustment reaction? Ms. White felt the BASC-2 could be especially useful because the child self-report version can be used with children as young as 9 years old, whereas the *Youth Self-Report* in the ASEBA system begins at age 11. Furthermore, the BASC-2 has scales (Hyperactivity, Anxiety, Depression, and Attention Problems) that are aligned with the DSM-IV diagnoses she wanted to rule out. Had Ms. White been clear about Samantha's diagnosis after the intake interview, she more than likely would have chosen a briefer unidimensional measure that could assess the severity of Samantha's symptoms. In addition to requiring much less time for the client to complete and for the clinician to score and interpret, unidimensional measures like the *Children's Depression Inventory* (CDI) or the *State–Trait Anxiety Inventory for Children* (STAIC) (see Chapter 9) are more applicable for monitoring counseling progress because they have a much briefer time frame: weeks versus months. Guidelines for incorporating standardized measures into the assessment of a child are summarized in the Practice Suggestion: Considerations when Assessing Children with Standardized Measures.

The results of the BASC-2 teacher, parent, and child scales helped to 1) clarify Samantha's diagnosis, 2) establish a problem focus for counseling, and 3) create a baseline measure of Samantha's distress. The scores on the *Teacher Rating Scale* indicated Sam was functioning in the "normal" range on all the scales, and both parents perceived her as having a significant level of anxiety. Sam's overall SRP profile was in the normal range on all scales, but her highest scale was anxiety, and she did endorse some critical items and indicate the presence of some problems that were not revealed during the intake interview.

The results of those rating scales were very helpful in several ways. First, along with other information, they helped to clarify that Sam was experiencing a stress reaction and difficulty adjusting to her parents' conflict, subsequent divorce and remarriages, and not ADHD. One of the criteria for a diagnosis of ADHD, either type, is that impairment in functioning is present in at least two environments, home and school. Given that the teacher rating on the Hyperactivity and Attention Problems scales were in the normal range, there was not evidence to support that Samantha was having an impairment in school functioning. Ms. White was able to confirm that there was not impairment at school by reviewing Samantha's report card, which revealed a slight drop in grades in two subjects but that she was "making progress" and "meeting expectations" in her Work Habits/Effort. Nor did she meet the DSM-IV criteria for a mood or anxiety disorder. In addition, the inclusion of several adaptive skills on the BASC-2 helped identify Samantha's strengths, and therefore a more comprehensive case conceptualization was developed. Samantha's strengths in Adaptability revealed her resiliency, which seemed to lessen the impact of her parents' discord and divorce on her emotional well-being. Furthermore, Sam's responses to certain items on the SRP revealed problem areas that had not been identified during clinical interviews with either Sam or her parents. Those included: "I hear voices in my head that

PRACTICE SUGGESTION
Considerations when Assessing Children with Standardized Measures

- When diagnostic clarification or more comprehensive case conceptualization is needed, consider using a multirater assessment system that has parallel parent, teacher, and self-report versions such as the ASEBA or BASC-2.
- Does a child's social competencies and adaptive functioning need to be evaluated as well? If so, some rating systems like the ASEBA and BASC-2 parent and teacher questionnaires include prosocial and adaptive scales as well as psychopathology scales.
- Only some questionnaires have validity scales to detect very biased or distorted responding.
- Determine where parents, teacher, and the child will complete rating scales or questionnaires.
- Determine whether scoring will be done by hand or by computer.
- Clearly understand the relationship between percentile and t scores and how they are interpreted with the specific measure being used.
- Present feedback to parents and other caregivers in language free of technical jargon. Use the feedback session as an opportunity to discuss how a child's behavior can change depending upon the environment.
- Clarify parent and teacher responses to critical items (several parent and teacher rating scales have a list of critical items).
- What cultural factors may have impacted a child's or adult's responses?
- If projective techniques (see Chapters 3 and 8) are being considered for use in the assessment of a child, then keep in mind the following points:
  a. Consider using projective techniques (human-figure drawings, sentence completion tests, and picture-story tests) as a way to engage preschool and elementary school age children in the assessment and counseling process.
  b. Projective techniques can be valuable counseling tools for case conceptualization purposes and identifying concerns, feelings, and beliefs a child is having that can become the focus of treatment.
  c. Be very cautious in using projective techniques as diagnostic tools for social, emotional, and behavioral disorders. Projective techniques have been found to be of limited value and questionable validity compared to adult behavior and child self-report rating scales.

no one else can hear," "Other kids hate to be with me," and "I have trouble standing in line." Ms. White went over those items with Samantha at her next counseling appointment. Samantha clarified that sometimes she hears a friend or her parents' voices in her head. Her perception that other kids "hate" her and her nervous feeling she gets when the class lines up for recess became areas to focus on in subsequent counseling sessions. Third, Ms. White now had a baseline measure of Sam's emotional functioning and when she readministered the SRP after the 12th session she found Sam reporting much less emotional distress. The parent, teacher, and self-report rating scales provided information that was both confirming of the respective adult and child perspectives and unique. Having these additional perspectives, obtained through standardized measures, Ms. White was able to be more effective in her counseling with Samantha.

PROVIDING FEEDBACK TO PARENTS AND CAREGIVERS   Many parents and caregivers view psychological tests as just that, a diagnostic test like a blood test or x-ray that can accurately reveal a child's disorder. When standardized measures are part of a child assessment process it is important that parents and other caregivers receive feedback about what the results of questionnaires and rating scales say and don't say about a child. It is important for them to understand that with the exception of mental retardation and learning disorders (see Chapter 13), there is not a questionnaire or test that by itself can reveal the presence of a psychiatric disorder like a throat culture can with strep throat. So what is it that will be helpful for the adults in the child's life to know about specific instruments used in the assessment process? Again, the case of Samantha can be illustrative.

Ms. White, the school counselor, began by reviewing with Samantha's parents why they, the teacher, and Samantha had completed the respective rating scales and why there might be different results. She explained that a child's behavior can vary in different settings, a reality that parents recognize and some find comfort in, while some are dismayed when noting, "She's an angel at school and would not dare do what she does when she comes home and tortures her sister." She also reminded Samantha's parents that everyone will have a somewhat different perspective because everyone has had different experiences with Samantha. Ms. White went on to discuss the scores and what it means for scores to be in the normal, clinical, or at-risk range. She made a point of telling the parents that the scores suggest how Samantha is doing compared to thousands of other girls her age. Her teacher, for example, did perceive Samantha as having some symptoms and behaviors that are seen in ADHD but the overall score suggested that the frequency of those symptoms and behaviors is typical for girls her age. On the other hand, Ms. White said, "As parents, you see her as having a significant amount of anxiety, more so than most girls her age." It can be helpful to then discuss a percentile, rather than the more technical *t* score, so that parents gain some perspective on how developmentally normative are the problems, behaviors, or symptoms. Ms. White explained to them the approximate guidelines that are used to determine normal, at-risk, and clinically significant: below the 90th percentile, between the 90th and 95th percentile, and greater than the 95th percentile. (Technically speaking, the actual percentiles will vary depending upon the scale but this gives some parameters in a way that most people can understand.) Last, she reminded the parents of what she told them at the outset, that the questionnaires would help provide a focus for counseling and provide a way to measure Samantha's progress. Ms. White made sure she gave the parents an opportunity to ask any questions about the questionnaire and the information they provide.

CULTURAL CONSIDERATIONS

The research and clinical use of child assessment rating scales, both adult questionnaires and youth self-report scales, has become a global phenomenon. A literature search through a large database such as *Psych Info* quickly reveals the magnitude of this trend. Studies have examined whether psychopathology constructs like depression or ADHD apply to youth in a variety of different cultures, and the ability of assessment measures standardized on a U.S. population to discriminate between "normal" and "disordered" youth in other cultures and countries. A cross-cultural research methodology utilizes child assessment measures to also understand how cultural factors influence the course and outcome of childhood disorders (Achenbach et al., 2008).

There has been a proliferation of multiple language versions of many of the existing youth assessment measures. Clients whose language is not English are likely to appreciate the opportunity to report their thoughts, behaviors, and feelings or their child's symptoms in their primary language. The language issue is complicated when children speak one language and their primary caregivers speak another. Fortunately, the growing number of multiple language measures provides clinicians with the ability to have children and their caregivers respond to a rating scale in different languages with reasonable assurance that the information obtained is comparable.

Notwithstanding this global phenomenon, clinicians still need to remain sensitive to the potential for cultural bias with some measures. Bias would occur if the use of an emotional or behavioral assessment measure resulted in a systematic inappropriate labeling or treating of a specific group of people. If, for example, self-report measure A or parent–teacher rating scale B resulted in Latino males scoring in the clinical range on scales suggestive of aggression and conduct problems, despite evidence from other sources indicating no higher rates of aggression and conduct problems in this group compared to other groups, then the instruments in question would have a potential biasing effect. If that biased instrument was then used with a Latino male, for example, and the results of that instrument then became the primary reason for deciding on diagnosis X (e.g., conduct disorder) and intervention Y (e.g., placement in a youth correctional facility), significant ethical and legal problems would arise. When a particular group of people routinely score in the deviant range—above the 95th or below the 5th percentiles, for example—then it is the obligation of test developers and users to discern whether those results are a function of a group of people, *on average,* possessing more or less of a specific problem or trait, or stem from something about how the test items are typically interpreted by members of that group.

Some general guidelines and recommendations for using adult behavior rating scales and youth self-report measures in culturally competent ways has been established and is likely to continue (Merrell, 2008). Merrell's recommendations include: 1) recognizing that even a measure whose standardization sample is proportionally representative of various minority groups may not be valid for a particular subgroup or population; 2) carefully reviewing a test manual for information about a measure's applicability for specific racial/ethnic minority youth; 3) examining studies that have demonstrated bias with a particular measure; and 4) discontinuing the use of a measure for treatment monitoring if the use of it during the initial assessment was found not to be appropriate for a given client. Cultural competency guidelines can provide a framework for clinicians who incorporate standardized measures into their overall assessment process to do so with sensitivity and respect for clients' cultural norms, practices, and values regarding what constitutes deviant child behavior.

Summary and Conclusions

The emotional, behavioral, and psychological assessment of children, preschool through adolescence, is a complex process requiring input from multiple perspectives: the youth, parent, teacher, and other knowledgeable adults. The gathering of those perspectives can be done through the use of standardized measures that young children, adolescents, parents, teachers, and other caregivers can complete. As with adult standardized assessments discussed in previous chapters, the results of child and adult rating scales can inform diagnostic, case conceptualization, and treatment planning decisions and serve as a measure of counseling progress. A procedure that efficiently and systematically helps clinicians identify a child's feelings, behaviors, thoughts, and symptoms that may not have been revealed during intake interviews is a necessary component to a well-done comprehensive assessment.

Several examples of the most widely used and researched ratings scales and inventories were discussed and evaluated. The chapter focused on multidimensional measures that have parallel youth self-report, parent, and teacher versions. Parental caregivers and educational professionals provide their perceptions of a child's behaviors, attitudes, moods, symptoms, and problems. The measures chosen for discussion in this chapter represent some of the best of what is available for clinicians in terms of psychometric quality and clinical usefulness.

Reflection Questions and Experiential Exercises

1. Think of a child you know. What factors might account for differences in symptoms and behaviors reported by the child, his or her parent, and his or her teacher on a questionnaire?

2. What factors will guide your selection of an assessment instrument for a child or adolescent client?

3. What is the difference between multidimensional and unidimensional child assessment measures?

4. What aspects of a measure would make it child friendly in general; preschool and adolescent friendly in particular?

5. What do scores in the "clinically significant" range say and not say about a child?

6. Complete one of the rating scales described in this chapter on a child you know well. What was easy and what was challenging about completing it?

7. Given the items or questions on the scale you completed in exercise 6, did you find any items possibly insensitive or offensive? Which items might someone else find offensive? Why do you think that?

COMPREHENSIVE RISK ASSESSMENTS: SUICIDE AND DANGEROUSNESS TO OTHERS

Chapter Objectives

After reading this chapter, you should be able to:

■ Identify risk and protective factors for assessing suicide and homicide risk.

■ Understand how standardized measures are combined with unstructured interviews, for the assessment of danger to self and others.

■ Explain how to integrate information gathered from a risk assessment interview and standardized measures.

■ Explain how to locate a client along a continuum of risk from none to imminent.

Juanita, a 27-year-old mother of two children, ages 2 and 4, arrived by herself at a local mental health clinic following her primary care doctor's referral. The physician had prescribed an antidepressant to her. Juanita appeared tired, worn, and despondent, telling the counselor she is feeling "lousy, down, and bored." She was not sure if the medicine—she could not recall the name—was helping, and she seemed discouraged about things in her life changing anytime soon. She reported later in the interview that she has been having trouble sleeping and difficulty enjoying playtime with her children. Her depression symptoms prompted the interviewer to ask, "Given what you've been experiencing, it's common for people to have thoughts about death. Have you had any thoughts in the past week about killing yourself?" Juanita hesitantly responded "yes" with a look of embarrassment. When asked about a plan, she replied, "I might swallow all of my pills" and "maybe I'll just cut my wrists." Further questioning revealed that although she had thoughts that she and her children would be better off if she killed herself, Juanita also could reason why she would not do that to her children. Juanita indicated that her children would "grow up better with my sister" and that her "depression was hurting them." She then added "but my children need a mother and if I kill myself Mark (the father) will get them not my sister and that would be awful for them."

Juanita and Mark separated two months ago. The separation followed Mark's arrest for assault and driving under the influence of alcohol. Juanita is bilingual in Spanish and English; English is her primary language. Juanita is enrolled in an associate's degree program in nursing and wants very much to complete it so she can help others. Her parents divorced when she was 10, and she has occasional contact with her mother, who lives in Puerto Rico. "I don't see my father anymore; he drank all the time and was horribly mean to us." She has an older sister living in the same town with whom she visits regularly and can rely on for help with her children.

OVERVIEW

Evaluating a client's potential for seriously harming self or others is one of the most vexing assessment challenges facing helping professionals and trainees. Even experienced counselors, faced with a client who is expressing a desire to commit suicide, can find themselves uncomfortable and anxious. Similarly, clients who appear threatening, volatile, and angry can impact a clinician's sense of security and concern for the safety of self and others. And when a client does commit suicide or seriously harms another person, mental health professionals are sometimes left with feelings of guilt and inadequacy.

A sense of responsibility for a client's life is fueled by both personal and professional factors. Values and beliefs, including views about the right to die, and professional standards of care developed by the mental health disciplines strongly influence not only how one undertakes a risk assessment, but also the emotional and psychological responses should death occur. Furthermore, how much a mental health professional does to prevent a suicide of a client can depend upon a number of factors, including one's own experiences with suicidal thoughts and behaviors, religious background and views on death, and whether there are circumstances when suicide might be considered the "rational" or best option (Rogers, Gueulette, Abbey-Hines, Carney, & Werth, 2001). When a client does commit suicide, mental health clinics and organizations often undergo "psychological autopsies" in part to review how ongoing risk assessments are done. What makes the assessment of self-harm, suicide, and violence toward others such a daunting task is that we can never know for sure who is going to go through with the act.

The task for a helping professional presented with a client like Juanita is to *estimate* how at-risk she is for suicide and danger to others. Once an estimate of risk is made, appropriate interventions can follow. Traditionally, clinicians have relied upon unstructured clinical interviews of clients and significant others and, when available, review pertinent records in order to estimate suicide and homicide risk. The current state of risk assessment practice has reached the point in which standardized measures, both semistructured interviews and self-reports, are used to supplement *but not replace* clinical interviews. The purpose of this chapter is to apply a risks and resources model discussed in Chapters 1 and 4 as an organizing framework for understanding when and how to evaluate risk of suicide and danger to others. Although the overall framework can be applied to both suicide and homicide risk, each will be discussed separately, beginning with suicide risk assessment.

A detailed discussion of the management and treatment of at-risk clients, although vital, is beyond the scope of this chapter. For those wanting more guidance on approaches to working with such clients, Marsha Linehan's *Cognitive Behavioral Treatment of Borderline Personality Disorder* (1993) is a very helpful source. Her section on managing and working with suicidal behaviors in clients with borderline personality disorders can be applied to just about all clients for whom frequent suicidal thinking and behaviors is a concern. Additional resources are listed at the American Association of Suicidology's website (***www.suicidology .org/web/guest/home***).

ASSESSING SUICIDE RISK

It has been suggested that suicide is a permanent solution to a temporary problem. That temporary problem is known as "psychache." Psychache has been described as unrelenting psychological pain and the individual experiencing it can come to see death as relief (Shneidman, 2001). The role of a clinician–evaluator is to assess the degree of likelihood that a client will act on the belief that suicide presents the best option available for alleviating psychological pain. The clinician will gather information about potential risk and protective factors in order to make that assessment. One of the more informative factors is a prior history of suicide attempts and the old adage, "The best predictor of future behavior is past behavior," aptly applies. What might be other risk factors to evaluate and which circumstances, if present, might lessen the risk? And what about assessing suicide risk with someone who has never engaged in any self-injurious behavior nor made a suicide attempt?

The difficulty in making predictions about suicide risk is that suicide is a very low-base-rate phenomenon. Even though in 2005 over 32,000 adults committed suicide and the rate in youth, ages 15 through 19, doubled from 1960 to 2005 (to 7.7 per 100,000), these figures constitute less than 0.013% of the general population (Centers for Disease Control and Prevention [CDC], 2009). The prevalence in psychiatric outpatients is much greater, about 100 times higher (Brown, Beck, Steer, & Grisham, 2000), but 1% is still a very low base. Obviously the prevalence of suicide attempts is greater than suicide deaths, but historically this has been difficult to ascertain because of competing definitions of *attempt, threat,* and *gesture.* Also, clinicians are likely to unwittingly inflate in their minds the base rate because of their professional experience (the availability heuristic) (see Chapter 5). Surveys have found that the vast majority of mental health counselors, psychologists, and psychiatrists have had at least one client attempt suicide (Rogers et al., 2001; Kleespies & Dettmer, 2000). Because of the severity and potential consequences for both client and clinician, suicidal events—although salient—become exaggerated in their estimated frequency by clinicians (except for those clinicians working predominantly with a high-risk population such as borderline personality disorder). The base-rate problem is illustrated by Brown et al.'s (2000) study of almost 7,000 outpatients, seen at a university outpatient center over a 20-year period. Fewer than 1% (49) eventually committed suicide even though 66% of the patients had a primary, secondary, or tertiary diagnosis of some type of mood disorder, one of the disorders considered a risk factor. As was discussed in Chapter 7, our ability to use assessment tools to make predictions about human behavior works reasonably well when the base rate of the behavior or phenomenon in question is close to 50% of the population. That is the case when measures like the BDI-II and BAI are used to predict whether a client coming into a community mental health center has an anxiety or affective disorder versus no disorder since combined those disorders have a lifetime prevalence of approximately 50% for adults (Kessler, Berglund, Demler, Jin, & Walters, 2005). Assessment tools are helpful when making predictions about moderate-level base rate phenomena, but they are not really useful when the base rate is very low.

Given that the ultimate type of harm to self, suicide, has such a low base rate, how do clinicians go about using the available assessment tools to make effective decisions when evaluating a client's danger to self? To begin, counselors and other professionals need to recognize that they cannot predict with any degree of accuracy whether or not any one specific person will commit suicide. What can be done, however, is to estimate the degree of risk someone poses for harming self or others and make management decisions based on that risk. With death from suicide being the 11th leading cause of all deaths (CDC, 2009), thorough risk assessments are clearly a public health need. A risks and resources model can provide a framework for evaluating potential for harm to self and others and to help locate a client in a zone of risk (see Figure 11.1). The goal for the assessor is to properly locate a client within this zone. It is also important to understand that a clinician could use all the available information at his or her disposal to estimate where along the risk continuum the client belongs and that judgment could still turn out to be inaccurate.

FIGURE 11.1   Zone of Risk

Harm to Self and Suicidal Behavior

A clinician's ability to estimate risk depends upon an understanding of the different behaviors she or he is evaluating. The preceding discussion included the terms **self-harm** and **suicide attempt**. These terms are not synonymous. Self-harm involves self-inflicted acts that may or may not cause bodily injury and for which there is either "direct or implicit evidence" that the person did not intend to kill him- or herself, but the intention driving the act was to alter consciousness, communicate, or regulate emotions such as pain, anxiety, sadness, and irritability (Silverman, Berman, Sanddal, O'Carroll, & Joiner, 2007, p. 272). Acts of self-harm have also been termed **parasuicidal behavior** and **instrumental suicide–related behavior** (Linehan, 1993; Silverman et al., 2007). Examples of these behaviors include burning, cutting, head banging, and starvation. Clearly, acts of self-harm by their very nature place individuals at risk for death even if that is not the intention. A suicide attempt, on the other hand, may or may not result in injury, but the person had the *intention,* at some level, to kill him or herself (Shea, 1998; Silverman et al., 2007). The distinction between intention and behavior are important because they will influence the words used when asking questions to estimate risk. A counselor could ask a suicidal client if she had any thoughts about wanting to harm herself and she could answer "no," not because she is being deceitful, but rather because she believes her intended act will be a harmless way to end her pain. Alternatively, one could inquire of someone who is chronically self-harming (without the counselor's knowledge) if he has any thoughts of wanting to "kill" himself and his truthful answer "no" does not reveal the harmful behavior. Therefore, the choice of words and language when assessing and distinguishing between acts of self-harm and suicidal behavior is critical.

ADDITIONAL SUICIDE TERMS   Other suicide assessment terms that have been defined, revised, and deleted are *threat, plan,* and *gesture.* A threat is any nonverbal or verbal communication that does not have a "self-injurious component that a reasonable person would interpret as communicating suicidal behavior might occur in the near future" (Silverman et al., 2007, p. 268). A plan is a systematically formulated action that has the potential to cause injury to self. Because of its pejorative connotations of presumed client motivation, "gesture" has been recommended for elimination in favor of terms such as *self-harm* or *parasuicidal* (Linehan, 1993; Silverman et al., 2007).

Suicide Risk and Protective Factors

There are a number of factors that, when occurring in tandem, increase a client's risk for suicide. Because these factors are numerous, acronyms were developed to assist the clinician in recalling them when conducting risk assessments. One frequently referenced acronym is SAD PERSONS: Sex, Age, Depression, Previous attempt, Ethanol abuse (alcohol), Rational thinking loss, Social support lacking, Organized plan, No spouse, Sickness (Patterson, Dohn, Bird, & Patterson, 1983; Shea, 1998). A more recent acronym is NO HOPE: No framework for meaning, Overt change in clinical condition, Hostile interpersonal environment, Out of hospital recently, Predisposing personality factors, Excuses for dying are present and strongly believed (Shea, 1998). Both acronyms are focused primarily on risk factors. Although the SAD PERSONS scale implies protective factors (e.g., social support being present), the primary focus is risk. Comprehensive suicide risk assessment will involve a determination of both risk, particularly suicidal thinking and related behavior, and protective factors. Furthermore, acronyms are useful mnemonics only if they indeed facilitate recall and bring to mind all the necessary pieces of the concept.

Alternatively, it may be helpful to think about three domains when assessing a client's current suicide risk: 1) predisposing factors, 2) risk factors (chronic and acute), and 3) protective factors (see Tables 11.1 and 11.2) (Bryan & Rudd, 2006; Rudd & Joiner, 1998). Predisposing factors consist of demographic, diagnostic, and family environment variables that apply to an individual but are based on data at the group level indicating differences in suicidal behavior.

Table 11.1 Suicide Risk Factors

Chronic and acute risk factors:

- Identifiable stressors:
  - Significant loss (e.g., financial, interpersonal relationship[s], identity)
  - Acute or chronic health problems
  - Relationship instability
- Current depressive symptoms (e.g., anhedonia, low self-esteem, sadness, insomnia, fatigue [increased risk when combined with anxiety and substance abuse])
- Bipolar disorder (increased risk early in disorder's course)
- Anxiety (increased risk with trait anxiety)
- Schizophrenia (increased risk after active phases)
- Borderline and antisocial personality features
- Presence of hopelessness
  - Severity of hopelessness
  - Duration of hopelessness
- Poor impulsivity and self-control
  - Subjective self-control
  - Objective control (e.g., substance abuse, impulsive behaviors, aggression)

Suicidal thinking and behavior:

- Current ideation
  - Frequency
  - Intensity
  - Duration
- Presence of suicide plan (increased risk with specificity)
  - Availability of means
  - Lethality of means
- Active suicidal behaviors
  - Working on the plan
  - Making preparations for death
  - Leaving a note
- Explicit suicidal intent

Previous history of suicidal behavior:

- Frequency and context of previously suicidal behaviors
- Perceived lethality and outcome
- Opportunity for rescue and help seeking
- Preparatory behaviors

Table 11.2 Suicide Protective Factors

- Presence of social support
- Problem-solving skills and history of coping skills
- Active participation in treatment
- Presence of hopefulness
- Children present in the home
- Pregnancy
- Religious commitment
- Life satisfaction
- Intact reality testing
- Fear of social disapproval
- Fear of suicide or death

Source: "The Assessment, Management, and Treatment of Suicidality: Toward Clinically Informed and Balanced Standards of Care," by M. D. Rudd and T. E. Joiner, 1998, *Clinical Psychology: Science and Practice, 5,* pp. 146–147. Adapted with permission.

The presence of one or more predisposing factors are data to consider, along with other information, that provide greater contextual understanding when assessing a client but are not meant to be used in some algorithmic way to calculate risk level. To put it another way, the presence of these factors can create a vulnerability for suicidal thinking and behavior (Bryan & Rudd). Acute and chronic risk factors, on the other hand, are used more directly to help distinguish between mild, moderate, and imminent risk (Shea, 2002). These risk factors include psychosocial stressors, certain dysphoric and psychotic symptoms, and thoughts and behaviors that are suicidal in nature. Both prior history and what the individual is experiencing at the time of the assessment should be evaluated. Protective factors are also cognitive, interpersonal, and demographic in nature, and are thought to potentially lower a client's risk level.

PREDISPOSING FACTORS   Research has identified the following predisposing factors: age, gender, a prior diagnosis of either depression, personality disorder, schizophrenia, substance abuse, history of suicidal behavior, family history of suicidal behavior, and history of physical, sexual, and emotional abuse. Research has also found that individuals with a homosexual orientation and those who have been recently discharged from an inpatient psychiatric facility are also at slightly elevated risk. Aging is associated with increased risk in Caucasian populations (Rudd & Joiner, 1998; Shea, 2002) and decreased risk in Black, Hispanic, and Native American populations (Linehan, 1993). In women, the risk levels out in midlife, whereas with men it continues to increase, with men over 70 having the highest rate (Shea, 2002). Although adult males are approximately three times more likely than females to commit suicide, females are one-and-a-half times more likely to attempt suicide (CDC, 2010). The choice of method has been suggested as an explanation for this gender difference. Men much more often use a more lethal method such as a firearm, whereas women more typically use methods that do not cause imminent death, for example, an overdose.

The psychiatric disorders that are considered predisposing risk factors are not considered so because of the disorders in and of themselves, but rather due to the particular symptoms and behaviors associated with the disorders that the individual was experiencing at the time of diagnosis. In the case of depression, having had symptoms of hopelessness, dysphoria, psychache, anhedonia, and thoughts of death can lead someone to consider suicide. Suicide risk becomes even higher if the symptoms are present at the time of the assessment (acute factor) and severe. Brown et al.'s (2000) prospective longitudinal study of psychiatric outpatients provided evidence of this relationship between depression symptoms and suicide, and found that those symptoms, rather than psychiatric diagnoses, were a better predictor of eventual suicide.

Similarly, a current or former diagnosis of schizophrenia is less of a risk factor than the presence of certain acute psychotic symptoms and the long-term psychological consequences that come from having schizophrenia such as hopelessness, despondency and diminished self-worth. The psychotic symptoms that present a risk include command hallucinations (hearing voices directing the person to do something, in this case harmful), delusions of alien control over self, and extreme religious delusions (Shea, 2002). Furthermore, when one is in a psychotic state, risk is elevated because the person cannot engage in problem solving and other rational thinking necessary to come up with options for one's pain, other than death. It is a myth, however, that all people with schizophrenia pose a danger to themselves and others, although a significant minority do (Bryan & Rudd, 2006; Shea, 2002).

The personality disorder most often associated with suicide risk is borderline personality disorder. Individuals diagnosed with borderline personality disorder (BPD) have a greater rate of suicidal threats, previous attempts, and suicide-related behavior relative to other disorders than the general population (Linehan, 1993). Those who attempt suicide and engage in suicide-related behavior are much more likely to try again. In fact, one study found that 46% of those who committed suicide had at least one prior attempt (Roy, 1982). The likelihood of attempting suicide is clearly associated with childhood sexual abuse, an experience that a majority of women diagnosed with BPD have had (Herman, 1992). The majority (55%) of childhood sexual abuse victims go on to attempt suicide (Linehan). When looking at the data on suicide attempts it is important to keep in mind that both prior history and current suicidal thoughts and talk are risk factors. It is another myth that those who talk about suicide will not attempt it. Likewise, it is a fallacy that an interviewer can "plant the seed" for suicidal thinking when asking direct questions about thoughts and plans.

ACUTE AND CHRONIC RISK FACTORS Abuse of alcohol and other drugs is considered a risk factor because of their behavioral and cognitive effects (Bryan & Rudd, 2006). Alcohol, in particular, is both a disinhibitor substance (meaning it can lower one's impulse control) and a central nervous system depressant that can exacerbate dysphoric symptoms. Furthermore, heavy use can impair judgment and problem-solving skills. Therefore, if a client is contemplating suicide, has a plan, and has some intent on acting on it, he or she is more likely to carry out the plan when under the influence of a disinhibitor. Any drug that can be hallucinogenic, such as LSD, can create greater risk if it causes someone to experience the kinds of auditory hallucinations or delusions previously mentioned.

Many of the acute and chronic risk factors identified in Table 11.1 can be organized around the concept of loss. The following types of losses are associated with increased risk for suicide: 1) loss of health (e.g., chronic illness); 2) loss of status with peers, teachers, parents, or significant others (e.g., a job demotion or being cut from a school sports team); 3) a relationship ending or loss of contact with social supports; 4) loss of control and personal safety; 5) financial loss; 6) loss of hope, self-concept, and self-worth, all of which can arise from perceiving rejection or experiencing victimization; 7) ongoing loss of pleasant feelings and moods; and 8) loss of self-control.

The loss of hope, or hopelessness, is one of the strongest predictors of future suicide attempts (Beck, Steer, Beck & Newman,1993; Brown et al., 2000). For those clients whose hopelessness is severe and constant, the risk of a suicide attempt becomes even higher (Brown et al.). Fortunately, feelings of hopelessness and the beliefs that foster it can be changed through counseling. The depth and breadth of a client's hopelessness can be assessed from interviews and quantified with the *Beck Hopelessness Scale,* a 20-item true–false measure of one's beliefs, expectations, and motivations about the future for the past week (Beck, 1978).

PROTECTIVE FACTORS Protective factors, both acute and chronic ones, are those that lessen risk, help to place a client in that zone of risk, and guide management and treatment of suicidal clients (Linehan, 1993; Rudd & Joiner, 1998). One of the factors identified in Table 11.2 is active participation in treatment or counseling. "Actively in counseling" implies that the client is participating in the process and is taking any medication as prescribed. It also means that the client is working on changing thoughts and behaviors, particularly those connected to psychache. A client may or may not enter counseling with the kind of cognitive flexibility or problem-solving skills required to solve her psychache. If she does not, then those skills can be developed through counseling.

Good problem solving, as was discussed in Chapter 4, means that an individual has the capacity to envision multiple qualitatively different solutions to a problem and then choose one to carry out. Someone who believes there is one and only one way to solve a problem has a rigid way of thinking. For example, a client like Juanita who is having difficulty enjoying playing with her preschool children would be viewed as having good problem-solving skills if she could identify playing "pretend," doing what she enjoyed as a child, or studying other parents who seem to be happy with their children—three qualitatively different approaches to alleviating her concern. On the other hand, if she was inflexible in her thinking (e.g., "there is just no time to play with them") or came up with multiple solutions that involved the same theme (e.g., play pretend, play dress-up, play dolls), she would be considered to have poorer problem-solving skills.

Available and accessible support is another key protective factor. A counselor can certainly be a source of support, but the availability is limited. Other emotionally and psychologically supportive individuals—friends, partners, family members, coworkers—with whom the client can talk and receive validation are resources that can help to lessen risk. An intact marriage, in particular, will serve as a protective factor as long at the client perceives his or her spouse as supportive. Having children, particularly minor age children, is also a protective factor if the children constitute a reason to live. Juanita indicated that she believed her children would "grow up better with my sister" and that her depression was hurting them. On the other hand, she believed strongly that "children need a mother" and if she killed herself, then their father, Mark, rather than her sister, would get them, and he would be "awful for them."

Other protective factors include responsibility to other family members, beliefs about God and moral values, one's ability to cope with any adversity, and fear of disapproval. The identification of a client's reasons for living, or deterrents to suicide, can be assessed both through clinical interview and standardized measures, and are covered later in the chapter.

Identifying an individual's risk and protective factors is typically done through a combination of screening information, an interview with the client, and interviews with significant others who may accompany the client. Identification of these factors in combination with an assessment of the most critical risk factors—suicidal thoughts and related behaviors—will help to locate where in the zone of risk the client falls, and to plan management and treatment accordingly.

Inquiring about Suicide Risk

A clinician needs to possess a set of desirable attitudes and approaches (i.e., core competencies) in order to effectively assess a client's suicidal thoughts and behaviors (American Association for Suicidology, 2009; Shea, 2002). As with all assessment and counseling endeavors, an empathic stance is critical. Therefore, helping professionals must understand the values and beliefs they hold about suicide; otherwise, those beliefs may unconsciously interfere with an open, neutral, validating approach designed to maximize information gathering. Beliefs that suicide is sinful, a weakness, or done by only the most disturbed clients will hinder a nonjudgmental and objective inquiry. An empathic approach combines communicating in a caring, concerned voice that suicidal thoughts and behaviors are understandable, with a message of hope that other options for psychache are available. As was discussed in Chapter 3, balancing specific questions with statements of validation will promote client openness and further disclosure (e.g., "Juanita, given what has happened to you with all these losses and the amount of pain you are in, it's understandable that you are having serious thoughts about killing yourself."). The ability to understand the concept of psychache and suicide as a solution to that psychological pain—rather than as manipulative and attention seeking—will help the clinician to further uncover the function and meaning of suicidal thoughts and behaviors. Finally, it is important to again dispel the myth that asking about suicidal thoughts and behaviors can plant a seed. When asking about ideation and plans, clinicians are not providing ideas that clients have not already thought about. Instead, they are providing relief by sending a message that it is okay to talk about suicidal thoughts and feelings, often considered shameful. Questions delivered in the context of understanding and validation will help to lessen risk, not elevate it.

INTERVIEW QUESTIONS   When information obtained from a screening or intake interview suggests that a thorough suicide risk assessment is needed (i.e., the presence of chronic and acute risk factors), three points need to be considered. First, questions should be asked directly and without the use of euphemisms. Second, normalizing a question about suicidal ideation, and making a bridge between a client's expressed concerns and an initial question pertaining to ideation will foster a comfort level for both clinician and client. Third, this type of assessment is guided by the use of a flowchart model in which yes–no answers direct the interviewer to either stop inquiring or to continue to probe further. What specific information warrants the need, in an outpatient setting, for a suicide risk assessment? Any of the previously identified risk factors occurring in combination, particularly client reports of depression symptoms (including hopelessness, dysphoria, and recent losses) and psychotic symptoms involving command hallucinations and alien control should prompt a series of risk assessment questions. Furthermore, in most outpatient mental health facilities, it is often the case that one question regarding thoughts about killing oneself is part of a standard intake interview, regardless of the presenting problems. It is also a question on some standardized measures, such as the SCL-90-R or BDI-II, which may also be used as part of all client intakes. An affirmative response to an interview question or standard measure item regarding suicidal thoughts would prompt further inquiry about plan and method. In non-outpatient settings—emergency rooms, hospital, jails, and residential settings—every patient is likely to have a risk assessment, and the sample interview questions discussed next can be used as well. Prior to asking directly about suicidal thinking and behavior, the clinician will typically have asked about presenting problems, recent stressors, and easier but related topics such as thoughts about death in general and feelings of hopelessness. This more gradual approach to gathering information about suicidal thinking is strongly recommended (Bryan & Rudd, 2006; Shea, 2002).

The following are examples of how to begin a suicide risk interview:

a.   When someone is experiencing or feeling _____, it is common to have thoughts about killing himself or herself. Have you ever had any of those thoughts?

b.   As part of the initial assessment, one question we ask everyone who comes here is whether he or she has ever had thoughts of killing himself or herself.

c.   Given what we've been talking about, have you ever had thoughts of taking your life?

If the client denies suicidal ideations and his or her affect appears congruent, then further suicide risk questions are usually unnecessary. Often, clients who are not thinking about suicide find relief and gain perspective when asked about suicidal ideation. A client may respond, for example, "I'm glad it's not that bad." On the other hand, if the client's response to one of those initial suicide risk questions is either affirmative or noncommittal, or if the affective response appears incongruent with a verbal denial, then a series of additional questions will follow. Those questions will focus on the nature of suicidal ideation (frequency, duration, intensity, degree of intent), plans or methods (lethality, availability), history of thoughts and behaviors (attempts), reasons for living, situational triggers, and self-control (see Table 11.3). It is also possible that a client will allude to suicidal thinking during an initial interview or screening. Phrases such as "I don't think I can take it much longer" or "Things would be better if I weren't here anymore" are suggestive of suicidal ideation, and should be followed up with the types of questions shown in Table 11.3.

DETERMINING LEVEL OF RISK   Although no clinician can know for sure whether or not a client like Juanita will kill herself, determining an *estimate* of her level of risk needs to take place. Using the notion of a zone of risk and criteria established by Rudd and Joiner (1998), the clinician can attempt to locate Juanita along this continuum. It is the estimate of risk that will guide management and treatment decisions. The first factor to consider is whether or not Juanita has **active suicidal ideation**, as opposed to **passive ideation**, or self-harm behavior, with neither an intent nor plan to kill herself. Passive ideation involves thoughts about dying, such as "If I did not wake up tomorrow, that would be good," but does not include a desire and intention to kill oneself. Juanita did disclose active suicidal ideation; she had experienced thoughts of killing herself in the past week. Furthermore, she has several predisposing risk factors (possible emotional and physical abuse and possible prior history of depression) and chronic and acute factors (significant interpersonal losses, frequent feelings of hopelessness, and feeling "lousy, down"). All of these factors combined would place her at least in the moderate, possibly severe range, but what about her protective factors?

Juanita indicated a future orientation and reasons to live when she noted a desire to finish her nursing program and her children's need for their mother. She also appeared ready to engage in therapy and make some changes in her thinking. Juanita's risk factors, particularly hopelessness and depression symptoms, along with frequent suicidal ideation and a specific available lethal plan (swallowing pills or cutting her wrists), would place Juanita in the severe or extreme range. However, her protective factors, in a sense, counteract or balance out the risk factors, placing her in the moderate range. Further assessment revealed that when she had suicidal thoughts, they passed quickly, and although she has considered a lethal plan she did not intend to act on it, particularly because of her children. Her risk would be elevated to extreme were there no protective factors, particularly if she indicated a strong intention to act on her plan (Bryan & Rudd, 2006). It is Juanita's willingness to continue in therapy to address her strong feelings of sadness and pain that is the most encouraging sign. Other clients who engage in self-harming behavior,

Table 11.3 Suicide Risk Assessment Questions

Suicidal ideation: frequency, duration, intensity:

1. How often do you have these thoughts?
2. How long do they last?
3. On a scale of 1 to 10, 1 being very mild and 10 being very strong, how strong are these thoughts?
4. On a scale of 1 to 10, 10 being very likely, how likely are you to act on these thoughts?
5. When do these thoughts occur?**
6. Have you thought about **how** you would kill yourself?

If the answer to question six is yes, then inquire about:

Plans or methods:

1. What are the ways you have thought about ending your life?
2. Any other ways?
3. How long have you been working on this plan?
4. Do you have _____ (the method identified, e.g., a gun, a car, etc.)?
5. What things have you already done to try and _____ (plan mentioned)?
6. What else have you done to prepare for your death?
7. What are you hoping to accomplish by killing yourself (e.g., ending the pain, having a sense of identity, fantasies about how others will react)?

History of thoughts and behaviors:

1. Have there been other times in your life when you have thought about suicide?
2. Have you ever tried to kill yourself before? *If yes, then proceed to the next questions.*
3. When was the most recent time?
4. Tell me what was going on in your life that led you to attempt suicide.
5. What did you do?
6. What happened that you did not die?

Reasons for living:

1. What prevents you from killing yourself now?
2. Is there anything else that might stop you from acting on these thoughts?
3. How do you think significant others will react?
4. What do you think will happen to _____ (e.g., family members and significant others) if you kill yourself?
5. How are you hoping _____ (e.g., family members/significant others) will feel?

Self-control and impulsive behavior:

1. How much control do you think you have over these thoughts?
2. Have there been times when you felt out of control?
3. Have you tried to hurt yourself for the purpose of changing your feelings?
4. Are there times when you do things without thinking about what can happen?

**Situational Triggers questions to consider or address further based on the "when" question above:

1. How often do the thoughts occur when you are alone?
2. Does your suicidal thinking occur in response to a specific behavior or activity?
3. Are the situations predictable or random?
4. Do the situations favor self-control vs. impulsivity? (*i.e., most work or school settings favor self-control*)
5. Are you able to avoid the situation(s) that reinforces the thoughts?

even if not presenting active suicidal ideation, are at least at a mild level of risk because they may be already engaging in behavior—cutting or combining alcohol with certain prescription medications—that could have a fatal consequence:

Zone of Risk Criteria   The criteria contained within each zone of risk (see Figure 11.1) are meant to serve as clinical guidelines. Listing these criteria is not meant to convey that they may be somehow mathematically combined in order to accurately place a client along this continuum. "None" is when a client denies suicidal ideation and there is no other sign of ideation (e.g., a family member reporting the client had made statements about wanting to kill him- or herself). The criteria for establishing level of risk are provided in the Practice Suggestion: Estimating Level of Suicide Risk and are based on Bryan and Rudd's (2006, p. 198) guidelines.

It is the increase in ideation and psychache symptoms, along with the report of a plan, that moves an individual from the mild to the moderate range. Moreover, it is the intention to act on thoughts *and* a plan with the desire to end one's life that is the central defining marker between extreme and less-than-extreme risk. Therefore, when a client indicates he or she has thought of a plan, additional questions beyond those identified in Table 11.3 are needed. The next phase of a risk assessment interview involves open and closed questions. Open questions can be styled in the manner, "Tell me about a specific time when you were working on your plan. How far along

PRACTICE SUGGESTION
Estimating Level of Suicide Risk

1. Risk is estimated as **mild** when:
   a. suicidal ideation is present, but its frequency, duration, and intensity is "limited" and there is no intent to act on those thoughts
   b. plans are absent
   c. few dysphoria or psychache symptoms are present (sadness, pain, despondency, and hopelessness)
   d. good self-control exists
   e. only a few risk factors are present
   f. identifiable protective factors are occurring
2. Risk is considered **moderate** when:
   a. the ideation becomes frequent though still limited in duration and intensity, and no intention of acting on the thoughts, but a specific plan exists
   b. limited dysphoria symptoms are present
   c. good self-control exists
   d. some (rather than few) risk factors are present
   e. there are fewer identifiable protective factors
3. Risk is considered **severe** or greater when:
   a. ideation is frequent and persistent, but still no subjective or objective intention to act on a specific plan
   b. hopelessness is pervasive
   c. self-control is limited
   d. there are no protective factors and reasons for living

did you get, and what stopped you from carrying it out?" This can be followed with inquiries about other specific plans the client did not mention, such as "What about _____ (hanging self, overdosing, and so on)?" (Shea, 2002). Because intent is a key factor in locating clients in the zone of risk, conceptualizing intent as a continuum, rather than simply as being present or absent, will enhance the overall accuracy of the risk assessment. Clients' intention to kill themselves tends to wax and wane, like other thoughts and feelings, rather than being on or off.

Standardized Suicide Measures

Many standardized suicide measures now exist, but only a few have been recommended as part of an overall risk assessment (Nock, Wedig, Janis, & Deliberto, 2008; Range, 2005; Range & Knott, 1997). Those recommended for clinical use with adults include *Modified Scale for Suicidal Ideation, Scale for Suicide Ideation* (interview and self-report versions), *Self-Injurious Thoughts and Behavior Interview, Suicide Attempt Self-Injury Interview, Suicide Behaviors Questionnaire*, and Linehan's *Reasons for Living Inventory*. Like the measures reviewed in Chapters 9 and 10, these instruments are a combination of semistructured or structured interviews and self-report questionnaires with child and adolescent versions. None of these instruments is intended to be used *exclusively* as predictors of suicide risk. They can, however, be used to gather more in-depth information about suicidal ideation, including thoughts about plans and reasons for living. They are meant to supplement the interview and guide the clinician in making an estimate of risk.

Semistructured interviews enable the clinician to assess for all relevant risk factors and have the added advantage of a relatively precise scoring system. The SAD PERSONS was one of the first semistructured interviews to use a simple scoring system (0 or 1) for the presence of 10 risk factors, and high scores were intended to suggest a course of intervention or management for suicidal clients. Although a modified version was used in a study exploring its utility in guiding treatment decisions (e.g., hospital admissions), it did not fare as well as other measures, such as the *Scale for Suicide Ideation* (Cochrane-Brink, Lofchy, & Sakinofsky, 2000). Furthermore, its psychometric qualities have been criticized, and for those reasons it is not included in more recent and substantive reviews of suicide assessment measures (Juhnke, 1994; Nock et al., 2008; Range, 2005).

SCALE FOR SUICIDE IDEATION (SSI)   Aaron Beck and his colleagues (see Chapter 9) developed the *Scale for Suicide Ideation* (SSI), a 19-item measure for clinicians to complete following a semi-structured interview (Beck, Kovacs, & Weisman, 1979). Their goal was to have a tool to help quantify the intensity and nature of suicidal thinking where traditional measures such as the MMPI and Rorschach had not fared well. Rather than focusing on demographic risk factors, the SSI focuses on psychological variables, particularly the characteristics of suicidal thinking. It can be completed in less than 10 minutes. Specific items the clinician rate include the intensity and duration of ideation, wish to live and die (intent), plans, and reasons for living. There are also behavioral items, such as making a suicidal note, "final acts," and attempts. Each interview item is rated on a 3-point scale from 0 to 2, with 2 indicating the most intensity. For example, item 4 on the SSI, "Desire to make an active suicide attempt," is scored 2 if the desire is "moderate to strong." Item 12, "Method: specificity/planning of contemplated attempt," is also scored 2 if "details worked out/well formulated" (Beck et al., 1979, p. 346). When using the SSI, the clinician is expected to probe further any non-zero items. Thus the SSI helps the clinician evaluate the answers to standard risk assessment interview questions, such as the ones described earlier, so as to better locate clients in the zone of risk. A clinician who asked all of the questions described in Table 11.3 could use the SSI system to score the responses. Although it was initially conceived as a research tool with the hope of clinical applications, a number of studies have borne out that hope, finding the SSI to have good reliability, validity, and clinical usefulness with diverse psychiatric groups and settings (Nock et al., 2008). A 21-item version, along with a Spanish translation, is now distributed by Pearson at **www.pearson.assess.com**. The two additional items in this longer version address the number of previous attempts and the intent to die of the last attempt.

A modified version of the SSI was created for the purpose of adding suicidal ideation items not covered in the original SSI (Miller, Norman, Bishop, & Dow, 1986). There are five new items, including talking and writing about death. This semistructured interview functions like a structured interview in that specific questions for each item were designed so that paraprofessionals could also use it. It, too, is considered a measure with strong psychometric qualities (Clum & Yang, 1995; Range & Knott, 1997). It is used effectively in both inpatient and outpatient settings with adolescents and adults (Nock et al., 2008).

Beck, Steer, and Ranieri (1988) developed a self-report version of the SSI with the same 19 items and scoring system. Both a paper and pencil and computer version were created. Interestingly, when individuals complete the computer version they tend to get higher scores than they would on the paper and pencil version, suggesting that some people may be more inclined to answer affirmatively to questions regarding suicide when the questionnaire is computer based (Range, 2005). The self-report version correlated highly ($r > 0.90$) with the clinician-rated interview version, and subsequent studies found it is an effective measure with various populations (Nock et al., 2008). An inspection of the PsycINFO database reveals a significant number of cross-cultural studies and clinical applications with the self-report version. Examples include the translation and evaluation of its psychometric properties in Spanish, Urdu, Chinese, and Japanese versions, as well as its use as an assessment tool in Norway, India, and Uganda. The self-report version is also available from Pearson.

SUICIDE BEHAVIOR QUESTIONNAIRE (SBQ)   Another very brief self-report measure—it can be completed in less than five minutes—is the shortened version of the *Suicide Behavior Questionnaire* (SBQ), consisting of four questions for use with adolescent and adult outpatients (Range, 2005). The original SBQ, developed by Marsha Linehan, consists of 90 items; there are several four-item versions based on Linehan's original that have been used for clinical and research purposes. One recent validated revision of the SBQ contains the following questions (Osman et al., 2001, p. 454):

1. Have you ever thought about or attempted to kill yourself?
2. How often have you thought about killing yourself in the past year?
3. Have you ever told someone you were going to commit suicide or that you might do it?
4. How likely is it that you will attempt suicide someday?

Each of the four questions on the Osman et al. SBQ-R has a different response format. The reliability and validity of the longer SBQ and the abbreviated versions have been demonstrated with inpatient and outpatient samples (Nock et al., 2008; Range, 2005). A children's version, requiring a third-grade reading level, also was developed.

REASONS FOR LIVING INVENTORY (RFL)   Marsha Linehan and her colleagues expanded upon the SBQ to create a 48-item inventory of reasons for living or reasons not to commit suicide.

The inventory comprises six primary factors: Survival and Coping Beliefs, Responsibility to Family, Child-Related Concerns, Fear of Suicide, Fear of Social Disapproval, and Moral Objections (Linehan, Goodstein, Neilson, Chiles, 1983). Individuals rate the importance of each statement on a 6-point Likert scale, from 1 being "extremely unimportant," to 6 being "extremely important." Many of the items are related to specific risk and protective factors, such as intent, wish to die or live, hopelessness, problems-solving skills, and a belief that "only God has the right to end a life."

A total score and subscale scores can be obtained with higher scores indicating stronger reasons for living (Range, 2005). Its psychometric properties are strong: internal reliability estimates are in the adequate to excellent range, and it has good construct validity in that scores have differentiated individuals with only suicidal ideation from those who have attempted suicide (Nock et al., 2008; Range). Like the SSI, the *Reasons for Living Inventory* (RFL) has been translated into several languages and has been modified for specific settings and populations. It has been noted that completing the RFL can have a beneficial effect on clients because of its focus on strengths (Range).

In addition to the original RFL, there are several population-specific versions, including the *Reasons for Living Adolescents* (32 items), the *College Students Reasons for Living Inventory* (46 items), the *Reasons for Living for Young Adults* (32 items, for ages 17–30), and the Brief RFL (12 items, for inmates or those who would have difficulty with the original two-page questionnaire). These adaptations of the RFL also have sound psychometric qualities (Range, 2005; Nock et al., 2008).

SUICIDE ASSESSMENT CHECKLIST-R (SAC-R)   One other measure of note is the *Suicide Assessment Checklist-R* (SAC-R), a mixed format, suicide risk scale that is completed following a semistructured interview (Rogers, Lewis, & Subich, 2002). It was designed for crisis line workers but can be used by mental health professionals in emergency and outpatient settings. A secondary purpose of the SAC-R is to enable clinicians to have a standardized form on which a risk assessment rating (from low to high risk) and intervention is documented. As a documentation tool, it is a helpful checklist to consider using. Like the SSI, a scoring system exists whereby points are given for both demographic risk factors (e.g., male, 15–35) and behavioral risks (e.g., method). A second part of the scale asks clinicians to rate the client on nine psychological and psychosocial factors using a 5-point scale from "none" to "extreme." The factors include "sense of worthlessness," "sense of hopelessness," "social isolation," "intent to die," and "future time perspective" (Rogers et al., 2002, p. 501). Separate scores for parts 1 and 2, along with a total score, can be calculated. Total scores range from 11 to 108. The SAC-R appears in the appendix of the Rogers et al. (2002) article in the *Journal of Counseling and Development*.

The SAC-R has adequate internal reliability and good construct and criterion validity (Rogers et al., 2002). In one study, individuals referred to the emergency center because of a prior attempt scored the highest, followed by those referred for suicidal ideation, and those who were nonsuicidal referrals scored the lowest. There was, however, only a 7-point difference between the average scores of the first and third groups. Similarly, those who were hospitalized scored higher than those sent home or referred for outpatient treatment, although the differences were relatively small. The authors caution that the scores are meant to offer guidelines regarding disposition and are not intended in any way to be predictive of future behavior (i.e., a suicide attempt).

Advantages and Limitations of Standardized Measures

There are several advantages to using standardized suicide risk assessment measures in clinical settings, but these are by no means meant to be a substitute for thorough clinical interviewing and the management decisions that are based upon that process (Range, 2005). When rapid assessment and treatment decisions are required—for example, in emergency services—a self-report such as the SSI is an effective supplemental tool to the clinical interview (Cochrane-Brink et al., 2000). For some clients, answering questions posed on paper is a more comfortable format than responding to an interviewer, particularly with such a sensitive topic as suicide. Second, a semistructured interview helps the clinician to cover all the bases that a standard of care would indicate. The items on the interview can prompt clinicians to inquire what they may have forgotten or overlooked given the volume of questions needed at times. Additionally, semistructured interview scales and self-report measures provide documentation of the information gathered upon which disposition and treatment decisions are made.

Even when used as supplemental tools, standardized suicide report measures have several limitations. First, they can overestimate the degree of risk, resulting in a false positive: labeling someone as a severe suicide risk who is not. Secondly, they tend to be ineffective in estimating acute severe risk because they suggest a static quality to suicide risk when just the opposite is the case (Range, 2005). Finally, their generalizability tends to be limited because of the specific settings in which they were created and the narrow populations used to assess their utility, primarily White youth and young adults (Bryan & Rudd, 2006). Given the costs and time required, some may question whether there is added clinical utility in using them instead of relying solely on interview and observation to ensure that all the necessary questions are covered. In some cases, the addition of a standardized measure may not seem clinically necessary, but it is essential for risk management and liability purposes that whichever suicide risk assessment format is used, it is well documented.

Treatment Planning and Managing Risk

When a clinician determines that a client poses high or severe suicide risk, no-suicide contracts have often been used with limited and uncertain effectiveness (Berman 2006; Rudd, Mandrusiak, & Joiner, 2006). Contracts are an agreement between client and clinician whereby the client agrees orally and in writing not to harm or kill self. Alternatively, counselors and clinicians can work collaboratively on ways to reduce psychache, increase tolerance for emotional pain, and broaden the repertoire of coping skills for emotional pain. Just as there is a continuum of risk, so is a spectrum of interventions also available, from weekly outpatient treatment to brief hospitalization, with increased therapy and phone contacts in between. In general, maintaining this collaborative approach with clients about how to go about managing suicidal thoughts, impulses, and behavior is a recommended alternative to contracts, which can have an infantilizing quality to them and set up an adversarial client–therapist relationship. Having said that, there may be some clients for whom collaborating on a contract in terms of an agreed-upon safety plan is worthwhile. Additionally, when possible, the involvement of significant others can help maintain a client's safety. In the case of Juanita, for example, she and her counselor developed an "emergency plan," which included steps she would take if her suicidal thoughts became too overwhelming, with the last step being "call my counselor." She was also willing to meet twice a week for the first three weeks of treatment to focus on developing alternatives to suicide for coping with her hopelessness, pain, and sorrow.

ASSESSING DANGEROUSNESS TO OTHERS

The assessment of an individual's potential to harm someone else is a more complex task than assessing danger to self. In part, this is because those who have been violent have a tendency to minimize and underreport their behavior, and in part because danger to others encompasses a wider range of behaviors and terms than suicide risk. It also has an added dimension to it, given that mental health professionals have ethical obligations and legal requirements for warning potential victims of violence. Given these complexities, it is not surprising that clinicians have a history of being poor predictors of a client's future violent behavior (Litwack, Zapt, Groscup, & Hart, 2006; Mossman, 1994). Clinicians, however, are somewhat better predictors of *imminent* violence (Litwack et al., 2006). Consequently, the assessment of injury to others involves gathering data in multiple ways from different sources: prior legal and psychiatric records, interviews with family members and significant others, interviews with representatives of correctional and legal systems, and client interview. The use of standardized measures for assessing dangerousness and homicide risk are not on a par with suicide risk measures, but a few pertaining to aggression are available and will be discussed briefly. As with suicide risk, risk assessment of dangerousness to others (including homicide) is driven by an understanding of risk and protective factors.

Risk and Protective Factors

The best predictor of one's potential for violent behavior is a prior history of aggressive behavior (Amore et al., 2008; Gardner, Lidz, Mulvey, & Shaw, 1996; Mossman, 1994). What is meant by a history of aggressive behavior? Aggression has been defined as "goal-directed motor behavior that has a deliberate intent to harm or injure another object or others" (Suris & Coccaro, 2008, p. 732). This definition is somewhat narrow and does not take into account other types of aggression, including verbal aggression, which may not have the "deliberate" intent to harm but nevertheless can cause emotional or psychological harm. The definition of aggression could be applied to violent behavior—an extreme form of it. Aggression can also be thought of as any forceful verbal or physical behavior that violates the rights and feelings of others and results in some type of physical, emotional, or psychological harm (Michelson, Sugai, Wood, & Kazdin, 1983). This definition includes both verbal and physical behavior and focuses on the consequence of the behavior (harm) rather than underlying motivation, which at times can be difficult to discern. Verbal aggression can include threats to harm, harassment, and demeaning or insulting language. Physical aggression includes any behavior that is *potentially* harmful to someone else—hitting, punching, shoving, kicking, throwing of objects, and using a weapon or an object as a weapon (e.g., a baseball bat). The relationship between a prior history of aggression and future aggressive behavior, documented for several decades with many groups in various settings, was demonstrated once again in a recent study of 374 psychiatric inpatients over a one-year period (Amore et al., 2008). Similar to suicide assessment, intent is a key factor when attempting to estimate the level of risk a client poses to someone else. Individuals can, however, display behaviors considered aggressive, as in the case of a child having a temper tantrum (consisting of kicking, throwing objects, or punching a wall), but the child does not necessarily have the intention of harming someone or something else. When the behavior includes intent to harm, the behavior is considered violent, and when the intent is ultimate harm or injury, then assessing homicide risk becomes necessary.

Shea (1998) suggests that the assessment of one's risk for violent behavior is enhanced by an understanding of the three types of violence: affective, predatory, and biologically induced.

Affective violence is the kind seen in intimate relationships, such as spousal or parent and child. It usually occurs impulsively, in a fit of rage, and can be influenced by alcohol intoxication (Stover, Meadows, & Kaufman, 2009). Clinicians are most likely to come in contact with clients whose aggressive behavior is the affective type, particularly when working with couples. Routine screening in outpatient settings both for victims and perpetrators of intimate partner violence is critical given its documented prevalence (Soglin, Bauchat, Soglin, & Martin, 2009). *Predatory violence* is the kind that involves long, detailed planning and is found in people with antisocial personalities and some serial rapists and child abusers. *Biologically induced violence* refers to behavior that stems either from substances like alcohol, LSD, and other hallucinogens; to a psychotic process involving command hallucinations, alien control, and extreme religious delusions; or to brain disease, as in the case of Alzheimer's, tumors, and complex seizures (Shea, 1998).

Who, then, is likely to engage in violent behavior, especially lethal behavior? Although under certain circumstance almost anyone can commit an isolated aggressive act, certain additional risk factors are associated with patterns of aggressive and violent behavior. These include age, gender, exposure to violence, poor impulse control, and possibly psychiatric diagnosis.

Age and gender differences in violent behavior are striking. Most violent behavior is committed by males, particularly those under age 35 (Shea, 1998). If a male has witnessed violence such as spousal abuse or has been a victim of violence (e.g., physical abuse), his risk for engaging in violent behavior is somewhat greater than the general population (Byrd & Davis, 2009). Females, on the other hand, are no more likely to commit violent behaviors than are nonvictims of violence, but are at greater risk for being revictimized. Although for the adult females who do commit violence, the frequency of physical abuse experienced as a child seems to be a factor related to their later violence.

Having poor impulse control is a risk factor for acting out feelings of frustration and anger. Impulse control problems are associated with certain psychiatric disorders: childhood disorders (attention deficit–hyperactivity disorder and conduct disorder), personality disorders (antisocial and borderline), and alcohol abuse and addiction. As previously noted, substances that are disinhibitory, such as alcohol, can lower one's impulse control and increase the potential for acting on harmful desires and fantasies. Therefore, alcohol abuse or dependence is the DSM disorder most frequently seen in individuals with a history of violent behavior, with the risk increasing in relation to the severity of usage, particularly for males (Melnicks, Sacks, & Banks, 2006; Shea, 1998). If a client appears at risk for violence, then a comprehensive substance abuse assessment should be considered as well (see Chapter 12).

Risk for violence is also associated with conduct disorder in children (the precursor to antisocial personality disorder), antisocial personality disorder, and borderline personality disorder based on some of the core features of these disorders. Antisocial personality and conduct disorders feature a "pattern of disregard for, and violation of, the rights of others" (American Psychiatric Association, 2000, p. 701), and include aggressive acts to people, property, and objects. Often, individuals with borderline personality disorder have problems with regulating and expressing anger leading to aggressive behavior (Linehan, 1993). Although the diagnosis of schizophrenia is commonly associated with the probability of dangerousness, most clients with schizophrenia pose little or no risk for harming others. It is, as noted, an active psychotic process that involves command hallucinations, alien control, and extreme religious or paranoid delusions where the potential for violence is elevated, and that occurs only in a small percentage of cases of schizophrenia (Shea, 1998).

Determining Risk

The process for determining whether a client poses an imminent danger to someone else is similar to the interview approach for suicide risk. The questions are designed to uncover ideation, intent, and plan. As with suicide risk, a client who has formulated a plan, is intent on acting on it, and has multiple risk factors present and little if any protective factors, is at the highest risk level. Typically this type of an assessment calls for a more immediate attention to the safety of others, including the interviewer, than suicide risk assessment. Consequently the interviewer should be attuned to warning signs of agitation and loss of control and have a security plan in place prior to conducting the assessment, especially if it is being done in an outpatient setting.

INTERVIEW QUESTIONS   Similar to the process for getting to suicide risk questions, the interviewer will want to set the stage for asking questions related to violence (Shea, 1998). This can be done by inquiring about less sensitive and threatening topics first and then making a bridge between one of these topics and violence. Questions regarding arguments, feelings of anger, expression of anger, and prior history of school or legal problems can provide that pathway to this type of risk assessment inquiry. The following case example, from Chapter 9, illustrates when an assessment of this type will occur.

> Fred, a 22-year-old Caucasian male was referred to a community mental health center by his probation officer. Fred was arrested two weeks prior to this appointment because of a domestic violence incident with his live-in girlfriend. Fred had punched his girlfriend and threatened to steal her car and take her children. Fred had told the arresting officer, "She dresses like a whore from the islands, I need to do God's work and punish her for her sins, peace my friendly man, save you." The arresting officer believed Fred was intoxicated when he arrested him.
>
> Fred's parents divorced when he was 6 years old and Fred's father used to "beat me with a strap." Fred has a GED and an erratic work history. This is his first time being brought to the attention of mental health services.

Fred is likely to be more open and less threatened about the domestic violence incident if he is led to it by earlier questions regarding work history and problems getting along with coworkers or bosses and how those conflicts were handled. Questions regarding interpersonal conflicts can provide material for a bridge to the violence risk assessment questions contained in Table 11.4. Information can also be gathered from his probation officer, a police record if available, and any other valuable collateral sources.

Standardized Aggression Measures

Two semistructured interviews and several self-report measures have been found to be helpful tools for assessing aggressive behavior, and therefore providing indirect evidence for the potential of violent, including lethal, behavior. The *Overt Aggression Scale Modified* is a semistructured interview designed to assess current aggressive behavior in clients in outpatient settings. The *Life History of Aggression* is also a semistructured interview that assesses aggressive incidents from the age of 13 onward (Suris & Coccaro, 2008). The *Aggression Questionnaire*, the *MMPI-2 Anger Content Scale,* the *Revised Conflict Tactics Scale's Physical Assault Subscale,* the *SCL-90-R Hostility Scale,* and the *State–Trait Anger Expression Inventory-2* are all self-report measures that assess various aspects of aggressive behavior, feelings of anger and hostility, and aggressive thinking.

Table 11.4 Dangerousness to Others: Risk Assessment Questions

Ideation:

1. Have you ever had thoughts of wanting to harm someone else? (*As with suicide risk, assess frequency, duration, and severity, and intent.*)
2. Have you thought of ways you would act on those thoughts?
3. What has stopped you from acting on these thoughts?

Plans:

4. What are the ways you've thought about harming (killing) _____?
5. How far have you gotten with _____ (specific plans)?
6. What has stopped you from carrying it out so far?

History:

7. Have you ever gotten into a physical fight with someone?
    If the answer is yes, then ask "What happened?"; "Was anyone injured?") *followed up with* "How did you feel about what you did?" (*Is the person feeling guilt or remorse versus externalizing blame?*)
    Explore in detail any aggressive or violent event that led to the referral.
8. When was the most recent time you acted violently? (*May need to give examples such as hit, punched, grabbed, kicked or used a weapon*)
9. What was the worst time?
10. Have you ever been arrested for fighting, assault, or destroying property?
11. Were you ever suspended from school for fighting?
12. Have you ever used a weapon to harm someone?
13. Have there been times when you've lost your temper and broken things?
14. Have you ever threatened to hurt someone?
15. Have you ever physically hurt someone?
16. Have you ever forced someone to have sex with you?

OVERT AGGRESSION SCALE MODIFIED   The *Overt Aggression Scale Modified* is a behavioral checklist typically used in restrictive settings, and is completed by a clinician after reviewing a patient's record and interviewing staff who have observed an aggressive episode. The clinician records the severity of the most serious observed aggressive episode over the past week based on four different types: verbal aggression, physical aggression against objects, physical aggression against self, and physical aggression against others (Bowers, 1999).

LIFE HISTORY OF AGGRESSION (LHA)   The *Life History of Aggression* (LHA) is an 11-item semistructured interview measure for assessing the frequency of various verbal and physical acts and their consequences on a 6-point scale, from 0 to 5, with 0 being "no occurrences" and 5 being "more events than can be counted" (Coccaro, Berman, & Kavoussi, 1997). The LHA is a modification of earlier interview versions that assess aggression over the lifetime. Individuals are asked how many times five specific types of aggressive acts have occurred since age 13: 1) verbal, 2) indirect (aggression against objects), 3) "non-specific fighting," 4) physical assaults against people with intent to harm, and 5) temper tantrums. The LHA includes four items related to consequences of aggressive behavior and antisocial behavior (such as school suspensions, problems with supervisors, and illegal activities with and without police involvement) and two items related to self-harm and suicide. The interrater reliability and test–retest reliabilities of the total score and the three subscores (aggression, consequences/anti-social behaviors, and self-directed) are in the good to excellent range and its construct validity has been established (Coccaro et al., 1997). The authors of the LHA suggest that a clinician will want to evaluate further specific aggressive incidents and behaviors when either the total LHA score exceeds 15, or when the aggression subscale is greater than 12 (the 98th percentile for nondiagnosed individuals).

AGGRESSION QUESTIONNAIRE (AQ)   The *Aggression Questionnaire* (AQ) was designed to be a psychometric improvement over the *Hostility Inventory,* one of the first self-report measures for assessing specific aspects of aggression (verbal and physical), anger, and hostility (Buss & Perry, 1992). The AQ consists of 29 items rated on a 5-point scale from 1 ("extremely uncharacteristic of me") to 5 ("extremely characteristic of me"). Positively worded items are reverse scored. Items include the statements (p. 454):

> Once in awhile I can't control the urge to strike another person.
>
> I have become so mad I have broken things.
>
> I have trouble controlling my temper.
>
> When people are especially nice I wonder what they want.

The internal reliability of the total scale is good (r = 0.89), and the four subscale internal reliabilities range from adequate to good (r = 0.72 to 0.85) (Buss & Perry, 1992; Harris, 1997). The AQ's construct validity has been demonstrated in a number of studies (Suris & Coccaro, 2008).

REVISED CONFLICT TACTICS SCALES: PHYSICAL ASSAULT SUBSCALE   The Physical Assault Subscale of the *Revised Conflict Tactics Scales* (CTS2) is an eight-item self-report measure of the frequency and severity of aggression and violence in intimate partner relationships. It is used as a tool to measure both physical abuse episodes a person has experienced as well as has committed (Byrd & Davis, 2009). The types of aggressive and violent acts include slapping and using a gun, and their frequency is rated on a 8-point scale ranging from "never" to "daily." The internal reliability and construct validity of all the scales have been established cross-culturally with university populations (Straus, 2004). The CTS2 is distributed by Western Psychological Services.

Does one's tendency to be prone to anger and hostility pose an additional risk factor for dangerousness to others? Although the link between chronic anger and overt acts of physical aggression toward others continues to be debated, recent studies have found that some individuals scoring higher on anger and hostility measures have exhibited significantly higher levels of some types of violent behavior, particularly with intimate partners (Deffenbacher, et al., 1996; Murphy, Taft, & Ekhardt, 2007; Suris & Coccaro, 2008). Even though high scores on self-report measures of anger and hostility are limited in their predictive validity (i.e., a significant percentage of clients will score low on these measures but engage in violent behavior and, conversely, score high and not act violently), several are worth mentioning because they contain scales and items related to acts of physical aggression and urges to harm others. Clinicians will want to interview further those clients scoring high by asking about what led them to endorse specific items as true or frequent, and also to inquire further about critical items even if a total scale score is within the normal range.

STATE–TRAIT ANGER EXPRESSION INVENTORY-2 (STAXI-2)   The *State–Trait Anger Expression Inventory-2* (STAXI-2) (Spielberger, 1999) is a revision of the original 44-item STAXI based on state–trait theory of personality and emotion (see Chapter 8). It is a 57-item self-report measure designed to evaluate different aspects of anger expression and control in individuals age 16 and older. Although it was intended primarily to assess the relationship between anger and physical conditions (such as hypertension and heart disease), it is used as an outcome measure for anger management treatment and domestic violence interventions. It is made up of six scales (State Anger, Trait Anger, Anger Expression-out, Anger Expression-in, Anger Control-Out, and Anger Control) and five subscales for the State and Trait anger scales: Feeling Angry, Feel Like Expressing Anger Verbally, Feel Like Expressing Anger Physically, Angry Temperament, and Angry Reaction. The State Anger scale assesses anger intensity for specific situations and times; the Trait Anger scale measures the frequency of angry feelings over time. The Expression and Control scales assess whether anger is acted out physically against people and objects, or if it is suppressed. Individuals respond to the items using a 4-point scale from "almost never" to "almost always."

The STAXI-2 was normed on a large sample made up of psychiatric patients and nondiagnosed participants. There is, however, no information about the racial and ethnic composition of the normative sample, which limits its use (Freeman, 2003). Based on a number of studies, the psychometric qualities—reliability and validity estimates—of both the original and STAXI-2 are very good (Deffenbacher, et al., 1996; Suris & Coccaro, 2008). The STAXI-2 is a level B measure requiring a sixth-grade reading level and is distributed by PAR (***www3.parinc.com***).

In addition to the AQ and STAXI-2, there are subscales on the MMPI-2 and SCL-90-R (see Chapter 8) that assess aggressive behaviors and traits. If these scores are significantly elevated, they should prompt a clinician to probe further about aggressive behaviors and intent to harm others. The Anger content scale on the MMPI-2 consists of six critical items, three of which focus on becoming angry and breaking things when drinking, hurting someone in a fight, and loss of self-control. The Hostility scale on the SCL-90-R includes items such as temper outbursts, violent urges, and urges to break things. Intent to harm is a key factor in determining a client's risk for danger to others, and therefore items related to urges—although not the same as intention and plan—should be probed further. Clients whose Anger or Hostility scale scores on either the MMPI-2 Anger Scale or the SCL-90-R Hostility scale are in the clinically significant range should undergo a more extensive clinical interview regarding their history of aggression.

As with suicide risk self-report measures, these aggression measures are meant to supplement, not replace, clinical interviews when assessing for the risk of harm to others. They are of particular value when formulating a case conceptualization and treatment plan. In addition to helping assess risk, these measures can be used to identify a treatment focus—for example, anger, poor impulse control, and aggressive urges—and modality of treatment: individual versus group.

Summary and Conclusions

The assessment of danger to self and others is one of the most daunting challenges facing helping professionals. The goal is to rapidly gather enough information regarding intention, prior behavior, current thinking and plans, and reasons for not killing self, or harming others, in order to *estimate* a client's level of risk so that appropriate management and treatment decisions can be made. Predicting an eventual suicide or homicide is not the objective, nor is it possible. Using information gathered from interviews and standardized measures to make predictions about suicide is an unrealistic task because it is such a low-base-rate phenomenon. If a counselor gathered no information about a client but predicted the client would not kill himself, the prediction would be right about 99 times out of 100. Making easy but unconstructive predictions, and conducting informative comprehensive assessments are two very different tasks. Clinicians can take solace in the fact that comprehensive risk assessment interviews based on a risks and protective factors framework, along with psychometrically sound measures, facilitate locating a client in a zone of risk. Once a clinician has made a judgment about risk level, a collaborative approach for deciding necessary interventions can take place. An understanding of suicide as a permanent solution to a temporary problem will facilitate an empathic uncovering of thoughts, intentions, and plans in order to promote a collaborative search for alternative coping strategies.

Several recommended semistructured and self-report suicide and violence assessment measures were reviewed. That said, state-of-the-art risk assessment practice continues to rely foremost on comprehensive interviews; standardized measures play a more limited but supplemental role. The measures reviewed, however, are of sufficient psychometric quality so that their use may become more widespread among counseling professionals. In addition, many of these measures provide a means by which a standard of care for risk assessment can be followed and documented.

Reflection Questions and Experiential Exercises

1. Do you think there are ever circumstances in which suicide is a rational choice for a person to make? Why or why not? If so, what are those circumstances?
2. What is the difference between acts of self-harm and suicide attempts?
3. What will help you recall risk and protective factors when interviewing clients about danger to self and others?
4. What are the advantages and limitations of standardized measures of aggression and anger for assessing danger to others?
5. In small groups, identify the risk and protective factors in the following case. What is your estimate of suicide risk? What other information would you want to collect to feel more confident about your estimate of risk?

   A 17-year-old boy named Jeff was in trouble. His mother, Mrs. Smith, called the counselor at the nearby high school, where Jeff was a senior, who then referred Mrs. Smith to the local community mental health center. Mrs. Smith was concerned that Jeff might have "ADD" and added almost as an aside that she and Jeff's father had considered asking Jeff to leave home because of "aggressive behavior," but decided not to.

   Jeff's history was fairly uneventful until he entered 10th grade. That was when an anger cycle began, which his mother described as his "stuffing things down that bother him until he erupts two to four weeks later." Tenth grade was also the year he became a "skinhead," began abusing alcohol and marijuana, and at times "needed to be physically restrained." Jeff has a younger sister with whom he has a close relationship.

   Jeff told the counselor he was feeling bummed out and hopeless. He reported that his father "intimidates" him. Jeff disclosed that he has the following things going for him: a girlfriend, an aunt with whom he's close, a talent for poetry, and a desire to get into a good college where he could develop his already excellent writing abilities.
6. Role-play in groups of three a suicide risk assessment interview with Jeff. One person will be Jeff, one the counselor/therapist who will conduct the interview, and one will observe. The observer notes which risk assessment questions are asked, paying particular attention to the phrasing and the answers they elicit.

12 ASSESSING SUBSTANCE USE DISORDERS

Chapter Objectives

After reading this chapter, you should be able to:

■ Understand a framework for the screening of substance use disorders.

■ Identify common interview questions.

■ Identify standardized measures most often used and recommended for clinical practice.

■ Understand the advantages and limitations of the common substance use assessment measures.

■ Explain how to incorporate standardized measures into the assessment of substance usage.

Tanya, a 47-year-old African American woman, was referred to the local mental health clinic through her Employee Assistance Program (EAP) because of "job stress" and was experiencing some anxiety and depression symptoms following the recent deaths of two family members.

At the intake interview, Tanya reported a history of "nervousness, agitation, and depression." Over the past month she had become overwhelmed with her new job responsibilities as a supervisor in a manufacturing plant and was having trouble coping with the loss of her sister and mother within the past year. She was experiencing "heart palpitations," "difficulty concentrating," and "frequent rashes." One of her fears was that she had a serious "mental illness" because her father was either "bipolar or something else" and was in and out of hospitals when she was growing up. He was also an "alcoholic." When Melanie, the intake clinician, asked, "What sorts of things have you tried already before coming here to cope with your anxiety?" Tanya spontaneously replied, "I go through bouts of drinking." Then she quickly added, "It's the only thing that relaxes me." She also reported overeating, having gained 15 pounds in the past six months, and smoking a pack a day.

Tanya's difficulties with alcohol and other drugs were long-standing. At 15 she was sent to a "rehab" place but didn't "stick with it." She had one year of sobriety following outpatient treatment at a substance abuse clinic when she was 31, but has continued to drink on and off since then along with episodic participation in AA. She reported that her consumption over the past month has been a "12-pack" every three to four days with "things" getting progressively worse over the past few months: two episodes of passing out, breaking a set of plates in a rage, and frequent headaches and feelings of guilt and depression. She denied use of any other drugs besides tobacco. She had, however, been prescribed Ambien for insomnia, which she takes on an as-needed basis.

Tanya appeared open about her alcohol consumption, negative consequences, treatment, and family history but was not ready to engage in treatment for alcohol dependence. She was ambivalent about stopping her drinking and did not want to go back to AA or try "detox" again—"I have my reasons," she added. Her perception that it was her only way to relax was in part fueling this ambivalence. She was hoping counseling would help, however. Melanie suggested she make a chart of the advantages and disadvantages of getting sober and, after explaining her rationale, gave Tanya the *Alcohol Use Disorders Identification Test* (AUDIT) in order to get a better understanding of the severity of her alcohol use and possible treatment options.

OVERVIEW

Daily American life provides countless examples of the ubiquity of drug usage: from advertisements and celebrity confessionals, to wine's putative benefits; from social customs and rituals, to prescribed use and prescription misuse. When does use become abuse or dependency is a question that all counselors, regardless of setting and population served, will consider as part of a clinical assessment. Although the specialty practice of drug abuse counselor has given rise to formal evaluations of substance abuse, all counseling professionals—community, mental health, organizational, rehabilitation, and school—have multiple reasons for needing, at a minimum, screening tools for substance abuse problems. Following an initial screening, helping professionals may want to conduct or refer out clients for more in-depth assessment. The counselor who interfaces with a client who is not using any drug—be it legal drugs such as caffeine, nicotine, or alcohol; illicit ones such as marijuana, cocaine, heroin, ecstasy, and others; or prescription medications for pain, attention, depression, anxiety, or sexual dysfunction—is an extreme rarity. Consequently, an understanding of the spectrum of substance abuse assessment tools available to all helping professionals is essential.

There are multiple reasons why helpers will want to conduct substance abuse screenings. As discussed in Chapter 1, screening is a type of secondary prevention method whereby individuals who are at risk for particular problems or disorders can be identified. Those individuals who receive services from mental health counselors are one such at-risk group when it comes to substance use disorders. Although substance use disorders are not as prevalent as mood and anxiety disorders, they still affect a significant number of individuals in the United States. A nationally representative interview survey estimated the lifetime prevalence of any substance use disorder to be about 15% (Kessler, Berglund, Demler, Jin, & Walters, 2005). In 2007 alone, over 22 million individuals age 12 and over were classified as having either a substance abuse or dependence disorder within the past year, using DSM-IV criteria, according to the Substance Abuse and Mental Health Services Administration's annual structured in-person interview of a large nationally representative sample (Substance Abuse and Mental Health Services Administration [SAMHSA], 2008). In mental health settings the rates of substance use disorders are much greater. It has been estimated that psychiatric and substance use disorders co-occur about 60% of the time (National Institute on Drug Abuse [NIDA], 2007). Specific comorbidity rates vary depending on gender and the particular disorders, but those with anxiety and mood disorders are twice as likely to have a substance use disorder as the general population, and those with any form of "serious psychological distress" are three times more likely than those without distress to have a substance abuse problem (SAMHSA, 2008). These numbers indicate that a large cadre of well-trained professionals—primary care, mental health, and substance abuse specialists—is needed for identifying and treating substance use disorders.

Identifying those at risk of, or who have developed, substance abuse problems is cost-effective. For every dollar spent on substance abuse prevention, $7 is saved in reduced criminal, justice, and health care costs. In just one year, 1992, businesses lost $82 billion in substance abuse–related costs (NIDA, National Institutes of Health [NIH], & U.S. Department of Health and Human Services, 2009). Untreated substance use disorders are more expensive than the combined costs of cancer, diabetes, and heart disease treatments. Substance abuse treatment is a significant driver of overall health care costs and substance addictions create major financial burdens for employers, educational systems, and the legal system (Prochaska, 2004).

Screening specifically for alcohol problem use, abuse, and dependency is very important. On average, individuals with untreated alcohol problems incur health care costs that are twice as high as those without problems (SAMHSA, 2009). Alcohol is the most widely used psychoactive drug in the United States and those who begin using prior to the age of 15 are at significantly higher risk for developing alcoholism than those who begin after 21.

Furthermore, abuse of alcohol and other drugs not only has significant health and business costs but social and psychological ones as well. Families are particularly adversely affected by substance abuse. Alcohol abuse has been found to be one of several causal factors in divorces of young American adults when at least one spouse drinks heavily during the marriage (Collins, Ellickson, & Klein, 2007). There is a strong relationship between substance abuse and domestic violence for both men and women (Stuart et al., 2008) and the link between substance abuse and child abuse and neglect is no longer in doubt (Sheridan, 1995). Although the studies regarding substance abuse and domestic violence and child abuse are not causal in nature, they suggest that substance abuse is a significant contributing factor. That is, the more frequently one abuses substances, the more likely those violent behaviors will occur. Additionally, substance abuse is a risk factor for psychological and psychiatric problems. Alcohol and other drugs, because of their effect on the central nervous system, can interfere with medications designed to treat disorders from hypertension to depression and worsen conditions such as mood disorders, personality disorders, and schizophrenia, as well as problems with impulse control and anger. Therefore, when screening suggests the presence of a substance abuse problem, further assessment of other problem areas will be needed if not already conducted. The interrelationship between the abuse of various substances and family and psychological disorders along with the cost-effectiveness of early identification of substance abuse problems speaks to the critical need for helping professionals of various disciplines to understand how to screen for substance use disorders.

The purpose of this chapter is to present a process for using interviews and standardized measures for assessing substance abuse and dependency. Although it has become commonplace for alcohol to be referred to and distinguished from other "drugs" and at times assessed and treated separately from other drug problems, the fact is, alcohol is a psychoactive substance (i.e., a drug that affects the central nervous system like any other chemical: caffeine, nicotine, marijuana, cocaine, and so on). The DSM-IV framework recognizes this reality and therefore classifies alcohol as one of 11 classes of substances for which the concepts of abuse and dependence are applied. Therefore, in this chapter the terms *drugs* and *substances* will be used generically to refer to any type of psychoactive drug, including alcohol. Also, the overall assessment process described here can be readily applied to any specific drug.

Tanya's story, in the chapter case study, is typical of those with substance abuse and dependence disorders in that 1) she has had multiple treatments followed by relapse; 2) she is currently in a contemplative stage of change with respect to her alcohol abuse; and 3) she is experiencing symptoms suggestive of other Axis I disorders anxiety and depression, the two most common Axis I disorders that co-occur with substance use disorders. Substance use disorders are often chronic conditions with multiple treatment episodes at different levels of care. Data from 1999 indicated that 60% of individuals with substance use disorders have had two treatment episodes and that most will need three to four episodes before abstinence can be maintained without relapse (Dennis, Scott, & Funk, 2003). The stages of change model (Prochaska, DiClemente, & Norcross, 1992) would classify Tanya as being in the contemplative stage of change with respect to alcohol abuse because she acknowledges problems with her use but is ambivalent about changing her use because of the perceived benefits of continuing to drink. The goal of further evaluation, providing information, and motivational interviewing would be to facilitate a process whereby Tanya better understands her ambivalence and choices and decides to enter the preparation stage of change, indicating greater readiness to make changes in her usage. Strategies and treatment interventions for helping clients like Tanya move further along in their readiness for change have been researched and reviewed (Babor et al., 2007) and described in detail in *Motivational Interviewing*, 2nd edition (Miller & Rollnick, 2002).

SUBSTANCE ABUSE INTERVIEWS

Framing the Inquiry

As with other assessment topics, consumption and abuse of drugs will typically begin with either unstructured or semistructured interviews and proceed to standardized self-report measures and in some cases laboratory tests (e.g., urine analyses). The latter is typically conducted in specialized substance abuse treatment facilities where measures described here may be used first as part of a screening and evaluation process.

Like suicide and sex, substance usage is a sensitive topic for many people. That does not mean obtaining accurate and valuable client self-reports is unlikely. What it suggests is that forethought and care about how to frame this assessment should precede jumping into it. A clinician's understanding of when and how to inquire about consumption patterns will enhance the likelihood of client openness and forthrightness. That being said, some adult clients have been found to be open and appreciative of this kind of inquiry without any special framing of the topic when screened by a familiar and trusted professional such as their primary care physician (Miller, Thomas, & Mallin, 2006). Normalizing statements, bridges, and a sequential process of inquiring first about drugs that are easier for clients to talk about and moving on to those that are harder will facilitate obtaining useful information when a relative stranger (e.g., an intake clinician) is conducting the assessment. Normalizing statements can be similar in content to those mentioned in previous chapters. For example, "One of the things we ask *everyone* who comes here is how much he or she is using different types of drugs, starting with caffeine." A bridge statement connects the beginning of an inquiry, in this case substance usage, to problems previously discussed and provides a rationale for doing so. For example, "Given what you told me about your anxiety and trouble sleeping [prior problems provide rationale for asking], I'm wondering about drugs you might be using that could make that better or worse; what about _____ [a risks–resources inquiry]?" A sequential process of beginning with relatively less sensitive drugs to more difficult ones typically will begin with caffeine or nicotine consumption and proceed to prescription medications (if this information is not already obtained) with a focus on whether the drugs are being taken as prescribed. Then questions related to alcohol and illicit drugs will follow. Sometimes it may make more sense to get to consumption patterns indirectly by asking first about family history and then proceeding directly to client use. For example, "Before, you were telling me about your family and I'm wondering if anyone in your family has had any problems with alcohol or other drugs?" A discussion of family history can sometimes create a greater readiness for a client to talk openly about his or her usage.

Defining Problem Use, Abuse, and Dependence

Once the stage has been set, a series of questions designed to screen for substance abuse or dependency will follow. One way to consider the distinction between abuse and dependence is a continuum of problematic usage with dependence representing the more severe and compulsive end of the continuum (Rohsenow, 2008). A continuum model can be very useful for helping clients to locate where along a problematic dimension they fit. A continuum approach has the added benefit of providing a normalizing context for clinicians and clients to openly discuss usage and its consequences that often does not occur when substance usage is conceptualized in black or white terms: either you're an addict or you don't have a problem.

The DSM-IV-TR defines abuse as a "maladaptive pattern" of substance use that causes "recurrent and significant adverse consequences" in social, physical, legal, vocational and/or educational functioning in the past 12 months (American Psychiatric Association, 2000, p. 195). Therefore, interview questions or self-report measures aimed at uncovering the negative consequences of usage will be more helpful than information about frequency and quantity of use in making a diagnosis of substance abuse. Since the modern DSM system was introduced in 1980, the DSM has recognized multiple classes of substances that an individual could be abusing or dependent on. Currently, DSM-IV-TR recognizes 11 types of substances: alcohol, amphetamines, caffeine, cannabis, cocaine, hallucinogens, inhalants, nicotine, opioids, phencyclidine, (PCP), and sedatives, hypnotics, or anxiolytics (anti-anxiety medications).

The diagnosis of substance dependence, given it is conceptualized as a more severe disorder, requires more stringent criteria, which include but are not limited to the physiological concepts of **tolerance** and **withdrawal**. Individuals who are dependent upon a particular substance continue to use and "crave" it despite having the knowledge that repeated use causes problems. The DSM-IV-TR defines substance dependence as a "maladaptive pattern of substance use leading to significant impairment" in functioning as evident by "three or more symptoms occurring in the same 12-month period." Those symptoms include tolerance, withdrawal, efforts to cut down or control usage, taking larger amounts than intended, significant time spent in activities necessary to obtain the substance, and important social, occupational, or recreational activities are given up or reduced because of the usage (American Psychiatric Association, 2000, p. 197). This definition of dependence represents a change from DSM-III in which either withdrawal or tolerance needed to be present for the diagnosis to be made, rather than being 2 out of 7 possible but not necessary symptoms. This revised conceptualization means that psychological dependence typically includes a physiological component but that physiological symptoms are not necessary for dependence to occur. Tolerance is a physiological concept that applies to any drug, meaning that it takes increasingly larger amounts of the substance to produce the desired effect, or less of the effect occurs with the same dosage. Withdrawal is also a physiological concept that means specific symptoms (e.g., headaches, tremors, and/or restlessness) occur when the substance is discontinued. The DSM-IV-TR dependence criteria apply to all of the substances noted previously with the exception of caffeine.

Although the DSM-IV does not consider binge or at-risk drinking as a separate disorder, the National Institute on Alcohol and Alcoholism (NIAAA) has defined **risky drinking** as five or more standard drinks per occasion or more than 14 drinks per week in males and four or more per occasion or more than seven drinks per week in females (U.S. Department Health and Human Services [HHS], NIH, & NIAAA, 2005). Individuals who are consuming alcohol at those levels are at risk for alcohol abuse and dependence and health and mental health related problems, as well as exacerbating existing health conditions. Where along the continuum of use "normal" drinking ends and "excessive" begins is culturally bound, however, which will affect to some extent the assessment of alcohol abuse in different societies (e.g., Italy and Spain) (Agabio, Marras, Gessa, & Carpiniello, 2007; Escobar, Espi, & Canteras, 1995). Cultural factors will also affect the negative consequences in the home, the workplace, and social situations. Cultural considerations when conducting substance use assessments will be discussed more fully in a later section.

Interview Questions and Referral

If one of the previous normalizing or bridge statements and questions elicits an affirmative response from a client, then quantity, frequency, situational determinants, and history of consequences can be obtained (see Table 12.1).

It is the physical, health, interpersonal, and legal consequences, and not merely the frequency of consumption, that determines whether a client's usage will fall on this continuum of problematic use to dependency. As Table 12.1 illustrates, these questions can be adapted for particular substances and client situations. If the answers to these questions indicate that an individual appears at risk for abuse, or may already be abusing, then the clinician may opt to gather more history regarding when usage began, efforts to stop, periods of diminished use or abstinence, reasons for use and readiness to change this behavior, other negative consequences of usage, and previous treatment history. Alternatively, the clinician may then want to refer the individual for a more formal substance abuse evaluation that is likely to cover these areas along with the administering of one or more self-report measures. Keep in mind that the goal of this type of assessment interview, like the assessment of other types of problems, is to help decide what, if any, additional action needs to be taken by the clinician or client, such as the following:

- Completing standardized self-report questionnaire(s)
- Maintaining a self-monitoring log, diary, or journal
- Referral to drug counselor or specialist
- Informing parents if the client is a minor (see Chapter 2)

Table 12.1 Substance Abuse Screening Questions

1. Do you sometimes drink wine, beer or other alcoholic beverages?[1]
2. *Assess quantity:* How often do you drink/use/smoke in a day/week?
3. What is the most you have ever had in one day?
4. When you begin (drinking, smoking, using) how many _____ (drinks, joints, etc.) do you have?
5. *Assess whether drug usage has led to any problems: interpersonal, physical, legal, financial, etc.:* Has anyone ever been concerned about your (drug/alcohol) use?
6. *If the answer to 5 is yes, then ask,* What is/was their concern? or What does _____ (spouse, parent, boss, friend, and so on) think about your drug/alcohol use?
7. *Assess attempts to control usage:* Have there ever been times when you tried to stop or cut down your _____?[2]
8. Have you ever gotten help for your _____ (drinking, smoking, etc.)?[3]
9. Have you ever gotten arrested or had legal trouble because of your _____ (specific drug)?
10. Have you ever passed out or blacked out from too much _____?
11. Have you ever needed medical help because of your _____ (specific drug)?
12. When do you _____ (drink, smoke, etc.) the most? When do you do it the least?

[1]National Institute on Alcohol and Alcoholism Clinician's Guide initial screening question
[2] Similar to the first question on the CAGE (see Standardized Measures section)
[3]Similar to question 25 on the Drug Abuse Screening Test (see Standardized Measures section). Can also inquire about specific types of help (hospitalization, doctor appointment, mental health clinic).

- Brief intervention (1–2 sessions of providing information or advice, motivational interviewing, teaching behavior skills)
- Brief treatment (time-limited substance abuse treatment with either cognitive–behavioral or motivation enhancement therapy)
- Medically managed detox, outpatient or residential
- Long-term treatment (individual, group, and/or family therapy), or self-help (AA/NA, Rational Recovery, Smart Recovery)

The decision about what type of further intervention or assessment to suggest is just as important, if not more so, in the case of suspected substance use disorders as with other psychiatric disorders. Studies have shown that matching the appropriate level of treatment to the severity of the alcohol-related problems significantly improves treatment outcomes (Green, Worden, Menges, & McGrady, 2008). The research on the relationship between level of treatment, problem severity, and treatment outcome for other substances is less straightforward, however. That is, the research on matching the level of treatment to the severity of the usage with illicit drugs, marijuana being one exception, is less substantial than alcohol use studies and has yielded mixed results: a few positive, some negative, and some no-difference. Despite this varied research literature, a screening followed by brief intervention or referral for treatment for those identified at moderate to high risk for abuse or dependence is now a public health model and a standard of care for the identification and treatment of any substance use disorder (Babor et al., 2007). This model promotes ongoing risk assessment and follow-up in order to match the level of risk with the appropriate level of intervention.

SUBSTANCE ABUSE SCREENING MEASURES

A range of standardized substance abuse assessment measures are available but it is those designed for screening purposes that helping professionals are likely to find advantageous in identifying the presence of substance abuse disorders in community, college, mental health, and primary care settings. A screening tool is one that identifies individuals who are at risk for having a targeted problem or disorder, in this case a substance use disorder, based on a score that has been demonstrated to have predictive validity. Screening methods have evolved significantly in the field of substance abuse over the past three decades, from measures that were developed to see if they could accurately identify those individuals who had already been diagnosed and were considered "active cases" to instruments intended to detect individuals who are at risk for a substance use disorder (Babor et al., 2007). Beyond screening measures there are a wealth of instruments designed for more comprehensive and specific evaluations and problems. Examples of those include questionnaires and inventories designed to assess the following: cravings, drug history, drinking patterns, negative consequences of usage, readiness to changes, attitudes toward treatment, relapse situations, other situational factors, and treatment outcomes (Adesso, Cisler, Larus, & Hayes, 2004; Green et al., 2008). Depending upon the instrument, it can be used for either a specific drug (e.g., alcohol or marijuana) or multiple substances. Six widely used, researched, and recommended screening tools for alcohol and other drug use are CAGE, a four-item questionnaire for alcohol use; *Michigan Alcohol Screening Test* (MAST) and its multiple versions; *Alcohol Use Disorders Identification Test* (AUDIT); the *Drug Abuse Screening Test* (DAST); the *Drug Use Screening Inventory-Revised* (DUSI-R), a relatively lengthy but comprehensive self-report measure; and the *Substance Abuse Subtle Screening Inventory*—3rd Edition (SASSI-3).

	Table 12.2 Screening Measures			
Name	**Focus[1]**	**Format[2]**	**# Items**	**Timeframe**
AUDIT	AlU, patterns of use, dependence symptoms, adults	Q, mult	10/5/3	past year
CAGE	AlU, negative consequences, adults	I & Q	4	lifetime
DAST	msubs, adults & adolescents, social, legal, & medical problems, efforts to cut down or stop	Q	28/10	lifetime
DUSI-R	msubs, validity and lie scale, adults & adolescents	I	140	current/life
GAIN	adults & adolescents, substance abuse scale part of biopsychosocial Patterns of use, problem, risk situations	I, mult	varies*	past month, past 90 days, lifetime
MAST	AlU & msub version; severity of Use, negative consequences, adults, adolescents, elderly	Q, mult	25/10	current, lifetime
SASSI-3	msubs; dependence, and indirect adolescent	version Q	93	lifetime, past 6 month; 6 months before or after critical event

[1]The specific focus and intended population: AlU = alcohol use; msubs = multiple substances
[2]I = interview; Q = self-report questionnaire; mult = multiple versions exist; * = number of questions (depends on positive responses to questions)

In addition, the *Global Appraisal of Individual Needs* (GAIN) is commonly used and well recommended, but it is a lengthy semistructured interview. Each questionnaire or interview has its advantages and disadvantages depending upon the drug, purpose (e.g., assessing current vs. lifetime usage or screening for abuse vs. dependence), and setting and population (e.g., adolescents, adults, elderly). The ones reviewed and compared in Table 12.2 have received multiple and enthusiastic endorsements as general purpose screening tools for alcohol and other substance use disorders. The SASSI-3 has been the subject of more criticism and debate than the others but is included here because of its continued popularity among counseling professionals as well as its unique features.

Alcohol Use Measures

CAGE The CAGE is a four-item questionnaire, and the letters *C, A, G,* and *E* serve as a prompt for the interview questions (Cut down, Annoyed, Guilty, and Eye-opener) (Ewing, 1984). It is designed for screening alcohol abuse and dependency in primary care and community mental health settings. It is one of the more popular alcohol abuse screening tools and consists of the following four questions:

1. Have you ever tried to **C**ut down on your drinking?
2. Have people **A**nnoyed you by criticizing your drinking?
3. Have you ever felt bad or **G**uilty about your drinking?
4. Have you ever had a drink first thing in the morning to settle your nerves or to get rid of a hangover? (**E**ye-opener)

The questions are administered as part of a clinical interview, and they are intended to assess the consequences of drinking rather than the quantity. Any affirmative response ("yes," "sometimes," or "often") is given 1 point. Using a cutoff score of 1 (i.e., answering yes to just one question), the CAGE was found to have adequate sensitivity and specificity (Green et al., 2008). *Sensitivity* is a measure of a test's ability to correctly identify those having the problem or disorder, and *specificity* the ability of the test to identify those who do not have a problem (see Chapter 7). Keep in mind that a positive screen does not necessarily mean that the individual meets the diagnostic criteria for an alcohol use disorder (i.e., a false positive), and conversely, a negative screen could be a false negative, meaning the individual could be found to have an alcohol use disorder based on more extensive evaluation. A clinician always needs to weigh the costs and benefits of using particular cutoff scores in particular settings with specific populations. The sensitivity and specificity of the CAGE has varied depending upon gender and age and setting. Its sensitivity and specificity has been adequate with primary care populations but somewhat less so with college students, certain female groups, and the elderly (Culberson, 2006; Dhalla & Kopec, 2007). Its brevity and ability to accurately identify those with and without alcohol problems in outpatient settings is what has made it such a popular screening tool. As a screening tool it is not designed to assess other aspects of alcohol abuse and dependence such as bingeing, other consequences, readiness to change, and so on.

MICHIGAN ALCOHOL SCREENING TEST (MAST)   The *Michigan Alcohol Screening Test* (MAST), one of the oldest substance abuse screening measures (Selzer, 1971), is designed to assess the severity of and insight about both current alcohol and lifetime usage. Over the past four decades several other versions have been developed: Brief Mast (10 items) (Pokorny, Miller, Kaplan, 1972); Geriatric Version (MAST-G, 24 items) (Blow, 1991); and the MAST/AD for alcohol and drugs (Westermeyer, Yargic, & Thuras, 2004). The original MAST consists of 25 yes/no items; the majority of which ask if the person has ever experienced physical and health, social and interpersonal, and legal consequences because of alcohol use. A few items pertain to control over current drinking. The MAST uses a weighted scoring system, and the higher the score, the more severe the alcohol problem. Both hand and computer scoring is available. It can be completed in just a few minutes. The MAST is available at ***www.projectcork.org***. Sample questions include:

Have you ever attended a meeting of Alcoholics Anonymous (AA)?

Have you ever gone to anyone for help about your drinking?

Have you ever been in a hospital because of your drinking?

Those three items are given 5 points if answered yes, and are the only 5-point items; the remaining ones are scored 1 or 2. Questions 9, 20, and 21 are also included in the Brief MAST along with seven other 2-point items such as "Do friends or relatives think you are a normal drinker?" Scores on the MAST range from 0 to 53, with scores of 5 or greater suggesting alcohol dependence (Hedlund & Vieweg, 1984).

The MAST was developed, however, prior to the DSM-IV, when the DSM conceptualization of dependence was more narrowly defined as consisting of either withdrawal or tolerance. It has been found to have good psychometric qualities. Its internal consistency reliability, test–retest reliability, and validity for screening for alcohol abuse in many different populations ranges from adequate to excellent (Green et al., 2008). On the other hand, its usefulness has been questioned when assessing clients who are highly defensive or motivated to deny alcohol problems such as those involved with the legal system (Laux, Newman, & Brown, 2004; Otto & Hall, 1998). If a clinician does suspect a high degree of minimization or denial with the client, then another substance abuse assessment tool and/or a measure of client defensiveness would be helpful. The SASSI-3, which will be discussed shortly, is one such measure.

The *Michigan Assessment Screening Test/Alcohol-Drug* (MAST/AD) is a modified version of the MAST in which the phrase "or drug use" or "use drugs" is added to each item (Westermeyer et al., 2004). This modified version enables the clinician to use one brief measure for any type of substance use with little additional time to complete than the original MAST. Furthermore, the clinician would not need to rely on two or more separate screening measures if alcohol *and* other substances are a concern. Although the MAST/AD was found to correlate highly with other measures, its utility as a screening measure in clinical settings where substance abuse has not already been identified was not demonstrated (Westermeyer et al., 2004).

***ALCOHOL USE DISORDERS IDENTIFICATION TEST* (AUDIT)** The *Alcohol Use Disorders Identification Test* (AUDIT) is a 10-item, multiple-choice questionnaire developed by the World Health Organization (WHO) in 1989 as a screening tool for excessive alcohol consumption, dependence symptoms, and loss of control (Babor, Higgins-Biddle, Saunders, & Monteiro, 2001). It is designed for use in various settings, including primary care, inpatient and outpatient mental health, emergency, and workplace. It can be given either as a self-report questionnaire or as a structured interview and can be completed within 3 minutes. There is also a 3-item version, the AUDIT-C, which contains the first three consumption questions of the full audit related to binge and risky drinking and has been validated with veteran and primary care populations (Bradley et al., 2007). The AUDIT-C was found to be as effective as the full AUDIT and the CAGE in accurately identifying alcohol abuse in a large representative primary care population. Unlike the CAGE and MAST, the AUDIT measures the frequency and quantity of alcohol consumption. In addition, the questions pertaining to control and dependency have a one-year time frame, as opposed to an unlimited time frame in the case of the MAST.

Each version of the AUDIT has a 5-point scoring system for each question ranging from 0 to 4 for a maximum possible score of 40 on the full AUDIT. The cutoff score is 8 on the AUDIT for indicating a "strong likelihood" of alcohol abuse (Babor et al., 2001). Others have suggested using lower cutoff scores and different ones for males (4) and females (2), or using the AUDIT-C in outpatient community populations when wanting to accurately identify those with alcohol use disorders in the past year (Bradley et al., 2007). The WHO has recommended using the following four levels of risk zones along with suggested interventions:

- Level 1: 0–7 points—Intervention: Alcohol education
- Level 2: 8–15 points—Intervention: Simple advice
- Level 3: 16–19 points—Intervention: Simple advice plus brief counseling and continued monitoring
- Level 4: 20 and above—Intervention: Referral evaluation of alcohol dependence (Babor et al., 2001, p. 22).

WHO recognizes that these zones are guidelines, which will vary some depending upon the country and definitions of standard drinks and other information the clinician may have about the individual undergoing the screening.

The AUDIT is in the public domain and can be obtained from WHO at ***http://www.who.int/substance_abuse/publications/alcohol/en/index.html*** or ***www.projectcork.org***. Sample questions include the following:

- How often do you have a drink containing alcohol?
  (Never, monthly or less, 2 to 4 times a month, 2 to 3 times a week, 4 or more times a week)

- How often do you have 6 or more standard drinks on one occasion?
  (Never, less than monthly, monthly, weekly, daily or almost daily)

- How often during the last year have you failed to do what was normally expected of you because of your drinking?
  (Never, less than monthly, monthly, weekly, daily or almost daily)

Like the CAGE, the AUDIT or AUDIT-C can be easily woven into a clinical interview or intake assessment and readily scored. It has been shown to have excellent sensitivity and specificity in various adult populations, including geriatric, college, and community and has been adopted as an international screening test for alcohol abuse and dependence (Babor et al. 2001). It is also the recommended self-report screening measure to be used by primary care and mental health professionals either alone or in combination with a screening interview (HHS, NIH, & NIAAA, 2009). On the other hand, it is not designed to assess for alcohol use disorders over one's lifetime, but just within the past year. Furthermore, like the CAGE and the MAST, its usefulness is limited for those individuals who are likely to minimize or deny consumption and consequences of abuse because of the straightforward nature of the questions.

General Substance Use Measures

DRUG ABUSE SCREENING TEST **(DAST)**   The *Drug Abuse Screening Test* (DAST), a modification of the MAST, is a self-report screening measure for any type of substance use disorder, including alcohol. The DAST (Skinner, 1982), developed at the Addiction Research Foundation in Toronto, consists of 28 items focused on the social and legal consequences of usage rather than frequency and quantity. But it does assess drug use in the past year and inability to control usage as well. There are also briefer (10-item, 20-item) and adolescent versions (Yudko, Lozhkina, & Fouts, 2007). The 28-item DAST can be completed in 5 to 10 minutes and can be also administered by interview. Each item is answered yes/no, and all but three yes items are scored 1 point for a total score ranging from 0 to 28. A cutoff score of 6 has been typically used to indicate a drug abuse or dependence problem (Yudko et al., 2007).

Sample items include the following:

- Do you ever feel bad about your drug use?
- Have you engaged in illegal activities to obtain drugs?
- Have you ever experienced withdrawal symptoms as a result of heavy drug intake?

A literature review of studies evaluating the psychometric properties of all versions of the DAST found that all four versions had excellent reliabilities—internal consistency and test–retest—and high sensitivity and specificity for use in clinical practice (Yudko et al., 2007). The DAST can also be obtained at ***www.projectcork.org*** or from the author at ***Harvey.skinner@utoronto.ca***.

DRUG USE SCREENING INVENTORY—REVISED (DUSI-R)   The *Drug Use Screening Inventory—Revised* (DUSI-R) is a relatively long self-report measure, 140 yes/no items, and like the GAIN (discussed next), assesses domains other than substance abuse, including health, psychiatric disorders, school and work adjustment, interpersonal and family functioning (Tarter & Kirisci, 1997). It is one of only two self-report measures of substance use that contains a validity check and lie scale. This is an important feature since individuals with substance abuse problems may deny or minimize their frequency and quantity of use as well as the consequences. The DUSI-R has good psychometric properties and is designed to identify individuals who will benefit from more in-depth evaluation.

GLOBAL APPRAISAL OF INDIVIDUAL NEEDS—INITIAL (GAIN)   The *Global Appraisal of Individual Needs—Initial* (GAIN-I) is a semistructured biopsychosocial, evidenced-based interview that covers eight core areas including substance use, and is designed for adolescents and adults in a variety of inpatient and outpatient settings (Dennis, White, Titus, & Unsicker, 2008). Developed originally between 1993 and 1995, the GAIN-I is now in its fifth version with more detailed coverage of substance usage. In addition to substance usage it assesses the following domains: Physical health, Risk behaviors, Mental Health, Legal issues, and Family/Living situation. It comprises over 100 subscales. Paper and computer administrations are available and can take approximately one to two hours to complete, depending upon whether the "core" GAIN or full GAIN is used. There are, however, two briefer versions: the GAIN-SS (Short Screener) with 20 items, which is designed to identify individuals with a DSM-IV diagnosis including substance use disorder, and the GAIN-Quick (Q) (Dennis et al., 2008). The GAIN-Q can be self-administered or used as an interview and the self-administered version can be completed within 20 minutes. A Spanish language version of the full GAIN is also available. All versions can be downloaded from Chestnut Health Systems at *www.chestnut.org/li/gain*.

The substance use section covers alcohol, marijuana, heroin, cocaine, amphetamines, tobacco, and other drugs, and assesses self-reported frequency use (i.e., lifetime, past month, and past 90 days); most recent use; highest quantity ever and past 90 days; number of days with problems from substance use withdrawal symptoms and the consequences of those symptoms; where substances were used (e.g., work, home, or school) and with whom (e.g., family, friends, or coworkers); lifetime treatment episodes; and reasons for quitting. There are five substance usage and related scales: Substance Frequency, Substance Problem scale—Lifetime, Current Withdrawal scale, Treatment Resistance, and Treatment Motivation. The GAIN-I begins with a screening for cognitive impairment, which is helpful when assessing individuals who may have had heavy and prolonged substance usage. Sample questions include the following:

- During the past 90 days on how many days did you **go without using any** alcohol, marijuana, or other drugs?
- During the past 90 days what is the **most days** you have gone in a row without using alcohol, marijuana, or other drugs?
- During the past 90 days did you use alcohol or other drugs while or within an hour prior to . . . (*Six activities are listed, such as "being at a paid job or work."*)

The GAIN-I has undergone considerable research in substance abuse treatment facilities and outpatient clinics. Its most recent norms (2008) are based on over 2,000 adults and 16,000 adolescents, though only the adolescent sample includes racial–ethnicity breakdowns and it is unclear how closely they match the latest U.S. Census data (Modisette, Hunter, Ives, Funk, & Dennis, 2009). The internal consistency and test–retest reliabilities for the overall GAIN-I and specific scales range from good to excellent. The GAIN-I has been validated in numerous studies of adolescents and adults (Dennis et al., 2008). Adolescents' self-report of frequency of substance usage correlated significantly with "family members and others" reports as well as biological markers such as urine analysis. In an adult outpatient and residential, predominantly African American sample, self-report of frequency of usage correlated moderately with biological markers (urine and saliva) for opiates and cocaine, less so for marijuana (Dennis et al., 2003).

Because of its depth and breadth, the GAIN-I is more often used for research purposes or as part of a diagnostic evaluation in substance abuse treatment facilities where the co-occurrence of substance use disorders and other Axis I disorders is very prevalent. Clearly it is the most comprehensive instrument of the ones reviewed in this chapter. The abbreviated version could be used as a screening tool in other types of mental health settings. The main limitation of the GAIN-I is the time required to complete it and therefore the added cost relative to briefer and equally efficient screening measures.

SUBSTANCE ABUSE SUBTLE SCREENING INVENTORY—THIRD EDITION (SASSI-3)   The *Substance Abuse Subtle Screening Inventory*—Third Edition (SASSI-3) is a self-report questionnaire for adults ages 18 and older with a 3.2-grade reading level and takes approximately 15 minutes to complete (Miller, 1999). It is designed to identify individuals who have a high probability of having a substance dependence disorder but are not necessarily going to openly acknowledge usage and symptoms. There are also adolescent (ages 12 to 18) and Spanish versions (for adults 18 and older with a fifth-grade reading level) of the SASSI-3. The first version of SASSI was published in 1985 and the third came out 14 years later. The SASSI-3 is unique among the substance abuse self-report questionnaires described in this section in its use of questions that are not directly related to substance usage but are predictive of substance dependence in individuals who are not forthcoming about their usage and symptoms (Lazowsi, Miller, Boye, & Miller, 1998). The development of the third edition was based on a need to remove two objectionable items from the second edition, while at the same time maintain and improve the test's predictive accuracy (Lazowski et al., 1998).

The SASSI-3 consists of two parts: 67 true–false items that are not directly related to substance usage and 26 face-valid or direct questions about alcohol and other drug use. The alcohol and other drug questions can be answered based on one of four time frames: entire lifetime, past six months, or six months before or after a critical event. The manual, however, recommends using the lifetime option (Miller, 1999). It comprises the following scales: Face Valid Alcohol, Face Valid Other Drugs, Symptoms, Obvious Attributes, Subtle Attributes, Defensiveness, Supplemental Addiction Measure, Family vs. Controls, and Correctional. There is also a scale to detect random responding. The Subtle Attributes, Defensiveness, and Supplemental Addiction scales complement one another in identifying individuals who deny, minimize, or lie about their usage in various ways. From a technical standpoint, it is a solid instrument. It has very good internal reliability (alpha = 0.93) and stability (test–retest coefficients ranged from 0.92 to 1.00 in a small sample of 40) (Lazowski et al., 1998).

The SASSI-3's purported predictive accuracy has been seen as its major benefit. The initial validation study, using a sample in which 35% of the group came from treatment settings for substance abuse and dependence, found a 97% sensitivity rate and 95% specificity rate (Lazowski et al., 1998). That is, the SASSI-3 correctly identified 97% of the sample as having substance use dependence, and it identified as not having dependence 95% of those who did not meet criteria for that disorder. Those statistics look impressive but the accuracy of the SASSI-3 may not be as good in settings where the base rate of substance dependency is much less. Although the validation sample included other settings where substance use disorders are not the primary focus of treatment, the base rate of substance use disorders in those settings—general psychiatric hospital, vocational rehabilitation, and sex offender treatment programs—is also high. The improvement in diagnostic accuracy that any test can provide beyond what a clinician might achieve using an informal assessment method is a function of the base rate of the disorder in the population, as was discussed in Chapter 7. Some reviewers and researchers have suggested that the diagnostic accuracy of SASSI-3 may be more limited in populations where the base rate of substance dependence is much lower and no better than the other measures described earlier (Feldstein & Miller, 2007; Fernandez, 2001; Pittenger, 2001). Therefore, they have argued that this may call into question the need for a relatively long substance use assessment measure that focuses on individuals who are more apt to be defensive and dishonest when shorter, straight-forward measures like the CAGE, AUDIT, or DAST will suffice. In fact, Feldstein and Miller (2007) concluded that there is a pretty high correlation between those measures and the SASSI-3. On the other hand, if a clinician has reason to suspect that a client may be inclined to respond to substance use questionnaires in a defensive or dishonest fashion, then the SASSI-3 may prove to be very helpful (Lazowski & Miller, 2007). Notwithstanding this scholarly debate over the SASSI-3's utility, it is important to keep in mind that it, like other measures, is really meant to be a screening tool and not by itself a diagnostic one.

Screening and Brief Intervention for Tanya

Melanie elected to use the AUDIT, full version, with Tanya for the following reasons: 1) it is highly recommended as an alcohol use disorder's screening tool in mental health settings; 2) it is brief and readily scored and interpreted; 3) the clinical interview indicated alcohol was the primary substance use problem; nicotine use, though heavy, was causing fewer immediate negative consequences; and 4) Tanya's acknowledgment of how much alcohol she was consuming and treatment history suggested she might be alcohol dependent (see Practice Suggestion: Guidelines for using Substance Usage Screening Measures). The AUDIT contains questions designed to identify those with dependence symptoms: efforts to cut down, role impairment, and cravings. Melanie elected to incorporate a standardized measure into her assessment, even though further interviewing might have obtained the necessary information to differentiate abuse from dependence, because Tanya was minimizing the severity of her usage and the negative consequences for herself. "My father was an alcoholic and I'm not like him," she stated. Nor did she feel her drinking affected her like it did other people in her life, including past boyfriends. As the intake interview was drawing to a close, Melanie raised with Tanya the possibility of her filling out a questionnaire that could help both of them better understand how her usage was affecting her and how it compared to others who have received counseling for alcohol problems. Melanie stated, "Given what we've talked about so far with your history and your drinking, I'm thinking it would be also helpful to have you fill out a short questionnaire that could help both of us better understand how you are doing, how your drinking compares with lots of others who have gotten help, and what would be some counseling options. Is that something you would be interested in doing?" A test score could show Tanya how she was doing compared to others and this normative type of information might help her see that her reference group, family and friends, was a biased group, and might also help her resolve her ambivalence about drinking. Tanya agreed to complete the AUDIT. She scored 23 on the AUDIT, well beyond a score of 8, which indicates an alcohol abuse disorder is very likely. She was told that individuals who do not have problems with alcohol usually score below 8. Tanya agreed to follow up with the clinic's substance abuse

PRACTICE SUGGESTION
Guidelines for Using Substance Use Screening Measures

- Begin using a very brief screening tool that can be readily scored and interpreted such as the CAGE, AUDIT, or brief versions of the MAST or DAST.
- Consider the purpose for conducting a standardized assessment: evaluate history of use, assess current usage, identify interpersonal, physical, emotional, or legal consequences of usage, or a combination of these reasons.
- Given that many clients find this a sensitive topic and may be defensive, provide a rationale for the screening that may enhance compliance and honest responding.
- If you have reason to suspect that a client may respond in a guarded, distorted, or dishonest fashion, consider using the SASSI-3.
- Consider the screening as an intervention: a client's willingness to take part in it may suggest that he or she is at least in the contemplation stage of change by virtue of wanting to learn more about his or her usage and associated problems relative to others.
- Provide feedback to the client about a continuum of use and what the screening tool says about where along the continuum he or she falls.
- Tailor the next intervention to where the client is at along both a readiness-for-change and substance usage continuum.
- Consider using longer, more comprehensive measures if the initial screening is suggestive of abuse or dependence.
- Gather client feedback about the suggested next steps (e.g., more intensive evaluation, brief psychoeducational sessions, referral to AA, individual or group counseling, or more intensive treatment).

counselor for further evaluation and possible treatment but that appointment would not occur for another two weeks. The counselor agreed to see her one or two more times prior to that appointment for a brief psychoeducational intervention. This involved going over her list of pros and cons about continued drinking, hearing further her concerns about AA, educating her about other types of interventions, and providing her information about coping with anxiety and how alcohol can affect her rages and interfere with her prescribed sleeping aid.

Additional Measures

A variety of additional general substance abuse and alcohol-specific measures have been developed for diagnostic, case conceptualization, and treatment planning and monitoring purposes. Given the staggering economic, social, and personal costs of substance use disorders, documenting treatment outcome and effectiveness via standardized measures has become a high priority not just for researchers but mainstream clinical practice as well. A list of those measures along with their purpose and format can be found in Table 12.3. Some of these measures can be used with relatively little training while others require considerably more training than the measures reviewed here. Although there are dozens of more comprehensive diagnostic measures than Table 12.3 contains, they are rarely used outside of research studies because of the additional time, training, and costs required relative to screening measures (Adesso et al., 2004).

Table 12.3 Additional Substance Abuse & Dependence Measures

Name	Focus	Format[1]	Items
Alcohol only:			
Alcohol Abstinence Self-Efficacy Scale*	Relapse situations	Questionnaire	40
Alcohol Dependence Scale	Diagnosis	Questionnaire	25
Alcohol Urge Questionnaire	Cravings	Questionnaire	8
Drinker Inventory of Consequences	Negative consequences	Questionnaire or Interview	15/50
Fast Alcohol Screening Test (FAST)	Screening	Interview	4
Form-90 (Quick)	Drinking patterns	Interview	10
Recovery Attitude and Treatment Evaluator	Readiness for change level of care	Interview	35
Short Inventory of Problems	Negative consequences	Questionnaire	15
Stages of Change Readiness & Treatment Eagerness Scale (SOCRATES)	Readiness for change	Questionnaire	39
Timeline Followback Treatment History	Drinking patterns	Interview	Varies
TWEAK (CAGE + 1)	Screening	Interview	5
Multiple substances:			
Addiction Severity Index	Case conceptualization	Interview	133
Drug Taking Confidence Questionnaire			
Form 90 Comprehensive Timeline of Alcohol & Other Drug Use	Treatment monitoring	Interview	58
Inventory of Drug Use Consequences	Negative consequences	Questionnaire	50
Inventory of Drug Taking Situations	Self-efficacy in high-risk situations	Questionnaire	50
Short Inventory of Alcohol and Drugs (SIP-AD)	Dependence, adverse consequences	Questionnaire	15

*Self-efficacy is the belief that my actions can produce a desired outcome (e.g., refrain from drinking in a specific situation).

Cultural Considerations when Using Screening Measures

Definitions of what constitutes substance abuse and dependence are inextricably related to societal norms and customs (Fals-Stewart & Klostermann, 2008). Therefore, the cultural beliefs, values, and practices regarding any kind of substance one is exposed to will impact not only the use of various substances but how one responds to assessment questions regarding that behavior. Furthermore, definitions of what constitutes a typical amount of alcohol or other substances and what is considered a harmful or adverse reaction will also vary from culture to culture. To complicate matters, many individuals may identify themselves as having multiple ethnic identities and varying levels of acculturation into the majority culture and enculturation into minority groups. The existing research, however, on the relationship between acculturation–enculturation status and substance dependence is very limited (Blume, Morera, & de la Cruz, 2008).

The cross-cultural applications of substance abuse screening measures, although progressing over the past 25 years, are not yet on a par with the work that has been done on the cultural utility of other types of tests and measures covered in earlier chapters. The validity of substance use screening measures with different ethnic, racial, and other cultural groups depends in part on the normative sample the measure was developed on, and part on subsequent research with specific minority groups. Therefore, specific measures vary in their applicability for different racial–ethnic groups. On the one hand, the SASSI-3 was validated on a sample that was 20% Black and 6% Hispanic (Lazowski et al., 1998); on the other hand, the MAST was not normed on a representative sample and subsequent research has found it may have limited applicability for minorities in general (Piazza, Martin, & Dildine, 2000). In addition, one study concluded that the Short-MAST is not a valid screening tool for some American Indian tribes (Robin et al., 2004).

Although some measures have been translated into Spanish and other non-English languages, specific concepts used on an English language version may not exist in other languages and cultures. One example of this is the concept of "craving," which does not translate readily into Spanish, and many individuals of Mexican descent do not comprehend that idea (Blume et al., 2008). Although cravings are not asked about on the brief measures reviewed earlier, it is a concept that could be introduced in an interview, and is specifically assessed with certain standardized measures such as the *Alcohol Craving Questionnaire* and the *Penn Alcohol Craving Scale* (Cooney, Kadden, & Steinberg, 2008).

Among the measures reviewed in this chapter the research is mixed with regard to their cross-cultural utility. Only the AUDIT was developed with the aim of using it globally, but it is limited to alcohol use. The AUDIT was validated on groups of primary care patients from six different countries: Australia, Bulgaria, Kenya, Mexico, Norway, and the United States. Subsequent research has found that by adjusting the cutoff score of 8, mentioned earlier, it can be a highly sensitive tool for detecting problematic alcohol use in various populations (Babor et al., 2001). Although other measures have been translated into Spanish and other languages, several problems have been noted in general with translated standardized assessments for addictive behaviors: weaker psychometric properties, difficult-to-understand items, and changes in meaning from the English version (Blume et al., 2008). For example, a study assessing high-risk drinking in pregnant females using a Portuguese version of the CAGE found that its internal reliability was weaker than the English version (Moraes, Viellas, & Reichenheim, 2005). Given the concerns that have been raised about ethnic minorities in the United States not receiving adequate treatment for substance use problems (Lowman & Le Fauve, 2003; NIDA, 2007; Tucker, 1985), it is likely that ongoing research will continue regarding the applicability of screening measures for various cultural groups in order to improve methods for identifying those in need of treatment and providing culturally sensitive interventions.

Summary and Conclusions

Although many helping professionals may not consider themselves primarily substance abuse specialists, it is essential that all kinds of counselors become familiar with substance use disorders' screening tools. Individuals who present in mental health, college counseling, and EAP settings are much more likely than the general population to be at risk for, or already experiencing, some kind of substance use disorder. Therefore, knowledge of the spectrum of assessment tools available—from simple screening measures to comprehensive diagnostic interview schedules and specific problem assessments, (e.g., negative consequences of drug usage)—is essential for any type of helping professional to possess. This chapter focused on screening measures that require minimal training to use, are available for free, and can be downloaded from several websites. Some of the measures reviewed are relatively brief (10 items or less); they are all psychometrically sound with good sensitivity and specificity for many different populations; and do not require special user qualifications to score and interpret. The 10-item AUDIT is one such measure that has been translated into non-English languages and has become the international gold standard for screening of alcohol abuse and dependence. With the exception of the AUDIT, the cross-cultural research of these screening measures lags behind older traditional personality and mental health tests. Additional self-report measures designed to assess specific aspects of a substance use problem (e.g., relapse situations) are also available but often require more advanced training to score and interpret.

Clinical lore would suggest that client self-reports about substance usage, whether obtained from interviews or standardized measures, are often distorted. There appears to be a widespread belief amongst clinicians that individuals with substance abuse problems tend to deny or minimize the frequency, quantity, and negative consequences of using psychoactive drugs. How pervasive an issue this is may be more myth than reality. Accurate client self-reports can be obtained under certain conditions: 1) confidentiality is assured, 2) the clinician emphasizes the importance of honest responding and uses clear and straightforward questions, 3) the client is not under the influence of alcohol at the time of the assessment, and 4) biological markers are obtained (Adesso et al., 2004). Similar concerns about the validity of client self-reports have been raised with adolescents but there is mounting evidence supporting the use of interview and standardized self-report measures with this population (Winters, Newcomb, & Fahnhorst, 2004). The clinician's ability to use interview techniques discussed in Chapters 3 and 4 for substance use problems will enhance the usefulness of standardized screening measures.

Reflection Questions and Experiential Exercises

1. What views do you hold about drug consumption? Do your views differ depending upon the drug? What are your values, beliefs, and attitudes about drug consumption for recreational or treatment purposes?
2. How open do you think clients will be when interviewed about drug consumption? Do you think clients will be more honest about drug consumption during an interview or in response to a questionnaire? Why might there be a difference?
3. What is the difference between a screening and a diagnostic measure for substance use disorders?
4. Obtain a copy of one of the measures reviewed (all are in the public domain) and in small groups review the items and discuss the advantages and limitations of that measure.
5. In groups of three, role-play a substance abuse/dependence screening interview for a few minutes. Have one person be an observer, one the client, and one the counselor. Process the role play when completed by having the observer give feedback to the counselor about which questions were asked and how they were posed (e.g., open vs. closed, time frame included vs. not included).

13 ASSESSMENT OF INTELLECTUAL AND COGNITIVE ABILITIES AND ACHIEVEMENT

Chapter Objectives

After reading this chapter, you should be able to:

■ Understand various theoretical perspectives on intelligence and cognitive abilities.

■ Identify common intelligence, cognitive ability, and achievement tests.

■ Explain how common intelligence and achievement tests are used and what they can reveal about a person's cognitive functioning.

■ Identify the features of commonly used intelligence and achievement tests and their cultural limitations.

Joshua, an 8-year-old second-grade student, came to the attention of his school's special education team because he had made marginal progress in understanding what he was reading, despite intensive specialized reading instruction. In the spring of second grade his reading comprehension was still at a first-grade level and his parents had become increasingly concerned about his lack of progress. Joshua was described by both his first- and second-grade teachers as a "quiet, shy" boy who "never caused any problems in the classroom" but would often complain of "stomachaches" and other vague somatic concerns in the morning around the time reading instruction would begin. His second-grade teacher shared with Joshua's parents her concern that Joshua seemed to have a lot of difficulty paying attention and got distracted easily. She thought he should be evaluated for ADD and suggested the parents contact Joshua's pediatrician. Dr. Jones, Joshua's pediatrician, gave Joshua's mother the *Conners' Rating Scales* for her and the teacher to complete. Based on the results of the Conners' and Joshua's developmental and school history, Dr. Jones helped the parents get in touch with the special education team and requested that an evaluation of Joshua's learning style and cognitive abilities be done.

Joshua's parents divorced when he was in kindergarten and he lives primarily with his mother and her current boyfriend. The parents have a cooperative relationship and Joshua visits with his father on Wednesday evenings and weekends. His mother is a college graduate who found school to be easy. She works full-time as a bank manager. His father, on the other hand, struggled through school and ended up getting a GED. He works part-time in construction. Joshua has a 4-year-old brother.

Joshua was described by his mother as "the perfect baby" who was "easygoing and never fussy." He reached his developmental milestones on time and his parents and pediatrician did not have any concerns about Joshua until he entered kindergarten. Joshua ended up repeating kindergarten because he had problems with following and remembering directions, attention span, and learning the alphabet his first year. In first grade it became apparent that he was having trouble recognizing words and his reading fluency was poor. The school then provided 30 minutes a day of small-group instruction in a new reading tutorial program.

Joshua was referred by the special education team to the school psychologist to assess what may account for his difficulties with reading comprehension. The psychologist administered the *Wechsler Intelligence Scale for Children*—Fourth Edition, the *Wechsler Individual Achievement Test*, Third Edition, the *Woodcock–Johnson-III Test of Achievement* (selected subtests) and the *Test of Word Reading Efficiency*. The results of that evaluation indicated Joshua had a wide range of cognitive abilities despite his overall intellectual functioning being in the average range. His test scores were pieces of a puzzle that were put together to gain a better understanding of why he was having difficulties with reading despite intensive, specialized instruction.

OVERVIEW

Joshua was evaluated with a traditional intelligence test and academic achievement tests to determine whether he might have a learning disability. Intelligence and achievement tests are two separate but interrelated categories of psychological tests that the majority of professional counselors and other helping professionals do not typically administer and interpret. Your understanding, however, of the basic abilities assessed by these tests will facilitate referring clients for this kind of assessment and help you and your clients to better understand and navigate this type of testing. Although many tests belong to these two categories, this chapter will focus on the intelligence and achievement tests most commonly used by counselors and psychologists.

The *Wechsler Intelligence Scale for Children*—Fourth Edition (WISC-IV), one of the tests administered to Joshua, is one example of a test from the category known as intelligence or cognitive ability tests. What types of questions, items, and tasks are included on intelligence tests like the WISC-IV? How can the results from a test like the WISC-IV be used to both better understand Joshua's academic difficulties and design educational strategies to help him learn? How do different theoretical perspectives on the nature of intelligence and cognitive abilities influence and shape the content of currently used tests? The answers to these questions will be discussed in this chapter.

The assessment of an individual's intelligence, cognitive processes, and academic aptitudes is an interrelated and complex process. Most commonly the assessment of intelligence is completed in educational settings as part of an evaluation to determine whether a student, like Joshua, has a learning disability. This type of testing is also used to evaluate whether an individual has mental retardation, or a pervasive developmental disorder, like autism or Asperger's disorder. Intelligence tests may be also used as part of other kinds of diagnostic evaluations when injury to the brain has occurred or is suspected. Brain functioning could be impacted by a head injury, a disease process like Alzheimer's, or chronic and severe substance use. Intelligence testing may also be done in community, rehabilitation, and VA settings in order to assess an individual's cognitive strengths and weaknesses for the purpose of identifying remediation strategies that can help the person function better in the workplace, home, or community. It is also conducted in forensic settings when knowledge of a client's intellectual functioning is necessary for addressing a legal question. In order to administer, score, and interpret the requisite tests used in those diagnostic evaluations, substantial training in the construct of intelligence and the specific tests are required. Therefore, all of the tests reviewed in this chapter are level C tests and should be administered, scored, and interpreted only by those with the requisite training.

Practically speaking, both intelligence and achievement tests measure cognitive abilities (Kaufman, Johnson, & Liu, 2008; McGrew, 2009; Sternberg & Kaufman, 1998) that are critical for successful academic and vocational performance. Cognitive abilities are mental traits or capacities that individuals have more or less of (Das, Naglieri, & Kirby, 1994) and are thought to be arranged in a hierarchal fashion with the broadest ability at the top and the more narrow abilities at the bottom (McGrew, 2009). Those tests labeled as intelligence tests typically assess the broad abilities and processes such as verbal and quantitative reasoning and memory, and achievement tests measure the specific abilities subsumed by those broader abilities such as reading, spelling, and math skills. Some tests, like the ones Joshua was given—the WISC-IV and the Woodcock–Johnson-III—consist of multiple subtests, some of which assess those broad abilities and others the narrow ones like vocabulary and math knowledge.

Another way to think about the interrelationship between these two types of tests is that intelligence tests are used to *predict* what someone is likely to learn, and achievement tests measure what has already been learned (Reynolds & Kaumphaus, 2003). For example, the WISC-IV is used to determine whether a child will have difficulty learning in a traditional American classroom, but also contains subtests that measures specific knowledge the child has already acquired such as vocabulary and arithmetic. Tests that are strictly achievement tests measure the knowledge in a particular subject area an individual has acquired relative to others in his or her peer group. The overlap between traditional intelligence and achievement tests has been demonstrated statistically by the very high correlation found between the overall score on the WISC-IV and scores on an achievement test: the *Wechsler Individual Achievement Test,* 2nd Edition (Kaufman, Flanagan, Alfonso, & Mascolo, 2006). You may recall from Chapter 7 that when two tests are highly correlated they are likely measuring similar but not identical constructs.

On the other hand, there are important conceptual distinctions between those tests traditionally thought of as intellectual and those that are achievement oriented. Tests belonging to the intelligence or cognitive ability category measure latent abilities; in other words, underlying abilities that are critical for successful outcomes, such as academic achievement (Gottfredson & Saklofske, 2009). To put it another way, the cognitive abilities found on intelligence tests can be considered the cause, and the specific abilities found on achievement tests are thought of as the effect, or result, of those causal abilities. Processes such as memory, perception, problem solving, and verbal and quantitative reasoning are examples of these latent or hidden abilities assessed by intelligence tests but not by most achievement tests. One important difference, therefore, between intelligence or cognitive ability tests and achievement is that the former are much broader in scope.

Intelligence and cognitive ability tests deemphasize the assessment of acquired knowledge related to specific academic subjects and stress learning with novel stimuli and information. This difference is important to recognize because successful performance on an achievement test is heavily dependent upon the knowledge set a particular culture values and teaches. On the other hand, performing well on intelligence and ability tests is more a result of underlying abilities and processes that are not quite as culturally bound. The similarities and differences between cognitive ability and achievement tests will be illuminated further as the chapter unfolds.

NATURE OF INTELLIGENCE: MULTIPLE PERSPECTIVES

An understanding of the various theories of intelligence informs one's grasp of the subtests and test items that make up intelligence or cognitive ability tests like the one Joshua was given. Intelligence is a multifaceted construct, like personality, with many definitions and no consensus about the "right" one. Despite a lack of agreement about the construct intelligence, Alfred Binet and Theodore Simon embarked on the construction of the first practical intelligence test in 1905. More than 100 years have gone by since their test was created, but multiple definitions and a lack of consensus remains.

One early definition of intelligence described it as "a fundamental faculty . . . this faculty is judgment, otherwise called good sense, practical sense, the faculty of adapting one's self to circumstances" (Matarazzo, 1972, p. 66). Other definitions included "an overall competency or global capacity which in one way or another enables a sentient individual to comprehend the world and to deal effectively with its challenges" (Wechsler, 1981, p. 8) and "the ability to solve problems or to fashion products that are valued in one or more cultural or community settings" (Gardner, 1993, p. 7). Although there is still not a consensus on how to define intelligence, these varied definitions share a common theme according to Sternberg (1997), which is adaptation to one's environment. Acting intelligently means behaving in ways that promote adaptation to one's environment.

If one's environment is a traditional American elementary school classroom, as is the case with Joshua, then having good verbal and quantitative reasoning skills would likely be adaptive. What about the ability to get along with others, regulate one's emotions, and be creative—might that be adaptive? Classrooms are filled with people who have to deal with each other and yet standardized tests of interpersonal intelligence do not yet exist. An ability test of emotional intelligence has been developed based on a four-branch model of intelligence—managing, understanding, and accurately perceiving emotions, and using emotions to facilitate thinking (Mayer, Salovey, & Caruso, 2008), but for all intents and purposes the *Mayer-Salovey-Caruso Emotional Intelligence Test* is a research work in progress and has not yet been adopted by practitioners in mental health and educational settings. The same can be said about a test of creativity, the *Torrance Tests of Creative Thinking* (Kaplan & Saccuzzo, 2005). Traditional intelligence tests do not assess practical ways in which an individual is successfully adapting to his or her environment but rather assess cognitive abilities and processes—such as verbal and quantitative reasoning, abstract thinking, working memory, problem solving, and visual–spatial reasoning—that may be indirectly related to adaptation in specific contexts. The similarities and differences in definitions and the relevant skills measured on intelligence or cognitive ability tests stem from particular theoretical conceptualizations of intellectual, cognitive, and neuropsychological abilities and functioning.

Traditionally, tests of broad cognitive abilities have been labeled as intelligence tests and produce an intelligence quotient, or IQ, score. Relative to the tests covered in this text, intelligence tests and testing has the longest history and has been fraught with significant controversy over how IQ scores have been used and misused. Tests of cognitive abilities, although there is a good deal of overlap between the two in terms of the specific skills and processes measured, do not produce IQ scores but yield scores that have a similar meaning as will be discussed later. Currently, however, some traditional "IQ" tests, such as the WISC-IV, produce both an IQ score and an overall cognitive ability score. In fact, with the latest revisions of other tests commonly thought of as IQ tests, the trend has been toward generating overall scores that are labeled as general ability scores or something similar and deemphasizing the overall IQ score. Classifications—mentally retarded, learning disabled, and gifted—are still made in many settings from the overall IQ scores on intelligence tests, however, and that is what has fomented debate and controversy about the purpose and consequences of intelligence testing.

Conceptualizations of intelligence are not unique to Western societies but Eastern perspectives have emphasized abilities such as introspective knowledge and depth of processing, which are not considered by traditional Western theories (Sternberg & Kaufman, 1998). Within Western subcultures and ethnic groups there is a good deal of variability in what are considered "intelligent" abilities, with some groups favoring cognitive abilities while others view characteristics such as communication and social skills as markers of intelligence (Neisser et al., 1996).

Traditional Western models of intelligence are based on a **factor analytic** process (see Chapter 7) and a **hierarchical** theory; newer theories are based on **information processing** models (Daniel, 1997) and some models are a hybrid of hierarchical and information processing theories. Factor analysis, as you may recall from Chapter 7, involves calculating the correlations among various tests and subtests to determine statistically which tests are related and which ones are unrelated. For example, factor analytic studies have shown that at the top of a hierarchy is overall ability; at the midlevel are abilities such as memory, verbal reasoning, and learning from novel stimuli; and at the lower level are abilities such as spelling and decoding words (see Figure 13.1) (McGrew, 2009). Intelligence and cognitive ability tests such as the *Stanford–Binet Intelligence Scales,* the *Wechsler Scales, Differential Abilities Scales* (DAS), and the *Woodcock–Johnson Tests of Cognitive Ability* are based on some type of multifactor hierarchal model of intelligence. Other tests, such as the *Kaufman Assessment Battery for Children—2nd Edition* (KABC-II) and the *Das–Naglieri Cognitive Assessment System,* are based in part on an information processing model. The KABC-II and the DAS-II are hybrid tests in that they are based on both a factor analytic and an information processing model.

Factor Analytic and Hierarchical Theories

Factor analytic theories of intelligence include the original two-factor model developed by Charles Spearman, who helped construct the statistical technique, factor analysis, and multiple factor models developed by Thorndike, Thurstone, Guilford, Vernon, and Cattell and Horn

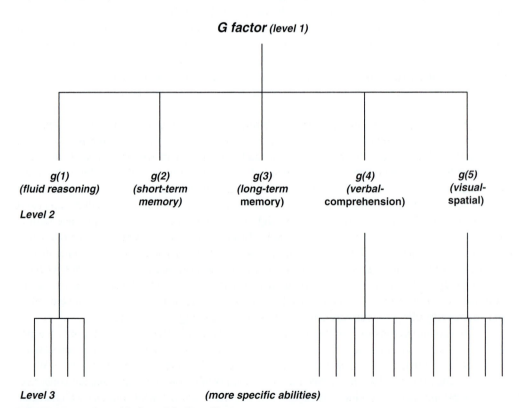

FIGURE 13.1 Hierarchical Model of Intelligence

(Sattler, 1988) and most recently Carroll (McGrew, 2009). The Cattell and Horn and Carroll models have been combined into one, the CHC model, and this model has influenced the revisions to current intelligence tests such as the WISC-IV and Stanford–Binet—Fifth Edition.

SPEARMAN'S MODEL   Spearman proposed that intelligence comprises an overarching ability, the *g factor,* and subordinate abilities or specifics, *s* factors (Sternberg & Kaufman, 1998). This is a hierarchical model (Figure 13.1) that establishes high- or broad- and low- or narrow-level intellectual skills or abilities. The *g* factor was hypothesized to be present in any type of cognitive ability. The cognitive processes Spearman thought were most highly correlated with general intelligence were abstract reasoning—the relationship between two or more ideas—deductive reasoning, judgment, and comprehension, which made up most of the original *Binet–Simon Intelligence Scales*. On the other hand, cognitive tasks having a low correlation with overall intelligence were thought to be those involving speed, visual–motor, and memory skills. Spearman's was the most parsimonious of the factor analytic theories.

GUILFORD'S MODEL   The most complex factor analytic theory was the one developed by J. P. Guilford. Guilford's Structure of Intellect Model, a revision of his original theory, is a three-dimensional model consisting of 180 elements (Guilford, 1988). According to the model there are three higher-order factors—content, operations, and products—and five to six subfactors so that any one cognitive task involves the interrelationship between three subfactors. For example, an individual could be asked to work on a visual problem (content) and perform a certain thinking operation such as recognition in order to produce a "product" (e.g., organizing colored blocks to produce a specific design [relationship between stimuli]). In revising his model, Guilford recognized the different types of memory processes involved in cognition—storage or retention and retrieval, either short or long term, and the need to separate out the "figural" content dimension into auditory and visual content. Guilford's model has been used for labeling the different types of abilities assessed by the Wechsler and Stanford–Binet tests (Kaufman, 1979).

CATTELL, HORN, AND CARROLL'S MODEL   The factor analytic theory that has had a significant impact on the development of newer intelligence tests and the revisions of traditional ones is Cattell and Horn's fluid-crystallized model (Horn, 1968; Matarazzo, 1972; McGrew, 2009). In this model, fluid intelligence represents accidental learning from novel stimuli, particularly nonverbal. Crystallized intelligence is acquired through the formal teaching of knowledge and skills—typically the kind obtained from acculturation. Examples of tests designed to measure crystallized intelligence would be ones where an individual is asked to define vocabulary words, solve arithmetic problems, or answer questions about historical and scientific information such as the Vocabulary, Arithmetic, and Information subtests on the WISC-IV. An example of a test designed to measure fluid intelligence might be one where the individual needs to detect patterns in a series of unfamiliar designs in order to figure out which designs from a group are needed to make a puzzle (see Figure 13.2). Measures of fluid intelligence are thought to be more culturally fair or neutral because successful performance is not dependent upon having acquired specific knowledge or information a culture values. Whereas crystallized intelligence tests reflect what is valued, taught, and reinforced within specific cultures. Theoretically, fluid intelligence is thought to be more a product of innate physiological structures, and crystallized intelligence a product of culture. These intelligences were thought to become separate and independent abilities as the individual develops. And as one grows older, fluid intelligence declines and is more impacted by brain damage than crystallized intelligence, according to their theory.

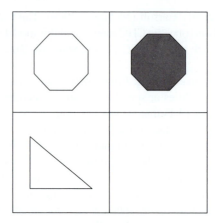

Which of these shapes goes in the empty box?

FIGURE 13.2   Sample Fluid Reasoning Item

A recent analysis has provided support for the notion that fluid cognitive abilities decline with age, but so do some crystallized abilities such as quantitative and writing skills (Kaufman, Johnson, & Liu, 2008).

The Horn and Cattell model was both influenced by and a response to the works of earlier theorists, and along with Carroll's three-stratum model has shaped the development and interpretation of the second generation of intelligence tests such as *Kaufman Assessment Battery for Children, Woodcock–Johnson Tests of Cognitive Abilities*, and the fifth edition of the Stanford–Binet (Bain & Allin, 2005; Bain & Gray, 2008; Kaufman & Kaufman, 1983; Keith, Kranzler, & Flanagan, 2001; McGrew, 2009). Cattell and Horn's fluid and crystallized model of intelligence has been updated and is similar to Carroll's three-stratum model. Carroll's (2005) hierarchical theory, which is based on large factor analytic studies of existing intelligence test data, posits a *g* factor, eight midlevel domains of cognitive abilities, and a third level of 80 more narrow abilities.

Although factor analytic theories have contributed significantly to how the results of intelligence tests are interpreted, there still is debate and ongoing research about what a particular factor or dimension on any given intelligence test is measuring (Daniel, 1997). McGrew (2009) and others (Daniel, 1997; Jensen, 2004) have strongly advocated for a blending of the Cattell–Horn and Carroll models for purposes of having a common classification scheme of cognitive abilities as one way of having a more uniform system for interpreting the results of intelligence tests. The two models share a conceptual framework and use very similar terms for eight domains of cognitive ability: fluid reasoning, comprehension knowledge (crystallized abilities), visual and auditory processing, long- and short-term memory processes, cognitive processing speed, and decision and reaction speed. The blended Cattell–Horn–Carroll (CHC) model has been validated in a number of studies (Kaufman, Johnson, & Liu, 2008) and shares some similarities to the other major theoretical school of intellectual and cognitive assessment: information processing theory.

Information Processing Theory

As with the factor analytic model, there are multiple and competing paradigms within information processing theory. Information processing theories have drawn upon neuropsychological and developmental principles and concepts, particularly those of the Russian neuropsychologist A. R. Luria and the Swiss developmental psychologist Jean Piaget. Luria (1973) articulated three kinds of interacting systems, or what he called "principal functional units," in the brain that enable human beings to attend and perceive, process, and respond to stimuli in the environment. In order to achieve a goal, whether it is finishing this chapter or writing a paragraph, the systems need to be working in tandem. The first functional system is the one that regulates wakefulness and sleep and, as such, plays a role in the processes of arousal, attention, and concentration. The more awake and alert one is, the better one can stay focused on a task, but only to a point. When arousal becomes too high, concentration wanes. The second system is an analytical and memory system. This system receives some type of sensory input (e.g., a melody), analyzes it ("that sounds like 'Happy Birthday'"), and stores the information for later retrieval. According to the model, information can be processed either simultaneously or sequentially (i.e., one piece after another in a linear fashion). Simultaneous processing, for example, might consist of an auditory input like a song, and a visual input, the face of the person singing the song, which are processed at the same time. Not only can information be input in a serial or concurrent manner, but it can also be output either way. This idea of information processing occurring in a sequential or concurrent fashion has been supported by a significant amount of research, including studies in culturally diverse settings (Das et al., 1994).

The third system is a planning, problem-solving, and evaluating system. Although Luria's model has been modified over the years, it is the dominant information processing model shaping the design of specific subtests and items on several of the current test of cognitive and intellectual abilities, such as the KABC-II and the *Cognitive Assessment System* (Das et al., 1994; Kaufman & Kaufman, 2004a). His model has also been incorporated into the CHC theory.

COMPUTER METAPHOR OF INFORMATION PROCESSING   Another way to think about Luria's information processing theory is to use a computer metaphor. Data are entered into a computer, and an output is produced such as a document, a drawing, or a multimedia presentation. Similarly, humans input data through their sensory channels—auditory, visual, tactile, olfactory, and kinesthetic—and produce a response. The response may or may not occur through the same sensory channel. Consider this example: A teacher orally instructs a class of elementary school students to take out their spelling books and write down the week's new list of words (auditory input) and the students respond by writing the words, a visual–motor (tactile and kinesthetic) task. Alternatively, the teacher could also write the instructions on the blackboard for those who have difficulty processing auditory stimuli so that they can use their visual channel. Additionally, the teacher could select a different output or response for the students with underdeveloped fine-motor skills; they spell the words out loud. Any given task requires multiple sensory inputs that need to be processed, and according to Luria's model they can be done in a successive, or step-wise fashion, or simultaneously, though clearly there are limits to how much information a human can process simultaneously even if one considers him or herself a great multitasker. Most complex cognitive tasks (e.g., reading) involve both sequential processing (e.g., inputting a series of letters to form a word and a series of words to form a sentence) and simultaneous processing (e.g., comparing and contrasting the letters and words on the page with knowledge stored in memory and retrieving those memories). Intelligence and cognitive ability tests based on information processing theory are designed to measure different aspects of how, primarily, auditory, visual, and kinesthetic stimuli are perceived, processed, recalled, evaluated, and acted on. The notion of the mind functioning like a computer came about through developments in the fields of cognitive psychology and artificial intelligence and has continued to shape ongoing theorizing about the nature of information processing in humans (Lohman, 1989).

Now consider the operating system in a computer: the software responsible for how various applications function and how those applications are stored and retrieved on the hard drive, or computer's memory. One concept various information processing theories have identified is some type of central operating system or processor (Das et al., 1994) responsible for coding incoming stimuli, matching it against what is already stored in long-term memory, and then using that information to plan in order to complete a task or achieve a goal. According to the Das, Naglieri, and Kirby's model, the brain's central processor coordinates five interrelated brain activities: perceiving, organizing, and integrating stimuli, and planning and problem solving. Imagining a scene where "Happy Birthday" is sung illustrates how these control processes come into play. A cake with lit candles is perceived and the syllable "hap" is heard accompanied by a tune. Once the visual and auditory stimuli are perceived they are organized and integrated whereby the current stimuli are compared and contrasted with what has been stored in long-term memory. The individual can now plan (e.g., "I will sing along") or problem solve (e.g., "My throat is sore, but I will smile and clap when the song is over, but not sing along"). This processing can happen in less than a second. This control system has more recently been referred to as the executive system, and the control of these processes is termed **executive functioning** (McCabe, Roediger, McDaniel, Balota, & Hambrick, 2010). Therefore, the central, or executive, system regulates processes that involve strategies a person uses to attend, understand, and organize and retrieve information necessary for learning, problem solving, and planning. The executive system is believed to be responsible for other cognitive processes such as shifting one's mind-set or cognitive flexibility, selective attention, monitoring thoughts and actions, and behavioral processes such as impulse control or the ability to prevent oneself from acting without thinking. Joshua, for example, was having difficulties with organization and staying on track when problem solving. He was experiencing executive functioning weaknesses, and executive functioning problems are thought to be at the core of certain disorders such as attention deficit–hyperactivity disorder (Barkley, 2006). Cognitive ability testing can help to identify which of those processes are strong and weak for a client and then use that information to teach the client strategies that can facilitate the learning of particular tasks or subjects.

ADDITIONAL INFORMATION PROCESSING AND COGNITIVE ABILITY CONCEPTS

Metacognition   Metacognition is the ability to reflect upon and think about one's thoughts. For example, a counselor is using metacognition when he or she thinks about his or her intention underlying a counselor statement (e.g., "What was I trying to accomplish when I said 'how are you feeling'?") (Martin, Martin, Meyer, & Slemon, 1986). Metacognition is one process that is controlled by the executive functioning system and is essential for the kind of planning involved with most tasks of daily life (Das et al., 1994). It is also related to motivation and has a developmental component to it. Metacognitive abilities, however, are rarely if ever assessed with standardized intelligence or cognitive ability tests unless the evaluator chooses to explore with the test taker how he or she arrived at his or her answer.

Schemas   Schemas, a term Piaget introduced, are theoretical structures used for perceiving, filtering, organizing, and classifying stimuli and are similar in concept to scripts or frames (Nisbett & Ross, 1980). The schema is like a template that is stored in memory and is used to see if the incoming stimuli has certain feature and attributes that either match or do not match the template. Schemas enable human beings to classify and categorize any kind of stimuli, whether it is visual, auditory, olfactory, tactile, or kinesthetic. So that when one sees, for example, an object with four legs, fur, a tail, and has a certain size and shape, the dog schema enables the person to figure out the object is indeed a dog and not a cat.

Memory Processes   Information processing theory posits three main **memory processes**: sensory, short-term (or what is now often referred to as *working memory*), and long-term memory (Mayer, 2003). Sensory memory holds information from different sensory inputs very briefly and is sometimes referred to as *immediate memory*. Working memory is the ability to temporarily store and process a limited number of pieces of information in one's mind to solve a task or accomplish a goal (Baddeley, 2003; 2007; Baddeley & Hitch, 1974). Have you ever had the experience of walking to a refrigerator, opening it up, and not remembering what it is you want to take out? That is a working memory problem. According to Baddeley and Hitch's model, the working memory system is divided into three subsystems. One system is responsible for storing verbal information; another for visual–spatial and possibly kinesthetic information; and a third system, the central executive, affects attention. This multimodal system also includes the rehearsal process. There is a good deal of variation in how much a person can hold and store in working memory and this ability is thought to be related to other cognitive abilities. Once information is encoded and processed it gets stored in long-term memory, where large quantities of information are retained for a significant length of time, years.

These various cognitive processes are related to different structures in the brain. For example, the frontal cortex is the area of the brain responsible for executive functioning: planning, problem solving, and abstract thinking. The hippocampus is one of the places where memories are stored. Other areas of the brain are responsible for processing sensory input. The visual cortex, at the back of the brain, receives and begins to process visual stimuli, and separate areas of the brain are involved with the other senses: auditory, kinesthetic, tactile, and olfactory.

Regardless of how intelligence is conceptualized, any test that purports to measure it can provide only an estimate, based on one performance, of how much of a set of skills a person has, compared to some normative group. And a number of factors beyond one's intelligence can affect performance on an intelligence test at any given time, such as motivation, fatigue, concentration, anxiety, depression, and the content of the test. Therefore, the task of the evaluator, when interpreting scores on an intelligence test's subtests, is to assess to what extent the scores represent how much of a specific ability an individual possesses and to what extent the scores underestimate that ability because other noncognitive ability factors affected performance.

TESTS OF INTELLECTUAL AND COGNITIVE ABILITIES

Referral for Testing

When might a counselor or other professional refer a client for the type of intelligence testing that produces IQ or similar kinds of scores? (See Practice Suggestion: When to Refer for Cognitive Ability Testing.) One prompt might be a concern about *why* an individual's educational or vocational performance is not on target or below one's peer group. Who might have that concern about an individual's intellectual functioning? Typically parents and other caregivers, educators, physicians, vocational and rehabilitation counselors, or employers are the ones likely to make a referral for intellectual testing prior to the individual entering a mental health system. It is much

PRACTICE SUGGESTION
When to Refer for Cognitive Ability Testing

- When an individual's educational or vocational performance is not on target or below one's peer group
- When cognitive developmental milestones are significantly below average (e.g., a 4-year-old using only two-word sentences)
- When an educator suspects a learning disability
- For identification of cognitive strengths and weaknesses that could impact learning or be a focus of remediation and training
- To rule out the presence of some type of dementia
- To determine impairments in cognitive functioning as a result of:
  - Traumatic brain injury or other serious head injury
  - A disease process known to impact cognitive functioning (e.g., Alzheimer's)
  - Chronic alcohol abuse
- To make a differential diagnosis (psychiatric or emotional disorder versus cognitive disorder)

less common that a mental health professional is the first one to raise the need for intellectual testing. Joshua, in the chapter case study, was referred for intellectual evaluation by his teacher and parents because of concern that he was not progressing in his reading skills relative to his peers. The purpose of assessing his intellectual or cognitive abilities is to determine his pattern of strengths and weaknesses, which could shed light on why his reading skills are lagging. The assessment would provide information upon which to design instructional interventions in order to improve his reading skills and potentially other skills that are identified as being weak.

In addition to assessing a pattern of strengths and weaknesses, another reason a referral for intelligence testing or assessment of cognitive processing might be made is when other assessment information, such as a mental status exam, suggests that a person's cognitive functioning may be significantly impaired. Individuals who have experienced some type of traumatic brain injury or have a neurological disease, such as Alzheimer's dementia, may display the kinds of cognitive deficits that lead to a referral for cognitive ability testing. As part of a comprehensive diagnostic evaluation, information obtained from traditional intellectual tests can help to sort out different diagnostic possibilities. Examples of the kinds of diagnostic uncertainties cognitive or intellectual assessments can help resolve include the following:

- Alzheimer's versus major depression in an elderly client
- Traumatic brain injury versus post-traumatic stress disorder in a combat veteran
- Attention deficit–hyperactivity disorder versus learning disability versus emotional problems in a child

As with any type of assessment, the goal of an intellectual or cognitive assessment is to gather information that will lead to the design of effective interventions. Therefore, a test of intellectual or cognitive abilities is helpful only if it can provide information about an individual's cognitive processing strengths and weaknesses and learning styles, which then forms the foundation for effective remedial interventions. Given the array of intellectual and cognitive tests and subtests available, the selection of either an overall test or subtests from different tests depends upon the specific abilities in need of assessment and the potential for the results of a single test or group of tests to guide intervention strategies. Those who receive the more specialized training in the construct of intelligence and the administering, scoring, and interpreting of various intellectual and cognitive ability tests recognize that the selection of a particular intelligence, cognitive ability, or achievement test is based on the specific referral question(s) and needs of the client. For example with a client like Joshua who had adequate language skills but has already demonstrated problems with reading, a test that includes those types of abilities necessary for effective reading—verbal reasoning, word knowledge, sequential processing, and memory—would be a good choice. On the other hand, if a child was having difficulty learning to read and that child was known to have a history of significant speech and language problems, then a test with minimal language demands would be a better choice.

Also, as will been seen later, some tests do not assess particular abilities that the assessor might decide are important to evaluate. One such example is processing speed: how quickly information is analyzed and responded to. Therefore, a test might be selected because of its capacity to assess processing speed. Tests overlap a good deal in the specific abilities and processes that they assess, but the specific aspects of those processes can vary from test to test. Memory processes is one example of that. Some tests evaluate long-term, short-term, and working memory, others only short-term and working memory. Furthermore, memory processes can be assessed in a visual context, an auditory context, or both, and the assessment methods may vary as well. Is the individual asked to recall a series of numbers or the names of pictures, or perform some other task in order to assess short-memory functioning, for example? Therefore, one's familiarity with the ability or process in need of assessment and how a specific test goes about evaluating that process will influence the selection of a test.

Beyond the referral question, certain pragmatic considerations guide the selection of a particular intellectual or cognitive ability test. Experience with a particular test is often the primary factor guiding the selection process. Typically psychologists and other professionals who administer and interpret these types of tests have had training and professional experience with one specific test and tend, therefore, to rely on that test for many cognitive assessments. Cost, length of time to administer, and ease in which the test can be scored and interpreted are other factors that will influence the choice of a specific test, as is the case with other types of assessment instruments such as personality inventories.

Wechsler Scales

David Wechsler was a clinical practitioner with a strong interest in diagnostic tools that could better serve his clients than the ones in existence when he began his career as a psychologist in 1922 at the Bureau of Child Guidance in New York City (Matarazzo, 1972). His grand vision of a test that could both assess intellectual abilities and diagnosis psychiatric conditions was never realized, but the tests he created—the *Wechsler Adult Intelligence Scale* (WAIS), the *Wechsler Intelligence Scale for Children* (WISC), and the *Wechsler Pre-school and Primary Scale of Intelligence* (WPPSI)—have become the most popular tests in the field of intellectual assessment (Kaufman et al., 2006; Tulsky & Ledbetter, 2000). Each of his scales has been revised several times since 1939 when the first intelligence scale—the *Wechsler–Bellevue Test*—was published, and have continued to be revised since his death in 1981, including the publication of Spanish language versions of the WAIS and WISC fourth editions. One of the most important contributions Wechsler made was the calculation of an intelligence quotient, or IQ score, from an individual's performance on his test. The IQ score was based on normative population data and replaced the Binet–Simon method of using a mental age score to measure overall intelligence.

The latest editions of the Wechsler scales are based on the multidimensional hierarchical (Cattell–Horn–Carroll [CHC]) model of intelligence and information processing theory discussed earlier. The impact both the CHC and information processing theories have had on the revisions to the Wechsler intelligence tests can be seen by the abilities that are now emphasized. The current tests emphasize CHC constructs such as fluid reasoning abilities (i.e., the ability to learn from and reason with novel or unfamiliar stimuli) more so than crystallized abilities (i.e., demonstrating knowledge acquired prior to taking the test) and information processing concepts like working memory and processing speed. Each of the Wechsler Scales—the adult, child, and pre-school versions—comprises multiple subtests and measures a unique or narrow ability. One example is auditory working memory. Each subtest is also measuring broad or shared abilities: two or more subtests measuring the same process or ability such as verbal comprehension or fluid reasoning. In addition, abilities are assessed in different contexts.

WECHSLER ADULT INTELLIGENCE SCALE—FOURTH EDITION (WAIS-IV) The *Wechsler Adult Intelligence Scale—Fourth Edition* (WAIS-IV) (Wechsler, 2008) is the sixth revision of the original *Wechsler–Bellevue Scale*. Published in 2008, the WAIS-IV consists of 15 subtests (10 core and 5 supplemental) that make up four primary factors or indexes: Verbal Comprehension (VCI), Perceptual Reasoning (PRI), Working Memory (WMI), and Processing Speed (PSI) (see Table 13.1). The verbal comprehension subtests measure the ability to reason with and understand verbal stimuli such as analogies and vocabulary items. Perceptual reasoning subtests examine the ability to process and analyze visual–spatial stimuli such as reproducing a model from randomly arranged blocks or arranging abstract jigsaw-like puzzle pieces to complete a geometric design. Working memory, as previously noted, is the ability to temporarily hold and process a limited number of pieces of information in one's mind to solve a task or accomplish a goal. The processing speed subtests measure how quickly certain types of visual stimuli are perceived and analyzed in order to accomplish a visual–motor task such as copying abstract symbols. The WAIS-IV has been normed for individuals 16 to 90 years old and changes have been made from the WAIS-III (1997) to better incorporate current theories and concepts regarding intellectual functioning. Those changes include a new subtest to measure fluid reasoning or intelligence, improved ways to measure working memory, a new subtest to measure processing speed, the deletion of four WAIS-III performance subtests, and modifications of the subtests that were retained in the fourth edition.

The WAIS-IV produces five primary scores: a full-scale IQ (FSIQ) based on the 10 core subtests and a score for each of the four indexes: VCI, PRI, WMI, and PSI. An optional General Abilities index can also be calculated by combining the Verbal Comprehension and Perceptual Reasoning indices. The calculation of a general abilities index is also new to the WAIS-IV. In previous editions, three separate IQ scores were calculated: Full-scale, Verbal, and Performance. An FSIQ between 85 and 115 is considered to be in the average range (mean = 100; standard deviation = 15). The FSIQ is calculated from the scores on the 10 core subtests (see Table 13.1). Similarly, on the four composite indexes, average scores are equal to 100 with a standard deviation of 15. On the individual subtests, 10 is an average score with a standard deviation of 3.

The psychometric properties of the WAIS-IV are excellent, and the standardization group is more representative of the United States population than earlier versions of the WAIS (Hartman, 2009). The national standardization group consisted of 2,200 individuals between the

Table 13.1 Wechsler Scales

	Test		
	WAIS-IV (16–90)	WISC-IV (6–16.11)	WPPSI[1] (2.6–7.3)
(Scales)/Subtests[2]:			
(Verbal Comprehension)			
Similarities	•	•	•
Vocabulary	•	•	•
Information	•	•	•
Comprehension	•	•	•
Word Reasoning		•	•
(Perceptual Reasoning)			
Block Design	•	•	•
Matrix Reasoning	•	•	•
Visual puzzles:	•		
Picture Concepts:		•	•
Picture Completion	•	•	•
Figure weights:	•		
(Working Memory[3])			
Digit Span	•	•	
Arithmetic	•	•	
Letter–Number Sequencing	•	•	
(Processing Speed)			
Symbol Search	•	•	•
Coding	•	•	•
Cancellation:	•	•	

[1]WPPSI core and supplemental subtests vary depending upon the age range.

[2]Supplemental tests are in italics and new tests in bold (Information is a supplemental test and Comprehension is a core test on the WISC-IV).

[3]Arithmetic is a supplemental test and Letter–Number Sequencing is a core test for the Working Memory Scale on the WISC-IV.

ages of 16 and 90, who were selected to match the 2005 U.S. census data for gender, education level, ethnicity, and geographic region (Wechsler, 2008). The internal reliability estimates for the FSIQ and the four primary indexes are in the excellent range. The test manual presents ample evidence of its construct and predictive validity. A recent review praised the WAIS-IV for its clinical usefulness and flexibility in educational and neuropsychological assessment (Hartman).

WECHSLER INTELLIGENCE SCALE FOR CHILDREN—FOURTH EDITION (WISC-IV) The *Wechsler Intelligence Scale for Children*—Fourth Edition (WISC-IV) (Wechsler, 2003) is designed for children and adolescents ages 6 to 16 years, 11 months and is very similar in structure to the WAIS-IV (see Table 13.1). The alignment of the subtests in the WISC and WAIS is now closer than in any other previous versions of these tests. There are, however, slight differences in what are considered core versus supplemental tests and two subtests that do not match. The changes in the WISC-IV from previous versions are the most significant of all the prior revisions with an emphasis on assessing fluid reasoning and working memory (Burns & O'Leary, 2004).There are, like the WAIS-IV, a total of 15 subtests (10 core and 5 supplemental), and the four scales on the WISC-IV match the four indices on the WAIS-IV: VCI, PRI, WMI, and PSI. In addition to the four scale scores, an FSIQ is calculated. The meaning and interpretation of the IQ score has changed fundamentally with the WISC-IV because of the different subtests used to calculate the FSIQ score so that a WISC-IV FSIQ score reflects more the CHC theory of intellectual abilities than any prior version of the WISC (Kaufman et al., 2006). Like the WAIS-IV, the WISC-IV FSIQ is based on the scores from the 10 core subtests. The other substantial changes from WISC-R and WISC-III to IV include 1) greater use of items that the evaluator can teach and enhanced "user friendly" administration, and 2) improved psychometric properties (Burns & O'Leary, 2004). Another important change in the WISC-IV is a simpler, more objective scoring system (Kaufman et al., 2006). Although the scoring of subtest items is more objective than in previous versions, there is still an element of subjectivity that goes into deciding whether a child's response to a particular subtest item is a 0 or no-credit response versus a 1- or 2-point response.

The 10 core subtests can be administered in just over one hour on average with an additional 20–25 minutes for the five supplemental tests. Each subtest measures both unique and shared cognitive abilities. Brief descriptions of those abilities can be found in Table 13.2. Starting points on specific subtests are determined by the child's age. As is the case with the WAIS-IV, the subtest will be stopped if the test taker gets a certain number of incorrect responses in a row. The number of consecutive incorrect responses that results in the subtest no longer being administered varies from two to five, depending on the subtest.

Reviews of the WISC-IV have praised its excellent psychometric properties (Burns & O'Leary, 2004; Kaufman et al., 2006). The normative sample consisted of 2,200 children and closely matched the 2002 U.S. Census data in terms of age, gender, ethnicity, parent's educational level, and geographic regions. The reliability estimates, both internal consistency and test–retest, for the four index scores and the FSIQ are in the good to excellent range. Although there is debate as to whether the WISC-IV is based on four factors or five Cattell–Horn–Carroll factors, a number of studies have shown that it correlates well but not perfectly with measures of academic achievement and cognitive abilities demonstrating its construct validity (Kaufman et al., 2006).

WECHSLER PRE-SCHOOL AND PRIMARY SCALE OF INTELLIGENCE (WPPSI)   The *Wechsler Pre-school and Primary Scale of Intelligence* is now in its third edition (WPPSI-III) and is intended for children ages 2 years, 6 months to 7 years, 3 months. The overall structure and content of the WPPSI-III is similar to the WISC-IV (see Table 13.1), particularly for the older age range. The WPPSI-III has two age ranges—2 years, 6 months to 3 years, 11 months; and 4 years to 7 years, 3 months—and the amount and nature of the subtests administered depends upon which age range the child is in. For children in the younger range there are four core subtests and one supplemental designed to assess verbal comprehension and perceptual organizational abilities, whereas for the older children there are seven core, five supplemental, and two optional subtests so that processing speed in addition to verbal and perceptual abilities can be assessed. All of the subtests now have teaching and practice items, a significant change from earlier versions. That is, the administrator of the test is allowed to demonstrate how to answer or solve the first one or two items if the child answers incorrectly on his or her first try. For children ages 6 to 7 and 3 months, evaluators have a choice between using either the WPPSI-III or the WISC-IV, but the WPPSI-III does not contain subtests designed to assess working memory skills so if there is a need to assess working memory, then the WISC-IV is a better choice. On the other hand, if there is reason to suspect prior to the testing that the child may have underdeveloped working memory abilities, then the WPPSI would be a helpful test because the FSIQ would not be negatively

Table 13.2 Wechsler Subtests: Unique and Shared Abilities Measured		
Subtest	**Unique Ability**	**Shared Abilities**
Similarities	Abstract reasoning with verbal concepts	Abstract reasoning, word knowledge, language development, & acquired knowledge
Vocabulary	Word definition	Verbal comprehension, acquired knowledge, language development
Information	Knowledge of people, places, & objects	Acquired knowledge
Comprehension	Understanding social rules & concepts	Verbal reasoning, language development
Word Reasoning	Verbal concept formation	Word knowledge, inductive reasoning
Block Design	Reproducing a geometric pattern	Perceptual–organizational & fluid, visual processing
Matrix Reasoning	Analyzing patterns and relationships with visual-spatial stimuli	Fluid reasoning, sequential reasoning
Visual puzzles:	Visual perceptual reasoning	Fluid reasoning
Picture concepts:	Non-verbal concept formation	Perceptual–organizational & fluid reasoning
Picture Completion	Analyzing part–whole relationships with pictures	Perceptual–organizational reasoning, visual processing
Digit Span	Immediate recall of numbers	Working memory
Arithmetic	Math knowledge	Fluid (quantitative) reasoning
Letter-Number Sequencing	Recall with verbal/quantitative stimuli	Working memory
(Processing Speed)		
Symbol Search	Visual scanning	Processing speed, rapid performance
Coding	Visual–motor copying	Processing speed, rapid performance
Cancellation:	Visual scanning	Processing speed, rapid performance

Source: Based on *Essentials of WISC-IV Assessment,* by D. P. Flanagan and A. S. Kaufman, 2004 (Hoboken, NJ: Wiley).

impacted. On the WISC-IV, as noted, the FSIQ is impacted by the working memory scores. For the younger age range a Receptive Vocabulary subtest replaces the Vocabulary subtest, which is an expressive language skills and word knowledge test. The Receptive Vocabulary subtest requires the child to point to one of four pictures, which matches the word spoken by the evaluator.

INTERPRETING WECHSLER SCALES   What can the results of an intelligence test like the Wechsler reveal about a person's cognitive functioning and abilities? The analysis and interpretation of Wechsler scores occurs at three levels: 1) overall intellectual or cognitive ability (e.g., full-scale IQ score), 2) major factor or scale scores, and 3) intra-individual or subtest level.

Although many people—clients, family members, educators, and medical and mental health professionals—are often interested in "how intelligent" a person is, that question is more misleading than illuminating. Measures of overall intelligence (e.g., full-scale intellectual quotient [FSIQ] scores) are like baseball batting averages: they represent a summary statistic about an individual's performance and give a general idea of how well a performer he or she is, relative to his or her peer group, but not the factors that together make up the performance. Consequently, full-scale IQ scores tend to mask *intra*-individual differences that represent a person's pattern of strengths and weaknesses. Furthermore, there can be extensive variability among specific cognitive abilities for two people with the exact same FSIQ. Therefore, an FSIQ score is used less often than scale and subtest scores for the purpose of both understanding an individual's cognitive ability and designing interventions. The reason why the FSIQ is limited in its ability to drive interventions can be illustrated by a baseball analogy. Let's take two baseball players with the exact same subpar batting average. Player A and Player B both have .200 batting averages, meaning that they get one hit every five times at bat. But Player A strikes out and hits into double plays every four out of five times at bat and his hits are all singles, whereas Player B gets mostly doubles and home runs when making hits and, when not, produces runs with sacrifice flies. So although the averages are the same, the specific talents, or lack thereof, of each player are not revealed by the hitting statistic. Overall IQ scores are a similar kind of statistic in that they provide a general idea about a person's intellectual functioning compared to his or her peer group, but not how well he or she performed on tests of specific abilities that determine the FSIQ. For example, an individual could have an FSIQ in the average range but some subtest scores could be below average, some average, and others above average.

A more useful approach to interpretation is to examine *intra*-individual subtest differences in order to identify a person's cognitive strengths and weaknesses based on the unique and shared abilities of the different subtests. This has been referred to as "profile analysis" with the goal being to find clues about a person's abilities, which can generate hypotheses about why the individual performed the way he or she did; but not to classify the individual (Flanagan & Kaufman, 2004; Kaufman, 1979; Sattler, 1988). Briefly, profile analysis determines whether there are statistically significant differences among the index scores: Verbal Comprehension, Perceptual Reasoning, Working Memory, and Processing Speed. The Wechsler manuals provide information about how much of an index or subtest score difference is considered significant. If differences do exist, then the next step is to determine whether there are common and/or unique cognitive abilities accounting for those differences. For example, although all of an individual's subtest scores might fall within the average range, there could be a significant difference in how the person performs on tests involving working memory versus those involving comprehension and reasoning with words and other verbal stimuli.

The process of interpreting WISC-IV scores and profile analysis can be illustrated with the case of Joshua from the beginning of the chapter.

BOX 13.1
Joshua's WISC-IV Composite and Subtest Scores Summary

Scale[1]	Composite Score	Percentile Rank
VCI	83	13
PRI	90	27
WMI	88	21
PSI	86	18
FSIQ	85	16
VCI Subtest Scores		
Similarities	5	5
Vocabulary	7	16
Comprehension	9	38
PRI Subtest Scores		
Block Design	11	63
Picture Concepts	9	37
Matrix Reasoning	5	5
WMI Subtest Scores		
Digit Span	10	50
Letter–Number Seq.	6	9
Arithmetic	5	5
PSI Subtest Scores		
Coding	8	23
Symbol Search	7	16

[1] VCI = Verbal Comprehension Index; PRI = Perceptual Reasoning Index; WMI = Working Memory Index; PSI = Processing Speed Index; and FSIQ = Full-Scale IQ

Of the four index scores, the verbal comprehension index is the lowest, falling at the low end of the low-average range (80–89). Joshua's ability to understand and reason with verbal material is relatively weak compared to others in his age group, which may account for the limited progress he has made in reading. Profile analysis revealed that Similarities and Matrix Reasoning subtests were relative weaknesses for Joshua. Those two tests involve abstract reasoning and the ability to understand relationships between conceptually similar objects or material. Reading comprehension, in part, involves abstract reasoning skills and given this cognitive weakness it is not surprising that Joshua has had a history of comprehension difficulties. On the other hand, Block Design was the one test where he displayed a relative strength compared to his performance on the other subtests. Block Design involves the ability to understand part–whole relationships in a visual–spatial context. Reading intervention for Joshua could build on this strength to help bring his reading comprehension up to grade level. Intervention strategies that incorporate visual–spatial strategies such as mapping and breaking down the whole concept (e.g., paragraph main topic) into its parts (i.e., sentences that relate to the topic) could facilitate the goal of improved reading comprehension.

Performance on cognitive ability tests can be affected by factors other than the cognitive abilities being assessed. Those factors include motivation, effort, anxiety, and depression. When subtest and index or scale scores fall below the average range for that test, it is important to consider what contribution, if any, these emotional and psychological factors played. Anxiety appeared to be a factor with Joshua's lowest performance: Matrix Reasoning and Arithmetic. On both those subtests, the evaluator noted that Joshua exhibited a good deal of muscle tension and displayed a pattern of responding that often suggests emotional factors are playing a role. For example, he answered incorrectly on the second item on both subtests, then had two correct answers, another incorrect one, followed by correct answers. When an individual displays uneven performance like Joshua did, rather than answering items correctly until they become too difficult and the subtest is stopped, emotionality or attention may be a factor. Observations of the test taker along with an examination of the pattern of performance within particular subtests can provide clues about the possible influence of noncognitive factors. Therefore, interpretation of the Wechsler Scales is a holistic process based on both quantitative and qualitative data.

Kaufman Scales

KAUFMAN ASSESSMENT BATTERY FOR CHILDREN—SECOND EDITION (KABC-II)   Alan Kaufman, a licensed school psychologist, who wrote one of the more influential books on interpreting the WISC-R (Kaufman, 1979) developed along with his wife, Nadeen Kaufman, the *Kaufman Assessment Battery for Children* (K-ABC) in 1983, and 10 years later the *Kaufman Adolescent and Adult Intelligence Test* (KAIT). The original K-ABC consisted of 10 cognitive ability subtests and six achievement-like subtests (Kaufman & Kaufman, 1983). The revision, KABC-II, published in 2004 (Kaufman & Kaufman, 2004a) is for ages 3 to 18 and differs from the original in terms of subtests, theoretical design, and interpretation. Other changes seem more cosmetic in that the names of a couple of subtests have been changed but the basic content and the abilities being assessed remain unchanged (Bain & Gray, 2008). The KABC-II consists of 18 subtests, but the overall mental processing score for children 4 years, 6 months and older, is determined by only nine core subtests, and for those between the ages 3 and 4 years, 5 months only five tests determine that overall score. The evaluator now has the choice of interpreting the KABC-II results using either the Luria information processing model (sequential vs. simultaneous) or the CHC hierarchical model. This allows for greater flexibility in interpreting test scores to gain a fuller understanding of an individual's cognitive functioning and abilities.

The KABC-II is designed for the purpose of having a cognitive ability test for children and adolescents that is firmly grounded in both information processing theory and the CHC theory of intelligence, particularly the fluid versus crystallized distinction. The information processing, or *mental processing subtests,* as the Kaufmans labeled them, measure the following processes and abilities: sequential and simultaneous information processing, planning, short-term memory, and learning. The specific subtests used to assess these processes are based on Luria's model and some of them resemble his original neuropsychological tests (Kaufman & Kaufman, 2004a). Depending upon the model used, either a Mental Processing Index (MPI) or Fluid-Crystallized Index (FCI) is calculated, rather than IQ scores, with average scores equal to 100 and standard deviation of 15. Like the Wechsler Scales, the subtests have a mean of 10 and a standard deviation of 3. There are five scales on the KABC-II when the CHC model is used: Short-Term Memory, Visual Processing, Learning Ability, Fluid Reasoning, and Crystallized

Ability. The specific subtests names stay the same but the names of the overall scales are different when using an information processing model of interpretation: Short-term Memory becomes Sequential Processing, Visual Processing becomes Simultaneous Processing, Learning remains the same, Fluid Reasoning is Planning, and Crystallized Ability is simply Knowledge. The Knowledge scale is not, however, included in the calculation of the MPI because the two subtests that scale comprises are not given if the information processing model is being used.

The KABC–II mental processing subtests share some similarities to the WISC-IV subtests but also have some unique features. The sequential processing skills are measured by two subtests, one requiring recall of words in a particular order and the other involves immediate recall of numbers in a series, similar to Digit Span on the Wechsler Scales. Digit span, however, assesses the ability to recall numbers in the reverse sequence, whereas Number Recall on the KABC-II measures only the ability to recall numbers in the same sequences as presented by the evaluator. One other subtest that measures sequential processing is a supplemental test and involves the ability to recall a series of hand movements made by the examiner and reproduce them in the same sequence. The simultaneous processing scale contains more subtests overall and more changes from the original test. The simultaneous processing scale contains "Triangles," which is similar to Block Design on the Wechsler Scales. There are an additional seven subtests but typically five are administered. These subtests assess a variety of abilities such as pattern reasoning with geometric forms, analyzing similarities and differences in pictures, and understanding the elements of a story. Although many complex cognitive tasks such as reading and writing require both sequential and simultaneous processing skills, the Kaufmans strove to develop tests that were purely sequential or simultaneous measures. As described previously, sequential processing involves perceiving stimuli that are in a "serial or temporal order" and analyzing those stimuli in a linear fashion in order to solve a problem (Kaufman & Kaufman, 1983). For example, being required to repeat a series of numbers in the same order as was given to you, like with a telephone number, is a sequential processing task. On the other hand, simultaneous information processing is the ability to perceive and integrate various stimuli either verbally or visual–spatially in order to solve a problem such as an analogy.

The Kaufmans' primary goals in developing the K-ABC was to have a test that made up for the limitations in the existing popular intelligence tests at that time (WISC-R and Stanford–Binet) and whose scores could be more productively used in designing educational interventions. One of the limitations in those earlier tests was that there was no allowance made for modeling how to go about solving problems or answering items on subtests. A major advance in intelligence testing, with the KABC-II, is that for most of the mental processing subtests, the first two items are teaching items whereby the evaluator can demonstrate how the item is done correctly if the child initially answers incorrectly. On a practical note, the administration of the KABC-II is made relatively easy by including all the subtests within three easel-like booklets, with few additional materials needed. Another advance is the reduced language demands compared to the WISC-IV. For a long time, a test that could measure overall and specific intellectual abilities free from the demands of language was sought for those individuals who either had receptive or expressive language delays or for whom English was not their primary language.

The KABC-II was standardized with a stratified random sample of 3,025 children who closely matched the 2001 U.S. Census in terms of gender, age, ethnicity, parental education, and geographic region (Kaufman & Kaufman, 2004a). Internal reliability estimates for the MPI and FCI are in the excellent range (0.90 or greater) and test–retest reliabilities are in the adequate range. There is ample evidence supporting the construct validity of the KABC-II and it is briefly summarized in the test manual. One illustrative piece of evidence is that the MPI was found to correlate 0.88 with the WISC-IV FSIQ for 56 children ages 7–16, and different diagnostic groups—learning disability, mental retardation, and autistic—had significantly lower MPI scores, as would be expected. Some reviewers (Kaplan & Saccuzzo, 2005) have strongly criticized the KABC-II because its definition of intelligence and the manner in which it measures intelligence has limited correspondence, but that is a criticism that also applies to the Wechsler Scales and other tests of cognitive abilities currently in use.

KAUFMAN ADOLESCENT AND ADULT INTELLIGENCE TEST (KAIT)   The *Kaufman Adolescent and Adult Intelligence Test* (KAIT) is for individuals ages 11 to 85 and consists of six core subtests designed, like the KABC-II, to measure crystallized and fluid intelligences and assess an individual's cognitive strengths and weaknesses (Kaufman & Kaufman, 1993). The core subtests measure these specific abilities: word knowledge and verbal reasoning, fluid reasoning with visual–spatial symbols and associate learning, logical reasoning with syllogisms, auditory sequencing and comprehension, planning speed, and abstract reasoning with verbal concepts. The KAIT also includes four supplemental subtests that make up the "extended" battery and a mental status test. The expanded battery comprises four tests, which are designed to measure short- and long-term memory, or what the Kaufmans call *primary and secondary memory*. These additional subtests were designed for clinicians conducting neuropsychological evaluations of adolescents and adults when assessment of memory functions is needed. More specifically, two of the subtests are intended to assess recall of newly learned information without the effect of rehearsal. The KAIT can be administered, on average, in 65 minutes for the core battery and 91 minutes when the expanded battery is included.

Stanford–Binet Intelligence Scales

The Stanford–Binet Intelligence Scales—Fifth Edition (SB5) (Roid, 2003) is designed to assess intellectual and cognitive abilities in individuals ages 2 to 85 and produces a full-scale, nonverbal, and verbal IQ score. As an intelligence test covering the lifespan from toddler to older adult, the SB5 has a practical advantage over the Wechsler and Kaufman tests, which require different kits for different developmental stages. Like other tests of intellectual and cognitive functioning, it is used to assess learning disabilities, mental retardation, other developmental disorders, and neuropsychological problems (Bain & Allin, 2005). The SB5, like the KABC-II and to a lesser extent the current Wechsler Scales, is based on the CHC model of intelligence. The SB5 consists of two primary domains—verbal and nonverbal—with a total of 10 subtests (15 were in SB4) that make up the two domains. Given the theoretical model driving its development, the SB5 assesses abilities such as fluid reasoning, crystallized knowledge, working memory, quantitative reasoning, and visual–spatial processing. Each of those primary abilities or factors is assessed with two specific subtests, and the factor scores have a mean of 100 and standard deviation of 15, allowing for comparisons both within the SB5 and with other tests such as the WISC-IV or KABC-II. One of the unique features of the SB5, which was developed for the fourth edition, is the use of adaptive testing (Sattler, 1988). In adaptive testing, one's performance on two initial subtests determines where on subsequent subtests the test taker begins. For example, the SB5 has one verbal and one nonverbal "routing" test whereby the individual's performance on those tests, along with his or her chronological age, dictates the starting point (e.g., item 5 rather than item 1) on the remaining verbal and nonverbal subtests. Therefore, the time to administer the SB5 is highly variable, ranging from 15 to 75 minutes.

The SB5 was normed with a group of 4,800 individuals ages 2 to 85 who were selected so that the standardization sample could match, as closely as possible, the 2001 U.S. Census data for age, gender, ethnicity, geographical region, and parents' educational level (Roid, 2003).

The standardization group does match closely the U.S. Census data with the exception of over-representing individuals whose parents had less than 12 years of education compared to those with more than 12 years (Bain & Allin, 2005). Its psychometric properties in terms of representative norms and reliability and validity estimates are comparable to other cognitive ability tests. Internal consistency reliability estimates for the 10 subtests across all age groups are good (0.80 to 0.89) and excellent (0.90 or better) for the FSIQ, NVIQ, VIQ, and the factor scores (Roid). And test–retest reliabilities were adequate or better depending upon the age group. The SB5 manual presents substantial evidence of its construct and concurrent validities (Bain & Allin). One of the several ways in which its construct validity was established, as was the case with the KABC-II and Wechsler Scales, was to compare the scores for different groups—gifted children, children with mental retardation, with ADHD, and with learning disabilities—to see if their average scores fall within the predicted range and are significantly different from one another in the expected directions. The average scores for those clinical groups are different from one another and those differences are in the expected direction, for example gifted children having significantly higher mean scores than the learning disability group.

The previous version of the Stanford–Binet, SB4, had been criticized for a number of limitations, the most serious being difficulty making comparisons in intellectual functioning throughout the ages because the subtests administered at different ages are too variable (Sattler, 1988). Other criticisms have been both technical—lack of uniformity in the high and low scores that are possible at different age ranges—and practical—relatively long time for administration, too many materials, and difficulty scoring atypical responses. Over the past 30 years, the SB has been dwarfed in popularity by the Wechsler and other scales that have been developed over that time and it remains to be seen whether the fifth edition of the oldest standardized test developed in the United States for assessing intellectual and cognitive abilities will see a resurgence in popularity with its fifth edition.

Differential Abilities Scale—2nd Edition

The *Differential Abilities Scale—2nd Edition* (DAS-II) is designed to assess the major CHC abilities in children ages 2.5–17 in order to develop educational interventions for children who are exhibiting learning problems (Elliot, 2007). The DAS-II consists of 20 subtests and two different core batteries for younger children (ages 2.5–6.11) and school age (7–17) assessing the following areas: verbal and visual working memory, immediate and delayed recall, visual–spatial relationships and processing, phonological awareness, math concepts, and processing speed. Both specific cognitive abilities and overall cognitive processes or thinking styles are assessed with the DAS-II. The original DAS had a complex administration and scoring system but was considered a "state of the art" instrument (Anastasi & Urbina, 1997). A review of the DAS-II (Beran, 2007) praised it for its strengths, including strong psychometric properties, clinical usefulness, cross-cultural applicability, and level of detail in its manual. More specifically, there are many teaching items, the option of Spanish and American Sign Language translations for the nonverbal subtests, and a design feature that allows for more tailored administration of items within subtests than other cognitive ability tests provide. This is particularly helpful because children are less likely to get fatigued and experience too much failure like what can happen on a more traditional test like the WISC-IV.

Like the KABC-II, the DAS-II provides an overall estimate of cognitive ability rather than an IQ score. In addition to the General Conceptual Ability score, there are three major scales or "cluster" scores: Verbal Ability, Nonverbal Ability, and Spatial Ability. The supplemental

Table 13.3 CHC Model and Cognitive Ability Tests

	Tests			
	KABC-II	**SB5**	**WISC-IV/WAIS-IV**	**DAS-II**
CHC Level II Ability:				
Fluid Reasoning	•	•	•	•
Comprehension Knowledge	•	•	•	•
Short-Term Memory (Working)	•	•	•	•
Visual Processing	•	•	•	•
Auditory Processing	x	x	x	•
Long-Term Memory Storage & Retrieval	•	x	•	•
Cognitive Processing Speed	x	x	•	•
Decision and Reaction Speed	x	x	x	•
Quantitative Knowledge	•	•	•	•
Reading and Writing	x	x	x	•

diagnostic subtests assess working memory and processing speed. Although a scaled score is not produced, the test, like the KABC-II, assesses sequential and simultaneous information processing. As with other intelligence and cognitive ability tests, the DAS-II can be used to assess an individual's pattern of strengths and weakness by comparing scores on the three clusters as well as specific subtest scores. The core battery for school-age children consists of six subtests and typically can be administered within an hour. The more specific abilities those subtests assess include knowledge of word definitions, verbal abstract reasoning, visual–spatial reasoning, inductive reasoning with visual symbols, quantitative reasoning, immediate recall with geometric designs, and visual–spatial deductive reasoning, One aspect of the DAS-II that is unique among intelligence and cognitive ability tests is that *t* scores are generated for the subtests. Together, the results from the core and additional diagnostic subtests can facilitate a better understanding of a child's information processing and learning styles.

Having now summarized the four prominent tests of intelligence and cognitive ability and their multiple components, how do those tests compare? One way to compare these four tests—Wechsler Scales, KABC-II, SB5, and DAS-II—is the degree to which they assess CHC midlevel abilities. Although theories of intelligence will continue to evolve, the CHC model has gained tremendous support and has guided the revisions to these tests. Table 13.3 lists the midlevel CHC abilities and whether or not there are subtests within these four major tests that assess those abilities. Keep in mind, however, that the precise methods and items for assessing these CHC abilities will vary, to some degree, from test to test.

Cognitive Assessment System (CAS)

One other relatively recent noteworthy contribution to the field of cognitive and intellectual assessment is the *Das–Naglieri Cognitive Assessment System* (CAS) (Naglieri & Das, 1997). Das, Kirby, and Jarman (1975) built on the work of Luria and expanded and revised his model as an alternative to the prevailing hierarchical models of intelligence. This model, as described previously, posits four primary, nonhierarchical, and interrelated information processes: attention, successive processing, simultaneous processing, and planning. Jack Naglieri was also a significant contributor to the development of some of the K-ABC subtests (Kaufman & Kaufman, 1983). Together, Naglieri and Das (1990) developed their PASS theory of cognitive processing, and the CAS is designed to measure those four cognitive processes in children ages 5 to 17 using eight subtests. Their analysis of the earlier versions of the WISC-IV (WISC-R) and KABC-II K-ABC led them to conclude that both tests were adequate for assessing successive and simultaneous information processing capabilities but deficient in assessing attention and planning. As with other new theories and tests, the hope with the CAS is that it will have better clinical utility in terms of helping children with learning disabilities and other cognitive problems such as attention deficit–hyperactivity disorder.

Cognitive Ability Screening Tests

There are several other less commonly used tests of cognitive and intellectual abilities that are often used as screening instruments. Two of these are brief versions of the Wechsler and Kaufman tests to be used across the lifespan. In addition to their use as screening tools for more comprehensive cognitive assessments, they are both designed as reevaluation tools and supplements to a comprehensive psychiatric evaluation, especially where detailed quantitative information about cognitive functioning is needed, but not necessarily an IQ score. The *Wechsler Abbreviated Scale of Intelligence* (WASI) (Wechsler, 1999) is for individuals ages 6 to 89 and the *Kaufman Brief Intelligence Test*—Second Edition (KBIT-2) (Kaufman & Kaufman, 2004b) is for ages 4 to 90. The WASI has two and four subtest versions and the two-subtest version can be completed in 15 minutes. The four subtests are parallel versions of the WISC-III and WAIS-III subtests: Vocabulary, Similarities, Block Design, and Matrix Reasoning. In addition to screening for more comprehensive evaluation, the WASI can be used for reevaluating individuals who were originally tested with a full Wechsler Scale. The KBIT-2 consists of three subtests, two crystallized (vocabulary and abstract reasoning) and one fluid (visual–spatial reasoning), and can be completed in approximately 20 minutes. It too is designed for screening and reevaluation purposes. Other brief screening tests include *McCarthy Screening Test,* an abbreviated version of the *McCarthy Scales of Children's Abilities* for ages 2½ to 8½; *Reynolds Intellectual Screening Test* (RIST), ages 3–94, with a verbal and nonverbal subtest; *Shipley-2,* ages 7–89, and consisting of two subtests: a 40-item vocabulary test and a multiple-choice test of fluid reasoning test involving block patterns; and the *Slosson Intelligence Test Revised for Children and Adults,* ages 4–65, a test of verbal knowledge, comprehension, and reasoning and abstract and quantitative reasoning.

Cognitive ability screening tests have their advantages and limitations. Their primary purpose is to identify clients who would benefit from a more comprehensive cognitive ability test. They are relatively easy and quick to administer and can identify those who may have weaknesses in two primary areas: verbal reasoning and visual–perceptual reasoning without the time it takes to administer an entire intelligence test. On the other hand, they are limited because they do not assess major domains of cognitive ability such as short-term or working memory and processing speed. In addition, they are not intended to be used for diagnostic and placement decisions and should not be used for those purposes.

Neuropsychological Tests

Neuropsychological tests are related to cognitive ability tests in that they assess specific aspects of brain functioning and are used when there is suspicion of brain impairment or disease. In cases of traumatic brain injury and stroke, or when dementia or specifically Alzheimer's disease is unfolding, a neuropsychological test may be used, especially when results of medical imaging and functioning tests (PET and CAT scans, MRI, and EEG) are inconclusive or negative.

To a lesser extent, neuropsychological testing may be used in cases of chronic substance abuse or schizophrenia because of the impact those disorders can have on brain functioning. A neuro-psychological assessment can include tests that are multidimensional cognitive ability tests like those found on the WAIS-IV or KABC-II, or unidimensional tests that assess one aspect of brain functioning such as memory. The *Wechsler Memory Scale*—Fourth Edition (WMS-IV) is an example of an unidimensional neuropsychological test that measures working and long-term memory using a variety of stimuli. The WMS-IV assesses visual–spatial and logical memory and to a lesser extent, auditory memory. Other aspects of brain functioning that can be assessed with neuropsychological tests include processes such as attention and speed of information processing, verbal comprehension, planning and problem solving, visual–spatial perception, organization, and reasoning, and visual–motor coordination and planning (Groth-Marnat, 2003). Some of the more frequently used neuropsychological tests, in addition to the WMS-IV include *Halstead–Reitan Neuropsychological Test Battery* and specific subtests (Finger-Tapping Test and Grooved Pegboard) and the *FAS Word Fluency Test and Category Test* (Camara, Nathan, & Puente, 2000). Typically, a neuropsychological evaluation will consist of two or more tests or subtests from a multidimensional ability test or a neuropsychological test battery, like the Halstead–Reitan. The choice of instruments is related to the specific referral question(s). For example, if the question is, "What are my client's current memory strengths and weaknesses?" then tests of memory processes will be selected.

THE NATURE OF INTELLIGENCE AND IQ TESTING: CONTROVERSIES, KNOWNS, AND UNKNOWNS

Controversies and Questions

Controversies have swirled around the use of intelligence tests and IQ scores since the U.S. Army began using them as a screening tool in World War I. Debate has focused on whether intelligence is mostly a product of genetics and the social implications for racial–ethnic groups who, on average, have scored lower on standardized intelligence tests (Gottfredson & Saklofske, 2009; Jensen, 1980). If intelligence is essentially genetically determined, and groups on average are found to have lower IQ scores, then claims of racial and ethnic superiority and inferiority arise. Arthur Jensen's *Bias in Mental Testing* was the seminal research in this area. He and others (Neisser et al., 1996) have found that African Americans score about 15 IQ points less than Whites, and Hispanic groups in between the two. What accounts for these ethnic group differences in overall IQ scores remains a matter of research and scholarly debate but does not appear to be related to one single factor (Neisser et al., 1996). It is important for counselors and other mental health professionals to bear in mind that differences in full-scale IQ scores found among various groups is not a result of test bias or test administration and that membership in a particular group cannot predict one's level of intelligence. When it comes to intelligence, there is more variation within any one racial–ethnic group than there is between two groups (Neisser et al., 1996).

Other challenging questions that have been raised are 1) Does intelligence change over the lifespan? 2) Do IQ scores have predictive value? 3) What impact do different environmental and cultural factors—education and teaching, exposure to chemicals, poverty, and family system—have on intelligence test scores? The answers to those questions have been summarized along with the supporting research by a task force of the American Psychological Association (Neisser et al., 1996). Briefly, their report provided the following conclusions: intelligence as measured by IQ scores is pretty stable during development. That is, IQ scores obtained at different stages, elementary school age, middle school, and late adolescence are highly correlated with one another. Although an individual's performance on repeated measures of intelligence may fluctuate significantly over time, his or her relative standing with respect to the peer group remains fairly stable. That is, if an individual is found to have overall intelligence in the average range in elementary school, the likelihood that his or her intellectual functioning will still be in that range by adolescence is high. The relationship between IQ scores and academic and vocational scores is not as strong, however, as the developmental relationship. There is some moderate relationship between full-scale IQ and academic achievement but much less of a relationship between IQ and occupational success. Specifically, FSIQ scores have been shown through substantial research to correlate reasonably well (0.50) with academic performance (i.e., grades) in traditional school settings and number of years of education, somewhat less so with occupational performance, and very little with future negative outcomes such as involvement in crime. In addition, much is still unknown regarding environmental influences on intelligence, which continues to be an ongoing field of study.

Although IQ scores have been found to be fairly stable during development, an unexplained phenomenon has been found: IQ scores were rising worldwide between the late 1950s and early 1980s by approximately 3 IQ points per decade. James Flynn (1987, 1999) was the first researcher to systematically analyze the data documenting this phenomenon, which was subsequently labeled the "Flynn effect." This finding further fueled the nature–nurture debate and led some to speculate about which environmental factors—more complex lifestyles or nutritional changes—may be playing a significant role in determining intelligence, at least the kind measured by intelligence tests. These documented gains in IQ scores were occurring during a time when measures of academic achievement were mixed. SAT scores declined from the mid-1960s to 1980, whereas other tests of reading and math achievement showed no gain or some improvement for certain ethnic groups (Neisser et al., 1996). This led Flynn (1999, p. 6) to wonder, "How could American students be getting so much brighter, as measured by IQ tests, and yet be learning no more in school as measured by achievement tests?"

The IQ debates and controversies have been played out for decades both in scholarly peer-reviewed journals and popular magazines such as the *Atlantic Monthly* and *New Republic*. Long-standing arguments about the nature of intelligence and the interpretation of IQ scores were rekindled with the publication in 1994 of *The Bell Curve: Intelligence and Class Structure in American Life* by Herrnstein and Murray. Those who have defended the use of intelligence tests stress that it is not the tests themselves that are problematic but how IQ scores are interpreted (Gottfredson & Saklofske, 2009; Kaufman, 1979). Defenders of intelligence tests, such as Kaufman, recognize the limitations and shortcomings of intelligence tests but believe they are the best tools available for understanding an individual's cognitive functioning, predicting academic achievement in a traditional educational setting, and gathering information that can lead to beneficial individualized educational interventions. Some who have criticized the shortcomings of traditional intelligence tests have developed their own theories of the nature of intelligence. The two most prominent critics to espouse alternative theories have been Robert Sternberg and Howard Gardner.

Are the Existing Models Incomplete?

STERNBERG'S TRIARCHIC THEORY   Another theory of intellectual and cognitive abilities that incorporates an information processing model is Sternberg's triarchic theory (Sternberg, 1988).

Sternberg, however, views information processing and factor analytic models of intellectual and cognitive functioning as incomplete. He has advocated for a more comprehensive and contextual model of intelligence that returns to the concept of adaptation formulated decades earlier by Binet, Simon, and Wechsler. According to Sternberg (1997, p. 1030), "intelligence comprises the mental abilities necessary for adaptation to, as well as shaping and selection of, any environmental context." A more complete model of intelligence, he believes, examines the mind of the individual, that is, what he or she is thinking when acting intelligently, the external world the individual lives in, and how experience mediates the relationship between the internal and external contexts (Sternberg, 1988). By formulating a broader contextual model of intelligence that includes concepts traditional theories have ignored, his model only partially resembles traditional information processing models discussed earlier.

Sternberg's (1985, 1988, 1997) triarchic model is based on the interaction of the environmental context and internal context, which consists of three interrelated parts that form a feedback loop: metacognition, performance, and knowledge acquisition. The environmental context defines what intelligent behavior is—intelligent people are those who adapt to and shape their environment. The metacognitive component is called upon in novel situations and is a kind of analytical ability similar to aspects of fluid intelligence, which traditional IQ tests have measured. Metacognitive abilities are in essence effective problem-solving skills and include 1) awareness that a problem exists, 2) problem definition, 3) constructing problem-solving strategies, 4) ways to mentally represent information about the problem, 5) using mental energy to solve the problem, 6) monitoring how problem solving is going, and 7) evaluating whether or not a solution worked (Sternberg, 1988). The performance component involves the steps used to carry out metacognition, and knowledge acquisition is the learning that occurs through engaging in problem-solving thoughts and behaviors. These core analytic abilities are necessary for adaptation in any environmental context, although the specific strategies one acquires are culturally dependent.

Sternberg in his writings and research has emphasized the aspect of intelligence that traditional intelligence tests have ignored: practical or commonsense smarts. Sternberg and his colleagues (1995) have argued that practical intelligence is not just job or situation specific, and that it is unrelated to one's IQ as measured by traditional cognitive ability tests. The test they developed, the *Sternberg Triarchic Abilities Test* assesses analytical, creative, and practical intelligences with multiple-choice and essay questions and has been used for research purposes, but has not yet been published for clinical or educational assessment purposes.

GARDNER'S THEORY OF MULTIPLE INTELLIGENCES   Howard Gardner's theory of multiple intelligences or "frames of mind" (1993) is based on his research with children and brain-damaged adults and the work of Jean Piaget and is also a response to what he saw as the limitations with traditional theories and tests of intelligence. Gardner proposed a "preliminary list" of seven independent intelligences: linguistic, logical–mathematical, spatial, musical, bodily–kinesthetic, interpersonal, and intrapersonal. The linguistic and logical–mathematical are conceptually similar to cognitive abilities described as verbal and quantitative reasoning. Spatial intelligence as Gardner defines it may also be similar to visual–spatial abilities identified in the CHC model (Gottfredson & Saklofske, 2009). The other types of intelligence broaden the conceptualization of intelligence to include social—the ability to cooperate, understand, and empathize with other people—and intrapersonal (the ability to self-reflect and understand self) intelligences as well as the abilities that musicians, athletes, dancers, and other professionals possess. According to his multidimensional model, all of these intelligences have equal value, but the strength and weakness of a particular intelligence is what varies among human beings. Like Sternberg, Gardner defined intelligence in terms of cultural adaptation: "the ability to solve problems or fashion products that are of consequence in a particular cultural setting or community" (Gardner, 1993, p. 15). Gardner's main criticism of existing cognitive ability tests is that they favor linguistic and logical intelligences and that assessment of those abilities is detached from the environments in which they are utilized. With this view of intelligence in mind, Gardner advocated for a more ecologically valid or naturalistic form of assessment whereby multiple intelligences are measured in ways that better correspond to how these abilities are manifested in daily life. To date, however, no formal or informal tests have been developed to assess all seven intelligences.

CULTURAL CONSIDERATIONS

Several of the intelligence tests currently on the market are advertised as "culturally fair." What does it mean for a cognitive ability test to be culturally fair? Is it even possible for one test to be "fair" to peoples of all cultures? Historically, intelligence tests like the Wechsler Scales were seen as disadvantaging those whose primary language was not English, given the receptive and expressive language demands of the test, as well as those whose educational environment provided less exposure and learning of concepts depicted on specific subtests. For example, earlier versions of the Wechsler Scales included items and pictures on several subtests that reflected the values and learning experiences of the mainstream American culture in the 1950s and 1960s that individuals from minority cultures may not have been exposed to.

With those problems in mind, several intelligence tests were developed that significantly reduced or eliminated language demands. The *Leiter International Performance Scale,* published in 1948 and revised in 1997, is an individually administered test for ages 2 to 20 with virtually no verbal or mimed instructions and does not require speech responses (Hooper & Bell, 2006). There are 20 subtests that measure the following abilities: visual–spatial reasoning, memory, and attention processes. It was developed with various ethnic groups—Native American, Hispanic, and African American, and it is predominantly a nonverbal test that produces an IQ score (Roid & Miller, 1997). Other tests were developed that were either predominantly or exclusively tests of visual–spatial reasoning and included tasks involving visual–spatial: analogies, classification, relationships, and sequential processing. *Raven's Progressive Matrices, Cattell's Culture Fair Intelligence Test,* the *Test of Nonverbal Intelligence-3* (TONI-3), and the *Universal Nonverbal Intelligence Test* (UNIT) are examples of intelligence tests with minimal or no language demands (Drummond & Jones, 2006). Tests like the TONI-3, the *Leiter International Performance Scale—Revised* and the UNIT are often used with children with hearing impairments and speech and language disabilities.

Individuals with other kinds of disabilities—visual or motor impairments—may also be given a test like the Leiter–Revised where their physical disabilities will not interfere with their performance as much as they would on a test like the KABC-II, which has more motor demands. Alternatively, the individual, depending upon the disability, may be given a portion of a test like the WISC-IV. A child who has a serious visual impairment would likely be administered only the verbal comprehension and working memory subtests on the WISC-IV. If a child has some type of physical handicap, whether it be hearing, vision, or movement, then the Individuals with Disabilities Educational Act requires, and *Standards for Educational and Psychological Testing* (APA, AERA, & NCME, 1999) (see Chapter 2) endorses, that the person be tested with a modification of an existing test or use a test whereby the individual's performance will not be adversely affected by his or her disability.

As with other tests discussed in previous chapters, the trend with intelligence test revisions has been to obtain a standardization sample that closely matches U.S. Census data for race-ethnicity, gender, and socioeconomic status, develop separate language versions, and do validation studies with different cultures from various countries. For example, the WISC-III and WAIS-III were adapted for use and standardized in 16 different European and Asian countries and a Spanish version of the WISC-IV is available with a French version in development. As part of the development of the KABC-II, a cross-cultural validation study with a group of Pueblo Indian children from New Mexico, who had significant cultural differences from the standardization sample in terms of language, socioeconomic status, diet, and religious practices, was found to have similar average scores on all of the KABC-II subtests (Fletcher-Janzen, 2009). This was an unexpected finding given that studies comparing the performance of relatively less acculturated groups and the standardization sample with the original K-ABC found the less acculturated groups to have lower average performances.

Speed is one other dimension that cultures value and promote differently. Yet processing speed is considered a core intellectual ability in different Western theories of intelligence, and performance on some intelligence tests is either increased because of quick and accurate responding, or penalized for slow but accurate responding. Although as Table 13.3 illustrates, not all cognitive ability tests assess processing and decision-making speed.

These are just a few examples of the trend toward revising existing cognitive and intellectual ability tests with an emphasis on broader cultural usefulness. In addition, tests that minimize or eliminate language demands will continue to play an important role in the cognitive assessments of individuals who have speech, language, or hearing impairments, visual or motor impairments, and a primary language other than English.

ASSESSING ACHIEVEMENT

Overview

Achievement tests measure knowledge and skills acquired in specific subject areas, especially the "3 R's," reading, writing, and arithmetic. Some achievement tests cover just one subject area, though most are broader in scope. Reading subtests on these various achievement tests might include the various components necessary for successful reading: vocabulary knowledge, word recognition and decoding, comprehension, and fluency (ease and speed in reading and understanding). Math subtests focus on quantitative knowledge and skills such as computational skills, fluency, and quantitative reasoning and relationships. Writing tests typically involve spelling tests or sentence composition. There are also narrow, one-subject achievement tests such as the *Peabody Vocabulary Test*.

As discussed earlier, one way to distinguish between intelligence and achievement tests is that achievement tests measure knowledge gained through a specific structured program, like a math class, whereas intelligence tests measure underlying or latent abilities an individual possesses that might be thought of as requisite skills for mastering the content of achievement tests. Also, successful performance on intelligence tests is less dependent upon formal instruction or what has been termed *crystalized intelligence*. Though keep in mind that some intelligence or cognitive ability tests have a small set of subtests that do assess crystallized intelligence or acquired knowledge and are similar in content to an achievement test of the same subject such as vocabulary knowledge (Nagileri & Bornstein, 2003). This distinction reflects a difference in how these two types of tests are often used. Achievement tests are used to *evaluate* what someone has learned, and intelligence or cognitive ability tests are used to *predict* learning (Reynolds & Kamphaus, 2003). Therefore, any classroom test designed by a teacher is considered an achievement test even if it has not been normed and evaluated psychometrically.

One of the most common reasons to administer an achievement test is for identifying a student, as in the case study of Joshua, as having some type of learning disability. Other reasons why achievement tests are used include assessing the effect of remedial intervention or instruction strategies, selecting students for specific interventions or programs, and evaluating the effectiveness of entire educational programs. Achievement tests are most often used in educational settings K–12 and to a lesser extent in postsecondary and organizational settings. They are also used sometimes in career counseling and vocational settings to help identify an individual's academic strengths and weaknesses that can facilitate job and career placement decisions. The following achievement tests are some of the more commonly used ones for individuals, particularly when there is reason to suspect a learning disability or below-grade-level academic functioning (see Table 13.4): *Kaufman Test of Educational Achievement,* Second Edition (KTEA-II), *Woodcock–Johnson-III Tests of Achievement* (WJ-III, AcH), *Wide Range Achievement Test-4* (WRAT-4), *Wechsler Individual Achievement Test,* Third Edition (WIAT-III) and *Peabody Individual Aptitude Test* (PIAT). In general, achievement tests do not require as much specialized training to administer, score, and interpret as intelligence and cognitive ability tests, and therefore test user qualifications tend to be at the second or B level.

Common Achievement Tests

WOODCOCK–JOHNSON TEST OF ACHIEVEMENT—THIRD EDITION (WJ-III-Ach)

Of the tests listed in Table 13.4, the *Woodcock–Johnson Tests of Achievement*—Third Edition (WJ-III-Ach) (Woodcock, McGrew, & Mather, 2001) is the broadest and has become one of the most popular in K–12 settings. The companion test to the WJ-III-Ach is the *WJ-III Tests of Cognitive Abilities* (WJ-III-Cog), which was normed with the WJ-III-Ach and drew upon the CHC model for revising subtests and the respective test items. One criticism, however, of WJ-III-Ach is that some of the subtests are redundant with the cognitive abilities counterpart (Naglieri & Bornstein, 2003). For example, the verbal comprehension cognitive ability subtest and the reading vocabulary— Synonyms Achievement subtest—contain nearly identical items. The WJ-III-Ach comprises

Table 13.4 Achievement Tests

Name	Age Range	Content[1]
Kaufman Test of Educational Achievement, Second Edition (KTEA-II)	4–25	R, M, WL, & OL
Peabody Individual Aptitude Test (PIAT)	5–22	GK, R, M, WL, & S
Wechsler Individual Achievement Test, Third Edition (WIAT-III)	4–19	R, M, WL, OL, & S
Woodcock–Johnson-III (WJ-III)	2–90	GK, R, M, WL, & OL
Wide Range Achievement Test-4 (WRAT-4)	5–94	R, M, & S

[1]GK = general knowledge; M = math and computational skills; OL = oral language skills; R = reading related skills; S = spelling; WL = written language skills

22 subtests covering not only reading, writing, and arithmetic, but grammar, science, social studies, and humanities knowledge, awareness of sounds (e.g., rhymes), and comprehending directions as well. The Understanding Directions subtest consists of items measuring auditory processing and short-term memory and again reflects the overlap between some of the WJ-III achievement and ability subtests. The WJ-III-Ach consists of a standard battery (subtests 1–12) and an extended battery (subtests 13–22) and has been normed for ages 2 to 90. The number of items per subtest varies widely from 9 on the Sound Awareness to 160 on Math Fluency and becomes increasingly more difficult as the subtest progresses. Each subtest can be administered in approximately five minutes.

The psychometric properties of the WCJ-III are excellent and the normative sample was recently updated. The normative sample consisted of 8,818 individuals from over 100 different communities across the United States and was selected based on 13 socioeconomic variables (Woodcock et al., 2001). Both age- and grade-based norms are available for interpreting test scores. Internal reliability estimates for the subtests are 0.80 and higher, with some 0.90 or greater. The Woodcock–Johnson tests have been popular in educational settings because of their comprehensive coverage of a broad array of subjects not typically covered on other achievement tests.

WECHSLER INDIVIDUAL ACHIEVEMENT TEST—THIRD EDITION (WIAT-III) The *Wechsler Individual Achievement Test*—Third Edition (WIAT-III) is another popular and commonly used achievement test. The WIAT-III is designed for ages 4 to 50 and consists of 16 subtests (Pearson, 2009). The subtests are similar in content to the WJC-III and include Reading Comprehension, Oral Reading Fluency, Early Reading Skills, Listening Comprehension, Oral Expression, Written Expression (Spelling and Sentence and Essay Composition), Math Fluency (Addition and Subtraction), and Math Problem Solving. The time to administer the subtest is somewhat variable.

The technical properties of the WIAT-III are adequate (Miller, 2010) The test was normed on 3,000 individuals throughout the United States. Internal reliabilities range from 0.69 to 0.87, averaged over grade (pre-kindergarten–12) for the oral language and written expression subtests (Breaux & Frey, 2010).

KAUFMAN TESTS OF EDUCATIONAL ACHIEVEMENT—SECOND EDITION The *Kaufman Tests of Educational Achievement*—Second Edition (KTEA-II) consist of two parts: the comprehensive form for individuals ages 4 years 6 months to 25 years and a brief form that can be used up to age 90 (Kaufman & Kaufman, 2005). The KTEA-II, comprehensive form, consists of four major domains or composites: reading, math, oral and written language, for a total of 14 subtests. The KTEA-II was normed along with the *Kaufman Ability Scales,* KABC-II and KIAT, and those norms closely match the 2000 U.S. Census data (Kaufman & Kaufman, 2005). The internal reliability estimates for the 14 subtests are in the adequate range (Erford, 2006).

Interpreting Achievement Tests

Scores on achievement tests, like cognitive ability tests, can be analyzed at three levels: subtest, composite or scale, and overall score. As with ability tests, overall scores are less useful for assessing an individual's pattern of strengths and weaknesses than subtest and composite scores. In addition to standard scores like percentiles, most achievement tests produce age- and grade-equivalent scores. As you may recall from Chapter 6, those latter scores are based on the average scores at specific age and grade levels from the normative sample. Therefore, these tests can provide information about the degree to which an individual's performance in particular areas is consistent with age or grade peers, but does not indicate the actual grade level at which the test taker is performing. Similar to ability tests, standard scores between 85 and 115 are in the average range for subtests and composite scores on the WCJ-III, WIAT-III, and KTEA-II. Significant differences among subtest and composite or scale scores are the basis for determining an individual's relative strengths and weaknesses. The manual for a specific test (e.g., the WCJ-III) typically provides information about how much of a difference in standard scores is needed to call the discrepancy significant.

The interpretation of achievement test scores can be illustrated with the case study of Joshua. The school psychologist who tested Joshua administered some of WCJ-III subtests, the entire WIAT-III, and the *Test of Word Reasoning Efficiency* (TOWRE), a measure of fluency and phonemic decoding skills. His scores on the WIAT-III ranged from low-average to average (see Table 13.5). The results from the two WCJ-III subtests (Reading Fluency and Math Fluency) were consistent with his WIAT-III scores. Both tests revealed a weakness for Joshua with mathematical operational and reasoning skills and overall math fluency. His writing skills were a relative strength; all were in the average range. Reading skills, however, were more variable. The WIAT-III and WCJ-III results showed that he does better with reading decoding and fluency than he does with understanding what he reads. Reading comprehension is particularly challenging for him when the length of the material is several paragraphs.

Joshua's achievement test scores were also interpreted in the context of his WISC-IV scores, which were in the average range for his FSIQ and three of the four index scores: Perceptual Reasoning, Working Memory, and Processing Speed. Verbal Comprehension was in the low-average range but that was due to Joshua's relative weak performance on a test of abstract verbal reasoning. His math achievement scores, fluency, and numerical operations were significantly less than his cognitive ability index scores. Comparisons between achievement and cognitive ability, particularly IQ scores, have been the traditional procedure for evaluating learning

Table 13.5 Joshua's Achievement Test Scores

Subtest	Standard Score	Percentile Rank
WIAT-III:		
Listening Comprehension	93	32
Reading Comprehension	80	9
Word Reading	87	18
Pseudoword Decoding	93	32
Oral Reading Fluency	89	23
Oral Expression	96	39
Math Problem Solving	80	9
Numerical Operations	69	2
Math Fluency—Addition	77	6
Math Fluency—Subtraction	75	5
Sentence Composition	94	34
Essay Composition	89	23
Spelling	89	23
WCJ-III:		
Reading Fluency	94	34
Math Fluency	77	6

disabilities. One method for assessing for the presence of a learning disability is to determine if there is a statistically significant difference between achievement and ability scores. That method, however, is problematic, as will be discussed shortly. Although there were not statistically significant differences between his reading achievement test scores and his cognitive ability scores, he did demonstrate a weakness in the area of reading comprehension when compared to his same age peers. This weakness was found despite a year and a half of intensive evidenced-based reading instruction. Math skills were also below average but Joshua had not received intensive instruction in that area. The school psychologist and Joshua's education team needed to unravel this puzzle and figure out what was accounting for these lower-than-average scores. Are they a result, perhaps, of a learning disability, emotional factors that affected his performance on the testing day as well as his day-to-day learning in the classroom, or possibly inattentiveness and distractibility?

Assessing Learning Disabilities

The WCJ-III Ach, WIAT-III, and KTEA-II are designed to be aligned with the 2004 revision of the Individuals with Disabilities Education Act (IDEA), a set of federal government regulations pertaining to special education practices and procedures, including how learning disabilities are defined and evaluated. IDEA was first enacted in 1975 as public law 94-142, the Education for All Handicapped Children Act, and renamed in 1990. It was intended to improve the practices of identifying, evaluating, and educating children with various special needs. The 2004 IDEA recognizes the following eight categories of academic abilities: oral expression, listening comprehension, written expression, basic reading skills, reading comprehension, reading fluency, and mathematics calculations and reasoning (U.S. Department of Education, 2004). An individual can now, according to federal law, be diagnosed with a learning disability if he or she displays inadequate academic achievement given his or her age and grade level despite appropriate experience and instruction in the subject matter. This is the concept of **response to intervention (RTI)**. Students, like Joshua, who are provided intensive evidence-based educational intervention in one or more of the eight academic areas cited previously, and still lag behind as evidenced from grade-level benchmarks (i.e., standardized achievement tests), can be diagnosed with a learning disability. If a student, despite receiving instruction in a method that has been shown empirically to raise academic performance for representative groups of children, is not responding to that intervention, then some kind of learning problem is likely accounting for that lack of progress. In other words, if the teaching method has previously been shown to be effective and therefore is not in question, then the problem may lie within the individual's brain or manner in which he processes information. This is a significant change from the traditional definition of learning disability, which required a severe discrepancy between ability, typically measured by an intelligence test, and aptitude, as measured by an achievement test, in order to call someone learning disabled. A major problem with that definition was that "severe discrepancy" was arbitrary (i.e., how much of a difference in IQ and achievement scores was needed to be severe). Some states required that schools diagnose a learning disability only if the IQ-achievement discrepancy was at least two standard deviations, and others had a less stringent requirement, 1.5 standard deviations. That lack of a consistent standard resulted in huge variations across the country in learning disability diagnoses. A second problem with the traditional learning disability definition was that it excluded many children who displayed significant cognitive processing weaknesses but did not demonstrate the ability–achievement discrepancy. In other words, if a child had lower-than-average cognitive abilities and lower-than-average achievement scores there might not be a difference between the two sets of scores, but the low scores may indeed reflect some kind of information processing problem. The RTI process, in essence, is a solution to the problematic discrepancy model. School districts still have the option of using the discrepancy model if they so choose, but RTI is considered a more effective way to assess for learning disabilities (U.S. Department of Education, 2006).

Take a student like Joshua who was having difficulty with reading skills and immerse him in a scientifically based instruction program. Then provide that instruction intensively and measure his achievement with standardized tests. Theoretically, he will make sufficient progress and catch up to his peers if he does not have some type of information processing problem. If progress is not occurring, then there exists the possibility that his brain is processing information in such a way that makes, in this case, reading, a very difficult task. It is not, however, only a matter of instructional method or information processing abilities that determines achievement test performance. As has been stressed throughout this text, test scores cannot be viewed in isolation, and good assessment practice requires a contextual examination and understanding of scores. When low scores on an achievement test are found, the assessor's job is to explain the scores and in this case determine whether this is the result of a learning disability, limited academic exposure and instruction, or some other contributing factors. Other factors such as anxiety, attention, fatigue, and motivation can all play a role, and therefore the assessment of a learning disability, like other diagnoses, needs to integrate multiple pieces of data from different sources: test scores, student observation, teacher and parent reports, and classroom performance.

Summary and Conclusions

Traditional tests of cognitive abilities have undergone numerous revisions so that the two oldest tests—Wechsler and Stanford–Binet—are more similar in theoretical foundation and content than ever before. The Cattell–Horn–Carroll (CHC) three-level hierarchical model of cognitive abilities has emerged as the major model influencing the revisions of both traditional and newer tests such as the KABC-II. The CHC model posits a g factor, or overall cognitive ability, ten midlevel factors or abilities, and 80 narrow abilities. The midlevel factors include fluid reasoning (reasoning with novel stimuli), comprehension knowledge (learned or acquired information), visual and auditory processing, long- and short-term memory processes, cognitive processing speed, and decision and reaction speed. The tests being used in clinical and educational settings assess primarily these core abilities and processes that make up this CHC model. How those broad abilities are measured, along with whether or not other cognitive abilities such as planning, problem solving, and sequential and simultaneous processing are assessed, is what differentiate the various cognitive ability

tests. Those tests designated as intellectual or cognitive ability tests assess a broad range of abilities—both fluid and crystallized—whereas those labeled as achievement or aptitude tests tend to be narrower in scope, measuring only acquired knowledge or what has been learned from some type of formal instruction. Consequently, some cognitive ability tests have achievement-like subtests on them, such as Vocabulary on the Wechsler Scales. In general, however, cognitive ability tests assesses underlying capacities or abilities necessary for successful learning and daily functioning, whereas achievement tests assess the outcome of that learning.

Despite what may appear to be a convergence and unification in the field of intelligence testing, some researchers and theorists have suggested that little has changed over the past century of revisions and that important aspects of what might be considered "intellectual" abilities are not being assessed. Tests of emotional, practical, and creative intelligence have emerged more recently, but to date have been the province of research investigations, not mainstream clinical and educational practice.

Notwithstanding that criticism, cognitive abilities tests are likely to continue to play an important role in the assessment of learning disabilities and cognitive functioning that has been impacted by brain injury or disease. Ultimately, as with any assessment tool, tests of cognitive abilities are only as good as their capacity to predict future functioning and inform intervention, instructional, and remediation efforts. Developments in neuroscience, brain imaging techniques, and statistical modeling are likely to have an impact on future revisions of tests as well as the development of new ones such as the *Cognitive Assessment System*.

Cognitive ability tests have their greatest value when used to identify patterns of individual strengths and weaknesses rather than tools for classification and global predictions. Pattern or profile analysis has assessment utility in that it provides a pathway for intervention: instructional and remediation efforts. A sophisticated understanding of those patterns and the theoretical constructs underlying them requires advanced training beyond what a single graduate assessment course can provide and is why cognitive ability tests are appropriately designated as level C instruments. This is probably apparent when one compares what knowledge is required to understand a relatively straightforward self-report measure like the BDI-II with that required for a test like the WISC-IV. Even if one is not going to perform a cognitive assessment, an understanding of what cognitive ability tests do and do not measure can facilitate referrals for this type of assessment and help clients, family members, and other stakeholders understand the nature of, and reasons for, this kind of assessment.

Reflection Questions and Experiential Exercises

1. What are the similarities and differences between achievement and ability tests?
2. Which cognitive abilities do you think should be assessed on a test that purports to be a comprehensive measure of intelligence?
3. When might you refer a client for assessment of intellectual functioning, cognitive processing abilities, or neuropsychological testing?
4. What information can an intelligence test provide about a client beyond a description of overall intellectual level (e.g., average)?
5. Some ability tests are marketed as being "culturally fair." What types of questions do you think belong and don't belong on a culturally fair test?
6. Think of three people whom you consider intelligent or smart. What is it about those people that makes them smart? What similarities and differences do they share in their "smarts"? Share your answers to these two questions with two other classmates.
7. How would you go about explaining to a parent whose child received an overall cognitive ability score of 90 what that means? What is the limitation of an overall ability score and what other test scores would you want the parent to understand?

14 ASSESSING THE THERAPEUTIC ALLIANCE

Chapter Objectives

After reading this chapter, you should be able to:

- Identify standardized therapeutic alliance questionnaires.
- Explain the benefits and limitations of those questionnaires.
- Understand the cultural implications of using alliance questionnaires.
- Understand how research findings impact the use of these questionnaires in counseling settings.

Amy, a 19-year-old college sophomore, was seeing Dr. Samson for counseling at a local university counseling center because of things "not feeling real." This was her fourth experience with counseling since her senior year in high school but her first with a male therapist. Amy described a sense of living in a dream state, of feeling detached, and lacking energy to study. She was also troubled by stress and conflict with her roommate. Amy reported that things had changed after her senior year in high school following a family trip to China. Her parents had suspected she had medical complications stemming from a flu virus she caught while in China. Medical testing was done but proved to be negative. When asked about her previous counseling, Amy appeared uncomfortable and looked away. When she looked back she said, "It did not help. The last counselor I saw was weird—she kept telling me to think positive, and that lady I saw first just listened but never told me what to do." She saw the other therapists only one or two times and did not recall anything significant about those experiences.

In subsequent counseling sessions, Dr. Samson continued exploring Amy's feelings, history of intimate relationships, and sources of stress. He was aware, however, of an active–passive dynamic between him and Amy. He found himself overcompensating for Amy's desire for him to "just tell me what I should do to feel better." And he was aware of her view that none of her previous counseling experiences were helpful. At the end of the fourth session, a session in which he had felt more challenged with communicating empathically and had suggested that Amy could try self-monitoring the time during the day she feels "most stressed," he asked Amy if she would be willing to fill out a brief questionnaire. He explained to her the purpose in filling out the questionnaire: "So I can make sure you are getting the help you need. This will help me understand better how you are feeling about our sessions."

Amy replied, "Is this because you think you can't help me anymore?"

"No, it's just that I can be more helpful to you if I have a better sense of how you feel about our sessions."

Amy agreed and was given the *Session Rating Scale, Version 3* (SRS V.3.0), which she completed in the waiting room of the counseling center immediately following the session.

OVERVIEW

During a speech at Oberlin College in 1954, Carl Rogers made this prescient statement: "If I can provide a certain type of relationship, the other person will discover within himself the capacity to use that relationship for growth, and change and personal development will occur" (Rogers, 1961, p. 33). What type of relationship did Rogers think was beneficial for individuals seeking professional counseling? He stressed the importance of therapist as facilitator by communicating empathy, unconditional positive regard, warmth, caring, and respect. Freud, on the other hand, argued for a neutral, detached relationship in order to promote transference; and Aaron Beck and other cognitive–behavioral theorists emphasized an educator role for the counselor. Might different types of relationships work better than others depending upon the client and his or her presenting problems? And what about a conceptualization of a therapeutic relationship that takes into account multiple perspectives? In searching for answers to those questions, psychotherapy researchers over the past 30 years have discovered that the therapeutic relationship is an essential, if not *the* key, ingredient affecting client progress and overall outcome. When compared to other factors—technique, theoretical orientation, and therapist experience—it is the quality of the counseling relationship that has been consistently shown to have the largest impact on client improvement (Bachelor & Horvath, 1999; Lambert & Barley, 2001; Orlinsky, Ronnestad, & Willutzki, 2003; Prochaska & Norcross, 2010). Although experts in the fields of counseling and psychology will continue to debate Roger's belief that the therapeutic relationship is both *necessary* and *sufficient* for bringing about improvement in the problems people bring to therapy, these research findings have helped to create a consensus that a strong positive counselor–client relationship is a necessary condition if change is to occur.

One specific conceptualization of the therapeutic relationship that has received a considerable amount of research and clinical attention is the notion of a counselor–client **alliance**. This chapter will discuss the concept of therapeutic alliance and questionnaires designed to measure the strength of the alliance. It will examine several specific standardized client self-report questionnaires, their advantages, disadvantages, and cultural considerations. Guidelines for using alliance questionnaires in clinical settings will also be discussed. The chapter will include a brief discussion of the current research findings on the relationship between the alliance and treatment outcome.

THE THERAPEUTIC ALLIANCE

The term *therapeutic alliance* has its roots in Freudian psychoanalysis and includes the psychoanalytic concept of transference. Greenson, another prominent psychoanalyst, expanded the notion of a therapeutic alliance to a "working" alliance between the analyst and his patient. By the mid-1970s, as other psychotherapy theories gained prominence, alternative perspectives on the alliance emerged. Edward Bordin and Lester Luborsky and his colleagues at Penn State reconceptualized the alliance to include concepts relevant to diverse theoretical orientations, including psychodynamic, cognitive–behavioral, humanistic–experiential and family systems, and possibly any professional helping relationship (Horvath, 2001). Alliance includes the facilitative aspects of the relationship Rogers spoke about: empathy, warmth, and a nonjudgmental stance, and broadens it to include the idea of a collaborative partnership (Bordin, 1979; Cecero, Fenton, Nich, Frankforter, & Carroll, 2001). The therapeutic alliance has been alternately called the "working and helping alliance" and has been operationally defined and measured differently by researchers. Their decisions to label the alliance as "working" or "helping" suggest perhaps slightly different beliefs about the fundamental nature of counselor–client collaboration. One unifying definition that has gained significant acceptance and has spawned the development of several commonly used alliance questionnaires is Bordin's conceptualization. The alliance, according to Bordin (1979) consists of three parts: 1) an emotional bond between client and therapist, 2) an agreement between client and therapist on the therapy goals, and 3) an agreement on how to achieve those goals. Bordin proposed that his working alliance construct could be generalized to any type of helping relationship where one person is seeking change and the other is an agent of change, and this alliance can develop in many places besides a therapy setting, such as the classroom.

COLLABORATIVE JOURNEY   The relationship as an alliance can be illustrated with this image. Two people, one the counselor, the other the client, Amy, are walking side by side in the woods. As they go down the trail conversing about what they are seeing, an emotional connection involving trust, respect, and caring begins to develop. Every so often they pause in their journey to examine the surrounding landscape. Together they will decide what to look at and how to look. Will they take pictures? And if so what type of camera and lens might they choose? Or perhaps they will get off the path they have been on to examine some tree or vegetation more closely. Again they will together figure out where and how to focus their attention. If Amy's ideas on where to look and how closely they should inspect things are received in a respectful, understanding, and caring manner, then further emotional bonding is likely to happen.

Now consider the landscape as Amy's thoughts, feelings, behaviors, struggles, and dilemmas. The counselor can unilaterally decide what this landscape looks like and how it will be explored. Alternatively, the counselor and Amy can come together in partnership, deciding how they will venture through this psychological landscape and what the destination will be. To put it more directly, counselor and client collaborate on the counseling goals and methods for achieving the goals. The concept of the alliance as collaboration can be further illustrated with the case of Amy. Dr. Samson might have as his goal for Amy to change her core belief about her self-worth, whereas Amy's goal is to simply stop feeling so lousy and have more energy. Amy desires symptom relief, while Dr. Samson wants his client to achieve a new set of personal beliefs. In this case, counselor–client agreement on therapy goals is missing. On the other hand, if they both agree that a change in self-concept from worthless to worthwhile is the goal, then theoretically the alliance is strengthened. But agreement on goals is just one part of the alliance. They also need to agree on the tasks, the methods by which the goals will be achieved. The counselor's preferred methods could be directing client's attention to childhood experiences and dream interpretation, directing clients to talk to an empty chair and focusing awareness on bodily sensations, instructing a client in how to keep a diary that includes situations, thoughts, and feelings, or some combination of these and other methods. The counselor's way of doing things may or may not fit with the client's view of how to work on her problems. Once again, alliance is theoretically strengthened when counselor and client act as partners coming to agreement on which methods will be used.

STANDARDIZED ALLIANCE INVENTORIES AND RATING SCALES

Since Bordin's conceptualization of alliance as part emotional bonding and part active collaboration, several standardized questionnaires and inventories have been developed to assess the quality and strength of the therapeutic alliance. A strong therapeutic alliance has been shown to be an important and powerful predictor of therapy outcome in mental health settings (Asay & Lambert, 1999; Hilsenroth, Peters, & Ackerman, 2004; Martin, Garske, & Davis, 2000).

Like measures of other constructs such as personality, psychiatric disorders, or intelligence, there is no single agreed-upon measurement tool for assessing the therapeutic alliance. Unlike those measures, however, measures for assessing therapeutic alliance have not been developed using large representative samples, and might be considered works in progress. Notwithstanding that limitation, their inclusion in a counseling assessment text is valuable given the importance of the alliance in determining client progress and as a standardized way to measure the counseling skill of relationship building and maintenance (Summers & Barber, 2003).

Research Findings

In research studies, the client's perception of the alliance, the therapist's perception of the alliance, and some outside observer's perception have all been measured, but it appears that it is the client's perception that is the best predictor of whether the client will improve (Horvath & Symonds, 1991; Martin et al., 2000). The connection between the therapeutic relationship and therapy progress and outcome has been well established through dozens of individual studies and a number of reviews of studies or meta-analyses (Asay & Lambert, 1999; Garfield & Bergin 1994; Martin et al., 2000). In reviewing the psychotherapy outcome literature, Asay and Lambert have found that the relationship is responsible for 30% of client improvement, whereas techniques account for only 15% (the remaining 55% is due to factors such as expectancy and client factors).

Horvath (2001, p. 366) has concluded that "over half the beneficial effects of psychotherapy accounted for in previous meta-analyses are linked to the quality of the alliance." More specifically, he found the following:

- The relationship between the strength of the therapeutic alliance and client outcome is relatively the same regardless of which alliance measure is used.
- The alliance is more predictive of a client's overall perception that therapy was successful than it is of specific symptomatic improvement. This finding has been supported by other research as well (Safran & Wallner, 1991).
- The correlation between alliance measured early on (sessions 1–5) and client outcome is 0.22 and is roughly the same as when the alliance is measured later on in therapy.
- There is no significant difference among the different counseling theories when it comes to the alliance and client outcome relationship (i.e., the relationship is the same whether one uses person-centered, cognitive–behavioral, psychodynamic, or integrative therapy).

In addition, it has been found that alliance ratings obtained during psychological assessment are strongly related to alliance ratings obtained later on in therapy (Hilsenroth et al., 2004). This suggests, contrary to popular wisdom, that the information-gathering tasks of assessment do not interfere with relationship building between client and counselor. During assessment, a strong alliance can be formed if the assessment is therapeutic in focus rather than purely information gathering in nature. Although many clinicians have found it challenging to balance the information-gathering tasks of an assessment with relationship building, this study suggests that it is certainly possible, and an alliance formed as early as an intake can set the stage for and maintain a strong therapeutic alliance.

Lastly, it is important to recognize that clients enter counseling relationships with prior relationship, attachment, and sometimes counseling histories. Research has shown, not surprisingly, that individuals with borderline and other personality disorders have had more difficult times developing a therapeutic alliance. Similarly, certain attachment styles (i.e., a predominant behavioral tendency toward interpersonal relationships) may be related to poor initial alliance formation. Especially challenging is the forming of an alliance with a client who does not come seeking counseling voluntarily.

Typically, a therapy client completes an alliance inventory or questionnaire following a single therapy session and might complete it multiple times during the course of therapy. Similarly, a counselor could complete a parallel version of the questionnaire, and those ratings can be compared. What follows is an examination of four standardized therapeutic alliance measures: the *Revised Helping Alliance Questionnaire* (HAq-II) (Luborsky et al., 1996); the *Working Alliance Inventory* (WAI) (Horvath & Greenberg, 1989); *California Psychotherapy Alliance Scale* (CALPAS) (Gaston, 1991), and the *Session Rating Scale Version 3.0* (SRS V.3.0) (Duncan et al., 2003). Although other measures exist, the first three listed here have been studied the most (Martin et al., 2000), and the Session Rating Scale is the only one designed specifically for use in counseling, as opposed to research settings.

HELPING ALLIANCE QUESTIONNAIRE (HAq) The original *Helping Alliance Questionnaire,* an 11-item questionnaire measuring the strength of the therapeutic alliance, was developed in 1983. It was revised 13 years later because of a realization that several of its items were assessing symptom improvement rather than the strength of the therapist–client alliance and because all items were positively phrased (Luborsky et al., 1996). The HAq-II consists of 19 items on a 6-point Likert scale. Clients are asked to rate the degree to which they "strongly disagree" versus "strongly agree" with items. Sample items include:

- I feel I can depend upon the therapist.
- I feel the therapist wants me to achieve my goals.
- The procedures used in my therapy are not well suited to my needs.

There is both a client and therapist version with an equal number of positive and negatively worded items. The scoring is reversed for the negatively worded items. Both versions are in the public domain and can be obtained at ***http://www.med.upenn.edu/cpr/instruments.html***.

Based on one large, multisite pilot study, the HAq-II was found to have good internal consistency (Cronbach's alpha = 0.90 or greater for sessions 2, 5, and 24) and test–retest reliability (r = 0.78), and good convergent validity (correlations between the HAq-II and the CALPAS range from 0.59 at session 2 to 0.69 at session 24). The study found little relationship between pretreatment level of symptom severity and the HAq-II demonstrating good discriminant validity as well. That is, the degree of symptom severity should not, theoretically, influence the strength of the alliance and therefore the correlation between two unrelated constructs should be lower than between two related ones.

Although the HAq-II was found to have adequate reliability and validity for a standardized questionnaire, its usefulness at this point may be limited because of the small homogenous group of clients who completed it. All of the clients had a DSM-III-R diagnosis of cocaine dependence and were disproportionately male (69%). Its generalizability to diverse client populations and problems still awaits further research.

WORKING ALLIANCE INVENTORY (WAI) The *Working Alliance Inventory* (WAI) was developed in 1989, and like the HAq-II has both a client and therapist version. The WAI contains 36 items and provides an overall alliance score and three subscale scores: goal, task, and bond

(Horvath & Greenberg, 1989). Each of the three scales has 12 items, six worded in the positive directions and six in the negative (Hatcher & Barends, 1996). Each item is rated on a 7-point Likert scale ranging from "never" to "always." Sample item stems include the following (Horvath & Greenberg, 1989, p. 226):

- I feel uncomfortable with _____.
- _____ and I understand each other.
- _____ perceives accurately what my goals are.
- I believe the time _____ and I are spending together is not spent efficiently.
- _____ and I collaborate on setting goals for my therapy.
- I believe the way we are working with my problem is correct.

The reliability of the overall alliance score is good: Cronbach's alpha = 0.92 (Tracey & Kokotovic, 1989). Its validity has been established in three separate correlational studies (Kivlighan, 2007). Tichenor and Hill (1989) developed an observer version of the WAI, which enables a trained observer to rate the presence of these three components of the alliance: agreement on goals, agreement on how to achieve the goals, and the client–therapist connection.

CALIFORNIA PSYCHOTHERAPY ALLIANCE SCALE (CALPAS)   The *California Psychotherapy Alliance Scale* (CALPAS) developed in 1991 is a 24-item scale designed to assess four alliance dimensions: Patient Commitment, Patient Working Capacity, Therapist Understanding and Involvement, and Working Strategy Consensus (Gaston, 1991). Parallel client, therapist, and trained rater versions of the CALPAS are available. On the patient version, patients are asked to rate for each item the degree to which it describes his or her experience in the therapy session just completed, from "not at all" to "very much so." Sample items (Hatcher & Barends, 1996, pp. 1330–1332) include:

- Did you feel that you disagreed with your therapist about changes you would like to make in your therapy?
- Did you feel pressured by your therapist to make changes before you were ready?
- How much did your therapist help you gain a deeper understanding of your problems?
- Did you feel that your therapist understood what you hoped to get out of this session?

Studies have shown the CALPAS to have good reliability for the total score (Cronbach's alpha = 0.83) but much lower internal consistency for the four subscales: Cronbach's alpha ranges from 0.43 to 0.73 (Gaston, 1991). Both criterion and construct validity for the CALPAS have been established in several studies (Cecero et al., 2001; Gaston, 1991; Tichenor & Hill, 1989).

The four CALPAS scales measure the collaborative aspect of the alliance, agreement on goals and task, the emotional connection between client and therapist, as well as specific client abilities such as dedication and commitment and the ability to self-reflect. For example, the Patient Working Capacity scale has items designed to assess a client's ability to "disclose intimate and salient information, self-observe one's reactions, . . . and deepen exploration of salient themes" (Gaston, 1991, p. 69).

The HAq-II, the WAI, and the CALPAS inventories have been the most extensively researched standardized alliance questionnaires (Horvath, 2001). Their use, however, has been limited to psychotherapy research studies, and their adoption by counselors and therapists in outpatient mental health settings has been met with some resistance because of the questionnaires' length and complexity (Duncan et al., 2003).

SESSION RATING SCALE VERSION 3.0 (SRS V.3.0) The *Session Rating Scale Version 3.0* (SRS V.3.0) was developed with the hope that counselors in daily practice with large client case-loads would find it both a useful and practical tool (Duncan et al., 2003). Like the other alliance inventories, it was based on Bordin's pan-theoretical definition of alliance. It is, however, the least researched of the available alliance measures. Despite its lack of a strong research foundation, its inclusion in this chapter is valuable given that it is designed to be used by counselors in everyday practice.

The SRS V.3.0 is unique in its brevity and visual format (see Figure 14.1). Four items—relationship, goals and topics agreement, approach or method fit, and overall session rating—are measured on a 10-cm spatial continuum. Clients are asked to "Rate today's session by placing a hash mark on the line nearest to the description that best fits your experience." Each item has a negative verbal description as the left anchor point for the scale and a positive description as the right anchor point. For example, on the first item, clients place a mark between "I did not feel heard, understood, and respected" and "I felt heard, understood, and respected" (Duncan et al., 2003).

The Session Rating Scale Version 3.0

Name _____   Age (Yrs): _____

ID # _____   Sex: M/F

Session # _____   Date: _____

Please rate today's session by placing a hash mark on the line nearest to the description that best fits your experience.

I did not feel heard, Understood, and respected.	Relationship I--------------------------------I	I felt heard, understood, and respected.
We did not work on or talk about what I Wanted to work on and talk about	Goals and Topics I--------------------------------I	We worked on and talked about what I wanted to work on and talk about.
The therapist's approach is not a good fit for me.	Approach or Method I--------------------------------I	The therapist's approach is a good fit for me.
There was something Missing in the session today	Overall I--------------------------------I	Overall, today's session was right for me.

From: S. D. Miller (©2000) www.scottdmiller.com reprinted with permission from the author. Working copies are available free of charge to clinicians who register and agree to the licensing terms at: www.scottdmiller.com

FIGURE 14.1   SRS V3.0

One preliminary study of the SRS V.3.0 found both its internal consistency and test–retest reliability estimates to be comparable to or exceed those of the HAq-II (Cronbach's alpha = 0.88 vs. 0.90 for the HAq-II, and test–retest = 0.64 vs. 0.63). Concurrent validity was established by obtaining correlations for 70 clients over six administrations of the SRS and the HAq-II. The correlation between the two measures is 0.48 (Duncan et al., 2003). The authors suggest, based on a total possible score of 40, that an overall score of less than 36 or an individual item score of less than 9 should prompt a counselor to explore the rating with his or her client.

APPLYING ALLIANCE QUESTIONNAIRES IN COUNSELING SETTINGS

Reflections on the Case Study

Prior to Amy's fifth session, Dr. Samson inspected her SRS V.3.0 ratings, noticing that although all four items were toward the high end, or right side, of the scale each one was below the cutoff point, suggestive of further exploration with the client. In the next session, Amy and Dr. Sampson explored her ratings, which centered around Amy's belief that her therapist did not understand how difficult it is for her to feel the way she does when everyone else thinks she should "just get over it."

Dr. Samson responded to Amy's concern as sensitively as he knew how. He suggested to Amy that if at any point during her counseling sessions, she felt like she was not being under-stood, to let him know. This discussion prompted Dr. Samson to pay even closer attention to how he communicates empathy to Amy and for him to ask clarifying questions when uncertain about how Amy is feeling and thinking.

Advantages and Disadvantages of Using Therapeutic Alliance Questionnaires

The main benefit in using a therapeutic alliance questionnaire is that it provides a systematic and quantifiable way of assessing the most important aspect of the counseling process. By giving your client an alliance questionnaire, you send the message to the client that his or her input about the relationship is valuable. And when a questionnaire reveals an area of concern (e.g., a perceived lack of therapist understanding), this concern is out in the open and can be addressed in subsequent sessions. Three additional advantages include cost, ease and speed of administration, and no specific user qualifications. All of the existing alli-ance questionnaires are currently available for free from journal articles, books, or websites. Even the longer questionnaires, the WAI and CALPAS, can be typically completed by cli-ents in under 10 minutes and the SRS V.3.0 can be completed within one minute. Clients, therefore, are not unduly burdened by the additional time commitment. Finally, despite on-going research into the components of an alliance, the central construct is not difficult to understand. Counselors and therapists in training would be acting within the boundaries of their competency when using alliance questionnaires.

The major limitation of client–therapist alliance measures reviewed in this chapter is the lack of meaningful interpretation systems for clinical practice. Although a substantial body of research has demonstrated that the alliance may be the most significant predictor of client out-comes, clinicians do not have a benchmark for deciding at what point an alliance score should be cause for concern. Widespread use of alliance measures is more likely to happen if therapists know what to do with scores obtained at different times during the course of therapy. As a clinical tool, any particular item rated by a client at the midpoint or lower on a Likert scale would merit follow-up, as would low overall average scores for the entire questionnaire. For example, a recent study comparing therapeutic alliance measures found the mean scores on the WAI and CALPAS to be 5.74 and 5.2, respectively, out of a possible 7 (the authors revised the questionnaires' existing Likert scales so both would be on a 7-point scale for comparison purposes) (Cecero et al., 2001). The evolution of alliance measures has not yet, however, reached the point where a range of scores may be predictive of specific outcomes such as dropout or premature termination, or successful treatment in terms of symptom reduction or improved interpersonal functioning.

Guidelines for Using Standardized Alliance Measures

Introducing an alliance questionnaire and responding to client questions about the questionnaire is just as important as the discussion with a client about any other assessment measure. When psychotherapy clients in outpatient mental health settings complete therapeutic alliance measures, they tend to give high overall ratings of the alliance and there is typically small variation in their ratings. Average scores for the total alliance rating and specific subscale ratings are typically close to the high point on a Likert scale regardless of whether it is a 5-, 6-, or 7-point scale. Given those findings, a client whose average score is 2 points or more below the high point on the measures reviewed in this chapter is someone with whom the therapist would want to explore in session his or her feelings and attitudes about the therapeutic relationship and the process of the therapy. These clients may be at risk of prematurely dropping out or continuing to experience a weak connection to the therapist. Clients who experience a weak therapeutic alliance are less likely to demonstrate improvement and may pose significant clinical challenges for the therapist. Therefore, assessing the alliance early on in treatment (i.e., prior to the fifth session) would be a helpful clinical practice. Research studies have shown that alliance ratings obtained after the second and third sessions correlate highly with ratings obtained much later on in treatment, for example, the 24th session (Luborksy et al., 1996).

PRACTICE SUGGESTION
Guidelines for Using Standardized Alliance Measures

- Assess alliance formation between the second and fourth counseling session following the intake session.
- Consider measuring the alliance with clients for whom you suspect a personality disorder, who are mandated, who report previous negative counseling experiences, or who have a chronic history of maladaptive interpersonal relationships.
- Clients should complete an alliance scale or inventory immediately following the session.
- Remember to frame the presentation of the alliance measure as a way "to make sure this counseling or therapy is helping you and that you and I are working together to address your needs."
- Explore in the next session with your client any items that are 2 or more points away from the highest rating on the Likert scale.

These guidelines are based on the author's review of the alliance literature and his own clinical practice and are summarized in Practice Suggestion: Guidelines for Using Standardized Alliance Measures. Of the four alliance measures reviewed in this chapter, only the SRS V.3.0 contains specific cutoff scores for clinicians to follow. For those counselors, therapists, and clinicians working with individuals in hospital, residential, or partial-hospitalization facilities or allied fields, the existing alliance measures may seem wanting. Recently, however, efforts have been made to modify the CALPAS for use in nonpsychotherapy settings (c.f. Sherer et al., 2007; Westreich, Rosenthal, & Muran, 1996).

Cultural Considerations

Alliance measures have been developed and researched on adult outpatient mental health populations receiving a variety of therapy approaches, including psychodynamic, cognitive–behavioral, humanistic–experiential, and family systems. Child versions of these measures have not yet been developed and it's unclear how valid these tools are with adolescent clients. In general, someone with a sixth-grade reading level is likely to understand these alliance measures but some of the language may be confusing even for some adult clients. For example, two items on the HAq-II, "The therapist and I have meaningful *exchanges* (italics added)" and "The therapist and I sometimes have *unprofitable* exchanges" ask clients to rate a more abstract idea, an exchange.

One effort was made to translate the HAq-II, WAI, and CALPAS into French (Bachelor & Salamé, 2000). Other language versions of these questionnaires have not yet been developed. Furthermore, when an alliance measure has been translated into another language, similarities and differences between alternate language versions have not been reported.

The most significant limitation of the existing therapeutic alliance measures is the lack of cross-cultural information. The client samples used for the development of alliance questionnaires or the ones used in subsequent alliance research have tended to be homogenous with respect to presenting problem, DSM diagnosis, and ethnicity. Client data have typically not included racial and ethnic information, or when studies have reported that information the sample was almost entirely Caucasian (95%) (Hatcher & Barends, 1996). The one notable exception was the sample used for the revision of the *Helping Alliance Questionnaire,* which was 41% African American and 3% Hispanic or American Indian (Luborsky et al., 1996).

More cross-cultural research on therapeutic alliance measures is needed in order to address a number of questions. Do clients of different cultural, racial, or ethnic groups respond in ways to therapeutic alliance questionnaires that are somehow different than Caucasians? Might alliance questionnaire items reflect a particular cultural bias? As noted in previous chapters, individuals from certain cultures (e.g., Asian) may have difficulty measuring their distress, tending to provide midpoint ratings on self-report scales (Comas-Díaz, 2006). This bias could equally apply to rating one's interpersonal attitudes and feelings toward a person in a position of power, the counselor. The alliance construct of emotional bond and collaboration may be incongruent with certain cultural beliefs about emotional connection with professionals in a perceived position of power and having a collaborative involvement with an "expert."

The impact cross-cultural client–therapist factors have on alliance formation and maintenance is just beginning to be addressed. For example, will alliance scores be significantly different than what has been reported in existing studies, when client and therapist are of the same versus different gender, racial identity, or sexual orientation? One preliminary study of counselors in training was conducted to examine the influence of racial identity on working alliance ratings but was limited to analogue situations (Burkard, Ponterotto, Reynolds, & Alfonso, 1999).

Summary and Conclusions

Hundreds of studies spanning more than 30 years of research have demonstrated what may seem intuitive: clients who report a strong emotional connection to and collaborate with their therapist are more likely to rate themselves as having improved when therapy ends. What may be less obvious is that the strength of the client–therapist alliance is a better predictor of client outcome than specific counseling approaches or techniques in outpatient mental health settings. The relationship between client–therapist alliance and therapy outcome has been established through the use of standardized therapeutic alliance measures.

This chapter focused on the client self-report versions of four standardized therapeutic alliance rating scales: the *Revised Helping Alliance Questionnaire* (HAq-I), the *Working Alliance Inventory* (WAI), the *California Psychotherapy Alliance Scale* (CALPAS), and the *Session Rating Scale Version 3.0* (SRS V.3.0). A common transtheoretical framework underlying the development of these alliance measures was reviewed along with relevant research findings. These alliance measures, though different in length and format, are conceptually similar in that they are based on Bordin's three-part definition of alliance as consisting of 1) an emotional bond; 2) client–therapist agreement on therapy goals; and 3) agreement on how to achieve those goals. Guidelines for incorporating these relatively recent assessment measures into clinical practice were discussed, as were important cross-cultural considerations.

Reflection Questions and Experiential Exercises

1. What factors might affect how a client responds to a therapeutic alliance questionnaire?
2. In addition to questionnaires, how else might you evaluate the quality of the therapeutic alliance?
3. How comfortable would you feel exploring with your client a low rating on an alliance questionnaire item?
4. What do you think about the fundamental concept of therapy relationship as a mutual partnership or collaboration? When might you find yourself as a therapist acting without input from your client?
5. Are there particular clients for whom formal assessment of the therapeutic alliance might be beneficial?
6. In small groups of three to four students, brainstorm a list of counselor attitudes, qualities, and skills that would help a counselor establish and maintain a therapeutic alliance, and the attitudes, qualities, and skills that would interfere with establishing and maintaining a strong alliance.
7. Identify with your practicum or internship supervisor a client you would like to have complete a therapeutic alliance questionnaire or inventory. Obtain a copy of one of the measures reviewed in this chapter and consider using it after the third, fourth, or fifth counseling session. Discuss your reactions to using an alliance measure with your supervisor and how you might integrate the results of the measure into your next counseling session.

15 PUTTING IT ALL TOGETHER

Chapter Objectives

After reading this chapter, you should be able to:

■ Describe a process for selecting assessment methods based on psychometric and practical considerations.

■ Identify cultural considerations when selecting and using assessment instruments.

■ Explain a process for communicating assessment results orally and through reports.

■ Understand trends impacting the development and future uses of standardized assessments.

Tomas had a challenging and stressful childhood. His Latin American parents had brought him to the United States from Guatemala when he was an infant. He was removed from his parents' home the fall he began third grade following several reports that were made to child protective services. A teacher and a neighbor had independently called a help line, on more than one occasion, because of concerns that Tomas was being mistreated: coming to school hungry with unexplained bruises, and he was left alone to care for his two younger siblings for extended periods of time during the evening. Tomas spent the remainder of the school year in foster care, apart from his two younger brothers, but returned the following year to live with his father and stepmother, with whom he had a very conflict-riddled relationship. These changes resulted in him spending his elementary school years in three different schools in separate districts. Additionally, his biological mother had moved to another part of the country and he had only limited contact with her until he entered high school.

Tomas is currently 15 years old and a sophomore in high school and his life has become relatively stable. However, his father and stepmother have been concerned about his continuing academic struggles with homework and long-term projects. Despite his above-average performance on statewide achievement tests, Tomas's school grades have widely fluctuated since late elementary school. His father and stepmother are concerned that Tomas is not "working up to his potential" and feel like his schools have overlooked his academic difficulties because teachers have often said, "He is a joy to have in class." Tomas's stepmother, Mrs. Ramon, contacted the local mental health center to get Tomas help because of his "anxiety and attention problems." Tomas had received counseling services once before, in third grade when his father remarried, but he and his stepmother were not sure if the sessions had helped.

Tomas told his current counselor, Melanie, that he was a "fair to poor student" in elementary and high school and that he had received a lot of tutoring, which had helped him to be more organized with his studies. Mrs. Ramon conveyed her concerns as well: "He's not finishing tasks on time, he's never organized, has a really messy desk and piles of papers all over the place." Both Tomas and his stepmother had additional concerns. Tomas seemed to be nervous a lot, especially when he was in group situations. Tomas had gone online and thought that he might have "social anxiety." As a result he tended to avoid going out or would only reluctantly attend social gatherings, which led to his feeling "down and lonely." But Mrs. Ramon thought he had "that ADD" like his cousin and that's why school had been so hard for him.

Tomas also had some confusion about his cultural identity. When asked on forms to check off a racial box, he was often unsure what to select and usually picked "other." Both of his biological parents were from Latin American countries but he believed that he assimilated well, having grown up in the United States with English as his primary language, and almost all of his friends growing up had been "Anglos." On the other hand, he yearned for greater connection with his mother and her native practices.

OVERVIEW

The first task for any counselor or helping professional prior to engaging in the assessment process is to make a decision about how to approach it. Melanie is apt to ask herself, "Of the many informal and formal methods available to me, which ones am I going to use with Tomas in order to answer my questions and arrive at a decision?" As you may recall from long ago, in Chapter 1, there are multiple reasons why helping professionals engage in assessment: clarifying a diagnosis, screening, developing a case conceptualization, understanding the nature of presenting problems, estimating risk of danger to self or others, planning treatments, evaluating the course of counseling or other kinds of interventions, and therapeutic benefit. Therefore, the selection of a particular assessment method or combination of methods is guided first and foremost by the clinician's purpose for carrying out the assessment. Some methods, for example, like structured interviews, because of their depth and comprehensiveness, are well suited for diagnosing but because of their length and time to administer are not helpful tools for evaluating whether a counseling intervention is helping a client to get better. Brief self-report questionnaires, in general, are more appropriate for that latter purpose. A school counselor may need to select an instrument to screen potential students for a social skills group, but her colleague, the school psychologist, may need to evaluate one of those same students with cognitive ability and achievement tests to determine if the student has a learning disability. Simultaneously, a helping professional will be guided by psychometric, practical, and cultural considerations when choosing from among the various methods and instruments. At some point after assessment information is gathered and analyzed, the results will need to be presented to the client. The purpose of this final chapter is to describe a process for selecting and integrating assessment data and communicating assessment results. The chapter will also explore some future trends in assessment that appear to be on the horizon. So how did Melanie go about selecting which assessment methods to use with Tomas, and how might she inform him about what she learned?

SELECTING AND USING ASSESSMENT METHODS

Identifying the Purposes of the Assessment

CLARIFYING DIAGNOSES AND FORMULATING CASE CONCEPTUALIZATIONS   Melanie approached the overall assessment of Tomas from both a monothetic and idiographic perspective. Practically speaking, she began the assessment process with reading information a colleague at her agency had obtained from an initial telephone screening. Based on that screening, Melanie thought Tomas was likely to be presenting with multiple problems, a complex history, and different diagnostic possibilities. Given the potential complexities with this client, she wanted to obtain additional information with an unstructured intake interview, which would allow her to tailor the direction of the interview to Tomas's presenting concerns and problems. By the end of the intake, she had gathered the information presented in the case study at the opening of the chapter and some additional data. Melanie, Tomas, and his parents were now in the position of wanting to rule out diverse diagnoses, including a learning disability, attention deficit–hyperactivity disorder (ADHD), some type of anxiety disorder, and possibly depression as well. When an unstructured interview alone appears to be an inadequate tool for arriving at a DSM diagnosis, then a structured interview or standardized measures can often help to clarify the diagnostic picture.

Melanie's decision to include standardized measures into a comprehensive assessment of Tomas was guided by both an understanding of what can be accomplished by using them and the ethical and regulatory guidelines pertaining to the use of psychological tests that was discussed in Chapter 2. Melanie believed she was competent, given her graduate school training and post-graduate work experience and supervision, to administer a couple of self-report questionnaires to better understand the nature of Tomas's anxiety, trauma, and depression symptoms, but arranged for a colleague to rule out the possibility of ADHD and a learning disability. In collaboration with Tomas's father and stepmother they decided to involve the school psychologist at Tomas's school, someone Melanie had collaborated with before. The psychologist was qualified to administer and interpret cognitive ability and achievement tests (Chapter 13) to determine if Tomas has a learning disability, as well as interpret parent and teacher rating scales that are commonly used to assess for ADHD. Although those two disorders are more typically identified when a child is in elementary school, they sometimes get missed in cases like this when a child has been in multiple schools and locations.

As the counselor, Melanie's role in the diagnostic process was more circumscribed than the psychologist's but just as important. After her initial interview with Tomas they discussed and he agreed that it would be helpful for him to fill out two brief self-report questionnaires: the *Revised Children's Manifest Anxiety Scale—Second Edition* (RCMAS-2) and the *Brief Symptom Inventory* (BSI), two of the questionnaires discussed in Chapter 9. Both measures can be used with adolescents. These questionnaires could help clarify, along with the information gathered from the intake and the psychologist's evaluation, whether or not Tomas met the diagnostic criteria for an anxiety disorder, particularly PTSD, ADHD, or both. A diagnosis by itself, however, despite its potential for informing treatment planning—targeting symptoms and goals for treatment—is limited to a description of *what* the client is experiencing, not *why* the disorder is present.

Hypotheses about why a client is experiencing psychological problems and symptoms are the essence of a case conceptualization or formulation (Hersen & Porzelius, 2002). As was stated in Chapter 1, a case conceptualization is an integration of the client's presenting problems with client background information—family and cultural history, development, psychosocial stressors, coping strategies and personal strengths, social supports, and psychological and physical functioning—so that a hypothesis about why the presenting problems are occurring can be stated. Diagnoses describe conditions, whereas case conceptualizations offer explanations. By having more standardized information at her disposal, Melanie can begin to formulate hypotheses that connect client history to specific symptoms and behaviors. For example, knowing Tomas's responses to standardized measures such as the RCMAS-2 and the BSI helps to provide additional context for understanding Tomas, his perceptions, and specific features of the anxiety he is experiencing. This knowledge facilitates Melanie's ability to begin to formulate hypotheses about why Tomas is experiencing his problems. These measures, along with Tomas's verbal self-report, served the dual purpose of facilitating case conceptualization and gauging his progress throughout the course of counseling.

In addition to helping with case conceptualizations and establishing counseling goals, standardized measures can quantify progress toward and attainment of those goals. Tomas's scores on the BSI, for example, can serve as a baseline of his symptom severity, intensity, or frequency. Readministering the BSI at later times—for example, his fifth session, 12th session, and 6 months after the first session—enables comparisons with his baseline score. This also provides a structure to help Tomas reflect on his progress and for Tomas and Melanie to collaboratively look at whether counseling is helping and whether or not changes need to be made. Those changes might include a referral for medication, more intensive counseling (twice a week rather than weekly), or a change in therapy modality (individual, group, or family). Standardized measures also help clients and clinicians visualize progress, or the lack thereof, in ways that are different than verbal self-reports or counselor observations.

Promoting Counseling Engagement

Another reason why Melanie chose to use standardized measures in her ongoing assessment of Tomas was to promote counseling engagement and provide additional therapeutic benefit (Finn & Tonsager 1997; Ackerman, Hilsenroth, Baity, & Blagys, 2000). As was discussed in Chapter 1, assessment and intervention are complementary processes. When Melanie gave Tomas the RCMAS-2 and BSI, she was, in essence, performing an intervention. The act of using these measures as both assessment and intervention tools has multiple intentions behind it. One intention is to engage Tomas in the acts of self-reflection (*What am I experiencing?*) and perspective taking (*I guess things are not as bad as I thought, there are more zeros and ones than twos and threes on this form*). A second intention is to help Tomas see the importance of working on tasks (completing the inventory) in between the counseling sessions. If the counseling process is intended to go beyond the provision of emotional support and promote change, then the client will need to engage in some type of action, even if at only the cognitive level, outside of the sessions. Thirdly, the assessment measure becomes a vehicle for facilitating a collaborative discussion about Tomas's concerns and symptoms, their frequency or intensity, and which ones to focus on in subsequent counseling sessions.

A client's engagement in the counseling process is partly dependent upon his or her stage of readiness for change. In addition to Tomas's response to interview questions discussed in Chapter 4, his readiness for change can be gauged indirectly through his attitude and response to the standardized measures. Whether or not Tomas completed the inventories in their entirety, or got partway through and stopped, is data. His compliance with, or difficulty, completing this task is a likely predictor of how he might respond to other interventions, at least those requiring minimal sustained attention, effort, and reading. Melanie can take those data along with other information—Tomas's specific responses and overall style of responding to the inventory (e.g., almost all items are given either the lowest or highest rating)—in order to establish ideas about subsequent interventions. By administering a standardized measure, the clinician promotes client engagement, and by doing so activates and helps maintain the cyclical relationship between assessment and intervention.

Melanie had a clear understanding of the reasons why she wanted to incorporate standardized measures into the initial and ongoing assessment with her client, Tomas, but despite her clarity of purpose she still had a multitude of possible instruments at her disposal. What other factors did she need to consider in order to narrow her pool of choices and finally decide upon the ones she did? Knowledge of the psychometric properties of various instruments, their multicultural applications, and the practicalities of using them were the remaining considerations for her. Questions a counselor can ask to guide the selection and use of assessment instruments are listed in Practice Suggestion: Guidelines for Selecting and Using Assessment Methods.

PRACTICE SUGGESTION
Guidelines for Selecting and Using Assessment Methods

SELECTION QUESTIONS

1. What is my purpose?
   a. Diagnosis?
   b. Screening?
   c. Case conceptualization
   d. Monitoring counseling interventions
   e. Evaluating counseling outcome
   f. Engaging the client
2. Do I need to use a standardized test or measure? If so:
   a. What cultural factors—language, values, beliefs, and practices—would be an impediment to using it?
   b. Does the age range of the test apply to my client?
   c. How representative are the test's norms?
   d. Is there another test with better norms if the first test selected has norms that don't fit for my client?
3. What are the costs involved with a formal or informal measure?
   a. Training, time to administer, score, and interpret
   b. Client acceptance
4. What are the potential benefits of using this assessment method?

ETHICAL AND ADMINISTRATION QUESTIONS

1. Am I competent to administer, score, and interpret this test?
2. Am I emotionally prepared to begin the assessment?
3. Have I provided informed consent? If the client is a minor, has a parent or guardian provided consent for the assessment?
4. Was information about the following provided?
   a. Assessment methods to be used
   b. Time involved
   c. Cost
   d. How the results will be communicated and to whom
5. Do I have a private, confidential, and interruption-free environment in which to administer the test?
6. Do I have the necessary materials: writing implement, computer, timing device, test manual, and answer sheets or response forms?
7. Is the reading level of the test appropriate for my client? Does the client understand the directions?
8. Upon completion of the test, where will it be stored?

> **QUESTIONS TO CONSIDER BEFORE COMMUNICATING ASSESSMENT RESULTS**
>
> 1. How and when will the results be communicated?
> 2. How can the results be provided in language that is relatively free of technical jargon and difficult constructs?
> 3. What might be the therapeutic benefit of providing assessment results to this client?
> 4. How might the communication of the assessment results facilitate the client or a family member taking some action on the part of the client?
> 5. Will the results be documented? If so, in what format?

Psychometric Considerations

RELIABILITY AND VALIDITY   Several psychometric factors should guide the selection of an assessment measure in mental health settings (Newman, Rugh, & Ciarlo, 2004), and those same factors can apply equally as well to other settings: educational, organizational, rehabilitation, and forensic. The primary factors are the complementary psychometric concepts: reliability and validity that were discussed in Chapter 7. Again, *reliability* refers to the internal stability or consistency of a measure, and *validity* to the ability of a measure to assess what it purports to measure and how well it does that. An abundance of formal assessment measures have both, adequate or better levels of reliability, and demonstrated validity and clinical usefulness or utility. Therefore, there is no longer a reason to choose one that is lacking in acceptable psychometric standards when the purposes are screening, clarifying a diagnosis, identifying traits or abilities, or predicting future behavior. However, what constitutes acceptable or minimum levels of reliability and validity continues to be a matter of debate and research. Although a consensus on minimum standards for a measure's reliability and validity has not yet been achieved, work has begun on developing criteria by which a measure's usefulness can be judged. One such effort was that developed by Hunsley and Mash (2008), who produced a three-level system for evaluating any standardized measure's reliability, validity, norms, and clinical usefulness. Criteria were used to determine, for example, whether a measure's reliability and validity were "adequate," "good," or "excellent" (Hunsley & Mash). They proposed that a minimum degree of reliability would be internal reliability estimates or alpha coefficients equal to or greater than 0.70, interrater reliability of 0.60 to 0.74, and test–retest reliability of 0.70 or better. More subjective criteria were provided for content and construct validity as well as validity generalization. Their minimum standard for validity generalization was, "some evidence supports the use of this instrument with (a) more than one specific group (based on sociodemographic characteristics such as age, gender, and ethnicity) or (b) in multiple settings (e.g., home, school, primary care)" (Hunsley & Mash, p. 9). It is up to other researchers and reviewers of assessment instruments to decide how much and what kind of evidence is needed to judge a measure as having acceptable validity for use with different groups in various settings, but at least this constitutes a starting point for creating common benchmarks by which assessment measures can be evaluated.

Another selection factor to consider is whether or not a norm-referenced test or measure is needed. A valid norm-referenced measure is essential to use if the purpose of the assessment is to determine a diagnosis, level of functioning, or when conducting programs or treatment evaluation studies (Achenbach, 2001). This was the case with the school psychologist who would be using cognitive ability and achievement tests to gauge Tomas's performance relative to other children as way to see if he might have a learning disability. He would also be using norm-referenced questionnaires to rule out ADHD. On the other hand, if one's purpose is idiographic—developing a case conceptualization, monitoring an individual client's course of counseling, or measuring response to an educational or pharmacological intervention—then using an inadequately normed or informal un-normed measure such as a client diary or log or a teacher's chart or checklist can suffice. Melanie's assessment role with Tomas was idiographic and therefore she could have relied on informal instruments to develop her case conceptualization and evaluate how the counseling process was going. She was, however, aware of these two brief standardized questionnaires that have items regarding many of the symptoms found in anxiety and depression, and having Tomas complete them would be an easy, reliable, efficient, and low-cost way to help him report on his emotional and psychological functioning.

What Are the Test's Norms?

If a test is to be used to clarify a diagnosis or level of functioning, how does a helping professional go about deciding if its norms are appropriate? An understanding of who comprises the normative group is essential in order to use standardized measures in an ethical and responsible fashion. Remember, the normative or standardization group serves as a reference group from which an individual client's score can be compared. Two factors need to be considered: the process for selecting the normative sample and its demographic makeup (Achenbach, 2001; Malgady & Colon-Malgady, 2008). Some samples are chosen out of convenience, such as when a group of people is readily available to the test developer or researcher. Others are carefully chosen to be representative of a large population; for example, all elementary school age children in the United States.

Representativeness is perhaps a minimum qualitative standard for considering the use of a standardized measure. A common criterion used to judge the adequacy of a particular demographic group being represented in the standardization sample is the extent to which that group's percentage in the sample matches that of the population of interest. Typically, test manuals or review articles will provide the information about the standardization group's demographic profile. Therefore a test's normative sample may or may not include the ethnic or racial group for a particular client. Even if the ethnic or racial group of interest is proportionally represented in the sample, there are not usually separate norms in the manual for that group (Malgady & Colon-Malgady, 2008). Does that matter? It depends on the inferences and conclusions one is attempting to draw from test scores.

Another way to assess a test's cultural fit for a particular client is whether or not separate norms exist for that group. That is, separate tables are used for converting raw scores to standardized scores based on one's age or gender, but rarely are any other demographic variables of interest used such as race, ethnicity, religious affiliation, or other cultural factors. Some cultural specific tests have been developed, but those too are not without their limitations (Dana, 2008; Ridley, Li, & Hill, 1998). There is, for example, the TEMAS, a narrative picture-story test for children with separate stimulus cards for minorities and non-minorities and norms for Black, Other Hispanic, Puerto Rican, and White children ages 5 to 13 (Flanagan, Costantino, Cardalda, & Costantino, 2008). There is also the *Handbook of Tests and Measurements for Black Populations* (Jones, 1996). Tests with cultural specific norms are, however, the exception. Since most assessment instruments do not provide separate normative tables based on ethnic or racial factors or other demographic factors and do not take into account multiracial identity and acculturation status, clinicians need to proceed with caution when making interpretation from the test data (Dana). This is why, despite the fact that clinicians use standardized measures as part of the assessment process, the measure should be considered as only one source of information

(AERA, APA, & NCME, 1999) and that judgments about a client, for example, is depressed or is not depressed, are always probabilistic in nature. It can be hard to remain tentative in one's thinking, but easy to commit a logical fallacy when using standardized instruments: the test is a valid measure of depression, the client scored at the 98th percentile on the depression scale; therefore the client must have depression. Furthermore, the ethical guidelines of the respective professional codes—ACA, ASCA, AMHCA, and APA—*require* clinicians to consider the impact of cultural factors on test performance, an issue that will be taken up further in the next section.

Cultural Considerations when Selecting and Using Standardized Measures

Although Euro-American science and measurement concepts, including psychological measurement, have been transported to and taught in many other societies, the notion of measuring and quantifying one's feelings, thoughts, and behaviors is alien to many individuals (Comas-Díaz, 2006). When an individual is being asked to respond and perform in a way that is incongruent with his or her cultural beliefs, values, and attitudes, performance on and response to psychological tests will be impacted. Culture, therefore, can be conceptualized as a set of worldviews and values and adaptive behaviors that are shared by a group of people in multiple contexts (Breunlin, Schwartz, & Mac Kune-Karrer, 1992). Although there are other definitions of culture in the counseling literature, this is one the author is partial to and believes promotes an understanding of the influence of culture on assessment. Culture is one of several lenses one can look through to understand a person or group's behaviors, emotional expression, and beliefs. Therefore, how one behaves during a psychological test or responds to an interview or measure will, in part, be culturally determined since worldviews influence and shape personal behavior.

Culture obviously shapes one's understanding and expression of language and almost all psychological tests will be partly an assessment of language skills, rather than the construct of interest: psychopathology, personality, cognitive ability, and so on (AERA et al., 1999). In a counseling context, for example, one's cultural norms can influence whether or not a type of question or the style in which it is posed is responded to (Hays, 2008). Some questions may seem offensive or answering them could be perceived as being disloyal in some way to one's cultural values and beliefs. How one goes about reporting experiences, identifying symptoms, and judging normal from abnormal behavior is also culturally determined (Ridley, Li, & Hill, 1998; Ridley, Tracy, Pruitt-Stephens, Wimsatt, & Beard, 2008).

The degree to which culture is influencing behavioral expression and a client's report of it at any given moment can be difficult to know. The challenge is to explain how both the client's personal and shared worldviews come together to impact responses during the assessment process (Ridley et al., 2008). That ambiguity is compounded by two competing viewpoints about the determinants of human behavior: universal principles applicable across groups and within group specificity (Lopez, 2002). The former stipulates that behavior is driven by general laws of human nature—for example, having a fight or flight response—regardless of one's cultural background and views. The latter tends to neglect the influence of generalizing principles in favor of cultural determinism. A multicultural assessment is an attempt to reconcile those competing theories in order to understand and hypothesize about why an individual did what he or she did at that moment (Fields, 2010; Hays, 2008; Lopez; Ridley et al., 2008; Ridley et al., 1998). Maintaining a multicultural assessment perspective is so critical that entire texts have been devoted just to this topic (see Appendix B: Additional Resources).

As with the counseling relationship, it also possible that when the assessor and client differ on some demographic variable—gender, race–ethnicity, sexual orientation, religious identification, or developmental stage—that difference may impact the client's behavior during the assessment. Some research has found that when clinician and client are of similar ethnic backgrounds, the clinician is better able to understand the client's expression of symptoms that may be culturally related and how thoughts and feelings are connected to specific experiences (Malgady & Costantino, 1998). As with the counseling relationship, it is often not practical or necessary to match client and assessor on all possible demographic factors. Furthermore, cultural sensitivity can bias a clinician in either direction (Fields, 2010). A review of the multicultural counseling literature has summarized studies showing that clinicians can overpathologize symptoms, behaviors, and experience when cultural factors are not taken into consideration and, conversely, underdiagnosis pathology by being too focused on cultural determinism (Ridley et al., 1998). Given that a client's culture will impact, to varying degrees, how she or he understands and responds to test questions and items, a clinician will fundamentally be concerned with how to interpret statistically deviant test scores, especially if those scores will be used to justify diagnostic or treatment decisions. Anytime deviant scores are obtained, the assessor needs to ask, Does the score reflect a high or low level of the construct being measured?; Is it a reflection of a culturally determined response set?; or Is the score somehow a product of both?

Interpretation of Scores

A standardized score on a psychological measure indicates only *how* an individual performed, not *why*. In order to properly interpret statistically deviant test scores that could indicate serious psychopathology, low intelligence, or some other construct, a clinician needs to take into account the individual's background and language, the test's normative sample, observations about the client, cultural factors such as identity, orientation, and acculturation status, and stress and any other relevant information about the client (Acevedo-Polakovich et al., 2007; AERA et al., 1999; Cuellar, 1998; Geisinger, 2003). For example, if a measure designed to screen for the presence of psychosis is given to an individual from an American Indian culture and that culture believes in and reinforces hallucinatory and other kinds of paranormal experiences, she may agree with items such as, "I see things that others do not"; "I have experienced people who are no longer alive communicating to me"; and "Other people are aware of my thoughts." Her endorsement of a sufficient number of test items could result in an abnormally high score on a scale indicative of psychosis or schizophrenia, but that score could very well be a function of culturally sanctioned beliefs and practices, not a psychotic process. It is also possible that the high score on a psychosis scale does reflect an emerging psychiatric disorder for that same individual. The question, again, is whether the test score represents pathology, cultural influences, or both. Regardless of the specific construct being measured—schizophrenia, depression, introversion, or intelligence—the generalizability of a construct, developed and measured in one specific culture, to others is an open question and usually the focus of ongoing research.

Alternative Language Versions

Many of the psychological tests and measures developed over the past 60 years have been translated into various languages and researched in many diverse cultures. This has led to a better understanding of the cross-cultural applicability of the constructs psychological tests measure. The translation of a test from its original language into another language does not, however, guarantee that the test is valid for a specific population (AERA et al., 1999; Hambleton & Zenisky, 2011). The question the assessor needs to grapple with is whether a test has been sufficiently researched with the population of interest in order to make predictions or decisions about a client on the basis of the test results. Standard 9.7 from the *Standards for Educational and Psychological Testing* states:

> When a test is translated from one language to another, the methods used in establishing the adequacy of the translation should be described, and empirical and logical evidence should be provided for score reliability and validity of the translated test's score inferences for the uses intended in the linguistic groups to be tested. (AERA et al., 1999, p. 99)

As the standard indicates, translation alone is not a sufficient benchmark for judging a test's suitability for a client whose primary language differs from that of the original version of the test. The translation of standardized test response choices such as "true" or "false" or occurring "often" or "not at all," let alone entire questions or items, from English into another language can convey slightly or radically different meanings than intended in the original version. Therefore, a translated version of a test is not necessarily equivalent to the original version. Future research is necessary to evaluate how a translated test compares to the original version in terms of the standard scores obtained. An example of that kind of research has been conducted with the *Achenbach System for Empirically Based Assessment* (ASEBA) (see Chapter 10). The ASEBA has been translated into multiple languages and its administration in 23 cultures found the cross-cultural generalizability of the construct of internalizing and externalizing childhood disorders (Ivanova et al., 2007). That is, the average problem scale scores in different cultures on the *Youth Self-Report* and parent and teacher rating scales in the ASEBA are similar to the cross-cultural overall mean scores: the average of many different cultures' scores (Achenbach, 2011). To put it another way, regardless of the language version of the test and the country in which it was used, youth, parents, and teachers have similar understandings of different types of problems and, on average, report similar levels of severity of those identified problems. It is this kind of cross-cultural research that provides support for the use of this particular set of questionnaires and the translated versions of them for diverse groups of clients. A cross-cultural study with a slightly different focus illustrates some of the complexities involved with different languages. The study had a counterintuitive finding: symptom severity, using a clinician symptom rating scale, was found to be higher when clinician and client spoke the same language (Spanish) than when their primary languages (English and Spanish) were different (Malady & Costantino, 1998). The researchers speculated on possible clinician biases and dynamic factors that may have produced these results without a definitive conclusion, but these results highlighted the role language and other cultural factors can have in the diagnostic process. Ongoing research can provide some clues as to the advantages and limitations of using translated tests with particular language or cultural groups.

When possible, clients should be given tests in their primary or dominant language, and when this is not possible then clinicians are advised to not use the test of interest and rely on other sources of information for an assessment. To do otherwise would represent a violation of psychologists and counselors' ethical guidelines for selecting and administering tests (American Counseling Association, 2005; American Psychological Association, 2002) as well as Standard 9, "Testing Individuals of Diverse Linguistic Background" of the *Standards for Educational and Psychological Testing* (AERA et al., 1999). The standards state: "Some tests are inappropriate for use with individuals whose knowledge of the language of the test is questionable" (p. 97).

Given the changing demographics of the United States and the influx of individuals for whom English is not their primary language, clinicians are going to need measures with applicable norms and reliable and valid alternative language versions. Fortunately, tremendous work has been done over the past two decades to create or update measures that have cross-cultural applicability (Fabri, 2008). Most of the measures reviewed in this text and elsewhere have English and Spanish editions available, and the majority of them have been translated into multiple languages and have been researched in various non-English-speaking cultures.

Despite the availability of Spanish and other language versions of some of the more common psychological tests, concerns have been voiced that the normative samples for these tests developed in the United States have not adequately, if at all, addressed issues of cultural diversity (Dana, 2008; Wood, Garb, Lilienfeld, & Nezworski, 2002). When tests have included samples of Hispanic, Asian Americans, and other minority groups, those samples are typically based only on the percentage of those racial groups or ethnicities in the general population but are not necessarily representative of their respective, gender, geography, bilingual characteristics, education level, and acculturation differences. The problem, however, in obtaining such a stratified standardization sample for particular ethnic or racial groups, let alone subgroups (female Hispanics, for example), is the sheer geographic diversity and ethnic heterogeneity within any one group (Malgady & Colon-Malgady, 2008). Asian and Pacific Islander Americans, for example, represent over two dozen separate cultures, each with its own language, values, customs, and history (Okazaki, 1998).

Cultural Guidelines for Using Psychological Tests

Multistep guidelines and recommendations for selecting, administering, and interpreting tests with Hispanic populations have been developed (Fernandez, Boccaccini, & Noland, 2007) and can apply to other groups as well (Ridley et al., 2008). The first step Fernandez et al. recommend is to determine the client's language preference, if bilingual, and use a test that has been translated into the client's preferred language, if available. Simultaneously, the clinician needs to determine if he or she is qualified to administer a test or measure to a client whose language differs from the clinician. If a test is not available in the client's primary language, then a clinician might consider using an interpreter but needs to keep in mind that any results gained from a nonstandardized administration of a test or measure must be interpreted with a great deal of caution (Acevedo-Polakovich et al., 2007). If an interpreter is going to be used, that person should be professionally trained and be able to converse in the client's dialect, not just language, and understand issues related to interpreter bias (AERA et al., 1999; Hays, 2008). Hays has provided some practical guidance for using interpreters during an assessment. Those guidelines range from how to handle ethical issues such as confidentiality and client autonomy, to practical matters such as having a preassessment meeting, allowing extra time for the assessment, and being mindful of class issues potentially affecting the conversation.

Fernandez et al. (2007) provided three additional guidelines for culturally sensitive assessment. First, the clinician should attempt to assess whether the client's reading level meets the minimum level established for the test. Most test manuals indicate the necessary reading level. An individual, however, may be proficient in speaking a language but less so with reading it and vice versa. Second, a translated test does not necessarily mean that the test had been researched and normed on the cultural group in question, and even if some research has been done with the specific group, other cultural variables such as acculturation status and stress and immigration history may not have been considered. As indicated earlier, a multicultural assessment will attempt to account for the multiple demographic and cultural variables that may be contributing to the responses obtained from an assessment method, be that an unstructured interview or a standardized test. Third, clinicians should attempt to determine if the existing research is applicable for the client. If Tomas, the client in the chapter's case study, was bilingual but not acculturated, and a more recent immigrant, then whatever research is available regarding the measures used—the BSI and RCMAS-2—might shed light on interpreting them. Although Fernandez et al. found 30 measures of adult personality or psychopathology that had been translated into Spanish, only two of those measures—the MMPI-2 and the BDI—had been researched with Latin American populations. A counselor interested in assessing a bilingual client who recently arrived in the United States from Haiti with another measure, the SCL-90-R for example, would find the research base to be wanting. Adherence to these guidelines will help clinicians to select, administer, score, and interpret psychological measures in a culturally sensitive and competent manner in accordance with professional standards and ethical codes discussed in Chapter 2. There are not, however, more specific procedures for determining what type of research is adequate for deciding that a specific test is or is not appropriate for a particular client. It will be a matter of clinical judgment as to whether it makes sense to test the client or rely solely on other methods—interviews and observations—to answer the assessment question.

Selecting Culturally Fair Tests

One remaining cultural consideration is the notion of test fairness and bias. Since test scores are typically used to classify or predict an individual's future status, the issue of tests unfairly and improperly identifying a person as disabled, disturbed, or unfit has a long and controversial history. The concern about test bias and fairness has typically revolved around tests such as ability and aptitude commonly used for selection purposes in educational and employment contexts and to a much lesser extent in clinical settings (Padilla & Borsato, 2008). Test fairness and test bias are sometimes used interchangeably, but *fairness* is a professional and societal value, and *bias* is a technical term (AERA et al., 1999), even though one definition of a fair test is a test free from bias. Test bias occurs when there are systematically high or low scores for certain groups of test takers because of some problem in test content (AERA et al.). If the content of a test is biased in some way, it can sometimes be detected by merely reviewing test items. For example, a review of a hypothetical national professional counselor licensing exam might reveal that the test contains a number of questions pertaining to information that trainees in the Northeast and West had been exposed to in their graduate school programs, but students in the South had not. If Southern counselors were found to score lower than other counselors, on average, this may well reflect a test biased in favor of those exposed to all the information on the licensing exam, not that Southern counselors are potentially substandard. Content bias can also happen when items elicit responding in a systematic way for one group and not another. For example, a behavior rating scale that asks respondents to rate items as "not true," "somewhat true," or "often true" may be problematic for some cultures that sees "truth" as present or absent rather than on a continuum.

In addition to content review, test bias can be determined by statistical procedures that evaluate the validity coefficients for two groups: the majority and a minority (Anastasi & Urbina, 1997). If the correlations between a test, for example the Graduate Record Exam, and a criterion, grade point average after the first year of graduate school, are significantly different for two groups, then the test is considered to have bias. Keep in mind that the mean scores on the GRE for two racial–ethnic groups—for example, Asians and Caucasian—could be significantly different but that by itself would not make it a biased test. It is the statistical relationship between the predictor (GRE) and the criterion (GPA) that matters. A test could also be statistically biased if it predicts significantly different performance levels on the criterion variable. That is, a test, like the GRE, would be biased if it predicted one racial or ethnic group would perform significantly worse or better in graduate school, despite there not being evidence of this difference. How much of a problem has test bias been? Large-scale review studies with Black and Hispanic populations have generally concluded that ability tests used to predict future performance in occupational and industrial, military, and postsecondary settings have not found significant validity coefficient differences between the minority and Caucasian groups (Anastasi & Urbina). Consequently, subsequent research has focused on decision models for selecting culturally fair test batteries.

Decision theory models have examined how individual tests or combinations of them are used for selection or prediction purposes even if the test in question does not contain biased content. If a test score is used in such a way that systematically results in the majority group being selected (e.g., graduate school admission) and a minority group not selected, then the use of the test for selection purposes is apt to be considered unfair. This can be illustrated by returning to the example of GRE scores and graduate school performance. Let's say the average GRE score for Asian grad school applicants to counseling programs is higher than Caucasian applicants but both groups are found to perform equally well once in counseling programs, based on final GPAs. In that case, using the mean score for Asians, the higher GRE score, as a cutoff score for admission would be unfair to Caucasian applicants. Even though the GRE is not thought to be biased in its content, if a cutoff score is established for admission purposes and individuals from a particular group are more likely on average to score lower on the test and therefore denied admission despite the likelihood that they will perform equally well as the majority group, then unfairness, not test bias, is likely to be determined.

Practical Considerations when Selecting Assessment Instruments

When the rationale for conducting an assessment has been identified and the relevant cultural factors addressed, a number of practical considerations will inform which particular test, measure, interview, or observation is decided upon. These practical issues include cost of the method, training required to competently use and interpret it, administration, scoring, and interpretation time, age range, and *utility*. A test's **utility** refers to its ability to deliver practical clinical decision-making information and enhance client outcomes above and beyond what another method (e.g., an interview) can provide, given the relative costs involved (Hunsley & Mash, 2008). It is also the ability of a measure to augment clinical decision making while simultaneously being user friendly, having client acceptability, and providing value and added benefit beyond what other methods offer. Specifically in mental health settings, professionals' willingness to incorporate a psychological test or another standardized method into the assessment process will depend upon having one that is short, practical, and treatment-centered and predictive of how a client is likely to respond to counseling (Beutler, Malik, Talebi, Flemming, & Moleiro, 2004). When compared to other kinds of tests—medical and educational—psychological tests have been found to be equally, if not more, valid in terms of predicting diagnosis, behavior, and treatment response (Meyer et al., 2001).

The amount of time spent using a standardized measure is a cost for the clinician—as is training time and the price of the measure—and the benefit of using an instrument should at least equal, if not exceed, the cost (Yates & Taub, 2003). Those benefits include improved assessment outcomes: better case conceptualization, diagnostic accuracy, and treatment planning. A measure's utility, therefore, is a kind of cost–benefit ratio, and time is always a critical cost. Surveys of clinical and neuropsychologists found that the average times to score and interpret measures routinely used for the assessment of individuals suspected having some type of psychopathology were relatively brief, ranging from 15 to 30 minutes for unidimensional measures and 26 to 34 minutes for multidimensional measures, whereas measures of personality typically take 46 to 58 minutes, depending on the test (Camara, Nathan, & Puente, 2000).

How does Melanie, our counselor, go about applying the concept of utility when selecting measures to use with her client? She wants to get a more complete picture of the kinds of symptoms and problems related to thinking, feeling, and behavior that Tomas is experiencing. Having considered cultural and psychometric factors, Melanie has narrowed down her choice to two measures, A and B. Measure A can be competently scored and interpreted after one assessment course and supervised clinical experience with it. Measure B, on the other hand, requires multiple courses to adequately interpret, is four times as long, twice the cost, and offers little information beyond what measure A does for case conceptualization and treatment planning purposes. Melanie is likely to choose A. She also wants to have a measure of Tomas's symptom severity at the onset, in the middle, and at the end of counseling. Clinicians are more likely to value and use measures that are relatively inexpensive, brief, efficient, and provide clinically relevant information. The ones she chose, the BSI and the RCMAS-2, meet those criteria and their administration, scoring, and interpretation is relatively straightforward compared to a costlier and more complex instrument like the MMPI-II.

Administrating Formal Assessments

Like any counseling session, assessment needs to be conducted in a comfortable, safe, private, and secure setting that will be free of interruption. Some assessments, such as a brief self-report questionnaire, will require little additional preparation to administer other than familiarity with the instrument, knowing where and how it will be completed—with pen, pencil, or keyboard—and where it will be kept. Other kinds of assessments, for example a psychoeducational assessment that includes cognitive ability and achievement testing, will require a table or desk, and other materials such as a stopwatch, test recording forms, and other materials specific to the test. In both cases the assessor will need to 1) be familiar with the test's directions and accompanying manual; 2) provide an explanation to the client or clients about the purpose of the assessment, the time involved, and what will happen once the assessment is completed (how and when results will be communicated); and 3) respond to client questions about the procedure.

   As just mentioned, an important requirement is to be familiar with the manual that typically is purchased separately from a test, questionnaire, or structured interview. The manual provides the administration instructions and it is essential that those instructions are followed. Otherwise the procedure is administered in a nonstandardized manner, which then means the results cannot be properly interpreted. For example, imagine that a school counselor has an 8-year-old second-grade student who she suspects may be suffering from depression because of the recent death of the student's mother. The counselor, as part of her assessment, decides to administer a depression questionnaire to the student but decides to read the questions to the student because she knows the student is still reading at a beginning first-grade level and may not understand some of the items. The manual probably makes no mention of administering the questionnaire orally, because the standardization group participants read the questions. Therefore, this would be a nonstandardized administration and the child might pick up certain cues from the counselor's tone of voice when reading that could subtly or not so subtly affect the child's responses in either direction (endorsing more or fewer items indicative of depression). Comparing the score of a child who had the questionnaire read to him or her with those who read it themselves would be problematic.

   Many psychological tests and even some structured interviews and observation forms can be administered and/or scored via computer. The counselor will need to decide ahead of time which method will be used, computer version or paper and pencil. If a computer administration or scoring is decided upon, make sure ahead of time that the machine is ready and that the scoring system is set up. In some cases a form may be sent electronically to another site for scoring. The logistics of that should be considered and established before the client arrives. How will client privacy be protected and how and when will the clinician receive the feedback from the site?

Assessment documents—test answer sheets, questionnaires, or interview notes—must be kept in a confidential and secure place like any other client information that is recorded. Wherever the assessment is done—a clinic, school, organizational or private practice setting—the counselor needs to be aware of who else might have access to where assessment documents and materials will be kept. What safeguards are in place to ensure that the material can be accessed by only those professionals who have a right to view that information? If a test or questionnaire is going to be sent via the Internet or by postal mail for scoring, what identifying information, if any, will be attached to it? It is the responsibility of the assessor to ensure that a test sent somewhere else for scoring has only a code number or some other anonymous method to protect the client's privacy. The counselor will want to verify before the assessment begins that there is indeed a procedure like that in place if scoring will be done elsewhere.

COMMUNICATING WITH CLIENTS ABOUT PSYCHOLOGICAL MEASURES

Collaboration and Verbal Feedback

The process of discussing the use of standardized measures in the assessment and counseling process and providing feedback to clients can be illustrated with the chapter case study. Once Melanie has decided on a measure she thinks would be a useful inclusion in the assessment process, she needs to communicate this idea to Tomas. How might Melanie approach Tomas about completing a standardized measure? Melanie would want to be mindful of her intention or purpose behind giving Tomas a standardized measure. Her intention will guide how she goes about explaining what Tomas will be doing and more importantly *why* she wants him to complete this task. If Melanie's purpose is to clarify a diagnosis or formulate a case conceptualization, she might say something like:

> One of the things that will help me understand what you are experiencing and figure out what is going on would be for you to fill out this checklist.

And if Melanie keeps in mind that assessment is a collaborative process, she may want to follow up her statement to Tomas with, "How does that sound to you?" If Tomas believes completing some type of measure will be helpful, he is more likely to complete the task. If he has concerns or does not understand what is going to happen, he has an opportunity to ask Melanie questions. This discussion also illustrates how the ethical guidelines regarding informed consent that were covered in Chapter 2 can be adhered to.

Alternatively, if Melanie's intention is to better target treatment goals or have a quantifiable measure of progress and outcome, she might say,

> Given what we have discussed today I think it would be helpful if we could come up with more specific goals and a way to see if we are making progress toward those goals. How would you feel about completing a brief questionnaire that would help with that?

Once a client has agreed to complete a rating scale, checklist, or inventory, the next step would be a brief simple discussion of the following logistical and other ethical issues:

- Typical length of time required to complete it
- Where the measure will be completed (home, office, waiting room, other location)
- When it will be completed (immediately, sometime before the next visit)
- Who, if anyone else besides the clinician, will see the measure.

Discussing assessment results with a client can also be therapeutic by providing a client validation and relief. When Tomas and Melanie sat down to review his BSI responses, Tomas mentioned a few things that Melanie was curious about. Tomas, timidly and quietly said, "I wasn't sure how to answer some of the questions." Melanie reassured him that that was common and then they proceeded to discuss the ones Tomas was unsure about. When that process ended, Tomas noted in a more upbeat tone, "Others must feel this way too, or I guess it would not be on a questionnaire. I'm not the only one with these problems." "That's right," Melanie responded, "many people who come here struggle with the same concerns you have." By normalizing Tomas's experiences and providing reassurance, Melanie helps to strengthen their therapeutic alliance, which is likely to build further client engagement in the counseling process and enhance the likelihood of a beneficial outcome (Asay & Lambert, 1999).

In some mental health clinics and organizations, standardized assessment measures may be routinely given to clients, along with insurance and consent forms, prior to an intake interview. This practice has the advantage of sensitizing clients to the need for reflecting on and rating the frequency and severity of one's problems and symptoms and can help to focus the client when presenting his or her concerns to the clinician. Furthermore, with the measure at hand, the clinician can probe during the intake items that may raise a red flag such as "feeling hopeless about the future." Given that a significant number of outpatient clients come for only one to three visits, especially when depressed (Meredith, Sturm, & Wells, 1999; Watkins et al., 2009), having as much information as possible about client problems can guide a discussion of options: medication, therapies (individual, group, family) and self-help (books, exercise, relaxation strategies). The disadvantage of this approach is that the first assessment measure selected is not customized for the particular client. With some clients the chosen pre-intake assessment measure may be a good fit and for others not. And many clients, particularly those from non-Western cultures, need to begin with a more interpersonal process than completing a standardized measure can provide (Hays, 2008). They need to tell their story and get it out to an empathic, nonjudgmental listener. Once a connection or bond is formed with the counselor, then an appraisal of how the client is thinking, feeling, and behaving can take place. Unfortunately there is no available research that can shed light on whether the order of administration (pre- or post-intake) of a standardized measure makes a difference in terms of client satisfaction or therapy outcome.

Documenting Assessment Findings

The results and interpretations from a psychological assessment can be documented in a variety of ways. The document is a vehicle for organizing and synthesizing the clinician's impressions, conceptualizations, or diagnostic formulations. Its content and style will vary depending on the purpose of the assessment, the referral question, and the intended recipients. Sometimes a letter summarizing the key findings is sent to a parent, physician, or other health care provider, the legal system (probation officer, guardian ad litum, lawyer, or judge), or another helping professional. Letters are helpful ways to communicate with other professionals involved in the client's care so that services can be coordinated. Primary care providers, in particular, who are often on the front line in identifying and treating—with medication—psychological disorders value and rely on assessments about their patients that counselors and other helping professionals have conducted. Other times a lengthier document such as a diagnostic, psychoeducational, or psychological evaluation is produced. How long should these documents be? That depends in part on the nature of the assessment and the potential reader. Typically, reports based on traditional psychological tests—cognitive ability, achievement, or personality—tend to be longer than those that contain formulations about psychiatric diagnoses or interview summaries. Many reports are read by people other than the client and therefore keeping them relatively brief is a useful rule of thumb. Other helping professionals, judges, medical professionals, and employers, are more apt to prefer documents that are no more than several pages long and even then may skip over the bulk of the report, reading only the bottom line: the summary and recommendations. Furthermore, the report should have minimal technical jargon that may simply confuse the reader. The goal is to provide clients, family members, and other helpers with information that enhances rather than clouds their understanding of the client.

In whatever format assessment findings are conveyed to someone other than the client, it is important that the client's informed consent is obtained prior to the start of the assessment. That is, as was discussed in Chapter 2, the client understands the purpose in sending the results to a third party and what the document contains. This consent needs to be documented, usually on an "authorization to release" form the client or parent–guardian, in the case of a minor, signs.

Although there is not a standard format for documenting a psychological assessment, there are some common elements that any letter or report should include. The following sections are typically found in assessment or evaluation documents: Reason for Referral, Background Information, Procedures Performed, Behavioral Observations, Results, and Summary and Recommendations (see Appendix A: Sample Assessment Documents). A letter to another helping or medical professional, parent, or legal entity will be helpful to the extent that it contains these elements, albeit in a more condensed format.

REASON FOR REFERRAL The Reason for Referral section of a psychological report or evaluation is relatively brief and contains who, why, and when information. This includes a sentence or two about who made the referral and why that referral was made, which usually presents the purpose of the current assessment: clarify diagnosis, facilitate treatment planning, gain greater understanding of abilities, traits, or presenting problems. It is also important to document when the referral was made because some aspects of the client's life may have changed from the time the referral was made to the date the assessment began.

BACKGROUND INFORMATION The background information provides a context for understanding the presenting concerns, problems, or questions that led to the evaluation. Typically this section will include pertinent developmental, family, educational, interpersonal, and work or military history, as well as physical and mental health conditions that may have or are currently impacting the referral problem. This section also serves the purpose of providing a contextual understanding for the assessment results. It brings scores and results to life so that the client and readers of the report can make sense of them.

PROCEDURES PERFORMED Any and all of the methods used in the assessment are listed in this section, from standardized tests to informal procedures such as reviewing prior records. When standardized measures or tests are used, the specific name of the instrument rather than the general category—intelligence test, for example—should be noted. The procedures are generally listed in the order in which they were administered (see Appendix A: Sample Assessment Documents).

BEHAVIORAL OBSERVATIONS The behavioral observation section, as discussed in Chapter 5, should contain what the assessor observed and avoid stating inferences about those observations.

Therefore, the section should use neutral, objective language that describes what was seen or heard. If an inference is made in this section, it should be stated tentatively, given that it is a hypothesis, along with the supporting data. For example, the author had completed an assessment of a preschool girl and wrote: "She had looked toward the door one time to see if her father had left the room." The phrase "to see if . . ." is an inference; there are multiple reasons why the daughter may have looked toward the door. Upon reflection, he changed the latter part of the sentence to read: "*as if she may have been* looking to see if her father was still there." In this section inferences should be kept to a minimum, with the focus being a description of what was noticed during the assessment. Larger inferences or hypotheses belong in the Summary and Conclusion section of the report.

This section of the report may be based either on informal or formal observations or both, but the report writer just needs to be clear about which type is the basis of this section. As noted in Chapter 5, this is generally where the mental status observations—general appearance, speech, motor activity, and engagement with and attitude toward the interviewer—belong.

RESULTS   The Results section, sometimes titled "Findings," presents the data from standardized tests or measures. Like much of the counseling field, there is no consensus among professionals about what properly belongs in this section and the best format for describing the data. As noted earlier, it is more helpful for the consumer of the report to have technical information explained in terms that are more readily understandable. Terms such as *standard scores, standard error of measurement,* and *confidence intervals* can be confusing even to those who have had courses in statistics or psychological measurement, let alone those who have not. Similarly, a subtest or scale label can be equally confusing to those unfamiliar with the test. Therefore, an alternative to presenting scales or subtest names and their respective scores is to be descriptive of what the scale is measuring. For example, rather than simply listing subtests on the WISC-4—Vocabulary, Block Design, Digit Span, and so on—a brief description of the ability or process being measured is more helpful. The clinician might state, "On a task requiring defining words orally, Tomas performed in the average range." The content and organization of this section will vary depending upon the ability or trait being assessed, the purpose of the assessment, and the referral question. In general, skills, abilities, traits, or problems that were found to fall outside the normal range, for that particular test, will be the focus of this section. In addition, the specific test data need to be discussed in some fashion, and there are pros and cons to presenting them in different ways.

Some reports include standard scores from all scales or subtests within the test, while others include only overall scores; some provide both. On the other hand, a report may omit standard scores in favor of descriptive language—average range, above or below average range, clinical or normal range—or percentiles. The descriptive labels for scores are found in the manual for that specific test, and it is those labels that should be applied. Another approach is to provide labels and percentiles in this section and include an appendix section in the report where all test standard scores are provided. The advantage of including all standard scores in this section is that the report then becomes a document in which those scores are contained and can be readily accessed by other professionals whose knowledge of the scores could potentially help a client, family, or third party. Keep in mind that to fully understand how standard scores are, in reality, probability estimates requires a particular kind of mathematical aptitude that some report readers will not have. To think of this in another context, standard scores are technical data in the same way an EKG printout is. And like an EKG, a patient relies on a cardiologist to interpret the data. So too will counseling clients and their family members need a professional to help them make sense of the technical information. Perhaps psychological scores are not as abstruse as medical data and can be presented in ways that the typical consumer of the report can understand. Many people do understand the concepts of average, range, and percentiles and can make sense of that information, especially when given the context for understanding those terms. Furthermore, if a results section omits the standard scores in favor of descriptive labels or percentiles, the scores can be sent, with the proper release, to whomever would have reason to use them. That, however, can be time-consuming and may result in further assessment or intervention being delayed. By placing the technical data in an appendix, the results section can stay focused on what was learned about the client's specific strengths and weakness, high or low traits, or level of symptoms, problems, or psychopathology in language that is illuminating rather than confusing. Regardless of the specific style of data presentation, this section should clearly address the referral question and focus on the information that enhances an understanding of the person being assessed—an understanding that was not available prior to the assessment.

SUMMARY AND RECOMMENDATIONS   The Summary and Recommendations section is where the key findings and conclusions are highlighted. The main results and the interpretations drawn from them are presented in such a way that they pave the way for the recommendations that follow. This section provides the clinician's integration and synthesis of all assessment data—both informal and formal—in order to provide some tentative conclusions. Those conclusions may include diagnostic impressions or formulations, a case conceptualization, or the rationale for a particular decision or course of action. Generally, this is done within one paragraph. The report will conclude with a list of recommendations, which may be somewhat generic or highly specific and geared toward the intervention setting. A more general counseling recommendation might state, "Tomas would benefit from weekly individual therapy," or more specifically, "Tomas would benefit from a therapy approach that focuses on the mismatch between his personality style and the family environment he resides in." Similarly, an educational intervention could be stated more generically, "Tomas would benefit from weekly individual study skills training," or better yet, "Tomas would benefit from a study skills approach that emphasizes his strength in visual–spatial processing and memory and targets his weakness in sequential processing." Ultimately, the recommendations should flow logically from the results and summary and describe a course of action that is based on the new knowledge gained from the assessment.

It is considered a best practice for the assessor or evaluator to review the report in person with the client and in some cases, such as with students, with others (family members, an educational team, or other helpers). This provides them with an opportunity to ask questions about the results; the assessor has a chance to see that they understand the data; and collectively they have a place to discuss their views about the recommendations and any potential barriers to implementing them.

THE NEXT GENERATION OF FORMAL ASSESSMENTS

The combined total of the current child, adolescent, and adult standardized tests and measures was, at the time of this writing, in excess of 3,500 and filled 18 volumes of the *Mental Measurements Yearbook* (Buros Institute, 2010). New assessment measures are coming into the marketplace and the counseling field at a very rapid pace, exceeding the capacity for counselors, psychologists, social workers, educators, and other helping professionals to keep up. In the most recent volume (18) of the *Mental Measurements Yearbook* (Buros Institute) there were reviews of 159 new tests, some of which were revisions of existing tests discussed in earlier chapters, but the vast majority were new measures covering a broad spectrum such as *Business Critical*

Thinking Skills Test, Chronic Pain Coping Inventory, Cigarette Use Questionnaire, Five-Factor Personality Inventory—Children, and the *Fitness Interview Test—Revised*. The assessment field has reached the stage where standardized measures are available for just about any dimension of human experience and functioning a helping professional is likely to encounter—from abilities and traits to problems and habits. Paradoxically, at the same time in which professionals have a cornucopia of measures to choose from, restrictions on psychological testing have been imposed, in mental health settings and elsewhere, despite the mounting evidence that psychological assessment in general, and testing in particular, is useful and effective for a number of practical problems in educational, industrial–organizational, physical and mental health care, and vocational settings (Garb, 2003; Kubiszyn et al., 2000; Meyer et al., 2001).

Beyond increasing the sheer volume and breadth of assessment instruments, other kinds of changes are likely to take place over the next 20 years if history is a window into the future. The next generation of standardized measures will probably reflect trends that were observed during the first decade of the 21st century (Kamphaus, Petoskey, & Rowe, 2000; Krishnamurthy, 2008; Norcross, Karpiak, & Santoro, 2005; Wood et al., 2002). First, the instruction in, and use of, behavioral assessment methods will continue to increase while simultaneously the use of other methods such as projective assessments will decline. That trend is, in part, a reflection of economic pressures, which will likely result in clinicians using formal standardized assessments less often, but when doing so, utilizing those that are briefer and less costly (Wood et al.). Surveys of one group of professional assessors, psychologists, have found that to be the case already (Archer & Newsom, 2000; Piotrowski, 1999). Another likely trend will be the increased use of evidence-based measures. Researchers and scholars will likely expand on preliminary efforts to develop criteria for judging the psychometric quality and clinical usefulness of assessment methods. Furthermore, studies examining the incremental validity of old and new measures will continue to appear in mainstream journals (see Special Section of *Psychological Assessment,* December, 2003) and more specialized journals such as *Journal of Anxiety Disorders.* A third trend will be an expansion of the globalization of measures—translation of existing and new measures into non-English languages and replication of the reliability and validity of measures for various cultures. Fourth, technological innovations—using the Internet to obtain standardization samples and to administer, score, and interpret measures—will probably continue to grow. Fifth, child versions of adult therapy outcome and therapist–client alliance measures will be further developed and refined. Sixth, primary prevention efforts—using standardized measures to screen populations such as a community or school district—aimed at identifying those at risk for particular problems will become more widespread. The Affordable Care Act of 2010 recognizes the importance of prevention screenings for a number of problems and conditions, including autism, alcohol misuse, childhood behavior problems, depression, domestic violence, and which government and commercial insurers will reimburse (U.S. Department of Health and Human Services, 2011). Finally, more work will be done with aligning measures with DSM-5 criteria, the development of measures for all DSM disorders, and development of measures for non-DSM constructs such as spirituality, acculturation status, readiness for change, and so on.

As discussed earlier in this chapter, preliminary efforts have been made to develop evidence-based criteria that clinicians can use when selecting assessment measures. These efforts are a useful starting point for clinicians when deciding upon which of the available measures to incorporate into the assessment process. Yet what is still needed are assessment satisfaction data, analogous to therapy or therapist satisfaction measures that could further inform the selection of standardized measures. For example, having information on how easy, understandable, and helpful clients find a measure to be could further help the clinician in the selection process, especially when trying to decide upon two similar and psychometrically sound measures like the *Self-Report of Personality* from the BASC-2 or the *Youth Self-Report* from the ASEBA.

Evidence-Based Measures

Evidence for the effectiveness of assessment measures has been traditionally based more on clinical impressions than on scientific knowledge (Beutler et al., 2004). The practice of choosing measures based on clinical impression rather than empirical data is slowly dissipating. As the overall health care delivery system has adopted evidence-based principles and practices, so too have the fields of counseling and psychology. As was mentioned earlier, *Guide to Assessments That Work* (Hunsley & Mash, 2008) is one example of a preliminary step in compiling evidence-based criteria for mental health assessment measures. Building on a couple of isolated prior attempts at establishing criteria for the selection and use of measures for clinical purposes, Hunsley and Mash developed "criteria that would indicate the minimum evidence that would be sufficient to warrant the use of a measure for specific clinical purposes" (p. 6). Their work resembles a *Consumer Reports*-type rating system whereby assessment methods, rather than automobiles, electronics, and other products, are endorsed because they meet or exceed certain benchmarks. Furthermore, separate rating tables exist for different assessment purposes so that one could look at depression measures, for example, and find a list of measures and the recommendation ratings for diagnostic, case conceptualization and treatment planning, and treatment monitoring and treatment outcome evaluation purposes. Although future scholars and researchers may come up with cogent arguments for faulting the methodology and the ratings given to specific instruments, it is an important step in moving the assessment field in the direction of greater public and professional acceptability and usage, a direction that a number of other assessment professionals, researchers, and scholars have strongly advocated (Groth-Marnat, 1999; Hunsley & Meyer, 2003; Maruish, 1999; Nelson-Gray, 2003; Wood et al., 2002; Yates & Taub, 2003).

It is likely that similar efforts to develop criteria for evidence-based measures will take place with tests of intellectual and neuropsychological functioning, academic abilities, and vocational performance. As parents, governmental entities, and professional groups place greater demands on school systems to demonstrate student learning, so too will there be a need for more valid measures of predicting learning potential and outcomes for diverse groups of individuals. This is likely to result in greater professional and public scrutiny of existing tests, as happened in health care regarding mammograms and prostate-specific antigen tests (PSAs) and the ability of those screening tests to detect different types of cancers. This has been the case with projective instruments, particularly the Rorschach, with some advocating that these tests become a much smaller focus of assessment courses and, when covered, that educators should emphasize their significant limitations (Lilienfeld, Wood, & Garb, 2000). Only those standardized instruments that can pass scientific muster will assessment stakeholders—consumers, clients, clinicians, and third-party payers—be willing to utilize and pay for. Ironically, formal standardized assessment measures are still used only by a minority of helping professionals in educational and mental health settings (Nelson-Gray, 2003). In part, formal assessments may be underutilized (Yates & Taub, 2003) because a number of practical questions about the use of assessment instruments remain unanswered; despite the research that has shown that various ones have contributed to important client outcomes such as more effective treatment, greater understanding of self, improved functioning, and reduction of risk (Kubiszyn et al., 2000; Meyer et al., 2001).

If there is one question that counselors and other helping professionals would want to know and not be afraid to ask that would likely increase their use of standardized assessment tools, it would be this: Given a particular client's demographic profile and presenting problems or concerns, which assessment method or combination of methods will be most helpful for this assessment purpose (case conceptualization, diagnosis, and treatment planning or evaluation)? Information about an instrument's utility (its cost, benefit, and effectiveness relative to another standardized measure or a nonstandardized one—an unstructured clinical interview, for example) will be highly sought after by potential assessors as well as other stakeholders. Increasingly, assessment scholars and researchers are providing some preliminary information about assessment utility (Garb, 2003), but a good deal of research is still needed from which clinicians can make practical decisions (Johnston & Murray, 2003; Nelson-Gray, 2003; Yates & Taub, 2003). As new measures are developed, it will be necessary but not sufficient for them to have acceptable levels of reliability and validity. There will also need to be empirical evidence that the incorporation of a particular measure within the overall assessment process provide important additional information to the clinician and that supplemental data can be acquired in a cost-effective manner (Haynes & Lench, 2003). A trend toward using only measures with demonstrated utility has begun in the educational field as evidenced by the increasing number of colleges and universities that have dropped the standardized tests as an application requirement over the past decade. As of fall 2011, almost 850 four-year postsecondary institutions no longer require applicants to take a standardized test (Fair Access Coalition on Testing, n.d.). Why is that? Increasingly, colleges have found that the information gained from standardized tests—the SAT and ACT—relative to other types of information such as high school performance (grade point average and class rank), extracurricular activities, and personal essays may contribute only marginally to predictions about a given applicant's likelihood of staying in and graduating from that school (Rooney & Schaefer, 1998). In other words, many schools were finding those tests to be lacking in utility.

The use of relatively brief self-report multidimensional and unidimensional measures may become more commonplace in behavioral health care despite the lack of solid research on assessment utility. This probably will occur as the calls for evidence-based health care mount from multiple spheres, and the resources for treatment and prevention remain precious. The use of standardized measures has already become standard operating procedure for the treatment and monitoring of mental health problems in one of the larger national managed care organizations, United Behavioral Health (UBH). UBH expects that all clients will complete a Wellness Assessment Inventory after the first session and again between the third and fifth sessions. Sometimes the questionnaire is sent directly to the client or parent, in the case of a minor, or to the clinician who is expected to give it to the client to complete. This brief assessment tool consists of 24 items taken from other established measures such as the SCL-90-R (see Chapter 8) and the CAGE (see Chapter 13) and is designed to measure anxiety and depression symptoms, level of functioning and self-efficacy, and substance abuse. Other managed care organizations, health insurers, and federal and state governments are likely to require standardized measures be used for assessment or treatment outcome purposes, or both, if they have not done so already. Furthermore, this process is occurring with the DSM-5 field trials and may be incorporated into the DSM-5 itself when it is scheduled for arrival in spring of 2013.

Computerized Adaptive Testing and Item Response Theory

A combination of item response theory (IRT) and computerized adaptive testing has also impacted assessment practice, particularly test construction and administration, and will probably continue to do so for the foreseeable future. IRT is based on the notion that responses to specific items reflect an underlying trait or ability, and sophisticated statistical procedures are used to analyze how individual items discriminate between groups of people or level of ability. Most psychological tests have been developed from classical test theory (see Chapter 6), which focuses on the overall test properties: reliability and standard error of measurement. Alternatively, *modern test theory,* the term now used in reference to IRT, or what is also referred to a *latent trait theory,* focuses on individual test item analysis. IRT has enhanced test development and scoring by providing information about test items that classical test theory does not. Simply put, IRT is a collection of mathematical models that describe the relationship between the amount of an underlying ability or construct a group of people has and the probability of answering a test item correctly or in a certain direction. For example, given a personality test like the NEO-PI-R, items on the five major trait dimensions can be dichotomously scored 1 or 0, with a 1 indicating that the response to the item is keyed to one end of a trait, such as extraversion, and a 0 to the other end, in this case, introversion. According to IRT, the probability of an individual answering the items on the NEO-PI-R Extraversion scale "correctly," meaning indicative of extraversion, is a function of how much of that trait the test taker possesses. That probability function produces what is known as an item response or characteristic curve (see Figure 15.1), which describes the ability of an item to discriminate between individuals with varying degrees of the underlying or latent trait or ability (Harvey & Hammer, 1999).

IRT was initially applied to the construction of ability and achievement tests, but more recently it has been applied to personality and psychopathology measures, thanks to the advent of high-powered computers and statistical software packages in the 1980s (Harvey & Hammer, 1999; Thissen & Steinberg, 2010). The *Differential Aptitude Scale–*Second Edition (DAS-II) is an example of a cognitive ability test that was developed using IRT (Davis, 2010). By applying a particular IRT model, the developers of the DAS-II produced a test whereby the sequence of items, from easy to hard, was based on analyses of the item's difficulty for various age levels. This enables the administration of the test to be more tailored to a child's age and estimated ability level (Davis, 2010).

IRT, like classical test theory, is based on certain assumptions that may or may not be met given the test performance data (Thissen & Steinberg, 2010). One assumption is that the scale or subtest on a test is unidimensional, that is, it measures only one factor or trait, when in reality test scales often measure multiple dimensions. This is the case with most ability, personality, and psychopathology tests. Another assumption is that of local independence. This assumption states that for a group of people having a certain level of a trait, for example, extraversion, the only thing that affects their responses to individual items is how much of the trait they possess rather

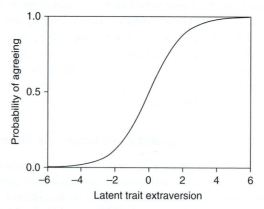

FIGURE 15.1 Hypothetical Item Characteristic Curve

than the qualities of the item itself. Those item characteristics that are assumed to be irrelevant to measuring the trait in question are things such as its wording or how the words are interpreted (Thissen & Steinberg, 2010). Advances in mathematically modeling have meant that IRT can be applied even when those fundamental assumptions are not met (Harvey & Hammer, 1999). These statistical models have now been applied to a wide range of tests, including the kind of adaptive and customized assessments being developed by the National Institutes of Health (NIH).

The *Patient-Reported Outcome Measures Information System* (PROMIS) developed by NIH is a recent application of IRT and adaptive testing in the area of psychopathology. NIH developed an item data bank using IRT and then selected items from the bank to create various measures including ones to assess anger, anxiety, and depression. Large banks of test items were developed through reviews of exiting measures and interviews with experts and patients. The initial item pool was then winnowed down and IRT was used for the final selection of a relatively small number of items for the domains comprised in the PROMIS system: pain, fatigue, emotional distress, physical function, and social function (DeWalt, Rothrock, Yount, & Stone, 2007).

Adaptive assessment is based on the concept of routing clients to specific test questions based on previous responses rather than completing an entire questionnaire or series of questionnaires in order to make the process more efficient and customized for the client. Rather than having an individual start at the beginning of a test or measure, the individual begins with an item that has been shown to discriminate between people who are low and high on some kind of ability, trait, or psychological dimension. Item response curves based on IRT are developed, which enable test developers to identify those items with the maximum potential for discriminating between those who are low and high on some variable. If that discriminating item is passed, then the person is routed to the next item that tends to differentiate people at the next level of the dimension; if not, then the person is routed to an item with less discriminating power. PROMIS is based on a two-tiered adaptive testing model. At stage one, an individual is given a brief (six to eight items) questionnaire, and the responses to specific items will determine if further questions are asked. Stage two consists of a longer, more in-depth questionnaire to further assess responses that raised a red flag in stage one. For example, by responding to the item "I felt sad at least some of the time in the past seven days," the individual would be routed to another series of questions in order to assess the possibility of depression. Conversely, the individual who indicated that sadness was never occurring would not be taken to the second tier. The PROMIS questionnaires are being used in the DSM-5 field trials and they can be viewed at ***www.nihpromis.org*** along with a demonstration of adaptive testing for depression and eight other health domains. One of the potential benefits of a measure designed in part, or entirely, through a process that makes it suitable for adaptive testing is that the time and cost to clinician and client can be reduced because the client is routed only to those items necessary—often half the usual number—for accurately predicting where along a psychological trait or ability dimension the person falls (Smith, Fischer, & Fister, 2003).

Summary and Conclusions

Assessment is an ongoing process of gathering, organizing, and synthesizing information in order to answer a question or make a decision. That process begins by the counselor identifying his or her purpose in conducting an assessment and then selecting the proper tools for the information-gathering phase. At times the task of choosing from an array of potential instruments can seem overwhelming, but attending to psychometric, multicultural, and pragmatic considerations can help make selecting the appropriate one(s) more manageable. This chapter presented an overview of those selection factors and how to apply them with a case study illustration.

Once the assessment data have been collected and assembled, the helping professional needs to communicate the findings and conclusions to others: clients, family members, other professionals, and so on. Some practice guidelines for documenting and communicating assessment findings were also presented.

Professional counseling assessment is not a recent phenomenon. The practice of assessment has evolved substantially since it was first introduced thousands of years ago in Ancient Chinese and Greek civilizations. This evolution will continue as more and more research unfolds and new technological innovations that have been infused in all modern societies shape the assessment process. This chapter briefly discussed trends in the development and use of standardized measures that researchers and scholars in the field envisioned for the 21st century. One direction in particular that was emphasized was the use of evidence-based measures, which parallels developments in the fields of medicine and education. Another was the use of item response theory and its application to adaptive testing: a more efficient assessment process.

FINAL NOTE

Assessment and intervention are ongoing, complementary processes that are guided by a few core principles: valuing a multicultural and ethically sensitive approach; applying only those tools that one is competent to use by virtue of education, training, and professional experience; and understanding that the context of the assessment—setting and purpose—drives the process. Since the moment you were born, you have been assessing the world around you informally, and now you have learned how to conduct more formal analyses. Hopefully, this text has enhanced your understanding of the current state of assessment practice and will help you to apply its principles, concepts, and methods in your daily professional endeavors.

Reflection Questions and Experiential Exercises

1. What does the concept of a test's *utility* mean?
2. What factors guide a helping professional when selecting an assessment method?
3. What are some factors to consider when selecting a standardized test or measure that is in a language different than the client's primary language?
4. When using a norm-based test, how do you determine if the normative sample is adequate for your client?
5. In what ways does the communication of test results to a client provide therapeutic benefit?
6. Identify an assessment measure you are interested in learning more about and go the *Mental Measurements Yearbook* database and read the reviews. What about the review was helpful, unhelpful, or unclear? Was there any information you were looking for that you did not find?
7. Compose a sample assessment document—letter or report—for a client with whom you are helping at your practicum or internship. Review the document with your supervisor.

APPENDIX A

SAMPLE ASSESSMENT DOCUMENTS
Sample Letter

09/30/11
Re: S.
D.O.B. 04/24/2002

Dear Dr. M.,

Thank you for referring S., a 9-year-old male, for counseling because of your and his parents' concerns about anxiety symptoms and panic attacks. I met with S. and his parents for an initial assessment interview on 8/14/11 and they were very concerned about S.'s emotional state, particularly the anxiety he had been experiencing since April.

Based on that intake interview and subsequent two additional interviews with S. and his responses to the *How I Feel Questionnaire,* an anxiety scale for children, it was my diagnostic impression that S. was experiencing anxiety, including obsessive thinking, worry, and rumination. He appeared to have an obsessive–compulsive disorder, obsessions only, however. His obsessions, worry, nervousness, and physical symptoms of anxiety appeared to have been triggered in part from experiencing a severe car accident last winter in which his mother was seriously injured.

Following the initial assessment, S. was seen for seven counseling sessions that included both individual and family sessions. He made significant improvement and at the last session on 9/23/11 he and his mother were reporting that he was not having any more panic attacks, that his nervousness was much less, and when intrusive thoughts arose he was better able to manage them.

Please feel free to contact me if you would like any additional information about S.'s therapy.

Regards,

Melanie Grenvue, M.Ed.
Licensed Mental Health Counselor

SAMPLE PSYCHOLOGICAL EVALUATION

Name: T.J.
Date of Birth: 03/10/77
Date of Evaluation: 11/16/2011, 11/28/2011

REASON FOR REFERRAL

T. J. ("T."), a 31-year-old female, was referred for psychological evaluation by her counselor, Melanie Grenvue, M.Ed., because of a history of depression, and a possible diagnosis of attention deficit hyperactivity disorder. T. was interested in ruling out whether or not she had attention deficit hyperactivity disorder and a learning disability. She also wondered if those disorders could be causing her problems at work or whether it was all "due to my depression."

BACKGROUND INFORMATION

T. is employed full-time as an administrative assistant in a large manufacturing company. She has been at her current job for four years and has held other jobs, including a telemarketing job and an office manager in a small medical practice. T. reported that she has "terrible" organizational skills. She has difficulties with finding papers and folders—often misplacing things, following through with tasks, and leaving jobs unfinished. She also reported some social anxiety, and indicated that she has had difficulty with organization for years. Additional problems that she noted, which also have been occurring for years, include difficulty retaining information when she reads, focusing on conversations, and keeping her attention from wandering when engaged in conversations with coworkers and family members.

T. has an associate's degree from a local community college. Following high school she took a couple of courses at a local vocational technological institute, where she was in a certificate program for environmental services but was unable to find a job in that field. She denies a history of behavioral problems in elementary or high school. She does recall that either in second or third grade she was told that she "needed to pay attention more." As far as she can recall, T. has had problems with disorganization in elementary and high school. She added that elementary school was easier than high school. She received a lot of tutoring in math when she was in middle school, which she felt helped her.

T. is the third child in a family of four children. She reported that a maternal uncle was diagnosed with schizophrenia and her younger brother has had "a lot of issues" and had been in trouble a lot because of "drug problems." Her parents divorced when she was 12 and she and her siblings were split up: she and her brother went to live with her father, and her two older sisters were almost out of the home but stayed with their mother. T. has a somewhat distant relationship with both her parents presently. T. lives with her boyfriend of six months and they are engaged to be married.

T. reported a significant mental health history beginning at age 13. She has had two prior episodes of outpatient counseling, each of which lasted about six months. She has never been hospitalized. She suffers from irritable bowel syndrome and sometimes takes medication for that but could not recall which medication. She was once prescribed Prozac when she was 16 but wasn't sure if it helped. At the time of this evaluation she was not on any medications.

PROCEDURES PERFORMED

Conners' Adult ADHD Diagnostic Interview for DSM-IV (CAADID)

Kaufman Adolescent and Adult Intelligence Test (KAIT)

Wide Range Achievement Test—4 (WRAT-4)

Conners' Continuous Performance Test (CPT)

Telephone conversation with Melanie Grenvue, M.Ed.

BEHAVIORAL OBSERVATIONS

T. presents as a tall, slender female, who is neatly and casually dressed. She is cooperative, pleasant, easy to engage, and responds openly to questions. She displays a wide range of affect that is consistent with the topic at hand. She is soft-spoken and a couple of times this evaluator needed to ask her to repeat what she said in order to hear her. Initially she would shift back and forth in her seat but became more still as the interview progressed.

On cognitive tasks, she persists in the face of failure but does not offer a guess when she is unsure. At times she displays impulsive behaviors. She has most difficulty staying focused when she is required to listen to an audiotape of simulated newscasts and stories. She seems aware of her performance on the cognitive tasks, by remarking on how she had done, but awareness does not appear to change her affect or impact her performance on subsequent tasks.

TEST RESULTS

Overall, intellectual functioning as assessed with the KAIT is in the average range, composite IQ equal to 95 (+/−5). Her performance on both tasks of crystallized intelligence and fluid intelligence are in the average range as well. Crystallized IQ score equals 93 (+/−6), fluid IQ score equals 99 (+/−6). There is not a significant difference between these two IQs. Crystallized intelligence tasks tend to measure ability that is based on information that has been acquired over time, usually in an educational setting. Fluid intelligence measures performance in problem solving and responding to new information. All of T.'s subtest scores are in the average range. She displays a relative strength on a verbal comprehension task that requires her to demonstrate cognitive flexibility with the meanings of words. T. displays a relative weakness on an auditory comprehension task and a logical reasoning task. Both of those tasks can be affected by a diminished attention span. Her performance on those tasks also suggests a weakness with numerical reasoning and more complex reasoning such as the kind required to solve syllogisms.

Academic functioning as assessed with the WRAT-4 ranges from the seventh-grade to high school level. On both screening of reading and spelling, T. is performing at a high school grade level; however, on a screening of arithmetic functioning, she is performing at the seventh-grade level.

In response to the semistructured interview for adult ADHD (CAADID), T. endorses a clinically significant number of items indicative of attention deficit–hyperactivity disorder. These symptoms include being easily distracted, difficulty following through on or completing tasks, sustaining attention, and losing important things.

Her performance on the Conners' CPT, a computer based test of sustained attention and impulsivity, indicates commission errors, indicative of impulsive responding, and a large number of omission errors indicating poor attention to the task. She also gave more variable responses at the end of the test than at the beginning, indicating an impaired ability to sustain attention. Those errors were in the markedly atypical range for adults.

SUMMARY AND RECOMMENDATIONS

The significant difference between T.'s overall intellectual functioning found to be in the average range and her arithmetic functioning, which was found to be at the sixth-grade level, suggest the presence of a learning disability in arithmetic. T.'s history and responses to the semistructured interview, the CAADID, her performance on the Conners', as well as her performance on the cognitive tasks suggest the presence of an attention deficit–hyperactivity disorder. Her psychiatric history also indicates that she has suffered from major depression, which currently seems to be in remission based on her response to questions on the CAADID and the report of her therapist.

DIAGNOSTIC IMPRESSION

Axis I: 314.01, attention deficit–hyperactivity disorder, 296.35, major depression in remission, 315.1, learning disorder in mathematics

Axis II: V71.09 No diagnosis

Axis III: none

Axis IV: Current stressors: work and family

Axis V: GAF = 60

RECOMMENDATIONS INCLUDE THE FOLLOWING

1. Given the current diagnosis of ADHD and major depression, T. would benefit from psychiatric consultation to determine an appropriate medication that could help with both ADHD and depression symptoms.

2. T. would possibly benefit from some individual coaching or counseling that could help her with organizational and self-monitoring strategies that would facilitate her sustaining attention, and task completion. This could be accomplished through a cognitive–behavioral approach in her current counseling. This could also include teaching self-talk and mindfulness techniques that can improve focusing and sustained attention.

3. T. could explore with her therapist how much of her current job involves mathematical skills and whether those skills are at a level that is higher than her current functioning. If that is the case, she may need to allow extra time for those tasks and maybe discuss with her employer ways to assist her in that regard.

APPENDIX B

ADDITIONAL RESOURCES

Books and Websites

ETHICS AND STANDARDS

American Educational Research Association, American Psychological Association, & National Council on Measurement in Education. (1999). *Standards for psychological and educational tests*. The latest edition of the standards includes sections on test construction, fairness in testing, and applications (user qualifications and responsibilities and testing in specific settings: educational, and employment).

Association for Assessment in Counseling and Education (AACE)—
http://www.theaaceonline.com/resources.htm
   The AACE website contains a treasure trove of assessment information, documents, and links. The following documents can be downloaded for free: *Standards for Qualification of Test Users*, *Responsibilities of Users of Standardized Tests*, and *Test Taker Rights and Responsibilities*. The site also contains standards for assessment in specialty areas: career counseling, marriage and family, mental health, school, and substance abuse. There are links to assessment-related organizations and reviews of specific tests and measures.

Ken Pope's Website—*http://www.kspope.com*
   The site contains the ethical codes of dozens of professional disciplines, including ACA, AMCHA, ASCA, NASW, APA, and AAMFT. There are additional resources on ethical decision making and an assessment section. The assessment section includes publisher statements regarding HIPAA and test materials.

The National Fair Access Coalition on Testing (FACT)—*http://www.fairaccess.org/home*
   FACT is an organization that supports public awareness about access to competent assessment professionals and promotes the development of ethics and practice standards and legislation related to assessment. The site provides a link to the International Test Commission Guidelines on testing.

MULTICULTURAL ASSESSMENT

Dana, R. H. (2005). *Multicultural assessment principles, applications, and examples*. Erlbaum. Provides a model for evaluating common assessment tests from a multicultural perspective as well as guidelines for using these tests with specific populations.

Association for Assessment in Counseling. (2003). *Standards for multicultural assessment* (2nd ed.). Author. This can be downloaded from *http://www.theaaceonline.com/multicultural.pdf*

Suzuki, L. A., & Ponterotto, J. G. (2008). *Handbook of multicultural assessment: Clinical, psychological, and educational applications* (3rd ed.). Wiley. Covers general assessment issues, specific populations, and personality and cognitive ability assessments with various groups.

Research Literature on Multilingual Versions of Psychiatric Assessment Instruments
   http://www.vtpu.org.au/resources/translated_instruments/researchliterature.html
   The Victorian Transcultural Psychiatry Unit, a division of the Australian government, is dedicated to providing mental health resources. The site contains research and reviews of largely mental health self-report instruments that have been translated into multiple languages. Measures can be accessed by title or language.

INTERVIEWING

Hill, Clara. (2004). *Helping skills: Facilitating exploration, insight, and action* (2nd ed.). American Psychological Association. Although this is a book on fundamental helping and counseling skills and how to apply them with intention, the exploration stage section features basic interviewing skills that can be applied with any informal or formal interview.

Ivey, Allen E., & Ivey, Mary B. (2007). *Intentional interviewing and counseling: Facilitating client development in a multicultural society* (6th ed.). Similar to Hill's book in content and scope, it covers the use of questions, observations, and the other counseling skills that are needed for effective interviewing.

Morrison, James R. (2008). *The first interview* (3rd ed.). Guilford Press. Although written from a medical perspective, it thoroughly and specifically covers the content and questions of an intake interview.

TESTS AND MEASURES

Buros Institute—*Mental Measurements Yearbook (MMY.)* The MMY contains reviews of new tests and measures. Each test is reviewed by two independent reviewers who are selected on the basis of their expertise in the subject area, contributions to the literature, and peer reviews, and they represent various assessment settings. In addition, test reviews are now available online at *http://buros.unl.edu/buros/jsp/search.jsp*. They can also be obtained through the MMY database that is often part of EbscoHost©.

Fischer, J., & Corcoran, K. (2007). *Measures for clinical practice and research: A sourcebook* (4th ed., Vol. 1 [Couples, Families, and Children] and Vol. 2 [Adults]). Oxford University Press. A compendium of brief, mostly self-report instruments for use with problems typically seen in mental health and similar settings. The volumes include reproductions of each instrument with a brief description and psychometric information: norms, reliability, and validity. Also includes a reference and information section about obtaining the measure. Many instruments can be copied from the book or can be obtained from the author. The problem topics are widespread, ranging from acculturation to substance abuse, and include areas such as treatment satisfaction, self-concept and esteem, social support, interpersonal behavior, ethnic identity, and eating problems.

Hebben, N., & Milberg, W. (2009). *Essentials of neuropsychological assessment* (2nd ed.). Wiley. Helpful reviews of commonly used neuropsychological tests and their purposes and applications.

Hunsley, J., & Mash, E. J. (2008). *A guide to assessments that work.* Oxford. Features assessments by diagnostic category and criteria for judging the applicability of them.

Maruish, M. E. (2004). *The use of psychological testing for treatment planning and outcomes assessment* (3rd ed., Vols. 1–3). Erlbaum. Volume 1 focuses on general considerations; Volume 2 covers instruments for children and adolescents. and Volume 3 is on adult measures. Each chapter covers a specific instrument and is typically authored by either the developer of the instrument or someone with expertise in the use and interpretation of the measure.

Project Cork—*http://www.projectcork.org/*

A site devoted to gathering and disseminating information and research on substance abuse measures. The primary substance use screening measures reviewed in Chapter 12 can be downloaded for free from the site.

PUBLISHER WEBSITES

Consulting Psychologists Press—*https://www.cpp.com/en/index.aspx*
    CPP distributes the *Myers–Briggs*® and *Strong Interest Inventory*® and other tests often used for career and vocational counseling purposes.

Psychological Assessment Resources, Inc. (PAR, Inc.)—*http://www4.parinc.com/*
    PAR carries a wide range of tests including achievement, career, cognitive ability, behavior, and personality.

Multi-Health Systems *http://www.mhs.com/*
    MHS carries a range of educational and clinical tests including popular ones such as *Conners'-3*™, *Children's Depression Inventory-2*™, and *SASSI*™.

Pearson—*http://www.pearsonassessments.com/pai/*
    Pearson distributes and publishes a very large collection of tests since its merger with the Psychological Corporation and NCS. Its collection includes ability tests (*Wechsler Scales,* K-ABC-2), achievement tests, behavior personality and psychopathology tests (BASC-2, CDI-2,MMPI-2, and *Beck Depression and Anxiety Inventories:* BDI-2 and BAI), and vocational tests.

Pro-Ed—*http://www.proedinc.com/customer/default.aspx*
    A publisher specializing in tests used primarily in education and rehabilitation settings: ability, achievement, and developmental.

Riverside—*http://www.riverpub.com/*
    Riverside carries a variety of ability and achievement tests for assessing cognitive development, learning, and educational abilities. Their collection includes the *Stanford–Binet Intelligence Scales,* 5th Edition, and *Woodcock–Johnson III*®.

Western Psychological Services—*http://www.wpspublish.com*
    WPS distributes tests for use in clinical, school, and industrial/organizational settings.

REFERENCES

Abramowitz, J. S. (2008). Obsessive-compulsive disorder. In J. Hunsley & E. J. Mash (Eds.), *Assessments that work* (pp. 275–292). New York, NY: Oxford.

Acevedo-Polakovich, I. D., Reynaga-Abiko, G., Garriott, P. O., Derefinko, K. J., Wimsatt, M. K., Gudonis, L. C., . . . Brown, T. L. (2007). Beyond instrument selection: Cultural considerations in the psychological assessment of U.S. Latinas/os. *Professional Psychology: Research and Practice, 38*(4), 375–384.

Achenbach, T. M. (1982). *Developmental psychopathology* (2nd ed.). New York, NY: Wiley.

Achenbach, T. M. (1991). *Manual for the Youth Self-Report* and 1991 profile. Burlington: University of Vermont, Department of Psychiatry.

Achenbach, T. M. (2001). What are norms and why do we need valid ones? *Clinical Psychology: Science and Practice, 8*(4), 446–450.

Achenbach, T. M. (2011). *ASEBA® Achenbach System of Empirically Based Assessment*. Retrieved from http://aseba.org/research/reserach.html

Achenbach, T. M., Becker, A., Döpfner, M., Heiervang, E., Roessner, V., Steinhausen, H.-C, et al. (2008). Multicultural assessment of child and adolescent psychopathology with ASEBA and SDQ instruments: Research findings, applications, and future directions. *Journal of Child Psychology and Psychiatry, 49*(3), 251–275.

Achenbach, T. M., Dumenci, L., & Rescorla, L. A. (2002). Ten-year comparisons of problems and competencies for national samples of youth: Self, parent, and teacher reports. *Journal of Emotional and Behavioral Disorders. 10,* 194–203.

Achenbach, T. M. & Rescorla, L. A. (2001). Manual for the ASEBA school-age forms and profiles. Burlington, VT: University of Vermont Research Center for Children, Youth and Families.

Achenbach, T. M., & Rescorla, L. A. (2006). Developmental issues in assessment, taxonomy, and diagnosis of psychopathology: Life-span and cross-cultural perspectives. In D. Cicchetti (Ed.), *Handbook of developmental psychopathology* (2nd ed). New York, NY: Wiley.

Achenbach, T. M., & Rescorla, L. A. (2007). *Multicultural supplement to the manual for the ASEBA school-age forms and profiles.* Burlington: University of Vermont, Research Center for Children, Youth & Families.

Ackerman, S., Hilsenroth, M., Baity, M., & Blagys, M. (2000). Interaction of therapeutic process and alliance during psychological assessment. *Journal of Personality Assessment, 75,* 82–109.

Adams, K. M. (2000). Practical and ethical issues pertaining to test revisions. *Psychological Assessment, 12*(3), 281–286.

Adesso, V. J., Cisler, R. A., Larus, B. J., & Hayes, B. B. (2004). Substance abuse. In M. Hersen (Ed.), *Psychological assessment in clinical practice: A pragmatic guide* (pp. 147–174). New York, NY: Brunner-Routledge.

Agabio, R., Marras, P., Gessa, G. L., & Carpiniello, B. (2007). Alcohol use disorders, and at–risk patients affected by mood disorder, in Cagliari, Italy. Sensitivity and specificity of different questionnaires. *Alcohol and Alcoholism, 42,* 575–581.

Albanese, M. A. (2003). Test review of the Mini-Mental State Examination. In B. S. Plake, J. C. Impara, & R. A. Spies (Eds.), *The fifteenth mental measurements yearbook.* Retrieved from the Buros Institute's *Test Reviews online* website: http://www.unl.edu/buros

Albemarle Paper Co. v. Moody, 422 U.S. 405 (1975).

Allen, A., Montgomery, M., Tubman, J., Frazier, L., & Escovar, L. (2003). The effects of assessment feedback on rapport-building and self-enhancement processes. *Journal of Mental Health Counseling, 25*(3), 165–182.

Allport, G. W. (1937). *Personality: A psychological interpretation.* New York, NY: Holt.

Allport, G. W., & Odbert, H. S. (1936). Trait-names: A psycho-lexical study. *Psychological Monographs, 47*(211).

American Association of Suicidology. (2009). *Core competencies for the assessment and management of individuals at risk for suicide.* Washington, DC: Author.

American Counseling Association. (2003). *Standards for qualifications of test users.* Alexandria, VA: Author.

American Counseling Association. (2005). *Code of ethics and standards of practice.* Alexandria, VA: Author.

American Educational Research Association, American Psychological Association, & National Council on

Measurement in Education. (1999). *Standards for educational and psychological testing.* Washington, DC: American Educational Research Association.

American Mental Health Counseling Association. (2010). *AMHCA Code of Ethics.* Alexandria, VA: Author.

American Psychiatric Association. (1994). *Diagnostic and statistical manual of mental disorders* (4th ed.). Washington, DC: Author.

American Psychiatric Association. (2000). *Diagnostic and statistical manual of mental disorders* (4th ed., text rev.). Washington, DC: Author.

American Psychiatric Association. (2010). *American Psychiatric Association DSM-5 development.* Retrieved from http://www.DSM5-org

American Psychoanalytic Association & Alliance of Psychoanalytic Organizations. (2006). *Psychodynamic diagnostic manual.* Bethesda, MD: Alliance of Psychoanalytic Organizations.

American Psychological Association. (2002). *Ethical principles of psychologists and code of conduct.* Washington, DC: Author.

American Psychological Association, American Educational Research Association, & National Council on Measurement in Education. (1974). *Standards for educational & psychological tests.* Washington, DC: American Psychological Association.

American School Counselor Association. (2010). *Ethical standards for school counselors.* Alexandra, VA: Author.

Amore, M., Menchetti, M., Tonti, C., Scarlatti, F., Lundgren, E., Esposito, W., et al. (2008). Predictors of violent behavior among acute psychiatric patients: Clinical study. *Psychiatry and Clinical Neurosciences, 62,* 247–255.

Anastasi, A. (1988). *Psychological testing* (6th ed.). New York: Macmillan.

Anastasi, A., & Urbina, S. (1997). *Psychological testing* (7th ed.). Upper Saddle River, NJ: Prentice Hall.

Ancoli-Israel, S. (2005). Sleep and aging: Prevalence of disturbed sleep and treatment considerations of older adults. *Journal of Clinical Psychiatry, 66*(9), 24–30.

Anderson, D. A., Burton, D. B., Parker, J. D., & Godding, P. R. (2001). A confirmatory factor analysis of the cognitive capacity screening examination in a clinical sample. *International Journal of Neuroscience, 111,* 221–233.

Archer, R. P. (2005). *MMPI-A: Assessing adolescent psychopathology* (3rd ed.). New York, NY: Routledge Press.

Archer, R. P. (2006). A perspective on the Restructured Clinical (RC) Scale project. *Journal of Personality Assessment, 87,* 179–185.

Archer, R. P., Handel, R. W., & Lynch, K. D. (2001). The effectiveness of MMPI-A items in discriminating between normative and clinical samples. *Journal of Personality Assessment, 77*(3), 420–435.

Archer, R. P., & Newsom, C. R. (2000). Psychological test usage with adolescent clients: Survey update. *Assessment, 7,* 227–235.

Archer, R. P., Tirrell, C. A., & Elkins, D. E. (2001). An evaluation of an MMPI-A short form: Implications for adaptive testing. *Journal for Personality Assessment, 76,* 76–89.

Armstrong, P. I., Day, S. X., McVay, J. P., & Rounds, J. (2008). Holland's RIASEC model as an integrative framework for individual differences. *Journal of Counseling Psychology, 55,* 1–18.

Asay, T. P., & Lambert, M. J. (1999). The empirical case for the common factors in therapy: Qualitative findings. In M. A. Hubble, B. L. Duncan, & S. D. Miller (Eds.), *The heart and soul of change: What works in therapy* (pp. 33–56). Washington, DC: American Psychological Association.

Asner-Self, K., Schreiber, J., & Marotta, S. (2006). A cross-cultural analysis of the Brief Symptom Inventory-18. *Cultural Diversity and Ethnic Minority Psychology, 12,* 367–375.

Association for Assessment in Counseling. (2003). *Responsibilities of users of standardized tests* (RUST). Alexandria, VA: Author.

Ayalon, L., & Young, M. A. (2005). Racial group differences in help-seeking behaviors. *Journal of Social Psychology, 145,* 391–403.

Ayalon, L., & Young, M. A. (2009). Using the SCL-90-R to assess distress in African Americans and Caucasian Americans. *Journal of Black Studies, 39,* 420–433.

Babor, T. F., Higgins-Biddle, J., Saunders, J., & Monteiro, M. (2001). *The alcohol use disorders identification test:*

Guidelines for use in primary health care (2nd ed). WHO/ MSD/MSBO1.6a. Geneva, Switzerland: World Health Organization. Retrieved from: http://whqlibdoc .who.int/hq/2001/who_msd_msb_01.6a.pdf

Babor, T. F., McRee, B. G., Kassebaum, P. A., Grimaldi, P. L., Ahmed, K., & Bray, J. (2007). Screening, Brief Intervention, and Referral to Treatment (SBIRT): Toward a public health approach to the management of substance abuse. *Substance Abuse, 28*(3), 7–30.

Bachelor, A., & Horvath, A. (1999). The therapeutic relationship. In M. A. Hubble, B. L. Duncan, & S. D. Miller (Eds.), *The heart and soul of change: What works in therapy* (pp. 133–178). Washington, DC: American Psychological Association.

Bachelor, A., & Salame, R. (2000). Participants' perceptions of dimensions of the therapeutic alliance over the course of therapy. *Journal of Psychotherapy Practice and Research, 9,* 39–53.

Baddeley, A. D. (2003). Working memory and language: An overview. *Journal of Communication Disorders, 36*(3), 189–208.

Baddeley, A. D. (2007). *Working memory, thought and action.* Oxford, England: Oxford University Press.

Baddeley, A. D., & Hitch, G. J. (1974). Working memory. In G.H. Bower (Ed.), *The psychology of learning and motivation,* (Vol. 8, pp. 47–90). New York: Academic Press.

Bagby, R. M., Ryder, A. G., Schuller, D. S., & Marshall, M. B. (2004). The Hamilton Rating Scale for Depression: Has the gold standard become a lead weight? *American Journal of Psychiatry, 161*, 2163–2177.

Bagby, R. M., Wild, N., & Turner, A. (2003). Psychological assessment in adult mental health settings. In J. R. Graham, J. A. Naglieri, & I. B. Weiner (Eds.), *Handbook of psychology: Assessment psychology* (Vol. 10, pp. 213–234). Hoboken, NJ: Wiley.

Bain, S. K., & Allin, J. D. (2005). Test review "Stanford-Binet Intelligence Scale, fifth edition". *Journal of Psychoeducational Assessment, 23,* 87–95.

Bain, S. K., & Gray, R. (2008). Review of *Kaufman Assessment Battery for Children–Second edition. Journal of Psychoeducational Assessment, 26,* 92–101.

Bandura, A. (1997). *Self-efficacy: The exercise of control.* New York: Freeman.

Barkley, R. A. (2006). *Attention deficit hyperactivity disorder: A handbook for diagnosis and treatment* (3rd ed.). New York, NY: Guilford Press.

Barnes, L. L. B., Harp, D., & Jung, W. S. (2002). Reliability generalization of scores on the Spielberger State-Trait Anxiety Inventory. *Educational and Psychological Measurement, 62,* 603–618.

Beck, A. T. (1967). *Depression: Clinical, experimental, and theoretical aspects.* New York, NY: Hoeber. Republished as *Depression: Causes and treatment.* Philadelphia: University of Pennsylvania Press.

Beck, A. T. (1978). *Beck Hopelessness Scale.* New York, NY: Psychological Corporation.

Beck, A. T., Epstein, N., Brown, G., & Steer, R. A. (1988). An inventory for measuring clinical anxiety: Psychometric properties. *Journal of Consulting and Clinical Psychology, 56,* 893–897.

Beck, A. T., Kovacs, M., & Weissman, A. (1979). Assessment of suicidal intention: The scale for suicidal ideation. *Journal of Consulting and Clinical Psychology, 47*(2), 343–352.

Beck, A. T., Steer, R. A., Beck, J. S., & Newman, C. F. (1993). Hopelessness, depression, suicidal ideation, and clinical diagnosis of depression. *Suicide and Life-Threatening Behavior, 23,* 139–145.

Beck, A. T., Steer, R. A., & Brown, G. K. (1996). *Manual for the Beck Depression Inventory,* (2nd ed.). San Antonio, TX: Psychological Corporation.

Beck, A. T., Steer, R. A., & Ranieri, W. F. (1988). Scale for suicide ideation: Psychometric properties of a self-report version. *Journal of Clinical Psychology, 44*(4), 499–505.

Beck, J. S. (1995). *Cognitive therapy: Basics and beyond.* New York, NY: Guilford Press.

Bekhit, N. S., Thomas, G. V., Lalonde, S., & Jolley, R. (2002). Psychological assessment in clinical practice in Britain. *Clinical Psychology and Psychotherapy, 9,* 285–291.

Ben-Porath, Y. S., & Tellegen, A. (2008). *MMPI-2-RF manual for administration, scoring, and interpretation.* Minneapolis: University of Minnesota Press.

Beran, T. N. (2007). Differential Abilities Scale Edition—Second Edition. *Canadian Journal of School Psychology, 22*(1), 128–132.

Berman, A. (2006). Risk management with suicidal patients. *Journal of Clinical Psychology, 62*(2), 171–184.

Bersoff, D. N. (2008). *Ethical conflicts in psychology* (4th ed.). Washington, DC: American Psychological Association.

Bersoff, D. N., & Hofer, P. T. (2008). The legal regulation of school psychology. In D. N. Bersoff, *Ethical conflicts in psychology* (4th ed.). Washington, DC: American Psychological Association.

Besser, A., & Priel, B. (2005). The apple does not fall far from the tree: Attachment styles and personality vulnerabilities to depression in three generations of women. *Personality and Social Psychology Bulletin, 31,* 1052–1073.

Beutler, L. E., Malik, M., Talebi, H., Fleming, J., & Moleiro, C. (2004). Use of psychological tests/instruments for treatment planning. In M. E. Maruish (Ed.), *The use of psychological testing for treatment planning and outcomes assessment: Vol. I. General considerations* (pp. 111–146). Mahwah, NJ: Erlbaum.

Black, D. W. (2011) Proposed DSM-5 revisions to personality disorder criteria need further scrutiny. *Annals of Clinical Psychiatry, 23*(3), 161.

Blake, R. J., & Sackett, S. A. (1999). Holland's typology and the five factor model: A rational empirical analysis. *Journal of Career Assessment, 7,* 249–279.

Block, J. (1995). A contrarian view of the five-factor approach to personality description. *Psychological Bulletin, 117*(2), 187–215. doi:10.1037/0033-2909.117.2.187

Blow, F. (1991). *Michigan Alcoholism Screening Test – Geriatric Version (MAST–G).* Ann Arbor: University of Michigan Alcohol Research Center.

Blume, A. W., Morera, O. F., & de la Cruz, B. G. (2008) Assessment of addictive behaviors in ethnic-minority cultures. In D. M. Donovan, & G. A. Marlatt (Eds), *Assessment of addictive behaviors* (2nd ed., pp. 49–70). New York, NY: Guilford Press.

Bordin, E. (1979). The generalizability of the psychoanalytic concept of the working alliance. *Psychotherapy: Theory, Research, and Practice, 16,* 252–260.

Boughner, S., Hayes, S. F., Bubenzer, D. L., & West, J. D. (1994). Use of standardized assessment instruments by marital and family therapists: A survey. *Journal of Marital and Family Therapy, 20,* 69–75.

Bowers, L. (1999). A critical appraisal of violent incident measures. *Journal of Mental Health, 8*(4), 339–349.

Bowman, M. L. (1989). Testing individual differences in china. *American Psychologist, 44,* 576–578.

Boyle, G. J. (1995). Myers-Briggs Type Indicator (MBTI): Some psychometric limitations. *Australian Psychologist, 30,* 71–74.

Bracken, B. A., & Keith, L. K. (2004). *Clinical Assessment of Behavior professional manual.* Lutz, FL: Psychological Assessment Resources.

Bradley, K. A., DeBenedetti, A. F., Volk, R. J., Williams, E. C., Frank, D., & Kivlahan, D. R. (2007). AUDIT-C as a brief screen for alcohol misuse in a non-VA primary care sample. *Alcoholism: Clinical and Experimental Research, 31*(7), 1–10.

Breaux, K. C., & Frey, F. E. (2010). Conducting ability-achievement discrepancy analyses using WISC-IV GAI and WIAT III technical report #1. Retrieved from http://www.pearsonassessments.com/NR/rdonlyres/EA31BB94-6F51-4343-9633-424380E9D75D/0/WIAT3_GAI_Tables_Final.pdf

Breslau, N., Roth, T., Rosenthal, L., & Andreski, P. (1996). Sleep disturbance and psychiatric disorders: A longitudinal epidemiological study of young adults. *Biological Psychiatry, 39,* 411–418.

Breunlin, D. C., Schwartz, R. C., & MacKune-Karrer, B. (1992). *Metaframeworks: Transcending the models of family therapy.* San Francisco, CA: Jossey-Bass.

Brooks, R., & S. Goldstein. (2004). *The power of resilience: Achieving balance, confidence and personal strength in your life.* Chicago, IL: Contemporary Books.

Brown, T. A., Antony, M. M., & Barlow, D. H. (1992). Psychometric properties of the Penn State Worry Questionnaire in a clinical anxiety disorders sample. *Behaviour Research and Therapy, 30,* 33–37.

Brown, G. K., Beck, A. T., Steer, R. A., & Grisham, J. R. (2000). Risk factors for suicide in psychiatric outpatients: A 20-year prospective study. *Journal of Consulting and Clinical Psychology, 68,* 371–377.

Bryan, C. J., & Rudd, M. D. (2006). Advances in the assessment of suicide risk. *Journal of Clinical Psychology: In Session, 62,* 185–200.

Bugental, J. F. T. (1990). Existential-humanistic psychology. In J. K. Zeig & W. M. Munion (Eds.), *What is psychotherapy? Contemporary perspectives* (pp. 189–192). San Francisco, CA: Jossey-Bass.

Buhr, K., & Dugas, M. J. (2002). The Intolerance of Uncertainty Scale: Psychometric properties of the English version. *Behaviour Research and Therapy, 40,* 931–945.

Buonomano, D. N. (2010). *Brain bugs: How the brain's flaws shape our lives.* New York, NY: Norton.

Burkard, A. W., Ponterotto, J. G., Reynolds, A. L., & Alfonso, V. C. (1999). White counselor trainees' racial identity and working alliance perceptions. *Journal of Counseling and Development, 77,* 324–329.

Burns, R. C., & Kaufman, S. H. (1970). Kinetic family drawings (K-F-D): An introduction to understanding children through kinetic drawings. New York, NY: Brunner/Mazel.

Burns, T. G., & O'Leary, S. D. (2004). Wechsler Intelligence Scale for Children—IV: Test review. *Applied Neuropsychology, 11*(4), 233–236.

Buros Institute. (2010). *Test Reviews Online.* Retrieved from http://buros.unl.edu/buros/jsp/search.jsp

Buss, A. H., & Perry, M. (1992). The Aggression Questionnaire. *Journal of Personality and Social Psychology, 63,* 452–459

Butcher, J. N. (1990). *The MMPI-2 in psychological treatment.* New York, NY: Oxford University Press.

Butcher, J. N. (2004). Personality assessment without borders: Adaptation of the MMPI-2 across cultures. *Journal of Personality Assessment, 83*(2), 90–104.

Butcher, J. N. (2006). Pathways to MMPI–2 use: A practitioner's guide to test usage in diverse settings. In J. N. Butcher (Ed.), *MMPI-2: A practitioner's guide* (pp. 3–13). Washington, DC: American Psychological Association.

Butcher, J. N., & Clark, L. A. (1979). Recent trends in cross-cultural MMPI research and application. In J. N. Butcher (Ed.), *New developments in the use of the MMPI* (pp. 69–112). Minneapolis: University of Minnesota Press.

Butcher, J. N., Graham, J. R., Ben-Porath, Y. S., Tellegen, A., Dahlstrom, W. G., & Kaemmer, B. (2001). *Minnesota Multiphasic Personality Inventory-2: Manual for administration, scoring, and interpretation* (rev. ed.). Minneapolis: University of Minnesota Press.

Butcher, J. N., Williams, C. L., Graham, J. R., Archer, R. P., Tellegen, A., Ben-Porath, Y. S., & Kaemmer, B. (1992). *MMPI–A: Minnesota Multiphasic Personality Inventory–A: Manual for administration, scoring, and interpretation.* Minneapolis: University of Minnesota Press.

Byrd, P. M., & Davis, J. L. (2009). Violent behavior in female inmates: Possible predictors. *Journal of Interpersonal Violence, 24,* 379–392.

Camara, W., Nathan, J., & Puente, A. (2000). Psychological test usage: Implications in professional psychology. *Professional Psychology: Research and Practice, 31*(2), 141–154.

Campbell, M. H. (2001). Test Review of the Reynolds Depression Screening Inventory. In B. S. Plake & J. C. Impara (Eds.), *The fourteenth mental measurements yearbook.* Retrieved from the Buros Institute's *Test Reviews Online* website: http://www.unl.edu/buros

Campbell, D. T., & Fiske, D. W. (1959). Convergent and discriminant validation by the multitrait-multimethod matrix. *Psychological Bulletin, 56,* 81–105.

Canadian Society for Exercise Physiology. (2009). Canadian physical activity guidelines. Retrieved from http://www.csep.ca/CMFiles/Guidelines/CSEP-InfoSheets-adults-ENG.pdf

Carlson, J. F. (1992). Review of the Reynolds Child Depression Scale. In J. J. Kramer & J. C. Conoley (Eds.), *The eleventh mental measurements yearbook.* Retrieved from the Buros Institute's *Test Reviews Online* website: http://www.unl.edu/buros

Carroll, J. B. (2005). The three-stratum theory of cognitive abilities. In D. P. Flanagan & P. L. Harrison (Eds.), Contemporary intellectual assessment: Theories, tests and issues (2nd ed., pp. 69–76). New York, NY: Guilford Press.

Cattell, R. B. (1947). Confirmation and clarification of the primary personality factors. *Psychometrika, 12,* 197–220.

Cattell, R. B., Cattell, A. K. S., & Cattell, H. E. P. (1993). *16PF Fifth Edition Questionnaire.* Champaign, IL: Institute for Personality and Ability Testing.

Cattell, R. B., & Eber, H. W. (1972). *Manual for forms A and B Sixteen Personality Factors questionnaire "The 16PF".* Champaign, IL: Institute for Personality and Ability Testing.

Cecero, J., Fenton, L., Nich, C., Frankforter, T., & Carroll, K. (2001). Focus on therapeutic alliance: The psychometric properties of six measures across three treatments. *Psychotherapy: Theory, Research, Practice and Training, 38*(1), 1–11.

Center for Applications of Psychological Type (CAPT). (2010). *CAPT: Training, books, research for MBTI, archetypes, leadership, psychological type..* Retrieved from http://www.capt.org/about-capt/contact-capt.htm

Centers for Disease Control and Prevention. (2008). Physical activity guidelines for Americans: Fact sheet for health professionals on physical activity guidelines for adults. Retrieved from http://www.cdc.gov/nccdphp/dnpa/physical/pdf/PA_Fact_Sheet_Adults.pdf

Centers for Disease Control and Prevention. (2009). *FASTSTATS – Homepage.* Retrieved from http://www.cdc.gov/nchs/fastats/default.htm

Centers for Disease Control and Prevention. (2010). Injury – WISQARS (Web-based Injury Statistics Query and Reporting System). Retrieved from http://www.cdc.gov/injury/wisqars/index.html

Chiesa, M., Fonagy, P., Bateman, A. W., & Mace, C. (2009). Psychiatric morbidity and treatment pathway outcomes of patients presenting to specialist NHS psychodynamic psychotherapy services: Results from a multi-centre study. *Psychology and Psychotherapy: Theory, Research and Practice, 82,* 83–98. British Psychological Society.

Choca, J. P. (2004). *Interpretative guide to the Millon Clinical Multiaxial Inventory* (3rd ed.). Washington, DC: American Psychological Association.

Chorpita, B. F., Tracey, S. A., Brown, T. A., Collica, T. J., & Barlow, D. H. (1997). Assessment of worry in children and adolescents: An adaptation of the Penn State Worry Questionnaire. *Behaviour Research and Therapy, 35*(6), 569–581.

Clum, G. A., & Yang, B. (1995). Additional support for the reliability and validity of the Modified Scale for Suicide Ideation. *Psychological Assessment, 7*(1), 122–125.

Coccaro, E. F., Berman, M. E., & Kavoussi, R. J. (1997). Assessment of life history of aggression: Development and psychometric characteristics. *Research Psychiatry, 73,* 147–157.

Cochrane-Brink, K. A., Lofchy, J. S., & Sakinofsky, I. (2000). Clinical rating scales in suicide risk assessment. *General Hospital Psychiatry, 22,* 445–451.

Cohen, S., & Herbert, T. B. (1996). Health psychology: Psychological factors and physical disease from the perspective of human psychoneuroimmunology. *Annual Review of Psychology, 47,* 113–142.

Cohen, S., & Wills, T. A. (1985). Stress, social support, and the buffering hypothesis. *Psychological Bulletin, 98,* 310–357.

Collins, R., Ellickson, P., & Klein, D. (2007). The role of substance use in young adult divorce. *Addiction, 102,* 786–794.

Comas-Díaz, L. (2006). Cultural variation in the therapeutic relationship. In C. Goodheart, A. Kazdin, & R. J. Sternberg (Eds.), *Evidence-based psychotherapy: Where practice and research meet* (pp. 81–105). Washington, DC: American Psychological Association.

Comer, J. S., & Kendall, P. C. (2005). High-end specificity of the children's depression inventory in a sample of anxiety-disordered youth. *Depression and Anxiety, 22*(1), 11–19.

Conners, C. K. (1997). *Conners' Rating Scales-Revised: Technical manual.* North Tonawanda, NY: Multi-Health Systems.

Cooney, N. L., Kadden, R. M., & Steinberg, H. R. (2008). Assessment of alcohol problems. In D. M Donovan & G. A Marlatt (Eds.), *Assessment of addictive behaviors* (2nd ed., pp. 71–112). New York, NY: Guilford Press.

Corey, G., Corey, M. S., & Callanan, P. (2007). *Issues and ethics in the helping professions.* Belmont, CA: Thomson Brooks/Cole.

Costa, P. T., & McCrae, R. R. (1985). *The NEO Personality Inventory Manual.* Odessa, FL: Psychological Assessment Resources.

Costa, P. T., & McCrae, R. R. (1992). *NEO PI-R. Professional manual.* Odessa, FL: Psychological Assessment Resources.

Crittendon, J., & Hopko, D. R. (2006). Assessing worry in older and younger adults: Psychometric properties of an abbreviated Penn State Worry Questionnaire (PSWQ-A). *Journal of Anxiety Disorders, 20,* 1036–1054.

Cronbach, L. J. (1951). Coefficient alpha and the internal structure of tests. *Psychometrika, 16,* 297–334.

Crone, D., & Horner, R. H. (2003). *Building positive behavior support systems in schools—Functional behavior assessment.* New York, NY: Guilford Press.

Cuellar, I. (1998). Cross-cultural clinical psychological assessment of Hispanic Americans. *Journal of Personality Assessment, 70*(1), 71–86.

Culberson, J. W. (2006). Alcohol use in the elderly: Beyond the CAGE Part 2: Screening instruments and treatment strategies. *Geriatrics, 61,* 20–26.

Cummings, J. A. (1986). Projective drawings. In H. M. Knoff (Ed.), *The assessment of child and adolescent personality.* New York, NY: Guilford Press.

Dailor, A. N., & Jacob, S. (2011). Ethically challenging situations reported by school psychologists: Implications for training. *Psychology in the Schools, 48,* 619–631.

Dahl, R. E. (1996). The regulation of sleep and arousal: Development and psychopathology. *Development and Psychopathology, 8,* 3–27.

Dahlstrom, W. G., & Dahlstrom, L. E. (1980). *Basic readings on the MMPI: A new selection on personality measurement.* Minneapolis, MN: University of Minnesota Press.

Dahlstrom, W. G., Welsh, G. S., & Dahlstrom, L. E. (1972). *An MMPI Handbook: Vol. I: Clinical interpretations.* Minneapolis: University of Minnesota Press.

Dana, R. H. (2005). Multicultural assessment: *Principles, applications and examples.* Mahwah, NJ: Erlbaum.

Dana, R. H. (2008). Clinical diagnosis in multicultural populations. In L. A. Suzuki & J. G. Ponterotto (Eds.), *Handbook of multicultural assessment: Clinical, psychological, and educational applications* (3rd ed., pp. 107–131). San Francisco, CA: Jossey-Bass.

Daniel, M. H. (1997). Intelligence testing: Status and trends. *American Psychologist, 52*(10), 1038–1045.

Das, J. P., Kirby, J. R., & Jarman, R. F. (1975). Simultaneous and successive syntheses: An alternative model for cognitive abilities. *Psychological Bulletin, 82,* 87–103.

Das, J. P., Naglieri, J. A., & Kirby, J. R. (1994). *Assessment of cognitive processes.* Boston, MA: Allyn & Bacon.

Dattilio, F., Tresco, K., & Siegel, A. (2007). An empirical survey on psychological testing and the use of the term psychological: Turf battles or clinical necessity? *Professional Psychology: Research and Practice, 38*(6), 682–689.

Davidson, K. (2011). Changing the classification of personality disorders—An ICD-11 proposal that goes too far? *Personality and Mental Health, 5,* 243–245.

Davies, D. (2004). *Child development a practitioner's guide* (2nd ed.). New York, NY: Guilford Press.

Davis, A. S. (2010). Test review of the Differential Ability Scales-Second Edition. In R. A. Spies, J. F. Carlson, & K. F. Geisinger (Eds.), *The eighteenth mental measurements yearbook.* Retrieved from the Buros Institute's *Test Reviews Online* website: http://www.unl.edu/buros

Davis, R. D. (1999). Millon: Essentials of his science, theory, classification, assessment, and therapy. *Journal of Personality Assessment, 72,* 330–353.

Davis, R. D., Meagher, S. E., Goncalves, M., Woodward, M., & Millon, T. (1999). Treatment planning and outcome in adults: The Millon Clinical Multiaxial Inventory-III. In M. E. Maruish (Ed.), *The use of psychological testing for treatment planning and outcomes assessment* (2nd ed., pp. 359–380). Mahwah, NJ: Erlbaum.

Dawes, R. M. (1994). *House of cards: Psychology and psychotherapy built on myth.* New York, NY: Free Press.

Deffenbacher, J. L., Oetting, E. R., Thwaites, G. A., Lynch, R. S., Baker, D. A., Stark, P. S., Thacker, S., & Eiswerth-Cox, L. (1996). State-trait anger theory and the utility of the Trait Anger Scale. *Journal of Counseling Psychology, 43,* 131–148.

Dennis, M. L., Scott, C. K., & Funk, R. (2003). Main findings from an experimental evaluation of recovery management checkups and early re-intervention (RMC/ERI) with chronic substance users. *Evaluation and Program Planning, 26,* 339–352.

Dennis, M. L., White, M. K., Titus, J. C., & Unsicker, J. I. (2008). *Global Appraisal of Individual Needs (GAIN): Administration guide for the GAIN and related measures (Version 5).* Bloomington, IL: Chestnut Health Systems.

Denzine, G. M. (2008). Review of the Revised Children's Manifest Anxiety Scale: Second Edition. In R. A. Spies, J. F. Carlson, & K. F. Geisinger (Eds.), *The eighteenth mental measurements yearbook.* Retrieved from the Buros Institute's *Test Reviews Online* website: http://www.unl.edu/buros

Derksen, J. L. (2006). The contribution of the MMPI-2 to the diagnosis of personality disorders. In J. N. Butcher (Ed.), *MMPI-2: A practitioner's guide* (pp. 99–120). Washington, DC: American Psychological Association.

Derogatis, L. R. (1994). *SCL-90-R: Administration, Scoring and Procedures Manual.* Minneapolis: National Computer Systems.

Derogatis, L., & Savitz, K. (1999). The SCL-90-R, brief symptom inventory and matching clinical rating scales. In M. Maruish (Ed.), *The use of psychological testing for treatment, planning and outcomes Assessment* (2nd ed., pp. 41–80). Mahwah, NJ: Erlbaum.

DeWalt, D. A., Rothrock, N., Yount, S., & Stone, A. A. (2007). Evaluation of item candidates: The PROMIS qualitative item review. *Medical Care, 45,* S12–S21.

Dhalla, S., & Kopec, J. A. (2007). The CAGE questionnaire for alcohol misuse: A review of reliability and validity studies. *Clinical and Investigative Medicine—Medecine Clinique et Experimentale, 30*(1), 33–41.

Digman, J., & Takemoto-Chock, N. K. (1981). Factors in the natural language of personality: Re-analysis, comparison, and interpretation of six major studies. *Multivariate Behavioral Research, 16,* 1246–1256.

Donnay, D. A., Thompson, R. C., Morris, M. L., & Schaubhut, N. A. (2004). *Technical brief for the newly revised Strong Interest Inventory assessment.* Paper presented at the Annual Convention of the American Psychological Association, Honolulu, HI. Retrieved from http://www.ccp.com

Donoso, O. A., Hernandez, B., & Horin, E. V. (2010). Use of psychological tests within vocational rehabilitation. *Journal of Vocational Rehabilitation, 32*(3), 191–200.

Dougherty, L. R., Klein, D. N., Olino, T. M., & Laptook, R. S. (2008). Depression in children and adolescents. In J. Hunsely & E. Mash (Eds.), *A guide to assessments that work* (pp. 69–95). New York, NY: Oxford University Press.

Dreger, R. M. (1978). Review of the State-Trait Anxiety Inventory. In O. K. Buros (Ed.), *The eighth mental measurements yearbook* (pp. 1094–1095). Highland Park, NJ: Gryphon Press.

Drummond, R., & Jones, K. (2006). Assessment procedures for counselors and helping professionals (6th ed.). Upper Saddle River, NJ: Pearson Merrill Prentice Hall.

Dubois, P. H. (1970). *The history of psychological testing.* Boston, MA: Allyn & Bacon.

Dugas, M. J., Freeston, M. H., Provencher, M. D., Lachance, S., Ladouceur, R., & Gosselin, P. (2001). Le Questionnaire sur l'Inquiétude et l'Anxiété. Validation dans des échantillons non cliniques et cliniques [The Worry and Anxiety Questionnaire: Validation in non-clinical and clinical samples] *Journal de Thérapie Comportementale et Cognitive, 11,* 31–36.

Duke, M., Nowicki, S., & Martin, E. (1996). *Teaching your child the language of social success.* Atlanta, GA: Peachtree.

Duncan, B. L., Miller, S. D., Reynolds, L., Sparks, J., Claud, D., Brown, J., & Johnson, L. D. (2003). The session rating scale: Psychometric properties of a "working" alliance scale. *Journal of Brief Therapy, 3*(1), 3–12.

Edelbrock, C., & Achenbach, T. M. (1984). The teacher version of the child behavior profile: I. Boys aged 6–11. *Journal of Consulting and Clinical Psychology, 52,* 207–217.

Eisen, J. L., Phillips, K. A., Baer, L., Beer, D. A., Atala, K. D., & Rasmussen, S. A. (1998). The Brown Assessment of Beliefs Scale: Reliability and validity. *American Journal of Psychiatry, 155,* 102–108.

Eisen, J. L., Phillips, K. A., Coles, M. E., & Rasmussen, S. A. (2004). Insight in obsessive compulsive disorder and body dysmorphic disorder. *Comprehensive Psychiatry, 45*(1), 10–15.

Elliott, C. D. (2007). *Differential Ability Scales* (2nd ed.). San Antonio, TX: Harcourt Assessment.

Ellsworth, J. R., Lambert, M. J., & Johnson, J. (2006). A comparison of the Outcome Questionnaire-45 and Outcome Questionnaire-30 in classification and prediction of treatment outcome. *Clinical Psychology and Psychotherapy, 13*(6), 380–391. doi: 10.1002/cpp.503

Erard, R. E. (2004). Release of test data under the 2002 ethics code and the HIPAA privacy rule: A raw deal or just a half baked idea? *Journal of Personality Assessment, 82*(1), 23–30.

Erford, B. T. (2006). *Assessment for counselors.* Boston, MA: Houghton Mifflin.

Escobar, F., Espi, F., & Canteras, M. (1995). Diagnostic tests for alcoholism in primary health care: Compared efficacy of different instruments. *Drug and Alcohol Dependence, 40,* 151–158.

Ewing, J. A. (1984). Detecting alcoholism: The CAGE Questionnaire. *Journal of American Medical Association, 252,* 1905–1907.

Exner, J. E. (1974). *The Rorschach: A comprehensive system: Vol. 1.* New York, NY: Wiley.

Ey, S., & Hersen, M. (2004). Pragmatic issues of assessment in clinical practice. In M. Hersen (Ed.), *Psychological assessment in clinical practice: A pragmatic guide* (pp. 3–20). New York, NY: Brunner-Routledge.

Fabri, M. (2008). Cultural adaptation and translation of assessment instruments from diverse populations: The use of the Harvard Trauma Questionnaire in Rwanda. In L. A. Suzuki & J. G. Ponterotto (Eds.), *Handbook of multicultural assessment: Clinical, psychological, and educational applications* (3rd ed., pp. 195–221). San Francisco, CA: Jossey-Bass.

Fair Access Coalition on Testing. (n.d.). *Home - Fair Access Coalition on Testing.* Retrieved from http://www.fairaccess.org

Fals-Stewart, W., & Klostermann, K. (2008). Substance use disorders. In J. A. Maddux & B. A. Winstead (Eds.), *Psychopathology foundations for a contemporary understanding* (2nd ed., pp. 327–348). New York, NY: Routledge.

Feldstein, S. W., & Miller, W. R. (2007). Does subtle screening work? A review of the Substance Abuse Subtle Screening Inventory (SASSI). *Addiction, 102*(1), 41–50.

Fernández-Ballesteros, R. (2002). Psychological assessment is not only clinical. *American Psychologist, 57,* 138–139

Fernandez, E. (2001). The Substance Abuse Subtle Screening Inventory-3. In B. S. Plake & J. C. Impara (Eds.), *The fourteenth mental measurements yearbook.* Retrieved from the Buros Institute's *Test Reviews Online* website: http://www.unl.edu/buros

Fernandez, K., Boccaccini, M. T., & Noland, R. M. (2007). Professionally responsible test selection for Spanish speaking clients: A four-step approach for identifying and selecting translated tests. *Professional Psychology: Research and Practice, 38,* 363–374.

Fields, A. J. (2010). Multicultural research and practice: Theoretical issues and maximizing cultural exchange. *Professional Psychology: Research and Practice, 41,* 196–201.

Finch, A. J. Jr., Saylor, C. F., & Edwards G. L. (1985). Children's Depression Inventory: Sex and grade norms for normal children. *Journal of the Consulting and Clinical Psychology, 53,* 424–425.

Finn, S. E. (2007). *In our clients' shoes: Theory and techniques of therapeutic assessment.* Mahwah, NJ: Erlbaum.

Finn, S. E., & Tonsager, M. E. (1997). Information-gathering and therapeutic models of assessment: Complementary paradigms. *Psychological Assessment, 9,* 374–385.

Finn, S. E., & Kamphuis, J. H. (2006). Therapeutic assessment with the MMPI–2. In J. N. Butcher (Ed.), *MMPI–2: A practitioners guide* (pp. 165–191). Washington, DC: American Psychological Association Books.

First, M. B. (2010). Clinical utility in the revision of the Diagnostic and Statistical Manual of Mental Disorders (DSM). *Professional Psychology: Research and Practice, 41,* 465–473.

First, M. B., Spitzer, R. L., Gibbon, M., & Williams, J. B. (1996). *Structured clinical interview for the DSM-IV Axis I Disorders (SCID PTSD Module).* Arlington, VA: American Psychiatric Press.

Fischer, C. T. (2004). Individualized assessment moderates the impact of HIPAA privacy rules. *Journal of Personality Assessment, 82*(1), 35–38.

Fischer, C. T., & Finn, S. E. (2008). Developing the life meaning of psychological test data: Collaborative and therapeutic approaches. In R. P. Archer & S. R. Smith (Eds.), *Personality assessment* (pp. 379–404). New York, NY: Routledge.

Fiske, D. W. (1949). Consistency of the factorial structure of personality ratings from different sources. *Journal of Abnormal and Social Psychology, 44,* 329–344.

Fiske, A., & O'Riley, A. (2008). Late life depression. In J. D. Hunsley & A. J. Mash (Eds.), *A guide to assessments that work* (pp. 138–157). New York, NY: Oxford University Press.

Flanagan, R. (2001). Test review of the Reynolds Depression Screening Inventory. In B. S. Plake & J. C. Impara (Eds.), *The fourteenth mental measurements yearbook.* Retrieved from the Buros Institute's *Test Reviews Online* website: http://www.unl.edu/buros

Flanagan, E. H., & Blashfield, R. K. (2010). Increasing clinical utility by aligning the DSM and ICD with clinicians' conceptualizations. *Professional Psychology: Research and Practice, 41,* 474–481.

Flanagan, R., Costantino, G., Cardalda, E., & Costantino, E. (2008). TEMAS: A multicultural test and its place in an assessment battery. In L. A. Suzuki & J. G. Ponterotto (Eds.), *Handbook of multicultural assessment: Clinical, psychological, and educational applications* (3rd ed., pp. 323–345). San Francisco, CA: Jossey-Bass.

Flanagan, D. P., & Kaufman, A. S. (2004). *Essentials of WISC-IV assessment.* Hoboken, NJ: Wiley.

Fleenor, J. W. (2001). Review of the Myers-Briggs Type Indicator, Form M. In B. S. Plake & J. C. Impara (Eds.), *The fourteenth mental measurements yearbook* (pp. 816–818). Lincoln, NE: University of Nebraska Press.

Fletcher-Janzen, E. (2011). A validity study of the Kaufman Assessment Battery for Children, Second Edition (KABC-II) and the Taos Pueblo Indian children of New Mexico. Retrieved from http://www.pearsonassessments.com/pai/ca/RelatedInfo/KABC-IIValidityStudy.htm

Flynn, J. R. (1987). Massive IQ gains in 14 nations: What IQ tests really measure. *Psychological Bulletin, 101,* 171–191.

Flynn, J. R. (1999). Searching for justice: The discovery of IQ gains over time. *American Psychologist, 54,* 5–20.

Folstein, M. F., Folstein, S. E., & McHugh, P. R. (1975). Mini-mental state: A practical method for grading the cognitive state of patients for the clinician. *Journal of Psychiatric Research, 12*(3), 189–198.

Folstein, M. F., Folstein, S. E., McHugh, P. R., & Fanjiang, G. (2001). *Mini-Mental State Examination: User's guide.* Odessa, FL: Psychological Assessment Resources.

Frank, J. (1973). *Persuasion and healing.* New York, NY: Schocken.

Frauenhoffer, D., Ross, M., Gfeller, J., Searight, H., & Piotrowski, C. (1998). Psychological test usage among licensed mental health practitioners: A multidisciplinary survey. *Journal of Psychological Practice, 4*(1), 28–33.

Fredman, N., & Sherman, R. (1987). *Handbook of measurements for marriage and family therapy.* New York, NY: Brunner/Mazel.

Freeman, J. (2003). Review of the State-Trait Anger Expression Inventory-2. In B. S. Plake, J. C. Impara, & R. A. Spies (Eds.), *The fifteenth mental measurements yearbook.* Retrieved from the Buros Institute's *Test Reviews Online* website: http://www.unl.edu/buros

Fresco, D. M., Mennin, D. S., Heimberg, R. G., & Turk, C. L. (2003). Using the Penn State Worry Questionnaire to identify individuals with generalized anxiety disorder: A receiver operating characteristic analysis. *Journal of Behavior Therapy and Experimental Psychiatry, 34,* 283–291.

Frick, P. J., & McMahon, R. J. (2008). Child and adolescent conduct problems. In J. Hunsley & E. J. Mash (Eds.), *A guide to assessments that work* (pp. 41–66). New York, NY: Oxford University Press.

Friedman, A. F., Lewak, R., Nichols, D. S., & Webb, J. T. (2000). *Psychological Assessment with the MMPI-2* (2nd ed.). Upper Mahwah, NJ: Erlbaum.

Gallup Organization. (2011). *Religion.* Retrieved from http://www.gallup.com/poll/1690/Religion.aspx

Garb, H. N. (1999). Call for a moratorium on the use of the Rorschach Inkblot in clinical and forensic settings. *Assessment, 6,* 313–315.

Garb, H. N. (2003). Incremental validity and the assessment of psychopathology in adults. *Psychological Assessment, 15,* 508–520.

Garb, H. N., Lilienfeld, S. O., & Fowler, K. A. (2008). Psychological assessment and clinical judgment. In J. E. Maddux & B. A. Winstead (Eds.), *Psychopathology: Foundations for a contemporary understanding.* (2nd ed., pp. 103–124). New York, NY: Routledge.

Garb, H. N., Wood, J. M., Nezworski, M. T., Grove, W. M., & Stejskal, W. J. (2001). Toward a resolution of the Rorschach controversy. *Psychological Assessment, 13,* 433–448.

Gardner, H. (1993). *Multiple intelligences: The theory in practice.* New York: Basic Books.

Gardner, W., Lidz, C. W., Mulvey, E. P., & Shaw, E. C. (1996). Clinical versus actuarial predictions of violence in patients with mental illnesses. *Journal of Consulting and Clinical Psychology, 64,* 602–609.

Garfield, S. L., & Bergin, A. E. (1994). Introduction and historical overview. In A. E. Bergin & S. L. Garfield (Eds.), *Handbook of psychotherapy and behavior change* (4th ed., pp. 3–18). New York, NY: Wiley.

Gaston, L. (1991). Reliability and criterion-related validity of the California Psychotherapy Alliance Scales. Patient version. *Psychological Assessment, 3,* 68–74.

Gay, L. R., & Airasian, P. (2003). *Educational research: Competencies for analysis and application* (7th ed.). Upper Saddle River, NJ: Pearson Education.

Geisinger, K. (2003). Testing and assessment in cross-cultural psychology. *Handbook of psychology: Assessment psychology, Vol. 10* (pp. 95–117). Hoboken, NJ: Wiley.

Geisinger, K. F. (2000). Psychological testing at the end of the millennium: A brief historical review. *Professional Psychology: Research and Practice, 31*(2), 117–118.

Gervais, N. J., & Dugas, M. J. (2008). Generalized anxiety disorder. In J. Hunsley & E. J. Mash (Eds.), *A Guide to Assessments That Work* (pp. 254–274). New York, NY: Oxford University Press.

Ghassemzadeh, H., Mojtabai, R., Karamghadiri, N., & Ebrahimkhani, N. (2005). Psychometric properties of a Persian language version of the Beck Depression Inventory—Second Edition: *BDI-II* Persian. *Depression and Anxiety, 21*(4), 185–192. doi: 10.1002/da.20070.

Gillis, M. M., Haaga, D. A. F., & Ford, G. T. (1995). Normative values for the Beck Anxiety Inventory, Fear Questionnaire, Penn State Worry Questionnaire, and Social Phobia and Anxiety Inventory. *Psychological Assessment, 7,* 450–455.

Glasser, W. (2000). *Reality therapy in action.* New York, NY: Harper Collins.

Goldberg, L.R. (1992). Development of markers for the big-five factor structure. *Psychological Assessment, 4*(1) 26–42.

Goodman, W. K., Price, L. H., Rasmussen, S. A., Mazure, C., Delgado, P., Heninger, G. R., & Charney, D. S. (1989a). The Yale-Brown Obsessive Compulsive Scale: II. Validity. *Archives of General Psychiatry, 46,* 1012–1016.

Goodman, W. K., Price, L. H., Rasmussen, S. A., Mazure, C., Fleischmann, R. L., Hill, C. L., . . . & Charney, D. S. (1989b). The Yale-Brown Obsessive Compulsive Scale: I. Development, use, and reliability. *Archives of General Psychiatry, 46,* 1006–1011.

Gottfredson, L. S., & Saklofske, D. H. (2009). Intelligence: Foundations and issues in assessment. *Canadian Psychology, 50*(3), 183–195.

Graham, J. R. (1993). *MMPI2: Assessing personality and psychopathology* (2nd ed.). New York, NY: Oxford University Press.

Green, K., Worden, B., Menges, D., & McGrady, B. (2008). Alcohol use disorders. In J. Hunsley & E. J. Mash (Eds.), *A Guide to Assessments that work* (pp. 339–369). New York, NY: Oxford University Press.

Greene, R. L. (2006). Use of the MMPI-2 in outpatient mental health settings. In J. N. Butcher (Ed.), *MMPI-2: A practitioner's guide* (pp. 253–272). Washington, DC: American Psychological Association.

Greene, R. L., & Brown, R. C. (1998). *MMPI-2 Adult Interpretive System* (2nd ed.). Lutz, FL: Psychological Assessment Resources.

Greene, R. L., & Clopton, J. R. (1999). Minnesota Multiphasic Personality Inventory-2 (MMPI-2). In M. E. Maurish (Ed.), *The use of psychological testing for treatment, planning and outcomes assessment* (2nd ed., pp. 1023–1049). Mahwah, NJ: Erlbaum.

Griggs v. Duke Power Co., 420 F.2d 1225, 1236-1237 (4th Cir. 1970).

Groth-Marnat, G. (1999). *Handbook of psychological assessment* (3rd ed. Rev.) New York, NY: Wiley.

Groth-Marnat, G. (2003). *Handbook of psychological assessment* (4th ed.). Hoboken, NJ: Wiley.

Guilford, J. P. (1988). Some changes in the structure-of-intellect model. *Educational and Psychological Measurement, 48,* 1–4.

Haley, J. (1976). *Problem solving therapy.* San Francisco, CA: Jossey-Bass.

Hambleton, R., & Zenisky, A. (2011). Translating and adapting tests for cross-cultural assessments. In D. Matsumoto & F. J. R. Van de Vijver (Eds.), *Cross-cultural research methods in psychology* (pp. 46–73). Cambridge, UK: Cambridge University Press.

Hamilton, M. (1967). Development of a rating scale for primary depressive illness. *British Journal of Social and Clinical Psychiatry, 6,* 278–296.

Handler, M. W., & DuPaul, G. J. (2005). Assessment of ADHD: Differences across psychology specialty areas. *Journal of Attention Disorders, 9*(2), 402–412.

Handler, L., & Habenicht, D. (1994). The Kinetic Family Drawing Technique: A review of the literature. *Journal of Personality Assessment, 62*(3), 440–464.

Hanson, W. E. (2005). Test review of OQ-45 (Outcome Questionnaire). In R. A. Spies & B. S. Plake (Eds.), *The sixteenth mental measurements yearbook.* Retrieved from the Buros Institute's Test Reviews Online website: http://www.unl.edu/buros

Harkness, A. R. (2009). Theory and measurement of personality traits. In J. N. Butcher (Ed)., *Handbook of personality assessment* (pp. 150–162). New York, NY: Oxford University Press.

Hartman, D. E. (2009). *Applied neuropsychology, 16*(1), 85–87.

Harris, J. A. (1997). A further evaluation of the aggression questionnaire: Issues of validity and reliability. *Behaviour Research and Therapy, 35*(11), 1047–1053.

Harvey, R. J., & Hammer, A. L. (1999). Item response theory. *Counseling Psychologist, 27*(3), 353–383.

Hatcher, R. L., & Barends, A. W. (1996). Patients' view of the alliance in psychotherapy: Exploratory factor analysis of three alliance measures. *Journal of Consulting and Clinical Psychology, 64*, 1326–1336.

Hathaway, S. R., & McKinley, J. C. (1940). A multiphasic personality schedule (Minnesota): I. Construction of the schedule. *Journal of Psychology, 10*, 249–254.

Hathaway, S. R., & McKinley, J. C. (1980). Construction of the schedule. In W. G. Dahlstrom & L. Dahlstrom (Eds.), *Basic readings on the MMPI: A new selection on personality measurement* (pp. 7-1–1). Minneapolis: University of Minnesota Press.

Haynes, S. N., & Lench, H. (2003). Incremental validity of new clinical assessment measures. *Psychological Assessment, 15,* 456–466.

Hays, K. F. (1999). *Working it out: Using exercise in psychotherapy.* Washington, DC: American Psychological Association.

Hays, P. A. (2008). *Addressing cultural complexities in practice: Assessment, diagnosis, and therapy* (2nd ed.). Washington, DC: American Psychological Association.

Hays, W. L. (1981). *Statistics.* New York, NY: Holt, Rinehart and Winston.

Hebben, N., & Milberg, W. (2009). *Essentials of neuropsychological assessment* (2nd ed.). Hoboken, NJ: Wiley.

Hedlund, J., & Vieweg, B. (1984). The Michigan Alcoholism Screening Test (MAST): A comprehensive review. *Journal of Operational Psychiatry, 15*, 55–64.

Herman, J. L. (1992). *Trauma and recovery.* U.S.: Basic Books.

Hersen, M. (2003). *Comprehensive handbook of psychological assessment volume 2: Personality assessment.* Hoboken, NJ: Wiley.

Hersen, M., & Porzelius, L. K. (Eds.). (2002). *Diagnosis, conceptualization, and treatment planning for adults: A step-by-step guide.* Mahwah, NJ: Erlbaum.

Hess, A. K. (2001). Review of Conners' Rating Scales-Revised. In B. S. Plake & J. C. Impara (Eds.), *The fourteenth mental measurements yearbook* (pp. 331–333). Lincoln, NE: Buros Institute of Mental Measurements.

Hill, C. E. (2004). *Helping skills: Facilitating exploration, insight, and action* (2nd ed.). Washington, DC: American Psychological Association.

Hilsenroth, M., Peters, E., & Ackerman, S. (2004). The development of therapeutic alliance during psychology assessment: Patient and therapist perspectives across treatment. *Journal of Personality Assessment, 83*, 331–344.

Hoelzle, J., & Meyer, G. (2008). The factor structure of the MMPI-2 Restructured Clinical (RC) scales. *Journal of Personality Assessment, 90*, 443–455.

Hojnoski, R., Morrison, R., Brown, M., & Matthews, W. (2006). Projective test use among school psychologists: A survey and critique. *Journal of Psychoeducational Assessment, 24*(2), 145–159.

Holland, J. L. (1997). *Making vocational choices: A theory of vocational personalities and work environments* (3rd ed.). Odessa, FL: Psychological Assessment Resources.

Holland, J. L. (1999). Why interest inventories are also personality inventories. In M. L. Savickas & A. R. Spokane (Eds.), *Vocational interests: Meaning, measurement, and use in counseling* (pp. 87–101). Palo Alto, CA: Davies-Black.

Hood, A. B., & Johnson, R. W. (2007). *Assessment in counseling: A guide to the use of psychological assessment procedures* (4th ed.). Alexandria, VA: American Counseling Association.

Hooper, V. S., & Bell, S. M. (2006). Concurrent validity of the universal nonverbal intelligence test and the Leiter International Performance Scale-Revised. *Psychology in the Schools, 43*(2), 143–148.

Hopko, D. R., Lejuez, C. W., Armento, M. E. A., & Bare, R. L. (2004). Depressive disorders. In M. Hersen (Ed.), *Psychological assessment in clinical practice: A pragmatic guide* (pp. 85–116). New York, NY: Taylor & Francis.

Horn, J. L. (1968). Organization of abilities and the development of intelligence. *Psychological Review, 75*(3), 242–259.

Horvath, A. O. (2001). The alliance. *Psychotherapy: Theory/Research/Practice/Training, 38*(4), 365–372.

Horvath, A. O., & Greenberg, L. S. (1989). Development and validation of the Working Alliance Inventory. *Journal of Counseling Psychology, 36*, 223–233.

Horvath, A. O., & Symonds, B. D. (1991). Relation between working alliance and outcome in psychotherapy: A meta-analysis. *Journal of Counselling Psychology, 38*, 139–149.

Hoyer, J., Ruhl, U., Scholz, D., & Wittchen, H. (2006). Patients' feedback after computer-assisted diagnostic interviews for mental disorders. *Psychotherapy Research, 16*(3), 357–363.

Hunsley, J., & Bailey, J. M. (2001). Whither the Rorschach? An analysis of the evidence. *Psychological Assessment, 13,* 472–485.

Hunsley, J., & Mash, E. J. (2008). *A guide to assessments that work*. New York, NY: Oxford University Press.

Hunsley, J., & Meyer, G. J. (2003). The incremental validity of psychological testing and assessment: Conceptual, methodological, and statistical issues. *Psychological Assessment, 15*(4), 446–455.

Imel, Z. E., & Wampold, B. E. (2008). The importance of treatment and the science of common factors in psychotherapy. In S. D. Brown & R. W. Lent (Eds.), *Handbook of counseling psychology* (4th ed., pp. 249–256). New York, NY: Wiley.

Ingram, R., & Smith, L. T. (2008). Mood disorders. In J. A. Maddux & B. A. Winstead (Eds.), *Psychopathology foundations for a contemporary understanding* (2nd ed., pp. 171–198). New York, NY: Routledge.

International Test Commission. (1999). *International guidelines for test use*. Stockholm, Sweden: Author. Retrieved from http://www.intestcom.org/guidelines/index.php

Ivanova, M. Y., Achenbach, T. M., Rescorla, L. A., Dumenci, L., Almqvist, F., Bilenberg, N . . . Verhulst, F. C. (2007). The generalizability of the Youth Self-Report Syndrome Structure in 23 societies. *Journal of Consulting and Clinical Psychology, 75*(5), 729–738.

Ivarsson, T. (2006). Normative data for the Multidimensional Anxiety Scale for Children (MASC) in Swedish adolescents. *Nordic Journal of Psychiatry, 60*(2), 107–113.

Ivey, A. E., & Ivey, M. B. (2007). *Intentional interviewing and counseling: Facilitating client development in a multicultural society* (7th ed.) Pacific Grove, CA: Brooks/Cole.

Jensen, A. R. (1980). *Bias in mental testing*. New York, NY: Free Press.

Jensen, A. R. (2004). Obituary. *Intelligence, 32,* 1–5. doi:10.1016/j.intell.2003.10.001

Johnson, S. L., Miller C. J., & Eisner L. R. (2008). Bipolar disorder. In J. Hunsley & E. J. Mash (Eds.). *A guide to assessments that work* (pp. 121–137). New York, NY: Oxford University Press.

Johnston, C., & Mah, J. W. (2008). Child attention deficit/hyperactivity disorder. In J. Hunsley & E. J. Mash (Eds.). *A guide to assessments that work* (pp. 17–40). New York, NY: Oxford University Press.

Johnston, C., & Murray, C. (2003). Incremental validity in the psychological assessment of children and adolescents. *Psychological Assessment, 15,* 496–507.

Joint Committee on Testing Practices. (2004). *Code of Fair Testing Practices in Education*. Washington, DC: Author. Retrieved from http://www.apa.org/science/programs/testing/committee.aspx

Joint Committee on Testing Practices. (1999). *Rights and responsibilities of test takers: Guidelines and expectations*. Washington, DC: Author. Retrieved from http://www.apa.org/science/programs/testing/committee.aspx

Jones, R. L. (1996). *Handbook of tests and measurements for black populations*. Hampton, VA: Cobb & Henry.

Jones, D. E., Doty, S., Grammich, C., Horsch, J. E., Houseal, R., Lynn, M. . . . Taylor, R. H. (2002). *Religious congregations and membership in the United States 2000: An enumeration by region, state and county based on data reported by 149 religious bodies*. Retrieved from http://www.glenmary.org/grc/RMS_2000/findings.htm

Juhnke, G. A. (1994). Teaching suicide risk assessment to counselor education students. *Counselor Education and Supervision, 34*(1), 52–57.

Kamphaus, R. W., & Frick, P. J. (2005). *Clinical assessment of child and adolescent personality and behavior* (2nd ed.). New York, NY: Springer Science and Business Media.

Kamphaus, R. W., Petoskey, M. D., & Rowe, E. W. (2000). Current trends in psychological testing of children. *Professional Psychology: Research and Practice, 31,* 155–164.

Kaplan, D. M., Kocet, M. M., Cottone, R. R., Glosoff, H. L., Miranti, J. G., Moll, E. C., . . . Tarvydas, V. M. (2009). New mandates and imperatives in the revised ACA code of ethics. *Journal of Counseling and Development*, 87, 241–256.

Kaplan, R. M., & Saccuzzo, D. P. (2005). *Psychological testing: Principles, applications, and Issues* (6th ed.). Belmont, CA: Wadsworth/Thomson Learning.

Katkin, E. S. (1978). Review of the State-Trait Anxiety Inventory. In O. K. Buros (Ed.), *The eighth mental measurements yearbook* (pp. 1095–1096). Highland Park, NJ: Gryphon Press.

Kaufman, A. S. (1979). *Intelligent testing with the WISC-R.* New York, NY: Wiley.

Kaufman, A. S., Flanagan, D. P., Alfonso, V. C., & Mascolo, J. T. (2006). Review of Wechsler Intelligence Scale for Children, Fourth Edition (WISC-IV). *Journal of Psychoeducational Assessment, 24*(3), 278–295.

Kaufman, A. S., & Kaufman, N. L. (1983). *K-ABC interpretative manual.* Circle Pines, MN: American Guidance Service.

Kaufman, A. S., & Kaufman, N. L. (1993). *Kaufman Adolescent & Adult Intelligence Test Manual.* Circle Pines, MN: American Guidance Service.

Kaufman, A. S., & Kaufman, N. L. (2004a). *Kaufman Assessment Battery for Children, Second Edition* (KABC-II). Circle Pines, MN: American Guidance Services.

Kaufman, A. S., & Kaufman, N. L. (2004b). *Kaufman Brief Intelligence Test, Second Edition* (K-BIT-2). Minneapolis, MN: Pearson Assessment.

Kaufman, A. S., & Kaufman, N. L. (2005). *Kaufman test of educational achievement - second edition.* Circle Pines, MN: American Guidance Service.

Kaufman, A. S., Johnson, C. K., & Liu, X. (2008). A CHC theory-based analysis of age differences on cognitive abilities and academic skills at ages 22 to 90 years. *Journal of Psychoeducational Assessment, 26,* 350–381.

Keane, T., Silberbogen, A. K., & Weierich, M. R. (2008). Assessment of posttraumatic stress disorder. In J. Hunsley & E. J. Mash (Eds.), *A guide to assessments that work* (pp. 293–318). New York, NY: Oxford University Press.

Keith, T. Z., Kranzler, J. H., & Flanagan, D. P. (2001). What does the Cognitive Assessment System (CAS) measure? Joint confirmatory factor analysis of the CAS and the Woodcock-Johnson Tests of Cognitive Ability (3rd ed.). *School Psychology Review, 30,* 89–119.

Kessler, R. C., Berglund, P., Demler, O., Jin, R., & Walters, E. E. (2005). Lifetime prevalence and age-of-onset distributions of DSM-IV disorders in the National Comorbidity Survey Replication. *Archives of General Psychiatry, 62,* 593–602.

Kirsch, I. (2010). *The emperor's new drugs.* New York, NY: Basic Books.

Kivlighan, D. M., Jr. (2007). Where's the relationship in research on the alliance? Two methods for analyzing dyadic data. *Journal of Counseling Psychology, 54,* 423–433.

Kleespies, P. M., & Dettmer, E. L. (2000). An evidence-based approach to evaluating and managing suicidal emergencies. *Journal of Clinical Psychology, 56,* 1109–1130.

Kline, P. (1995). New objective ratings scales for child assessment, II: Self-report scales for children and adolescents: Self-report of personality of the Behavior Assessment System for Children, the Youth Self-Report, and the Personality Inventory for Youth. *Journal of Psychoeducational Assessment, 13,* 16–193.

Knoff, H. M. (2001). Review of Conners' Rating Scales-Revised. In B. S. Plake & J. C. Impara (Eds.), *The fourteenth mental measurements yearbook* (pp. 334–337). Lincoln, NE: Buros Institute of Mental Measurements.

Koocher, G. P., & Keith-Spiegel, P. (1998). *Ethics in psychology: Professional standards and cases* (2nd ed.). New York, NY: Oxford University Press.

Kottler, J. A. (2010). *On being a therapist* (4th ed.). San Francisco, CA: Jossey-Bass.

Kovacs, M. (1992). *Children's Depression Inventory.* North Tonawanda, NY: Multi-Health Systems.

Krishnamurthy, R. (2008, August). Competency-focused psychological assessment training. In R. Archer (Chair), *Current directions in psychological assessment practice, research, and training.* Symposium conducted at the meeting of the American Psychological Association Convention, Boston, MA.

Kubiszyn, T. W., Meyer, G. J., Finn, S. E., Eyde, L. D., Kay, G. G., Moreland, K. L., et al. (2000). Empirical support for psychological assessment in clinical health care settings. *Professional Psychology: Research and Practice, 31,* 119–130.

Kuder, G. F., & Richardson, M. W. (1937). The theory of the estimation of test reliability. *Psychometrika, 2,* 151–160.

Kwan, K. K., & Maestas, M. L. (2008). MMPI-2 and MCMI-III performances of non-white people in the United States: What we (don't) know and where we go from here. In L. A. Suzuki & J. G. Ponterotto (Eds.),

Handbook of multicultural assessment: Clinical, psychological, and educational applications (pp. 425–446). San Francisco, CA: Jossey-Bass.

Lachar, D., & Gruber, C. P. (1995). *Personality Inventory for Youth (PIY) Manual: Technical guide.* Los Angeles, CA: Western Psychological Services.

Lambert, M. J., & Barely, D. E. (2001). Research summary on the therapeutic relationship and psychotherapy outcome. *Psychotherapy, 38,* 357–361.

Lambert, M .J., & Finch, A. E. (1999). The Outcome Questionnaire. In M. E. Maruish (Ed.), *The use of psychological testing for treatment planning and outcomes assessment* (2nd ed., pp. 831–869). Mahwah, NJ: Erlbaum.

Lambert, M. J., Masters, K. S., & Astle, D. (1988). An effect-size comparison of the Beck, Zung, & Hamilton rating scales for depression: A three-week and twelve-week analysis. *Psychological Reports, 63,* 467–470.

Lambert, M. J., & Ogles, B. M. (2004). The efficacy and effectiveness of psychotherapy. In M. J. Lambert (Ed.), *Bergin and Garfield's handbook of psychotherapy and behavior change* (5th ed., pp. 139–193). New York, NY: Wiley.

Lambert, M. J., & Shimokawa, K. (2011). Collecting client feedback. *Psychotherapy, 48*(1), 72–79.

Larry P. v. Riles 793 F.2d 969 (9th Cir. 1979).

Laux, J. M., Newman, I., & Brown, R. (2004). The Michigan Alcoholism Screening Test (MAST): A statistical validation analysis. *Measurement Evaluation in Counseling Development, 36,* 209–225.

Lazowski, L. E., & Miller, G. A. (2007). SASSI: A reply to the critique of Feldstein & Miller [Letter to the editor]. *Addiction, 102,* 1001–1002.

Lazowksi, L. E., Miller, F. G., Boye, M. W., & Miller, G. A. (1998). Efficacy of the Substance Abuse Subtle Screening Inventory—3 (SASSI-3) in identifying substance dependence in disorders in clinical setting. *Journal of Personality Assessment, 71,* 114–128.

Léger, D., Scheuermaier, K., Philip, P., Paillard, M., & Guilleminault, C. (2001). SF-36: Evaluation of quality of life in severe and mild insomniacs compared with good sleepers. *Psychosomatic Medicine, 63,* 49–55.

Leong, F. T. L., Okazaki, S., & Tak, J. (2003). Assessment of depression and anxiety in East Asia. *Psychological Assessment, 15*(3), 290–305.

Lilienfeld, S. O., Wood, J. M., & Garb. H. N. (2000). The scientific status of projective techniques. *Psychological Science in the Public Interest, 1,* 27–66.

Lim, D., Sanderson, K., & Andrews, G. (2000). Lost productivity among full-time workers with mental disorders. *Journal of Mental Health Policy and Economics, 3,* 139–146.

Linehan, M. (1993). *Cognitive-behavioral treatment of borderline personality disorder.* New York, NY: Guilford Press.

Linehan, M. M., Goodstein, J. L., Nielsen, S. L., & Chiles, J. A. (1983). Reasons for staying alive when you are thinking of killing yourself: The Reasons for Living Inventory. *Journal of Consulting and Clinical Psychology, 51,* 276–286.

Litwack, T. R., Zapf, P. A, Groscup, J. L., & Hart, S. D. (2006). Violence risk assessments: Research, legal, and clinical considerations. In A. Hess & I. Weiner (Eds.), *Handbook of forensic psychology* (3rd ed., pp. 487–533). New York, NY: Wiley.

Logue, P. E., Tupler, L. A., D'Amico, C., & Schmitt, F. A. (1993). The Neurobehavioral Cognitive Status Examination: Psychometric properties in use with psychiatric inpatients. *Journal of Clinical Psychology, 49,* 80–89.

Lohman, D. F. (1989). Human intelligence: An introduction to advances in theory and research. *Review of Educational Research, 59,* 333–373.

López, S. R. (2002). Teaching culturally informed psychological assessment: Conceptual issues and demonstrations. *Journal of Personality Assessment, 79*(2), 226–234.

Lowe, J. R., & Widiger, T. A. (2008). Personality disorders. In J. Maddux & B. Winstead (Eds.), *Psychopathology: Foundations for a contemporary understanding* (2nd ed., pp. 223–249). New York, NY: Routledge.

Lowman, C., & Le Fauve, C. E. (2003). Health disparities and the relationship between race, ethnicity, and substance abuse treatment outcomes. *Alcoholism: Clinical and Experimental Research, 27*(8), 1324–1326.

Luborsky, L., Barber, J. P., Siqueland, L., Johnson, S., Najavits, L. M., Frank, A., & Daley, D. (1996). The revised Helping Alliance Questionnaire (HAQ-II): Psychometric properties. *Journal of Psychotherapy Practice and Research, 6,* 260–271.

Luria, A. R. (1973). *The working brain: An introduction to neuropsychology* (B. Haigh, Trans.). New York, NY: Basic Books.

Lynam, D. R., & Widiger, T. (2001). Using the five factor model to represent the personality disorders: An expert consensus approach. *Journal of Abnormal Psychology, 110,* 401–412.

Maddux, J. E., Gosselin, J. T., & Winstead, B. A. (2008). Conceptions of psychopathology. In J. E. Maddux & B. A. Winstead (Eds.), *Psychopathology: Foundations for a contemporary understanding* (2nd ed. pp. 3–18). New York, NY: Routledge.

Malgady, R. G., & Costantino, G. (1998). Symptom severity in bilingual Hispanics as a function of interviewer ethnicity and language of interview. *Psychological Assessment, 10*(2), 120–127.

Malgady, R. G., & Colon-Malagady, G. (2008). Building community test norms: Considerations for ethnic minority. In L. A. Suzuki & J. G. Ponterotto (Eds.), *Handbook of multicultural assessment: Clinical, psychological, and educational applications* (3rd ed., pp. 34–51). San Francisco, CA: Jossey-Bass.

Mangold, D. L., Veraza, R., Kinkler, L., & Kinney, N. (2007). Neuroticism predicts acculturative stress in Mexican-American college students. *Hispanic Journal of Behavioral Sciences, 29*(3), 366–383.

Marks, P. A., Seeman, W., & Haller, D. L. (1974). *The actuarial use of the MMPI with adolescents and adults.* Baltimore, MD: Williams & Wilkins.

Martin, D. J., Garske, J. P., & Davis, M. K. (2000). Relation of the therapeutic alliance with outcome and other variables: A meta-analytic review. *Journal Consulting and Clinical Psychology, 68,* 438–450.

Martin, J., Martin, W., Meyer, M., & Slemon, A. (1986). Empirical investigation of the cognitive mediational paradigm for research on counseling. *Journal of Counseling Psychology, 33*(2), 115–123.

Martinez, S., Stillerman, L., & Waldo, M. (2005). Reliability and validity of the SCL-90-R with Hispanic college students. *Hispanic Journal of Behavioral Sciences, 27,* 254–264.

Maruish, M. E. (1999). Introduction. In M. E. Maruish (Ed.) *The use of psychological testing for treatment planning and outcomes assessment* (2nd ed., pp. 1–40). Mahwah, NJ: Erlbaum.

Maslow, A. H. (1943). A theory of human motivation. *Psychological Review, 50*(4), 370–396.

Mastrangelo, P. M. (2001). Review of the Myers-Briggs Type Indicator, Form M. In B. S. Plake & J. C. Impara (Eds.), *The fourteenth mental measurements yearbook* (pp. 818–820). Lincoln, NE: University of Nebraska Press.

Matarazzo, J. D. (1972). *Wechsler's measurement and appraisal of adult intelligence* (5th ed.). New York, NY: Oxford University Press.

Matarazzo, J. D. (1990). Psychological assessment versus psychological testing: Validation from Binet to the school, clinic, and courtroom. *American Psychologist, 45*(9), 999–1017.

Mattia, J. L., & Zimmerman, M. (2001). Epidemiology. In W. J. Livesley (Ed.), *Handbook of personality disorders* (pp. 107–123). New York, NY: Guilford Press.

Maulik, P. K., Eaton, W. W., & Bradshaw C. P. (2011). The effect of social networks and social support on mental health services use, following a life event, among the Baltimore Epidemiologic Catchment Area cohort. *Journal of Behavioral Health Services & Research, 38*(1), 29–50.

May, R., & Yalom, I. (2000). Existential therapy. In R. Corsini & D. Wedding (Eds.), *Current psychotherapies.* (6th ed., pp. 273–302.). Itasca, IL: Peacock.

Mayer, J. D., Salovey, P., & Caruso, D. R. (2008). Emotional intelligence: New ability or eclectic mix of traits? *American Psychologist, 63,* 503–517.

Mayer, R. (2003). Memory and information processes. In W. M. Reynolds & G. E. Miller (Eds.). *Handbook of psychology, Volume 7, Educational Psychology.* Hoboken, NJ: Wiley.

McCabe, D. P., Roediger, H. L., McDaniel, M. A., Balota, D. A., & Hambrick, D. Z. (2010). The relationship between working memory capacity and executive functioning: Evidence for an executive attention construct. *Neuropsychology, 24,* 222–243.

McClough, J. F., & Clarkin, J. F. (2004). Personality disorders. In M. Hersen (Ed.), *Psychological assessment in clinical practice* (pp. 117–146). New York, NY: Brunner-Routledge.

McConaughy, S. H. (1993). Advances in empirically based assessment of children's behavioral and emotional problems. *School Psychology Review, 22,* 285–307.

McConaughy, S. H., & Achenbach, T. M. (2004). *Manual for the Test Observation Form for Ages 2–18.* Burlington: University of Vermont, Center for Children, Youth & Families.

McConaughy, S. H., & Achenbach, T. M. (2009). *Manual for the Direct Observation Form.* Burlington: University of Vermont, Center for Children, Youth & Families.

McCrae, R. R., & Costa, P. T. (1985). Updating Norman's "Adequate" Taxonomy: Intelligence and personality dimensions in natural language and in questionnaires. *Journal of Personality and Social Psychology, 49*(3), 710–721.

McCrae, R. R., & Costa, P. T. (1997). Personality trait structures as a human universal. *American Psychologist, 52,* 509–516.

McCrae, R. R., & Costa, P. T. (2010). *NEO™ Inventories for the NEO™ Personality Inventory-3, NEO™ Five-Factor Inventory-3, NEO™ Personality Inventory-Revised Professional Manual.* Lutz, FL: PAR.

McGoldrick, M., Gerson, R., & Petry, S. S. (2008). *Genograms: Assessment and intervention* (3rd ed.). New York, NY: Norton.

McGrew, K. S. (2009). CHC theory and the human cognitive abilities project: Standing on the shoulders of the giants of psychometric intelligence research. *Intelligence 37,* 1–10.

McIntire, S. A., & Miller, L. A. (2007). *Foundations of psychological testing: A practical approach* (2nd ed.). Thousand Oaks, CA: Sage.

Meehl, P. E. (1954). *Clinical vs. statistical prediction a theoretical analysis and a review of the evidence.* Minneapolis: University of Minnesota Press.

Meichenbaum, D. (1985). *Stress inoculation training.* New York, NY: Pergamon Press.

Meichenbaum, D., & Turk, D. C. (1982). *Stress, coping, and disease: A cognitive-behavioral perspective.* New York, NY: McGraw-Hill.

Meier, S. T. (2008). *Measuring Change in Counseling and Psychotherapy.* New York, NY: Guilford Press.

Melnick, G., Sacks, S., & Banks, S. (2006). Use of the COVR in violence risk assessment. Letter to the editor. *Psychiatric Services, 57*(1), 142.

Meredith, L. S., Sturm, R., & Wells, K. B. (1999). A naturalistic study of psychotherapy: The medical outcomes study approach. In N. E. Miller & K. M. Magruder (Eds.), *Cost-effectiveness of psychotherapy: A guide for practitioners, researchers, and policymakers* (pp. 52–62). New York, NY: Oxford University Press.

Merrell, K. W. (2008). *Behavioral, social, and emotional assessment of children and adolescents* (3rd ed.). Mahwah, NJ: Erlbaum.

Meyer, G. J. (Ed.). (2006). The MMPI-2 Restructured Clinical Scales [Special issue]. *Journal of Personality Assessment, 87*(2).

Meyer, G. J., Finn, S. E., Eyde, L. D., Kay, G. G., Moreland, K. L., Dies, R. R., . . . Reed, G. M. (2001). Psychological testing and psychological assessment: A review of evidence and issues. *American Psychologist, 56,* 128–165.

Meyer, T. J., Miller, M. L., Metzger, R. L., & Borkovec, T. D. (1990). Development and validation of the Penn State Worry Questionnaire. *Behaviour Research and Therapy, 28,* 487–495.

Michelson, L., Sugai, D. P., Wood, R. P., & Kazdin, A. E. (1983). *Social skills assessment and training with children: An empirically based approach.* New York, NY: Plenum.

Miller, C., & Evans, B. B. (2004). Ethical issues in assessment. In M. Hersen (Ed.), *Psychological assessment in clinical practice* (pp. 21–32). New York, NY: Brunner-Routledge.

Miller, D. E. (2010). Test review of Wechsler Individual Achievement Test-Third Edition (*WIAT-III.*) In R. A. Spies, J. F. Carlson, & K. F. Geisinger (Eds.), *The eighteenth mental measurements yearbook.* Retrieved from the Buros Institute's *Test Reviews Online* website: http://www.unl.edu/buros

Miller, G. A. (1999). *The Substance Abuse Subtle Screening Inventory (SASSI) Manual, Second Edition.* Springville, IN: SASSI Institute.

Miller, I. W., Norman, W. H., Bishop, S. B., & Dow, M. G. (1986). The Modified Scale for Suicide Ideation: Reliability and validity. *Journal of Consulting and Clinical Psychology, 54*(5), 724–725.

Miller, J. D., Maples, J., Few, L. R., Morse, J. Q., Yaggi, K. E., & Pilkonis, P. A. (2010). Using clinician-rated five-factor model data to score the DSM-IV personality disorders. *Journal of Personality Assessment, 92*(4), 296–305.

Miller, P. M., Thomas, S., & Mallin, R. (2006) Patient attitudes towards self- report and biomarker alcohol screening by primary care physicians. *Alcohol and Alcoholism, 41,* 3, 306–310.

Miller, W. R., & Rollnick, S. (2002). *Motivational interviewing: Preparing people to change addictive behavior* (2nd ed.). New York, NY: Guilford Press.

Millon, T. (1994). *Millon Index of Personality Styles (MIPS) manual*. San Antonio, TX: Psychological Corporation.

Millon, T., & Davis, R. D. (1993). The Millon Adolescent Personality Inventory and the Millon Adolescent Clinical Inventory. *Journal of Counseling and Development, 71*, 570–573.

Millon, T., Davis, R. D., & Millon, C. (1997). *MCMI-III manual* (2nd ed.). Minneapolis, MN: National Computer Systems.

Millon, T., Millon, C., Davis, R., & Grossman, S. (2009). *MCMI-III Manual* (4th ed.). Bloomington, MN: NCS Pearson.

Mills, J., & Crowley, R. (1986). *Therapeutic metaphors for children and the child within*. Philadelphia, PA: Taylor & Francis.

Milstein, G., Manierre, A., & Yali, A. M. (2010). Psychological care for persons of diverse religions: A collaborative continuum. *Professional Psychology: Research and Practice, 41*(5), 371–381.

Minuchin, S. (1974). *Families and family therapy*. Cambridge, MA: Harvard University Press.

Modisette, K. C., Hunter, B. D., Ives, M. L., Funk, R. R. & Dennis, M. L. (2009). *NORMS including alpha, mean, N, sd, ICC for Adolescents (by demographics) and overall for Young Adults (18–25) and Adults (18+) using the CSAT 2008 V5 Dataset*. Normal, IL: Chestnut Health Systems. Retrieved from: http://www.gaincc.org/index.cfm?pageID=4

Molina, S., & Borkovec, T. D. (1994). The Penn State Worry Questionnaire: Psychometric properties and associated characteristics. In G. C. L. Davey & F. Tallis (Eds.), *Worrying: Perspectives on theory, assessment and treatment*. New York, NY: Wiley.

Moraes, C. L., Viellas, E. F., & Reichenheim, M. E. (2005). Assessing alcohol misuse during pregnancy: Evaluating psychometric properties of the CAGE, T-ACE and TWEAK in a Brazilian setting. *Journal of Studies on Alcohol, 66*(2), 165–173.

Morrison, J. R. (2008). *The first interview* (3rd ed.). New York, NY: Guilford Press.

Morriss, R., Leese, M., Chatwin, J., & Baldwin, D. (2008). Inter-rater reliability of the Hamilton Depression Rating Scale as a diagnostic and outcome measure of depression in primary care. *Journal of Affective Disorders, 111*, 204–213.

Mossman, D. (1994). Assessing predictions of violence: Being accurate about accuracy. *Journal of Consulting and Clinical Psychology, 62*, 783–792.

Mozley, S. L., Buckley, T. C., & Kaloupek, D. G. (2004). Acute and posttraumatic stress disorders. In M. Hersen (Ed.), *Psychological Assessment in clinical practice* (pp. 61–84). New York, NY: Brunner-Routledge.

Mullins-Sweatt, S. N., & Widiger, T. A. (2006). The five-factor model of personality disorder: A translation across science and practice. In R. Krueger & J. Tackett (Eds.), *Personality and psychopathology: Building bridges* (pp. 39–70). New York, NY: Guilford Press.

Murphy, C., Taft, C., & Eckhardt, C. I. (2007). Anger problem profiles among partner violent men: Differences in clinical presentation and treatment outcome. *Journal of Counseling Psychology, 54*, 189–200.

Myers, I. B., & McCaulley, M. H. (1985). *Manual: A guide to the development and use of the Myers-Briggs Type Indicator*. Palo Alto, CA: Consulting Psychologists Press.

Naglieri, J. A., & Bornstein, B. T. (2003). Intelligence and achievement: Just how correlated are they? *Journal of Psychoeducational Assessment, 21*(3), 244–260.

Naglieri, J, A., & Das, J. P. (1990). Planning, attention, simultaneous, and successive (PASS) cognitive processes as a model for intelligence. *Journal of Psychological Assessment, 8*, 303–337.

Naglieri, J. A., & Das, J. P. (1997). *Das-Naglieri Cognitive Assessment System administration and scoring manual*. Itasca, IL: Riverside.

Naglieri, J., Drasgow, F., Schmit, M., Handler, L., Prifitera, A., Margolis, A., & Velasquez, R. (2004). Psychological testing on the Internet: New problems, old issues. *American Psychologist, 59*, 150–162.

Naglieri, J., McNeish, T. J., & Bardos, A. N. (1991). *Draw A Person: Screening procedure for emotional disturbance (Draw A Person: SPED)*. San Antonio, TX: Pearson.

National Association of Social Workers. (1999). *Code of ethics of the national association of social workers*. Washington, DC: Author.

National Council of Schools and Programs of Professional Psychology. (2007). *Competency developmental achievement levels (DALs) of the National Council of Schools and Programs in Professional Psychology.* Washington, DC: Author. Retrieved from www.nscpp.info

National Institute on Drug Abuse. (2007). Topics in brief: Comorbid Drug Abuse and Mental Illness. Retrieved from http://www.drugabuse.gov/publications/topics-in-brief/comorbid-drug-abuse-mental-illness

National Institute on Drug Abuse, National Institute for Health, & U.S. Department of Health and Human Services. (2009). *Principles of drug addiction treatment: A research-based guide* (2nd ed.). Retrieved from http://www.drugabuse.gov/publications/principles-drug-addiction-treatment/drug-addiction-treatment-in-united-states

Neisser, U., Boodoo, G., Bouchard, T. J., Jr., Boykin, A. W., Brody, N., Ceci, S. J., . . . Urbina, S. (1996). Intelligence: Knowns and unknowns. *American Psychologist, 51,* 77–101.

Nelson-Gray, R. O. (2003). Treatment utility of psychological assessment. *Psychological Assessment, 15,* 521–531.

New Hampshire Board of Mental Health Practice. (2002). Administrative Rules: Chapter Mhp 500 ethical and professional standards, responsibilities of licensees. Retrieved from http://www.gencourt.state.nh.us/rules/state_agencies/mhp500.html

Newman, F. L., Rugh, D., & Ciarlo, J. A. (2004). Guidelines for selecting psychological instruments for treatment planning and outcomes assessment. In M. E. Maruish (Ed.), *The use of psychological testing for treatment planning and outcomes assessment* (3rd ed., Vol. 1, pp. 197–214). Mahwah, NJ: Erlbaum.

Newman, M. L., & Greenway, P. (1997). Therapeutic effects of providing MMPI-2 test feedback to clients at a university counseling service. *Psychological Assessment, 9,* 122–131.

Nichols, D. S. (2006). The trials of separating the bath water from the baby: A review and critique of the MMPI-2 Restructured Clinical Scales. *Journal of Personality Assessment, 87,* 121–138.

Nichols, D. S., & Crowhurst, B. (2006). Use of the MMPI-2 in inpatient mental health settings. In J. N. Butcher (Ed.), *The MMPI-2: A practitioner's guide* (pp. 195–252). Washington, DC: American Psychological Association.

Nisbett, R. E., & Ross, L. D. (1980). *Human inference: Strategies and shortcomings of social judgment.* Englewood Cliffs, NJ: Prentice Hall.

Nock, M. K., Wedig, M. M., Janis, I. B., & Deliberto, T. L. (2008). Self-injurious thoughts and behaviors. In J. Hunsley & E. J. Mash (Eds.), *A guide to assessments that work* (pp. 158–180) New York, NY: Oxford University Press.

Norcross, J. C., Karpiak, C. P., & Santoro, S. O. (2005). Clinical psychologists across the years: The division of clinical psychology from 1960 to 2003. *Journal of Clinical Psychology, 61,* 1467–1483.

Norcross, J. C., & Wampold, B. E. (2011). Evidence-based therapy relationships: Research conclusions and clinical practices. *Psychotherapy, 48*(1), 98–102.

Norman, W. T. (1963). Toward an adequate taxonomy of personality attributes: Replicated factor structure in peer nomination personality ratings. *Journal of Abnormal and Social Psychology, 66,* 574–583.

Novy, D., Stanley, M., Averill, P., & Daza, P. (2001). Psychometric comparability of English- and Spanish-language measures of anxiety and related affective symptoms. *Psychological Assessment, 13*(3), 347–355.

O'Hanlon, W. H., & Weiner-Davis, M. (1989). *In search of solutions: A new direction in psychotherapy.* New York, NY: Norton.

Okazaki, S. (1998). Psychological assessment of Asian Americans: Research agenda for cultural competency. *Journal of Personality Assessment, 70,* 54–70.

Okazaki, S., & Tanaka-Matsumi, J. (2006). Cultural considerations in cognitive-behavioral assessment. In P. A. Hays & G. Y. Iwamasa (Eds.), *Culturally responsive cognitive-behavioral therapy* (pp. 247–266). Washington, DC: American Psychological Association.

Okiishi, J. C., Lambert, M. J., Eggett, D., Nielsen, S. L., Dayton, D. D., & Vermeersch, D. A. (2006). An analysis of therapist treatment effects: Toward providing feedback to individual therapists on their patients' psychotherapy outcome. *Journal of Clinical Psychology, 20*(4), 17–29.

Okun, A., Stein, R. E., Bauman, L. J., & Silver, E. J. (1996). Content validity of the Psychiatric Symptom Index, CES-Depression Scale, and State-Trait Anxiety Inventory from the perspective of DSM-IV. *Psychological Reports, 79,* 1059–1069.

Orlinsky, D. E., Ronnestad, M. H., & Willutzki, U. (2003). Fifty years of process-outcome research: Continuity and change. In M. J. Lambert (Ed.), *Bergin and Garfield's handbook of psychotherapy and behavior change* (5th ed., pp. 307–390). New York, NY: Wiley.

Osman, A., Bagge, C. L., Gutierrez, P. M., Konick, L. C., Kopper, B. A., & Barrios, F. X. (2001). The Suicidal Behaviors Questionnaire - Revised (SBQ-R): Validation with clinical and non-clinical samples. *Assessment, 8,* 445–455.

Otto, P. K., & Hall, J. E. (1998). The utility of the Michigan Alcoholism Screening Test in the detection of alcohol dependents and problem drinkers. *Journal of Personality Assessment, 52,* 499–505.

Padilla, A. M., & Borsato, G. N. (2008). Issues in culturally appropriate psychoeducational assessment. In L. A. Suzuki & J. G. Ponterotto (Eds.), *Handbook of multicultural assessment clinical, psychological, and educational applications* (3rd ed., pp. 5–21). San Francisco, CA: Jossey-Bass.

Palmer, L., Fiorito, M., & Tagliareni, L. (2007). In M. Hersen & J. C. Thomas (Eds.), *Handbook of clinical interviewing with children* (pp. 62–76). Thousand Oaks, CA: Sage.

Papay, J. P., & Spielberger, C. D. (1986). Assessment of anxiety and achievement in kindergarten and first and second grade children. *Journal of Abnormal Child Psychology, 14*(2), 279–286.

Patterson, W. M., Dohn, H. H., Bird, J., & Patterson, G. A. (1983). Evaluation of suicidal patients: The SAD PERSONS scale. *Psychosomatics, 24,* 343–349.

Pauker, J. D. (1985). Review of SCL-90-R. In J. V. Mitchell, Jr. (Ed.), *The ninth mental measurements yearbook.* Retrieved from the Buros Institute's *Test Reviews Online* website: http://www.unl.edu/buros

Payne, R. W. (1985). Review of SCL-90-R. In J. V. Mitchell, Jr. (Ed.), *The ninth mental measurements yearbook.* Retrieved from the Buros Institute's *Test Reviews Online* website: http://www.unl.edu/buros

Pearson. (2009). *Wechsler Individual Achievement Test - Third Edition.* San Antonio, TX: Author.

Pearson. (2010). Qualifications. Retrieved http://psychcorp.pearsonassessments.com/haiweb/Cultures/en-US/Site/ProductsAndServices/HowToOrder/Qualifications.htm

Pekarik, G. (1992). Post treatment adjustment of clients who drop out early vs. late in treatment. *Journal of Clinical Psychology, 48*(3), 379–387.

Penk, W. E., Rierdan, J., Losardo, M., & Robinowitz, R. (2006). The MMPI-2 and Assessment of Posttraumatic Stress Disorder (PTSD). In J. N. Butcher (Ed.), *MMPI-2: A practitioner's guide* (121–142). Washington, DC: American Psychological Association.

Perry, J. N., Miller, K. B., & Klump, K. (2006). Treatment planning with the MMPI-2. In Butcher, J. N. (Ed.), *MMPI-2: A practitioner's guide* (pp. 143–164). Washington, DC: American Psychological Association.

Persons, J. B., & Fresco, D. M. (2008). Adult depression. In J. Hunsley & E. J. Mash (Eds.) *A guide to assessments that work* (pp. 96–120). New York, NY: Oxford University Press.

Persons, J. B., Roberts, N. A., & Zalecki, C. A. (2003). Anxiety and depression change together during treatment. *Behavior Therapy, 34*(2), 149–163.

Pfeiffer, S. I. (2005). Review of the OQ-45 (Outcome Questionnaire). In R. A. Spies & B. S. Plake (Eds.), *The sixteenth mental measurements yearbook.* Retrieved from the Buros Institute's *Test Reviews Online* website: http://www.unl.edu/buros

Phelps, E. A., & Sharot, T. (2008). How (and why) emotion enhances the subjective sense of recollection. *Current Directions in Psychological Science, 17*(2), 147–152.

Piazza, N. J., Martin, N., & Dildine, R. J. (2000). Screening instruments for alcohol and other drugs problems. *Journal of Mental Health Counseling, 22*(3), 218–227.

Pierce, R., Frone, M., Russell, M., Cooper, M., & Mudar, P. (2000). A longitudinal model of social contact, social support, depression, and alcohol use. *Health Psychology, 91,* 28–38.

Piotrowski, C. (1999). Assessment practices in the era of managed care: Current status and future directions. *Journal of Clinical Psychology, 55*(7), 787–796.

Pittenger, D. J. (2001). The Substance Abuse Subtle Screening Inventory-3. In B. S. Plake & J. C. Impara (Eds.), *The fourteenth mental measurements yearbook* (Vol. 14, pp. 916–918). Lincoln, NE: Buros Institute of Mental Measurements.

Pokorny, A. D., Miller, B. A., & Kaplan, H. B. (1972). The brief MAST: A shortened version of the Michigan Alcoholism Screening Test. *American Journal of Psychiatry, 129,* 118–121.

Polanski, P. J., & Hinkle, J. S. (2000). The Mental Status Examination: Its use by professional counselors. *Journal of Counseling and Development, 78*(3), 357–364.

Pope, K. S. (2009). *Harcourt Assessment's HIPAA Position Statement*. Retrieved from http://www.kspope .com/assess/harcourt-hipaa.php

Pope, K. S., & Vetter, V. A. (1992). Ethical dilemmas encountered by members of the American Psychological Association: A national survey. *American Psychologist, 47*(3), 397–411.

Porzelius, L. K. (2002). In M. Hersen & L. K. Porzelius (Eds.). (2002). *Diagnosis, conceptualization, and treatment planning for adults: A step-by-step guide* (pp. 1–13). Mahwah, NJ: Erlbaum.

Price, R. H., Choi, J., & Vinokur, A. D. (2002). Links in the chain of adversity following job loss: How financial strain and loss of personal control lead to depression, impaired functioning and poor health. *Journal of Occupational Health Psychology, 7*(4), 302–312.

Prochaska, J. O. (2004). Population treatment for addictions. *Current Directions in Psychological Science, 13,* 242–246.

Prochaska, J., DiClemente, C., & Norcross, J. (1992). In search of how people change: Applications to addictive behaviors. *American Psychologist, 47*(9), 1102–1114.

Prochaska, J. O., & Norcross, J. C. (2010). *Systems of psychotherapy: A transtheoretical analysis* (7th ed.). Pacific Grove, CA: Brooks Cole.

Prochaska, J. O., Norcross, J., & DiClemente, C. C. (1994). *Changing for good: The revolutionary program that explains the six stages of change and teaches you how to free yourself from bad habits.* New York, NY: Avon Books.

Prochaska, J. O., Norcross, J. C., Fowler, J. L., Follick, M. J., & Abrams, D. B. (1992). Attendance and outcome in a work site weight control program: Processes and stages of change as process and predictor variables. *Addictive Behaviors, 17,* 35–45.

Range, L. (2005). The family of instruments that assess suicide risk. *Journal of Psychopathology and Behavioral Assessment, 27*(2), 133–140.

Range, L. M., & Knott, E. C. (1997). Twenty suicide assessment instruments: Evaluations and recommendations. *Death Studies, 21,* 25–58.

Ranson, M. L., Nichols, D. S., Rouse, S. V., & Harrington, J. (2009). Changing or replacing an established standard: Issues, goals, and problems, with special reference to recent developments in the MMPI-2. In J. N. Butcher (Ed.), *Oxford handbook of personality assessment* (pp. 112–139). New York, NY: Oxford University Press.

Rastogi, S., Johnson, T. D., Hoeffel, E. M., & Drewery, M. P. (2011). *The Black population: 2010. Census briefs.* Retrieved from http://www.census.gov/prod/ cen2010/briefs/c2010br-06.pdf

Ravensberg, H. V., & Tobin, T. J. (2008). *IDEA 2004: Final regulations and the reauthorized functional behavioral assessment.* Retrieved from http://www .ssrn.com/abstract=1151394

Reed, G. M. (2010). Toward ICD-11: Improving the clinical utility of WHO's international classification of mental disorders. *Professional Psychology: Research and Practice, 41,* 457–464.

Rescorla, L. A. (2009). Rating Scale Systems for Assessing Psychopathology: The Achenbach System of Empirically Based Assessment (ASEBA) and the Behavior Assessment System for Children-2 (BASC-2). In J. Matson et al. (Eds.), *Assessing childhood psychopathology and developmental disabilities* (pp. 117–149). doi: 10.1007/978-0-387-09528-8

Rettew, D. C., Lynch, A. D., Achenbach, T. M., Dumenci, L., & Ivanova, M. Y. (2009). Meta-analyses of agreement between diagnoses made from clinical evaluations and standardized diagnostic interviews. *International Journal of Methods in Psychiatric Research, 18,* 169–184.

Reynolds, C. R., & Kamphaus, R. W. (Eds.). (2003). *Handbook of psychological and educational assessment of children: Personality, behaviors, and context* (2nd ed.). New York, NY: Guilford Press.

Reynolds, C. R., & Kamphaus, R. W. (2004). *Behavior Assessment System for Children* (2nd ed.). Circle Pines, MN: American Guidance Service.

Reynolds, C. R., & Richmond, B. O. (1979). Factor structure and construct validity of "what I think and feel": The Revised Children's Manifest Anxiety Scale. *Journal of Personality Assessment, 43,* 281–283.

Reynolds, C. R., & Richmond, B. O. (2008). *Revised Children's Manifest Anxiety Scale* (2nd ed.). Torrance, CA: Western Psychological Services.

Reynolds, W. M., & Kobak, K. A. (1995). Reliability and validity of the Hamilton Depression Inventory: A paper and pencil version of the Hamilton Depression Rating Scale clinical interview. *Psychological Assessment, 7,* 472–483.

Reynolds, W. M., & Kobak, K. A. (1998). *Reynolds Depression Screening Inventory: Professional Manual.* Odessa, FL: Psychological Assessment Resources.

Ridley, C. R., Li, L. C., & Hill, C. L. (1998). Multicultural assessment: Reexamination, reconceptualization, and practical application. *Counseling Psychologist, 26*(6), 939–947.

Ridley, C. R., Tracy, M. L., Pruitt-Stephens, L., Wimsatt, M. K., & Beard, J. (2008). Multicultural assessment validity: The preeminent ethical issue in psychological assessment. In L. A. Suzuki & J. G. Ponterotto (Eds.), *Handbook of multicultural assessment: Clinical, psychological, and educational applications* (3rd ed., pp. 22–33). San Francisco, CA: Jossey-Bass.

Robin, R. W., Saremi, A., Albaugh, B., Hanson, R. L., Williams, D., & Goldman, D. (2004). Validity of the SMAST in two American Indian tribal populations. *Substance Use & Misuse, 39*(4), 601–624. doi:10.1081/JA-120030062

Rogers, C. R. (1951). *Client-centered therapy; its current practice, implications, and theory.* Oxford, England: Houghton Mifflin.

Rogers, C. R. (1961). On becoming a person: A therapist's view of psychotherapy. Boston, MA: Houghton Mifflin.

Rogers, J. R., Gueulette, C. M., Abbey-Hines, J., Carney, J. V., & Werth, W. L. (2001). Rational suicide: An empirical investigation of counselor attitudes. *Journal of Counseling and Development, 79*(3), 365–372.

Rogers, J. R., Lewis, M. M., & Subich, L. M. (2002). Validity of the suicide assessment checklist in an emergency crisis center. *Journal of Counseling and Development, 80,* 493–502.

Rogers, R. (2001). *Handbook of diagnostic and structured interviewing.* New York, NY: Guilford Press.

Rogers, R. (2004). APA 2002 Ethics, amphibology, and the release of psychological test records a counterperspective to Erard. *Journal of Personality Assessment, 82*(1), 31–34.

Rohsenow, D. J. (2008). Substance use disorders. In J. Hunsley & E. J. Mash (Eds.), *A guide to assessments that work* (pp. 319–338). New York, NY: Oxford University Press.

Roid, G. H. (2003). *Stanford-Binet Intelligence Scales, Fifth Edition.* Itasca, IL: Riverside.

Roid, G. H., & Miller, L. J. (1997). *Leiter International Performance Scale – Revised: Examiner's Manual.* Wood Dale, IL: Stoelting.

Rooney, C., & Schaeffer, B. (1998). *Test scores do not equal merit: Enhancing equality & excellence in college admissions by deemphasizing SAT and ACT results.* Retrieved from http://www.fairtest.org/sites/default/files/optrept.pdf

Rorschach, H. (1975). *Psychodiagnostics* (8th ed.). (P. Lemkau & B. Kronenberg, Trans.). New York, NY: Grune & Stratton (original work published 1932).

Roth, T. (2005). Prevalence: Associated risks, and treatment patterns of insomnia. *Journal of Clinical Psychiatry, 66*(9), 10–13.

Rouse, S. V., Greene, R. L., Butcher, J. N., Nichols, D. S., & Williams, C. L. (2008). What do the MMPI-2 Restructured Clinical Scales reliably measure? Answers from multiple research settings. *Journal of Personality Assessment, 90,* 435–442.

Rowa, K., McCabe, R. E., & Antony, M. M. (2008). Specific phobia and social phobias. In J. Hunsley & E. J. Mash (Eds.), *A guide to assessments that work* (pp. 207–228). New York, NY: Oxford University Press.

Roy, A. (1982). Risk factors for suicide in psychiatric patients. *Archives of General Psychiatry, 39,* 1089–1095.

Rubial-Álvarez, S., Machado, M. C., Sintas, E., de Sola, S., Böhm, P., & Peña-Casanova, J. (2007). A preliminary study of the Mini Mental State Examination in a Spanish child population. *Journal of Child Neurology, 22,* 1269–1273.

Rudd, M. D., & Joiner, T. E. (1998). The assessment, management, and treatment of suicidality: Toward clinically informed and balanced standards of care. *Clinical Psychology: Science and Practice, 5,* 135–150.

Rudd, M. D., Mandrusiak, M., & Joiner, T. E. (2006). The case against no-suicide contracts: The commitment to treatment statement as a practice alternative. *Journal of Clinical Psychology, 62,* 243–251.

Rush, A. J., Trivedi, M. H., Ibrahim, H. M., Carmody, T. J., Arnow, B., Klein, D. N, . . . Keller, M. B.

(2003). The 16-item Quick Inventory of Depressive Symptomatology (QIDS) Clinician Rating (QIDS-C) and Self-Report (QIDS-SR): A psychometric evaluation in patients with chronic major depression. *Biological Psychiatry, 54,* 573–583.

Ryngala, D. J., Shields, A. L., & Caruso, J. C. (2005). Reliability generalization of the Revised Children's Manifest Anxiety Scale. *Educational and Psychological Measurement, 65*(2), 259–271.

Sadeghi, M., Fischer, J. M., & House, S. G. (2003). Ethical dilemmas in multicultural counseling. *Journal of Multicultural Counseling and Development, 31*(3), 179–192.

Safran, J. D., & Wallner, L. K. (1991). The relative predictive validity of two therapeutic alliance measures in cognitive therapy. *Psychological Assessment: A Journal of Consulting and Clinical Psychology, 3,* 188–195.

Sattler, J. M. (1988). *Assessment of Children* (3rd ed.). San Diego, CA: Author.

Saucier, G. (1994). Mini-markers: A brief version of Goldberg's unipolar big-five markers *Journal of Personality Assessment, 63*(3), 506–516.

Saunders, S. M., Miller, M. L., & Bright, M. M. (2010). Spiritually conscious psychological care. *Professional Psychology: Research and Practice, 41*(5), 355–362.

Savickas, M. L. (1999). The psychology of interests. In M. Savickas & A. Spokane (Eds.), *Vocational interests: Meaning, measurement, and use in counseling* (pp. 19–56). Palo Alto, CA: Davies–Black.

Savickas, M. L. (2000). Renovating the psychology of careers for the 21st century. In A. Collin & R. A. Young (Eds.), *The future of career* (pp. 53–68). Cambridge, UK: Cambridge University Press.

Scheflen, A. E. (1978). Susan smiled: An explanation in family therapy. *Family Process, 17,* 59–68.

Schroeder, C. S., & Gordon, B. N. (2002). *Assessment and treatment of childhood problems; A clinician's guide.* New York, NY: Guilford Press.

Scott, E. L., Eng, W., & Heimberg, R. G. (2002). Ethnic differences in worry in a nonclinical population. *Depression and Anxiety, 15,* 79–82.

Screening for Mental Health - Home. (n.d.). *Screening for mental health - Home.* Retrieved from http://www .mentalhealthscreening.org

Seligman, L. D., Ollendick, T. H., Langley, A. K., & Baldacci, H. B. (2004). The utility of measures of child and adolescent anxiety: A meta-analytic review of the Revised Children's Manifest Anxiety Scale, the State-Trait Anxiety Inventory for Children, and the Child Behavior Checklist. *Journal of Clinical Child and Adolescent Psychology, 33,* 557–565.

Sellbom, M., Ben-Porath, Y. S., & Bagby, R. M. (2008). Personality and psychopathology: Mapping the MMPI-2 restructured clinical (RC) scales onto the five factor model of personality. *Journal of Personality Disorders, 22*(3), 291–312.

Selzer, M. L. (1971). The Michigan Alcoholism Screening Test (MAST): The quest for a new diagnostic instrument. *American Journal of Psychiatry, 127,* 1653–1658.

Shea, S. C. (1998). *Psychiatric interviewing the art of understanding: A practical guide for psychiatrists, psychologists, counselors, social workers, nurses, and other mental health professionals.* Philadelphia, PA: Saunders.

Shea, S. C. (2002). *The practical art of suicide assessment a guide for mental health professionals and substance abuse counselors.* Hoboken, NJ: Wiley.

Shedler, J., Beck, A., & Bensen, S. (2000). Practical mental health assessment in primary care. *Journal of Family Practice, 49,* 614–662.

Sherer, M., Evans, C. C., Leverenz, J., Stouter, J., Irby, J. M, Jr., Lee, J. E., et al. (2007). Therapeutic alliance in post-acute brain injury rehabilitation: Predictors of strength of alliance and impact of alliance on outcome. *Brain Injury, 21,* 663–672.

Sheridan, M. (1995). A proposed intergenerational model of substance abuse, family functioning, and abuse/ neglect. *Child Abuse and Neglect, 19,* 519–530.

Shneidman, E. (2001). *Comprehending suicide: Landmarks in 20th century suicidology.* Washington, DC: American Psychological Association.

Silverman, M. M., Berman, A. L., Sanddal, N. D., O'Carroll, P. W., & Joiner, T. E. (2007). Rebuilding the Tower of Babel: A revised nomenclature for the study of suicide and suicidal behaviors part 2: Suicide-related ideations, communications, and behaviors. *Suicide and Life-Threatening Behavior, 37,* 264–277.

Silverman, W. K., & Ollendick, T. H. (2008). Assessment of child and adolescent anxiety disorders. In J. Hunsley &

E. Mash (Eds.), *A guide to assessments that work* (pp. 181–206). New York, NY: Oxford University Press.

Skiba, R., Simmons, A., Ritter, S., Gibb, A., Rausch, M., Cuadrado, J., et al. (2008). Achieving equity in special education: History, status, and current challenges. *Exceptional Children, 74*(3), 264–288.

Skinner, H. A. (1982). The Drug Abuse Screening Test. *Addictive Behaviors*, 7, 363–371.

Skodol, A. E. (2011). Scientific issues in the revision of personality disorders for DSM-5. *Personality and Mental Health, 5,* 97–111.

Smith, J. D. (2010). Therapeutic assessment with children and families: Current evidence and future directions. *Emotional & Behavioral Disorders in Youth,* 39–43.

Smith, G. T., Fischer, S., & Fister, S. M. (2003). Incremental validity principles of test construction. *Psychological Assessment, 15*(4), 467–477.

Smith, G. T., & Zapolski, T. C. B. (2009). Construction validation of personality measures. In J. N. Butcher (Ed.). *Handbook of personality assessment* (pp. 81–98). New York, NY: Oxford University Press.

Smith, R. F. (2008). Biological bases of psychopathology. In J. A. Maddux & B. A. Winstead (Eds.), *Psychopathology foundations for a contemporary understanding* (2nd ed., pp. 67–82). New York, NY: Routledge.

Snyder, C. R., Michael, S. T., & Cheavens, J. S. (1999). Hope as a psychotherapeutic foundation of common factors, placebos, and expectancies. In M. A. Huble, B. Duncan, & S. Miller (Eds.), *Heart and soul of change* (pp. 179–201). Washington, DC: American Psychological Association.

Soglin, L. F., Bauchat, J., Soglin, D. F., & Martin, G. J. (2009). Detection of intimate partner violence in a general medical practice. *Journal of Interpersonal Violence, 24*(2), 338–348.

Spengler, P. M., Strohmer, D. C., Dixon, D. N., & Shivy, V. A. (1995). A scientist-practitioner model of assessment: Implications for training, practice and research. *The Counseling Psychologist, 23*(3), 506–534.

Spielberger, C. D. (1999). *State-Trait Anger Expression Inventory-2 (STAXI-2)*. Odessa, FL: Psychological Assessment Resources.

Spielberger, C. D., Gorsuch, R. C., & Lushene, R. E. (1970). *Manual for the State Trait Anxiety Inventory*. Palo Alto, CA: Consulting Psychologists Press.

Startup, H. M., & Erickson, T. M. (2006). The Penn State Worry Questionnaire (PSWQ). In G. C. L. Davey & A. Wells (Eds.), *Worry and its psychological disorders: Theory, assessment and treatment* (pp. 265–283). Chichester, England: Wiley.

Stein, M. B. (2008). Review of the Revised Children's Manifest Anxiety Scale: Second Edition In R. A. Spies, J. F. Carlson, & K. F. Geisinger (Eds.), *The eighteenth mental measurements yearbook*. Retrieved from the Buros Institute's *Test Reviews Online* website: http://www.unl.edu/buros

Steketee, G. S. (1998). *Overcoming OCD: A behavioral and cognitive protocol for the treatment of OCD*. New York, NY: New Harbinger.

Sternberg, R. J. (1985). *Beyond IQ: A triarchic theory of human intelligence*. New York, NY: Cambridge University Press.

Sternberg, R. J. (1988). *The triarchic mind: A new theory of human intelligence*. New York, NY: Viking.

Sternberg, R. J. (1997). The concept of intelligence and its role in lifelong learning and success. *American Psychologist, 52,* 1030–1037.

Sternberg, R. J., & Kaufman, J. C. (1998). Human abilities. *Annual Review of Psychology, 49,* 479–502.

Sternberg R. J., Wagner R. K., Williams W. M., Horvath J. (1995). Testing common sense. *American Psychologist.* 50, 912–927

Stewart, W. F., Ricci, J. A., Chee, E., Hahn, S. R., & Morganstein, D. (2003). Cost of lost productive work time among US workers with depression. *JAMA: The Journal of the American Medical Association, 289*(23), 3135–3144.

Stover, C. S., Meadows, A., & Kaufman, J. (2009). Interventions for Intimate Partner Violence: Review and Directions for Evidence Based Practice. *Professional Psychology: Research and Practice, 40,* 223–233.

Straus, M. A. (2004). Cross-cultural reliability and validity of the Revised Conflict Tactics Scales: A study of university student dating couples in 17 nations. *Cross-Cultural Research, 38*(4), 407–432.

Stuart, G. L., Temple, J. R., Follansbee, K. W., Bucossi, M. M., Hellmuth, J. C., & Moore, T. M. (2008). The role of drug use in a conceptual model of IPV in men and women arrested for domestic violence. *Psychology of Addictive Behaviors, 22*(1), 12–24.

Substance Abuse and Mental Health Services Administration, Office of Applied Studies. (2008). *Results from the 2007 National Survey on Drug Use and Health: National Findings* (NSDUH Series H-34, DHHS Publication No. SMA 08-4343). Rockville, MD: Author.

Substance Abuse and Mental Health Services Administration, Office of Applied Studies. (2009). The NSDUH report: *Worker substance abuse by industry*. Retrieved from http://www.drugabusestatistics.samhsa.gov/2k7/industry/worker.pdf

Sulkowski, M. L., Storch, E. A., Geffken, G. R., Ricketts, E., Murphy, T. K., & Goodman, W. K. (2008). Concurrent validity of the Yale-Brown Obsessive-Compulsive Scale-Symptom Checklist. *Journal of Clinical Psychology, 64,* 1338–1351.

Summers, R. F., & Barber, J. P. (2003) Therapeutic alliance as a measurable psychotherapy skill. *Academic Psychiatry, 27,* 160–165.

Suppiger, A., In-Albon, T., Hendriksen, S., Hermann, E., Margraf, J., & Schneider, S. (2009). Acceptance of structured diagnostic interviews for mental disorders in clinical practice and research settings. *Behavior Therapy, 40,* 272–279.

Suris, A., & Coccaro, E. F. (2008). Aggression measures. In A. J. Rush, M. B. First, & D. Blacker, (Eds.), *Handbook of psychiatric measures* (2nd ed., pp. 731–744). Arlington, VA: American Psychiatric Publishing.

Tarter, R., & Kirisci, L. (1997). The Drug Use Screening Inventory for Adults: Psychometric Structure and Discriminative Sensitivity. *American Journal of Drug and Alcohol Abuse, 23,* 207–219.

Tellegen, A., Ben-Porath, Y. S., McNutly, J. L., Arbisi, P. A., Graham, J. R., & Kaemmer, B. (2003). *The MMPI-2 restructured clinical (RC) scales: Development, validation, and interpretation.* Minneapolis: University of Minnesota Press.

Tellegen, A., Ben-Porath, Y. S., Sellbom, M., Arbisi, P. A., McNulty, J. L., & Graham, J. L. (2006). Further evidence of the validity of the MMPI–2 Restructured Clinical (RC) scales: Addressing questions raised by Rogers et al. and Nichols. *Journal of Personality Assessment, 87,* 148–171.

Teng, E. L., & Chui, H. C. (1987). The Modified Mini-Mental State (3MS) examination. *Journal of Clinical Psychiatry, 48,* 314–318.

Thissen, D., & Steinberg, L. (2010). Using item response theory to disentangle constructs at different levels of generality. In S. Embretson (Ed.), *Measuring psychological constructs: Advances in model-based approaches* (pp. 123–144). Washington, DC: American Psychological Association.

Thomas, M. L., & Locke, D. E. C. (2010). Psychometric properties of the MMPI-2-RF Somatic Complaints (RC1) Scale. *Psychological Assessment, 22,* 492–503.

Tichenor, V., & Hill, C. E. (1989). A comparison of six measures of the working alliance. *Psychotherapy: Research and Practice, 26,* 195–199.

Tombaugh, T. N., McDowell, I., Kristjansson, B., & Hubley, A. M. (1996). Mini-Mental State Examination (MMSE) and the Modified MMSE (3MS): A psychometric comparison and normative data. *Psychological Assessment, 8,* 48–59.

Tracey, T. J., & Kokotovic, A. M. (1989). Factor structure of the Working Alliance Inventory. *Psychological Assessment, 1,* 207–210.

Trzepacz, P. T., & Baker, R. W. (1993). *The Psychiatric Mental Status Examination.* Oxford, UK: Oxford University Press.

Tucker, M. B. (1985). U.S. ethnic minorities and drug abuse: An assessment of the science and practice. *International Journal of the Addictions, 20*(6–7), 1021–1047.

Tulsky, D. S., & Ledbetter, M. F. (2000). Updating the WAIS-III and WMS-III: Considerations for research and practice. *Psychological Assessment, 12,* 253–262.

Tupes, E. C., & Christal, R. E. (1961). Recurrent personality factors based on trait ratings (ASD-TR-61-97). Lackland Air Force Base, TX: U.S. Air Force.

Turner, S. M., DeMers, S. T., Fox, H. R., & Reed, G. (2001). APA Guidelines for test user qualifications: An executive summary. *American Psychologist, 56,* 1099–1113.

U.S. Department of Education. (2004). Building the legacy: IDEA 2004. Retrieved from http://idea.ed.gov/explore/home

U.S. Department of Education. (2006). Response to Intervention—Special Education Research. Retrieved from http://www2.ed.gov/programs/specedintervention/legislation.html

U.S. Department of Education. (2011). Family educational rights and privacy act. Washington, DC: Author. Retrieved from http://www2.ed.gov/policy/gen/guid/fpco/ferpa/index.html

U.S. Department of Health and Human Services. (2009). OCR privacy brief summary of the HIPAA privacy rule. Retrieved from http://www.hhs.gov/ocr/privacy/hipaa/understanding/summary/privacysummary.pdf

U.S. Department of Health and Human Services. (2011). HealthCare.gov. Retrieved from http://www.healthcare.gov/law/features/index.html

U.S. Department of Health and Human Services, National Institute for Health, & National Institute on Alcohol Abuse and Alcoholism. (2005). *Helping patients who drink too much: A clinician's guide* (2005 ed.). Washington, DC: Author.

van Gorp, W. G., Altshuler, L., Theberge, D. C., & Mintz, J. (1999). Declarative and procedural memory in bipolar disorder. *Biological Psychiatry, 46,* 525–531.

Viglione, D. J., & Hilsenroth, M. (2001). The Rorschach: Facts, fiction, and future. *Psychological Assessment, 13,* 452–471.

Walker, E., Bollini, A., Hochman, K., Kestler, L., & Mittal, V. (2008). Schizophrenia. In J. E. Maddux & B. A. Winstead (Eds.), *Psychopathology: Foundations for a contemporary understanding* (pp. 199–222). New York, NY: Routledge.

Wampold, B. E. (2001). *The great psychotherapy debate: Model, methods, and findings.* Mahwah, NJ: Erlbaum.

Ward, S. B. (2003). Test review of the Mini-Mental State Examination. In B. S. Plake, J. C. Impara, & R. A. Spies (Eds.), *The fifteenth mental measurements yearbook.* Retrieved from the Buros Institute's *Test Reviews Online* website: http://www.unl.edu/buros

Washington v. Davis, 426 U.S. 229 (1976).

Watkins, C. E., Campbell, V. L., Nieberding, R., & Hallmark, R. (1995). Contemporary practice of psychological assessment by clinical psychologists. *Professional Psychology: Research and Practice, 26,* 54–60.

Watkins, K. E., Burnam, A., Orlando, M., Escarce, J. J., Huskamp, H. A., & Goldman, H. H. (2009). The health value and cost of care for major depression. *Value in Health, 12,* 65–72.

Watzlawick, P., Beavin, J. H., & Jackson, D. D. (1967). *Pragmatics of human communication: A study of interactional patterns, pathologies, and paradoxes.* New York, NY: Norton.

Wechsler, D. (1981). *Manual for the Wechsler Adult Intelligence Scale—Revised.* New York, NY: Psychological Corporation.

Wechsler, D. (1999). *Wechsler Abbreviated Scale of Intelligence (WASI).* San Antonio, TX: Harcourt Assessment.

Wechsler, D. (2003). *Wechsler Intelligence Scale for Children* (4th ed.) (WISC-IV). San Antonio, TX: Psychological Corporation.

Wechsler, D. (2008). *The Wechsler Adult Intelligence Scale—Fourth Edition.* San Antonio, TX: Pearson.

Westen, D., & Morrison, K. (2001). A multidimensional meta-analysis of treatments for depression, panic, and generalized anxiety disorder: An empirical examination of the status of empirically supported therapies. *Journal of Consulting and Clinical Psychology, 69,* 875–899.

Westermeyer, J., Yargic, I., & Thuras, P. (2004). Michigan Assessment-Screening Test for Alcohol and Drugs (MAST/AD): Evaluation in a clinical sample. *American Journal on Addictions,* 13, 151–162.

Westreich, L. M., Rosenthal, R. N., & Muran, J. C. (1996). A preliminary study of therapeutic alliance and dually diagnosed inpatients. *American Journal on Addictions, 5,* 81–86.

Whipple, J. L., & Lambert, M. J. (2011). Outcome measures for practice. *Annual Review of Clinical Psychology, 7,* 87–111.

Whiston, S. C. (2009). *Principles and applications of assessment in counseling* (3rd ed.). Belmont, CA: Brooks/Cole Cengage Learning.

Widiger, T. A. (2008). Personality disorder. In J. Hunsley & E. J. Mash (Eds.), *A guide to assessments that work* (pp. 413–435). New York, NY: Oxford University Press.

Wiebe, J. S., & Penley, J. A. (2005). A psychometric comparison of the Beck Depression Inventory-II in English and Spanish. *Psychological Assessment, 17*(4), 481–485.

Wiggins, J. S. (1973). *Personality and prediction: Principles of personality assessment.* Reading, MA: Addison-Wesley.

Williams, S. L. (2008). Anxiety disorders. In J. A. Maddux & B. A. Winstead (Eds.), *Psychopathology foundations for a contemporary understanding* (2nd ed., pp. 141–170). New York, NY: Routledge.

Winters, K. C., Newcomb, M. D., & Fahnhorst, T. (2004). Substance-use disorders. In M. Hersen (Ed.), *Psychological assessment in clinical practice* (pp. 393–408). New York, NY: Brunner-Routledge.

Wolraich, M., Lambert, W., Doffing, M., Bickman, L., Simmons, T., & Worley, K. (2003). Psychometric properties of the Vanderbilt ADHD Diagnostic Parent Rating Scale in a referred population. *Journal of Pediatric Psychology, 28,* 559–568.

Wood, J. M., Garb, N. H., Lilienfeld, O. S., & Nezworski, M. T. (2002). Clinical Assessment. *Annual Review of Psychology, 53,* 519–543.

Woodcock, R. W., McGrew, K. S., & Mather, N. (2001). Examiner's manual. *Woodcock-Johnson III Tests of Achievement.* Itasca, IL: Riverside.

World Health Organization (1992). *The ICD-10 Classification of mental and behavioral disorders. Clinical descriptions and diagnostic guidelines.* Geneva, Switzerland: Author. Retrieved from http://who.int/classifications/icd/en/index.html

Wubbolding, R. E. (1991). *Understanding reality therapy: A metaphorical approach.* New York, NY: Harper Perennial.

Wyss, C., Voelker, S., Cornock, B., & Hakim-Larson, J. (2003). Psychometric properties of a French-Canadian Translation of Achenbach's Youth Self-Report. *Canadian Journal of Behavioural Science, 35,* 67–71.

Yang, J., Dai, X., Yao, S., Cai, T., Gao, B., McCrae, R. R., & Costa, P. T., Jr. (2002). Personality disorders and the Five-Factor Model of personality in Chinese psychiatric patients. In P. T. Costa, Jr. & T. A. Widiger (Eds.), *Personality disorders and the Five-Factor Model of personality.* (pp. 215–221). Washington, DC: American Psychological Association.

Yates, B. T., & Taub, J. (2003). Assessing the costs, benefits, cost-effectiveness, and cost-benefit of psychological assessment: We should, we can, and here's how. *Psychological Assessment, 15,* 478–495.

Youngstrom, E. A., Wolpaw, J. M., Kogos, J. L., Schoff, K. M., Ackerman, B. P., & Izard, C. E. (2000). Interpersonal problem solving in preschool and first grade: Developmental change and ecological validity. *Journal of Clinical Child Psychology, 29,* 589–602.

Yudko, E., Lozhkina, O., & Fouts, A. (2007). A comprehensive review of the psychometric properties of the Drug Abuse Screening Test. *Journal of Substance Abuse Treatment, 32*(2), 189–198.

INDEX